Diodorus Siculus

II

The Historical Library
of
DIODORUS the SICILIAN
in Forty Books

Edited by
Giles Laurén

Volume Two
Books 15-40

SOPHRON IMPRIMIT
2014

ISBN 13: 978-0-9897836-3-7
ISBN 10: 0989783634

Design by Sophron Editeur

CONTENTS

BOOK XV

1. Throughout our entire treatise our practice has been to employ the customary freedom of speech enjoyed by history, and we have added just praise of good men for their fair deeds and meted out just censure upon bad men whenever they did wrong. By this means, as we believe, we shall lead men whose nature fortunately inclines them to virtue to undertake, because of the immortality fame accords them, the fairest deeds, whereas by appropriate obloquies we shall turn men of the opposite character from their impulse to evil. Consequently, since we have come in our writing to the period when the Lacedaemonians fell upon deep distress in their unexpected defeat at Leuctra, and again in their unlooked-for repulse at Mantineia lost the supremacy over the Greeks, we believe that we should maintain the principle we have set for our writing and set forth the appropriate censure of the Lacedaemonians.

For who would not judge men to be deserving of accusation who had received from their ancestors a supremacy with such firm foundations and that too preserved by the high spirit of their ancestors for over five hundred years, and now beheld it, as the Lacedaemonians of that time did, overthrown by their own folly? And this is easy to understand.

For the men who had lived before them won the glory they had by many labours and great struggles, treating their subjects the while fairly and humanely; but their successors used their allies roughly and harshly, stirring up, besides, unjust and insolent wars against the Greeks, and so it is quite to be understood that they lost their rule because of their own acts of folly. For the hatred of those they had wronged found in their disasters an opportunity to retaliate upon their aggressors, and they who had been unconquered from their ancestors' time were now attended by such contempt as, it stands to reason, must befall those who obliterate the virtues that characterised their ancestors. This explains why the Thebans, who for many generations had been subjects of their superiors, when they defeated them to everyone's surprise, became supreme among the Greeks, but the Lacedaemonians, when once they had lost the supremacy, were never at any time able to recover the high position enjoyed by their ancestors.

Now that we have sufficiently censured the Lacedaemonians, we shall in turn pass on to the further course of our history, after we have first set the time-limits of this section. The preceding Book, which is the fourteenth of our narrative, closed with the events concerned with the enslaving of the Rhegians by Dionysius and the capture of Rome by the Gauls, which took place in the year preceding the campaign of the Persians in Cyprus against Evagoras the king. In this Book we shall begin with this war and close with the year preceding the reign of Philip the son of Amyntas.

How the Persians fought against Evagoras in Cyprus (2-4, 8-9).

2. When Mystichides was archon in Athens, [486] the Romans elected in place of consuls three military tribunes, Marcus Furius, Gaius, and Aemilius. This year Artaxerxes, the King of the Persians, made war upon Evagoras, the king of Cyprus. He busied himself for a long time with the preparations for the war and gathered a large armament, both naval and land; his land force consisted

1

of three hundred thousand men including cavalry, and he equipped more than three hundred triremes. As commanders he chose for the land force his brother-in-law Orontes, and for the naval Tiribazus, a man who was held in high favour among the Persians. These commanders took over the armaments in Phocaea and Cyme, repaired to Cilicia, and passed over to Cyprus, where they prosecuted the war with vigour.

Evagoras made an alliance with Acoris, the king of the Egyptians, who was an enemy of the Persians, and received a strong force from him, and from Hecatomnus, the lord of Caria, who was secretly co-operating with him, he got a large sum of money to support his mercenary troops. Likewise he drew on such others to join in the war with Persia as were at odds with the Persians, either secretly or openly. He was master of practically all the cities of Cyprus, and of Tyre and some others in Phoenicia. He also had ninety triremes, of which twenty were Tyrian and seventy were Cyprian, six thousand soldiers of his own subjects, and many more than this number from his allies. In addition to these he enlisted many mercenaries, since he had funds in abundance, and not a few soldiers were sent him by the king of the Arabs and by certain others of whom the King of the Persians was suspicious.

3. Since Evagoras had such advantages, he entered the war with confidence. First, since he had not a few boats of the sort used for piracy, he lay in wait for the supplies coming to the enemy, sank some of their ships at sea, drove off others, and captured yet others. Consequently the merchants did not dare to convey food to Cyprus; and since large armaments had been gathered on the island, the army of the Persians soon suffered from lack of food and the want led to revolt, the mercenaries of the Persians attacking their officers, slaying some of them, and filling the camp with tumult and revolt. It was with difficulty that the generals of the Persians and the leader of the naval armament, known as Glōs, put an end to the mutiny. Sailing off with their entire fleet, they transported a large quantity of grain from Cilicia and provided a great abundance of food. As for Evagoras, King Acoris transported an adequate supply of grain from Egypt and sent him money and adequate supplies for every other need. Evagoras, seeing that he was much inferior in naval strength, fitted out sixty additional ships and sent for fifty from Acoris in Egypt, so that he had in all two hundred triremes. These he fitted out for battle in a way to cause terror and by continued trials and drill got ready for a sea engagement. Consequently, when the King's fleet sailed past toward Citium, he fell upon the ships unexpectedly and had a great advantage over the Persians. For he attacked with his ships in compact array ships in disorder, and since he fought with men whose plans were prepared against men unready, he at once at the first encounter won a prearranged victory. For, attacking as he did with his triremes in close order triremes that were scattered and in confusion, he sank some and captured others. Still the Persian admiral Glōs and the other commanders put up a gallant resistance, and a fierce struggle developed in which at first Evagoras held the upper hand. Later, however, when Glōs attacked in strong force and put up a gallant fight, the result was that Evagoras turned in flight and lost many of his triremes.

4. The Persians after their victory in the sea-fight gathered both their sea and land forces at the city of Citium. From this as their base they organised a siege of Salamis and beleaguered the city both by land and by sea. Meantime Tiribazus crossed over to Cilicia after the sea-fight and continued thence to the King, reported the victory, and brought back two thousand talents for the prosecution of the war. Before the sea-fight, Evagoras, who had fallen in with a body of the land force near the sea and defeated it, had been confident of success, but when he suffered defeat in the sea-fight and found himself besieged, he lost heart. Nevertheless, deciding to continue the war, he left his son Pnytagoras behind as supreme commander in Cyprus and himself took ten triremes, eluded the enemy, and got away from Salamis. On arriving in Egypt he met the king and urged him to continue the war energetically and to consider the war against the Persians a common undertaking.

How the Lacedaemonians, contrary to the common agreements, deported the Mantineians from their native land (5, 12).

5. While these events were taking place, the Lacedaemonians determined to make war upon Mantineia, without regard to the standing treaty [of Antalcidas], for the following reasons. The Greeks were enjoying the general peace of Antalcidas, in accordance with which all the cities had got rid of their garrisons and recovered by agreement their autonomy. The Lacedaemonians, however, who by their nature loved to command and by policy preferred war, would not tolerate the peace which they considered to be a heavy burden, and longing for their past dominance over Greece, they were poised and alert to begin a new movement. At once, then, they stirred up the cities and formed partisan groups in them with the aid of their friends, being provided in some of the cities with plausible grounds for interference. For the cities, after having recovered their autonomy, demanded an accounting of the men who had been in control under the Lacedaemonian supremacy; and since the procedure was harsh, because the people bore enmity for past injuries and many were sent into exile, the Lacedaemonians took it upon themselves to give support to the defeated faction. By receiving these men and dispatching a force with them to restore them to their homes, they at first enslaved the weaker cities, but afterward made war on and forced the more important cities to submit, s having preserved the general peace no longer than two years.

Seeing that the city of the Mantineians lay upon their borders and was full of valiant men, the Lacedaemonians were jealous of its growth which had resulted from the peace and were bent on humbling the pride of its citizens. First of all, therefore, they dispatched ambassadors to Mantineia, commanding them to destroy their walls and all of them to remove to the original five villages from which they had of old united to form Mantineia. When no one paid any attention to them, they sent out an army and laid siege to the city. The Mantineians dispatched ambassadors to Athens, asking for aid. When the Athenians did not choose to make a breach of the common peace, the Mantineians none the less with stood the siege on their own account and stoutly resisted the enemy. In this way, then, fresh wars got a start in Greece.

On the poems of Dionysius the tyrant (6-7).

6. In Sicily Dionysius, the tyrant of the Syracusans, now that he was relieved of wars with the Carthaginians, enjoyed great peace and leisure. Consequently he devoted himself with much seriousness to the writing of poetry, and summoning men of repute in this line, he accorded them special honours and resorted to them, making use of them as instructors and revisers of his poems. Elated by the flattering words with which these men repaid his benefactions, Dionysius boasted far more of his poems than of his successes in war. Among the poets in his company was Philoxenus [of Cythera] the writer of dithyrambs, who enjoyed very high repute as a composer in his own line. After dinner, when the compositions of the tyrant, which were wretched, had been read, he was asked what was his judgement of the poetry. When he replied with a good deal of frankness, the tyrant, offended at his words, found fault with him that he had been moved by jealousy to use scurrilous language and commanded his servants to drag him off forthwith to the quarries. On the next day, however, when Philoxenus' friends made petition for a grant of pardon, Dionysius made up with him and again included the same men in his company after dinner. As the drinking advanced, again Dionysius boasted of the poetry he had written, recited some lines which he considered to be happily composed, and then asked, "What do you think of the verses?" To this Philoxenus said not a word, but called Dionysius' servants and ordered them to take him away to the quarries. Now at the time Dionysius, smiling at the ready wit of the words, tolerated the freedom of speech, since the joke took the edge off the censure, but when some time later his acquaintances and Dionysius as well asked him to desist from his untimely frankness, Philoxenus made a paradoxical offer. He would, he said, in his answer both respect the truth and keep the favour of Dionysius. Nor did he fail to make his word good. For when the tyrant produced some lines that described harrowing events, and asked, "How do the verses strike you?", he replied, "Pitiful!", keeping his double promise by the ambiguity. For Dionysius took the word "pitiful" as signifying harrowing and deeply moving, which are successful effects of good poets, and therefore rated him as having approved them; the rest, however, who caught the real meaning, conceived that the word "pitiful" was only employed to suggest failure.

7. Much the same thing, as it happened, also occurred in the case of Plato the philosopher. Dionysius summoned this man to his court and at first deigned to show him the highest favour, since he saw that he practised the freedom of speech that philosophy is entitled to. Later, being offended at some of his statements, he became altogether alienated from him, exposed him in the market, and sold him as a slave for twenty minas. Those who were philosophers, however, joined together, purchased his freedom, and sent him off to Greece with the friendly admonition that a wise man should associate with tyrants either as little as possible or with the best grace possible.

Dionysius did not renounce his zeal for poetry but dispatched to the Olympic Games actors with the most pleasing voices who should present a musical performance of his poems for the assembled throng. At first their pleasing voices filled the hearers with admiration, but later, on further reflection, the reciters were despised and rewarded with laughter. Dionysius, on learning of the slight that was cast upon his poems, fell into a fit of melancholy. His condition grew constantly worse and a madness seized his mind, so that he kept saying that he was the victim of jealousy and suspected all his friends of plotting against him. At last his frenzy and madness went so far that he slew many of his friends on false charges, and he drove not a few into exile, among whom were Philistus and his own brother Leptines, men of outstanding courage who had rendered him many important services in his wars. These men, then, passed their banishment in Thurii in Italy where they were cordially welcomed by the Italian Greeks.

Later, at the request of Dionysius, they were reconciled with him and returned to Syracuse where they enjoyed his former goodwill, and Leptines married Dionysius' daughter. These, then, were the events of this year.

On the arrest of Tiribazus and his acquittal (8, 10-11).

8. When Dexitheüs was archon in Athens, [385] the Romans elected as consuls Lucius Lucretius and Servius Sulpicius. This year Evagoras, the king of the Salaminians, arrived in Cyprus from Egypt, bringing money from Acoris, the king of Egypt, but less than he had expected. When he found that Salamis was closely besieged and that he was deserted by his allies, he was forced to discuss terms of settlement. Tiribazus, who held the supreme command, agreed to a settlement upon the conditions that Evagoras should withdraw from all the cities of Cyprus, that as king of Salamis alone he should pay the Persian King a fixed annual tribute, and that he should obey orders as slave to master. Although these were hard terms, Evagoras agreed to them all except that he refused to obey orders as slave to master, saying that he should be subject as king to king. When Tiribazus would not agree to this, Orontes, who was the other general and envious of Tiribazus' high position, secretly sent letters to Artaxerxes against Tiribazus. The charges against him were first, that although he was able to take Salamis, he was not doing so, but was receiving embassies from Evagoras and conferring with him on the question of making common cause; that he was likewise concluding a private alliance with the Lacedaemonians, being their friend; that he had sent to Pytho [at Delphi] to inquire of the god regarding his plans for revolt; and, most important of all, that he was winning for himself the commanders of the troops by acts of kindness, bringing them over by honours and gifts and promises. On reading the letter the King, believing the accusations, wrote to Orontes to arrest Tiribazus and dispatch him to him. When the order had been carried out, Tiribazus, on being brought to the King, asked for a trial and for the time being was put in prison. After this the King was engaged in a war with the Cadusians and postponed the trial, and so the legal action was deferred.

9. Orontes succeeded to the command of the forces in Cyprus. But when he saw that Evagoras was again putting up a bold resistance to the siege and, furthermore, that the soldiers were angered at the arrest of Tiribazus and so were insubordinate and listless in pressing the siege, Orontes became alarmed at the surprising change in the situation. He therefore sent men to Evagoras to discuss a settlement and to urge him to agree to a peace on the same terms Evagoras had agreed to with Tiribazus. Evagoras, then, was surprisingly able to dispel the menace of capture, and agreed to peace on the conditions that he should be king of Salamis, pay the fixed tribute annually, and obey as a king the orders of the King. So the Cyprian war, which had lasted for approximately ten years, although the larger part of the period was spent in preparations and there were in all but two years of continuous warfare, came to the end [380] we have described.

Glos, who had been in command of the fleet and was married to the daughter of Tiribazus, fearful that it might be thought that he had co-operated with Tiribazus in his plan and that he would be punished by the King, resolved to safeguard his position by a new project of action. Since he was well supplied with money and soldiers and had furthermore won the commanders of the triremes to himself by acts of kindness, he resolved to revolt from the King. At once, then, he sent ambassadors to Acoris, the king of the Egyptians, and concluded an alliance with him against the King. He also wrote the Lacedaemonians and incited them against the King, promising to give them a large sum of money and offering other great inducements. He pledged himself to full co-operation with them in Greece and to work with them in restoring the supremacy their fathers had exercised. Even before this the Spartans had made up their minds to recover their supremacy, and at the time were already throwing the cities into confusion and enslaving them, as was clear to all men. Moreover, they were in bad repute because it was generally believed that in the agreement they had made with the King they had betrayed the Greeks of Asia, and so they repented of what they had done and sought a plausible excuse for a war against Artaxerxes. Consequently they were glad to enter the alliance with Glōs.

10. After Artaxerxes had concluded the war with the Cadusians, he brought up the trial of Tiribazus and assigned three of the most highly esteemed Persians as judges. At this time other judges who were believed to have been corrupt were flayed alive and their skins stretched tight on judicial benches. The judges rendered their decisions seated on these, having before their eyes an example of the punishment meted out to corrupt decisions. Now the accusers read the letter sent by Orontes and stated that it constituted sufficient cause for accusation. Tiribazus, with respect to the charge in connection with Evagoras, presented the agreement made by Orontes that Evagoras should obey the King as a king, whereas he had himself agreed upon a peace on the terms that Evagoras should obey the King as a slave his master. With respect to the oracle he stated that the god as a general thing gives no response regarding death, and to the truth of this he invoked all the Greeks present as witnesses. As for the friendship with the Lacedaemonians, he replied in defence that he had formed the friendship not for any advantage of his own but for the profit of the King; and he pointed out that the Greeks of Asia were thereby detached from the Lacedaemonians and delivered captive to the King. At the conclusion of his defence he reminded the judges of the former good services he had rendered the King.

It is related that Tiribazus pointed out many services to the King, and one very great one, as a result of which he was highly regarded and became a very great friend. Once during a hunt, while the King was riding in a chariot, two lions came at him, tore to pieces two of the four horses belonging to the chariot, and then charged upon the King himself; but at that very moment Tiribazus appeared, slew the lions, and rescued the King from the danger. In wars also, men say, he excelled in valour, and in council his judgement was so good that when the King followed his advice he never made a mistake. By means of such a defence Tiribazus was cleared of the charges by the unanimous vote of the judges.

On the death of Glōs and the condemnation of Orontes (11, 18).

11. The King summoned the judges one by one and asked each of them what principles of justice he had followed in clearing the accused. The first said that he observed the charges to be debatable, while the benefactions were not contested. The second said that, though it were granted that the charges were true, nevertheless the benefactions exceeded the offences. The third stated that he did not take into account the benefactions, because Tiribazus had received from the King in return for them favours and honours many times as great, but that when the charges were examined apart by themselves, the accused did not appear to be guilty of them. The King praised the judges for having rendered a just decision and bestowed upon Tiribazus the highest honours, such as were customary. Orontes, however, he condemned as one who had fabricated a false accusation, expelled him from his list of friends, and subjected him to the utmost marks of degradation.

Such was the state of affairs in Asia.

How the Lacedaemonians, contrary to the common agreements, deported the Mantineians from their native land (12).

12. In Greece the Lacedaemonians continued the siege of Mantineia, and through the summer the Mantineians maintained a gallant resistance against the enemy. For they were considered to surpass the other Arcadians in valour, and it was for this reason that the Lacedaemonians had formerly made it their practice in battle to place them, as their most trustworthy allies, on their flank. But with the coming of winter the river which flows beside Mantineia received a great increase from the rains and the Lacedaemonians diverted the flow of the river with great dikes, turned the river into the city, and made a pool of all the region round about. Consequently, as the houses began to fall, the Mantineians in despair were compelled to surrender the city to the Lacedaemonians. After they received the surrender, they imposed no other hardship on the Mantineians than the command that they should move back to their former villages. Consequently they were compelled to raze their own city and return to their villages.

The settlement of the island of Pharos in the Adriatic (13).

13. While these events were taking place, in Sicily Dionysius, the tyrant of the Syracusans, resolved to plant cities on the Adriatic Sea. His idea in doing this was to get control of the Ionian Sea, in order that he might make the route to Epeirus safe and have there his own cities which could give haven to ships. For it was his intent to descend unexpectedly with great armaments upon the regions about Epeirus and to sack the temple at Delphi, which was filled with great wealth. Consequently he made an alliance with the Illyrians with the help of Alcetas the Molossian, who was at the time an exile and spending his days in Syracuse. Since the Illyrians were at war, he dispatched to them an allied force of two thousand soldiers and five hundred suits of Greek armour. The Illyrians distributed the suits of armour among their choicest warriors and incorporated the soldiers among their own troops. Now that they had gathered a large army, they invaded Epeirus and would have restored Alcetas to the kingship over the Molossians. When no one paid any attention to them, they first ravaged the country, and after that, when the Molossians drew up against them, there followed a sharp battle in which the Illyrians were victorious and slew more than fifteen thousand Molossians. After such a disaster befell the inhabitants of Epeirus, the Lacedaemonians, as soon as they had learned the facts, sent a force to give aid to the Molossians, by means of which they curbed the barbarians' great audacity.

While these events were taking place, the Parians, in accordance with an oracle, sent out a colony to the Adriatic, founding it on the island of Pharos, as it is called, with the co-operation of the tyrant Dionysius. He had already dispatched a colony to the Adriatic not many years previously and had founded the city known as Lissus. From this as his base Dionysius . . . Since he had the leisure, he built dockyards with a capacity for two hundred triremes and threw about the city a wall of such size that its circuit was the greatest possessed by any Greek city. He also constructed large gymnasia along the Anapus River, and likewise temples of the gods and whatever else would contribute to the growth and renown of the city.

The campaign of Dionysius against Tyrrhenia and the plundering of the temple (14).

14. At the conclusion of the year, in Athens; [384] Diotrephes was archon and in Rome the consuls elected were Lucius Valerius and Aulus Mallius, and the Eleians celebrated the Ninety-ninth Olympiad, that in which Dicon of Syracuse won the "stadion." This year the Parians, who had settled Pharos, allowed the previous barbarian inhabitants to remain unharmed in an exceedingly well fortified place, while they themselves founded a city by the sea and built a wall about it. Later, however, the old barbarian inhabitants of the island took offence at the presence of the Greeks and called in the Illyrians of the opposite mainland. These, to the number of more than ten thousand, crossed over to Pharos in many small boats, wrought havoc, and slew many of the Greeks. The governor of Lissus appointed by Dionysius sailed with a good number of triremes against the light craft of the Illyrians, sinking some and capturing others, and slew more than five thousand of the barbarians, while taking some two thousand captive.

Dionysius, in need of money, set out to make war against Tyrrhenia with sixty triremes. The excuse he offered was the suppression of the pirates, but in fact he was going to pillage a holy temple, richly provided with dedications, which was located in the seaport of the Tyrrhenian city of Agylle, the name of the port being Pyrgi. Putting in by night, he disembarked his men, attacked at daybreak, and achieved his design; for he overpowered the small number of guards in the place, plundered the temple, and amassed no less than a thousand talents. When the men of Agylle came out to bring help, he overpowered them in battle, took many prisoners, laid waste their territory, and then returned to Syracuse. From the booty which he sold he took in no less than five hundred talents. Now that Dionysius was well supplied with money, he hired a multitude of soldiers from every land, and after bringing together a very considerable army, was obviously preparing for a war against the Carthaginians.

These, then, were the events of this year.

The campaign of Dionysius against the Carthaginians; his victory and defeat (15-17).

15. When Phanostratus was archon in Athens, [383] the Romans elected instead of consuls four military tribunes, Lucius Lucretius, Sentius Sulpicius, Lucius Aemilius, and Lucius Furius. This year Dionysius, the tyrant of the Syracusans, after preparations for war upon the Carthaginians, looked about to find a reasonable excuse for the conflict. Seeing, then, that the cities subject to the Carthaginians were favourable to a revolt, he received such as wished to do so, formed an alliance with them, and treated them with fairness. The Carthaginians at first dispatched ambassadors to the ruler and asked for the return of their cities, and when he paid no attention to them, this came to be the beginning of the war.

Now the Carthaginians formed an alliance with the Italian Greeks and together with them went to war against the tyrant; and since they wisely recognised in advance that it would be a great war, they enrolled as soldiers the capable youth from their own citizens, and then, raising a great sum of money, hired large forces of mercenary troops. As general they chose their king Magon and moved many tens of thousands of soldiers across to Sicily and Italy, planning to wage war on both fronts. Dionysius for his part also divided his forces, on the one front fighting the Italian Greeks and on the other the Phoenicians. Now there were many battles here and there between groups of soldiers and minor and continuous engagements, in which nothing of consequence was achieved. But there were two important and famous pitched battles. In the first, near Cabala, as it is called, Dionysius, who put up an admirable fight, was victorious, slaying more than ten thousand of the barbarians and capturing not less than five thousand. He also forced the rest of the army to take refuge on a hill which was fortified but altogether without water. There fell also Magon their king after a splendid combat. The Phoenicians, dismayed at the magnitude of the disaster, at once sent an embassy to discuss terms of peace, but Dionysius declared that his only terms were conditional upon their retiring from the cities of Sicily and paying the cost of the war.

16. This reply was considered by the Carthaginians to be harsh and arrogant and they outgeneralled Dionysius with their accustomed knavery. They pretended that they were satisfied with the terms, but stated that it was not in their power to hand over the cities; and in order that they might discuss the question with their government, they asked Dionysius to agree to a truce of a few days. When the monarch agreed and the truce took effect, Dionysius was overjoyed, supposing that he would forthwith take over the whole of Sicily. The Carthaginians meanwhile gave their king Magon a magnificent funeral and replaced him as general with his son, who, though he was young indeed, was full of ambition and distinguished for his courage. He spent the entire period of the truce drilling and exercising his troops, and what with laborious exercise, hortatory speeches, and training in arms, he rendered the army obedient and competent. At the expiration of the period agreed upon both sides deployed their forces and entered the battle with high spirit. There followed a sharp pitched battle at Cronium, as it is called, and the deity redressed by victory turn for turn the defeat of the Carthaginians. The former victors, who were loudly boasting because of their military success, were unexpectedly tripped up, and they who, because of their defeat, were crestfallen at the outlook, won an unexpected and important victory.

17. Leptines, who was stationed on one wing and excelled in courage, ended his life in a blaze of glory, righting heroically and after slaying many Carthaginians. At his fall the Phoenicians were emboldened and pressed so hard upon their opponents that they put them to flight. Dionysius, whose troops were a select band, at first had the advantage over his opponents; but when the death of Leptines became known and the other wing was crushed, his men were dismayed and took to flight. When the rout became general, the Carthaginians pursued the more eagerly and called out to one another to take no one captive; and so all who were caught were put to death and the whole region close at hand was heaped with dead. So great was the slaughter, as the Phoenicians recalled past injuries, that the slain among the Sicilian Greeks were found to number more than fourteen thousand. The survivors, who found safety in the camp, were preserved by the coming of night. After their great victory in a pitched battle the

Carthaginians retired to Panormus.

The Carthaginians, bearing their victory as men should, dispatched ambassadors to Dionysius and gave him the opportunity to end the war. The tyrant gladly accepted the proposals, and peace was declared on the terms that both parties should hold what they previously possessed, the only exception being that the Carthaginians received both the city of the Selinuntians and its territory and that of Acragas as far as the river called Halycus. And Dionysius paid the Carthaginians one thousand talents.

This was the state of affairs in Sicily.

18. In Asia Glōs, the Persian admiral in the Cyprian War, who had deserted from the King and had called upon both the Lacedaemonians and the king of the Egyptians to make war upon the Persians, was assassinated by certain persons and so did not achieve his purpose. After his death Tachōs took over his operations. He gathered a force about him and founded on a crag near the sea a city which bears the name of Leucê and contains a sacred shrine of Apollo. A short time after his death a dispute over this city arose between the inhabitants of Clazomenae and those of Cymae. Now at first the cities undertook to settle the matter by recourse to war, but later someone suggested that the god be asked which one of the two cities should be master of Leucê. The Pythia decided that it should be the one which should first offer sacrifice in Leucê, and that each side should start from his own city at the rising of the sun on a day upon which both should agree. When the day was set, the Cymaeans assumed that they would have the advantage because their city lay the nearer, but the Clazomenians, though they were a greater distance away, devised the following scheme to get the victory. Choosing by lot colonists from their own citizens, they founded near Leucê a city from which they made their start at the rising of the sun and thus forestalled the Cymaeans in performing the sacrifice. Having become masters of Leucê by this scheme, they decided to hold an annual festival to bear its name which they called the Prophthaseia [the anticipation]. After these events the rebellions in Asia came of themselves to an end.

How Amyntas and the Lacedaemonians made war upon the Olynthians (19, 21-23).

19. After the death of Glōs and Tachōs the Lacedaemonians renounced their undertakings in Asia, but they went on organising affairs in Greece for their own interest, winning over some of the cities by persuasion and getting others into their hands by force through the return of the exiles. From this point they began openly to bring into their own hands the supremacy of Greece, contrary to the common agreements adopted in the time of Antalcidas after intervention by the King of the Persians. In Macedonia Amyntas the king had been defeated by the Illyrians and had relinquished his authority; he had furthermore made a grant to the people of the Olynthians of a large part of the borderland because of his abandonment of political power. At first the people of the Olynthians enjoyed the revenues from the land given them, and when later the king unexpectedly recovered strength and got back his entire kingdom, the Olynthians were not inclined to return the land when he asked for it. Consequently Amyntas gathered an army from his own people, and forming an alliance with the Lacedaemonians persuaded them to send out a general and a strong force against the Olynthians. The Lacedaemonians, having decided to extend their control to the regions about Thrace, enrolled soldiers both from their citizens and from their allies, more than ten thousand in all; the army they turned over to Phoebidas the Spartan with orders to join forces with Amyntas and to make war together with him upon the Olynthians. They also sent out another army against the people of Phlius, defeated them in battle, and compelled them to accept the rule of the Lacedaemonians.

At this time the kings of the Lacedaemonians were at variance with each other on matters of policy. Agesipolis, who was a peaceful and just man and, furthermore, excelled in wisdom, declared that they should abide by their oaths and not enslave the Greeks contrary to the common agreements. He pointed out that Sparta was in ill repute for having surrendered the Greeks of Asia to the Persians and for organising the cities of Greece in her own interest, although she had sworn in the common agreement that she would preserve their autonomy. Agesilaüs, who was by nature a man of action, was fond of war and yearned for dominance over the Greeks.

How the Lacedaemonians seized the Cadmeia (20).

20. When Evander was archon at Athens, [382] the Romans elected six military tribunes with consular power, Quintus Sulpicius, Gaius Fabius, Quintus Servilius, Publius Cornelius. During their term of office, the Lacedaemonians took possession of the Cadmeia in Thebes for the following reasons. Seeing that Boeotia had a large number of cities and that her inhabitants were men of outstanding valour, while Thebes, still retaining her renown of ancient times, was, generally speaking, the citadel of Boeotia, they were mindful of the danger that Thebes, if a suitable occasion arose, might claim the leadership of Greece. Accordingly the Spartans gave secret instructions to their commanders, if ever they found an opportunity, to take possession of the Cadmeia. Acting under these instructions, Phoebidas the Spartan, who had been assigned to a command and was leading an expeditionary force against Olynthus, seized the Cadmeia. When the Thebans, resenting this act, gathered under arms, he joined battle with them and after defeating them exiled three hundred of the most eminent Thebans. Then after he had terrorised the rest and had stationed a strong garrison in the Cadmeia, he went off on his own business. For this act the Lacedaemonians, being now discredited in the eyes of the Greeks, punished Phoebidas with a fine but would not remove the garrison from Thebes. So the Thebans in this way lost their independence and were compelled to take orders from the Lacedaemonians. As the Olynthians continued the war against Amyntas [III], king of the Macedonians, the Lacedaemonians relieved Phoebidas of his command, and installed Phoebidas' brother Eudamidas as general. Giving him three thousand hoplites, they dispatched him to carry on the war against the Olynthians.

21. Eudamidas struck into the territory of the Olynthians and, in conjunction with Amyntas, continued to wage war upon the Olynthians. Thereupon the Olynthians, who had collected a considerable force, had the better in the field because they had more soldiers than the enemy; but the Lacedaemonians, having made ready a considerable force, appointed Teleutias general in charge of it. Teleutias was brother of King Agesilaüs and was greatly admired for his valour by his fellow citizens. He accordingly set out from the Peloponnese with an army and on arriving near the territory of the Olynthians took over the soldiers commanded by Eudamidas. Being now a match for the enemy, he began by plundering the Olynthian territory and dividing among his troops the booty that he had collected; but when the Olynthians and their allies in full force took the field, he gave battle. At first they drew apart after an even contest, but later a stubborn battle was fought in which Teleutias himself fell after a splendid fight and the Lacedaemonians lost more than twelve hundred men, After the Olynthians had met with so remarkable a success, the Lacedaemonians, wishing to repair the loss they had sustained, prepared to send out more numerous forces, while the Olynthians, judging that the Spartans would come with larger forces and that the war would last for a long time, prepared large supplies of grain and procured additional soldiers from their allies.

22. When Demophilus was archon at Athens, [381/0] the Romans elected as military tribunes with consular power Publius Cornelius, Lucius Verginius, Lucius Papirius, Marcus Furius, Valerius, Aulus Manlius, Lucius and Postumius. During their term of office the Lacedaemonians appointed as general Agesipolis their king, gave him an adequate army, and voted to make war on the Olynthians. On his arrival in Olynthian territory, he took under his command the soldiers previously encamped there and continued the war against the inhabitants. The Olynthians, however, engaged in no important battle this year, but to the end fought only by exchanges of missiles and short engagements, being in awe of the strength of the king's army.

How they enslaved the Greek cities contrary to the covenants (23).

23. At the close of the year Pythias was archon [380/79] at Athens, and at Rome six military tribunes with consular power were elected, Titus Quinctius, Lucius Servilius, Lucius Julius, Aquilius, Lucius Lucretius, and Servius Sulpicius; and in this year the Eleians celebrated the hundredth Olympiad, at which Dionysodorus of Tarentum won the stadium race. During their term of office Agesipolis, king of the Lacedaemonians, died of illness after a reign of fourteen years; Cleombrotus his brother succeeded to the throne and reigned for nine years. The Lacedaemonians appointed Polybiadas general and sent him to the war against the Olynthians. He took over the forces, and, prosecuting the war vigorously and with able generalship, was often superior. With ever-increasing success, after several victories, he reduced the Olynthians to a state of siege. In the end he thoroughly cowed his enemies and forced them to become subjects of the Lacedaemonians. With the enrolment of the Olynthians in the Spartan alliance many other states likewise were eager to enlist under the Lacedaemonian standard. As a result the Lacedaemonians at this particular juncture reached their greatest power and won the overlordship of Greece on both land and sea. For the Thebans were secured by a garrison; the Corinthians and the Argives were safely humbled as a result of the previous wars; the Athenians, because of their policy of occupying with colonists the lands of those whom they subdued, had a bad reputation with the Greeks; the Lacedaemonians, however, had given their constant attention to securing a large population and practice in the use of arms, and so were become an object of terror to all because of the strength of their following. Consequently the greatest rulers of that time, the Persian King and Dionysius the tyrant of Sicily, paid court to the Spartan overlordship and sought alliance with them.

How the Carthaginians were endangered when afflicted by a plague (24).

24. When Nicon was archon at Athens, [379/8] the Romans elected six

military tribunes with consular power, Lucius Papirius, Gaius Servilius, Lucius Quinctius, Lucius Cornelius, Lucius Valerius, and Aulus Manlius. During their term of office the Carthaginians invaded Italy and restored their city to the Hipponiatae who had been exiled from it, and, having gathered together all the refugees, they showed themselves very solicitous of their welfare. After this a plague broke out among the inhabitants of Carthage which was so violent and took off so many of the Carthaginians that they risked losing their commanding position. For the Libyans, undervaluing them, seceded, and the Sardinians, thinking they now had an opportunity to oppose the Carthaginians, revolted, and, making common cause, attacked the Carthaginians. About the same time a supernatural disaster befell Carthage; for turmoils and fears and panicky disturbances constantly occurred throughout the city defying explanation; and many men rushed from their houses in arms, having the impression that enemies had burst into the city, and they fought constantly with one another as if with enemies, killing some and wounding others. Finally, after having propitiated the deity by sacrifices and with difficulty rid themselves of their misfortunes, they quickly subdued the Libyans and recovered the island of Sardinia.

How the Thebans recovered the Cadmeia (25-27).

25. When Nausinicus was archon at Athens, [378/7] the Romans elected four military tribunes with consular power, Marcus Cornelius Quintus Servilius, Marcus Furius, and Lucius Quinctius. During their term of office what is known as the Boeotian War broke out between the Lacedaemonians and the Boeotians for the following reasons. When the Lacedaemonians maintained a garrison unjustly in the Cadmeia and had exiled many important citizens, the exiles gathered together, secured the support of the Athenians, and returned by night to their native city. Having first slain in their own houses those who favoured the Lacedaemonian cause, whom they surprised while still asleep, they next rallied the citizens to the cause of freedom and obtained the co-operation of all the Thebans. When the populace had quickly assembled under arms, at daybreak they attempted to assault the Cadmeia. The Lacedaemonians who formed the garrison of the citadel, numbering with their allies not less than fifteen hundred, sent men to Sparta to announce the insurrection of the Thebans and to urge them to send help as soon as possible. Favoured by their position, they slew many of the attackers and wounded severely no small number. The Thebans, anticipating the arrival of a large army from Greece to aid the Lacedaemonians, dispatched envoys to Athens to remind them that they too once aided in restoring the democracy of the Athenians at the time when the Athenians had been enslaved by the Thirty Tyrants, and to request the Athenians to come with all their forces and assist them in reducing the Cadmeia before the arrival of the Lacedaemonians.

26. The Athenian people heard the ambassadors through to the end and voted to dispatch immediately as large a force as possible for the liberation of Thebes, thus repaying their obligation for the former service and at the same time moved by a desire to win the Boeotians to their side and to have in them a powerful partner in the contest against the superiority of the Lacedaemonians. For the Boeotian was reputed to be inferior to none of the Greek nations in the number of its men and in military valour. Finally Demophon, who had been made general, and had immediately raised a levy of five thousand hoplites and five hundred horse, on the following day at dawn led forth his troops from the city,

13

and pressed on at full speed in an effort to outstrip the Lacedaemonians; but the Athenians none the less went on with their preparations for an expedition into Boeotia with all their forces in case of need. Demophon by taking cross-country paths appeared unexpectedly before Thebes. Since many soldiers likewise came hurriedly together from the other cities of Boeotia, there was quickly assembled a great army for the support of the Thebans. For not less than twelve thousand hoplites and more than two thousand horse were assembled. And since they were one and all eager for the siege, dividing their forces they kept making their assaults in relays, maintaining a persistent attack at all times both day and night.

27. The garrison in the Cadmeia under the exhortations of their commanders stoutly defended themselves against their adversaries, expecting that the Lacedaemonians would come shortly with a large army. Now as long as they had sufficient food, they held out stubbornly against the attacks and slew and wounded many of their besiegers, supported by the strength of the citadel; but when the scarcity of provisions increased and the Lacedaemonians, occupied in mustering forces, were long in coming, dissension spread amongst them. For the Lacedaemonians among them thought they should hold out till death, while their partners in war from the allied cities, who were many times their number, declared themselves for surrendering the Cadmeia. Under such compulsion even the men from Sparta itself, who were but few, joined in the evacuation of the citadel. These therefore capitulated on terms and returned to the Peloponnese; but the Lacedaemonians advanced with a considerable force on Thebes, and, coming just too late, were unsuccessful in their attack. They put on trial the three officers of the garrison, sentenced two to death, and inflicted so heavy a fine upon the third that his estate could not pay it. Subsequently the Athenians returned home, and the Thebans assailed Thespiae but were unsuccessful in their attack.

While these things were taking place in Greece, the Romans dispatched five hundred colonists, who were to be exempt from taxes, to Sardinia.

On the Boeotian War and the events connected with it (28-35).

28. When Calleas was archon at Athens, [377/6] the Romans elected as military tribunes with consular power four men, Lucius Papirius, Marcus Publius, Titus Cornelius, and Quintus Lucius. During their term of office, following the failure of the Lacedaemonians at Thebes, the Boeotians, uniting boldly, formed an alliance and gathered a considerable army, expecting that the Lacedaemonians would arrive in Boeotia in great strength. The Athenians sent their most respected citizens as ambassadors to the cities which were subject to the Lacedaemonians, urging them to adhere to the common cause of liberty. For the Lacedaemonians, relying on the size of the force at their disposal, ruled their subject peoples inconsiderately and severely, and consequently many of those who belonged to the Spartan sphere of influence fell away to the Athenians. The first to respond to the plea to secede were the peoples of Chios and Byzantium; they were followed by the peoples of Rhodes and Mytilene and certain others of the islanders; and as the movement steadily gathered force throughout Greece, many cities attached themselves to the Athenians. The democracy, elated by the loyalty of the cities, established a common council of all the allies and appointed representatives of each state. It was agreed by common consent that, while the council should hold its sessions in Athens, every city great and small should be on an equal basis and enjoy but one vote, and that all should continue independent, accepting the Athenians as leaders. The Lacedaemonians, aware that the movement of their cities to secede could not be checked, nevertheless strove earnestly by means of diplomatic missions, friendly words and promises of benefits to win back the peoples who had become estranged. Likewise they devoted themselves assiduously to their preparations for war, for they expected the Boeotian War to be a hard and tedious affair for them, since the Athenians and the rest of the Greeks who participated in the council were allied with the Thebans.

29. While these things were going on, Acoris, the king of the Egyptians, being on unfriendly terms with the Persian King, collected a large mercenary force; for by offering high pay to those who enrolled and doing favours to many of them, he quickly induced many of the Greeks to take service with him for the campaign. Having no capable general, he sent for Chabrias the Athenian, a man distinguished both for his prudence as general and his shrewdness in the art of war, who had also won great repute for personal prowess. Now Chabrias, without first securing the permission of the Athenian people, accepted the appointment and took command of the forces in Egypt and with great dispatch made preparations to tight the Persians. Pharnabazus, who had been appointed by the King general of the Persian armies, prepared large supplies of war material, and also sent ambassadors to Athens, first to denounce Chabrias, who by becoming general of the Egyptians was alienating, so he said, the King's affection from the people of Athens, and, secondly, to urge them to give him Iphicrates as general. The Athenians, being eager to gain the favour of the Persian King and to incline Pharnabazus to themselves, quickly recalled Chabrias from Egypt and dispatched Iphicrates as general to act in alliance with the Persians.

The truce which the Lacedaemonians and Athenians had concluded in the earlier period remained unshaken up to this time. But now Sphodriades the Spartan, who had been placed in command and was by nature flighty and precipitate, was prevailed upon by Cleombrotus, the king of the Lacedaemonians, without the consent of the ephors to occupy the Peiraeus. Sphodriades with more than ten thousand soldiers attempted to occupy the Peiraeus at night, but he was detected by the Athenians and, failing in the attempt, returned without accomplishing anything. He was then denounced before the council of the Spartans, but since he had the kings to support him, he got off by a miscarriage of justice. As a result the Athenians, much vexed at the occurrence, voted that the truce had been broken by the Lacedaemonians. They then decided to make war on them and chose three of their most distinguished citizens as generals, Timotheus, Chabrias, and Callistratus. They voted to levy twenty thousand hoplites and five hundred cavalry, and to man two hundred ships. They likewise admitted the Thebans into the common council on terms equal in all respects. They voted also to restore the land settled by cleruchs to its former owners and passed a law that no Athenian should cultivate lands outside of Attica. By this generous act they recovered the goodwill of the Greeks and made their own leadership more secure.

30. Now many of the other cities for the aforesaid reason were prompted to fall away to Athens; and the first to join in the alliance and the most eager were the cities of Euboea excepting Hestiaea; for Hestiaea, having been treated most generously by the Lacedaemonians while she had suffered terribly in war with the Athenians, had very good reason for maintaining unabated her enmity to Athens and for continuing to observe inviolate her pledge to Sparta. Nevertheless seventy cities eventually entered into alliance with the Athenians and participated on equal footing in the common council. So with the constant increase in the strength of the Athenians and the diminution of that of the Lacedaemonians the two states were now well matched. The Athenians, seeing affairs proceeding to their liking, dispatched a force to Euboea to serve at once as a protection for their allies and to subdue the opposition. In Euboea a short time before this a certain Neogenes with the assistance of Jason of Pherae had gathered soldiers and occupied the citadel of Hestiaea, and so appointed himself tyrant of this country and of the city of the Oreitans. Because of his violent and arrogant rule the Lacedaemonians had then dispatched Theripides against him. Theripides at first endeavoured to prevail upon the tyrant by reasoning with him to leave the citadel; but when the tyrant paid no heed to him, he rallied the people of the district to the cause of freedom, took the place by storm, and restored their freedom to the people of Oreüs. For this reason the people who inhabit what is known as the country of the Hestiaeans continued to be loyal to the Spartans and preserved intact their friendship. Chabrias, in command of the force dispatched by the Athenians, laid waste Hestiacotis, and, fortifying its Metropolis, as it is called, which is situated on a naturally steep hill, left a garrison in it, and then sailed to the Cyclades and won over Peparethos and Sciathos and some other islands which had been subject to the Lacedaemonians.

31. The Spartans, perceiving that the impulse of their allies to secede was not to be checked, put an end to their former severity and began to treat the cities humanely. By this sort of treatment and by benefactions they rendered all their allies more loyal. And now that they saw that the war was becoming more serious and required strict attention, they set ambitiously to work on their various preparations for it, and in particular brought to greater perfection the organisation and distribution of their soldiers and the services. In fact they divided the cities and the soldiers that were levied for the war into ten parts. The first part included the Lacedaemonians, the second and third the Arcadians, the fourth the Eleians, the fifth the Achaeans. Corinthians and Megarians supplied the sixth, the seventh the Sicyonians and Phliasians and the inhabitants of the promontory called Acte, the eighth the Acarnanians, the ninth the Phocians and Locrians, and the last of all the Olynthians and the allies who lived in Thrace. They reckoned one hoplite to two light-armed, and one horseman as equivalent to four hoplites. Such was the organisation, and King Agesilaüs was put in command of the campaign. He was renowned for courage and shrewdness in the art of war and had been all but invincible in the former periods. For in all his wars he won admiration and especially when the Lacedaemonians were fighting the Persians. For he gave battle and won the victory over a force of many times his own number; then he overran a large part of Asia, mastering the open country, and finally would probably have succeeded, had not the Spartans recalled him because of political affairs, in reducing the whole Persian empire to the direst straits. For he was a man of energy, daring but highly intelligent, engaging in hazardous actions. Accordingly the Spartans, seeing that the magnitude of the war called for a first-rate leader, again appointed him commander of the whole war.

32. Agesilaüs led forth his army and reached Boeotia accompanied by all the soldiers, amounting to more than eighteen thousand, in which were the five divisions of Lacedaemonians. Each division contained five hundred men. The company known as Sciritae amongst the Spartans is not drawn up with the rest, but has its own station with the king and it goes to the support of the sections that from time to time are in distress; and since it is composed of picked men, it is an important factor in turning the scale in pitched battles, and generally determines the victory. Agesilaüs also had fifteen hundred cavalry. Passing on then to the city of Thespiae, which was garrisoned by the Lacedaemonians, he encamped near it and for several days rested his men from the hardships of the march. The Athenians, having become aware of the arrival of the Lacedaemonians in Boeotia, immediately went to the assistance of Thebes with five thousand foot-soldiers and two hundred cavalry. When these forces had assembled, the Thebans occupied an oblong crest about twenty stades from the city and, having transformed the obstacle into a bastion, awaited the attack of the enemy; for the reputation of Agesilaüs so overawed them that they were too timid to await his attack on equal terms in the level country. As for Agesilaüs, he led out his army in battle array against the Boeotians, and, when he had drawn near, in the first place launched his light-armed troops against his opponents, thus testing their disposition to fight him. When the Thebans had easily from their higher position thrust his men back, he led the whole army against them closely arrayed to strike them with terror. Chabrias the Athenian, however, leading his mercenary troops, ordered his men to receive the enemy with a show of contempt, maintaining all the while their battle lines, and, leaning their shields against their knees, to wait with upraised spear. Since they did what they were ordered as at a single word of command, Agesilaüs, marvelling at the fine discipline of the enemy and their posture of contempt, judged it inadvisable to force a way against the higher ground and compel his opponents to show their valour in a hand-to-hand contest, and, having learned by trial that they would dare, if forced, to dispute the victory, he challenged them in the plain. When the Thebans would not come down to meet him, he withdrew the phalanx of infantry, dispatched the cavalry and light-armed ranks to plunder the countryside unhampered, and so took a great quantity of spoil.

33. The Spartan advisers, who accompanied Agesilaüs, and his officers expressed to him their surprise that Agesilaüs, who reputedly was a man of energy and had the larger and more powerful force, should have avoided a decisive contest with the enemy. To them Agesilaüs made answer that, as it was, the Lacedaemonians had won the victory without the risk; for when the countryside was being sacked, the Boeotians had not dared to rally to its defence; but if, when the enemy themselves had conceded the victory, he had forced them to endure the risks of battle, perhaps through the uncertainty of fortune the Lacedaemonians might even have come to grief in the contest. Now at the time he was thought in this reply of his to have estimated the possible outcome fairly well, but later in the light of events he was believed to have uttered no mere human saying but a divinely inspired oracle. For the Lacedaemonians, having taken the field against the Thebans with a mighty army and having compelled them to fight for their freedom, met with a great disaster. They were defeated, namely, at Leuctra first, where they lost many of their citizen soldiers and their king Cleombrotus fell; and later, when they fought at Mantineia, they were utterly routed and hopelessly lost their supremacy. For fortune has a knack, when men vaunt themselves too highly, of laying them unexpectedly low and so teaching them to hope for nothing in excess. At any rate Agesilaüs, prudently satisfied with his first success, brought his army through unharmed.

After this Agesilaüs returned with his army to the Peloponnese, while the Thebans, saved by the generalship of Chabrias, marvelled at his skill in strategy. Chabrias, though he had performed many gallant deeds in war, was particularly proud of this bit of strategy and he caused the statues which had been granted to him by his people to be erected to display that posture. The Thebans after the departure of Agesilaüs, leading an expedition against Thespiae, destroyed the advance outpost consisting of two hundred men, but after making repeated assaults on the city itself and accomplishing nothing worthy of mention, led their army back to Thebes. Phoebidas, the Lacedaemonian, who had a considerable garrison in Thespiae, sallied forth from the city, fell rashly upon the retreating Thebans, and lost more than five hundred soldiers, while he himself, fighting brilliantly, after receiving many wounds in front, met a hero's death.

34. Not long after this the Lacedaemonians again took the field against Thebes in the same strength as before, but the Thebans, by occupying certain new obstacles, prevented the enemy from devastating the country, though they did not venture to offer battle in the plains face to face against the whole army of the enemy. As Agesilaüs advanced to the attack, they came out to meet him gradually. A bitter battle raged for a long time, in which at first Agesilaüs' men prevailed, but later, as the Thebans poured forth in full force from the city, Agesilaüs, beholding the multitude of men streaming down upon him, summoned his soldiers by trumpet to withdraw from the battle. The Thebans, who found themselves now for the first time not inferior to the Lacedaemonians, erected a trophy of victory and thereafter faced the army of the Spartans with confidence.

With regard to the fighting of the land forces, such was the issue. At sea about the same time occurred a great naval battle between Naxos and Paros, of which the cause was as follows. Pollis, the admiral of the Lacedaemonians, learning that a large shipment of grain was on its way to Athens in freighters, lay in wait watching for the grain fleet as it put in to port, intending to attack the freighters. The Athenian people, being informed of this, sent out a convoy to guard the grain in transit, which in fact brought it safe to the Peiraeus. Later Chabrias, the Athenian admiral, with the whole navy sailed to Naxos and laid it under siege. Bringing his siege-engines to bear against the walls, when he had shaken them, he then bent every effort to take the city by storm. While these things were going on, Pollis, the admiral of the Lacedaemonians, sailed into port to assist the Naxians. In eager rivalry both sides engaged in a sea-battle, and forming in line of battle charged each other. Pollis had sixty-five triremes; Chabrias eighty-three. As the ships bore down on one another, Pollis, leading the right wing, was first to attack the opposing triremes on the left wing, which Cedon the Athenian commanded. In a brilliant contest he slew Cedon himself and sank his ship; and, in similar fashion engaging the other ships of Cedon and tearing them open with the beaks of his ships, he destroyed some and others he forced to flee. When Chabrias beheld what was happening, he dispatched a squadron of the ships under his command and brought support to the men who were hard pressed and so retrieved the defeat of his own side. He himself with the strongest part of the fleet in a valiant struggle destroyed many triremes and took a large number captive.

35. Although he had thus won the upper hand and forced all the enemies'

ships to flee, he abstained altogether from pursuit. For he recalled the battle of Arginusae and that the assembly of the people, in return for the great service performed by the victorious generals, condemned them to death on the charge that they had failed to bury the men who had perished in the fight; consequently he was afraid, since the circumstances were much the same, that he might run the risk of a similar fate. Accordingly, refraining from pursuit, he gathered up the bodies of his fellow citizens which were afloat, saved those who still lived, and buried the dead. Had he not engaged in this task he would easily have destroyed the whole enemy fleet. In the battle eighteen triremes on the Athenian side were destroyed; on the Lacedaemonian twenty-four were destroyed and eight captured with their crews. Chabrias then, having won a notable victory, sailed back laden with spoils to the Peiraeus and met with an enthusiastic reception from his fellow citizens. Since the Peloponnesian War this was the first naval battle the Athenians had won. For they had not fought the battle of Cnidus with a fleet of their own, but had got the use of the King's fleet and won a victory.

While these things were going on, in Italy Marcus Manlius, who aspired to a tyranny in Rome, was overpowered and slain.

The campaign of the Triballi against Abdera (36).

36. When Charisander was archon at Athens, [376/5] the Romans elected four military tribunes with consular power, Servius Sulpicius, Lucius Papirius, Titus Quinctius; and the Eleians celebrated the one hundred first Olympiad, in which Damon of Thurii won the stadium race. During their term of office, in Thrace the Triballians, suffering from a famine, moved in full force into territory beyond their borders and obtained food from the land not their own. More than thirty thousand invaded the adjacent part of Thrace and ravaged with impunity the territory of Abdera; and after seizing a large quantity of booty they were making their way homeward in a contemptuous and disorderly fashion when the inhabitants of Abdera took the field in full force against them and slew more than two thousand of them as they straggled in disorder homewards. The barbarians then, enraged at what had happened and wishing to avenge themselves upon the Abderites, again invaded their land. The victors in the earlier conflict, being elated by their success and aided by the presence of the Thracians of the neighbouring region, who had sent out a body of men to assist them, drew up their lines opposite to the barbarians. A stubborn battle took place, and since the Thracians suddenly changed sides, the Abderites, now left to fight alone and surrounded by the superior number of the barbarians, were butchered almost to a man, as many as took part in the fight. Just after the Abderites had suffered so great a disaster and were on the point of being besieged, Chabrias the Athenian suddenly appeared with troops and snatched them out of their perils. He drove the barbarians from the country, and, after leaving a considerable garrison in the city, was himself assassinated by certain persons. Timotheus succeeded him as admiral, sailed to Cephallenia, won over the cities there, and likewise persuaded the cities of Acarnania to come over to Athens. After he had made a friend of Alcetas, king of the Molossians, and, speaking generally, had won over the areas belonging to the cities of those regions, he defeated the Lacedaemonians in a naval battle off Leucas. All this he accomplished quickly and easily, not only persuading men by his eloquence, but also winning battles by courage and good generalship. Consequently he won great acclaim, not only among his own fellow citizens but also among the Greeks at large. Thus stood the fortunes of

Timothetis.

37. While these things were going on, the Thebans made an expedition against Orchomenus with five hundred picked men and performed a memorable action. For as the Lacedaemonians maintained a garrison of many soldiers in Orchomenus and had drawn up their forces against the Thebans, a stiff battle took place in which the Thebans, attacking twice their number, defeated the Lacedaemonians. Never indeed had such a thing occurred before; it had seemed enough if they won with many against few. The result was that the Thebans swelled with pride, became more and more renowned for their valour, and had manifestly put themselves in a position to compete for the supremacy of Greece.

Of the historians, Hermeias of Methymne brought to a close with this year his narrative of Sicilian affairs, having composed ten books, or, as some divide the work, twelve.

38. When Hippodamas was archon at Athens, [375/4] the Romans elected four military tribunes with consular power, Lucius Valerius, Lucius Manlius, Servius Sulpicius, and Lucretius. During their term of office Artaxerxes, King of the Persians, intending to make war on the Egyptians and being busily engaged in organising a considerable mercenary army, decided to effect a settlement of the wars going on in Greece. For by this means he particularly hoped that the Greeks, once released from their domestic wars, would be more ready to accept mercenary service. Accordingly he sent ambassadors to Greece to urge the cities to enter into a general peace by agreement. The Greeks welcomed his proposal because they wearied of the uninterrupted series of wars, and all agreed to make peace on the condition that all the cities should be independent and free from foreign garrisons. Accordingly the Greeks appointed agents who, going from city to city, proceeded to evacuate all the garrisons. The Thebans alone would not agree that the ratification of the peace should be made city by city, but insisted that all Boeotia should be listed as subject to the confederacy of the Thebans. When the Athenians opposed this in the most contentious manner, Callistratus, their popular leader, reciting their reasons, while, on behalf of the Thebans, Epameinondas delivered the address before the general assembly with marvellous effect, the result was that though the terms of the peace were harmoniously concluded for all the other Greek states, the Thebans alone were refused participation in them; and, through the influence of Epameinondas, who by his own personal merits inspired his fellow citizens with patriotic spirit, they were emboldened to make a stand against the decision of all the rest. For the Lacedaemonians and Athenians, who had constantly been rivals for the hegemony, now yielded one to the other, the one being judged worthy to rule on land, the other on the sea. They were consequently annoyed by the claims to leadership advanced by a third contender and sought to sever the Boeotian cities from the Theban confederation.

39. The Thebans, who excelled in bodily strength and prowess and had already conquered the Lacedaemonians in numerous battles, were elated in spirit and eager to dispute the supremacy on land. Nor were they cheated of their hope, both for the aforesaid reasons and because they had more good commanders and generals during the period under consideration. Most famous were Pelopidas, Gorgidas, and Epameinondas. Epameinondas, indeed, far excelled not merely those of his own race but even all Greeks in valour and shrewdness in the art of war. He had a broad general education, being particularly interested in the philosophy of Pythagoras. Besides this, being well endowed with physical advantages, it is natural that he contributed very distinguished achievements. Hence even when compelled with a very few citizen soldiers to fight against all the armies of the Lacedaemonians and their allies, he was so far superior to these heretofore invincible warriors that he slew the Spartan king Cleombrotus, and almost completely annihilated the multitude of his opponents. Such were the remarkable deeds which he unexpectedly performed because of his astuteness and the moral excellence he had derived from his education.

However, we shall somewhat later explain these matters more fully in a special chapter; at present we shall turn to the thread of our narrative.

40. After autonomy had been conceded to the various peoples, the cities fell into great disturbances and internal strife, particularly in the Peloponnese. For having been used to oligarchic institutions and now taking foolish advantage of the liberties which democracy allows itself, they exiled many of their good citizens, and, trumping up charges against them, condemned them. Thus falling into internal strife they had recourse to exile and confiscations of property, particularly against those who during the Spartan hegemony had been leaders of their native cities. Indeed in those times the oligarchs had exercised authoritative control over their fellow citizens, and later as the democratic mob recovered its freedom it harboured a grudge. First, however, the exiles of Phialeia, rallying their forces, recovered Heraea, as it is called, a stronghold. And setting out from there, they swooped down upon Phialeia, and at a time when, as it happened, the festival of Dionysus was being celebrated, they fell unexpectedly upon the spectators in the theatre, killed many, persuaded not a few to participate in their folly, and retreated to Sparta. The exiles from Corinth, who, many in number, were living among the Argives, attempted to return, but though admitted into the city by some of their relatives and friends, they were denounced and surrounded, and, as they were about to be apprehended, fearful of the maltreatment their capture would entail, they slew one another. The Corinthians, having charged many of their citizens with assisting the exiles in the attack, put some to death and exiled others. Again, in the city of the Megarians, when some persons endeavoured to overturn the government and were overpowered by the democracy, many were slain and not a few driven into exile. Likewise among the Sicyonians as well a number who tried to effect a revolution but failed were killed. Among the Phliasians, when many who were in exile had seized a stronghold in the country and gathered a considerable number of mercenaries, a battle was fought against the city party, and, when the exiles won the victory, over three hundred of the Phliasians were slain. Later, as the sentinels betrayed the exiles, the Phliasians got the upper hand and executed more than six hundred exiles, while they drove the rest out of the country and compelled them to take refuge in Argos. Such were the disasters that afflicted the Peloponnesian cities.

The campaign of the Persians against Egypt (41-43).

41. When Socratides was archon at Athens, [374/3] the the Romans elected four military tribunes with consular power, Quintus Servilius, Servius Cornelius, and Spurius Papirius. During their term of office King Artaxerxes sent an expedition against the Egyptians, who had revolted from Persia. The leaders of the army were Pharnabazus, commanding the barbarian contingent, and Iphicrates the Athenian, commanding the mercenaries, who numbered twenty thousand. Iphicrates, who had been summoned for the campaign by the King, was given the assignment because of his strategic skill. After Pharnabazus had wasted several years making his preparations, Iphicrates, perceiving that though in talk he was clever, he was sluggish in action, frankly told him that he marvelled that anyone so quick in speech could be so dilatory in action. Pharnabazus replied that it was because he was master of his words but the King was master of his actions. When the Persian army had assembled at the city of Acê it numbered two hundred thousand barbarians under the command of Pharnabazus and twenty thousand Greek mercenaries led by Iphicrates. The triremes numbered three hundred and the thirty-oared vessels two hundred. The number of those conveying food and other supplies was great. At the beginning of the summer the King's generals broke camp with the entire army, and accompanied by the fleet sailing along the coast proceeded to Egypt. When they came near the Nile they found that the Egyptians had manifestly completed their preparations for the war. For Pharnabazus marched slowly and had given plenty of time for the enemy to prepare. Indeed it is the usual custom for the Persian commanders, not being independent in the general conduct of war, to refer all matters to the King and await his replies concerning every detail.

42. The Egyptian king Nectanebôs learned the size of the Persian armies, but was emboldened, chiefly by the strength of the country, for Egypt is extremely difficult of approach, and secondly by the fact that all points of invasion from land or sea had been carefully blocked. For the Nile empties into the Egyptian Sea by seven mouths, and at each mouth a city had been established along with great towers on each bank of the stream and a wooden bridge commanding its entrance. He especially fortified the Pelusiac mouth because it is the first to be encountered by those approaching from Syria and seemed to be the most likely route of the enemy approach. He dug channels connecting with this, fortified the entrances for ships at the most suitable points, and inundated the approaches by land while blocking the sea approaches by embankments. Accordingly it was not easy either for the ships to sail in, or for the cavalry to draw near, or for the infantry to approach. Pharnabazus' staff, finding the Pelusiac mouth so remarkably fortified and guarded by a multitude of soldiers, rejected utterly the plan of forcing a way through it and decided to make the invasion by ship through another mouth. Accordingly they voyaged on the open sea so that the ships should not be sighted by the enemy, and sailed in by the mouth known as Mendesian, which had a beach stretching over a considerable space. Landing here with three thousand men, Pharnabazus and Iphicrates pushed forward to the walled stronghold at the mouth. The Egyptians rushed out with three thousand horse and infantry, and a sharp battle ensued, but many men from their ships came to increase the number of the Persians, until finally the Egyptians were surrounded, many slain, and not a few captured alive; and the rest were driven in confusion into the city. Iphicrates' men dashed in with the defenders inside the walls, took possession of the fortress, razed it, and enslaved the inhabitants.

43. After this, discord set in amongst the commanders, causing the failure of the enterprise. For Iphicrates, learning from the captives that Memphis, the most strategically situated of the Egyptian cities, was undefended, advised sailing immediately up to Memphis before the Egyptian forces arrived there, but Pharnabazus thought they should await the entire Persian force; for in this way the campaign against Memphis would be less dangerous. When Iphicrates demanded that he be given the mercenaries that were on hand and promised if he had them to capture the city, Pharnabazus became suspicious of his boldness and his courage for fear lest he take possession of Egypt for himself. Accordingly when Pharnabazus would not yield, Iphicrates protested that if they let slip the exact moment of opportunity, they would make the whole campaign a failure. Some generals indeed bore a grudge against him and were attempting to fasten unfair charges upon him. Meanwhile the Egyptians, having had plenty of time to recuperate, first sent an adequate garrison into Memphis, and then, proceeding with all their forces against the ravaged stronghold at the Mendesian mouth of the Nile and being now at a great advantage owing to the strength of their position, fought constant engagements with the enemy. With ever-increasing strength they slew many Persians and gained confidence against them. As the campaign about this stronghold dragged on, and the Etesian winds had already set in, the Nile, which was filling up and flooding the whole region with the abundance of its waters, made Egypt daily more secure. The Persian commanders, as this state of affairs constantly operated against them, decided to withdraw from Egypt. Consequently, on their way back to Asia, when a disagreement arose between him and Pharnabazus, Iphicrates, suspecting that he might be arrested and punished as Conon the Athenian had been, decided to flee secretly from the camp. Accordingly, having secured a ship he covertly got away at night and reached port at Athens. Pharnabazus dispatched ambassadors to Athens and accused Iphicrates of being responsible for the failure to capture Egypt. The Athenians, however, replied to the Persians that if they detected him in wrongdoing they would punish him as he deserved, and shortly afterward appointed Iphicrates general in command of their fleet.

On the system of training of Iphicrates and his discoveries in the art of war (44).

44. It will not be out of place to set forth what I have learned about the remarkable character of Iphicrates. For he is reported to have possessed shrewdness in command and to have enjoyed an exceptional natural genius for every kind of useful invention. Hence we are told, after he had acquired his long experience of military operations in the Persian War, he devised many improvements in the tools of war, devoting himself especially to the matter of arms. For instance, the Greeks were using shields which were large and consequently difficult to handle; these he discarded and made small oval ones of moderate size, thus successfully achieving both objects, to furnish the body with adequate cover and to enable the user of the small shield, on account of its lightness, to be completely free in his movements. After a trial of the new shield its easy manipulation secured its adoption, and the infantry who had formerly been called "hoplites" because of their heavy shield, then had their name changed to "peltasts" from the light *pelta* they carried. As regards spear and sword, he made changes in the contrary direction: namely, he increased the length of the spears by half, and made the swords almost twice as long. The actual use of these arms confirmed the initial test and from the success of the experiment won great fame for the inventive genius of the general. He made soldiers' boots that were easy to untie and light and they continue to this day to be called "iphicratids" after him. He also introduced many other useful improvements into warfare, but it would be tedious to write about them. So the Persian expedition against Egypt, for all its huge preparations, disappointed expectations and proved a failure in the end.

45. Throughout Greece now that its several states were in confusion because of unwonted forms of government, and many uprisings were occurring in the midst of the general anarchy, the Lacedaemonians gave assistance to such as were trying to establish oligarchies, while the Athenians supported those groups which clung to democracy. For both these states did maintain the truce for a short time, but then, acting in co-operation with their affiliated cities renewed the war, no longer respecting the general peace that had been agreed upon. So it came about that in Zacynthos the popular party, being angry and resentful toward those who had held control of the government during the domination of the Lacedaemonians, drove them all into exile. . . . These Zacynthians, having taken refuge with Timotheüs the Athenian in charge of the fleet, joined his naval force and fought with him. Accordingly they made him their confederate, were transported by him to the island, and seized a stronghold by the sea which they called Arcadia. With this as their base and having the support of Timotheüs they inflicted damage upon those in the city. And when the Zacynthians asked the Lacedaemonians to help them, these latter at first sent envoys to Athens to denounce Timotheüs; but then, seeing that the Athenian people favoured the exiles, they organised a fleet, and manning twenty-five triremes sent them to assist the Zacynthians, placing Aristocrates in command.

The campaign of the Lacedaemonians against Corcyra (46-47).

46. While these things were going on, some partisans of the Lacedaemonians in Coreyra revolted against the democracy and called upon the Spartans to dispatch a fleet, promising to betray Coreyra to them. The Lacedaemonians, aware of the great importance that Coreyra had for the aspirants to sea power, made haste to possess themselves of this city. So they immediately dispatched to Coreyra twenty-two triremes, having given the command to Alcidas. They pretended that this expedition was sent to Sicily, in order to be received as friends by the Corcyraeans and then with the assistance of the exiles to occupy the city. The Corcyraeans, discovering the design of the Spartans, kept careful guard over the city and sent envoys to Athens to get help. The Athenians voted help for the Corcyraeans and the Zacynthian exiles, sent to Zacynthos Ctesicles as general in command of the exiles, and prepared to dispatch a naval force to Coreyra.

While these things were going on, the Plataeans in Boeotia, clinging to the alliance with the Athenians, sent to them for soldiers, having decided to hand their city over to the Athenians. At this the Boeotarchs became incensed with the Plataeans, and, being eager to forestall the allied force from Athens, immediately brought a considerable army against the Plataeans. They reached the neighbourhood of Plataeae when the attack was not expected, so that a large number of the Plataeans were arrested in the fields and carried off by the cavalry, while the rest, who had escaped to the city, being helpless without any allies, were forced to make a covenant agreeable to their enemies; they were obliged, namely, to depart from the city with their movable possessions and never again to set foot on Boeotian soil. Thereupon the Thebans, having razed Plataeae completely, pillaged Thespiae as well, which was at odds with them. The Plataeans with their wives and children, having fled to Athens, received equality of civic rights as a mark of favour from the Athenian people.

Such was the state of affairs in Boeotia.

47. The Lacedaemonians appointed Mnasippus general and ordered him to proceed to Corcyra with sixty-five triremes, his forces consisting of fifteen hundred soldiers. Touching at the island, he picked up the exiles, then sailed into the harbour and captured four ships, the three remaining ships having fled to the shore, where they were burned by the Corcyraeans to prevent their falling into the hands of the enemy. He also defeated with his infantry a contingent on land which had seized a certain hill, and generally terrorised the Corcyraeans. The Athenians had some time previously dispatched Timotheüs, Conon's son, with sixty ships to aid Corcyra. He, however, before intervening in their favour, had sailed to the region of Thrace. Here he summoned many cities to join the alliance, and added thirty triremes to his fleet. At this point, because he was too late to assist Corcyra, he was at first deprived of his command as a result of his loss of popularity. Later, however, when he sailed along the Attic coast to Athens, bringing with him a great number of envoys from states which were ready to conclude an alliance with Athens, having added thirty triremes to his fleet and put the whole fleet in good trim for the war, the people repented and reinstated him in his command. They furthermore equipped forty additional triremes, so that altogether he had one hundred thirty; they also provided liberal stores of food, engines of war, and other supplies needed for war. To meet the immediate emergency, they chose Ctesicles general and sent him with five hundred soldiers to aid the Corcyraeans. He arrived there secretly by night and sailed into Corcyra undetected by the besiegers. Finding the inhabitants of the city at strife with one another and handling military matters badly, he composed the dissensions, devoted much attention to the city's business, and heartened the besieged. At first in an unexpected attack on the besiegers he slew about two hundred, and later in a great battle slew Mnasippus and not a few others. Finally he encircled and laid siege to the besiegers and won great approval. The war to possess Corcyra was practically at an end when the Athenian fleet sailed in with the generals Timotheus and Iphicrates. These, having arrived too late for the critical moment, accomplished nothing worth mentioning except that, falling in with some Sicilian triremes which Dionysius had dispatched under the command of Cissides and Crinippus to assist his allies the Lacedaemonians, they captured them with their crews, nine ships in all. By selling the captives as booty they collected more than sixty talents, with which they paid their forces.

While these things were going on, in Cyprus Nicocles the eunuch assassinated the king Evagoras and possessed himself of the royal power over the Salaminians; and in Italy the Romans, arrayed in battle against the Praenestini, defeated them and slew almost all their opponents.

On the earthquake and inundation that took place in the Peloponnesus and the torch that appeared in the heavens (48-50).

48. When Asteius was archon at Athens, [373/2] the Romans elected six military tribunes with consular power, Marcus Furius, Lucius Furius, Aulus Postumius, Lucius Lucretius, Marcus Fabius, and Lucius Postumius. During their term of office great earthquakes occurred in the Peloponnese accompanied by tidal waves which engulfed the open country and cities in a manner past belief; for never in the earlier periods had such disasters befallen Greek cities, nor had entire cities along with their inhabitants disappeared as a result of some divine force wreaking destruction and ruin upon mankind. The extent of the destruction was increased by the time of its occurrence; for the earthquake did not come in the daytime when it would have been possible for the sufferers to help themselves, but the blow came at night, so that when the houses crashed and crumbled under the force of the shock, the population, owing to the darkness and to the surprise and bewilderment occasioned by the event, had no power to struggle for life. The majority were caught in the falling houses and annihilated, but as day returned some survivors dashed from the ruins and, when they thought they had escaped the danger, met with a greater and still more incredible disaster. For the sea rose to a vast height, and a wave towering even higher washed away and drowned all the inhabitants and their native lands as well. Two cities in Achaïa bore the brunt of this disaster, Helice and Bura, the former of which had, as it happened, before the earthquake held first place among the cities of Achaïa. These disasters have been the subject of much discussion. Natural scientists make it their endeavour to attribute responsibility in such cases not to divine providence, but to certain natural circumstances determined by necessary causes, whereas those who are disposed to venerate the divine power assign certain plausible reasons for the occurrence, alleging that the disaster was occasioned by the anger of the gods at those who had committed sacrilege. This question I too shall endeavour to deal with in detail in a special chapter of my history.

49. In Ionia nine cities were in the habit of holding a common assemblage of all the Ionians and of offering sacrifices of great antiquity on a large scale to Poseidon in a lonely region near the place called Mycalê. Later, however, as a result of the outbreak of wars in this neighbourhood, since they were unable to hold the Panionia there, they shifted the festival gathering to a safe place near Ephesus. Having sent an embassy to Delphi, they received an oracle telling them to take copies of the ancient ancestral altars at Helicê, which was situated in what was then known as Ionia, but is known now as Achaïa. So the Ionians in obedience to the oracle sent men to Achatê to make the copies, and they spoke before the council of the Achaeans and persuaded them to give them what they asked. The inhabitants of Helicê, however, who had an ancient saying that they would suffer danger when Ionians should sacrifice at the altar of Poseidon, taking account of the oracle, opposed the Ionians in the matter of the copies, saying that the sanctuary was not the common property of the Achaeans, but their own particular possession. The inhabitants of Bura also took part with them in this. Since the Achaeans by common decree had concurred, the Ionians sacrificed at the altar of Poseidon as the oracle directed, but the people of Helicê scattered the sacred possessions of the Ionians and seized the persons of their representatives, thus committing sacrilege. It was because of these acts, they say, that Poseidon in his anger brought ruin upon the offending cities through the earthquake and the flood. That it was Poseidon's wrath that was wreaked upon these cities they allege that clear proofs are at hand: first, it is distinctly conceived that authority over earthquakes and floods belongs to this god, and also it is the ancient belief that the Peloponnese was an habitation of Poseidon; and this country is regarded as sacred in a way to Poseidon, and, speaking generally, all the cities in the Peloponnese pay honour to this god more than to any other of the immortals. Furthermore, the Peloponnese has beneath its surface huge caverns and great underground accumulations of flowing water. Indeed there are two rivers in it which clearly have underground courses; one of them, in fact, near Phalus, plunges into the ground, and in former times completely disappeared, swallowed up by underground caves, and the other, near

Stymphalus, plunges into a chasm and flows for two hundred stades concealed underground, then pours forth by the city of the Argives. In addition to these statements the pious say further that except for those who committed the sacrilege no one perished in the disaster. Concerning the earthquakes and floods which occurred we shall rest content with what has been said.

How the Thebans defeated the Lacedaemonians in the most famous battle of Leuctra and laid claim to the supremacy of Greece (50-56).

50. When Alcisthenes was archon at Athens, [372/1] the Romans elected eight military tribunes with consular power, Lucius and Publius Valerius, Gaius Terentius, Lucius Menenius, Gaius Sulpicius, Titus Papirius, and Lucius Aemilius, and the Eleians celebrated the hundred second Olympiad in which Damon of Thurii won the stadium race. During their term of office, after the Lacedaemonians had held the supremacy in Greece for almost five hundred years, a divine portent foretold the loss of their empire; for there was seen in the heavens during the course of many nights a great blazing torch which was named from its shape a "flaming beam," and a little later, to the surprise of all, the Spartans were defeated in a great battle and irretrievably lost their supremacy. Some of the students of nature ascribed the origin of the torch to natural causes, voicing the opinion that such apparitions occur of necessity at appointed times, and that in these matters the Chaldeans in Babylon and the other astrologers succeed in making accurate prophecies. These men, they say, are not surprised when such a phenomenon occurs, but rather if it does not, since each particular constellation has its own peculiar cycle and they complete these cycles through age-long movements in appointed courses. At any rate this torch had such brilliancy, they report, and its light such strength that it cast shadows on the earth similar to those cast by the moon.

At this time Artaxerxes the Persian King, seeing that the Greek world was again in a turmoil, sent ambassadors, calling upon the Greeks to settle their internecine wars and establish a common peace in accordance with the covenants they had formerly made. All the Greeks gladly received his proposal, and all the cities agreed to a general peace except Thebes; for the Thebans alone, being engaged in bringing Boeotia under a single confederacy, were not admitted by the Greeks because of the general determination to have the oaths and treaties made city by city. So, remaining outside of the treaties as formerly, the Thebans continued to hold Boeotia in a single confederacy subject to themselves. The Lacedaemonians, being exasperated by this, decided to lead a large army against them as common enemies, for they cast an extremely jealous eye upon their increase of power, fearing lest with the leadership of all Boeotia they might break up the Spartan supremacy, given a suitable opportunity. For they constantly practised gymnastics and had great bodily strength, and since they were naturally lovers of war, they were inferior to no Greek nation in deeds of valour. They had besides leaders conspicuous for their virtues, greatest among them being three men, Epameinondas, Gorgidas, and Pelopidas. The city of the Thebans was full of pride because of the glory of its ancestors in the heroic age and aspired to mighty deeds. In this year, then, the Lacedaemonians were making ready for war, levying armies both of their own citizens and from their allies as well.

51. When Phrasicleides was archon at Athens, [371/0] the Romans elected eight military tribunes with consular power, Publius Manius, Gaius Erenucius, Gaius Sextus, Tiberius Julius, Lucius Lavinius, Publius Tribonius, and Gaius Manlius, and besides Lucius Anthestius. During their term of office the Thebans, since they were not participants in the truce, were forced to undertake alone the war with the Lacedaemonians; for there was no city that could legally join them, because all had agreed to the general peace. The Lacedaemonians, since the Thebans were isolated, determined to fight them and reduce Thebes to complete slavery. Since the Lacedaemonians were making their preparations without concealment and the Thebans were destitute of allies, everyone assumed that they would easily be defeated by the Spartans. Accordingly some of the Greeks who were friendly to the Thebans sympathised with them at the prospect of defeat, while others who were at odds with them were overjoyed at the thought that Thebes would in a trice be reduced to utter slavery. Finally the Lacedaemonians, their huge army ready, gave command of it to Cleombrotus their king, and first of all sent envoys ahead to Thebes, directing the Thebans to permit all of the Boeotian cities to be independent, to people Plataeae and Thespiae, and to restore the land to its former owners. When the Thebans replied that they never meddled with affairs in Laconia and the Spartans had no right to touch those of Boeotia, such being the tenor of their answers, the Lacedaemonians sent Cleombrotus forth immediately with his army against Thebes; and the Spartan allies were eager for the war, confident that there would be no contest or battle but that they would master the Boeotians without a struggle.

52. The Spartans accordingly advanced till they came to Coroneia, where they encamped and waited for such of their allies as were tardy. The Thebans, in view of the presence of the enemy, first voted to remove their wives and children to safety in Athens, then chose Epameinondas general and turned over to him the command in the war, giving him as his advisers six boeotarchs. Epameinondas, having conscripted for the battle all Thebans of military age and the other Boeotians who were willing and qualified, led forth from Thebes his army, numbering in all not more than six thousand. As the soldiers were marching out from the city it seemed to many that unfavourable omens appeared to the armament. For by the gates Epameinondas was met by a blind herald, who, seeking recovery of runaway slaves, just as was usual, cried his warning not to take them from Thebes nor to spirit them away, but to bring them home and keep them secure. Now the older people amongst those who heard the herald considered it an omen for the future; but the younger folk kept quiet so as not to appear through cowardice to hold Epameinondas back from the expedition. Epameinondas replied to those who told him that he must observe the omens:

> One only omen is best, to fight for the land that is ours. [Homer: *Il.*,12.243]

Though Epameinondas astounded the cautious by his forthright answer, a second omen appeared more unfavourable than the previous one. For as the clerk advanced with a spear and a ribbon attached to it and signalled the orders from headquarters, a breeze came up and, as it happened, the ribbon was torn from the spear and wrapped itself around a slab that stood over a grave, and there were buried in this spot some Lacedaemonians and Peloponnesians who had died in the expedition under Agesilaüs. Some of the older folk who again chanced to be there protested earnestly against leading the force out in the face of the patent opposition of the gods; but Epameinondas, deigning them no reply, led forth his army, thinking that considerations of nobility and regard for justice should be preferred as motives to the omens in question. Epameinondas accordingly, who was trained in philosophy and applied sensibly the principles of his training, was at the moment widely criticised, but later in the light of his successes was considered to have excelled in military shrewdness and did contribute the greatest benefits to his country. For he immediately led forth his army, seized in advance the pass at Coroneia, and encamped there.

53. Cleombrotus, learning that the enemy had seized the pass first, decided against forcing a passage there, proceeded instead through Phocis, and, when he had traversed the shore road which was difficult, entered Boeotia without danger. In his passage he took some of the fortresses and seized ten triremes. Later, when he reached the place called Leuctra, he encamped there and allowed the soldiers to recover after their march. As the Boeotians neared the enemy in their advance, and then, after surmounting some ridges, suddenly caught sight of the Lacedaemonians covering the entire plain of Leuctra, they were astounded at beholding the great size of the army. When the boeotarchs held a conference to decide whether they ought to remain and fight it out with an army that many times outnumbered them, or whether they should retreat and join battle in a commanding position, it chanced that the votes of the leaders were equal. For of the six boeotarchs, three thought that they should withdraw the army, and three that they should stay and fight it out, and among the latter Epameinondas was numbered. In this great and perplexing deadlock, the seventh boeotarch came to vote, whom Epameinondas persuaded to vote with him, and thus he carried the day. So the decision to stake all on the issue of battle was thus ratified. Epameinondas, saw that the soldiers were superstitious on account of the omens that had occurred, earnestly desired through his own ingenuity and strategy to reverse the scruples of the soldiery. Accordingly, a number of men having recently arrived from Thebes, he persuaded them to say that the arms on the temple of Heracles had surprisingly disappeared and that word had gone abroad in Thebes that the heroes of old had taken them up and set off to help the Boeotians. He placed before them another man as one who had recently ascended from the cave of Trophonius, who said that the god had directed them, when they won at Leuctra, to institute a contest with crowns for prizes in honour of Zeus the king. This indeed is the origin of this festival which the Boeotians now celebrate at Lebadeia.

54. An aider and abettor of this device was Leandrias the Spartan, who had been exiled from Lacedaemon and was then a member of the Theban expedition. He was produced in the assembly and declared that there was an ancient saying amongst the Spartans, that they would lose the supremacy when they should be defeated at Leuctra at the hands of the Thebans. Certain local oracle-mongers likewise came up to Epameinondas, saying that the Lacedaemonians were destined to meet with a great disaster by the tomb of the daughters of Leuctrus and Scedasus for the following reasons. Leuctrus was the person for whom this plain was named. His daughters and those of a certain Scedasus as well, being maidens, were violated by some Lacedaemonian ambassadors. The outraged girls, unable to endure their misfortune, called down curses on the country that had sent forth their ravishers and took their lives by their own hands. Many other such occurrences were reported, and when Epameinondas had convened an assembly and exhorted the soldiers by the appropriate pleas to meet the issue, they all shifted their resolutions, rid themselves of their superstition, and with courage in their hearts stood ready for the battle. There came also at this time to aid the Thebans an allied contingent from Thessaly, fifteen hundred infantry, and five hundred horsemen, commanded by Jason. He persuaded both the Boeotians and the Lacedaemonians to make an armistice and so to guard against the caprices of Fortune. When the truce came into effect, Cleombrotus set out with his army from Boeotia, and there came to meet him another large army of Lacedaemonians and their allies under the command of Archidamus, son of Agesilaüs. For the Spartans,seeing the preparedness of the Boeotians, and taking measures to meet their boldness and recklessness in battle, had dispatched the second army to overcome by the superior number of their combatants the daring of the enemy. Once these armies had united, the Lacedaemonians thought it cowardly to fear the valour of the Boeotians. So they disregarded the truce and with high spirits returned to Leuctra. The Boeotians too were ready for the battle and both sides marshalled their forces.

55. Now on the Lacedaemonian side the descendants of Heracles were stationed as commanders of the wings, namely Cleombrotus the king and Archidamus son of the King Agesilaüs, while on the Boeotian side Epameinondas, by employing an unusual disposition of his own, was enabled through his own strategy to achieve his famous victory. He selected from the entire army the bravest men and stationed them on one wing, intending to fight to the finish with them himself. The weakest he placed on the other wing and instructed them to avoid battle and withdraw gradually during the enemy's attack. So then,by arranging his phalanx in oblique formation, he planned to decide the issue of the battle by means of the wing in which were the elite. When the trumpets on both sides sounded the charge and the armies simultaneously with the first onset raised the battle-cry, the Lacedaemonians attacked both wings with their phalanx in crescent formation, while the Boeotians retreated on one wing, but on the other engaged the enemy in double-quick time. As they met in hand-to-hand combat, at first both fought ardently and the battle was evenly poised; shortly, however, as Epameinondas' men began to derive advantage from their valour and the denseness of their lines, many Peloponnesians began to fall. For they were unable to endure the weight of the courageous fighting of the elite corps; of those who had resisted some fell and others were wounded, taking all the blows in front. Now as long as King Cleombrotus of the Lacedaemonians was alive and had with him many comrades-in-arms who were quite ready to die in his defence, it was uncertain which way the scales of victory inclined; but when, though he shrank from no danger, he proved unable to bear down his opponents, and perished in an heroic resistance after sustaining many wounds, then, as masses of men thronged about his body, there was piled up a great mound of corpses.

56. There being no one in command of the wing, the heavy column led by Epameinondas bore down upon the Lacedaemonians, and at first by sheer force caused the line of the enemy to buckle somewhat; then, however, the Lacedaemonians, fighting gallantly about their king, got possession of his body, but were not strong enough to achieve victory. For as the corps of elite outdid them in feats of courage, and the valour and exhortations of Epameinondas contributed greatly to its prowess, the Lacedaemonians were with great difficulty forced back; at first, as they gave ground they would not break their formation, but finally, as many fell and the commander who would have rallied them had died, the army turned and fled in utter rout. Epameinondas' corps pursued the fugitives, slew many who opposed them, and won for themselves a most glorious victory. For since they had met the bravest of the Greeks and with a small force had miraculously overcome many times their number, they won a great reputation for valour. The highest praises were accorded the general Epameinondas, who chiefly by his own courage and by his shrewdness as a commander had defeated in battle the invincible leaders of Greece. More than four thousand Lacedaemonians fell in the battle but only about three hundred Boeotians. Following the battle they made a truce to allow for taking up the bodies of the dead and the departure of the Lacedaemonians to the Peloponnese.

Such was the outcome of events relating to the battle of Leuctra.

How there took place among the Argives a great slaughter which was called the reign of club-law (57-58).

On Jason, the tyrant of Pherae, and his successors (57, 60, 80, 95).

57. When the year had ended, at Athens [370-69] Dysnicetus was archon, and in Rome military tribunes with consular power were elected, four in number: Quintus Servilius, Lucius Furius, Gaius Licinius, and Publius Coelius. During their term of office the Thebans, taking the field with a large army against Orchomenus, aimed to reduce the city to slavery, but when Epameinondas advised them that any who aimed at supremacy over the Greeks ought to safeguard by their generous treatment what they had achieved by their valour, they changed their mind. Accordingly they reckoned the people of Orchomenus as belonging to the territory of their allies, and later, having made friends of the Phocians, Aetolians, and Locrians, returned to Boeotia again. Jason, tyrant of Pherae, whose power was constantly increasing, invaded Locris, first took Heracleia in Trachinia by treachery, laid it waste, and gave the country to the Oetaeans and Malians; then later, moving into Perrhaebia, he won over some of the cities by generous promises, and subdued others by force. As his position of influence speedily became established, the inhabitants of Thessaly looked with suspicion on his aggrandisement and encroachments.

While these things were going on, in the city of Argos civil strife broke out accompanied by slaughter of a greater number than is recorded ever to have occurred anywhere else in Greece. Among the Greeks this revolutionary movement was called "Club-law," receiving this appellation on account of the manner of the execution.

58. Now the strife arose from the following causes: the city of Argos had a democratic form of government, and certain demagogues instigated the populace against the outstanding citizens of property and reputation. The victims of the hostile charges then got together and decided to overthrow the democracy. When some of those who were thought to be implicated were subjected to torture, all but one, fearing the agony of torture, committed suicide, but this one came to terms under torture, received a pledge of immunity, and as informer denounced thirty of the most distinguished citizens, and the democracy without a thorough investigation put to death all those who were accused and confiscated their property. Many others were under suspicion, and as the demagogues supported false accusations, the mob was wrought up to such a pitch of savagery that they condemned to death all the accused, who were many and wealthy. When, however, more than twelve hundred influential men had been removed, the populace did not spare the demagogues themselves. For because of the magnitude of the calamity the demagogues were afraid that some unforeseen turn of fortune might overtake them and therefore desisted from their accusation, whereas the mob, now thinking that they had been left in the lurch by them, were angry at this and put to death all the demagogues. So these men received the punishment which fitted their crimes as if some divinity were visiting its just resentment upon them, and the people, eased of their mad rage, were restored to their senses.

59. About the same time, Lycomedes of Tegea prevailed upon the Arcadians to form a single confederacy with a common council to consist of ten thousand men empowered to decide issues of war and peace. Since civil war broke out in Arcadia on a large scale and the quarrelling factions came to a decision by force of arms, many were killed and more than fourteen hundred fled, some to Sparta, others to Pallantium. Now these latter refugees were surrendered by the Pallantians and slaughtered by the victorious party, whereas those who took refuge in Sparta prevailed upon the Lacedaemonians to invade Arcadia. Accordingly King Agesilaüs with an army and the band of fugitives invaded the territory of the Tegeans, who were believed to have been the cause of the insurrection and the expulsions. By devastation of the countryside and assaults upon the city, he cowed the Arcadians of the opposing party.

60. While these things were going on, Jason, tyrant of Pherae, because of his superior shrewdness as a general and his success in attracting many of his neighbours into an alliance, prevailed upon the Thessalians to lay claim to the supremacy in Greece; for this was a sort of prize for valour open to those strong enough to contend for it. Now it happened that the Lacedaemonians had sustained a great disaster at Leuctra; that the Athenians laid claim to the mastery of the sea only; that the Thebans were unworthy of first rank; and that the Argives had been brought low by civil wars and internecine slaughter, so the Thessalians put Jason forward as leader of the whole country, and as such gave him supreme command in war. Jason accepted the command, won over some of the tribes near by, and entered into alliance with Amyntas king of the Macedonians.

A peculiar coincidence befell in this year, for three of those in positions of power died about the same time. Amyntas, son of Arrhidaeus, king of Macedonia, died after a rule of twenty-four years, leaving behind him three sons, Alexander, Perdiccas, and Philip. The son Alexander succeeded to the throne and ruled for one year. Likewise Agesipolis, king of the Lacedaemonians, died after ruling a year, the kingship going to Cleomenes his brother who succeeded to the throne and had a reign of thirty-four years. Thirdly, Jason of Pherae, who had been chosen ruler of Thessaly and was reputed to be governing his subjects with moderation, was assassinated, either, as Ephorus writes, by seven young men who conspired together for the repute it would bring, or, as some historians say, by his brother Polydorus. This Polydorus himself also, after succeeding to the position of leader, ruled for one year. Duris of Samos, the historian, began his History of the Greeks at this point.

These then were the events of this year.

61. When Lysistratus was archon at Athens, [389/8] civil strife arose among the Romans, one party thinking there should be consuls, others that military tribunes should be chosen. For a time then anarchy supervened on civil strife, later they decided to choose six military tribunes, and those elected were Lucius Aemilius, Gaius Verginius, Servius Sulpicius, Lucius Quintius, Gaius Cornelius, and Gaius Valerius. During their term of office Polydorus of Pherae the ruler of Thessaly was poisoned by Alexander his nephew, who had challenged him to a drinking bout, and the nephew Alexander succeeded to the rule as overlord and held it for eleven years. Having acquired the rule illegally and by force, he administered it consistently with the policy he had chosen to follow. For while the rulers before him had treated the peoples with moderation and were therefore loved, he was hated for his violent and severe rule. Accordingly, in fear of his lawlessness, some Larissaeans, called Aleuadae because of their noble descent, conspired together to overthrow the overlordship. Journeying from Larissa to Macedonia, they prevailed upon the King Alexander to join them in overthrowing the tyrant. While they were occupied with these matters, Alexander of Pherae, learning of the preparations against him, gathered such men as were conveniently situated for the campaign, intending to give battle in Macedonia, but the Macedonian king, accompanied by refugees from Larissa, anticipated the enemy by invading Larissa with the army, and having been secretly admitted by the Larissaeans within the fortifications, he mastered the city with the exception of the citadel. Later he took the citadel by siege, and, having also won the city of Crannon, at first covenanted to restore the cities to the Thessalians, but then, in contempt of public opinion, he brought into them garrisons of considerable strength and held the cities himself. Alexander of Pherae, hotly pursued and alarmed at the same time, returned to Pherae.

Such was the state of affairs in Thessaly.

The accomplishments of the Thebans during their invasions of the Peloponnesus (62-66, 69, 75, 82-88 passim).

62. In the Peloponnese, the Lacedaemonians dispatched Polytropus as general to Arcadia with a thousand citizen hoplites and five hundred Argive and Boeotian refugees. He reached the Arcadian Orchomenus and guarded it closely since it was on friendly terms with Sparta. Lycomedes of Mantineia, general of the Arcadians, with five thousand men styled the elite, came to Orchomenus. As the Lacedaemonians led forth their army from the city a great battle ensued in which the Lacedaemonian general was killed and two hundred others, while the rest were driven into the city. The Arcadians, in spite of their victory, felt a prudent respect for the strength of Sparta and believed that they would not be able by themselves to cope with the Lacedaemonians. Accordingly, associating Argives and Eleians with themselves, they first sent envoys to Athens requesting them to join in an alliance against the Spartans, but as no one heeded them, they sent an embassy to the Thebans and persuaded them to join an alliance against the Lacedaemonians. Immediately, then, the Boeotians led out their army, taking some Locrians and Phocians along as allies. Now these men advanced against the Peloponnese under the boeotarchs Epameinondas and Pelopidas, for the other boeotarchs had willingly relinquished the command to these in recognition of their shrewdness in the art of war and their courage. When they reached Arcadia, the Arcadians, Eleians, Argives,and all the other allies joined them in full force. When more than fifty thousand had gathered, their leaders sitting in council decided to march upon Sparta itself and lay waste all Laconia.

63. As for the Lacedaemonians, since they had cast away many of their young men in the disaster at Leuctra and in their other defeats had lost not a few, and were, taking all together, restricted by the blows of fortune to but few citizen soldiers, and, furthermore, since some of their allies had seceded and others were experiencing a shortage of men for reasons similar to their own, they sank into a state of great weakness. Hence they were compelled to have recourse to the aid of the Athenians, the very people over whom they had once set up thirty tyrants, whom they had forbidden to rebuild the walls of their city, whose city they had aimed utterly to destroy, and whose territory, Attica, they wished to turn into a sheep-walk. Yet, after all, nothing is stronger than necessity and fate, which compelled the Lacedaemonians to request the aid of their bitterest enemies. Nevertheless they were not disappointed of their hopes, for the Athenian people, magnanimous and generous, were not terrified by the power of Thebes, and voted to aid with all their forces the Lacedaemonians now that they were in danger of enslavement. Immediately they appointed Iphicrates general and dispatched him with twelve thousand young men the self-same day. Iphicrates, then, whose men were in high spirits, advanced with the army at top speed. Meanwhile the Lacedaemonians, as the enemy took up quarters on the borders of Laconia, issued in full force from Sparta and marched on to meet them, weakened in military force but strong in inward courage. Now Epameinondas and the others, perceiving that the country of the Lacedaemonians was difficult to invade, thought it not to their advantage to make the invasion with such a large force in a body, and so decided to divide their army into four columns and enter at several points.

64. Now the first contingent, composed of the Boeotians, took the middle route to the city known as Sellasia and caused its inhabitants to revolt from the Lacedaemonians. The Argives, entering by the borders of Tegeatis, engaged in battle the garrison set to guard the pass, slew its leader Alexander the Spartan and about two hundred of the rest, amongst whom were the Boeotian refugees. The third contingent, composed of the Arcadians and containing the largest number, invaded the district called Sciritis, which had a large garrison under Ischolas, a man of conspicuous valour and shrewdness. Himself one of the most distinguished soldiers, he accomplished an heroic and memorable deed. Seeing that, because of the overwhelming number of the enemy, all who joined battle with them would be killed, he decided that while it was not in keeping with Spartan dignity to abandon his post in the pass, yet it would be useful to his country to preserve the men. He therefore in an amazing manner provided for both objects and emulated the courageous exploit of King Leonidas at Thermopylae. For he picked out the young men and sent them back to Sparta to be of service to her in her hour of deadly peril. He himself, keeping his post with the older men, slew many of the enemy, but finally, encircled by the Arcadians, perished with all his corps. The Eleians, who formed the fourth contingent, marching by other unguarded regions, reached Sellasia, for this was the locality designated to all as the rendezvous. When all the army had gathered in Sellasia, they advanced upon Sparta itself, sacking and burning the countryside.

65. Now the Lacedaemonians, who for five hundred years had preserved Laconia un-devastated, could not then bear to see it being sacked by the enemy, hot-headedly were ready to rush forth from the city; but being restrained by the elders from advancing too far from their native land, lest some one attack it, they were finally prevailed upon to wait quietly and keep the city safe. Now Epameinondas descended through the Taygetus into the Eurotas valley and was engaged in crossing the river, whose current was swift since it was the winter season, when the Lacedaemonians, seeing their opponents' army thrown into confusion by the difficulty of the crossing, seized the opportunity favourable for attack. Leaving the women, children, and the old men as well in the city to guard Sparta, they marshalled in full force the men of military age, streamed forth against the enemy, fell upon them suddenly as they crossed, and wrought heavy slaughter. As the Boeotians and Arcadians fought back and began to encircle the enemy with their superior numbers, the Spartans, having slain many, withdrew to the city, for they had clearly displayed their own courage. Following this, as Epameinondas in full force made a formidable assault on the city, the Spartans with the aid of their strong natural defences slew many of those who pressed rashly forward, but finally the besiegers applied great pressure and thought at first they had overcome Sparta by force; but as those who tried to force their way were some slain, some wounded, Epameinondas recalled the soldiers with the trumpet, but the men of their own accord would approach the city, and would challenge the Spartans to a pitched battle, bidding them otherwise admit their inferiority to the enemy. When the Spartans replied to the effect that when they found a suitable occasion they would stake everything on one battle, they departed from the city, and when they had devastated all Laconia and amassed countless spoils, they withdrew to Arcadia.

Thereupon the Athenians, who had arrived on the scene too late for action, returned to Attica without accomplishing anything of note; but others of their allies, to the number of four thousand men, came to reinforce the Lacedaemonians. Besides these they attached to their numbers the Helots who had been newly emancipated, a thousand, and two hundred of the Boeotian fugitives, and summoned no small number from the neighbouring cities, so that they created an army comparable to that of the enemy. As they maintained these in one body and trained them, they gained more and more confidence and made themselves ready for the decisive contest.

The synoecismos of Messenê by the Thebans (66-67).

66. Now Epameinondas, whose nature it was to aim at great enterprises and to crave everlasting fame, counselled the Arcadians and his other allies to resettle Messenê, which for many years had remained stripped of its inhabitants by the Lacedaemonians, for it occupied a position well suited for operations against Sparta. When they all concurred, he sought out the remnants of the Messenians, and registering as citizens any others who so wished he founded Messenê again, making it a populous city. Among them he divided the land, and reconstructing its buildings restored a notable Greek city and gained the widespread approbation of all men.

Here I think it not unsuitable, since Messenê has so often been captured and razed, to recapitulate its history from the beginning. In ancient times the line of Neleus and Nestor held it down to Trojan times; then Orestes, Agamemnon's son, and his descendants down to the return of the Heracleidae; following which Cresphontes received Messenê as his portion and his line ruled it for a time; but later when Cresphontes' descendants had lost the kingship, the Lacedaemonians became masters of it. After this, at the death of the Lacedaemonian king Teleclus, the Messenians were defeated in a war by the Lacedaemonians. This war is said to have lasted twenty years, for the Lacedaemonians had taken an oath not to return to Sparta unless they should have captured Messenê. Then it was that the children called partheniae were born and founded the city of Tarentum. Later, however, while the Messenians were in slavery to the Lacedaemonians, Aristomenes persuaded the Messenians to revolt from the Spartans, and he inflicted many defeats upon the Spartans at the time when the poet Tyrtaeus was given by the Athenians as a leader to Sparta. Some say that Aristomenes lived during the twenty-year war. The last war [464-455] between them was on the occasion of a great earthquake; practically all Sparta was destroyed and left bare of men, and the remnants of the Messenians settled Ithome with the aid of the Helots who joined the revolt, after Messenê had for a long time been desolate. When they were unsuccessful in all their wars and were finally driven from their homes, they settled in Naupactus, a city which the Athenians had given them for an abode. Furthermore some of their number were exiled to Cephallenia, while others settled in Messana in Sicily, which was named after them. Finally at the time under discussion the Thebans, at the instigation of Epameinondas, who gathered together the Messenians from all quarters, settled Messenê and restored their ancient land to them.

Such then were the many important vicissitudes of Messenian history.

The campaign of the Boeotians against Thessaly (67).

67. The Thebans, having accomplished in eighty-five days all that is narrated above, and having left a considerable garrison for Messenê, returned to their own land. The Lacedaemonians, who had unexpectedly got rid of their enemies, sent to Athens a commission of the most distinguished Spartans, and came to an agreement over the supremacy: the Athenians should be masters of the sea, the Lacedaemonians of the land; but after this in both cities they set up a joint command. The Arcadians now appointed Lycomedes their general, gave him the corps they called their élite, five thousand in number, and took the field against Pellene in Laconia. Having taken the city by force, they slew the Lacedaemonians who had been left behind there as a garrison, over three hundred men, enslaved the city, devastated the countryside, and returned home before assistance came from the Lacedaemonians. The Boeotians, summoned by the Thessalians to liberate their cities and to overthrow the tyranny of Alexander of Pherae, dispatched Pelopidas with an army to Thessaly, after giving him instructions to arrange Thessalian affairs in the interests of the Boeotians. Having arrived in Larissa and found the acropolis garrisoned by Alexander of Macedon, he obtained its surrender. Then proceeding into Macedon, where he made an alliance with Alexander the Macedonian king, he took from him as a hostage his brother Philip, whom he sent to Thebes. When he had settled Thessalian affairs as he thought fit in the interest of the Boeotians, he returned home.

68. After these events, Arcadians, Argives, and Eleians, making common cause, decided to take the field against the Lacedaemonians, and having sent a commission to the Boeotians prevailed on them to join in the war. They appointed Epameinondas commander along with other boeotarchs and dispatched seven thousand foot and six hundred horse. The Athenians, hearing that the Boeotian army was about to pass into the Peloponnese, dispatched an army and Chabrias as general against them. He arrived in Corinth, added to his number Megarians, Pellenians, and also Corinthians, and so gathered a force of ten thousand men. Later, when the Lacedaemonians and other allies arrived at Corinth, there were assembled no less than twenty thousand men all told. They decided to fortify the approaches and prevent the Boeotians from invading the Peloponnese. From Cenchreae to Lechaeum they fenced off the area with palisades and deep trenches, and since the task was quickly completed owing to the large number of men and their enthusiasm, they had every spot fortified before the Boeotians arrived. Epameinondas came with his army, inspected the fortifications, and, perceiving that there was a spot very easy of access where the Lacedaemonians were on guard, first challenged the enemy to come forth to a pitched battle, though they were almost three times his number, then when not a man dared to advance beyond the fortified line, but all remained on the defensive in their palisaded camp, he launched a violent attack upon them. Accordingly, throughout the whole area heavy assaults were made, but particularly against the Lacedaemonians, for their terrain was easily assailed and difficult to defend. Great rivalry arose between the two armies, and Epameinondas, who had with him the bravest of the Thebans, with great effort forced back the Lacedaemonians, and, cutting through their defence and bringing his army through, passed into the Peloponnese, thereby accomplishing a feat no whit inferior to his former mighty deeds.

69. Having proceeded straightway to Troezen and Epidaurus, he ravaged the countryside but could not seize the cities, for they had garrisons of considerable strength, yet Sicyon, Phlius, and certain other cities he so intimidated as to bring them over to his side. When he invaded Corinth, and the Corinthians sallied forth to meet him, he defeated them in battle, and drove them all back inside their walls, but when the Boeotians were so elated by their success that some of them rashly ventured to force their way through the gates into the city, the Corinthians, frightened, took refuge in their houses, but Chabrias the Athenian general made an intelligent and determined resistance, and succeeded in driving the Boeotians out of the city, having also struck down many of them. In the rivalry which followed, the Boeotians gathered all their army in line of battle and directed a formidable blow at Corinth; but Chabrias with the Athenians advanced out of the city, took his station on superior terrain and withstood the attack of the enemy. The Boeotians, however, relying upon the hardihood of their bodies and their experience in continuous warfare, expected to worst the Athenians by sheer might, but Chabrias' corps, having the advantage of superior ground in the struggle and of abundant supplies from the city, slew some of the attackers and severely wounded others. The Boeotians, having suffered many losses and being unable to accomplish anything, beat a retreat. So Chabrias won great admiration for his courage and shrewdness as a general and got rid of the enemy in this fashion.

70. From Sicily, Celts and Iberians to the number of two thousand sailed to Corinth, for they had been sent by the tyrant Dionysius to fight in alliance with the Lacedaemonians, and had received pay for five months. The Greeks, in order to make trial of them, led them forth; and they proved their worth in hand-to-hand fighting and in battles and many both of the Boeotians and of their allies were slain by them. Accordingly, having won repute for superior dexterity and courage and rendered many kinds of service, they were given awards by the Lacedaemonians and sent back home at the close of the summer to Sicily. Following this, Philiscus, who was sent on this mission by King Artaxerxes, sailed to Greece to urge the Greeks to compose their strife and agree to a general peace. All but the Thebans responded willingly; they, however, adhering to their own design, had brought all Boeotia into one confederation and were excluded from the agreement. Since the general peace was not agreed to, Philiscus left two thousand picked mercenaries, paid in advance, for the Lacedaemonians and then returned to Asia.

While these things were going on, Euphron of Sicyon, a particularly rash and crack-brained individual, with accomplices from Argos, attempted to set up a tyranny. Succeeding in his plan, he sent forty of the wealthiest Sicyonians into exile, first confiscating their property, and, when he had secured large sums thereby, he collected a mercenary force and became lord of the city.

71. When Nausigenes was archon at Athens, [368/7] in Rome four military tribunes with consular power were elected, Lucius Papirius, Lucius Menenius, Servius Cornelius, and Servius Sulpicius; and the Eleians celebrated the hundred third Olympiad, in which Pythostratus the Athenian won the stadium race. During their term of office Ptolemy of Alorus, son of Amyntas, assassinated Alexander, his brother-in-law, and was king of Macedon for three years. In Boeotia Pelopidas, whose military reputation rivalled that of Epameinondas, saw that the latter had arranged the Peloponnesian affairs to the advantage of the Boeotians, and was eager to be the instrument whereby districts outside of the Peloponnese were won for the Thebans. Taking along with him as his associate Ismenias, a friend of his, and a man who was admired for his valour, he entered Thessaly. There he met Alexander, the tyrant of Pherae, but was suddenly arrested with Ismenias, and placed under guard. The Thebans, incensed at what had been done, dispatched with all speed eight thousand hoplites and six hundred cavalry into Thessaly, so frightening Alexander that he dispatched ambassadors to Athens for an alliance. The Athenian people immediately sent him thirty ships and a thousand men under the command of Autocles. While Autocles was making the circuit of Euboea, the Thebans entered Thessaly. Though Alexander had gathered his infantry and had many times more horsemen than the Boeotians, at first the Boeotians decided to settle the war by battle, for they had the Thessalians as supporters; but when the latter left them in the lurch and the Athenians and some; other allies joined Alexander, and they found their provisions of food and drink and all their other supplies giving out, the boeotarchs decided to return home. When they had broken camp and were proceeding through level country, Alexander trailed them with a large body of cavalry and attacked their rear. A number of Boeotians perished under the continuous rain of darts, others fell wounded, until finally, being permitted neither to halt nor to proceed, they were reduced to utter helplessness, as was natural when they were also running short of provisions. When they had now abandoned hope, Epameinondas, who was at that time serving as a private soldier, was appointed general by the men. Quickly selecting the light-armed men and cavalry, he took them with him, and, posting himself in the rear, with their aid checked the enemy pursuers and provided complete security for the heavy-armed men in the front ranks; and by wheeling about and offering battle and using masterly formations he saved the army. By these repeated successes he more and more enhanced his own reputation and won the warm approbation of both his fellow citizens and allies. The Thebans brought judgement against the boeotarchs of the day and punished them with a heavy fine.

72. When the reason is asked why a man of such parts was serving as a private soldier in the expedition that was sent to Thessaly, we must give his own plea in defence. In the battle at Corinth Epameinondas, having cut through the guard of the Lacedaemonians on the outwork, though he might have slain many of the enemy, was satisfied with his advantage and desisted from further combat. A serious suspicion arose that he had spared the Lacedaemonians as a personal favour, and those who were jealous of his fame found an opportunity for plausible charges against him. They accordingly brought a charge of treason against him, and the populace, incensed, removed him from the board of boeotarchs, made him a private soldier, and sent him out with the rest. When he had by his achievements wiped out the feeling against him, the people then restored him to his former position of high repute. Shortly after this the Lacedaemonians fought a great battle with the Arcadians and defeated them signally. Indeed since the defeat at Leuctra this was their first stroke of good fortune, and it was a surprising one; for over ten thousand Arcadians fell and not one Lacedaemonian. The priestesses of Dodona had foretold to them that this war would be a tearless one for the Lacedaemonians. After this battle the Arcadians, fearful of the invasions of the Lacedaemonians, founded in a favourable location the city called Great, Megalopolis, by combining to form it twenty villages of the Arcadians known as Maenalians and Parrhasians.

Such were the events in Greece at this time.

73. In Sicily, Dionysius the tyrant having large armies, and perceiving that the Carthaginians were in no condition for war because of the plague which had raged in their midst and the defection of the Libyans, decided to take the field against them. Not having a reasonable excuse for strife, he alleged that the Phoenicians in the empire of Carthage had violated the territory subject to him. He therefore got ready an armament of thirty thousand foot, three thousand horse, three hundred triremes and the supply train appropriate for that force, and invaded Carthaginian territory in Sicily. He immediately won Selinus and Entella, laid waste the whole countryside, and, having captured the city of Eryx, besieged Lilybaeum, but there were so many soldiers in the place that he abandoned the siege. Hearing that the Carthaginians' dockyards had been burned and thinking their whole fleet had been destroyed, he conceived a contempt for them and dispatched only one hundred thirty of his best triremes to the harbour of Eryx, sending all the rest back to Syracuse. The Carthaginians, having unexpectedly manned two hundred ships, sailed against the fleet at anchor in the harbour of Eryx, and, as the attack was unforeseen, they made off with most of the triremes. Later when winter had set in, the two states agreed to an armistice and separated, each going to its own cities. A little later Dionysius fell sick and died, after ruling as overlord for thirty-eight years. His son Dionysius succeeded and ruled as tyrant twelve years.

74. It is not out of keeping with the present narrative to recount the cause of his death and the events which befell this dynast toward the end of his life. Now Dionysius had produced a tragedy at the Lenaea at Athens and had won the victory, and one of those who sang in the chorus, supposing that he would be rewarded handsomely if he were the first to give news of the victory, set sail to Corinth. There, finding a ship bound for Sicily, he transferred to it, and obtaining favouring winds, speedily landed at Syracuse and gave the tyrant news of the victory. Dionysius did reward him, and was himself so overjoyed that he sacrificed to the gods for the good tidings and instituted a drinking bout and great feasts. As he entertained his friends lavishly and during the bout applied himself overzealously to drink, he fell violently ill from the quantity of liquor he had consumed. Now he had an oracle the gods had given him that he should die when he had conquered "his betters," but he interpreted the oracle as referring to the Carthaginians, assuming that these were "his betters." So in the wars that he had many times waged against them he was accustomed to withdraw in the hour of victory and accept defeat willingly, in order that he might not appear to have proved himself "better" than the stronger foe. For all that, however, he could not in the end by his chicanery outwit the destiny Fate had in store for him; on the contrary, though a wretched poet and though judged on this occasion in a competition at Athens, he defeated "better" poets than himself. So in verbal consistency with the decree of the oracle he met his death as a direct consequence of defeating " his betters."

Dionysius the younger on his succession to the tyranny first gathered the populace in an assembly and urged them in appropriate words to maintain toward him the loyalty that passed to him with the heritage that he had received from his father; then, having buried his father with magnificent obsequies in the citadel by the gates called royal, he made secure for himself the administration of the government.

75. When Polyzelus was archon at Athens, [367/6] anarchy prevailed at Rome because of civil dissensions, and in Greece, Alexander, tyrant of Pherae in Thessaly, having lodged accusations about certain matters against the city of Scotussa, summoned its citizens to an assembly and, having surrounded them with mercenaries, slew them all, cast the bodies of the dead into the ditch in front of the walls, and plundered the city from end to end. Epameinondas, the Theban, entered the Peloponnese with an army, won over the Achaeans and some cities besides, and liberated Dymê, Naupactus, and Calydon, which were held by a garrison of the Achaeans. The Boeotians invaded Thessaly also and released Pelopidas from the custody of Alexander, tyrant of Pherae, and to the Phliasians upon whom the Argives were waging war, Chares brought assistance, having been sent with an army under his command by the Athenians; he defeated the Argives in two battles, and after securing the position of the Phliasians, returned to Athens.

76. When the year ended, Cephisodorus was archon at Athens, [366/5] and at Rome the people elected four military tribunes with consular power, Lucius Furius, Paulus Manlius, Servius Sulpicius, and Servius Cornelius. During their term of office, Themison, tyrant of Eretria, seized Oropus, but this city, which belonged to Athens, he quite unexpectedly lost; for when the Athenians took the field against him with far superior forces, the Thebans, who had come to aid him and had taken over from him the city for safekeeping, did not give it back.

While these things were going on, the Coans transferred their abode to the city they now inhabit and made it a notable place; for a large population was gathered into it, and costly walls and a considerable harbour were constructed. From this time on its public revenues and private wealth constantly increased, so much so that it became in a word a rival of the leading cities of Greece.

While these things were going on, the Persian King sent envoys and succeeded in persuading the Greeks to settle their wars and make a general peace with one another. Accordingly the war called Sparto-Boeotian was settled after lasting more than five years counting from the campaign of Leuctra.

In this period there were men memorable for their culture, Isocrates the orator and those who became his pupils, Aristotle the philosopher, and besides these Anaximenes of Lampsacus, Plato of Athens, the last of the Pythagorean philosophers, and Xenophon who composed his histories in extreme old age, for he mentions the death of Epameinondas which occurred a few years later. Then there were Aristippus and Antisthenes, and Aeschines of Sphettus, the Socratic.

77. When Chion was archon at Athens, [365/4] at Rome military tribunes with consular power were elected, Quintus Servilius, Gaius Veturius, Aulus Cornelius, Marcus Cornelius, and Marcus Fabius. During their term of office, though peace prevailed throughout Greece, clouds of war again gathered in certain cities and strange new outbreaks of revolution. For instance, the Arcadian exiles, setting out from Elis, occupied a stronghold known as Lasion of the country called Triphylia. For many years Arcadia and Elis had been disputing the possession of Triphylia, and according as the ascendancy shifted from one country to the other, they had alternately been masters of the district; but at the period in question, though the Arcadians were ruling Triphylia, the Eleians, making the refugees a pretext, took it from the Arcadians. As a result the Arcadians were incensed and at first dispatched envoys demanding a return of the district; but when no one paid any attention to them, they summoned an allied force from the Athenians and with it attacked Lasion. The Eleians coming to the rescue of the refugees, a battle ensued near Lasion in which, being many times outnumbered by the Arcadians, the Eleians were defeated and lost over two hundred men. When the war had started in this way, it came to pass that the disagreement between Arcadians and Eleians widened in scope, for immediately the Arcadians, elated by their success, invaded Elis and took the cities of Margana and Cronion, and Cyparissia and Coryphasium.

While these things were going on, in Macedon Ptolemy of Alorus was assassinated by his brother-in-law Perdiccas after ruling three years; and Perdiccas succeeded to the throne and ruled Macedon for five years.

78. When Timocrates was archon at Athens, [364/3] in Rome three military tribunes with consular power were elected, Titus Quinctius, Servius Cornelius, and Servius Sulpicius; and the hundred fourth Olympiad was celebrated by the Pisans and Arcadians, in which Phocides, an Athenian, won the stadium race. During their term of office the Pisans, renewing the ancient prestige of their country and resorting to mythical, antiquarian proofs, asserted that the honour of holding the Olympian festival was their prerogative. Judging that they had now a suitable occasion for claiming the games, they formed an alliance with the Arcadians, who were enemies of the Eleians. With them as supporters they took the field against the Eleians who were in the act of holding the games. The Eleians resisted with all their forces and a stubborn battle took place, having as spectators the Greeks who were present for the festival wearing wreaths on their heads and calmly applauding the deeds of valour on both sides, themselves out of reach of danger. Finally the Pisans won the day and held the games, but the Eleians later failed to record this Olympiad because they considered that it had been conducted by force and contrary to justice.

While these things were going on, Epameinondas the Theban, who enjoyed the highest standing amongst his fellow countrymen, harangued his fellow citizens at a meeting of the assembly, urging them to strive for the supremacy on the sea. In the course of the speech, which was the result of long consideration, he pointed out that this attempt was both expedient and possible, alleging in particular that it was easy for those who possessed supremacy on land to acquire the mastery of the sea. The Athenians, for instance, in the war with Xerxes, who had two hundred ships manned by themselves, were subject to the commands of the Lacedaemonians who provided only ten ships. By this and many other arguments suited to his theme he prevailed upon the Thebans to make a bid for the mastery at sea.

79. Accordingly the people immediately voted to construct a hundred triremes and dockyards to accommodate their number, and to urge the peoples of Rhodes, Chios, and Byzantium to assist their schemes. Epameinondas himself, who had been dispatched with a force to the aforementioned cities, so overawed Laches, the Athenian general, who had a large fleet and had been sent out to circumvent the Thebans, that he forced him to sail away and made the cities friendly to Thebes. Indeed if this man had lived on longer, the Thebans admittedly would have secured the mastery at sea in addition to their supremacy on land; when, however, a little while later, after winning a most glorious victory for his country in the battle of Mantineia, he died a hero's death, straightway the power of Thebes died with him. But this subject we shall set forth accurately in detail a little later. At that time the Thebans decided to take the field against Orchomenus for the following reasons. Certain refugees who wanted to change the constitution of Thebes to an aristocracy induced the knights of Orchomenus, three hundred in all, to join them in the attempt. These knights, who were in the habit of meeting with some Thebans on a stated day for a review under arms, agreed to make the attack on this day, and along with many others who joined the movement and added their efforts, they met at the appointed time. Now the men who had originated the action changed their minds, and disclosed to the boeotarchs the projected attack, thus betraying their fellow conspirators, and by this service they purchased safety for themselves. The officials arrested the knights from Orchomenus and brought them before the assembly, where the people voted to execute them, to sell the inhabitants of Orchomenus into slavery, and to raze the city. For from earliest times the Thebans had been ill-disposed towards them, having paid tribute to the Minyae in the heroic age, but later they had been liberated by Heracles. So the Thebans, thinking they had a good opportunity and having got plausible pretexts for punishing them, took the field against Orchomenus, occupied the city, slew the male inhabitants and sold into slavery the women and children.

80. About this time the Thessalians, who continued the war upon Alexander, tyrant of Pherae, and, suffering defeat in most of the battles, had lost large numbers of their fighting men, sent ambassadors to the Thebans with a request to assist them and to dispatch to them Pelopidas as general, for they knew that on account of his arrest by Alexander he was on very bad terms with the ruler, and besides, that he was a man of superior courage and widely renowned for his shrewdness in the art of war. When the common council of the Boeotians convened and the envoys had explained the matters on which they had been instructed, the Boeotians concurred with the Thessalians in every matter, gave Pelopidas seven thousand men and ordered him speedily to assist as requested; but as Pelopidas was hastening to leave with his army, the sun, as it happened, was eclipsed. Many were superstitious about the phenomenon, and some of the soothsayers declared that because of the withdrawal of the soldiers, the city's "sun" had been eclipsed. Although in this interpretation they were foretelling the death of Pelopidas, he notwithstanding set out for the campaign, drawn on by Fate. When he arrived in Thessaly, and found that Alexander had forestalled him by occupying the commanding positions and had more than twenty thousand men, he encamped opposite the enemy, and, strengthening his forces with allied troops from among the Thessalians, joined battle with his opponents. Although Alexander had the advantage by reason of his superior position, Pelopidas, eager to settle the battle by his own courage, charged Alexander himself. The ruler with a corps of picked men resisted, and a stubborn battle ensued, in the course of which Pelopidas, performing mighty deeds of valour, strewed all the ground about him with dead men, and though he brought the contest to a close, routed the enemy and won the victory, he yet lost his own life, suffering many wounds and heroically forfeiting his life. Alexander, after being worsted in a second battle and utterly crushed, was compelled by agreement to restore to the Thessalians the cities he had reduced, to surrender the Magnesians and the Phthiotian Achaeans to the Boeotians, and for the future to be the ruler over Pherae alone as an ally of the Boeotians.

81. Although the Thebans had won a famous victory, they declared to the world that they were the losers because of the death of Pelopidas; for having lost such a remarkable man, they rightly judged the victory of less account than the fame of Pelopidas. Indeed he had done many great services to his country and had contributed more than any other man to the rise of Thebes. For in the matter of the return of the refugees, whereby he recaptured the Cadmeia, all men agree in attributing to him the principal credit for its success. It turned out that this piece of good fortune was the cause of all the subsequent happy events. In the battle by Tegyra, Pelopidas alone of the boeotarchs won victory over the Lacedaemonians, the most powerful of the Greeks, the first occasion when on account of the importance of the victory the Thebans erected a trophy over the Lacedaemonians. In the battle of Leuctra he commanded the Sacred Band, with which he charged the Spartans first and thus was the primary cause of the victory. In the campaigns about Lacedaemon, he commanded seventy thousand men, and in the very territory of Sparta erected a trophy of victory over the Lacedaemonians, who never in all previous time had seen their land plundered. As ambassador to the Persian King he took Messenê under his personal charge in the general settlement, and though for three hundred years it had been stripped of inhabitants, the Thebans established it again. At the end of his life, in the contest with Alexander who had an army far outnumbering his, he not only gained a glorious victory, but also met his death with a courage that made it renowned. In his relations with his fellow citizens he was so favourably treated that from the return of the exiles to Thebes until his death he continued every year to hold the office of boeotarch, an honour accorded to no other citizen. So let Pelopidas, whose personal merits received the approbation of all, receive from us too the approbation of History.

At the same time, Clearchus, who was a native of Heracleia on the Black Sea, set out to win a tyranny, and when he had achieved his purpose, he emulated the methods of Dionysius tyrant of Syracuse, and after becoming tyrant of Heracleia ruled with conspicuous success for twelve years. While these things were going on Timotheiis, the Athenian general, commanding a force of both infantry and ships, besieged and took Torone and Potidaea, and brought relief to Cyzicus, which was undergoing a siege.

82. When this year had ended, at Athens [363/2] Charicleides became archon, and in Rome consuls were elected, Lucius Aemilius Mamercus and Lucius Sextius Lateranus. During their term of office the Arcadians collaborating with the Pisans administered the Olympian games, and were masters of the temple and the offerings deposited in it. Since the Mantineians had appropriated for their own private uses a large number of the dedications, they were eager as transgressors for the war against the Eleians to continue, in order to avoid, if peace were restored, giving an account of their expenditures. Since the rest of the Arcadians wished to make peace, they stirred up strife against their fellow countrymen. Two parties accordingly sprang up, one headed by Tegea, and the other by Mantineia. Their quarrel assumed such proportions that they resorted to a decision by arms, and the Tegeans, having sent ambassadors to the Boeotians, won assistance for themselves, for the Boeotians appointed Epameinondas general, gave him a large army, and dispatched him to aid the Tegeans. The Mantineians, terrified at the army from Boeotia and the reputation of Epameinondas, sent envoys to the bitterest enemies of the Boeotians, the Athenians and the Lacedaemonians, and prevailed upon them to fight on their side. When both peoples had quickly sent in response strong armies, many heavy engagements took place in the Peloponnesus. Indeed the Lacedaemonians, living near at hand, immediately invaded Arcadia, but Epameinondas, advancing at this juncture with his army and being not far from Mantineia, learned from the inhabitants that the Lacedaemonians, in full force, were plundering the territory of Tegea. Supposing then that Sparta was stripped of soldiers, he planned a great stroke, but fortune worked against him. He himself set out by night to Sparta, but the Lacedaemonian king Agis, suspecting the cunning of Epameinondas, shrewdly guessed what he would do, and sent out some Cretan runners and through them forestalling Epameinondas got word to the men who had been left behind in Sparta that the Boeotians would shortly appear in Lacedaemon to sack the city, but that he himself would come as quickly as possible with his army to bring aid to his native land. So he gave orders for those who were in Sparta to watch over the city and be terrified at nothing, for he himself would soon appear with help.

83. The Cretans speedily carried out their orders, and the Lacedaemonians miraculously avoided the capture of their native land; for had not the attack been disclosed in advance, Epameinondas would have burst into Sparta undetected. We can justly praise the ingenuity of both generals, but should deem the strategy of the Laconian the shrewder. It is true that Epameinondas, without resting the entire night, covered the distance at top speed and at daybreak attacked Sparta, but Agesilaüs, who had been left on guard and had learned only shortly before from the Cretans all about the enemy's plan, straightway devoted his utmost energy to the care of the city's defence. He placed the oldest children and the aged on the roofs of the houses and instructed them from there to defend themselves against the enemy if he forced a way into the city, while he himself lined up the men in the prime of life and apportioned them to the obstacles in front of the city and to the approaches, and, having blocked all places that could offer passage, he awaited the attack of the enemy. Epameinondas, after dividing his soldiers into several columns, attacked everywhere at once, but when he saw the disposition of the Spartans, he knew immediately that his move had been revealed. Nevertheless he made the assault on all the positions one after the other, and, though he was at a disadvantage because of the obstacles, closed in a hand-to-hand combat. Many a blow he received and dealt and did not call off the zealous rivalry until the army of the Lacedaemonians re-entered Sparta. Then as many came to the assistance of the besieged and night intervened, he desisted from the siege.

84. Having learned from his captives that the Mantineians had come in full force to assist the Lacedaemonians, Epameinondas then withdrew a short distance from the city and encamped, and having given orders to prepare mess, he left some of the horsemen and ordered them to burn fires in the camp until the morning watch, while he himself set out with his army and hurried to fall suddenly on those who had been left in Mantineia. Having covered much ground on the next day, he suddenly broke in on the Mantineians when they were not expecting it. However, he did not succeed in his attempt, although by his plan of campaign he had provided for every contingency, but, finding Fate opposed to him, contrary to his expectations he lost the victory. For just as he was approaching the unprotected city, on the opposite side of Mantineia there arrived the reinforcements sent by Athens, six thousand in number with Hegesileos their general, a man at that time renowned amongst his fellow citizens. He introduced an adequate force into the city and arrayed the rest of the army in expectation of a decisive battle. Presently the Lacedaemonians and Mantineians made their appearance as well, whereat all got ready for the contest which was to decide the issue and summoned their allies from every direction. On the side of the Mantineians were the Eleians, Lacedaemonians, Athenians, and a few others, who numbered all told more than twenty thousand foot and about two thousand horse. On the side of the Tegeans the most numerous and bravest of the Arcadians were ranged as allies, also Achaeans, Boeotians, Argives, some other Peloponnesians, and allies from outside, and all in all there were assembled above thirty thousand foot and not less than three thousand horse.

85. Both sides eagerly drew together for the decisive conflict, their armies in battle formation, while the soothsayers, having sacrificed on both sides, declared that victory was foreshadowed by the gods. In the disposition of forces the Mantineians with the rest of the Arcadians occupied the right wing with the Lacedaemonians as their neighbours and supporters, and next to these were Eleians and Achaeans; and the weaker of the remaining forces occupied the centre, while the Athenians filled the left wing. The Thebans themselves had their post on the left wing, supported by the Arcadians, while they entrusted the right to the Argives. The remaining multitude filled the middle of the line: Euboeans, Locrians, Sicyonians, Messenians, Malians, Aenianians, together with Thessalians and the remaining allies. Both sides divided the cavalry and placed contingents on each wing. Such was the array of the armaments, and now as they approached one another, the trumpets sounded the battle charge, the armies raised the battle shout, and by the very volume of their cries betokened their victory. At first they engaged in a cavalry battle on the flanks in which they outbid each other in keen rivalry. Now as the Athenian horse attacked the Theban they suffered defeat not so much because of the quality of their mounts nor yet on the score of the riders' courage or experience in horsemanship, for in none of these departments was the Athenian cavalry deficient; but it was in the numbers and equipment of the light-armed troops and in their tactical skill that they were far inferior to their opponents. Indeed they had only a few javelin-throwers, whereas the Thebans had three times as many slingers and javelin-throwers sent them from the regions about Thessaly. These people practised from boyhood assiduously this type of fighting and consequently were wont to exercise great weight in battles because of their experience in handling these missiles. Consequently the Athenians, who were continually being wounded by the light-armed and were harried to exhaustion by the opponents who confronted them, all turned and fled. Having fled beyond the flanks, they managed to retrieve their defeat, for even in their retreat they did not break their own phalanx, and encountering simultaneously the Euboeans and certain mercenaries who had been dispatched to seize the heights near by, they gave battle and slew them all. Now the Theban horse did not follow up the fugitives, but, assailing the phalanx opposing them, strove zealously to outflank the infantry. The battle was a hot one; the Athenians were exhausted and had turned to flee, when the Eleian cavalry-commander, assigned to the rear, came to the aid of the fugitives and, by striking down many Boeotians, reversed the course of the battle. So while the Eleian cavalry by their appearance in this fashion on the left wing retrieved the defeat their allies had sustained, on the other flank both cavalry forces lashed at one another and the battle hung for a short time in the balance, but then, because of the number and valour of the Boeotian and Thessalian horsemen, the contingents on the Mantineian side were forced back, and with considerable loss took refuge with their own phalanx.

86. Now the cavalry battle had the foregoing issue. When the infantry forces closed with the enemy in hand-to-hand combat, a mighty, stupendous struggle ensued. For never at any other time when Greeks fought Greeks was such a multitude of men arrayed, nor did generals of greater repute or men more competent ever display such gallantry in battle. For the most capable foot-soldiers of that time, Boeotians and Lacedaemonians, whose lines were drawn up facing one another, began the contest, exposing their lives to every risk. After the first exchange of spears in which most were shattered by the very density of the missiles, they engaged with swords, and although their bodies were all locked with one another and they were inflicting all manner of wounds, yet they did not leave off; and for a long time as they persisted in their terrible work, because of the superlative courage displayed on each side, the battle hung poised. For each man, disregarding the risk of personal hurt, but desirous rather of performing some brilliant deed, would nobly accept death as the price of glory. As the battle raged severely for a long time and the conflict took no turn in favour of either side, Epameinondas, conceiving that victory called for the display of his own valour also, decided to be himself the instrument to decide the issue. So he immediately took his best men, grouped them in close formation and charged into the midst of the enemy; he led his battalion in the charge and was the first to hurl his javelin, and hit the commander of the Lacedaemonians. Then, as the rest of his men also came immediately into close quarters with the foe, he slew some, threw others into a panic, and broke through the enemy phalanx. The Lacedaemonians, overawed by the prestige of Epameinondas and by the sheer weight of the contingent he led, withdrew from the battle, but the Boeotians kept pressing the attack and continually slaying any men who were in the rear rank, so that a multitude of corpses was piled up.

87. As for the Lacedaemonians, when they saw that Epameinondas in the fury of battle was pressing forward too eagerly, they charged him in a body. As the missiles flew thick and fast about him, he dodged some, others he fended off, still others he pulled from his body and used to ward off his attackers. While struggling heroically for the victory, he received a mortal wound in the chest. As the spear broke and the iron point was left in his body, he fell of a sudden, his strength sapped by the wound. About his body a rivalry ensued in which many were slain on both sides, but at last with difficulty by their superiority in bodily strength, the Thebans wore the Lacedaemonians out. As the latter turned and fled, the Boeotians pursued for a short time but turned back, considering it most essential to take possession of the bodies of the dead. So, when the trumpeters sounded recall for their men, all withdrew from battle and both sides set up trophies claiming the victory. In fact the Athenians had defeated the Euboeans and mercenaries in the battle for the heights and were in possession of the dead; while the Boeotians, because they had overpowered the Lacedaemonians and were in possession of the dead, were for awarding the victory to themselves. So for a long time neither side sent envoys to recover its dead, in order that it should not appear to yield the primacy; but later, when the Lacedaemonians were the first to have sent a herald to ask for the recovery of their dead, each side buried its own. Epameinondas, however, was carried back to camp still living, and the physicians were summoned, but when they declared that undoubtedly as soon as the spear-point should be drawn from his chest, death would ensue, with supreme courage he met his end. For first summoning his armour-bearer he asked him if he had saved his shield. On his replying yes and placing it before his eyes, he again asked, which side was victorious. At the boy's answer that the Boeotians were victorious, he said, "It is time to die," and directed them to withdraw the spear point. His friends present cried out in protest, and one of them said: "You die childless, Epameinondas," and burst into tears. To this he replied, "No, by Zeus, on the contrary I leave behind two daughters, Leuctra and Mantineia, my victories." Then when the spear point was withdrawn, without any commotion he breathed his last.

88. For us who are wont to accord to the demise of great men the appropriate meed of praise, it would be most unfitting, so we think, to pass by the death of a man of such stature with no word of note. For it seems to me that he surpassed his contemporaries not only in skill and experience in the art of war, but in reasonableness and magnanimity as well. For among the generation of Epameinondas were famous men: Pelopidas the Theban, Timotheüs and Conon, also Chabrias and Iphicrates, Athenians all, and, besides, Agesilaüs the Spartan, who belonged to a slightly older generation. Still earlier than these, in the times of the Medes and Persians, there were Solon, Themistocles, Miltiades, and Cimon, Myronides, and Pericles and certain others in Athens, and in Sicily Gelon, son of Deinomenes, and still others. All the same, if you should compare the qualities of these with the generalship and reputation of Epameinondas, you would find the qualities possessed by Epameinondas far superior. For in each of the others you would discover but one particular superiority as a claim to fame; in him, however, all qualities combined. For in strength of body and eloquence of speech, furthermore in elevation of mind, contempt of lucre, fairness, and, most of all, in courage and shrewdness in the art of war, he far surpassed them all. So it was that in his lifetime his native country acquired the primacy of Hellas, but when he died lost it and constantly suffered change for the worse and finally, because of the folly of its leaders, experienced slavery and devastation. So Epameinondas, whose valour was approved among all men, in the manner we have shown met his death.

89. The states of Greece after the battle, since the victory credited to them all was in dispute and they had proved to be evenly matched in the matter of valour, and, furthermore, were now exhausted by the unbroken series of battles, came to terms with one another. When they had agreed upon a general peace and alliance, they sought to include the Messenians in the compact, but the Lacedaemonians, because of the irreconcilable quarrel with them, chose not to be parties to the truce and alone of the Greeks remained out of it.

Among the historians Xenophon the Athenian brings the narrative of "Greek Affairs" down into this year, closing it with the death of Epameinondas, while Anaximenes of Lampsacus, who composed the "First Inquiry of Greek Affairs" beginning with the birth of the gods and the first generation of man, closed it with the battle of Mantineia and the death of Epameinondas. He included practically all the doings of the Greeks and non-Greeks in twelve volumes. Philistus brought his history of Dionysius the Younger down to this year, narrating the events of five years in two volumes.

90. When Molon was archon at Athens, [362/1] in Rome there were elected as consuls Lucius Genucius and Quintus Servilius. During their term of office the inhabitants of the Asiatic coast revolted from Persia, and some of the satraps and generals rising in insurrection made war on Artaxerxes. At the same time Tachos the Egyptian king decided to fight the Persians and prepared ships and gathered infantry forces. Having procured many mercenaries from the Greek cities, he persuaded the Lacedaemonians likewise to fight with him, for the Spartans were estranged from Artaxerxes because the Messenians had been included by the King on the same terms as the other Greeks in the general peace. When the general uprising against the Persians reached such large proportions, the King also began making preparations for the war. For at one and the same time he must needs fight the Egyptian king, the Greek cities of Asia, the Lacedaemonians and the allies of these, satraps and generals who ruled the coastal districts and had agreed upon making common cause with them. Of these the most distinguished were Ariobarzanes, satrap of Phrygia, who at the death of Mithridates had taken possession of his kingdom, and Mausolus, overlord of Caria, who was master of many strongholds and important cities of which the hearth and mother city was Halicarnassus, which possessed a famous acropolis and the royal palace of Caria; and, in addition to the two already mentioned, Orontes, satrap of Mysia, and Autophradates, satrap of Lydia. Apart from the Ionians were Lycians, Pisidians, Pamphylians, and Cilicians, likewise Syrians, Phoenicians, and practically all the coastal peoples. With the revolt so extensive, half the revenues of the King were cut off and what remained were insufficient for the expenses of the war.

91. The peoples who had revolted from the King chose as their general Orontes in charge of all branches of the administration. He, having taken over the command and funds needed for recruiting mercenaries, amounting to a year's pay for twenty thousand men, proceeded to betray his trust. For suspecting that he would obtain from the King not only great rewards but would also succeed to the satrapy of all the coastal region if he should deliver the rebels into the hands of the Persians, he first arrested those who brought the money and dispatched them to Artaxerxes; then afterward he delivered many of the cities and the soldiers who had been hired to the commanding officers who had been sent by the King. In a similar manner, betrayal occurred also in Cappadocia, where a strange and unexpected thing took place. Artabazus, the King's general, had invaded Cappadocia with a large army, and Datames, the satrap of the country, had taken the field against him, for he had collected many horsemen and had twenty thousand mercenary foot-soldiers serving with him. The father-in-law of Datames, who commanded the cavalry, wishing to acquire favour and at the same time having an eye to his own safety, deserted at night and rode off with the cavalry to the enemy, having the day before made arrangements with Artabazus for the betrayal. Datames then summoned his mercenaries, promised them largess, and launched an attack upon the deserters. Finding them on the point of joining forces with the enemy and himself attacking at the same time Artabazus' guard and the horsemen, he slew all who came to close quarters. Artabazus, at first unaware of the truth and suspecting that the man who had deserted Datames was effecting a counter-betrayal, ordered his own men to slay all the horsemen who approached. Mithrobarzanes, caught between the two parties, one group seeking revenge against him as a traitor; the other trying to punish him for counter-betrayal, was in a predicament, but since the situation allowed no time to deliberate, he had recourse to force, and fighting against both parties caused grievous slaughter. When, finally, more than ten thousand had been slain, Datames, having put the rest of Mithrobarzanes' men to flight and slain many of them, recalled with the trumpet his soldiers who had gone in pursuit. Amongst the survivors in the cavalry some went back to Datames and asked for pardon; the rest did nothing, having nowhere to turn, and finally, being about five hundred in number, were surrounded and shot down by Datames. As for Datames, though even before this he was admired for his generalship, at that time he won far greater acclaim for both his courage and his sagacity in the art of war; but King Artaxerxes, when he learned about Datames' exploit as general, because he was impatient to be rid of him, instigated his assassination.

92. While these things were going on, Rheomithres, who had been sent by the insurgents to King Tachôs in Egypt, received from him five hundred talents of silver and fifty warships, and sailed to Asia to the city named Leucae. To this city he summoned many leaders of the insurgents. These he arrested and sent in irons to Artaxerxes, and, though he himself had been an insurgent, by the favours that he conferred through his betrayal, he made his peace with the King. In Egypt King Tachôs, having completed his preparations for the war, now had two hundred triremes expensively adorned, ten thousand chosen mercenaries from Greece, and besides these eighty thousand Egyptian infantry. He gave the command of the mercenaries to the Spartan Agesilaüs, who had been dispatched by the Lacedaemonians with a thousand hoplites to fight as an ally, being a man capable of leading troops and highly regarded for his courage and for his shrewdness in the art of war. The command of the naval contingent he entrusted to Chabrias the Athenian, who had not been sent officially by his country, but had been privately prevailed upon by the king to join the expedition. The king himself, having command of the Egyptians and being general of the whole army, gave no heed to the advice of Agesilaüs to remain in Egypt and conduct the war through the agency of his generals, though the advice was sound. In fact when the armament had gone far afield and was encamped near Phoenicia, the general left in charge of Egypt revolted from the king, and having thereupon sent word to his son Nectanebos prevailed upon him to take the kingship in Egypt, and thereby kindled a great war. For Nectanebos, who had been appointed by the king commander of the soldiers from Egypt and had been sent from Phoenicia to besiege the cities in Syria, after approving of his father's designs, solicited the officers with bribes and the common soldiers with promises, and so prevailed upon them to be his accomplices. At last Egypt was seized by the insurgents, and Tachôs, panic-stricken, made bold to go up to the King by way of Arabia and beg forgiveness for his past errors. Artaxerxes not only cleared him of the charges against him but even appointed him general in the war against Egypt.

93. Shortly after, the King of Persia died, having ruled forty-three years, and Ochus, who now assumed a new name, Artaxerxes, succeeded to the kingdom and ruled twenty-three years; for since the first Artaxerxes had ruled well and had shown himself altogether peace-loving and fortunate, the Persians changed the names of those who ruled after him and prescribed that they should bear that name. When King Tachôs had returned to the army of Agesilaüs, Nectanebos, who had collected more than a hundred thousand men, came against Tachôs and challenged him to fight a battle for the kingship. Now Agesilaüs, observing that the king was terrified and lacked the courage to risk a battle, bade him take heart. "For," said he, "it is not those who have the advantage of numbers who win the victory, but those who excel in valour." Since the king paid no heed to Agesilaüs, he was obliged to withdraw with him to a large city. The Egyptians at first started to assault them once they were shut in it, but when they had lost many men in their attacks on the walls, they then began to surround the city with a wall and a ditch. As the work was rapidly nearing completion by reason of the large number of workers, and the provisions in the city were exhausted, Tachôs despaired of his safety, but Agesilaüs, encouraging the men and attacking the enemy by night, unexpectedly succeeded in bringing all the men out safely, and since the Egyptians had pursued close on their heels and the district was now flat, the Egyptians supposed that they had the enemy surrounded by superior numbers, and would utterly destroy them, but Agesilaüs seized a position which had on each side a canal fed by the river and thus halted the enemy's attack. Then having drawn up his force in conformity with the terrain and protected his army by the river channels, he joined battle. The superior numbers of the Egyptians had become useless, and the Greeks, who surpassed them in courage, slew many Egyptians and forced the rest to flee. Afterwards Tachôs easily recovered the Egyptian kingship, and Agesilaüs, as the one who single-handed had restored his kingdom, was honoured with appropriate gifts. On his journey back to his native land by way of Cyrenê Agesilaüs died, and his body packed in honey was conveyed to Sparta where he received kingly burial and honour.

So far did events in Asia progress to the end of the year.

94. In the Peloponnese, though the Arcadians had agreed on a general peace after the battle of Mantineia, they adhered to their covenant only a year before they renewed the war. In the covenant it was written that each should return to his respective native country after the battle, but there had come into the city of Megalopolis the inhabitants of neighbouring cities who had been moved to new homes and were finding transplantation from their own homes difficult to bear. Consequently when they had returned to the cities which had formerly been theirs, the Megalopolitans tried to compel them to abandon their homelands. And when for this reason a quarrel arose, the townsfolk asked the Mantineians and certain other Arcadians to help them, and also the Eleians and the other peoples that were members of the alliance with the Mantineians, whereas the Megalopolitans besought the Thebans to fight with them as allies. The Thebans speedily dispatched to them three thousand hoplites and three hundred cavalry with Pammenes as their commander. He came to Megalopolis, and by sacking some of the towns and terrifying others he compelled their inhabitants to change their abode to Megalopolis. So the problem of the amalgamation of the cities, after it had reached such a state of turmoil, was reduced to such calm as was possible.

Of the historians, Athanas of Syracuse wrote thirteen books beginning with the events attending and following Dion's expedition, but he prefixed, in one book, an account of the period of seven years not recorded in the treatise of Philistus and by recording these events in summary fashion made of the history a continuous narrative.

95. When Nicophemus was archon at Athens, [361/0] the consular office at Rome was assumed by Gaius Sulpicius and Gaius Licinius. During their term of office Alexander, tyrant of Pherae, sent pirate ships against the Cyclades, stormed some and took many captives, then disembarking mercenaries on Peparethos put the city under siege. And when the Athenians came to the assistance of the Peparethians and left Leosthenes in command of the mission, Alexander attacked the Athenians. Actually they were blockading such of Alexander's soldiers as were stationed in Panormus. Since the tyrant's men attacked unexpectedly, Alexander won a surprising success. For he not only rescued the detachment at Panormus from the greatest danger, but he also captured five Attic triremes and one Peparethian, and took six hundred captives. The Athenians, enraged, condemned Leosthenes to death as a traitor and confiscated his property, then choosing Chares as general in command and giving him a fleet, they sent him out, but he spent his time avoiding the enemy and injuring the allies. For he sailed to Corcyra, an allied city, and stirred up such violent civil strife in it that many murders and seizures took place, with the result that the Athenian democracy was discredited in the eyes of the allies. So it turned out that Chares, who did many other such lawless acts, accomplished nothing good but brought his country into discredit.

The historians Dionysodorus and Anaxis, Boeotians, closed their narrative of Greek history with this year. But we, now that we have narrated the events before the time of King Philip, bring this book to a close here in accordance with the plan stated at the beginning. In the following book which begins with Philip's accession to the throne, we shall record all the achievements of this king to his death, including in its compass those other events as well which have occurred in the known portions of the world.

BOOK XVI

How Philip, son of Amyntas, succeeded to the Macedonian throne (1-2).

1. In all systematic historical treatises it behooves the historian to include in his books actions of states or of kings which are complete in themselves from beginning to end; for in this manner I conceive history to be most easy to remember and most intelligible to the reader. Now incomplete actions, the conclusion of which is unconnected with the beginning, interrupt the interest of the curious reader, whereas if the actions embrace a continuity of development culminating naturally, the narrative of events will achieve a well-rounded perfection. Whenever the natural pattern of events itself harmonises with the task of the historian, from that point on he must not deviate at all from this principle. Consequently, now that I have reached the actions of Philip son of Amyntas, I shall endeavour to include the deeds performed by this king within the compass of the present Book. For Philip was king over the Macedonians for twenty-four years, and having started from the most insignificant beginnings built up his kingdom to be the greatest of the dominions in Europe, and having taken over Macedonia when she was a slave to the Illyrians, made her mistress of many powerful tribes and states. It was by his own valour that he took over the supremacy of all Hellas with the consent of the states, which voluntarily subordinated themselves to his authority. Having subdued in war the men who had been plundering the shrine at Delphi and having brought aid to the oracle, he won a seat in the Amphictyonic Council, and because of his reverence for the gods received as his prize in the contest, after the defeat of the Phocians, the votes which had been theirs. Then when he had conquered in war Illyrians, Paeonians, Thracians, Scythians, and all the peoples in the vicinity of these, he planned to overthrow the Persian kingdom, and, after transporting his armaments into Asia, was in the act of liberating the Greek cities; but, cut short by Fate in mid-career, he left armies so numerous and powerful that his son Alexander had no need to apply for allies in his attempt to overthrow the Persian supremacy. These deeds he accomplished, not by the favour of Fortune, but by his own valour. For King Philip excelled in shrewdness in the art of war, courage, and brilliance of personality; but, not to anticipate his achievements in my introduction, I shall proceed to the continuous thread of the narrative after first briefly retracing his early period.

2. When Callimedes was archon at Athens, [360/59] the one hundred fifth celebration of the Olympian games was held at which Porus of Cyrenê won the stadion race, and the Romans elected as consuls Gnaeus Genucius and Lucius Aemilius. During their term of office Philip, the son of Amyntas and father of Alexander who defeated the Persians in war, succeeded to the Macedonian throne in the following manner. After Amyntas had been defeated by the Illyrians and forced to pay tribute to his conquerors, the Illyrians, who had taken Philip, the youngest son of Amyntas, as a hostage, placed him in the care of the Thebans. They in turn entrusted the lad to the father of Epameinondas and directed him both to keep careful watch over his ward and to superintend his upbringing and education. Since Epameinondas had as his instructor a philosopher of the Pythagorean school, Philip, who was reared along with him,

acquired a wide acquaintance with the Pythagorean philosophy. Inasmuch as both students showed natural ability and diligence they proved to be superior in deeds of valour. Of the two, Epameinondas underwent the most rigorous tests and battles, and invested his fatherland almost miraculously with the leadership of Hellas, while Philip, availing himself of the same initial training, achieved no less fame than Epameinondas. For after the death of Amyntas, Alexander, the eldest of the sons of Amyntas, succeeded to the throne, but Ptolemy of Alorus assassinated him and succeeded to the throne and then in similar fashion Perdiccas disposed of him and ruled as king. But when he was defeated in a great battle by the Illyrians and fell in the action, Philip his brother, who had escaped from his detention as a hostage, succeeded to the kingdom, now in a bad way. For the Macedonians had lost more than four thousand men in the battle, and the remainder, panic-stricken, had become exceedingly afraid of the Illyrian armies and had lost heart for continuing the war. About the same time the Paeonians, who lived near Macedonia, began to pillage their territory, showing contempt for the Macedonians, and the Illyrians began to assemble large armies and prepare for an invasion of Macedonia, while a certain Pausanias, who was related to the royal line of Macedon, was planning with the aid of the Thracian king to join the contest for the throne of Macedon. Similarly, the Athenians too, being hostile to Philip, were endeavouring to restore Argaeus to the throne and had dispatched Mantias as general with three thousand hoplites and a considerable naval force.

How he defeated Argaeus, pretender to the throne (3).

3. The Macedonians because of the disaster sustained in the battle and the magnitude of the dangers pressing upon them were in the greatest perplexity. Yet even so, with such fears and dangers threatening them, Philip was not panic-stricken by the magnitude of the expected perils, but, bringing together the Macedonians in a series of assemblies and exhorting them with eloquent speeches to be men, he built up their morale, and, having improved the organisation of his forces and equipped the men suitably with weapons of war, he held constant manoeuvres of the men under arms and competitive drills. Indeed he devised the compact order and the equipment of the phalanx, imitating the close order fighting with overlapping shields of the warriors at Troy, and was the first to organise the Macedonian phalanx. He was courteous in his intercourse with men and sought to win over the multitudes by his gifts and his promises to the fullest loyalty, and endeavoured to counteract by clever moves the crowd of impending dangers. For instance, when he observed that the Athenians were centring all their ambition upon recovering Amphipolis and for this reason were trying to bring Argaeus back to the throne, he voluntarily withdrew from the city, after first making it autonomous. Then he sent an embassy to the Paeonians, and by corrupting some with gifts and persuading others by generous promises he made an agreement with them to maintain peace for the present. In similar fashion he prevented the return of Pausanias by winning over with gifts the king who was on the point of attempting his restoration. Mantias, the Athenian general, who had sailed into Methonê, stayed behind there himself but sent Argaeus with his mercenaries to Aegae. Argaeus approached the city and invited the population of Aegae to welcome his return and become the founders of his own kingship. When no one paid any attention to him, he turned back to Methonê, but Philip, who suddenly appeared with his soldiers, engaged him in battle, slew many of his mercenaries, and released under a truce the rest, who had fled for refuge to a certain hill, after he had first obtained from them the exiles, whom they delivered to him.

Now Philip by his success in this first battle encouraged the Macedonians to meet the succeeding contests with greater temerity. While these things were going on, the Thasians settled the place called Crenides, which the king afterward named Philippi for himself and made a populous settlement.

Among the writers of history Theopompus of Chios began his history of Philip at this point and composed fifty-eight books, of which five are lost.

How, having subdued the Illyrians and the Paeonians, he acquired the empire of his fathers (4).

4. When Eucharistus was archon at Athens, [359/8] the Romans elected as consuls Quintus Servilius and Quintus Genucius. During their term of office Philip sent ambassadors to Athens and persuaded the assembly to make peace with him on the ground that he abandoned for all time any claim to Amphipolis. Now that he was relieved of the war with the Athenians and had information that the king of the Paeonians, Agis, was dead, he conceived that he had the opportunity to attack the Paeonians. Accordingly, having conducted an expedition into Paeonia and defeated the barbarians in a battle, he compelled the tribe to acknowledge allegiance to the Macedonians. Since the Illyrians were still left as enemies, he was ambitious to defeat them in war also. So, having quickly called an assembly and exhorted his soldiers for the war in a fitting speech, he led an expedition into the Illyrian territory, having no less than ten thousand foot-soldiers and six hundred horsemen. Bardylis, the king of the Illyrians, having learned of the presence of the enemy, first dispatched envoys to arrange for a cessation of hostilities on the condition that both sides remained possessed of the cities which they then controlled, but when Philip said that he indeed desired peace but would not, however, concur in that proposal unless the Illyrians should withdraw from all the Macedonian cities, the envoys returned without having accomplished their purpose, and Bardylis, relying upon his previous victories and the gallant conduct of the Illyrians, came out to meet the enemy with his army; and he had ten thousand picked infantry soldiers and about five hundred cavalry. When the armies approached each other and with a great outcry clashed in the battle, Philip, commanding the right wing, which consisted of the flower of the Macedonians serving under him, ordered his cavalry to ride past the ranks of the barbarians and attack them on the flank, while he himself falling on the enemy in a frontal assault began a bitter combat. The Illyrians, forming themselves into a square, courageously entered the fray, and at first for a long while the battle was evenly poised because of the exceeding gallantry displayed on both sides, and as many were slain and still more wounded, the fortune of battle vacillated first one way then the other, being constantly swayed by the valorous deeds of the combatants; but later as the horsemen pressed on from the flank and rear and Philip with the flower of his troops fought with true heroism, the mass of the Illyrians was compelled to take hastily to flight. When the pursuit had been kept up for a considerable distance and many had been slain in their flight, Philip recalled the Macedonians with the trumpet and erecting a trophy of victory buried his own dead, while the Illyrians, having sent ambassadors and withdrawn from all the Macedonian cities, obtained peace. More than seven thousand Illyrians were slain in this battle.

On the pusillanimity of Dionysius the Younger and the flight of Dion (5-6).

5. Since we have finished with the affairs of Macedonia and Illyria, we shall now turn to events of a different kind. In Sicily Dionysius the Younger, tyrant of the Syracusans, who had succeeded to the realm in the period preceding this but was indolent and much inferior to his father, pretended because of his lack of enterprise to be peacefully inclined and mild of disposition. Accordingly, since he had inherited the war with the Carthaginians, he made peace with them and likewise pursued war listlessly for some time against the Lucanians and then, in the latest battles having had the advantage, he gladly brought to a close the war against them. In Apulia he founded two cities because he wished to make safe for navigators the passage across the Ionian Sea; for the barbarians who dwelt along the coast were accustomed to put out in numerous pirate ships and render the whole shore along the Adriatic Sea unsafe for merchants. Thereafter, having given himself over to a peaceful existence, he relieved the soldiers of their drills in warfare and though he had succeeded to the greatest of the realms in Europe, the tyranny that was said by his father to be bound fast by adamantine chains, yet, strange to say, he lost it all by his pusillanimity. The causes for its dissolution and the various events I shall attempt to record.

6. When Cephisodotus was archon at Athens, [358/7] the Romans elected as consuls Gaius Licinius and Gaius Sulpicius. During their term of office Dion, son of Hipparinus and the most distinguished of the Syracusans, escaped from Sicily and by his nobility of spirit set free the Syracusans and the other Sicilian Greeks in the following manner. Dionysius the Elder had begotten children of two wives, of the first, who was a Locrian by birth, Dionysius, who succeeded to the tyranny, and of the second, who was the daughter of Hipparinus, a Syracusan of great renown, two sons Hipparinus and Nysaeus. It chanced that the brother of the second wife was Dion, a man who had great proficiency in philosophy and, in the matter of courage and skill in the art of war, far surpassed the other Syracusans of his time. Dion, because of his high birth and nobility of spirit, fell under suspicion with the tyrant, for he was considered powerful enough to overthrow the tyranny. So, fearing him, Dionysius decided to get him out of the way by arresting him on a charge involving the death penalty. Dion, becoming aware of this, was at first concealed in the homes of some of his friends, and then escaped from Sicily to the Peloponnese in the company of his brother Megacles and of Heracleides who had been appointed commandant of the garrison by the tyrant. When he landed at Corinth, he besought the Corinthians to collaborate with him in setting free the Syracusans, and he himself began to gather mercenary troops and to collect suits of armour. Soon many gave ear to his pleas and he gradually accumulated large supplies of armour and many mercenaries, then, hiring two merchantmen, he loaded on board arms and men, while he himself with these transports sailed from Zacynthus, which is near Cephallenia, to Sicily, but he left Heracleides behind to bring up later some triremes as well as merchantmen to Syracuse.

The founding of Tauromenium in Sicily (7.1).

Events in Euboea and in the course of the Social War (7. 2-end).

7. While these things were going on, Andromachus of Tauromenium, who was the father of Timaeus, the author of the Histories, and distinguished for his wealth and nobility of spirit, gathered together the men who had survived the razing of Naxos by Dionysius. Having settled the hill above Naxos called Tauros and remained there a considerable time, he called it Tauromenium from his "remaining on Tauros." As the city made quick progress, the inhabitants laid up great wealth, and the city, which had won considerable repute, finally in our own lifetime, after Caesar had expelled the inhabitants of Tauromenium from their native land, received a colony of Roman citizens.

While these things were going on, the inhabitants of Euboea fell into strife among themselves, and when one party summoned the Boeotians to its assistance and the other the Athenians, war broke out over all Euboea. A good many close combats and skirmishes occurred in which sometimes the Thebans were superior and sometimes the Athenians carried off the victory. Although no important pitched battle was fought to a finish, yet when the island had been devastated by the intestinal warfare and many men had been slain on both sides, at long last admonished by the disasters, the parties came to an agreement and made peace with one another.

Now the Boeotians returned home and remained quiet, but the Athenians, who had suffered the revolt of Chios, Rhodes, and Cos and, moreover, of Byzantium, became involved in the war called the Social War which lasted three years. The Athenians chose Chares and Chabrias as generals and dispatched them with an army. The two generals on sailing into Chios found that allies had arrived to assist the Chians from Byzantium, Rhodes, and Cos, and also from Mausolus, the tyrant of Caria. They then drew up their forces and began to besiege the city both by land and by sea. Now Chares, who commanded the infantry force, advanced against the walls by land and began a struggle with the enemy who poured out on him from the city; but Chabrias, sailing up to the harbour, fought a severe naval engagement and was worsted when his ship was shattered by a ramming attack. While the men on the other ships withdrew in the nick of time and saved their lives, he, choosing death with glory instead of defeat, fought on for his ship and died of his wounds.

Siege of Amphipolis by Philip and its capture (8. 1-2).

How Philip, having reduced to slavery the people of Pydna, developed the gold mines (8. 3-end).

8. About the same time Philip, king of the Macedonians, who had been victorious over the Illyrians in a great battle and had made subject all the people who dwelt there as far as the lake called Lychnitis, now returned to Macedonia, having arranged a noteworthy peace with the Illyrians and won great acclaim among the Macedonians for the successes due to his valour. Thereupon, finding that the people of Amphipolis were ill-disposed toward him and offered many pretexts for war, he entered upon a campaign against them with a considerable force. By bringing siege-engines against the walls and launching severe and continuous assaults, he succeeded in breaching a portion of the wall with his battering rams, whereupon, having entered the city through the breach and struck down many of his opponents, he obtained the mastery of the city and exiled those who were disaffected toward him, but treated the rest considerately. Since this city was favourably situated with regard to Thrace and the neighbouring regions, it contributed greatly to the aggrandisement of Philip. Indeed he immediately reduced Pydna, and made an alliance with the Olynthians in the terms of which he agreed to take over for them Potidaea, a city which the Olynthians had set their hearts on possessing. Since the Olynthians inhabited an important city and because of its huge population had great influence in war, their city was an object of contention for those who sought to extend their supremacy. For this reason the Athenians and Philip were rivals against one another for the alliance with the Olynthians. However that may be, Philip, when he had forced Potidaea to surrender, led the Athenian garrison out of the city and, treating it considerately, sent it back to Athens, for he was particularly solicitous toward the people of Athens on account of the importance and repute of their city, but, having sold the inhabitants into slavery, he handed it over to the Olynthians, presenting them also at the same time with all the properties in the territory of Potidaea. After this he went to the city of Crenides, and having increased its size with a large number of inhabitants, changed its name to Philippi, giving it his own name, and then, turning to the gold mines in its territory, which were very scanty and insignificant, he increased their output so much by his improvements that they could bring him a revenue of more than a thousand talents. And because from these mines he had soon amassed a fortune, with the abundance of money he raised the Macedonian kingdom higher and higher to a greatly superior position, for with the gold coins which he struck, which came to be known from his name as Philippeioi, he organised a large force of mercenaries, and by using these coins for bribes induced many Greeks to become betrayers of their native lands. Concerning these matters the several events, when recorded, will explain everything in detail, and we shall now shift our account back to the events in the order of their occurrence.

How Dion, having liberated the Syracusans, defeated Dionysius (9-15).

9. When Agathocles was archon at Athens, [357/6] the Romans elected as consuls Marcus Fabius and Gaius Poplius. During their term of office, Dion son of Hipparinus sailed to Sicily intending to overthrow the tyranny of Dionysius, and with slenderer resources than those of any conqueror before his time he succeeded contrary to all expectation in overthrowing the greatest realm in all Europe. Who, indeed, would have believed that, putting ashore with two merchantmen, he could actually have overcome the despot who had at his disposal four hundred ships of war, infantry numbering nearly one hundred thousand, ten thousand horse, and as great a store of arms, food, and money as one in all probability possessed who had to maintain lavishly the aforesaid forces; and, apart from all we have mentioned, had a city which was the largest of the cities of Hellas, and harbours and docks and fortified citadels that were impregnable, and, besides, a great number of powerful allies? The cause for Dion's successes was, above all others, his own nobility of spirit, his courage, and the willing support of those who were to be liberated, but still more important than all these were the pusillanimity of the tyrant and his subjects' hatred of him; for when all these characteristics merged at a single critical moment, they unexpectedly brought to a successful close deeds which were considered impossible.

But we must forgo these reflections and turn to the detailed narrative of the events as they severally occurred. Dion, having sailed from Zacynthos, which lies by Cephallenia, with two merchantmen, put in at the harbour of Acragas named Minoa. This had been founded of olden time by Minos, king of the Cretans, on the occasion when, in his search for Daedalus, he had been entertained by Cocalus, king of the Sicanians, but in the period with which we are concerned this city was subject to the Carthaginians, and its governor, named Paralus, who was a friend of Dion, received him enthusiastically. Dion, having unloaded from the merchantmen five thousand suits of armour, handed them over to Paralus and requested him to transport them on wagons to Syracuse, while he himself, taking along the mercenaries numbering a thousand, led them against Syracuse. On the march he persuaded the peoples of Acragas, Gela, and some of the Sicanians and Sicels who dwelt in the interior, also the people of Camarina, to join in the liberation of the Syracusans, and then advanced to overthrow the tyrant. Since many men with their arms streamed in from all sides, soon more than twenty thousand soldiers were gathered. Likewise many also of the Greeks from Italy and of the Messenians were summoned, and all came in haste with great enthusiasm.

10. When Dion was on the borders of the Syracusan territory, there came to meet him a host of men without arms both from the countryside and from the city; for Dionysius, being suspicious of the Syracusans, had disarmed many of them. About this time the tyrant was sojourning in the newly founded cities along the Adriatic with large forces, and the commanders who had been left in charge of the garrison of Syracuse at first attempted to summon back the Syracusans from their revolt, but when the impulse of the mobs could not be checked they gave up in despair and gathered mercenaries and those who favoured the cause of the tyrant, and having filled their ranks decided to attack the insurgents. Dion distributed the five thousand suits of armour to such of the Syracusans as were unarmed, and equipped the rest as well as he could with weapons that came to hand. Then having brought them all to a general assembly, he disclosed that he had come for the liberation of the Greeks of Sicily, and he urged them to elect as generals those men who were well qualified to effect the restoration of their independence and the dissolution of the entire tyranny. The crowd as with one voice cried out that it chose Dion and his brother Megacles as generals with absolute power. Accordingly he drew up his army in line of battle immediately at the close of the assembly and advanced upon the city. Since no one disputed with him the open country, he entered fearlessly within the walls, and making his way through Achradina encamped in the market-place, no one daring to come out against him. The whole number of the soldiers with Dion was not less than fifty thousand. All of these with garlands on their heads came down to the city under the leadership of Dion and Megacles and with them thirty Syracusans who alone of the exiles in the Peloponnese were willing to share the battles with their fellow Syracusans.

11. Now that all the city had put on the garb of freedom in exchange for that of slavery and that fortune had changed the sullen looks of the tyranny to festival gaiety, every house was filled with sacrificing and rejoicing, as the citizens burnt incense on their own hearths, thanked the gods for their present blessings, and offered hopeful prayers for blessings to come. The women too raised great shouts of joy for the unexpected good fortune and gathered together in throngs throughout the whole city. There was no freeman, no slave, no stranger who did not hasten to gaze upon Dion, and all applauded the man's valour in terms too exalted for a mere mortal. And they had good reason for such feelings because of the magnitude and unexpected nature of the change; for after having experienced fifty years of slavery and forgotten the meaning of freedom through the lapse of time, they were suddenly released from their misfortune by the valour of a single man.

Dionysius himself at this time chanced to be sojourning near Caulonia in Italy, and he sent for Philistus his general, who was cruising the Adriatic, to come with his fleet and ordered him to sail to Syracuse. Both men made haste to reach the same spot, but Dionysius arrived seven days after the return of Dion. Immediately, then, on his arrival, desirous of outmanoeuvring the Syracusans, he sent an embassy to make peace, and gave many indications that he would surrender his power as tyrant to the people and would accept of the people's government important privileges in exchange. He requested them to dispatch envoys to him so that he might sit in conference with them and bring the war to an end. The Syracusans, accordingly, elated with hopes, dispatched as envoys the most important of their men; but Dionysius, having placed them under guard, postponed the conference and, observing that the Syracusans because of their hope of peace were lax in the matter of garrisons and unprepared for a battle, suddenly opened the gates of the citadel on the Island, and issued forth with his army in battle array.

12. Since the Syracusans had constructed a cross-wall of their own from sea to sea, the mercenaries fell upon the wall with a loud and terrifying outcry, massacred many of the garrison and, getting inside the wall, engaged in a struggle with those who were coming out to the rescue. Dion, being unexpectedly tricked by the violation of the truce, came to meet the enemy with his best soldiers and joining battle wrought extensive slaughter. For when fighting took place, as if in a stadium, within the narrow interval afforded by the cross wall, a multitude of soldiers collected in a contracted space. For this reason on both sides men outstanding in gallantry met in the action and since Dionysius' mercenaries, by the size of the promised rewards, and the Syracusans, by the hope of freedom, were wrought up to a high pitch of rivalry, at first the battle stood equally poised, as the valour of both sides in the fight was equal. Many fell, and not a few were wounded, receiving all the blows in front; for on the one hand those in the front rank courageously met death defending the rest, and those arrayed behind them covering them with their shields as they fell and holding firm in the desperate peril took the most dangerous risks to win the victory. After this engagement Dion, wishing to display his valour in the battle and eager to win the victory by his own deeds, forced his way into the midst of the enemy and there in an heroic encounter slew many and having disrupted the whole battle line of the mercenaries was suddenly cut off and isolated in the crowd. Many missiles hurled at him fell upon his shield and helmet, but he escaped these owing to the protection of his armour, but receiving a wound on his right arm he was borne down by the weight of the blow and barely escaped capture by the enemy. The Syracusans, fearing for their general's safety, dashed into the mercenaries in heavy formation and rescued the distressed Dion from his perils, then overpowering the enemy, forced them to flee. Since likewise in the other part of the wall the Syracusans had the superiority, the tyrant's mercenaries were chased in a body inside the gates of the Island. The Syracusans, who had now won victory in a significant battle and had securely recovered their freedom, set up a trophy to signalise the tyrant's defeat.

13. After this, Dionysius, who had failed and by now despaired of his tyranny, left a considerable garrison in his citadels, while he himself, having secured permission to take up his dead, eight hundred in number, gave their bodies a magnificent burial, causing them to be crowned with golden crowns and wrapped in fine purple; for he hoped by his solicitude for them to incite the survivors to fight spiritedly in defence of the tyranny; and those who had behaved gallantly he honoured with rich gifts. He kept sending messengers to the Syracusans to confer about terms of a settlement. But Dion in the matter of his embassies, by constantly offering plausible excuses, kept making postponements, and, when he had meanwhile constructed the remainder of the wall at his leisure, he then called for the embassies, having outmanoeuvred the enemy by encouraging their hopes of peace. When discussion arose concerning the terms of settlement, Dion replied to the ambassadors that only one settlement was possible, namely that Dionysius should resign his position as tyrant and then deign to accept certain privileges. Dionysius, since Dion's reply had been arrogant, assembled his commanders and began to deliberate on the best means of defending himself against the Syracusans. Having plenty of everything but grain and being in control of the sea, he began to pillage the countryside and, finding it difficult to provide subsistence from his foraging parties, he dispatched merchantmen and money to purchase grain. The Syracusans, who had many ships of war and kept putting in an appearance at opportune places, made off with many of the supplies which were being brought in by the traders.

This was the situation of affairs in Syracuse.

14. In Greece Alexander, tyrant of Pherae, was assassinated by his own wife Thebe and her brothers Lycophron and Tisiphonus. The brothers at first received great acclaim as tyrannicides, but later, having changed their purpose and bribed the mercenaries, they disclosed themselves as tyrants, slew many of their opponents, and, having contrived to make their forces imposing, retained the government by force. Now the faction among the Thessalians called Aleuadae, who enjoyed a far-flung reputation by reason of their noble birth, began to oppose the tyrants. Not being of sufficient strength to fight by themselves they took on Philip, the king of the Macedonians, as ally, and he, entering Thessaly, defeated the tyrants and, when he had vindicated the independence of their cities, showed himself very friendly to the Thessalians. Wherefore in the course of subsequent events not merely Philip himself but his son Alexander after him had the Thessalians always as confederates.

Among historians Demophilus, the son of the chronicler Ephorus, who treated in his work the history of what is known as the Sacred War, which had been passed over by his father, began his account with the capture of the shrine at Delphi and the pillaging of the oracle by Philomelus the Phocian. This war lasted eleven years until the annihilation of those who had divided amongst themselves the sacred property. Callisthenes wrote the history of the events in the Hellenic world in ten books and closed with the capture of the shrine and the impious act of Philomelus the Phocian. Diyllus the Athenian began his history with the pillaging of the shrine and wrote twenty-six books, in which he included all the events which occurred in this period both in Greece and in Sicily.

15. When Elpines was archon at Athens [356/5] the Romans elected as consuls Marcus Poplius Laenas and Gnaeus Maemilius Imperiosus, and the one hundred sixth celebration was held of the Olympian games, at which Porus the

Malian won the stadion race. During their term of office, in Italy there gathered in Lucania a multitude of men from every region, a mixture of every sort, but for the most part runaway slaves. These at first led a marauding life and as they habituated themselves to out-of-door life and making raids they gained practice and training in warfare; consequently, since they regularly had the upper hand with the inhabitants in their battles, they reached a state of considerably increased importance. First they took by siege the city Terina and plundered it completely; then, having taken Hipponium, Thurii, and many other cities, they formed a common government and were called Bruttians from the fact that most of them were slaves, for in the local dialect runaway slaves were called "bruttians."

Such, then, was the origin of the people of the Bruttians in Italy.

How, after being expelled from his native land, he again got control of Syracuse (16-20).

16. In Sicily Philistus, Dionysius' general, sailed to Rhegium and transported to Syracuse the cavalry, more than five hundred in number. When he had added to these other cavalry more numerous and two thousand infantry, he made an expedition against Leontini, which had revolted from Dionysius, and having succeeded in entering the walls by night captured a portion of the city. A sharp engagement ensued, and the Syracusans came to the aid of the Leontinians, so that he was defeated and was driven out of Leontini. Heracleides, who had been left behind by Dion as commander of his men-of-war, having been hindered by storms in the Peloponnese, was too late for Dion's return and the liberation of the Syracusans, but he now came with twenty men-of-war and fifteen hundred soldiers. Being a man of very great distinction and considered worthy of the position, he was chosen admiral by the Syracusans, and, having been assigned to the supreme command of the armed forces along with Dion, he participated in the war against Dionysius. After this Philistus, who had been appointed general and had fitted out sixty triremes, fought a naval battle with the Syracusans, who had about the same number. As the fight became sharp Philistus at first was superior because of his own gallantry, but later on, when he was intercepted by the enemy, the Syracusans, encircling the ships from all sides, put forth strenuous efforts to capture the general alive, but Philistus, with apprehensions of torture after his capture, slew himself after having performed a great many very important services to the tyrants and having proved himself the most faithful of their friends to the men in power. The Syracusans, after they had won the naval battle, dismembered the body of Philistus, dragged it through the whole city, and cast it forth unburied; and Dionysius, who had lost the most efficient of his friends and had no other general of repute, being himself unable to sustain the burden of the war, sent out ambassadors to Dion, first offering him the half of his power, but later consenting to place the whole of it in his hands.

17. When Dion replied that it was only fair to surrender to the Syracusans the acropolis with the reservation of certain property and privileges, Dionysius was ready to surrender the citadel to the people on the condition that he took his mercenaries and his property and went abroad to Italy, and Dion counselled the Syracusans to accept his offer, but the people, persuaded by their inopportune demagogues, refused, believing that they could forcibly make the tyrant surrender by siege. Thereafter Dionysius left the best of his mercenaries to guard the citadel, while he himself, putting his possessions and all his royal paraphernalia on board ship, sailed off secretly and put ashore in Italy. The Syracusans were divided into two factions, some being of the opinion that they should entrust the generalship and supreme power in the state to Heracleides because it was believed that he would never aim at tyrannical power, and the others declaring that Dion should have the supremacy over the entire government. Furthermore, large sums for wages were due to the Peloponnesian mercenaries who had liberated Syracuse and the city was short of funds, so the mercenaries, deprived of their money, banded together in excess of three thousand, and since all had been selected for meritorious conduct and because of their training in actual warfare were hardened veterans, they were far more than a match for the Syracusans in valour. As for Dion, when he was asked by the mercenaries to join their revolt and to take vengeance upon the Syracusans as a common enemy, he at first refused, but later, under compulsion of the critical circumstances, he accepted the command of the mercenaries, and with them marched off to Leontini. The Syracusans in a body set out to pursue the mercenaries, and, having engaged them on the way and lost many men, retreated. Dion, who had defeated them in a brilliant battle, harboured no grudge toward the Syracusans, for when they sent him a herald to arrange for the removal of the dead he granted them permission and set free without ransom the captives, who were numerous. For many who were on the point of being slain in their flight declared that they were on Dion's side and all for this reason escaped death.

18. After this Dionysius dispatched to Syracuse as general Nypsius the Neapolitan, a man who excelled in valour and in sagacity of generalship; and with him he sent merchantmen laden with grain and other supplies. Nypsius then set sail from Locri and completed the voyage to Syracuse. The tyrant's mercenaries, stationed on the acropolis, as their supply of grain failed at this time, were in dire distress for want of supplies, but for a time endured in good spirits their lack of food; then, when human nature succumbed to necessity and they despaired of saving their lives, they came together in an assembly at night and voted to surrender the citadel and themselves to the Syracusans at dawn. Night was just drawing to a close as the mercenaries sent heralds to the Syracusans to make terms, but, as dawn was just breaking, Nypsius sailed in with his fleet and anchored off Arethusa. Consequently, now that the scarcity had suddenly changed into a great abundance of supplies, the general Nypsius, after disembarking his soldiers, held a joint assembly, presented arguments suitable to the occasion and won the support of the men to meet the perils in store. Now the acropolis which was already on the point of being given over to the Syracusans was unexpectedly preserved in the aforesaid manner, but the Syracusans, manning all their triremes, sailed against the enemy while they were still occupied in unloading the supplies. Since the attack was unexpected and the mercenaries in the citadel could only be drawn up in confused fashion against the enemy triremes, a naval battle took place in which the Syracusans had the superiority, in fact they sank some of the ships, gained possession of others, and pursued the remnant to the shore. Elated by their success they offered magnificent sacrifice to the gods in honour of the victory, and, turning to banqueting and drink, with contempt for the men they had defeated, were negligent about their guards.

19. Nypsius, the commander of the mercenaries, wishing to renew the battle and retrieve the defeat, with his army which had been marshalled during the night unexpectedly attacked the wall which had been constructed, and, finding that the guards through contempt and drunkenness had betaken themselves to sleep, he placed against it the ladders that had been constructed in case they were needed. The bravest of the mercenaries climbed on the wall with these, slaughtered the guards, and opened the gates. As the men poured into the city, the generals of the Syracusans, becoming sober after their drunkenness, tried to bring aid, but, their efforts being hampered by the wine, some were slain and some fled. When the city had been captured and almost all the soldiers from the citadel had rushed inside the circuit-walls, since the Syracusans were panic-stricken by the suddenness and confusion of the attack, a great slaughter took place. The soldiers of the tyrant numbered more than ten thousand and their lines were so well marshalled that no one was able to withstand their sheer weight, inasmuch as the din and disorder and, furthermore, the lack of a commander, impeded the Syracusans in their hour of defeat. Once the market-place had come into possession of the enemy, the victors straightway attacked the residences. They carried off much property and took off as slaves many women and children and household servants besides. Where the Syracusans formed to meet them in narrow alleys and other streets, continuous engagements occurred and many were killed and not a few wounded. So they passed the night slaying one another at random in the darkness, and every quarter teemed with dead.

20. At daybreak the magnitude of the disaster was seen in its entirety, and the Syracusans, whose one hope of survival lay in help from Dion, sent horsemen to Leontini begging Dion not to suffer his native city to be captured by the spear point of the enemy, to forgive them the mistakes they had made, and in pity for their present misfortunes to come and retrieve his country's disaster. Dion, a man noble in spirit and civilised in his judgements because of his philosophical training, did not bear a grudge against his fellow citizens, but, after winning the mercenaries over, straightway set out and, having quickly traversed the road to Syracuse, arrived at the Hexapyla. After drawing up his soldiers at that point he advanced with all speed and encountered, fleeing from the city, children, women, and old men in excess of ten thousand. All of these as they met him besought him with tears to avenge their own misfortunes. The mercenaries from the citadel, having already obtained their objective, after plundering the houses by the market-place set them on fire and now, attacking the remaining residences, were in the act of plundering the possessions in these. At this very moment Dion, rushing into the city in several places and attacking the enemy as they were busily engaged in their looting, slew all whom he met as they were lugging furnishings of various sorts off on their shoulders, and because of the unexpectedness of his appearance and the disorder and confusion, all of those who were making off with their plunder were easily overpowered. Finally, after more than four thousand had been slain, some in the houses, and others in the streets, the rest fled in a body to the citadel and closing the gates escaped the danger.

Dion, having accomplished the finest of all the deeds ever performed by him, preserved the burning houses by extinguishing the flames, and, by restoring to good condition the circuit-wall, at one stroke fortified the city and by walling off the foe blocked their egress to the mainland. When he had cleansed the city of the dead and had erected a trophy of victory, he offered sacrifices to the gods for the deliverance of the city. An assembly was summoned, and the people, as an expression of their gratitude to him, elected Dion general with absolute power and accorded him honours suited to a hero, and Dion in harmony with his former conduct generously absolved all his personal enemies of the charges outstanding against them and having reassured the populace brought them to a state of general harmony. The Syracusans with universal praises and with elaborate testimonials of approval honoured their benefactor as the one and only saviour of their native land.

Such was the condition of affairs in Sicily.

Conclusion of the Social War (21-22. 2).

21. In Greece proper, where the Chians, Rhodians, Coans, and also the Byzantians were continuing the Social War against the Athenians, both sides were making great preparations, for they wished to decide the war by a naval battle. The Athenians had previously sent Chares forth with sixty ships, but now, manning sixty more and placing as generals in command the most distinguished of their citizens, Iphicrates and Timotheus, they dispatched this expedition along with Chares to continue war upon their allies who had revolted. The Chians, Rhodians, and Byzantians together with their allies manned one hundred ships and then sacked Imbros and Lemnos, Athenian islands, and having descended on Samos with a large contingent laid waste the countryside and besieged the city by land and by sea; and by ravaging many other islands that were subject to Athens they collected money for the needs of the war. All the Athenian generals now met and planned at first to besiege the city of the Byzantians, and when later the Chians and their allies abandoned the siege of Samos and turned to assist the Byzantians, all the fleets became massed in the Hellespont. Just at the time when the naval battle was about to take place a great wind fell upon them and thwarted their plans. When Chares, however, though the elements were against him, wished to fight, but Iphicrates and Timotheüs opposed on account of the heavy sea, Chares, calling upon his soldiers to bear him witness, accused his colleagues of treason and wrote to the assembly about them, charging that they had purposely shirked the sea-fight. And the Athenians were so incensed that they indicted Iphicrates and Timotheüs, fined them many talents, and removed them from the generalship.

Combination of three kings against Philip (22. 3).

22. Chares, now that he had succeeded to the command of the whole fleet and was eager to relieve the Athenians of its expense, undertook a hazardous operation. Now Artabazus had revolted from the Persian King and with only a few soldiers was on the point of joining combat with the satraps who had more than seventy thousand. Chares with all his forces took part with Artabazus in a battle and defeated the King's army, and Artabazus, out of gratitude for his kindness, made him a present of a large sum of money, with which he was able to furnish his entire army with supplies. The Athenians at first approved Chares' action, but later, when the King sent ambassadors and denounced Chares, they changed their minds; for word had been spread abroad that the King had promised Athens' enemies that he would join them in their war against the Athenians with three hundred ships. The assembly, accordingly, taking a cautious attitude, decided to bring to a close the war against their revolted allies; and finding that they too desired peace they easily came to terms with them.

So the Social War, as it was called, came to such a close after lasting four years.

In Macedon three kings combined against Philip, the kings of the Thracians, Paeonians, and Illyrians. For these peoples, inasmuch as they bordered upon Macedonia, eyed with suspicion the aggrandisement of Philip; singly, however, they were not capable of sustaining a combat, each having suffered defeat in the past, but they supposed that, if they should join their forces in a war, they would easily have the better of Philip. So it was that, while they were still gathering their armies, Philip appeared before their dispositions were made, struck terror into them, and compelled them to join forces with the Macedonians.

How Philomelus the Phocian, having seized Delphi and its oracle, kindled the Sacred War (23-25).

23. When Callistratus was archon at Athens, [355/4] the Romans elected as consuls Marcus Fabius and Gaius Plautius. During their term of office the Sacred War, as it was called, began and lasted nine years. For Philomelus the Phocian, a man of unusual audacity and lawlessness, seized the shrine in Delphi and kindled the Sacred War for reasons somewhat as follows. When the Lacedaemonians had fought the Leuctrian War with the Boeotians and been defeated, the Thebans brought a serious charge against the Lacedaemonians in the Amphictyonic Council because of their seizure of the Cadmeia and obtained a judgement against them for a large indemnity; and the Phocians for having cultivated a large portion of the consecrated territory named Cirrhaean were arraigned in the Council and were fined a large number of talents. When they did not discharge the assessments, the hieromnemones of the Amphictyons brought charges against the Phocians and demanded of the Council that if the Phocians did not pay the money to the god, they should lay under a curse the land of those who were cheating the god. Likewise they declared that the others against whom judgements had been passed should discharge their fines, the Lacedaemonians being in this category, and if they did not obey, they should incur the common hatred of the Greeks for their knavery. When the Greeks all ratified the decisions of the Amphictyons and the territory of the Phocians was about to be placed under the curse, Philomelus, who had the highest reputation among the Phocians, harangued his fellow countrymen, explaining that they were unable to pay the money on account of the magnitude of the fine, and that to allow the territory to be cursed was not only cowardly but involved them in danger since it was the destruction of the means by which they all lived. He endeavoured also to prove that the judgements of the Amphictyons were unjust in the highest degree, since they had inflicted huge fines for the cultivation of what was a very small parcel of land. Accordingly he advised them to treat the fines as null and void and declared that the Phocians had strong grounds for their case against the Amphictyons: for in ancient times they had held control and guardianship of the oracle. As witness he offered the most ancient and greatest of all poets, Homer who said:

> Now over Phocians Schedius ruled and e'en Epistrophus,
> They dwelt in Cyparissus and in Pytho land of rocks. [Illiad, 2. 517-9]

On this account he said they should enter a claim for the guardianship of the oracle on the ground that this belonged to the Phocians as an inheritance from their fathers. He promised that he would succeed with the enterprise if they would appoint him general with absolute power for the entire programme and give him complete authority.

24. When the Phocians out of fear of the judgement elected him general with absolute power, Philomelus set about energetically to fulfil his promise. First he went to Sparta, where he conversed in private with Archidamus king of the Lacedaemonians, representing that the king had an equal interest in the effort to render null and void the judgements of the Amphictyons, for there existed serious and unjust pronouncements of that Council to the injury of the Lacedaemonians also. He accordingly disclosed to Archidamus that he had decided to seize Delphi and that if he succeeded in obtaining the guardianship of the shrine he would annul the decrees of the Amphictyons. Although Archidamus approved of the proposal, he said he would not for the present give assistance openly, but that he would co-operate secretly in every respect, providing both money and mercenaries. Philomelus, having received from him fifteen talents and having added at least as much on his own account, hired foreign mercenaries and chose a thousand of the Phocians, whom he called peltasts. Then, after he had gathered a multitude of soldiers and had seized the oracle, he slew the group of Delphians called Thracidae who sought to oppose him and confiscated their possessions; but, observing that the others were terror-stricken, he exhorted them to be of good cheer since no danger would befall them. When news of the seizure of the shrine was noised abroad, the Locrians, who lived near by, straightway took the field against Philomelus. A battle took place near Delphi and the Locrians, having been defeated with the loss of many of their men, fled to their own territory, and Philomelus, being elated by his victory, hacked from the slabs the pronouncements of the Amphictyons, deleted the letters recording their judgements, and personally caused the report to be circulated that he had resolved not to plunder the oracle nor had he purposed to commit any other lawless deed, but that in support of the ancestral claim to the guardianship and because of his desire to annul the unjust decrees of the Amphictyons, he was vindicating the ancestral laws of the Phocians.

25. The Boeotians, coming together in an assembly, voted to rally to the support of the oracle and immediately dispatched troops. While these things were going on, Philomelus threw a wall around the shrine and began to assemble a large number of mercenaries by raising the pay to half as much again, and selecting the bravest of the Phocians he enrolled them and quickly had a considerable army; for with no less than five thousand troops he took up a position in defence of Delphi, already a formidable adversary for those who wished to make war upon him. Later on, having led an expedition into the territory of the Locrians and laid waste much of the enemy's land, he encamped near a river that flowed past a stronghold. Though he made assaults upon this, he was unable to take it and finally desisted from the siege, but joining battle with the Locrians he lost twenty of his men, and not being able to get possession of their bodies, he asked through a herald the privilege of taking them up. The Locrians, refusing to grant this, gave answer that amongst all the Greeks it was the general law that temple-robbers should be cast forth without burial. Philomelus so resented this that he joined battle with the Locrians and, bending every effort, slew some of the enemy, and having got possession of their bodies compelled the Locrians to make an exchange of the dead. As he was master of the open country, he sacked a large portion of Locris and returned to Delphi, having given his soldiers their fill of the spoils of war. After this, since he wished to consult the oracle for the war, he compelled the Pythian priestess to mount her tripod and deliver the oracle.

On the original discovery of the oracle (26).

26. Since I have mentioned the tripod, I think it not inopportune to recount the ancient story which has been handed down about it. It is said that in ancient times goats discovered the oracular shrine, on which account even to this day the Delphians use goats preferably when they consult the oracle. They say that the manner of its discovery was the following. There is a chasm at this place where now is situated what is known as the "forbidden" sanctuary, and as goats had been wont to feed about this because Delphi had not as yet been settled, invariably any goat that approached the chasm and peered into it would leap about in an extraordinary fashion and utter a sound quite different from what it was formerly wont to emit. The herdsman in charge of the goats marvelled at the strange phenomenon and having approached the chasm and peeped down it to discover what it was, had the same experience as the goats, for the goats began to act like beings possessed and the goatherd also began to foretell future events. After this as the report was bruited among the people of the vicinity concerning the experience of those who approached the chasm, an increasing number of persons visited the place and, as they all tested it because of its miraculous character, whosoever approached the spot became inspired. For these reasons the oracle came to be regarded as a marvel and to be considered the prophecy-giving shrine of Earth. For some time all who wished to obtain a prophecy approached the chasm and made their prophetic replies to one another; but later, since many were leaping down into the chasm under the influence of their frenzy and all disappeared, it seemed best to the dwellers in that region, in order to eliminate the risk, to station one woman there as a single prophetess for all and to have the oracles told through her. For her a contrivance was devised which she could safely mount, then become inspired and give prophecies to those who so desired, and this contrivance has three supports and hence was called a tripod, and, I dare say, all the bronze tripods which are constructed even to this day are made in imitation of this contrivance. In what manner, then, the oracle was discovered and for what reasons the tripod was devised I think I have told at sufficient length. It is said that in ancient times virgins delivered the oracles because virgins have their natural innocence intact and are in the same case as Artemis; for indeed virgins were alleged to be well suited to guard the secrecy of disclosures made by oracles. In more recent times, however, people say that Echecrates the Thessalian, having arrived at the shrine and beheld the virgin who uttered the oracle, became enamoured of her because of her beauty, carried her away with him and violated her; and that the Delphians because of this deplorable occurrence passed a law that in future a virgin should no longer prophesy but that an elderly woman of fifty should declare the oracles and that she should be dressed in the costume of a virgin, as a sort of reminder of the prophetess of olden times. Such are the details of the legend regarding the discovery of the oracle; and now we shall turn to the activities of Philomelus.

The defeat and death of Philomelus the Phocian (27-31).

27. When Philomelus had control of the oracle he directed the Pythia to make her prophecies from the tripod in the ancestral fashion, but when she replied that such was not the ancestral fashion, he threatened her harshly and compelled her to mount the tripod. Then when she frankly declared, referring to the superior power of the man who was resorting to violence: "It is in your power to do as you please," he gladly accepted her utterance and declared that he had the oracle which suited him. He immediately had the oracle inscribed and set it up in full view, and made it clear to everyone that the god gave him the authority to do as he pleased. Having got together an assembly and disclosed the prophecy to the multitude and urged them to be of good cheer, he turned to the business of the war. There came to him an omen as well, in the temple of Apollo, namely an eagle which, after flying over the temple of the god and swooping down to earth, preyed upon the pigeons which were maintained in the temple precincts, some of which it snatched away from the very altars. Those versed in such matters declared that the omen indicated to Philomelus and the Phocians that they would control the affairs of Delphi. Elated accordingly by these events, he selected the best qualified of his friends for the embassies, and sent some to Athens, some to Lacedaemon, and some to Thebes; and he likewise sent envoys to the other most distinguished cities of the Greek world, explaining that he had seized Delphi, not with any designs upon its sacred properties but to assert a claim to the guardianship of the sanctuary; for this guardianship had been ordained in early times as belonging to the Phocians. He said he would render due account of the property to all the Greeks and expressed himself as ready to report the weight and the number of the dedications to all who wished an examination. He requested that, if any through enmity or envy were to engage in war against the Phocians, these cities should preferably join forces with him, or, if not, at least maintain peaceful relations. When the envoys had accomplished their appointed mission, the Athenians, Lacedaemonians, and some others arranged an alliance with him and promised assistance, but the Boeotians, Locrians, and some others passed decrees to the contrary intent and renewed the war in behalf of the god upon the Phocians.

Such were the events of this year.

28. When Diotimus was archon at Athens, [354/3] the Romans elected as consuls Gaius Marcius and Gnaeus Manlius. During their term of office Philomelus, foreseeing the magnitude of the war, began to gather a multitude of mercenaries and to select for active duty those of the Phocians who were fit. Although the war required additional funds, he kept his hands off the sacred dedications, but he did exact from the Delphians, who were exceptionally prosperous and wealthy, a sufficient sum of money to pay the mercenaries. Having accordingly prepared a large army, he led it into the open country and was obviously holding himself ready to join issue with any who were hostile to the Phocians. And when the Locrians took the field against him a battle was fought near the cliffs called Phaedriades, in which Philomelus won the victory, having slain many of the enemy and taken not a few alive, while some he forced to hurl themselves over the precipices. After this battle the Phocians were elated by their success, but the Locrians, being quite dejected, sent ambassadors to Thebes asking the Boeotians to come to their support and the god's. The Boeotians because of their reverence for the gods and because of the advantage they gained if the decisions of the Amphictyons were enforced, sent embassies to the Thessalians and the other Amphictyons demanding that they make war in common against the Phocians. But when the Amphictyons voted the war against the Phocians much confusion and disagreement reigned throughout the length and breadth of Greece. For some decided to stand by the god and punish the Phocians as temple-robbers, while others inclined toward giving the Phocians assistance.

29. As tribes and cities were divided in their choice, the Boeotians, Locrians, Thessalians, and Perrhaebians decided to aid the shrine, and in addition the Dorians and Dolopians, likewise the Athamanians, Achaeans of Phthiotis, and the Magnesians, also the Aenianians and some others; while the Athenians, Lacedaemonians, and some others of the Peloponnesians fought on the side of the Phocians. The Lacedaemonians co-operated most eagerly for the following reasons. In the Leuctrian War the Thebans, after defeating the enemy, brought suit before the Amphictyons against the Spartans, the charge being that Phoebidas the Spartan had seized the Cadmeia, and the Amphictyons assessed a fine of five hundred talents for the offence. Then when the Lacedaemonians had had judgement entered against them and failed to pay the fine during the period set by the laws, the Thebans again brought suit, this time for double damages. When the Amphictyons set the judgement at a thousand talents, the Lacedaemonians, on account of the large amount of the fine, made declarations similar to those of the Phocians, saying that an unjust judgement had been rendered against them by the Amphictyons. Wherefore, though their interests were now common, the Lacedaemonians hesitated to begin war by themselves on account of the adverse judgement, but thought that it was more seemly to annul the judgements of the Amphictyons through the agency of the Phocians. For these particular reasons they were very ready to fight on the side of the Phocians and they co-operated in securing for them the guardianship of the sanctuary.

30. When it was clear that the Boeotians would take the field with a large army against the Phocians, Philomelus decided to gather a great number of mercenaries. Since the war required ampler funds he was compelled to lay his hands on the sacred dedications and to plunder the oracle. By setting the base pay for the mercenaries at half as much again as was usual he quickly assembled a large number of mercenaries, since many answered the summons to the campaign on account of the size of the pay. Now no men of honourable character enrolled for the campaign because of their reverence for the gods, but the worst knaves, and those who despised the gods, because of their own greed, eagerly gathered about Philomelus and quickly a strong army was formed out of those whose object it was to plunder the shrine. So Philomelus, because of the magnitude of his resources, soon had prepared a considerable army. He immediately advanced into the territory of the Locrians with soldiers both foot and horse amounting to more than ten thousand. When the Locrians marshalled their forces to meet him and the Boeotians came to the support of the Locrians, a cavalry battle ensued in which the Phocians had the superiority. After this the Thessalians together with the allies from neighbouring districts, having assembled to the number of six thousand, arrived in Locris and joining battle with the Phocians met with a defeat by a hill called Argolas. When the Boeotians put in an appearance with thirteen thousand men and the Achaeans from the Peloponnesus came to the support of the Phocians with fifteen hundred, the armies encamped over against one another, both assembled in one place.

31. After this the Boeotians, who had taken captive on foraging parties a good many mercenaries, brought them out in front of the city and made an announcement by heralds that the Amphictyons were punishing with death these men present who had enlisted with the temple-robbers; and immediately, making the deed follow the word, shot them all down, but the mercenaries serving with the Phocians were so enraged by this that they demanded of Philomelus that he mete out the like punishment to the enemy, and then, when, bending every effort, they had taken captive many men who were straggling up and down the countryside where the enemy were, they brought them back and all these Philomelus shot. Through this punishment they forced the opposite side to give up their overweening and cruel vengeance. After this, as the armies were invading another district and were making a march through heavily wooded rough regions, both vanguards suddenly became intermingled. An engagement took place and then a sharp battle in which the Boeotians, who far outnumbered the Phocians, defeated them. As the flight took place through precipitous and almost impassable country many of the Phocians and their mercenaries were cut down. Philomelus, after he had fought courageously and had suffered many wounds, was driven into a precipitous area and there hemmed in, and since there was no exit from it and he feared the torture after capture, he hurled himself over the cliff and having thus made atonement to the gods ended his life. Onomarchus, his colleague in the generalship, having succeeded to the command and retreated with such of his force as survived, collected any who returned from the flight.

While these things were going on, Philip, king of the Macedonians, after taking Methonê by storm and pillaging it, razed it to the ground, and having subdued Pagasae forced it to submit. In the region of the Black Sea Leucon, the king of the Bosporus, died after ruling forty years, and Spartacus, his son, succeeding to the throne, reigned for five years. A war took place between the Romans and Faliscans and nothing important or memorable was accomplished; only raids and pillaging of the territory of the Faliscans went on. In Sicily after Dion the general had been slain by some mercenaries from Zacynthos, Callippus, (a member of the Academy) who had procured them for the assassination, succeeded him and ruled thirteen months.

Onomarchus' succession to the command and his preparations for war (32-33).

32. When Thudemus was archon at Athens, [353/2] the Romans elected as consuls Marcus Poplius and Marcus Fabius. During their term of office, now that the Boeotians had won a victory over the Phocians and were of the opinion that the fate of Philomelus, who was chiefly responsible for the plundering of the temple and who had been punished by gods and men, would deter the rest from like villainy, they returned to their own country. The Phocians, now freed from the war, for the present returned to Delphi and there meeting with their allies in a common assembly deliberated on the war. The moderate party inclined toward the peace, but the irreligious, the hot-headed and avaricious were of the opposite opinion and were looking around to find the proper spokesman to support their lawless aims. When Onomarchus arose and delivered a carefully argued speech urging them to adhere to their original purpose, he swung the sentiment of the gathering toward war, though he did so not so much with the intention of consulting the common welfare as with a view to his own interests, for he had been sentenced frequently and severely by the Amphictyons in the same manner as the rest and had not discharged the fines. Accordingly, seeing that war was more desirable for himself than peace, he quite logically urged the Phocians and their allies to adhere to the project of Philomelus. Having been chosen general with supreme command, he began to collect a large number of mercenaries, and, filling the gaps in his ranks caused by the casualties and having increased his army by the large number of allies and of everything else that is serviceable for war.

33. He was greatly encouraged in this undertaking by a dream which gave intimation of great increase of power and glory. In his sleep, namely, it seemed that he was remodelling with his own hands the bronze statue which the Amphictyons had dedicated in the temple of Apollo, making it much taller and larger. He accordingly assumed that a sign was being given to him from the gods that there would be an increase of glory because of his services as general. The truth turned out to be otherwise, rather the contrary was indicated because of the fact that the Amphictyons had dedicated the statue out of the fines paid by the Phocians who had acted lawlessly toward the shrine and had been fined for so doing. What was indicated was that the fine of the Phocians would take on an increase at the hands of Onomarchus; and such turned out to be the case. Onomarchus, when he had been chosen general in supreme command, prepared a great supply of weapons from the bronze and iron, and having struck coinage from the silver and gold distributed it among the allied cities and chiefly gave it as bribes to the leaders of those cities. Indeed he succeeded in corrupting many of the enemy too, some of whom he persuaded to fight on his side, and others he required to maintain the peace. He easily accomplished everything because of man's greed. In fact he persuaded even the Thessalians, who were held in highest esteem amongst the allies, by bribes to maintain the peace. In his dealings with the Phocians also he arrested and executed those who opposed him and confiscated their property. After invading the territory of the (Locrians) he took Thronion by storm and reduced its inhabitants to slavery, and having intimidated the Amphissans by threats he forced them to submit. He sacked the cities of the Dorians and ravaged their territory. He invaded Boeotia, captured Orchomenus, then, having attempted to reduce Chaeroneia by siege and being defeated by the Thebans, he returned to his own territory.

How the Boeotians, having come to the assistance of Artabazus, defeated the satraps of the Great King (34. 1-2).

How the Athenians, having gained the mastery of the Chersonesus, colonised it (34. 3-4).

How Philip, having captured Methonê, razed it (34. 4-end).

34. While these things were going on, Artabazus, who had revolted from the Persian King, continued the war against the satraps who had been dispatched by the King to take part in the war against him. At first when Chares the Athenian general was fighting with him, Artabazus resisted the satraps courageously, but when Chares had gone and he was left alone he induced the Thebans to send him an auxiliary force. Choosing Pammenes as general and giving him five thousand soldiers, they dispatched him to Asia. Pammenes, by the support he gave to Artabazus and by defeating the satraps in two great battles, won great glory for himself and the Boeotians. Now it seemed an amazing thing that the Boeotians, after the Thessalians had left them in the lurch, and when the war with the Phocians was threatening them with serious dangers, should be sending armies across the sea into Asia and for the most part proving successful in the battles.

While these things were going on, war broke out between the Argives and the Lacedaemonians, and in a battle that took place near the city of Orneae the Lacedaemonians won, and after they had taken Orneae by siege, returned to Sparta. Chares the Athenian general sailed to the Hellespont, captured Sestus, slew its adult inhabitants, and enslaved the rest. When Cersobleptes,son of Cotys, because of his hostility to Philip and his alliance of friendship with the Athenians, had turned over to the Athenians the cities on the Chersonese except Cardia, the assembly sent out colonists to these cities. Philip, perceiving that the people of Methonê were permitting their city to become a base of operations for his enemies, began a siege, and although for a time the people of Methonê held out, later, being overpowered, they were compelled to hand the city over to the king on the terms that the citizens should leave Methonê with a single garment each. Philip then razed the city and distributed its territory among the Macedonians. In this siege it so happened that Philip was struck in the eye by an arrow and lost the sight of that eye.

How Philip, having defeated the Phocians, drove them from Thessaly (35. 1).

How Onomarchus the Phocian, having defeated Philip in two battles, brought him into extreme peril (35. 2). How Onomarchus, having defeated the Boeotians, seized Coroneia (35. 3). How Onomarchus, in a pitched battle with Philip and the Thessalians in Thessaly, was defeated (35. 4-5). How Onomarchus himself was hanged and the rest of his faction were drowned in the sea as temple-robbers (35. 6).

35. After this Philip in response to a summons from the Thessalians entered Thessaly with his army, and at first carried on a war against Lycophron, tyrant of Pherae, in support of the Thessalians; but later, when Lycophron summoned an auxiliary force from his allies the Phocians, Phayllus, the brother of Onomarchus, was dispatched with seven thousand men. But Philip defeated the Phocians and drove them out of Thessaly. Then Onomarchus came in haste with his entire military strength to the support of Lycophron, believing that he would dominate all Thessaly. When Philip in company with the Thessalians joined battle against the Phocians, Onomarchus with his superior numbers defeated him in two battles and slew many of the Macedonians. As for Philip, he was reduced to the uttermost perils and his soldiers were so despondent that they had deserted him, but by arousing the courage of the majority, he got them with great difficulty to obey his orders. Later Philip withdrew to Macedonia, and Onomarchus, marching into Boeotia, defeated the Boeotians in battle and took the city of Coroneia. As for Thessaly, however, Philip had just at that time returned with his army from Macedonia and had taken the field against Lycophron, tyrant of Pherae. Lycophron, however, since he was no match for him in strength, summoned reinforcements from his allies the Phocians, promising jointly with them to organise the government of all Thessaly. So when Onomarchus in haste came to his support with twenty thousand foot and five hundred horse, Philip, having persuaded the Thessalians to prosecute the war in common, gathered them all together, numbering more than twenty thousand foot and three thousand horse. A severe battle took place and since the Thessalian cavalry were superior in numbers and valour, Philip won. Because Onomarchus had fled toward the sea and Chares the Athenian was by chance sailing by with many triremes, a great slaughter of the Phocians took place, for the men in their effort to escape would strip off their armour and try to swim out to the triremes, and among them was Onomarchus. Finally more than six thousand of the Phocians and mercenaries were slain, and among them the general himself; and no less than three thousand were taken captives. Philip hanged Onomarchus; the rest he threw into the sea as temple-robbers.

How Phayllus, having succeeded to the command, coined into money many of the silver and gold dedications at the shrine (36. 1). How, having raised the rate of pay, he gathered a multitude of mercenaries (36).

36. After the death of Onomarchus his brother Phayllus succeeded to the command of the Phocians. In an attempt to retrieve the disaster, he began to gather a multitude of mercenaries, offering double the customary pay, and summoned help from his allies. He got ready also a large supply of arms and coined gold and silver money.

About the same time Mausolus, the tyrant of Caria, died after ruling twenty-four years, and Artemisia, his sister and wife, succeeded to the throne and reigned for two years. Clearchus, the tyrant of Heracleia, was slain during the festival of Dionysus as he went to witness the spectacle, after ruling twelve years, and his son Timotheüs succeeded to the throne and ruled for fifteen years. The Etruscans, continuing their war with the Romans, sacked much of the enemy territory and after marauding as far as the Tiber returned to their own country. In Syracuse, civil strife having broken out between the friends of Dion and Callippus, Dion's friends were defeated, fled to Leontini, and, after a short time, when Hipparinus son of Dionysius had put ashore at Syracuse with troops, Callippus was defeated and driven from the city, and Hipparinus, having recovered his father's realm, ruled for two years.

How he raised the fortunes of the Phocians when they were at their lowest ebb (37. 1). How, by corrupting the cities and their chief men with bribes, he won many allies (37. 2-3). How the tyrants of the Pheraeans, having betrayed Pherae to Philip, became allies of the Phocians (37. 3). Battle of the Phocians with the Boeotians near Orchomenus and defeat of the Phocians (37. 4-5). Other battles of the same peoples by the Cephisus and Coroneia and victory of the Boeotians (37. 5-6).

37. When Aristodemus was archon at Athens, [352/1] the Romans elected as consuls Gaius Sulpicius and Marcus Valerius, and the one hundred seventh celebration of the Olympian games was held, in which Micrinas of Tarentum won the stadion race. During their term of office Phayllus, the general of the Phocians after the death and defeat of his brother, effected another revival of the affairs of the Phocians, then at a low ebb on account of the defeat and slaughter of their soldiers. For since he had an inexhaustible supply of money he gathered a large body of mercenaries, and persuaded not a few allies to co-operate in renewing the war. In fact, by making lavish use of his abundance of money he not only procured many individuals as enthusiastic helpers, but also lured the most renowned cities into joining his enterprise. The Lacedaemonians, for example, sent him a thousand soldiers, the Achaeans two thousand, the Athenians five thousand foot and four hundred horse with Nausicles as their general. The tyrants of Pherae, Lycophron and Peitholaüs, who were destitute of allies after the death of Onomarchus, gave Pherae over to Philip, while they themselves, being protected by terms of truce, brought together their mercenaries to the number of two thousand, and, having fled with these to Phayllus, joined the Phocians as allies. Not a few of the lesser cities as well actively supported the Phocians because of the abundance of money that had been distributed; for gold that incites man's covetousness compelled them to desert to the side which would enable them to profit from their gains. Phayllus accordingly with his army carried the campaign into Boeotia, and, suffering defeat near the city of Orchomenus, lost a great number of men. Later in another battle that took place by the Cephisus River the Boeotians won again and slew over five hundred of the enemy and took no fewer than four hundred prisoners. A few days later, in a battle that took place near Coroneia, the Boeotians were victorious and slew fifty of the Phocians, and took one hundred thirty prisoners.

Now that we have recounted the affairs of the Boeotians and Phocians we shall return to Philip.

How Phayllus, having made an expedition into Locris, captured many cities (38. 1-5). How Phayllus, having fallen ill of a wasting sickness, died a painful death (38. 6). How Phalaecus, having succeeded to the command, conducted the war disgracefully, and was driven into exile (38. 6-end and 59).

38. Philip, after his defeat of Onomarchus in a noteworthy battle, put an end to the tyranny in Pherae, and, after restoring its freedom to the city and settling all other matters in Thessaly, advanced to Thermopylae, intending to make war on the Phocians. But since the Athenians prevented him from penetrating the pass, he returned to Macedonia, having enlarged his kingdom not only by his achievements but also by his reverence toward the god. Phayllus, having made a campaign into the Locris known as Epicnemidian, succeeded in capturing all the cities but one named Naryx, which he had taken by treachery at night but from which he was expelled again with the loss of two hundred of his men. Later as he was encamped near a place called Abae, the Boeotians attacked the Phocians at night and slew a great number of them; then, elated by their success, they passed into Phocian territory, and, by pillaging a great portion of it, gathered a quantity of booty. As they were on their way back and were assisting the city of the Narycaeans, which was under siege, Phayllus suddenly appeared, put the Boeotians to flight, and having taken the city by storm, plundered and razed it, but Phayllus himself, falling sick of a wasting disease, after a long illness, suffering great pain as befitted his impious life, died, leaving Phalaecus, son of the Onomarchus who had kindled the Sacred War, as general of the Phocians, a stripling in years, at whose side he had placed as guardian and supporting general Mnaseas, one of his own friends. After this in a night attack upon the Phocians the Boeotians slew their general Mnaseas and about two hundred of his men. A short while later in a cavalry battle which took place near Chaeroneia, Phalaecus was defeated and lost a large number of his cavalry.

How the peoples of the Peloponnese broke out in civil strife (39).

39. While these things were going on, throughout the Peloponnese also disturbances and disorders had occurred for the following reasons. The Lacedaemonians, being at variance with the Megalopolitans, overran their country with Archidamus in command, and the Megalopolitans, incensed over their actions but not strong enough to fight by themselves, summoned aid from their allies. Now the Argives, Sicyonians, and Messenians in full force and with all speed came to their assistance; and the Thebans dispatched four thousand foot and five hundred horse with Cephision placed in charge as general. The Megalopolitans accordingly, having taken the field with their allies, encamped near the headwaters of the Alpheius River, while the Lacedaemonians were reinforced by three thousand foot-soldiers from the Phocians and one hundred fifty cavalry from Lycophron and Peitholaüs, the exiled tyrants of Pherae, and, having mustered an army capable of doing battle, encamped by Mantineia. Then having advanced to the Argive city of Orneae, they captured it before the arrival of the enemy, for it was an ally of the Megalopolitans. When the Argives took the field against them, they joined battle and defeated them and slew more than two hundred. Then the Thebans appeared, and since they were in number twice as many though inferior in discipline, a stubborn battle was engaged; and as the victory hung in doubt, the Argives and their allies withdrew to their own cities, while the Lacedaemonians, after invading Arcadia and taking the city Helissus by storm and plundering it, returned to Sparta. Some time after this the Thebans with their allies conquered the enemy near Telphusa and after slaying many took captive Anaxander, who was in command, along with more than sixty others. A short time later they had the advantage in two other battles and felled a considerable number of their opponents. Finally, when the Lacedaemonians proved victorious in an important battle, the armies on both sides withdrew to their own cities. Then when the Lacedaemonians made an armistice with the Megalopolitans the Thebans went back to Boeotia. Phalaecus, who was lingering in Boeotia, seized Chaeroneia and when the Thebans came to its rescue, was expelled from that city. Then the Boeotians, who now with a large army invaded Phocis, sacked the greater portion of it and plundered the farms throughout the countryside; and having taken also some of the small towns and gathered an abundance of booty, they returned to Boeotia.

How Artaxerxes, commonly called Ochus, again got possession of Egypt, Phoenicia, and Cyprus (40-52. 8).

40. When Theellus was archon in Athens, [351/0] the Romans elected as consuls Marcus Fabius and Titus Quintius. During their term of office the Thebans, growing weary of the war against the Phocians and finding themselves short of funds, sent ambassadors to the King of the Persians urging him to furnish the city with a large sum of money. Artaxerxes, readily acceding to the request, made a gift to them of three hundred talents of silver. Between the Boeotians and the Phocians skirmishes and raids on each other's territory occurred but no actions worth mentioning took place during this year.

In Asia the King of the Persians, who had in the period treated above made an expedition into Egypt with vast multitudes of soldiers and was unsuccessful, in the period with which we are now dealing again made war on the Egyptians and, after carrying out some remarkable feats by his own forceful activity, regained possession of Egypt, Phoenicia, and Cyprus. To make clear the history of these events I shall set forth first the causes of the war by reviewing again briefly the period to which these events properly belong. We recall that, when the Egyptians revolted from the Persians in the earlier period, Artaxerxes, known as Ochus, himself unwarlike, remained inactive, and though he sent out armies and generals many times, failed in his attempts because of the cowardice and inexperience of the leaders. So, though regarded with contempt by the Egyptians, he was compelled to be patient because of his own inertia and peace-loving nature. In the period now under discussion, when the Phoenicians and the kings in Cyprus had imitated the Egyptians and in contemptuous disregard of him made a move to revolt, he became enraged and decided to make war upon the insurgents. So he rejected the practice of sending out generals, and adopted the plan of carrying out in person the struggles to preserve his kingdom. Wherefore, having made great provision of arms, missiles, food, and forces, he assembled three hundred thousand foot-soldiers, thirty thousand horsemen, three hundred triremes, and five hundred merchantmen and other ships to carry the supplies.

41. He began to make war also on the Phoenicians for the following reasons. In Phoenicia there is an important city called Tripolis, whose name is appropriate to its nature, for there are in it three cities, at a distance of a stade from one another, and the names by which these are called are the city of the Aradians, of the Sidonians, and of the Tyrians. This city enjoys the highest repute amongst the cities of Phoenicia, for there, as it happens, the Phoenicians held their common council and deliberated on matters of supreme importance. Now since the King's satraps and generals dwelt in the city of the Sidonians and behaved in an outrageous and high-handed fashion toward the Sidonians in ordering things to be done, the victims of this treatment, aggrieved by their insolence, decided to revolt from the Persians. Having persuaded the rest of the Phoenicians to make a bid for their independence, they sent ambassadors to the Egyptian king Nectanebos, who was an enemy of the Persians, and after persuading him to accept them as allies they began to make preparations for the war. Inasmuch as Sidon was distinguished for its wealth and its private citizens had amassed great riches from its shipping, many triremes were quickly outfitted and a multitude of mercenaries gathered and, besides, arms, missiles, food, and all other materials useful in war were provided with dispatch. The first hostile act was the cutting down and destroying of the royal park in which the Persian Kings were wont to take their recreation; the second was the burning of the fodder for the horses which had been stored up by the satraps for the war; last of all they arrested such Persians as had committed the acts of insolence and wreaked vengeance upon them. Such was the beginning of the war with the Phoenicians, and Artaxerxes, being apprised of the rash acts of the insurgents, issued threatening warnings to all the Phoenicians and in particular to the people of Sidon.

42. In Babylon the King, after assembling his infantry and cavalry forces, immediately assumed command of them and advanced against the Phoenicians. While he was still on the way, Belesys, the satrap of Syria, and Mazaeus, the governor of Cilicia, having joined forces, opened the war against the Phoenicians. Tennes, the king of Sidon, acquired from the Egyptians four thousand Greek mercenary soldiers whose general was Mentor the Rhodian. With these and the citizen soldiery he engaged the aforementioned satraps, defeated them, and drove the enemy out of Phoenicia.

While these things were going on, a war broke out in Cyprus also, the actions in which were interwoven with the war we have just mentioned. For in this island were nine populous cities, and under them were ranged the small towns which were suburbs of the nine cities. Each of these cities had a king who governed the city and was subject to the King of the Persians. All these kings in common agreement and in imitation of the Phoenicians revolted, and having made preparations for the war, declared their own kingdoms independent. Incensed at these actions, Artaxerxes wrote to Idrieus, despot of Caria, who had just acquired his office and was a friend and ally of the Persians by inheritance from his ancestors, to collect an infantry force and a navy to carry on a war with the kings in Cyprus. Idrieus, after making ready immediately forty triremes and eight thousand mercenary soldiers, sent them to Cyprus, having placed in command as their generals Phocion the Athenian and Evagoras, who had in the former period been king in the island. So these two, having sailed to Cyprus, at once led their army against Salamis, the largest of the cities. Having set up a palisade and fortified the encampment, they began to besiege the Salaminians by land and also by sea. Since all the island had enjoyed peace for a long time and the territory was wealthy, the soldiers, who had possession of the open country, gathered much booty. When word of their affluence got abroad, many soldiers from the opposite coast of Syria and Cilicia flocked over voluntarily in the hope of gain. Finally, after the army with Evagoras and Phocion had been doubled in size, the kings throughout Cyprus fell into a state of great anxiety and terror.

Such was the situation in Cyprus.

43. After this the King of the Persians, who had begun his journey from Babylon, marched with his army against Phoenicia, the ruler of Sidon, Tennes, who was informed of the great size of the Persian army and thought that the insurgents were incapable of fighting against it, decided to provide for his personal safety. Accordingly, without the knowledge of the people of Sidon, he sent the most faithful of his own henchmen, Thettalion, to Artaxerxes with the promise that he would betray Sidon to him, would assist him in vanquishing Egypt, and would render him great service, since he was acquainted with the topography of Egypt and knew accurately the landing-places along the Nile. The King on hearing from Thettalion these particulars was extremely pleased and said that he would free Tennes of the charges relative to the revolt, and he promised to give him rich rewards if he performed all that he had agreed upon, but when Thettalion added that Tennes wished him also to confirm his promise by giving his right hand, thereupon the King, flying into a rage at the thought that he was not trusted, handed Thettalion over to his attendants and gave orders to take off his head. When, as Thettalion was being led off to his punishment, he simply said: "You, O King, will do as you please, but Tennes, though he is able to achieve complete success, since you refuse the pledge, will assuredly not perform any of his promises," the King, hearing what he said, again changed his mind and recalling the attendants directed them to release Thettalion, and then he gave him his right hand, which is the surest pledge amongst the Persians. Thettalion accordingly returned to Sidon and reported what had happened to Tennes without the knowledge of the people of Sidon.

44. The Persian King, accounting it a matter of great importance, in view of his former defeat, to overthrow Egypt, dispatched envoys to the greatest cities of Greece requesting them to join the Persians in the campaign against the

Egyptians. Now the Athenians and the Lacedaemonians replied that they continued to observe their friendship for the Persians, but were opposed to sending troops as allies, but the Thebans, choosing Lacrates as general, dispatched him with a thousand hoplites and the Argives sent three thousand men; they did not, however, choose a general themselves, but when the King requested Nicostratus specifically as general, they concurred. Now Nicostratus was good both in action and in counsel, but there was madness mingled with his intelligence; for since he excelled in bodily strength, he would imitate Heracles when on a campaign by wearing a lion's skin and carrying a club in battle. Following the example of these states, the Greeks who inhabited the sea-coast of Asia Minor dispatched six thousand men, making the total number of Greeks who served as allies ten thousand. Before their arrival the Persian King, after he had traversed Syria and reached Phoenicia, encamped not far from Sidon. As for the Sidonians, while the King had been slow to move, they attended assiduously to the preparation of food, armour, and missiles. Likewise they had encompassed their city with huge triple ditches and constructions of lofty walls. They had also an ample number of citizen soldiers well trained in exercises and hard work and of superior bodily condition and strength. In wealth and in other resources the city far excelled the other cities of Phoenicia and, most important of all, it had more than a hundred triremes and quinqueremes.

45. Tennes, having confided his scheme for betrayal to Mentor the commander of the mercenaries from Egypt, left him to guard a portion of the city and to act in concert with his agents handling the betrayal, while he himself, with five hundred men, marched out of the city, pretending that he was going to a common meeting of the Phoenicians, and he took with him the most distinguished of the citizens, to the number of one hundred, in the role of advisers. When they had come near the King he suddenly seized the hundred and delivered them to Artaxerxes. The King, welcoming him as a friend, had the hundred shot as instigators of the revolt, and when five hundred of the leading Sidonians carrying olive branches as suppliants approached him, he summoned Tennes and asked him if he was able to deliver the city to him; for he was very eager not to receive Sidon on the terms of a capitulation, since his aim was to overwhelm the Sidonians with a merciless disaster and to strike terror into the other cities by their punishment. When Tennes assured him that he would deliver up the city, the King, maintaining his merciless rage, had all five hundred shot down while still holding the suppliant branches. Thereupon Tennes, approaching the mercenaries from Egypt, prevailed upon them to lead him and the King inside the walls. So Sidon by this base betrayal was delivered into the power of the Persians; and the King, believing that Tennes was of no further use to him, put him to death. The people of Sidon before the arrival of the King burned all their ships so that none of the townspeople should be able by sailing out secretly to gain safety for himself, but when they saw the city and the walls captured and swarming with many myriads of soldiers, they shut themselves, their children, and their women up in their houses and consumed them all in flames. They say that those who were then destroyed in the fire, including the domestics, amounted to more than forty thousand. After this disaster had befallen the Sidonians and the whole city together with its inhabitants had been obliterated by the fire, the King sold that funeral pyre for many talents, for as a result of the prosperity of the householders there was found a vast amount of silver and gold melted down by the fire. So the disasters which had overtaken

Sidon had such an ending, and the rest of the cities, panic-stricken, went over to the Persians.

Shortly before this time Artemisia, who had held despotic rule over Caria, passed away after ruling two years, and Idrieus, her brother, succeeded to the despotism and ruled seven years. In Italy the Romans made an armistice with the people of Praeneste, and a treaty with the Samnites, and they put to death two hundred sixty inhabitants of Tarquinii at the hands of the public executioners in the Forum. In Sicily Leptines and Callippus, the Syracusans then in power, took by siege Rhegium, which was garrisoned by the tyrant Dionysius the younger, ejected the garrison, and restored to the people of llhegium their independence.

46. When Apollodorus was archon in Athens, [350/49] the Romans elected as consuls Marcus Valerius and Gaius Sulpicius. During their term of office, in Cyprus, while the people of Salamis were being besieged by Evagoras and Phocion, the rest of the cities all became subject to the Persians, and Pnytagoras, the king of Salamis, alone continued to endure the siege. Now Evagoras was endeavouring to recover his ancestral rule over the Salaminians and through the help of the King of the Persians to be restored to his kingship, but later, when he had been falsely accused to Artaxerxes and the King was backing Pnytagoras, Evagoras, after having given up hope of his restoration and made his defence on the accusations brought against him, was accorded another and higher command in Asia. But then when he had misgoverned his province he fled again to Cyprus and, arrested there, paid the penalty. Pnytagoras, who had made willing submission to the Persians, continued thenceforth to rule unmolested as king in Salamis.

After the capture of Sidon and the arrival of his allies from Argos and Thebes and the Greek cities in Asia, the King of the Persians assembled all his army and advanced against Egypt. As he came to the great marsh where are the Barathra or Pits, as they are called, he lost a portion of his army through his lack of knowledge of the region. Since we have discoursed earlier on the nature of the marsh and the peculiar mishaps which occur there in the first Book of our History, we shall refrain from making a second statement about it. Having passed through the Barathra with his army the King came to Pelusium. This is a city at the first mouth at which the Nile debouches into the sea. Now the Persians encamped at a distance of forty stades from Pelusium, but the Greeks close to the town itself. The Egyptians, since the Persians had given them plenty of time for preparation, had already fortified well all the mouths of the Nile, particularly the one near Pelusium because it was the first and the most advantageously situated. Five thousand soldiers garrisoned the position, Philophron the Spartiate being the general in command. The Thebans, being eager to show themselves the best of the Greeks that were taking part in the expedition, were the first to venture, unsupported and recklessly, to make a crossing through a narrow and deep canal. They had passed through it and were assaulting the walls when the garrison of Pelusium sallied forth from the city and engaged in battle with the Thebans. As the engagement proved severe because of the intense rivalry on both sides, they spent the whole of that day in the battle and were separated only by the night.

47. Then on the next day, as the King divided the Greek army into three contingents, each contingent had a Greek general, and stationed along beside him a Persian officer, a man preferred above the others for valour and loyalty. Now the forward position was held by the Boeotians, who had as general the Theban

Lacrates and as Persian officer Rhosaces. The latter was a descendant of one of the seven Persians who deposed the Magi; he was satrap of Ionia and Lydia, and he was accompanied by a large force of cavalry and no small body of infantry composed of barbarians. Next in line was the Argive contingent of which Nicostratus was general and with him as Persian colleague Aristazanes. The latter was an usher of the King and the most faithful of his friends after Bagoas; and assigned to him were five thousand elite soldiers and eighty triremes. Of the third contingent Mentor was general, he who had betrayed Sidon, having the mercenaries that were formerly under his command; and associated with him on the expedition was Bagoas, whom the King trusted most, a man exceptionally daring and impatient of propriety; and he had the King's Greeks and an ample force of barbarians and not a few ships. The King himself with the remainder of the army held himself in reserve for the whole operation. Such being the distribution of the army on the Persian side, the king of the Egyptians, Nectanebos, was dismayed neither by the multitude of the enemy nor by the general disposition of the Persian forces, though his numbers were far inferior. In fact he had twenty thousand Greek mercenaries, about the same number of Libyans, and sixty thousand Egyptians of the caste known amongst them as "The Warriors", and besides these an incredible number of river-boats suited for battles and engagements on the Nile. The bank of the river facing Arabia had been strongly fortified by him, being a region crowded with towns and, besides, all intersected by walls and ditches. Although he had ready also all the other preparations which were adequate for the war, yet because of his own poor judgement he soon met with complete disaster.

48. The reason for his defeat was chiefly his lack of experience as a general and the fact that the Persians had been defeated by him in the previous expedition. For he had then had as his generals men who were distinguished and superior both in valour and in sagacity in the art of war, Diophantus the Athenian and Lamius the Spartan, and it was because of them that he had been victorious in all respects. At this time, however, since he supposed that he himself was a competent general, he would not share the command with anyone and so, because of his inexperience, was unable to execute any of the moves that would have been useful in this war. Now when he had provided the towns here and there with considerable garrisons, he maintained a strict guard there, and having in his own command thirty thousand Egyptians, five thousand Greeks, and half the Libyans, he held them in reserve to defend the most exposed approaches. Such being the disposition of the forces on both sides, Nicostratus, the general of the Argives, having as guides Egyptians whose children and wives were held as hostages by the Persians, sailed by with his fleet through a canal into a hidden district and, disembarking his men and fortifying a site for a camp, encamped there. The mercenaries of the Egyptians who were keeping a strict guard in the neighbourhood, observing the presence of the enemy, straightway made a sally in number not less than seven thousand. Cleinius the Coan, their commander, drew up his force in line of battle. When those who had sailed in were drawn up opposite, a sharp battle ensued in the course of which the Greeks serving with the Persians, fighting brilliantly, slew the general Cleinius and cut down more than five thousand of the rest of the soldiers. Nectanebos the Egyptian king, on hearing of the loss of his men, was terror-stricken, thinking that the rest of the Persian army also would easily cross the river. Assuming that the enemy with their entire army would come to the very gates of Memphis, he decided first and foremost to take precautionary measures to protect the city. Accordingly he returned to Memphis with the army he had retained and began to prepare for the siege.

49. Lacrates the Theban, who was in command of the first contingent, hastened to begin the siege of Pelusium. First he diverted the stream of the canal to other directions, then when the channel had become dry he filled it with earth and brought siege engines against the city. When a large portion of the walls fell, the garrison in Pelusium quickly built others to oppose the advance and reared huge towers of wood. The battle for the walls continued for several days running and at first the Greeks in Pelusium vigorously warded off the besiegers; but when they learned of the king's withdrawal to Memphis they were so terror-stricken that they sent envoys to arrange for a settlement. Since Lacrates gave them pledges backed by oaths to the effect that if they surrendered Pelusium they would all be conveyed back to Greece with whatever they could carry on their backs, they delivered over the citadel. After this Artaxerxes dispatched Bagoas with barbarian soldiers to take over Pelusium, and the soldiers, arriving at the place as the Greeks were issuing forth, seized upon many of the articles they were carrying out. The victims of this injustice in their anger called loudly upon the gods who were guardians of their oaths, whereupon Lacrates became incensed, put the barbarians to flight, slaying a number of them, thus standing by the Greeks, the sufferers from the broken pledges. When Bagoas fled to the King and brought accusation against Laerates, Artaxerxes decided that Bagoas' contingent had met with their just deserts and put to death the Persians who were responsible for the robbery. So it was in this fashion that Pelusium was delivered over to the Persians.

Mentor, who was in command of the third contingent, captured Bubastus and many other cities and made them subject to the King by a single strategic device. For since all the cities were garrisoned by two peoples, Greeks and Egyptians, Mentor passed the word around to the soldiers that King Artaxerxes had decided to treat magnanimously those who voluntarily surrendered their cities, but to mete out the same penalty to those who were overcome by force as he had imposed on the people of Sidon; and he instructed those who guarded the gates to give free passage to any who wished to desert from the other side. Accordingly, since the captured Egyptians were leaving the barracks without hindrance, the aforementioned word was quickly scattered amongst all the cities of Egypt. Immediately, therefore, the mercenaries were everywhere at variance with the natives and the cities were filled with strife; for each side was privately endeavouring to surrender its posts and nursing private hopes of gain in exchange for this favour; and this is what actually happened in the case of the city of Bubastus first.

50. When, namely, the forces of Mentor and Bagoas were encamped near Bubastus, the Egyptians, without the knowledge of the Greeks, sent an envoy to Bagoas offering to deliver the city if he would consent to their safety. The Greeks, having knowledge of the mission, overtook the envoy and by dire threats extracted the truth, whereat they were much enraged and attacked the Egyptians, slew some, wounded others, and herded the rest into a quarter of the city. The discomfited men, having notified Bagoas of what had taken place, asked him to come with all speed and receive the city from themselves, but the Greeks had been privately treating with Mentor, who gave them secret encouragement, as soon as Bagoas should enter Bubastus, to attack the barbarians. Later on, when Bagoas with the Persians was entering the city without the sanction of the Greeks and a portion of his men had got inside, the Greeks suddenly closed the gates and attacked those who were inside the walls, and, having slain all the men, took Bagoas himself prisoner. The latter, seeing that his hopes of safety lay in Mentor, besought him to spare his life and promised in future to do nothing without his advice. Mentor, who now prevailed upon the Greeks to set Bagoas free and to arrange the surrender through himself, won credit himself for his success, but, having become responsible for Bagoas' life, he made an agreement with him for common action, and after an exchange of pledges on this matter kept the agreement faithfully till the end of his life. The result of this was that these two by their co-operation in the service of the King attained later on to the greatest power of all the friends and relatives at Artaxerxes' court. In fact Mentor, having been appointed to the chief command in the coastal districts of Asia, performed great services to the King in gathering mercenaries from Greece and sending them to Artaxerxes, and in the course of his activities administering all his duties courageously and loyally. As for Bagoas, after he had administered all the King's affairs in the upper satrapies, he rose to such power because of his partnership with Mentor that he was master of the kingdom, and Artaxerxes did nothing without his advice. After Artaxerxes' death he designated in every case the successor to the throne and enjoyed all the functions of kingship save the title. Of these matters we shall record the details in their proper chronological sequence.

51. At the time under consideration, after the surrender of Bubastus, the remaining cities, terror-stricken, were delivered to the Persians by capitulation. King Nectanebos, while still tarrying in Memphis and perceiving the trend of the cities toward betrayal, did not dare risk battles for his dominion. So giving up hope of his kingship and taking with him the greater part of his possessions, he fled into Aethiopia. Artaxerxes, after taking over all Egypt and demolishing the walls of the most important cities, by plundering the shrines gathered a vast quantity of silver and gold, and he carried off the inscribed records from the ancient temples, which later on Bagoas returned to the Egyptian priests on the payment of huge sums by way of ransom. Then when he had rewarded the Greeks who had accompanied him on the campaign with lavish gifts, each according to his deserts, he dismissed them to their native lands; and, having installed Pherendates as satrap of Egypt, he returned with his army to Babylon, bearing many possessions and spoils and having won great renown by his successes.

How Philip, having won the Chalcidian cities to his side, razed their most important one (52. 9-55).

52. When Callimachus was archon at Athens, [349-48] the Romans elected as consuls Gaius Marcius and Publius Valerius. During their term of office Artaxerxes, seeing that Mentor the general had performed great services for him in the war against the Egyptians, advanced him over and above his other friends. Esteeming him worthy of honour for his gallant actions, he gave him a hundred talents of silver and also the best of expensive decorations, and he appointed him satrap of the Asiatic coast and placed him in charge of the war against the rebels, having designated him general in supreme command. Since Mentor was related to Artabazus and Memnon, both of whom had warred against the Persians in the preceding period and at the time now under consideration were fugitives from

Asia residing at the court of Philip, he requested the King and prevailed upon him to dismiss the charges against them. Immediately afterwards he also summoned them both to come to his presence with all their families; for there had been born to Artabazus by the sister of Mentor and Memnon eleven sons and ten daughters. Mentor was so enchanted with the large number of children born to the marriage that he promoted the lads, giving them the most distinguished commands in the armed forces. He made his first campaign against Hermias the tyrant of Atarneus, who had revolted from the King and was master of many fortresses and cities. Having promised Hermias that he would prevail upon the King to dismiss the charges against him too, he met him at a conference and then, playing him false, arrested him. After getting possession of his signet-ring and writing to the cities that a reconciliation had been effected with the King through Mentor's intervention, he sealed the letters with Hermias' ring, and sent the letters and with them agents who were to take over the districts. The populations of the cities, trusting the documents and being quite content to accept the peace, all surrendered their fortresses and cities. Now that Mentor through deception had quickly and without risk recovered the towns of the rebels, he won great favour with the King, who concluded that he was capable of performing the duties of general realistically. Similarly with regard to the other commanders who were at odds with the Persians, whether by force or by stratagem, he soon subdued them all.

This was the state of affairs in Asia.

In Europe Philip, the Macedonian king, marched against the cities of Chalcidicê, took the fortress of Zereia by siege and razed it. He then intimidated some of the other towns and compelled them to submit. Then coming against Pherae in Thessaly he expelled Peitholaüs, who was in control of the city. While these things were going on, there occurred in Pontus the death of Spartacus king of Pontus after a rule of five years. His brother Paerisades succeeded to the throne and reigned for thirty-eight years.

53. When this year had elapsed, at Athens [348/7] Theophilus was archon, and at Rome Gaius Sulpicius and Gaius Quintius were elected as consuls, and the one hundred eighth celebration of the Olympian games was held at which Polycles of Cyrenê won the stadion race. During their term of office Philip, whose aim was to subdue the cities on the Hellespont, acquired without a battle Mecyberna and Toronê by treasonable surrender, and then, having taken the field with a large army against the most important of the cities in this region, Olynthus, he first defeated the Olynthians in two battles and confined them to the defence of their walls; then in the continuous assaults that he made he lost many of his men in encounters at the walls, but finally bribed the chief officials of the Olynthians, Euthycrates and Lasthenes, and captured Olynthus through their treachery. After plundering it and enslaving the inhabitants he sold both men and property as booty. By so doing he procured large sums for prosecuting the war and intimidated the other cities that were opposed to him. Having rewarded with appropriate gifts such soldiers as had behaved gallantly in the battle and distributed a sum of money to men of influence in the cities, he gained many tools ready to betray their countries. Indeed he was wont to declare that it was far more by the use of gold than of arms that he had enlarged his kingdom.

54. Since the Athenians viewed with alarm the rising power of Philip, they came to the assistance of any people who were attacked by the king, by sending envoys to the cities and urging them to watch over their independence and punish with death those citizens who were bent on treason, and they promised them all that they would fight as their allies, and, after publicly declaring themselves the king's enemies, engaged in an out-and-out war against Philip. The man who more than any other spurred them on to take up the cause of Hellas was the orator Demosthenes, the most eloquent of the Greeks of those times. Even his city was, however, unable to restrain its citizens from their urge toward treason, such was the crop, as it were, of traitors that had sprung up at that time throughout Hellas. Hence the anecdote that when Philip wished to take a certain city with unusually strong fortifications and one of the inhabitants remarked that it was impregnable, he asked if even gold could not scale its walls. For he had learned from experience that what could not be subdued by force of arms could easily be vanquished by gold. So, organising bands of traitors in the several cities by means of bribes and calling those who accepted his gold "guest" and "friends," by his evil communications he corrupted the morals of the people.

55. After the capture of Olynthus, he celebrated the Olympian festival to the gods in commemoration of his victory, and offered magnificent sacrifices; and he organised a great festive assembly at which he held splendid competitions and thereafter invited many of the visiting strangers to his banquets. In the course of the carousals he joined in numerous conversations, presenting to many guests drinking cups as he proposed the toasts, awarding gifts to a considerable number, and graciously making such handsome promises to them all that he won over a large number to crave friendship with him.

At one time in the course of the drinking bout, noticing Satyrus, the actor, with a gloomy look on his face, Philip asked him why he alone disdained to partake of the friendly courtesy he offered; and when Satyrus said that he wished to obtain a boon from him but he feared lest, if he disclosed the request he had decided upon, he should be refused, the king, exceedingly pleased, affirmed that he granted forthwith any favour he might ask. He replied that there were two virgin daughters of a friend of his who were of marriageable age among the captive women; these girls he wished to obtain, not in order to derive any profit if he were granted the gift, but to give them both a dowry and husbands and not permit them to suffer any indignity unworthy of their years. Thereupon Philip gladly acceded to his request and immediately made a present of the girls to Satyrus. By dispensing many other benefactions and gifts of every kind he reaped returns many times greater than his favour; for many who were incited by hopes of his beneficence outstripped one another in devoting themselves to Philip and in delivering their countries to him.

Investigation of the expenditure of the sacred monies and punishment of the pillagers (56-57).

56. When Themistocles was archon at Athens, [347/6] at Rome Gaius Cornelius and Marcus Popilius succeeded to the consular office. During their term of office the Boeotians, after sacking much of the Phocian territory about the city named Hya, defeated their enemies and slew about seventy of them. After this the Boeotians, having come to grips near Coroneia with the Phocians, were defeated and lost many men. When the Phocians now seized several cities of considerable size in Boeotia, the Boeotians took the field and destroyed the grain in enemy territory, but were defeated on the return journey. While these things were going on, Phalaecus, the general of the Phocians, who was accused of stealing many of the sacred properties, was removed from his command. Three generals having been chosen to replace him, Deinocrates, Callias, and Sophanes, an investigation into the sacred property took place and the Phocians called upon those who had administered it to render an accounting. The man who had been in charge of most of it was Philon. Since he was unable to render a proper accounting, he was adjudged guilty, and after being tortured by the generals disclosed the names of his accomplices in the theft, while he himself, after being subjected to the utmost torments, obtained the kind of death that suited his impiety. Those who had diverted the properties to their own use restored whatever balance they still possessed of the stolen property and were themselves put to death as temple-robbers. Of the generals who had been in office previously, the first to hold the office, Philomelus, had kept his hands off the dedications, but the second, named Onomarchus, brother of Philomelus, squandered much of the god's money, while the third, Phayllus, the brother of Onomarchus, when he became general, struck into coin a large number of the dedications in order to pay the mercenaries. He coined for currency one hundred twenty gold bricks which had been dedicated by Croesus king of the Lydians weighing two talents each, and three hundred sixty golden goblets weighing two minae each, and golden statues of a lion and of a woman, weighing in all thirty talents of gold, so that the sum total of gold that was coined into money, referred to the standard of silver, is found to be four thousand talents, while of the silver offerings, those dedicated by Croesus and all the others, all three generals had spent more than six thousand talents' worth, and if to these were added the gold dedications, the sum surpassed ten thousand talents. Some of the historians say that the pillaged property was not less than the sums acquired by Alexander in the treasure chambers of the Persians. The generals on the staff of Phalaecus took steps even to dig up the temple, because some one said that there was a treasure chamber in it containing much gold and silver, and they zealously dug up the ground about the hearth and the tripod. The man who gave information about the treasure offered as witness the most famous and ancient of poets Homer, who says in a certain passage:

> "Nor all the wealth beneath the stony floor that lies Where
> Phoebus, archer god, in rocky Pytho dwells." [*Il.* 9,404-5]

As the soldiers attempted to dig about the tripod, great earthquakes occurred and roused fear in the hearts of the Phocians, and since the gods clearly indicated in advance the punishment they would visit upon the temple-robbers, the soldiers desisted from their efforts. The leader of this sacrilege, the aforementioned Philon, was promptly punished as lie deserved for his crime against the god.

57. Although the loss of the sacred property was ascribed entirely to the Phocians, the Athenians and the Lacedaemonians, who were fighting on the side of the Phocians and received pay out of all proportion to the number of soldiers they sent out, shared in the seizure. This period brought it to pass for the Athenians that they sinned against the divine powers to such an extent that, shortly before the Delphian affair, as Iphicrates was tarrying near Corcyra with a naval force and Dionysius the tyrant of Syracuse had shipped to Olympia and to Delphi statues cunningly wrought in gold and ivory, Iphicrates, chancing to fall in with the ships that were conveying these statues, seized them and sent word to the Athenian people inquiring what he should do with them; whereat the Athenians instructed him not to raise questions about what concerned the gods, but to give his attention to seeing that his soldiers were well fed. Now Iphicrates, obeying the decision of his country, sold as booty the works of art belonging to the gods. The tyrant, filled with rage at the Athenians, wrote them a letter of the following tenor:

> "Dionysius to the Senate and Assembly of the Athenians: It is inappropriate to wish you to do well since you are committing sacrilege against the gods both on land and on sea, and, having made off with the statues which had been sent by us to be dedicated to the gods, you have turned them into coin and have committed impiety toward the greatest of the gods, Apollo, whose abode is Delphi, and Olympian Zeus."

Such now was the conduct of the Athenians toward the divine powers, and that too though they boasted that Apollo was their tutelary god and progenitor. The Lacedaemonians, though they had consulted the oracle of Apollo at Delphi and through it come to possess their constitution which is admired of all the world, though even now they still interrogate the god on matters of supreme importance, had the effrontery to become partners in crime of those who pillaged the sanctuary.

How those who took refuge at the shrine of Apollo, Phocians all, five hundred in number, were miraculously to the last man burned to death (58).

58. In Boeotia the Phocians, who held three strongly fortified cities, Orchomenus, Coroneia, and Corsiae, conducted from these their campaign against the Boeotians. Being well supplied with mercenaries they pillaged the country and in their thrusts and engagements proved superior to the inhabitants of the place. As a consequence the Boeotians, feeling the pinch of war and the loss of great numbers of their men, but having no financial resources, sent envoys to Philip with a request for assistance. The king, pleased to see their discomfiture and disposed to humble the Boeotians' pride over Leuctra, dispatched few men, being on his guard against one thing only: lest he be thought to be indifferent to the pillaging of the oracle. As the Phocians were engaged in building a fortress near the place named Abae, at which is a holy shrine of Apollo, the Boeotians took the field against them. Some of the Phocians straightway fled to the nearest cities and dispersed, while others took refuge in the temple of Apollo and perished to the number of five hundred. Now many other divine visitations fell to the lot of the Phocians about this period, and in particular the one that I am about to relate. The men who had taken refuge in the temple supposed that their lives would be saved through the intervention of the gods, but on the contrary through some divine Providence they met with the punishment temple-robbers well deserve. For there was a quantity of rushes about the temple, and a fire had been left behind in the tents of the men who had fled, with the result that the rushes caught fire and such a great conflagration was touched off so miraculously that the temple was consumed and the Phocians who had fled to it for refuge were burned alive. Indeed it became apparent that the gods do not extend to temple-robbers the protection generally accorded to suppliants.

How the Phocian war was concluded (59-60).

59. When Archias was archon at Athens, [346/5] the Romans elected Marcus Aemilius and Titus Quinctius consuls. During their term of office the Phocian War, after lasting for ten years, was terminated in the following manner. Since the Boeotians and the Phocians were utterly dejected by the length of the war, the Phocians dispatched envoys to Lacedaemon asking for reinforcements, and the Spartans sent a thousand hoplites in charge of whom as general they placed their king Archidamus. Similarly the Boeotians sent an embassy to Philip proposing an alliance, and Philip, after taking over the Thessalians, entered Locris with a large army. When he had overtaken Phalaecus, who had again been granted the generalship and had the main body of the mercenaries, Philip prepared to decide the war by a pitched battle. Phalaecus, who was tarrying in Nicaea and saw that he was no match for Philip, sent ambassadors to the king to treat for an armistice. An agreement was reached whereby Phalaecus with his men should depart whithersoever he wished, and he then, under terms of the truce, withdrew to the Peloponnese with his mercenaries to the number of eight thousand, but the Phocians, whose hopes were now completely crushed, surrendered to Philip. The king, having without a battle unexpectedly terminated the Sacred War, sat in council with the Boeotians and the Thessalians. As a result he decided to call a meeting of the Amphictyonic Council and leave to it the final decision on all the issues at stake.

60. The members of the Council then passed a decree admitting Philip and his descendants to the Amphictyonic Council and according him two votes which formerly had been held by the Phocians, now defeated in war. They also voted that the three cities in the possession of the Phocians should have their walls removed and that the Phocians should have no participation in the shrine of Delphi or in the Council of the Amphictyons; that they should not be permitted to acquire either horses or arms until they should have repaid to the god the monies they had pillaged; that those of the Phocians who had fled and any others who had had a share in robbing the sanctuary were to be under a curse and subject to arrest wherever they might be; that all the cities of the Phocians were to be razed and the men moved to villages, no one of which should have more than fifty houses, and the villages were to be not less than a stade distant from one another; that the Phocians were to possess their territory and to pay each year to the god a tribute of sixty talents until they should have paid back the sums entered in the registers at the time of the pillaging of the sanctuary. Philip, furthermore, was to hold the Pythian games together with the Boeotians and Thessalians, since the Corinthians had shared with the Phocians in the sacrilege committed against the god. The Amphictyons and Philip were to hurl the arms of the Phocians and their mercenaries down the crags and burn what remained of them and to sell the horses. In similar tenor the Amphictyons laid down regulations for the custody of the oracle and other matters affecting due respect for the gods and the general peace and concord of the Greeks. Thereafter, when Philip had helped the Amphictyons give effect to their decrees and had dealt courteously with all, he returned to Macedonia, having not merely won for himself a reputation for piety and excellent generalship, but having also made important preparations for the aggrandisement that was destined to be his. For he was ambitious to be designated general of Hellas in supreme command and as such to prosecute the war against the Persians. This was what actually came to pass, but these events we shall record severally in their proper periods; we shall now proceed with the thread of our narrative.

How those who had participated with the Phocians in the pillaging of the shrine were all punished by some sort of divine agency (61-64).

61. First it is only right, so we think, to record the punishment which was visited by the gods upon those who had committed the outrage on the oracle. For, speaking generally, it was not merely the perpetrators of the sacrilege but all persons who had the slightest connection with the sacrilege that were hounded by the inexorable retribution sent of Heaven. In fact the man who first schemed for the seizure of the shrine, Philomelus, in a crisis of the war hurled himself over a cliff, while his brother Onomarchus, after taking over the command of his people, now become desperate, was cut to pieces in a battle in Thessaly, along with the Phocians and mercenaries of his command, and crucified. The third in succession and the one who coined into money most of the dedications, Phayllus, fell ill of a lingering disease and so was unable even to secure a quick release from his punishment. The last of all, Phalaecus, who had gathered the remnants of the pillaged property, passed his life for a considerable length of time wandering about in great fear and danger, though it was not Heaven's intent that he should be happier than those who participated with him in the sacrilege, but that by being tortured longer and by becoming known to many for his misfortunes, his sad fate might become notorious. For when he had taken flight with his mercenaries following the agreement, he first sojourned in the Peloponnese, supporting his men on the last remnants of the pillaging, but later he hired in Corinth some large freighters and with four light vessels prepared for the voyage to Italy and Sicily, thinking that in these regions he would either seize some city or obtain service for pay, for a war was in progress, as it chanced, between the Lucanians and the Tarentines. To his fellow passengers he said that he was making the voyage because he had been summoned by the people of Italy and Sicily.

62. When he had sailed out of the harbour and was on the high seas, some of the soldiers who were in the largest ship, on which Phalaecus himself was a passenger, conferred with one another because they suspected that no one had sent for them. For they could see on board no officers sent by the peoples who were soliciting aid, and the voyage in prospect was not short, but long and dangerous. Accordingly, since they not only distrusted what they had been told but also feared the overseas campaign, they conspired together, above all those who had commands among the mercenary troops. Finally drawing their swords and menacing Phalaecus and the pilot they forced them to reverse their course. When those who were sailing in the other boats also did the same, they put in again at a Peloponnesian harbour. Then they gathered at the Malean promontory in Laconia and there found Cnossian envoys who had sailed in from Crete to enlist mercenaries. After these envoys had conversed with Phalaecus and the commanders and had offered rather high pay, they all sailed off with them. Having made port at Cnossus in Crete, they immediately took by storm the city called Lyctus. To the Lyctians, who had been expelled from their native land, there appeared a miraculous and sudden reinforcement. For at about the same time the people of Tarentum were engaged in prosecuting a war against the Lucanians and had sent to the Lacedaemonians, who were the stock of their ancestors, envoys soliciting help, whereupon the Spartans, who were willing to join them because of their relationship, quickly assembled an army and navy and as general in command of it appointed King Archidamus, but as they were about to set sail for Italy, a request came from the Lyctians to help them first. Consenting to this, the Lacedaemonians sailed to Crete, defeated the mercenaries and restored to the Lyctians their native land.

63. After this Archidamus sailed to Italy and joined forces with the Tarentines but lost his life fighting gallantly in battle. He was praised for his ability as general and for his conduct on the whole, though in the matter of the Phocian alliance alone he was severely criticised as the one who was chiefly responsible for the seizure of Delphi. Now Archidamus was king of the Lacedaemonians for twenty-three years, and Agis his son succeeded to the throne and ruled for fifteen years. After the death of Archidamus his mercenaries, who had participated in plundering the shrine, were shot down by the Lucanians, whereas Phalaecus, now that he had been driven out of Lyctus, attempted to besiege Cydonia. He had constructed siege engines and was bringing them up against the city when lightning descended and these structures were consumed by the divine fire, and many of the mercenaries in attempting to save the engines perished in the flames. Among them was the general Phalaecus. Some say that he offended one of the mercenaries and was slain by him. The mercenaries who survived were taken into their service by Eleian exiles, were then transported to the Peloponnese, and with these exiles were engaged in war against the people of Elis. When the Arcadians joined the Eleians in the struggle and defeated the exiles in battle, many of the mercenaries were slain and the remainder, about four thousand, were taken captive. After the Arcadians and the Eleians had divided up the prisoners, the Arcadians sold as booty all who had been apportioned to them, while the Eleians executed their portion because of the outrage committed against the oracle.

64. Now the participants in the sacrilege met in this fashion with their just retribution from the deity, and the most renowned cities because of their part in the outrage were later defeated in war by Antipater, and lost at one and the same time their leadership and their freedom. The wives of the Phocian commanders who had worn the gold necklaces taken from Delphi met with punishment befitting their impiety. For one of them who had worn the chain which had belonged to Helen of Troy sank to the shameful life of a courtesan and flung her beauty before any who chose wantonly to abuse it, and another, who put on the necklace of Eriphyle, had her house set on fire by her eldest son in a fit of madness and was burned alive in it. Thus those who had the effrontery to flout the deity met just retribution in the manner I have described at the hands of the gods, while Philip who rallied to the support of the oracle added continually to his strength from that time on and finally because of his reverence for the gods was appointed commander of all Hellas and acquired for himself the largest kingdom in Europe.

Now that we have reported in sufficient detail the events of the Sacred War, we shall return to events of a different nature.

The voyage of Timoleon to Sicily and his fortunes up to his death (65-90 passim).

65. In Sicily the Syracusans, who were engaged in civil strife and were forced to live as slaves under many varied tyrannies, sent ambassadors to Corinth with the request that the Corinthians should dispatch to them as general a man who would administer their city and curb the ambitions of those who aimed to become tyrants. The Corinthians, concluding that it was only right to assist people who were offshoots of themselves, voted to send as general Timoleon, son of Timaenetus, a man of highest prestige amongst his fellow citizens for bravery and sagacity as a general and, in a word, splendidly equipped with every virtue. A peculiar coincidence befell him which contributed toward his being chosen to the generalship. Timophanes, his brother, a man of outstanding wealth and effrontery amongst the Corinthians, had for some time past been clearly aiming at a tyranny and at the moment was winning the poor to his cause and laying up a store of suits of armour and parading about the market-place accompanied by a band of ruffians, not actually claiming to be tyrant but practising the arts of tyranny. Timoleon, who was much averse to the rule of one man, first attempted to dissuade his brother from his overt attempt, but when the latter refused to heed and continued all the more his headstrong career, Timoleon, being unable by reasoning with him to make him mend his ways, put him to death as he was promenading in the market-place. A scuffle ensued and a mob of citizens came surging up stirred by the surprising character and the enormity of the deed, and dissension broke out. One side claimed that as the perpetrator of a kin-murder Timoleon should receive the punishment prescribed by the laws, whereas the other party asserted just the opposite, that they should applaud him as a tyrannicide. When the senate met to deliberate in the council chamber and the matter in dispute was referred to the session, Timoleon's personal enemies denounced him, while those more favourably inclined rallied to his cause and counselled letting him go free. While the investigation was still unsettled there sailed into the harbour from Syracuse the ambassadors who, having made known their mission to the senate, requested them to dispatch with all speed the general they needed. The session accordingly voted to send Timoleon and, in order to ensure the success of the project, they proposed a strange and amazing alternative to him. They affirmed categorically that if he ruled the Syracusans fairly, they adjudged him a tyrannicide, but if too ambitiously, a murderer of his brother. Timoleon, not so much in fear of the threat imposed on him by the senate as because of his native virtue, administered the government in Sicily fairly and profitably. For he subdued in war the Carthaginians, restored to their original state the Greek cities which had been razed by the barbarians, and made all Sicily independent; in a word, having found Syracuse and the other Greek cities depopulated when he took them over, he made them notably populous.

These matters, however, we shall record severally below in their proper periods; now we shall return to the thread of our narrative.

66. When Eubulus was archon at Athens, [345/4] the Romans elected as consuls Marcus Fabius and Servius Sulpicius. In this year Timoleon the Corinthian, who had been chosen by his fellow-citizens to command in Syracuse, made ready for his expedition to Sicily. He enrolled seven hundred mercenaries and, putting his men aboard four triremes and three fast-sailing ships, set sail from Corinth. As he coasted along he picked up three additional ships from the Leucadians and the Corcyraeans, and so with ten ships he crossed the Ionian Gulf.

During this voyage, a peculiar and strange event happened to Timoleon. Heaven came to the support of his venture and foretold his coming fame and the glory of his achievements, for all through the night he was preceded by a torch blazing in the sky up to the moment when the squadron made harbour in Italy. Now Timoleon had heard already in Corinth from the priestesses of Demeter and Persephone that, while they slept, the goddesses had told them that they would accompany Timoleon on his voyage to their sacred island. He and his companions were, in consequence, delighted, recognising that the goddesses were in fact giving them their support. He dedicated his best ship to them, calling it "The Sacred Ship of Demeter and Persephone."

Encountering no hazards, the squadron put in at Metapontum in Italy, and so, shortly after, did a Carthaginian trireme also bringing Carthaginian ambassadors. Accosting Timoleon, they warned him solemnly not to start a war or even to set foot in Sicily, but the people of Rhegium were calling him and promised to join him as allies, and so Timoleon quickly put out from Metapontum hoping to outstrip the report of his coming. Since the Carthaginians controlled the seas, he was afraid that they would prevent his crossing over to Sicily. He was, then, hastily completing his passage to Rhegium.

67. Shortly before this, the Carthaginians on their part had come to see that there would be a serious war in Sicily and began making friendly representations to the cities in the island which were their allies. Renouncing their opposition to the tyrants throughout the island, they established friendship with them, and particularly they addressed themselves to Hicetas, the most powerful of these, because he had the Syracusans under his control. They prepared and transported to Sicily a large sea and land force of their own, and appointed Hanno to the command as general. They had one hundred and fifty battleships, fifty thousand infantry, three hundred war chariots, over two thousand extra teams of horses, and besides all this, armour and missiles of every description, numerous siege engines, and an enormous supply of food and other materials of war.

Advancing first on Entella, they devastated the countryside and blockaded the country people inside the city. The Campanians who occupied the city were alarmed at the odds against them and appealed for help to the other cities that were hostile to the Carthaginians. Of these, none responded except the city of Galeria. These people sent them a thousand hoplites, but the Phoenicians intercepted them, overwhelmed them with a large force, and cut them all down. The Campanians who dwelt in Aetna were at first also ready to send reinforcements to Entella because of kinship, but when they heard of the disaster to the troops from Galeria, they decided to make no move.

68. Now at the time when Dionysius was still master of Syracuse, Hicetas had taken the field against it with a large force, and at first constructing a stockaded camp at the Olympieium carried on war against the tyrant in the city, but as the siege dragged on and provisions ran out, he started back to Leontini, for that was the city which served as his base. Dionysius set out in hot pursuit and overtook his rear, attacking it at once, but Hicetas wheeled upon him, joined battle, and having slain more than three thousand of the mercenaries, put the rest to flight. Pursuing sharply and bursting into the city with the fugitives, he got possession of all Syracuse except the Island.

Such was the situation as regards Hicetas and Dionysius.

Three days after the capture of Syracuse, Timoleon put in at Rhegium and anchored off the city. The Carthaginians promptly turned up with twenty triremes, but the people of Rhegium helped Timoleon to escape the trap. They called a general assembly in the city and staged a formal debate on the subject of a settlement. The Carthaginians expected that Timoleon would be prevailed upon to sail back to Corinth and kept a careless watch. He, however, giving no hint of an intention to slip away, remained close to the tribunal, but secretly ordered nine of his ships to put to sea immediately. Then, while the Carthaginians concentrated their attention on the intentionally long-winded Rhegians, Timoleon stole away unnoticed to his remaining ship and quickly sailed out of the harbour. The Carthaginians, though outmanoeuvred, set out in pursuit, but his fleet had gained a substantial lead, and as night fell it was able to reach Tauromenium before being overtaken. Andromachus, who was the leading man of this city and had constantly favoured the Syracusan cause, welcomed the fugitives hospitably and did much to ensure their safety.

Hicetas now put himself at the head of five thousand of his best soldiers and marched against the Adranitae, who were hostile to him, encamping near their city. Timoleon added to his force some soldiers from Tauromenium and marched out of that city, having all told no more than a thousand men. Setting out at nightfall, he reached Adranum on the second day, and made a surprise attack on Hicetas's men while they were at dinner. Penetrating their defences he killed more than three hundred men, took about six hundred prisoners, and became master of the camp. Capping this manoeuvre with another, he proceeded forthwith to Syracuse. Covering the distance at full speed, he fell on the city without warning, having made better time than those who were routed and fleeing.

Such were the events that took place in this year.

69. When Lyciscus was archon at Athens, [344/3] the Romans elected as consuls Marcus Valerius and Marcus Publius, and the one hundred and ninth Olympiad was celebrated, in which Aristolochus the Athenian won the foot-race. In this year the first treaty was concluded between the Romans and the Carthaginians. In Caria, Idrieus, the ruler of the Carians, died after ruling seven years, and Ada, his sister and wife, succeeding him, ruled for four years.

In Sicily, Timoleon took the Adranitae and the Tyndaritae into his alliance and received not a few reinforcements from them. Great confusion reigned in Syracuse, where Dionysius held the Island, Hicetas Achradina and Neapolis, and Timoleon the rest of the city, while the Carthaginians had put in to the Great Harbour with a hundred and fifty triremes and encamped with fifty thousand men on the shore. Timoleon and his men viewed the odds against them with dismay, but the prospect took a sudden and surprising change for the better. First Marcus, the tyrant of Catania, came over to Timoleon with a considerable army, and then many of the outlying Syracusan forts declared for him in a move to gain their independence. On top of all this, the Corinthians manned ten ships, supplied them with money, and dispatched them to Syracuse. Thereupon Timoleon plucked up courage, but the Carthaginians took alarm and unaccountably sailed out of the harbour, returning with all their forces to their own territory. Hicetas was left isolated, while Timoleon victoriously occupied Syracuse. Then he proceeded to recover Messana, which had gone over to the Carthaginians.

Such was the state of affairs in Sicily.

In Macedonia, Philip had inherited from his father a quarrel with the Illyrians and found no means of reconciling the disagreement. He therefore invaded Illyria with a large force, devastated the countryside, captured many towns, and returned to Macedonia laden with booty. Then he marched into Thessaly, and by expelling tyrants from the cities won over the Thessalians through gratitude. With them as his allies, he expected that the Greeks too would easily be won over also to his favour; and that is just what happened. The neighbouring Greeks straightway associated themselves with the decision of the Thessalians and became his enthusiastic allies.

70. When Pythodotus was archon at Athens, [343/2] the Romans elected as consuls Gaius Plautius and Titus Manlius. In this year Timoleon frightened the tyrant Dionysius into surrendering the citadel, resigning his office and retiring under a safe-conduct to the Peloponnese, but retaining his private possessions. Thus, through cowardice and meanness, he lost that celebrated tyranny which had been, as people said, bound with fetters of steel, and spent the remaining years of his life in poverty at Corinth, furnishing in his life and misfortune an example to all who vaunt themselves unwisely on their successes. He who had possessed four hundred triremes arrived shortly after in Corinth in a small tub of a freighter, conspicuously displaying the enormity of the change in his fortunes.

Timoleon took over the Island and the forts which had formerly belonged to Dionysius. He razed the citadel and the tyrant's palace on the Island, and restored the independence of the fortified towns. Straightway he set to work on a new code of laws, converting the city into a democracy, and specified in exact detail the law of contracts and all such matters, paying special attention to equality. He instituted also the annual office that is held in highest honour, which the Syracusans call the "amphipoly" of Zeus Olympius. To this, the first priest elected was Callimenes, the son of Alcadas, and henceforth the Syracusans continued to designate the years by these officials down to the time of my writing this history and of the change in their form of government. For when the Romans shared their citizenship with the Greeks of Sicily, the office of these priests became insignificant, after having been important for over three hundred years.

Such was the condition of affairs in Sicily.

71. In Macedonia, Philip conceived a plan to win over the Greek cities in Thrace to his side, and marched into that region. Cersobleptes, who was the king of the Thracians, had been following a policy of reducing the Hellespontine cities bordering on his territory and of ravaging their territories. With the aim of putting a stop to the barbarian attacks Philip moved against them with a large force. He overcame the Thracians in several battles and imposed on the conquered barbarians the payment of a tithe to the Macedonians, and by founding strong cities at key places made it impossible for the Thracians to commit any outrages in the future. So the Greek cities were freed from this fear and gladly joined Philip's alliance.

Theopompus of Chios, the historian, in his *History of Philip,* included three books dealing with affairs in Sicily. Beginning with the tyranny of Dionysius the Elder he covered a period of fifty years, closing with the expulsion of the younger Dionysius. These three books are XLI-XLIII.

72. When Sosigenes was archon at Athens, [342/1] the Romans elected as consuls Marcus Valerius and Marcus Gnaeus Publius. In this year, Arymbas king of the Molossians died after a rule of ten years, leaving a son Aeacides, Pyrrhus's father, but Alexander the brother of Olympias succeeded to the throne with the backing of Philip of Macedon.

In Sicily, Timoleon made an expedition against Leontini, for this was the city where Hicetas had taken refuge with a substantial army. He launched an assault on the part called Neapolis, but since the soldiers in the city were numerous and had an advantage in fighting from the walls, he accomplished nothing and broke off the siege. Passing on to the city Engyum, which was controlled by the tyrant Leptines, he assailed it with repeated attacks in the hope of expelling Leptines and restoring to the city its freedom. Taking advantage of his preoccupation, Hicetas led out his entire force and attempted to lay siege to Syracuse, but lost many of his men and hastily retreated back to Leontini. Leptines was frightened into submission, and Timoleon shipped him off to the Peloponnese under a safe-conduct, giving the Greeks tangible evidence of the results of his programme of defeating and expelling tyrants.

The city of Apollonia had also been under Leptines. On taking it, Timoleon restored its autonomy as well as that of the city of Engyum.

73. Lacking funds to pay his mercenaries, he sent a thousand men with his best officers into the part of Sicily ruled by the Carthaginians. They pillaged a large area, and, carrying off a large amount of plunder, delivered it to Timoleon. Selling this and realising a large sum of money, he paid his mercenaries for a long term of service. He took Entella also and, after putting to death the fifteen persons who were the strongest supporters of the Carthaginians, restored the rest to independence. As his strength and military reputation grew, all the Greek cities in Sicily began to submit themselves voluntarily to him, thanks to his policy of restoring to all their autonomy. Many too of the cities of the Sicels and the Sicanians and the rest who were subject to the Carthaginians approached him through embassies in a desire to be included in his alliance.

The Carthaginians recognised that their generals in Sicily were conducting the war in a spiritless manner and decided to send out new ones, together with heavy reinforcements. Straightway they made a levy for the campaign from among their noblest citizens and made suitable drafts among the Libyans. Furthermore, appropriating a large sum of money, they enlisted mercenaries from among the Iberians, Celts, and Ligurians. They were occupied also with the construction of battleships. They assembled many freighters and manufactured other supplies in enormous quantities.

The siege of Perinthus and Byzantium by Philip (74-77).

74. When Nicomachus was archon at Athens, [341/0] the Romans elected as consuls Gaius Marcius and Titus Manlius Torquatus. In this year, Phocion the Athenian defeated and expelled Cleitarchus, the tyrant of Eretria who had been installed by Philip. In Caria, Pizodarus, the younger of the brothers, ousted Ada from her rule as dynast and held sway for five years until Alexander's crossing over into Asia.

Philip, whose fortunes were constantly on the increase, made an expedition against Perinthus, which had resisted him and inclined toward the Athenians. He instituted a siege and advancing engines to the city assailed the walls in relays day after day. He built towers eighty cubits high, which far overtopped the towers of Perinthus, and from a superior height kept wearing down the besieged. He rocked the walls with battering rams and undermined them with saps, and cast down a long stretch of the wall. The Perinthians fought stoutly in their own defence and quickly threw up a second wall; many admirable feats were performed in the open and on the fortifications. Both sides displayed great determination. The king, for his part, rained destruction with numerous and varied catapults upon the men fighting steadfastly along the battlements, while the Perinthians, although their daily losses were heavy, received reinforcements of men, missiles, and artillery from Byzantium. When they had again become a match for the enemy, they took courage and resolutely bore the brunt of battle for their homeland. Still the king persevered in his determination. He divided his forces into several divisions and with frequent reliefs kept up a continuous attack on the walls both day and night. He had thirty thousand men and a store of missiles and siege engines besides other machines in plenty, and kept up a steady pressure against the besieged people.

75. So the siege dragged on. The numbers mounted of dead and wounded in the city and provisions were running short. The capture of the city was imminent. Fortune, however, did not neglect the safety of those in danger but brought them an unexpected deliverance. Philip's growth in power had been reported in Asia, and the Persian king, viewing this power with alarm, wrote to his satraps on the coast to give all possible assistance to the Perinthians. They consequently took counsel and sent off to Perinthus a force of mercenaries, ample funds, and sufficient stocks of food, missiles, and other materials required for operations.

Similarly the people of Byzantium also sent them their best officers and soldiers. So the armies were again well matched, and as the fighting was resumed, the siege was waged with supreme determination. Philip constantly battered the walls with his rams, making breaches in them, and as his catapults cleared the battlements of defenders, he would at the same moment drive through the breached walls with his soldiers in close formation and assail with scaling ladders the portions of the walls which he had cleared. Then hand-to-hand combat ensued and some were slain outright, others fell under many wounds. The rewards of victory challenged the daring of the contestants, for the Macedonians hoped to have a wealthy city to sack and to be rewarded by Philip with gifts, the hope of profit steeling them against danger, while the Perinthians had before their eyes the horrors of capture and sustained with great courage the battle for their deliverance.

76. The natural setting of the city greatly aided the besieged Perinthians towards a decisive victory. It lies by the sea on a sort of high peninsula with an isthmus one furlong across, and its houses are packed close together and very high. In their construction along the slope of the hill they overtop one another and thus give the city the general aspect of a theatre. In spite of the constant breaches in the fortifications, consequently, the Perinthians were not defeated, for they blocked up the alley-ways and utilised the lowest tier of houses each time as though it were a wall of defence. When Philip with much labour and hard fighting mastered the city wall, he found that the houses afforded a stronger one, ready made by Fortune. Since, in addition, the city's every need was promptly met by supplies coming to Perinthus from Byzantium, he split his forces in two, and leaving one division under his best officers to continue the operations before Perinthus, marched himself with the other and, making a sudden attack on Byzantium, enclosed that city also in a tight siege. Since their men and weapons and war equipment were all at Perinthus, the people of Byzantium found themselves seriously embarrassed.

Such was the situation at Perinthus and Byzantium.

Ephorus of Cymê, the historian, closed his history at this point with the siege of Perinthus, having included in his work the deeds of both the Greeks and the barbarians from the time of the return of the Heracleidae. He covered a period of almost seven hundred and fifty years, writing thirty books and prefacing each with an introduction. Diyllus the Athenian began the second section of his history with the close of Ephorus's and made a connected narrative of the history of Greeks and barbarians from that point to the death of Philip [son of Cassander].

77. When Theophrastus was archon at Athens, [340/39] the Romans elected as consuls Marcus Valerius and Aulus Cornelius, and the one hundred and tenth Olympiad was celebrated, in which Anticles the Athenian won the foot-race. In this year, seeing that Philip was besieging Byzantium, the Athenians voted that he had broken his treaty with them and promptly dispatched a formidable fleet to aid that city. Besides them, the Chians, Coans, Rhodians, and some others of the Greeks sent reinforcements also. Philip was frightened by this joint action, broke off the siege of the two cities, and made a treaty of peace with the Athenians and the other Greeks who opposed him.

In the west, the Carthaginians prepared great stores of war materials and transported their forces to Sicily. They had all told, including the forces previously on the island, more than seventy thousand infantry; cavalry, war-chariots, and extra teams of horses amounting to not less than ten thousand; two hundred battleships; and more than a thousand freighters carrying the horses, weapons, food and everything else. Timoleon was not daunted, however, although he learned the size of the hostile force while he himself was reduced to a handful of soldiers. He was still at war with Hicetas, but came to terms with him and took over his troops, thus materially increasing his own army.

78. He decided to commence the struggle with the Carthaginians in their own territory so as to keep intact the land of his allies while wasting that which was subject to the barbarians. He assembled his mercenaries immediately, together with the Syracusans and his allies, called a general assembly, and encouraged his audience with appropriate words to face the decisive struggle. When all applauded and shouted, urging him to lead them immediately against the barbarians, he took the field with not more than twelve thousand men in all.

He had reached the territory of Agrigentum when unexpected confusion and discord broke out in his army. One of his mercenaries named Thrasius, who had been with the Phocians when they plundered the shrine at Delphi and was remarkable for his mad recklessness, now perpetrated an act that matched his former outrages. While almost all the rest who had participated in the sacrilege against the oracle had received from the deity their due punishment, as we reported a little earlier, he who alone had eluded divine vengeance attempted to incite the mercenaries to desert. He said that Timoleon was out of his mind and was leading his men to certain destruction. The Carthaginians were six times their number and were immeasurably superior in every sort of equipment, but Timoleon was nevertheless promising that they would win, gambling with the lives of the mercenaries whom for a long time because of lack of funds he had not even been able to pay. Thrasius recommended that they should return to Syracuse and demand their pay, and not follow Timoleon any further on a hopeless campaign.

79. The mercenaries received his speech with enthusiasm and were on the point of mutiny, but Timoleon with some difficulty quieted the disturbance by urgent pleading and the offer of gifts. Even so, a thousand men did go off with Thrasius, but he put off their punishment till a later time, and by writing to his friends in Syracuse to receive them kindly and to pay them their arrears he brought the unrest to an end, but also stripped the disobedient men of all credit for the victory. With the rest, whose loyalty he had regained by tactful handling, he marched against the enemy who were encamped not far away. Calling an assembly of the troops, he encouraged them with an address, describing the cowardice of the Phoenicians and recalling the success of Gelon.

Just at the moment when all as with one voice were clamouring to attack the barbarians and to begin the battle, it chanced that pack animals came carrying wild celery for their bedding, and Timoleon declared that he accepted the omen of his victory, for the crown at the Isthmian games is woven of this. On his suggestion, the soldiers plaited crowns out of celery and with their heads wreathed advanced cheerfully in the confidence that the gods foretold their victory, and that, as a matter of fact, is how it was, for unpredictably, incredible to tell, they got the better of the enemy not only through their own valour but also through the gods' specific assistance.

Timoleon deployed his forces and advanced down from a line of little hills to the river Crimisus, where ten thousand of the enemy had already crossed. These he shattered at the first onset, taking his own position in the centre of his line. There was a sharp fight, but as the Greeks were superior both in bravery and in skill, there was great slaughter of the barbarians. The rest began to flee, but the main body of the Carthaginians crossed the river in the mean time and restored the situation.

80. As the battle was renewed, the Phoenicians were overwhelming the Greeks with their superior numbers when, suddenly, from the heavens sheets of rain broke and a storm of great hailstones, while lightning flashed and thunder roared and the wind blew in fierce gusts. All of this tempest buffeted the backs of the Greeks but struck the faces of the barbarians, so that, though Timoleon's soldiers were not much inconvenienced by the affair, the Phoenicians could not stand the force of circumstances, and as the Greeks continued to attack them, they broke into flight.

As all sought the river together - horse and foot intermingled, while the chariots added to the confusion - some perished helplessly trodden under foot or pierced by the swords or lances of their comrades, while others were herded by Timoleon's cavalry into the bed of the river and were struck down from behind. Many died without an enemy's stroke as the bodies piled up in the panic. There was crowding and it was difficult to keep one's feet in the stream. Worst of all, as the rain came down heavily, the river swept downstream as a raging torrent and carried the men with it, drowning them as they struggled to swim in their heavy armour.

In the end, even the Carthaginians who composed the Sacred Battalion, twenty-five hundred in number and drawn from the ranks of those citizens who were distinguished for valour and reputation as well as for wealth, were all cut down after a gallant struggle. In the other elements of their army, more than ten thousand soldiers were killed and no less than fifteen thousand were taken captive. Most of the chariots were destroyed in the battle but two hundred were taken. The baggage train, with the draught animals and most of the wagons, fell into the hands of the Greeks. Most of the armour was lost in the river, but a thousand breastplates and more than ten thousand shields were brought to the tent of Timoleon. Of these, some were dedicated later in the temples at Syracuse, some were distributed among the allies, and some were sent home by Timoleon to Corinth with instructions to dedicate them in the temple of Poseidon.

81. The battle yielded a great store of wealth also, because the Carthaginians had with them an abundance of silver and gold drinking vessels; these, as well as the rest of the personal property which was very numerous because of the wealth of the Carthaginians, Timoleon allowed the soldiers to keep as rewards for their gallantry. For their part, the Carthaginians who escaped from the battle made their way with difficulty to safety at Lilybaeum. Such consternation and terror possessed them that they did not dare embark in their ships and sail to Libya, persuaded that they would be swallowed up by the Libyan Sea because their gods had forsaken them.

In Carthage itself, when news of the extent of the disaster had come, all were crushed in spirit and took it for granted that Timoleon would come against them directly with his army. They wasted no time in recalling from exile Gisco the son of Hanno and appointing him general, for they thought that he best combined the qualities of boldness and military skill. They voted not to risk the lives of citizens in the future but to enlist foreign mercenaries, especially Greeks who, they thought, would answer the call in large numbers because of the high rate of pay and the wealth of Carthage; and they sent skilled envoys to Sicily with instructions to make peace on whatever terms proved possible.

82. At the end of this year, [339/8] Lysimachides became archon at Athens, and in Rome there were elected as consuls Quintus Servilius and Marcus Rutilius. In this year, Timoleon returned to Syracuse and promptly expelled from the city as traitors all the mercenaries who had abandoned him under the leadership of Thrasius. These crossed over into Italy, and coming upon a coastal town in Bruttium, sacked it. The Bruttians, incensed, immediately marched against them with a large army, stormed the place, and shot them all down with javelins. Those who had abandoned Timoleon were rewarded by such misfortune for their own wickedness.

Timoleon himself seized and put to death Postumius the Etruscan, who had been raiding sea traffic with twelve corsairs, and had put in at Syracuse as a friendly city. He received the new settlers sent out by the Corinthians kindly, to the number of five thousand. Then, when the Carthaginians sent envoys and pleaded with him urgently, he granted them peace on the terms that all the Greek cities should be free, that the river Lycus should be the boundary of their respective territories, and that the Carthaginians might not give aid to the tyrants who were at war with Syracuse.

After this, he concluded his war with Hicetas and put him to death, and then attacked the Campanians in Aetna and wiped them out. Likewise he overbore Nicodemus, tyrant of Centuripae, and ousted him from that city; and putting an end to the tyranny of Apolloniades in Agyrium he gave Syracusan citizenship to its freed inhabitants. In a word, all of the tyrants throughout the island were uprooted and the cities were set free and taken into his alliance. He made proclamation in Greece that:he Syracusans would give land and houses to those who wished to come and share in their state, and many Greeks came to receive their allotments. Ultimately forty thousand settlers were assigned to the vacant land of Syracuse and ten thousand to that of Agyrium, because of its extent and quality.

At this time, also, Timoleon revised the existing laws of Syracuse, which Diocles had composed. Those concerning private contracts and inheritance he allowed to remain unaltered, but he amended those concerned with public affairs in whatever way seemed advantageous to his own concept. Chairman and director of this legislative programme was Cephalus the Corinthian, a man distinguished for education and intelligence. When his hands were free of this matter, Timoleon transferred the people of Leontini to Syracuse, but sent additional settlers to Camarina and enlarged the city.

83. So, having established peaceful conditions everywhere throughout Sicily, he caused the cities to experience a vast growth of prosperity. For many years, because of domestic troubles and border wars, and still more because of the numbers of tyrants who kept constantly appearing, the cities had become destitute of inhabitants and the open country had become a wilderness for lack of cultivation, producing no useful crops. Now new settlers streamed into the land in great numbers, and as a long period of peace set in, the fields were reclaimed for cultivation and bore abundant crops of all sorts. These the Siceliot Greeks sold to merchants at good prices and rapidly increased their wealth.

It was by reason of the funds so acquired that many large constructions were completed in that period. There was, first, the structure in Syracuse on the Island called the "Hall of the Sixty Couches," which surpassed all the other buildings of Sicily in size and grandeur. This was built by Agathocles the despot, and since, in its pretentiousness, it went beyond the temples of the gods, so it received a mark of Heaven's displeasure in being struck by lightning. Then there were the towers along the shore of the Little Harbour with their mosaic inscriptions of varicoloured stones, proclaiming the name of their founder, Agathocles. Comparable to these but a little later, in the time of Hiero the king, there was built the Olympieium in the market and the altar beside the theatre, a stade in length and proportionally high and broad.

Among the lesser cities is to be reckoned Agyrium, but since it shared in the increase of settlers due to this agricultural prosperity, it built the finest theatre in Sicily after that of Syracuse, together with temples of the gods, a council chamber, and a market. There were also memorable towers, as well as pyramidal monuments of architectural distinction marking graves, many and great.

Philip's battle with the Athenians at Chaeroneia and the defeat of the Athenians (84-88).

84. When Charondes was archon at Athens, [338/7] Lucius J Aemilius and Gaius Plautius succeeded to the consulship. In this year, Philip the king, having won most of the Greeks over to friendship with him, was ambitious to gain the uncontested leadership of Greece by terrifying the Athenians into submission. Therefore he suddenly seized the city of Elateia, concentrated his forces there and adopted a policy of war with Athens. He expected to have no trouble in defeating them, since their reliance on the existing peace treaty made them unprepared for hostilities; and that is how it worked out. For after Elateia had been occupied, persons came at night to Athens reporting the occupation and stating that Philip would march immediately into Attica with his army. Taken aback by this unexpected development, the Athenian generals summoned the trumpeters and ordered them to keep blowing the alarm signal the whole night through.

The news spread into every household and the city was tense with terror, and at dawn the whole people flocked to the theatre even before the archons had made their customary proclamation. When the generals came and introduced the messenger and he had told his story, silence and terror gripped the assembly and none of the usual speakers dared propose a course of action. Again and again the herald called for someone to speak for the common safety, but no one came forward with a proposal. In utter perplexity and dismay, the crowd kept their eyes on Demosthenes. Finally he came down from his seat, and bidding the people take heart gave it as his opinion that they must straightway send envoys to Thebes and invite the Boeotians to join them to make a struggle for freedom. There was no time to send envoys to their other allies invoking the treaties of alliance, since in two days the king could be expected to enter Attica. As his way led through Boeotia, the support of the Boeotians was their only recourse, especially since Philip was at that time the friend and ally of the Boeotians and would evidently try to take them along as he marched past to the war against Athens.

85. When the people accepted the proposal and the decree authorising the embassy had been drafted by Demosthenes, they turned to the search for their most eloquent representative. Demosthenes willingly answered the call to service. He carried out the mission vigorously and returned to Athens at last having secured the adhesion of the Thebans.

Now that they had doubled their existing armed forces by the Boeotian alliance, the Athenians recovered their confidence. At once they designated Chares and Lysicles as generals and sent forth their entire army under arms into Boeotia. All their youth reported eager for battle and advanced with forced marches as far as Chaeroneia in Boeotia. Impressed by the promptness of the Athenian arrival and themselves no less ready to act decisively, the Boeotians joined them with their weapons and, brigaded together, all awaited the approach of the enemy. Philip's first move was to send envoys to the Boeotian League, the most eminent of whom was Pytho. He was celebrated for his eloquence, but judged by the Boeotians in this contest for their allegiance against Demosthenes, he surpassed all the other speakers, to be sure, but was clearly inferior to him. Demosthenes himself in his speeches parades his success against this orator as a great accomplishment, where he says: "I did not then give ground before Pytho in spite of his confidence and his torrent of words against you."

So Philip failed to get the support of the Boeotians, but nevertheless decided to fight both of the allies together. He waited for the last of his laggard confederates to arrive, and then marched into Boeotia. His forces came to more than thirty thousand infantry and no less than two thousand cavalry. Both sides were on edge for the battle, high-spirited and eager, and were well matched in courage, but the king had the advantage in numbers and in generalship. He had fought many battles of different sorts and had been victorious in most cases, so that he had a wide experience in military operations. On the Athenian side, the best of their generals were dead, Iphicrates, Chabrias, and Timotheüs too, and the best of those who were left, Chares, was no better than any average soldier in the energy and discretion required of a commander.

86. The armies deployed at dawn, and the king stationed his son Alexander, young in age but noted for his valour and swiftness of action, on one wing, placing beside him his most seasoned generals, while he himself at the head of picked men exercised the command over the other; individual units were stationed where the occasion required. On the other side, dividing the line according to nationality, the Athenians assigned one wing to the Boeotians and kept command of the other themselves. Once joined, the battle was hotly contested for a long time and many fell on both sides, so that for a while the struggle permitted hopes of victory to both.

Then Alexander, his heart set on showing his father his prowess and yielding to none in will to win, ably seconded by his men, first succeeded in rupturing the solid front of the enemy line and striking down many he bore heavily on the troops opposite him. As the same success was won by his companions, gaps in the front were constantly opened. Corpses piled up, until finally Alexander forced his way through the line and put his opponents to flight. Then the king also in person advanced, well in front and not conceding credit for the victory even to Alexander; he first forced back the troops stationed before him and then by compelling them t8o flee became the man responsible for the victory. More than a thousand Athenians fell in the battle and no less than two thousand were captured. Likewise, many of the Boeotians were killed and not a few taken prisoners. After the battle Philip raised a trophy of victory, yielded the dead for burial, gave sacrifices to the gods for victory, and rewarded according to their deserts those of his men who had distinguished themselves.

87. The story is told that in the drinking after dinner Philip downed a large amount of unmixed wine and forming with his friends a comus in celebration of the victory paraded through the midst of his captives, jeering all the time at the misfortunes of the luckless men. Now Demades, the orator, who was then one of the captives, spoke out boldly and made a remark able to curb the king's disgusting exhibition. He is said to have remarked: "O King, when Fortune has cast you in the role of Agamemnon, are you not ashamed to act the part of Thersites?" Stung by this well-aimed shaft of rebuke, Philip altered his whole demeanour completely. He cast off his garland, brushed aside the symbols of pride that marked the comus, expressed admiration for the man who dared to speak so plainly, freed him from captivity and gave him a place in his own company. with every mark of honour. Addressed by Demades with Attic charm, he ended by releasing all of the Athenian prisoners without ransom and, altogether abandoning the arrogance of victory, sent envoys to the people of Athens and concluded with them a treaty of friendship and alliance. With the Boeotian she concluded peace but maintained a garrison in Thebes.

88. After this defeat, the Athenians condemned to death the general Lysicles on the accusation of Lycurgus, the orator. Lycurgus had the highest repute of the politicians of his time, and since he had won praise for his conduct of the city's finances over a period of twelve years and lived in general a life renowned for rectitude, he proved to be a very stern prosecutor. One can judge of his character and austerity in the passage in his accusation where he says: "You were general, Lysicles. A thousand citizens have perished and two thousand were taken captive. A trophy stands over your city's defeat, and all of Greece is enslaved. All of this happened under your leadership and command, and yet you dare to live and to look on the sun and even to intrude into the market, a living monument of our country's shame and disgrace."

There was an odd coincidence in the period under review. At the same time as the battle took place at Chaeroneia, another battle occurred in Italy on the same day and at the same hour between the people of Tarentum and the Lucanians. In the service of Tarentum was Archidamus, the Lacedaemonian king, and it happened that he was himself killed. He had ruled the Lacedaemonians for twenty-three years; his son Agis succeeded to the throne and ruled for nine years.

At this time, also, Timothüs the tyrant of Heracleia-Pontica died after having been in power for fifteen years. His brother Dionysius succeeded to the tyranny and ruled for thirty-two years.

How the Greeks chose Philip as their lead general (89).

89. When Phrynichus was archon at Athens, [337/6] the Romans installed as consuls Titus Manlius Torquatus and Publius Decius. In this year King Philip, proudly conscious of his victory at Chaeroneia and seeing that he had dashed the confidence of the leading Greek cities, conceived of the ambition to become the leader of all Greece. He spread the word that he wanted to make war on the Persians in the Greeks' behalf and to punish them for the profanation of the temples, and this won for him the loyal support of the Greeks. He showed a kindly face to all in private and in public, and he represented to the cities that he wished to discuss with them matters of common advantage. A general congress was, accordingly, convened at Corinth. He spoke about the war against Persia and by raising great expectations won the representatives over to war. The Greeks elected him the general plenipotentiary of Greece, and he began accumulating supplies for the campaign. He prescribed the number of soldiers that each city should send for the joint effort, and then returned to Macedonia.

This was the state of affairs as regards Philip.

90. In Sicily, Timoleon the Corinthian died; he had put in order all the affairs of the Syracusans and the other Siceliot Greeks, and had been their general for eight years. The Syracusans revered him greatly because of his ability and the extent of his services to them and gave him a magnificent funeral. As the body was borne out in the presence of all the people the following decree was proclaimed by that Demetrius who had the most powerful voice of all the criers of his time: "The people of Syracuse have voted to bury this Timoleon son of Timaenetus, of Corinth, at a cost of two hundred minas, and to honour him to the end of time with musical, equestrian, and gymnastic games, because he destroyed the tyrants, defeated the barbarians, and resettled the mightiest of Greek cities, and so became the author of freedom for the Greeks of Sicily."

In this year, also, Ariobarzanes died after ruling for twenty-six years and Mithridates, succeeding him, ruled for thirty-five. The Romans were victorious in a battle against the Latins and Campanians in the vicinity of Suessa and annexed part of the territory of the vanquished. Manlius, the consul who had won the victory, celebrated a triumph.

How Philip was assassinated as he was about to cross into Asia (91-95).

91. When Pythodorus was archon at Athens, [330/29] the Romans elected as consuls Quintus Publius and Tiberius Aemilius Mamercus, and the one hundred and eleventh celebration of the Olympic Games took place, in which Cleomantis of Cleitor won the foot-race. In this year, King Philip, installed as leader by the Greeks, opened the war with Persia by sending into Asia as an advance party

Attalus and Parmenion, assigning to them a part of his forces and ordering them to liberate the Greek cities, while he himself, wanting to enter upon the war with the gods' approval, asked the Pythia whether he would conquer the king of the Persians. She gave him the following response:

> Wreathed is the bull. All is done. There is also
>
> the one who will smite him.

Now Philip found this response ambiguous but accepted it in a sense favourable to himself, namely that the oracle foretold that the Persian would be slaughtered like a sacrificial victim. Actually, however, it was not so, and it meant that Philip himself in the midst of a festival and holy sacrifices, like the bull, would be stabbed to death while decked with a garland. In any event, he thought that the gods supported him and was very happy to think that Asia would be made captive under the hands of the Macedonians.

Straightway he set in motion plans for gorgeous sacrifices to the gods joined with the wedding of his daughter Cleopatra, whose mother was Olympias; he had given her in marriage to Alexander king of Epirus, Olympias's own brother. He wanted as many Greeks as possible to take part in the festivities in honour of the gods, and so planned brilliant musical contests and lavish banquets for his friends and guests. Out of all Greece he summoned his personal guest-friends and ordered the members of his court to bring along as many as they could of their acquaintances from abroad. He was determined to show himself to the Greeks as an amiable person and to respond to the honours conferred when he was appointed to the supreme command with appropriate entertainment.

92. So great numbers of people flocked together from all directions to the festival, and the games and the marriage were celebrated in Aegae in Macedonia. Not only did individual notables crown him with golden crowns but most of the important cities as well, and among them Athens. As this award was being announced by the herald, he ended with the declaration that if anyone plotted against King Philip and fled to Athens for refuge, he would be delivered up. The casual phrase seemed like an omen sent by Providence to let Philip know that a plot was coming. There were other like words also spoken, seemingly divinely inspired, which forecast the king's death.

At the state banquet, Philip ordered the actor Neoptolemus, matchless in the power of his voice and in his popularity, to present some well-received pieces, particularly such as bore on the Persian campaign. The artist thought that his piece would be taken as appropriate to Philip's crossing and intended to rebuke the wealth of the Persian king, great and famous as it was, (suggesting) that it could some day be overturned by fortune. Here are the words that he first sang:

> Your thoughts reach higher than the air;
>
> You dream of wide fields' cultivation.
>
> The homes you plan surpass the homes
>
> That men have known, but you do err,
>
> Guiding your life afar.
>
> But one there is who'll catch the swift,
>
> Who goes a way obscured in gloom,
>
> And sudden, unseen, overtakes
>
> And robs us of our distant hopes -
>
> Death, mortals' source of many woes.

103

He continued with the rest of the song, all of it dealing with the same theme. Philip was enchanted with the message and was completely occupied with the thought of the overthrow of the Persian king, for he remembered the Pythian oracle which bore the same meaning as the words quoted by the tragic actor.

Finally the drinking was over and the start of the games set for the following day. While it was still dark, the multitude of spectators hastened into the theatre and at sunrise the parade formed. Along with lavish display of every sort, Philip included in the procession statues of the twelve gods wrought with great artistry and adorned with a dazzling show of wealth to strike awe in the beholder, and along with these was conducted a thirteenth statue, suitable for a god, that of Philip himself, so that the king exhibited himself enthroned among the twelve gods.

93. Every seat in the theatre was taken when Philip appeared wearing a white cloak, and by his express orders his bodyguard held away from him and followed only at a distance, since he wanted to show publicly that he was protected by the goodwill of all the Greeks, and had no need of a guard of spearmen. Such was the pinnacle of success that he had attained, but as the praises and congratulations of all rang in his ears, suddenly without warning the plot against the king was revealed as death struck. We shall set forth the reasons for this in order that our story may be clear.

There was a Macedonian Pausanias who came of a family from the district Orestis. He a was bodyguard of the king and was beloved by him because of his beauty. When he saw that the king was becoming enamoured of another Pausanias (a man of the same name as himself), he addressed him with abusive language, accusing him of being a hermaphrodite and prompt to accept the amorous advances of any who wished. Unable to endure such an insult, the other kept silent for the time, but,after confiding to Attalus, one of his friends, what he proposed to do, he brought about his own death voluntarily and in a spectacular fashion. For a few days after this, as Philip was engaged in battle with Pleurias, king of the Illyrians, Pausanias stepped in front of him and, receiving on his body all the blows directed at the king, so met his death.

The incident was widely discussed and Attalus, who was a member of the court circle and influential with the king, invited the first Pausanias to dinner and when he had plied him till drunk with unmixed wine, handed his unconscious body over to the muleteers to abuse in drunken licentiousness. So he presently recovered from his drunken stupor and, deeply resenting the outrage to his person, charged Attalus before the king with the outrage. Philip shared his anger at the barbarity of the act but did not wish to punish Attalus at that time because of their relationship, and because Attalus's services were needed urgently. He was the nephew of the Cleopatra whom the king had just married as a new wife and he had been selected as a general of the advanced force being sent into Asia, for he was a man valiant in battle. For these reasons, the king tried to mollify the righteous anger of Pausanias at his treatment, giving him substantial presents and advancing him in honour among the bodyguards.

94. Pausanias, nevertheless, nursed his wrath implacably, and yearned to avenge himself, not only on the one who had done him wrong, but also on the one who failed to avenge him. In this design he was encouraged especially by the sophist Hermocrates. He was his pupil, and when he asked in the course of his instruction how one might become most famous, the sophist replied that it would be by killing the one who had accomplished most, for just as long as he was remembered, so long his slayer would be remembered also. Pausanias connected this saying with his private resentment, and admitting no delay in his plans because of his grievance he determined to act under cover of the festival in the following manner. He posted horses at the gates of the city and came to the entrance of the theatre carrying a Celtic dagger under his cloak. When Philip directed his attending friends to precede him into the theatre, while the guards kept their distance, he saw that the king was left alone, rushed at him, pierced him through his ribs, and stretched him out dead; then ran for the gates and the horses which he had prepared for his flight. Immediately one group of the bodyguards hurried to the body of the king while the rest poured out in pursuit of the assassin; among these last were Leonnatus and Perdiccas and Attalus. Having a good start, Pausanias would have mounted his horse before they could catch him had he not caught his boot in a vine and fallen. As he was scrambling to his feet, Perdiccas and the rest came up with him and killed him with their javelins.

95. Such was the end of Philip, who had made himself the greatest of the kings in Europe in his time, and because of the extent of his kingdom had made himself a throned companion of the twelve gods. He had ruled twenty-four years. He is known to fame as one who with but the slenderest resources to support his claim to a throne won for himself the greatest empire in the Greek world, while the growth of his position was not due so much to his prowess in arms as to his adroitness and cordiality in diplomacy. Philip himself is said to have been prouder of his grasp of strategy and his diplomatic successes than of his valour in actual battle. Every member of his army shared in the successes which were won in the field but he alone got credit for victories won through negotiation.

Now that we have come to the death of Philip, we shall conclude this book here according to our original statement. Beginning the next one with Alexander's accession as king we shall try to include all of his career in one book.

BOOK XVII

How Alexander, having succeeded to the throne, disposed the affairs of his kingdom (1-7).

1. The preceding book, which was the sixteenth of the *Histories,* began with the coronation of Philip the son of Amyntas and included his whole career down to his death, together with those events connected with other kings, peoples and cities which occurred in the years of his reign, twenty-four in number. In this book we shall continue the systematic narrative beginning with the accession of Alexander, and include both the history of this king down to his death as well as contemporary events in the known parts of the world. This is the best method, I think, of ensuring that events will be remembered, for thus the material is arranged topically, and each story is told without interruption.

Alexander accomplished great things in a short space of time, and by his acumen and courage surpassed in the magnitude of his achievements all kings whose memory is recorded from the beginning of time. In twelve years he conquered no small part of Europe and practically all of Asia, and so acquired a fabulous reputation like that of the heroes and demigods of old. There is really no need to anticipate in the introduction any of the accomplishments of this king; his deeds reported one by one will attest sufficiently the greatness of his glory. On his father's side Alexander was a descendant of Heracles and on his mother's he could claim the blood of the Aeacids, so that from his ancestors on both sides he inherited the physical and moral qualities of greatness. Pointing out as we proceed the chronology of events, we shall pass on to the happenings which concern our history.

2. When Evaenetus was archon at Athens, [335/4] the Romans elected as consuls Lucius Furius and Gaius Manius. In this year Alexander, succeeding to the throne, first inflicted due punishment on his father's murderers, and then devoted himself to the funeral of his father. He established his authority far more firmly than any did in fact suppose possible, for he was quite young and for this reason not uniformly respected, but first he promptly won over the Macedonians to his support by tactful statements. He declared that the king was changed only in name and that the state would be run on principles no less effective than those of his father's administration. Then he addressed himself to the embassies which were present and in affable fashion bade the Greeks maintain towards him the loyalty which they had shown to his father. He busied his soldiers with constant training in the use of their weapons and with tactical exercises, and established discipline in the army.

A possible rival for the throne remained in Attalus, who was the brother of Cleopatra, the last wife of Philip, and Alexander determined to kill him. As a matter of fact, Cleopatra had borne a child to Philip a few days before his death. Attalus had been sent on ahead into Asia to share the command of the forces with Parmenion and had acquired great popularity in the army by his readiness to do favours and his easy bearing with the soldiers. Alexander had good reason to fear that he might challenge his rule, making common cause with those of the Greeks who opposed him, and selected from among his friends a certain Hecataeus and sent him off to Asia with a number of soldiers, under orders to bring back Attalus alive if he could, but if not, to assassinate him as quickly as possible. So he crossed over into Asia, joined Parmenion and Attalus and awaited an opportunity to carry out his mission.

3. Alexander knew that many of the Greeks were anxious to revolt, and was seriously worried. In Athens, where Demosthenes kept agitating against Macedon, the news of Philip's death was received with rejoicing, and the Athenians were not ready to concede the leading position among the Greeks to Macedon. They communicated secretly with Attalus and arranged to co-operate with him, and they encouraged many of the cities to strike for their freedom.

The Aetolians voted to restore those of the Acarnanians who had experienced exile because of Philip. The Ambraciots were persuaded by one Aristarchus to expel the garrison placed in their city by Philip and to transform their government into a democracy. Similarly, the Thebans voted to drive out the garrison in the Cadmeia and not to concede to Alexander the leadership of the Greeks. The Arcadians alone of the Greeks had never acknowledged Philip's leadership nor did they now recognize that of Alexander. Otherwise in the Peloponnesus the Argives and Eleians and Lacedaemonians, with others, moved to recover their independence. Beyond the frontiers of Macedonia, many tribes moved toward revolt and a general feeling of unrest swept through the natives in that quarter.

But, for all the problems and fears that beset his kingdom on every side, Alexander, who had only just reached manhood, brought everything into order impressively and swiftly. Some he won by persuasion and diplomacy, others he frightened into keeping the peace, but some had to be mastered by force and so reduced to submission.

4. First he dealt with the Thessalians, reminding them of his ancient relationship to them through Heracles and raising their hopes by kindly words and by rich promises as well, and prevailed upon them by formal vote of the Thessalian League to recognise as his the leadership of Greece which he had inherited from his father. Next he won over the neighbouring tribes similarly, and so marched down to Pylae, where he convened the assembly of the Amphictyons and had them pass a resolution granting him the leadership of the Greeks. He gave audience to the envoys of the Ambraciots and, addressing them in friendly fashion, convinced them that they had been only a little premature in grasping the independence that he was on the point of giving them voluntarily.

In order to overawe those who refused to yield otherwise, he set out at the head of the army of the Macedonians in full battle array. With forced marches he arrived in Boeotia and encamping near the Cadmeia threw the city of the Thebans into a panic. As the Athenians immediately learned that the king had passed into Boeotia, they too abandoned their previous refusal to take him seriously. So much the rapid moves and energetic action of the young man shook the confidence of those who opposed him. The Athenians, accordingly, voted to bring into the city their property scattered throughout Attica and to look to the repair of their walls, but they also sent envoys to Alexander, asking forgiveness for tardy recognition of his leadership.

Even Demosthenes was included among the envoys; he did not, however, go with the others to Alexander, but turned back at Cithaeron and returned to Athens, whether fearful because of the anti-Macedonian course that he had pursued in politics, or merely wishing to leave no ground of complaint to the king of Persia. He was generally believed to have received large sums of money from that source in payment for his efforts to check the Macedonians, and indeed Aeschines is said to have referred to this in a speech when he taunted Demosthenes with his venality: "At the moment, it is true, his extravagance has been glutted by the king's gold, but even this will not satisfy him; no wealth has ever proved sufficient for a greedy character." Alexander addressed the Athenian envoys kindly and freed the people from their acute terror.

Then he called a meeting at Corinth of envoys and delegates, and when the usual representatives came, he spoke to them in moderate terms and had them pass a resolution appointing him general plenipotentiary of the Greeks and undertaking themselves to join in an expedition against Persia seeking satisfaction for the offences which the Persians had committed against Greece. Successful in this, the king returned to Macedonia with his army.

5. Now that we have described what took place in Greece, we shall shift our account to the events in Asia. Here, immediately after the death of Philip, Attalus actually had set his hand to revolt and had agreed with the Athenians to undertake joint action against Alexander, but later he changed his mind. Preserving the letter which had been brought to him from Demosthenes, he sent it off to Alexander and tried by expressions of loyalty to remove from himself any possible suspicion. Hecataeus, however, following the instructions of the king literally, had him killed by treachery, and thereafter the Macedonian forces in Asia were free from any incitement to revolution, Attalus being dead and Parmenion completely devoted to Alexander.

As our narrative is now to treat of the kingdom of the Persians, we must go back a little to pick up the thread. While Philip was still king, Ochus ruled the Persians and oppressed his subjects cruelly and harshly. Since his savage disposition made him hated, the chiliarch Bagoas, a eunuch in physical fact but a militant rogue in disposition, killed him by poison administered by a certain physician and placed upon the throne the youngest of his sons, Arses. He similarly made away with the brothers of the new king, who were barely of age, in order that the young man might be isolated and tractable to his control, but the young king let it be known that he was offended at Bagoas's previous outrageous behaviour and was prepared to punish the author of these crimes, so Bagoas anticipated his intentions and killed Arses and his children also while he was still in the third year of his reign. The royal house was thus extinguished, and there was no one in the direct line of descent to claim the throne. Instead Bagoas selected a certain Dareius, a member of the court circle, and secured the throne for him. He was the son of Arsanes, and grandson of that Ostanes who was a brother of Artaxerxes [II, 405-359], who had been king. As to Bagoas, an odd thing happened to him and one to point a moral. Pursuing his habitual savagery he attempted to remove Dareius by poison. The plan leaked out, however, and the king, calling upon Bagoas, as it were, to drink to him a toast and handing him his own cup compelled him to take his own medicine.

6. Dareius's selection for the throne was based on his known bravery, in which quality he far surpassed the other Persians. Once when King Artaxerxes [III, 359-338] was campaigning against the Cadusians, one of them with a wide reputation for strength and courage challenged a volunteer among the Persians to fight in single combat with him. No other dared accept, but Dareius alone entered the contest and slew the challenger, being honoured in consequence by the king with rich gifts, while among the Persians he was conceded the first place in prowess. It was because of this prowess that he was thought worthy to take over the kingship. This happened about the same time as Philip died and Alexander became king.

Such was the man whom fate had selected to be the antagonist of Alexander's genius, and they opposed one another in many and great struggles for the supremacy. These our detailed narrative will describe in each case. We may now proceed with our story.

7. Dareius became king before the death of Philip and thought to turn the coming war back upon Macedonia, but when Philip died, Dareius was relieved of his anxiety and despised the youth of Alexander. Soon, however, when Alexander's vigour and rapidity of action had secured for him the leadership of all Greece and made evident the ability of the young man, then Dareius took warning and began to pay serious attention to his forces. He fitted out a large number of ships of war and assembled numerous strong armies, choosing at the same time his best commanders, among whom was Memnon of Rhodes, outstanding in courage and in strategic grasp. The king gave him five thousand mercenaries and ordered him to march to Cyzicus and to try to get possession of it. With this force, accordingly, Memnon marched on across the range of Mt. Ida.

Some tell the story that this mountain got its name from Ida, the daughter of Melisseus. It is the highest mountain in the region of the Hellespont and there is in its midst a remarkable cave in which they say the goddesses were judged by Alexander [Paris]. On this mountain are supposed to have lived the Idaean Dactyls who first worked iron, having learned their -kill from the Mother of the Gods. An odd occurrence has been observed in connection with this mountain which is known nowhere else. About the time of the rising of the Dog Star, if one stands upon the highest peak, the stillness of the surrounding atmosphere gives the impression that the summit is elevated above the motion of the winds, and the sun can be seen rising while it is still night. Its rays are not circumscribed in a circular orb but its flame is dispersed in many places, so that you would think that there were many patches of fire burning along the horizon. Presently, then, these draw together into one huge flame the width of which reaches three plethra. Finally, as the day dawns, the usually observed size of the sun's ball is attained and produces normal daylight.

Memnon traversed this mountain and suddenly falling upon the city of Cyzicus came within an ace of taking it. Failing in this, he wasted its territory and collected much booty. While he was thus occupied, Parmenion took by storm the city of Grynium and sold its inhabitants as slaves, but when he besieged Pitane. Memnon appeared and frightened the Macedonians into breaking off the siege. Later Callas with a mixed force of Macedonians and mercenaries joined battle in the Troad against a much larger force of Persians and, finding himself inferior, fell back on the promontory of Rhoeteium.

That was the situation in Asia.

How he recovered the tribes which revolted (8. 1-2).

*How he razed Thebes to the ground and terrified the Greeks
and was elected general plenipotentiary of Greece (8. 3-16).*

8. Now that the unrest in Greece had been brought under control, Alexander shifted his field of operations into Thrace. Many of the tribes in this region had risen but, terrified by his appearance, felt constrained to make their submission. Then he swung west to Paeonia and Illyria and the territories that bordered on them. Many of the local tribesmen had revolted, but these he overpowered, and established his control over all the natives in the area. This task was not yet finished when messengers reached him reporting that many of the Greeks were in revolt. Many cities had actually taken steps to throw off the Macedonian alliance, the most important of these being Thebes. At this intelligence, the king was roused to return in haste to Macedonia in his anxiety to put an end to the unrest in Greece.

The Thebans sought first of all to expel the Macedonian garrison from the Cadmeia and laid siege to this citadel; this was the situation when the king appeared suddenly before the city and encamped with his whole army near by. Before the king's arrival, the Thebans had had time to surround the Cadmeia with deep trenches and heavy stockades so that neither reinforcements nor supplies could be sent in, and they had sent an appeal to the Arcadians, Argives, and Eleians for help. They appealed for support from the Athenians also, and when they received from Demosthenes a free gift of weapons, they equipped all of their citizens who lacked heavy armour. Of those who were asked for reinforcements, however, the Peloponnesians sent soldiers as far as the Isthmus and waited to see what would happen, since the king's arrival was now expected, and the Athenians, under the influence of Demosthenes, voted to support the Thebans, but failed to send out their forces, waiting to see how the war would go. In the Cadmeia, the garrison commander Philotas observed the Thebans making great preparations for the siege, strengthened his walls as well as he could, and made ready a stock of missiles of all sorts.

9. So when the king appeared suddenly out of Thrace with all his army, the alliances of the Thebans had furnished them with only a hesitant support while the power of their opponents possessed an obvious and evident superiority. Nevertheless their leaders assembled in council and prepared a resolution about the war; they were unanimous in deciding to fight it out for their political freedom. The measure was passed by the assembly, and with great enthusiasm all were ready to see the thing through.

At first the king made no move, giving the Thebans time to think things over and supposing that a single city would never dare to match forces with such an army. For at that time Alexander had more than thirty thousand infantry and no less than three thousand cavalry, all battle-seasoned veterans of Philip's campaigns who had hardly experienced a single reverse. This was the army on the skill and loyalty of which he relied to overthrow the Persian empire. If the Thebans had yielded to the situation and had asked the Macedonians for peace and an alliance, the king would have accepted their proposals with pleasure and would have conceded everything they asked, for he was eager to be rid of these disturbances in Greece so that he might without distraction pursue the war with Persia.

Finally, however, he realized that he was despised by the Thebans, and so decided to destroy the city utterly and by this act of terror take the heart out of anyone else who might venture to rise against him. He made his forces ready for battle, then announced through a herald that any of the Thebans who wished might come to him and enjoy the peace which was common to all the Greeks. In response, the Thebans with equal spirit proclaimed from a high tower that anyone who wished to join the Great King and Thebes in freeing the Greeks and destroying the tyrant of Greece should come over to them. This epithet stung Alexander. He flew into a towering rage and declared that he would pursue the Thebans with the extremity of punishment. Raging in his heart, he set to constructing siege engines and to preparing whatever else was necessary for the attack.

10. Elsewhere in Greece, as people learned the seriousness of the danger hanging over the Thebans, they were distressed at their expected disaster but had no heart to help them, feeling that the city by precipitate and ill-considered action had consigned itself to evident annihilation. In Thebes itself, however, men accepted their risk willingly and with good courage, but they were puzzled by certain sayings of prophets and portents of the gods.

First there was the light spider's web in the temple of Demeter which was observed to have spread itself out to the size of an himation, and which all about shone iridescent like a rainbow in the sky. About this, the oracle at Delphi gave them the response:

> "The gods to mortals all have sent this sign; To the Boeotians first,
> and to their neighbours."

The ancestral oracle of Thebes itself had given this response:

> "The woven web is bane to one, to one a boon."

This sign had occurred three months before Alexander's descent on the city, but at the very moment of the king's arrival the statues in the market place were seen to burst into perspiration and be covered with great drops of moisture. More than this, people reported to the city officials that the marsh at Onchestus was emitting a sound very like a bellow, while at Dirce a bloody ripple ran along the surface of the water. Finally, travellers coming from Delphi told how the temple which the Thebans had dedicated from the Phocian spoils was observed to have bloodstains on its roof.

Those who made a business of interpreting such portents stated that the spider web signified the departure of the gods from the city, its iridescence meant a storm of mixed troubles, the sweating of the statues was the sign of an overwhelming catastrophe, and the appearance of blood in many places foretold a vast slaughter throughout the city. They pointed out that the gods were clearly predicting disaster for the city and recommended that the outcome of the war should not be risked upon the battlefield, but that a safer solution should be sought for in conversations.

Still the Thebans' spirits were not daunted. On the contrary they were so carried away with enthusiasm that they reminded one another of the victory at Leuctra and of the other battles where their own fighting qualities had won unhoped for victories to the astonishment of the Greek world. They indulged their nobility of spirit bravely rather than wisely, and plunged headlong into the total destruction of their country.

11. Now the king in the course of only three days made everything ready for the assault. He divided his forces into three parts and ordered one to attack the palisades which had been erected before the city, the second to face the Theban battle line, and the third as a reserve to support any hard pressed unit of his forces and to enter the battle in its turn. For their part, the Thebans stationed the cavalry within the palisades, assigned their enfranchised slaves, along with refugees and resident aliens, to face those who drove at the walls, and themselves made ready to fight before the city with the Macedonian force about the king which was many times their number. Their children and wives flocked to the temples and implored the gods to rescue the city from its dangers.

When the Macedonians approached and each division encountered the opposing force of Thebans, the trumpets blew the call to arms and the troops on both sides raised the battle cry in unison and hurled their missiles at the enemy. These were soon expended and all turned to the use of the sword at close quarters, and a mighty struggle ensued. The Macedonians exerted a force that could hardly be withstood because of the numbers of their men and the weight of the phalanx, but the Thebans were superior in bodily strength and in their constant training in the gymnasium. Still more, in exaltation of spirit they were lifted out of themselves and became indifferent to personal danger. Many were wounded in both armies and not a few fell facing the blows of the enemy. The air was filled with the roar of fighters locked in the struggle, moans and shouts and exhortations: on the Macedonian side, not to be unworthy of their previous exploits, and on the Theban, not to forget children and wives and parents threatened with slavery and their every household lying exposed to the fury of the Macedonians, and to remember the battles of Leuctra and of Mantineia and the glorious deeds which were household words throughout Greece. So for a long time the battle remained evenly poised because of the surpassing valour of the contestants.

12. At length Alexander saw that the Thebans were still fighting unflinchingly for their freedom, but that his Macedonians were wearying in the battle, and ordered his reserve division to enter the struggle. As this suddenly struck the tired Thebans, it bore heavily against them and killed many. Still the Thebans did not concede the victory, but on the contrary, inspired by the will to win, despised all dangers. They had the courage to shout that the Macedonians now openly confessed to being their inferiors. Under normal circumstances, when an enemy attacks in relays, it is usual for soldiers to fear the fresh strength of the reinforcements, but the Thebans alone then faced their dangers ever more boldly, as the enemy sent against them new troops for those whose strength nagged with weariness.

So the Theban spirit proved unshakable here, but the king took note of a postern gate that had been deserted by its guards and hurried Perdiccas with a large detachment of troops to seize it and penetrate into the city. He quickly carried out the order and the Macedonians slipped through the gate into the city, while the Thebans, having worn down the first assault wave of the Macedonians, stoutly faced the second and still had high hopes of victory. When they knew that a section of the city had been taken, however, they began immediately to withdraw within the walls, but in this operation their cavalry galloped along with the infantry into the city and trampled upon and killed many of their own men; they themselves rode into the city in disorder and, encountering a maze of narrow alleys and trenches, lost their footing and fell and were killed by their own weapons. At the same time the Macedonian garrison in the Cadmeia burst out of the citadel, engaged the Thebans, and attacking them in their confusion made a great slaughter among them.

13. So while the city was being taken, many and varied were the scenes of destruction within the walls. Enraged by the arrogance of the Theban proclamation, the Macedonians pressed upon them more furiously than is usual in war, and shrieking curses flung themselves on the wretched people, slaying all whom they met without sparing any. The Thebans, for their part, clinging desperately to their forlorn hope of victory, counted their lives as nothing and when they met a foeman, grappled with him and. drew his blows upon themselves. In the capture of the city, no Theban was seen begging the Macedonians to spare his life, nor did they in ignoble fashion fall and cling to the knees of their conquerors. Neither did the agony of courage elicit pity from the foe nor did the day's length suffice for the cruelty of their vengeance. All the city was pillaged. Everywhere boys and girls were dragged into captivity as they wailed piteously the names of their mothers.

In sum, households were seized with all their members, and the city's enslavement was complete. Of the men who remained, some, wounded and dying, grappled with the foe and were slain themselves as they destroyed their enemy; others, supported only by a shattered spear, went to meet their assailants and, in their supreme struggle, held freedom dearer than life. As the slaughter mounted and every corner of the city was piled high with corpses, no one could have failed to pity the plight of the unfortunates. For even Greeks, Thespians, Plataeans and Orchomenians and some others hostile to the Thebans who had joined the king in the campaign, invaded the city along with him and now demonstrated their own hatred amid the calamities of the unfortunate victims.

So it was that many terrible things befell the city. Greeks were mercilessly slain by Greeks, relatives were butchered by their own relatives, and even a common dialect induced no pity. In the end, when night finally intervened, the houses had been plundered and children and women and aged persons who had fled into the temples were torn from sanctuary and subjected to outrage without limit.

14. Over six thousand Thebans perished, more than thirty thousand were captured, and the amount of property plundered was unbelievable.

The king gave burial to the Macedonian dead, more than five hundred in number, and then calling a meeting of the representatives of the Greeks put before the common council the question what should be done with the city of the Thebans. When the discussion was opened, certain men who were hostile to the Thebans began to recommend that they should be visited with the direst penalties, and they pointed out that they had taken the side of the barbarians against the Greeks. For in the time of Xerxes they had actually joined forces with the Persians and campaigned against Greece, and alone of the Greeks were honoured as benefactors by the Persian kings, so that the ambassadors of the Thebans were seated on thrones set in front of the kings. They related many other details of similar tenor and so aroused the feelings of the council against the Thebans that it was finally voted to raze the city, to sell the captives, to outlaw the Theban exiles from all Greece, and to allow no Greek to offer shelter to a Theban. The king, in accordance with the decree of the council, destroyed the city, and so presented possible rebels among the Greeks with a terrible warning. By selling off the prisoners he realized a sum of four hundred and forty talents of silver.

15. After this he sent men to Athens to demand the surrender of ten political leaders who had opposed his interest, the most prominent of whom were Demosthenes and Lycurgus. So an assembly was convened and the ambassadors were introduced, and after they had spoken, the people were plunged into deep distress and perplexity. They were anxious to uphold the honour of their city but at the same time they were stunned with horror at the destruction of Thebes and, warned by the calamities of their neighbours, were alarmed in face of their own danger.

After many had spoken in the assembly, Phocion, the "Good," who was opposed to the party of Demosthenes, said that the men demanded should remember the daughters of Leos and Hyacinthus and gladly endure death so that their country would suffer no irremediable disaster, and he inveighed against the faint-heartedness and cowardice of those who would not lay down their lives for their city. The people nevertheless rejected his advice and riotously drove him from the stand, and when Demosthenes delivered a carefully prepared discourse, they were carried away with sympathy for their leaders and clearly wished to save them.

In the end, Demades, influenced, it is reported, by a bribe of five silver talents from Demosthenes's supporters, counselled them to save those whose lives were threatened, and read a decree that had been subtly worded. It contained a plea for the men and a promise to impose the penalty prescribed by the law, if they deserved punishment. The people approved the suggestion of Demades, passed the decree and dispatched a delegation including Demades as envoys to the king, instructing them to make a plea to Alexander in favour of the Theban fugitives as well, that he would allow the Athenians to provide a refuge for them. On this mission, Demades achieved all his objectives by the eloquence of his words and prevailed upon Alexander to absolve the men from the charges against them and to grant all the other requests of the Athenians.

16. Thereupon the king returned with his army to Macedonia, assembled his military commanders and his noblest Friends and posed for discussion the plan for crossing over to Asia. When should the campaign be started and how should he conduct the war? Antipater and Parmenion advised him to produce an heir first and then to turn his hand to so ambitious an enterprise, but Alexander was eager for action and opposed to any postponement, and spoke against them. It would be a disgrace, he pointed out, for one who had been appointed by Greece to command the war, and who had inherited his father's invincible forces, to sit at home celebrating a marriage and awaiting the birth of children. He then proceeded to show them where their advantage lay and by appeals aroused their enthusiasm for the contests which lay ahead. He made lavish sacrifices to the gods at Dium in Macedonia and held the dramatic contests in honour of Zeus and the Muses which Archelaüs, one of his predecessors, had instituted. He celebrated the festival for nine days, naming each day after one of the Muses. He erected a tent to hold a hundred couches and invited his Friends and officers, as well as the ambassadors from the cities, to the banquet. Employing great magnificence, he entertained great numbers in person besides distributing to his entire force sacrificial animals and all else suitable for the festive occasion, and put his army in a fine humour.

How he crossed into Asia and defeated the satraps at the river Granicus in Phrygia (17-21).

17. When Ctesicles was archon at Athens, [334/3] the Romans elected as consuls Gaius Sulpicius and Lucius Papirius. Alexander advanced with his army to the Hellespont and transported it from Europe to Asia. He personally sailed with sixty fighting ships to the Troad, where he flung his spear from the ship and fixed it in the ground, and then leapt ashore himself the first of the Macedonians, signifying that he received Asia from the gods as a spear-won prize. He visited the tombs of the heroes Achilles, Ajax, and the rest and honoured them with offerings and other appropriate marks of respect, and then proceeded to make an accurate count of his accompanying forces. There were found to be, of infantry, twelve thousand Macedonians, seven thousand allies, and five thousand mercenaries, all of whom were under the command of Parmenion. Odrysians, Triballians, and Illyrians accompanied him to the number of seven thousand; and of archers and the so-called Agrianians one thousand, making up a total of thirty-two thousand foot soldiers. Of cavalry there were eighteen hundred Macedonians, commanded by Philotas son of Parmenion; eighteen hundred Thessalians, commanded by Callas son of Harpalus; six hundred from the rest of Greece under the command of Erigyius; and nine hundred Thracian and Paeonian scouts with Cassander in command, making a total of forty-five hundred cavalry. These were the men who crossed with Alexander to Asia. The soldiers who were left behind in Europe under the command of Antipater numbered twelve thousand foot and fifteen hundred horse.

As the king began his march out of the Troad and came to the sanctuary of Athena, the sacrificant named Alexander noticed in front of the temple a statue of Ariobarzanes, a former satrap of Phrygia, lying fallen on the ground, together with some other favourable omens that occurred. He came to the king and affirmed that he would be victor in a great cavalry battle and especially if he happened to fight within the confines of Phrygia; he added that the king with his own hands would slay in battle a distinguished general of the enemy. Such, he said, were the portents the gods disclosed to him, and particularly Athena who would help him in his success.

18. Alexander welcomed the prediction of the seer and made a splendid sacrifice to Athena, dedicating his own armour to the goddess. Then, taking the finest of the panoplies deposited in the temple, he put it on and used it in his first battle. This he did in fact decide through his own personal fighting ability and won a resounding victory, but this did not take place till a few days later.

Meanwhile, the Persian satraps and generals had not acted in time to prevent the crossing of the Macedonians, but they mustered their forces and took counsel how to oppose Alexander. Memnon, the Rhodian, famed for his military competence, advocated a policy of not fighting a pitched battle, but of stripping the countryside and through the shortage of supplies preventing the Macedonians from advancing further, while at the same time they sent naval and land forces across to Macedonia and transferred the impact of war to Europe. This was the best counsel, as after-events made clear, but, for all that, Memnon failed to win over the other commanders, since his advice seemed beneath the dignity of the Persians. So they decided to fight it out, and summoning forces from every quarter and heavily outnumbering the Macedonians, they advanced in the direction of Hellespontine Phrygia. They pitched camp by the river Granicus, using the bed of the river as a line of defence.

19. When Alexander learned of the concentration of the Persian forces, he advanced rapidly and encamped opposite the enemy, so that the Granicus flowed between the encampments. The Persians, resting on high ground, made no move, intending to fall upon the foe as he crossed the river, for they supposed they could easily carry the day when the Macedonian phalanx was divided. Alexander at dawn boldly brought his army across the river and deployed in good order before they could stop him. In return, they posted their mass of horsemen all along the front of the Macedonians since they had decided to press the battle with these. Memnon of Rhodes and the satrap Arsamenes held the left wing each with his own cavalry; Arsites was stationed next with the horsemen from Paphlagonia; then came Spithrobates satrap of Ionia at the head of the Hyrcanian cavalry. The right wing was held by a thousand Medes and two thousand horse with Rheomithres as well as Bactrians of like number. Other national contingents occupied the centre, numerous and picked for their valour. In all, the cavalry amounted to more than ten thousand. The Persian foot soldiers were not fewer than one hundred thousand, but they were posted behind the line and did not advance since the cavalry was thought to be s sufficient to crush the Macedonians.

As the horse of each side joined battle spiritedly, the Thessalian cavalry posted on the left wing under the command of Parmenion gallantly met the attack of the troops posted opposite them; and Alexander, who had the finest of the riders on the right wing with him, personally' led the attack upon the Persians and closing with them, began to inflict substantial losses upon them.

20. But the Persians resisted bravely and opposed their spirit to the Macedonian valour, as Fortune brought together in one and the same place the finest fighters to dispute the victory. The satrap of Ionia Spithrobates, a Persian by birth and son-in-law of King Dareius, a man of superior courage, hurled himself at the Macedonian lines with a large body of cavalry, and with an array of forty companions, all Royal Relatives of outstanding valour, pressed hard on the opposite line and in a fierce attack slew some of his opponents and wounded others. As the force of this attack seemed dangerous, Alexander turned his horse toward the satrap and rode at him.

To the Persian, it seemed as if this opportunity for a single combat was god-given. He hoped that by his individual gallantry Asia might be relieved of its terrible menace, the renowned daring of Alexander arrested by his own hands, and the glory of the Persians saved from disgrace. He hurled his javelin first at Alexander with so mighty an impulse and so powerful a cast that he pierced Alexander's shield and right epomis and drove through the breastplate. The king shook off the weapon as it dangled by his arm, then applying spurs to his horse and employing the favouring momentum of his charge drove his lance squarely into the satrap's chest. At this, adjacent ranks in both armies cried out at the superlative display of prowess. The point, however, snapped off against the breastplate and the broken shaft recoiled, and the Persian drew his sword and drove at Alexander; but the king recovered his grip upon his lance in time to thrust at the man's face and drive the blow home. The Persian fell, but just at this moment, Rhosaces, his brother, galloping up brought his sword down on Alexander's head with such a fearsome blow that it split his helmet and inflicted a slight scalp wound. As Rhosaces aimed another blow at the same break, Cleitus, surnamed the Black, dashed up on his horse and cut off the Persian's arm.

21. The Relatives now pressed in a solid body about the two fallen men; at first they rained their javelins on Alexander, and then closing went all out to slay the king. Exposed as he was to many and fierce attacks he nevertheless was not overborne by the numbers of the foe. Though he took two blows on the breastplate, one on the helmet, and three on the shield which he had brought from the temple of Athena, he still did not give in, but borne up by an exaltation of spirit surmounted every danger. After this, several of the other noble Persians fighting against him fell, of whom the most illustrious were Atizyes and Pharnaces, brother of Dareius's queen, and also Mithrobuzanes who commanded the Cappadocians.

Now that many of their commanders had been slain and all the Persian squadrons were worsted by the Macedonians, those facing Alexander were put to flight first, and then the others also. Thus the king by common consent won the palm for bravery and was regarded as the chief author of the victory, and next to him the Thessalian cavalry won a great reputation for valour because of the skilful handling of their squadrons and their unmatched fighting quality. After the rout of the cavalry, the foot soldiers engaged one another in a contest that was soon ended. For the Persians, dismayed by the rout of the cavalry and shaken in spirit, were quick to flee. The total of the Persian infantry killed was more than ten thousand; of the cavalry not less than two thousand; and there were taken alive upwards of twenty thousand. After the battle the king gave magnificent obsequies to the dead, for he thought it important by this sort of honour to create in his men greater enthusiasm to face the hazards of battle.

Recovering his forces, Alexander led them down through Lydia and took over the city of the Sardians with its citadels and, what is more, the treasures stored therein, for Mithrines the satrap surrendered them without resistance.

How he took by siege Miletus and Halicarnassus (22-27).

22. Since the Persian survivors of the battle together with the general Memnon had taken refuge in Miletus, the king set up camp near the city and every day, using his men in relays, made continuous assaults on the walls. At first the besieged easily defended themselves from the walls, for many soldiers were gathered in the city, and they had abundant provision of missiles and other things useful for the emergency. When the king, in a more determined fashion, brought up siege engines and rocked the walls and pressed the siege very actively both by land and by sea, and the Macedonians forced an entry through the crumbling walls, then at last yielding to superior force, they took to flight. Immediately the Milesians, falling before the king with suppliant olive boughs, put themselves and their city into his hands. Some of the Persians were slain by the Macedonians, others, breaking out of the city, sought refuge in flight, and all the remainder were taken captive. Alexander treated the Milesians kindly but sold all the rest as slaves. Since the naval force was now useless and entailed great expense, he dismissed the fleet with the exception of a few ships which he employed for the transport of his siege engines. Among these was the Athenian contingent of twenty ships.

23. There are those who say that Alexander's strategic conception was sound, when he dismissed his fleet. For Dareius was still to be reckoned with and there was bound to be a great battle, and he judged that the Macedonians would fight more desperately if he deprived them of all hope of escape by flight. He employed the same device, they say, at the battle of the Granicus, where he placed the stream at his rear, for no one could think of flight when destruction of any who were followed into the bed of the river was a certainty. There is also, they note, in later years the case of Agathocles, king of the Syracusans, who copied the strategy of Alexander and won an unexpected and decisive victory. He had crossed to Libya with a small force and by burning his ships deprived his men of any hope of escape by flight, thus constraining them to fight like heroes and thereby win a victory over the Carthaginians, who had an army numbering many tens of thousands.

After the capture of Miletus, the bulk of the Persians and mercenaries, as well as the most enterprising of the commanders, concentrated their forces at Halicarnassus. This was the largest city in Caria, containing the palace of the kings of the Carians, and was well provided with interior fortresses. About the same time Memnon sent his wife and children to Dareius, because he calculated that leaving them in the king's care was a good way to ensure their safety, while at the same time the king, now that he had good hostages, would be more willing to entrust Memnon with the supreme command, and so it turned out. For Dareius straightway sent letters to those who dwelt next the sea, directing them one and all to take orders from Memnon. Accordingly, having assumed the supreme command, he made all the necessary dispositions for a siege in the city of the Halicarnassians.

24. King Alexander had his siege engines and provisions conveyed by sea to Halicarnassus while he himself with all his army marched into Caria, winning over the cities that lay on his route by kind treatment. He was particularly generous to the Greek cities, granting them independence and exemption from taxation, adding the assurance that the freedom of the Greeks was the object for which he had taken upon himself the war against the Persians. On his journey he was met by a woman named Ada, who belonged by blood to the ruling house of Caria. When she presented a petition to recover the position of her ancestors and requested his assistance, he gave orders that she should become the ruler of Caria. Thus he won the loyal support of the Carians by the favour that he bestowed on this woman. For straightway all the cities sent missions and presented the king with golden crowns and promised to co-operate with him in everything.

Alexander encamped near the city and set in motion an active and formidable siege. At first he made continued assaults on the walls with relays of attackers and spent whole days in active fighting. Later he brought up all sorts of engines of war, filled in the trenches in front of the city with the aid of sheds to protect the workers, and rocked the towers and the curtains between them with his battering rams. Whenever he overthrew a portion of the wall, he attempted by hand-to-hand fighting to force an entry into the city over the rubble, but Memnon at first easily beat off the Macedonians assaulting the walls, for he had large numbers of men in the city. Where the siege engines were attacking, he issued from the city at night with numbers of soldiers and applied fire to the machines. Fierce fights occurred in front of the city, in which the Macedonians showed far superior prowess, but the Persians had the advantage of numbers and of fire power. For they had the support of men who fought from the walls using engines to shoot darts, with which they killed some of the enemy and disabled others.

25. At the same moment, the trumpets sounded the battle signal on both sides and cheers came from all parts as the soldiers applauded in concert the feats of brave men on one side or the other. Some tried to put out the fires that rose aloft among the siege engines; others joined with the foe in close combat and wrought great slaughter; others erected secondary walls behind those which crumbled, heavier by far in construction than the preceding. The commanders under

Memnon took their places in the front line and offered great rewards to those who distinguished themselves, so that the desire for victory rose very high on both sides. There could be seen men encountering frontal wounds or being carried unconscious out of the battle, others standing over the fallen bodies of their companions and struggling mightily to recover them, while others who were on the point of yielding to the storm of terrors were again put in heart by the appeals of their officers and were renewed in spirit. At length, some of the Macedonians were killed at the very gates, among them an officer Neoptolemus, a man of distinguished family.

Presently two towers were levelled with the ground and two curtains overthrown, and some of Perdiccas's soldiers, getting drunk, made a wild night attack on the walls of the citadel. Memnon's men noticed the awkwardness of these attackers and issuing forth themselves in considerably larger numbers routed the Macedonians and killed many of them. As this situation became known, large numbers of Macedonians rushed up to help and a great struggle took place, and when Alexander and his staff came up, the Persians, forced back, were confined within the city, and the king through a herald asked for a truce to recover the Macedonians who had fallen in front of the walls. Now Ephialtes and Thrasybulus, Athenians fighting on the Persian side, advised not to give up the dead bodies for burial, but Memnon granted the request.

26. After this at a council of the commanders, Ephialtes advised them not to wait till the city was taken and they found themselves captives; he proposed that the leaders of the mercenaries should go out themselves in the front rank and lead an attack on the enemy. Memnon recognized that Ephialtes was eager to prove himself and, having great hopes of him because of his courage and bodily strength, allowed him to do as he wished. Accordingly he collected two thousand picked men and, giving half of them lighted torches and forming the others so as to meet the enemy, he suddenly threw all the gates wide open. It was daybreak, and sallying forth with his band he employed the one group to set fire to the siege engines, causing a great conflagration to flame up at once, while he personally led the rest deployed in a dense phalanx many ranks deep and charged the Macedonians as they issued forth to help extinguish the fire. When the king saw what was happening, he placed the best fighters of the Macedonians in front and stationed picked men in reserve. Behind these he posted a third group also consisting of others who had a good record for stout fighting. He himself at the head of all took command and made a stand against the enemy, who had supposed that because of their mass they would be invincible. He also sent men out to extinguish the fire and to rescue the siege engines.

As violent shouts arose at the same time on both sides and the trumpets sounded the attack, a terrific contest ensued because of the valour of the contestants and their consummate fighting spirit. The Macedonians prevented the fire from spreading, but Ephialtes's men had the advantage in the battle, and he himself, who had far greater bodily strength than the rest, slew with his own hand many who traded blows with him. From the top of the recently erected replacement wall, the defenders slew many of the Macedonians with dense showers of missiles, for there had been erected a wooden tower, a hundred cubits high, which was filled with dart-hurling catapults. As many Macedonians fell and the rest recoiled before the thick fire of missiles, Memnon threw himself into the battle with heavy reinforcements and even Alexander found himself quite helpless.

27. Just at that moment as the men from the city were prevailing, the tide of battle was surprisingly reversed. For the oldest Macedonians, who were exempt from combat duty by virtue of their age, but who had served with Philip on his campaigns and had been victorious in many battles, were roused by the emergency to show their valour, and, being far superior in pride and war experience, sharply rebuked the faintheartedness of the youngsters who wished to avoid the battle. Then they closed ranks with their shields overlapping and confronted the foe, who thought himself already victorious. They succeeded in slaying Ephialtes and many others, and finally forced the rest to take refuge in the city. Night had already fallen as the Macedonians pushed within the walls along with their fleeing enemies, but the king ordered the trumpeter to sound the recall and they withdrew to their camp. Memnon, however, assembled his generals and satraps, held a meeting, and decided to abandon the city. They installed their best men in the acropolis with sufficient provision and conveyed the rest of the army and the stores to Cos. When Alexander at daybreak learned what had taken place he razed the city and surrounded the citadel with a formidable wall and trench. A portion of his force under certain generals he dispatched into the interior with orders to subdue the neighbouring tribes.

These commanders, campaigning vigorously, subdued the whole region as far as greater Phrygia, supporting their men on the land. Alexander, for his part, overran the littoral as far as Cilicia, acquiring many cities and actively storming and reducing the strong points. One of these he captured surprisingly with such a curious reversal of fortune that the account of it cannot be omitted.

28. Near the frontiers of Lycia there is a great rock fortress of unusual strength inhabited by people named Marmares. As Alexander marched by, these people attacked the Macedonian rear guard and killed many, carrying off as booty numerous men and pack animals. The king was enraged at this, established a siege, and exerted every effort to take the place by force. The Marmares were very brave and had confidence in the strength of their fortifications, and manfully withstood the attack. For two whole days there were constant assaults and it was clear that the king would not leave until he had captured the "rock."

First, then, the older men of the Marmares advised their younger countrymen to end their resistance and make peace with the king on whatever terms were possible. They would have none of this, however, but all were eager to die together simultaneously with the end of the freedom of their state, so next the elders urged upon them that they should kill with their own hands their children and wives and aged relatives, and those who were strong enough to save themselves should break out through the midst of the enemy at night and take refuge in the neighbouring mountain. The young men agreed, and consequently gave orders to go each to his own house and there, enjoying the best of food and drink with their families, await the dread event. Some of them, however (these were about six hundred), decided not to kill their relatives with their own hands, but to burn them in the houses, and so issuing forth from the gates to make their way to the mountain. These carried out their decision and so caused each family to be entombed at its own hearth, while they themselves slipped through the midst of the enemy encamped about them and made their way to the near-by hills under cover of darkness.

This is what happened in this year.

29. When Nicocrates was archon at Athens, [333/32] Caeso Valerius and Lucius Papirius became consuls at Rome. In this year Dareius sent money to Memnon and appointed him commanding general of the whole war. He gathered a force of mercenaries, manned three hundred ships, and pursued the conflict vigorously. He secured Chios, and then coasting along to Lesbos easily mastered Antissa and Methymna and Pyrrha and Eressus. Mitylenê also, large and possessed of rich stores of supplies as well as plenty of fighting men, he nevertheless captured with difficulty by assault after a siege of many days and with the loss of many of his soldiers. News of the general's activity spread like wildfire and most of the Cyclades sent missions to him. As word came to Greece that Memnon was about to sail to Euboea with his fleet, the cities of that island became alarmed, while those Greeks who were friendly to Persia, notably Sparta, began to have high hopes of a change in the political situation. Memnon distributed bribes freely and won many Greeks over to share the Persian hopes, but Fortune nevertheless put an end to his career. He fell ill and died, seized by a desperate malady, and with his death Dareius's fortunes also collapsed.

The battle of Dareius against Alexander at Issus in Cilicia and the victory of Alexander (30-39).

30. The king had counted on Memnon's transferring the impact of the war from Asia into Europe, but learning of his death called a session of his Council of Friends and laid before them the alternatives, either to send generals with an army down to the coast or for himself, the king, to march down with all his armed forces and fight the Macedonians in person. Some said that the king must join in battle personally, and they argued that the Persians would fight better in that event. Charidemus, however, the Athenian, a man generally admired for his bravery and skill as a commander; he had been a comrade-in-arms of King Philip and had led or counselled all his successes, recommended that Dareius should on no account stake his throne rashly on a gamble, but should keep in his own hands the reserve strength and the control of Asia while sending to the war a general who had given proof of his ability. One hundred thousand men would be an adequate force, so long as a third of these were Greek mercenaries, and Charidemus hinted that he himself would assume the responsibility for the success of the plan.

The king was moved by his arguments at first but his Friends opposed them stoutly, and even brought Charidemus into suspicion of wanting to get the command so that he could betray the Persian empire to the Macedonians. At this, Charidemus became angry and made free with slurs on Persian lack of manliness. This offended the king, and as his wrath blinded him to his advantage, he seized Charidemus by the girdle according to the custom of the Persians, turned him over to the attendants, and ordered him put to death. So Charidemus was led away, but as he went to his death, he shouted that the king would soon change his mind and would receive a prompt requital for this unjust punishment, becoming the witness of the overthrow of the kingdom.

Charidemus's prospects had been high, but he missed their fulfilment because of his ill-timed frankness and he ended his life in this fashion. Once the king's passion had cooled he promptly regretted his act and reproached himself for having made a serious mistake, but all his royal power was not able to undo what was done. He was haunted by dreams of the Macedonian fighting qualities and the vision of Alexander in action was constantly before his eyes. He searched for a competent general to take over Memnon's command but could find no one, and finally felt constrained to go down himself to take part in the contest for the kingdom.

31. He wasted no time in summoning his forces from all directions and ordered them to muster in Babylon. He canvassed his Friends and Relatives and selected those who were suitable, giving to some commands suited to their abilities and ordering others to fight at his side as his personal staff. When the time set for the march had come, they had all arrived in Babylon. The number of the soldiers was over four hundred thousand infantry and not less than one hundred thousand cavalry.

This was the force with which Dareius marched out of Babylon in the direction of Cilicia; he had with him his wife and children, a son and two daughters, and his mother. As to Alexander, he had been watching how, prior to his death, Memnon had won over Chios and the cities in Lesbos and had taken Mitylenê by storm. He learned that Memnon planned to carry the war into Macedonia with three hundred ships of war and a land army also, while the greater part of the Greeks were ready to revolt. This caused him no little anxiety, but when persons came with the news of Memnon's death, he was relieved of this fear; but shortly thereafter he became seriously ill, and, afflicted by severe pain, sent for his physicians. All the rest were hesitant to treat him, but Philip the Arcarnanian offered to employ risky but quick-acting remedies and by the use of drugs to break the hold of the disease. This proposal the king accepted gladly, for he had heard that Dareius had already left Babylon with his army. The physician gave him a drug to drink and, aided by the natural strength of the sufferer as well as by Fortune, promptly relieved Alexander of the trouble. Making an astonishing recovery, the king honoured the physician with magnificent gifts and assigned him to the most loyal category of Friends.

32. Alexander's mother wrote at this time to him, giving him other useful advice and warning him to be on his guard against the Lyncestian Alexander. This was a man distinguished for bravery and high spirit who accompanied the king in the group of Friends in a trusted capacity. There were many other plausible circumstances joining to support the charge, and so the Lyncestian was arrested and bound and placed under guard, until he should face a court.

Alexander learned that Dareius was only a few days march away, and sent off Parmenion with a body of troops to seize the passage of the so-called . . . Gates. When the latter reached the place, he forced out the Persians who were holding the pass and remained master of it. Dareius decided to make his army mobile and diverted his baggage train and the non-combatants to Damascus in Syria; then, learning that Alexander was holding the passes and thinking that he would never dare to fight in the plain, made his way quickly to meet him. The people of the country, who had little respect for the small numbers of the Macedonians but were much impressed with the great size of the Persian army, abandoned Alexander and came over to Dareius. They brought the Persians food and other materials with great goodwill, and mentally predicted victory for them. Alexander, however, occupied Issus, a considerable city, which was terrified into submission.

33. When his scouts reported that Dareius was only thirty stades away and advancing in alarming fashion with his forces drawn up for battle, a frightening spectacle, Alexander grasped that this was a god-given opportunity to destroy the

Persian power in a single victory. He roused his soldiers with appropriate words for a decisive effort and marshalled the battalions of foot and the squadrons of horse appropriately to the location. He set the cavalry along the front of the whole army, and ordered the infantry phalanx to remain in reserve behind it. He himself advanced at the head of the right wing to the encounter, having with him the best of the mounted troops. The Thessalian horse was on the left, and this was outstanding in bravery and skill. When the armies were within missile range, the Persians launched at Alexander such a shower of missiles that they collided with one another in the air, so thickly did they fly, and weakened the force of their impact. On both sides the trumpeters blew the signal of attack and then the Macedonians first raised an unearthly shout followed by the Persians answering, so that the whole hillside bordering the battlefield echoed back the sound, and this second roar in volume surpassed the Macedonian war cry as five hundred thousand men shouted with one voice.

Alexander cast his glance in all directions in his anxiety to see Dareius, and as soon as he had identified him, he drove hard with his cavalry at the king himself, wanting not so much to defeat the Persians as to win the victory with his own hands. By now the rest of the cavalry on both sides was engaged and many were killed as the battle raged indecisively because of the evenly matched fighting qualities of the two sides. The scales inclined now one way, now another, as the lines swayed alternately forward and backward. No javelin cast or sword thrust lacked its effect as the crowded ranks offered a ready target. Many fell with wounds received as they faced the enemy and their fury held to the last breath, so that life failed them sooner than courage.

34. The officers of each unit fought valiantly at the head of their men and by their example inspired courage in the ranks. One could see many forms of wounds inflicted, furious struggles of all sorts inspired by the will to win. The Persian Oxathres was the brother of Dareius and a man highly praised for his fighting qualities; when he saw Alexander riding at Dareius and feared that he would not be checked, he was seized with the desire to share his brother's fate. Ordering the best of the horsemen in his company to follow him, he threw himself with them against Alexander, thinking that this demonstration of brotherly love would bring him high renown among the Persians. He took up the fight directly in front of Dareius's chariot and there engaging the enemy skilfully and with a stout heart slew many of them. The fighting qualities of Alexander's group were superior, however, and quickly many bodies lay piled high about the chariot. No Macedonian had any other thought than to strike the king, and in their intense rivalry to reach him took no thought for their lives.

Many of the noblest Persian princes perished in this struggle, among them Antixyes and Rheomithres and Tasiaces, the satrap of Egypt. Many of the Macedonians fell also, and Alexander himself was wounded in the thigh, for the enemy pressed about him. The horses which were harnessed to the yoke of Dareius's chariot were covered with wounds and terrified by the piles of dead about them. They refused to answer to their bridles, and came close to carrying off Dareius into the midst of the enemy, but the king himself, in extreme peril, caught up the reins, being forced to throw away the dignity of his position and to violate the ancient custom of the Persian kings. A second chariot was brought up by Dareius's attendants and in the confusion as he changed over to it in the face of constant attack he fell into a panic terror.

Seeing their king in this state, the Persians with him turned to flee, and as each adjacent unit in turn did the same, the whole Persian cavalry was soon in full retreat. As their route took them through narrow denies and over rough country, they clashed and trampled on one another and many died without having received a blow from the enemy. For men lay piled up in confusion, some without armour, others in full battle panoply. Some with their swords still drawn killed those who spitted themselves upon them. Most of the cavalry, however, bursting out into the plain and driving their horses at full gallop succeeded in reaching the safety of the friendly cities. Now the Macedonian phalanx and the Persian infantry were engaged only briefly, for the rout of the cavalry had been, as it were, a prelude of the whole victory. Soon all of the Persians were in retreat and as so many tens of thousands were making their escape through narrow passes the whole countryside was soon covered with bodies.

35. When night fell, the remainder of the Persian army easily succeeded in scattering in various directions while the Macedonians gave over the pursuit and turned to plunder, being particularly attracted by the royal pavilions because of the mass of wealth that was there. This included much silver, no little gold, and vast numbers of rich dresses from the royal treasure, which they took, and likewise a great store of wealth belonging to the King's Friends, Relatives, and military commanders. Not only the ladies of the royal house but also those of the King's Relatives and Friends, borne on gilded chariots, had accompanied the army according to an ancestral custom of the Persians, and each of them had brought with her a store of rich furniture and feminine adornment, in keeping with their vast wealth and luxury.

The lot of these captured women was pathetic in the extreme. They who previously from daintiness only with reluctance had been conveyed in luxurious carriages and had exposed no part of their bodies unveiled now burst wailing out of the tents clad only in a single chiton, rending their garments, calling on the gods, and falling at the knees of the conquerors. Flinging off their jewellery with trembling hands and with their hair flying, they fled for their lives over rugged ground and, collecting into groups, they called to help them those who were themselves in need of help from others. Some of their captors dragged these unfortunates by the hair, others, ripping off their clothing, drove them with blows of their hands or spear-butts against their naked bodies, thus outraging the dearest and proudest of the Persian possessions by virtue of Fortune's generosity to them.

36. Now the most prudent of the Macedonians looked on this reversal of fortune with compassion and felt pity for the case of those who had seen their former lot so violently changed; everything belonging to their high rank was far removed from them, and they were encompassed by what was foreign and hostile. (This, however, was not the attitude of most of the soldiery.) and the women were herded off into a luckless and humiliating captivity.

What particularly moved to tears of pity those who saw it was the family of Dareius, his mother, wife, two daughters of marriageable age, and a son who was a mere boy. In their case, the change in fortune and the magnitude of their loss of position, incredible as it was, was a spectacle that might well inspire compassion in those who beheld it. They knew nothing of Dareius, whether he lived and survived or had perished in the general disaster, but they saw their tent plundered by armed men who were unaware of the identity of their captives and committed many improper acts through ignorance. They saw the whole of Asia taken prisoner with them, and as the wives of the satraps fell at their feet and implored their help, they were not able to assist any one of of them, but themselves sought the assistance of the others in their own misfortunes.

The royal pages now took over the tent of Dareius and prepared Alexander's bath and dinner and, lighting a great blaze of torches, waited for him, that he might return from the pursuit and, finding ready for him all the riches of Dareius, take it as an omen for his conquest of the empire of all Asia.

In the course of the battle there died on the Persian side more than one hundred thousand infantry and not less than ten thousand cavalry; on the Macedonian side, the casualties were three hundred infantry and one hundred and fifty cavalry. This was the conclusion of the battle at Issus of Cilicia.

37. The kings, however, were still occupied. When he knew that he was decisively defeated, Dareius gave himself up to flight and mounting in turn one after another of his best horses galloped on at top speed, desperately seeking to escape from Alexander's grasp and anxious to reach the safety of the upper satrapies. Alexander followed him with the companion cavalry and the best of the other horsemen, eager to get possession of Dareius's person. He continued on for two hundred furlongs and then turned back, returning to his camp about midnight. Having dispelled his weariness in the bath, he turned to relaxation and to dinner.

Someone came to the wife and the mother of Dareius and told them that Alexander had come back from the pursuit after stripping Dareius of his arms. At this, a great outcry and lamentation arose among the women; and the rest of the captives, joining in their sorrow at the news, sent up a loud wail, so that the king heard it and sent Leonnatus, one of his Friends, to quiet the uproar and to reassure Sisyngambris [Sisigambis] by explaining that Dareius was still alive and that Alexander would show them the proper consideration. In the morning he would come to address them and to demonstrate his kindness by deeds. As they heard this welcome and altogether unexpected good news, the captive women hailed Alexander as a god and ceased from their wailing.

So at daybreak, the king took with him the most valued of his Friends, Hephaestion, and came to the women. They both were dressed alike, but Hephaestion was taller and more handsome. Sisyngambris took him for the king and did him obeisance. As the others present made signs to her and pointed to Alexander with their hands she was embarrassed by her mistake, but made a new start and did obeisance to Alexander. He, however, cut in and said, "Never mind, Mother. For actually he too is Alexander." By thus addressing the aged woman as "Mother," with this kindliest of terms he gave the promise of coming benefactions to those who had been wretched a moment before. Assuring Sisyngambris that she would be his second mother he immediately ratified in action what he had just promised orally.

38. He decked her with her royal jewellery and restored her to her previous dignity, with its proper honours. He made over to her all the former retinue of servants which she had been given by Dareius and added more in addition not less in number than the preceding. He promised to provide for the marriage of the daughters even more generously than Dareius had promised and to bring up the boy as his own son and to show him royal honour. He called the boy to him and kissed him, and as he saw him fearless in countenance and not frightened at all, he remarked to Hephaestion that at the age of six years the boy showed a courage beyond his years and was much braver than his father. As to the wife of Dareius, he said that he would see that her dignity should be so maintained that she would experience nothing inconsistent with her former happiness.

He added many other assurances of consideration and generosity, so that the women broke out into uncontrolled weeping, so great was their unexpected joy. He gave them his hand as pledge of all this and was not only showered with praises by those who had been helped, but won universal recognition through out his own army for his exceeding propriety of conduct. In general I would say that of many good deeds done by Alexander there is none that is greater or more worthy of record and mention in history than this. Sieges and battles and the other victories scored in war are due for the most part either to Fortune or valour, but when one in a position of power shows pity for those who have been overthrown, this is an action due only to wisdom. Most people are made proud by their successes because of their good fortune and, becoming arrogant in their success, are forgetful of the common weakness of mankind. You can see how very many are unable to bear success, just as if it were a heavy burden. Although Alexander lived many generations before our time, let him continue to receive in future ages also the just and proper praise for his good qualities.

39. Dareius hurried to Babylon and gathered together the survivors of the battle at Issus. He was not crushed in spirit in spite of the tremendous setback he had received, but wrote to Alexander advising him to bear his success as one who was only human and to release the captives in return for a large ransom. He added that he would yield to Alexander the territory and cities of Asia west of the Halys River if he would sign a treaty of friendship with him. Alexander summoned his Friends to a council and concealed the real letter. Forging another more in accord with his interests he introduced it to his advisers and sent the envoys away empty handed. So Dareius gave up the attempt to reach an agreement with Alexander by diplomatic means and set to work on vast preparations for war. He re-equipped those who had lost their armour in the defeat and he enlisted others and assigned them to military units. He sent for the levies from the upper satrapies, which he had previously left unemployed because of the haste of the last campaign. He took such pains over the constitution of the army that he ended up with one twice the size of that which had been engaged at Issus. He assembled eight hundred thousand infantry and two hundred thousand cavalry, and a force of scythe-bearing chariots in addition. These were the events of this year.

The siege of Tyre, the occupation of Egypt, and the journey of the king to Ammon (40-52).

40. When Niceratus was archon at Athens, [332/1] the Romans elected as consuls Marcus Atilius and Marcus Valerius, and the one hundred and twelfth Olympic Games were held, in which Grylus of Chalcis was the victor. In this year, Alexander buried the dead from his victory at Issus, including even those of the Persians who had distinguished themselves by courage. Then he performed rich sacrifices to the gods and rewarded those who had borne themselves well in battle with gifts appropriate to each, and rested the army for some days. Then he marched on towards Egypt, and as he came into Phoenicia, received the submission of all the other cities, for their inhabitants accepted him willingly.

At Tyre, however, when the king wished to sacrifice to the Tyrian Heracles, the people over hastily barred him from entering the city; Alexander became angry and threatened to resort to force, but the Tyrians cheerfully faced the prospect of a siege. They wanted to gratify Dareius and keep unimpaired their loyalty to him, and thought also that they would receive great gifts from the king in return for such a favour. They would draw Alexander into a protracted and difficult siege and give Dareius time for his military preparations, and at the same time they had confidence in the strength of their island and the military forces in it. They also hoped for help from their colonists, the Carthaginians.

The king saw that the city could hardly be taken by sea because of the engines mounted along its walls and the fleet that it possessed, while from the land it was almost unassailable because it lay four furlongs away from the coast. Nevertheless he determined to run every risk and make every effort to save the Macedonian army from being held in contempt by a single undistinguished city. Immediately he demolished what was called Old Tyre and set many tens of thousands of men to work carrying stones to construct a mole two plethra in width. He drafted into service the entire population of the neighbouring cities and the project advanced rapidly because the workers were numerous.

41. At first, the Tyrians sailed up to the mole and mocked the king, asking if he thought that he would get the better of Poseidon. Then, as the work proceeded with unexpected rapidity, they voted to transport their children and women and old men to Carthage, assigned the young and able-bodied to the defence of the walls, and made ready for a naval engagement with their eighty triremes. They did succeed in getting a part of their children and women to safety with the Carthaginians, but they were outstripped by the abundance of Alexander's labour force, and, not being able to stop his advance with their ships, were compelled to stand the siege with almost their whole population still in the city. They had a wealth of catapults and other engines employed for sieges and they had no difficulty in constructing more because of the engineers and artisans of all sorts who were in the city. All kinds of novel devices were fashioned by them, so that the entire circuit of the walls was covered with machines, especially on that side where the mole was approaching the city.

As the Macedonian construction came within range of their missiles, portents were sent by the gods to them in their danger. Out of the sea a tidal wave tossed a sea-monster of incredible size into the midst of the Macedonian operations. It crashed into the mole but did it no harm, remained resting a portion of its body against it for a long time and then swam off into the sea again. This strange event threw both sides into superstition, each imagining that the portent signified that Poseidon would come to their aid, for they were swayed by their own interest in the matter.

There were other strange happenings too, calculated to spread confusion and terror among people. At the distribution of rations on the Macedonian side, the broken pieces of bread had a bloody look. Someone reported, on the Tyrian side, that he had seen a vision in which Apollo told him that he would leave the city. Everyone suspected that the man had made up the story in order to curry favour with Alexander, and some of the younger citizens set out to stone him; he was, however, spirited away by the magistrates and took refuge in the temple of Heracles, where as a suppliant he escaped the people's wrath, but the Tyrians were so credulous that they tied the image of Apollo to its base with golden cords, preventing, as they thought, the god from leaving the city.

42. Now the Tyrians were alarmed at the advance of the mole, and they equipped many small vessels with both light and heavy catapults together with archers and slingers, and, attacking the workers on the mole, wounded many and killed not a few. As missiles of all sorts in large numbers rained upon unarmed and densely packed men, no soldier missed his mark since the targets were exposed and unsuspecting. The missiles struck not only from the front but also from the back, as men were working on both sides of a rather narrow structure and no one could protect himself from those who shot from two directions.

Alexander moved immediately to rectify what threatened to be a shocking disaster, and manning all his ships and taking personal command of them, made with all speed for the harbour of Tyre to cut off the retreat of the Phoenicians. They in turn were terrified lest he seize the harbour and capture the city while it was empty of soldiers, and rowed back to Tyre as fast as they could. Both fleets plied their oars at a fast stroke in a fury of determination, and the Macedonians were already nearing the entrance, but the Phoenicians, by a narrow margin, escaped losing their whole force and, thrusting their way in, got safely to the city with the loss only of the ships at the tail of the column.

So the king failed of this important objective, but nevertheless pushed on with the mole, protecting his workers with a thick screen of ships. As his engines drew close to the city and its capture seemed imminent, a powerful north-west gale blew up and damaged a large part of the mole. Alexander was at a loss to deal with the harm done to his project by the forces of nature and thought of giving up the siege attempt, but driven by ambition he sent to the mountain and felling huge trees, he brought them branches and all and, placing them beside the mole, broke the force of the waves. It was not long before he had restored the collapsed parts of the mole, and pushing on with an ample labour force until he came within missiles' range, he moved his engines out to the end of the causeway, and attacked the walls with his stone throwers, while he employed his light catapults against the men stationed along the battlements. The archers and slingers joined in the barrage, and wounded many in the city who rushed to the defence.

43. The Tyrians had bronze workers and machinists, and contrived ingenious counter-measures. Against the projectiles from the catapults they made wheels with many spokes, and, setting these to rotate by a certain device, they destroyed some of the missiles and deflected others, and broke the force of all. They caught the balls from the stone throwers in soft and yielding materials and so weakened their force. While this attack was going on from the mole, the king sailed around the city with his whole fleet and inspected the walls, and made it clear that he was about to attack the city alike by land and sea.

The Tyrians did not dare to put to sea again with their whole fleet but kept three ships moored at the harbour mouth. The king, however, sailed up to these, sank them all, and so returned to his camp. Wanting to double the security of their walls, the Tyrians built a second one at a distance of five cubits within the first; this was ten cubits in thickness, and the passage between the walls they filled with stones and earth, but Alexander lashed triremes together, mounted his various siege engines upon them, and overthrew the wall for the space of a plethron. Through this breach the Macedonians burst into the city, but the Tyrians rained on them a shower of missiles and managed to turn them back, and when night came, they rebuilt the fallen part of the wall.

Now the causeway had reached the wall and made the city mainland, and sharp fighting took place along the walls. The Tyrians had the present danger before their eyes and easily imagined what a disaster the actual capture of the city would be, so that they spent themselves so freely in the contest as to despise mortal danger. When the Macedonians moved up towers as high as the walls and in this way, extending bridges, boldly assaulted the battlements, the Tyrians fell back on the ingenuity of their engineers and applied many counter-measures to meet the assault. They forged great tridents armed with barbs and struck with these at close range the assailants standing on the towers. These stuck in the shields, and as ropes were attached to the tridents, they could haul on the ropes and pull them in. Their victims were faced with the alternative of releasing their arms and exposing their bodies to be wounded by the missiles which showered upon them, or clinging to their shields for shame and perishing in the fall from the lofty towers. Other Tyrians cast fishing nets over those Macedonians who were fighting their way across the bridges and, making their hands helpless, pulled them off and tumbled them down from bridge to earth.

44. They thought of another ingenious device also to offset the Macedonian fighting qualities, by which they involved the bravest of the enemy in a horrible torment which could not be avoided. They fashioned shields of bronze and iron and, filling them with sand, roasted them continuously over a strong fire and made the sand red hot. By means of a certain apparatus they then scattered this over those Macedonians who were fighting most boldly and brought those within its range into utter misery. The sand sifted down under breastplates and shirts, and scorching the skin with the intense heat inflicted upon them irremediable disaster. They shrieked supplications like those under torture and there was no one to help them, but with the excruciating agony they fell into madness and died, the victims of a pitiable and helpless lot.

At the same time, the Phoenicians poured down fire and flung javelins and stones, and by the volume of their missiles weakened the resolution of the attackers. They let down long poles or spars equipped with concave cutting edges and cut the ropes supporting the rams, thus rendering these instruments useless. With their fire-throwers they discharged huge red-hot masses of metal into the press of the enemy, and where so many men were packed together they did not miss their mark. With "crows" and "iron hands" they dragged over the edge many who were stationed behind the breastworks on the towers. With many hands at work they kept all their engines busy and caused many deaths among the besiegers.

45. They caused extreme terror by all of this and the fury of their fighting became hardly resistible, but the Macedonians did not lose their boldness. As those in front kept falling, those behind moved up and were not deterred by the sufferings of their comrades. Alexander mounted the stone-throwing catapults in proper places and made the walls rock with the boulders that they threw. With the dart-throwers on the wooden towers he kept up a constant fire of all kinds of missiles and terribly punished the defenders of the walls. In response, the Tyrians rigged marble wheels in front of the walls and causing these to rotate by some mechanism they shattered the flying missiles of the catapults and, deflecting them from their course, rendered their fire ineffective. In addition, they stitched up hides or pairs of skins and stuffed them with seaweed so as to receive the blows of the stones on these. As these were soft and yielding, the force of the flying stones was lessened. In sum, the Tyrians defended themselves strongly in all regards and showed themselves well provided with the means of defence. They were bold in face of their enemies, and left the shelter of the walls and their positions within the towers to push out onto the very bridges and match the courage of the Macedonians with their own valour. They grappled with the enemy and, fighting hand to hand, put up a stout battle for their city. Some of them used axes to chop off any part of the body of an opponent that presented itself.

There was one of the Macedonian commanders named Admetus who was a conspicuously brave and powerful man. He withstood the fury of the Tyrians with high courage and died heroically, killed instantly when his skull was split by the stroke of an axe.

Alexander saw that the Macedonians were held in check by the resistance of the Tyrians, and, as it was now night, recalled his soldiers by a trumpet call. His first impulse was to break off the siege and march on to Egypt, but he changed his mind as he reflected that it would be disgraceful to leave the Tyrians with all the glory of the operation. He found support in only one of his Friends, Amyntas the son of Andromenes, but turned again to the attack.

46. Alexander addressed the Macedonians, calling on them to dare no less than he. Fitting out all his ships for fighting, he began a general assault upon the walls by land and sea and this was pressed furiously. He saw that the wall on the side of the naval base was weaker than elsewhere, and brought up to that point his triremes lashed together and supporting his best siege engines. Now he performed a feat of daring which was hardly believable even to those who saw it. He flung a bridge across from the wooden tower to the city walls and crossing by it alone gained a footing on the wall, neither concerned for the envy of Fortune nor fearing the menace of the Tyrians. Having as witness of his prowess the great army which had defeated the Persians, he ordered the Macedonians to follow him, and leading the way he slew some of those who came within reach with his spear, and others by a blow of his sword. He knocked down still others with the rim of his shield, and put an end to the high confidence of the enemy.

Simultaneously in another part of the city the battering ram, put to its work, brought down a considerable stretch of wall; and when the Macedonians entered through this breach and Alexander's party poured over the bridge on to the wall, the city was taken. The Tyrians, however, kept up the resistance with mutual cries of encouragement and blocked the alleys with barricades, so that all except a few were cut down fighting, in number more than seven thousand. The king sold the women and children into slavery and crucified all the men of military age. These were not less than two thousand. Although most of the non-combatants had been removed to Carthage, those who remained to become captives were found to be more than thirteen thousand.

So Tyre had undergone the siege bravely rather than wisely and come into such misfortunes, after a resistance of seven months. The king removed the golden chains and fetters from Apollo and gave orders that the god should be called "Apollo Philalexander." He carried out magnificent sacrifices to Heracles, rewarded those of his men who had distinguished themselves, and gave a lavish funeral for his own dead. He installed as king of Tyre a man named Ballonymus, the story of whose career I cannot omit because it is an example of a quite astonishing reversal of fortune.

47. The former king, Straton, was deprived of his throne because of his friendship for Dareius, and Alexander invited Hephaestion to nominate as king of Tyre any personal guest-friend whom he wished. At first he favoured the host with whom he found pleasant lodging, and proposed that he should be designated master of the city. He was prominent among the citizens in wealth and position, but not being related to those who had been kings he would not accept the offer. Hephaestion then asked him to make a choice from among the members of the royal family, and he said that he knew a man of royal descent who was wise and good in all respects, but he was poor in the extreme. Hephaestion nevertheless agreed that he should be given the royal power, and the one who had been given the choice went off to find the man he had named, bearing with him the royal dress, and came upon him drawing water for hire in a garden, dressed in common rags. He informed him of the transformation in his position, dressed him in the king's robe, and gave him the other appropriate trappings of office. Then he conducted him to the market place and proclaimed him king of Tyre. Everyone accepted him with enthusiasm and marvelled at the vicissitudes of Fortune. Thus he became a Friend of Alexander's and took over the kingdom, an instructive example to those who do not know the incredible changes which Fortune can effect.

Now that we have described Alexander's activity, we shall turn our narrative in another direction.

48. In Europe, Agis king of Sparta engaged the services of those mercenaries who had escaped from the battle at Issus, eight thousand in number, and sought to change the political situation in Greece in favour of Dareius. He received from the Persian king ships and money and sailed to Crete, where he captured most of the cities and forced them to take the Persian side.

Amyntas who had fled from Macedonia and had gone up to Dareius had fought on the Persian side in Cilicia. He escaped, however, from the battle at Issus with four thousand mercenaries and got to Tripolis in Phoenicia before Alexander's arrival. Here he chose from the whole Persian fleet enough ships to transport his soldiers, and burned the rest. He sailed over to Cyprus, took on additional soldiers and ships, and continued on down to Pelusium. Becoming master of that city, he proclaimed that he had been sent by King Dareius as military commander because the satrap of Egypt had been killed fighting at Issus in Cilicia. He sailed up the river to Memphis and defeated the local forces in a battle before the city, but then, as his soldiers turned to plunder, the Egyptians issued out of the city, attacked his men as they were scattered looting estates located in the countryside, and killed Amyntas and all who came with him to the last man. That was the end of Amyntas, who had set his hand to great undertakings and failed when he had every prospect of success.

His experience was paralleled by those of the other officers and troop leaders who escaped at the head of their military units from the battle at Issus and attempted to maintain the Persian cause. Some got to important cities and held them for Dareius, others raised tribes and furnishing themselves with troops from them performed appropriate duties in the time under review.

The delegates of the League of Corinth voted to send fifteen envoys with a golden wreath as a prize of valour from Greece to Alexander, instructing them to congratulate him on his victory in Cilicia. Alexander, in the meantime, marched down to Gaza, which was garrisoned by the Persians, and took the city by storm after a siege of two months.

49. In the archonship of Aristophanes at Athens, [331/0] the consuls at Rome were Spurius Postumius and Titus Veturius. In this year King Alexander set in order the affairs of Gaza and sent off Amyntas [son of Andromenes] with ten ships to Macedonia, with orders to enlist the young men who were fit for military service. He himself with all his army marched on to Egypt and secured the adhesion of all its cities without striking a blow. For since the Persians had committed impieties against the temples and had governed harshly, the Egyptians welcomed the Macedonians.

Having settled the affairs of Egypt, Alexander went off to the Temple of Ammon, where he wished to consult the oracle of the god. When he had advanced half way along the coast, he was met by envoys from the people of Cyrenê, who brought him a crown and magnificent gifts, among which were three hundred chargers and five handsome four-horse chariots. He received the envoys cordially and made a treaty of friendship and alliance with them; then he continued with his travelling companions on to the temple. When he came to the desert and waterless part, he took on water and began to cross a country covered with an infinite expanse of sand. In four days their water had given out and they suffered from fearful thirst. All fell into despair, when suddenly a great storm of rain burst from the heavens, ending their shortage of water in a way which had not been foreseen, and which, therefore, seemed to those so unexpectedly rescued to have been due to the action of divine Providence. They refilled their containers from a hollow in the ground, and again with a four days' supply in hand marched for four days and came out of the desert. At one point, when their road could not be traced because of the sand dunes, the guide pointed out to the king that crows cawing on their right were calling their attention to the route which led to the temple. Alexander took this for an omen, and thinking that the god was pleased by his visit pushed on with speed. First he came to the so-called Bitter Lake, and then, proceeding another hundred furlongs, he passed by the Cities of Ammon. Then, after a journey of one day, he approached the sanctuary.

50. The land where this temple lies is surrounded by a sandy desert and waterless waste, destitute of anything good for man. The oasis is fifty furlongs in length and breadth and is watered by many fine springs, so that it is covered with all sorts of trees, especially those valued for their fruit. It has a moderate climate like our spring and, surrounded as it is by very hot regions, alone furnishes to its people a contrasting mildness of temperature. It is said that the sanctuary was built by Danaüs the Egyptian. The land, which is sacred to the god, is occupied on the south and west by Ethiopians, and on the north by the Libyans, a nomadic people, and the so-called Nasamonians who reach on into the interior.

All the people of Ammon dwell in villages. In the midst of their country there is a fortress secured by triple walls. The innermost circuit encloses the palace of the ancient rulers; the next, the women's court, the dwellings of the children, women, and relatives, and the guardrooms of the scouts, as well as the sanctuary of the god and the sacred spring, from the waters of which offerings addressed to the god take on holiness; the outer circuit surrounds the barracks of the king's guards and the guardrooms of those who protect the person of the ruler.

Outside of the fortress at no great distance there is another temple of Ammon shaded by many large trees, and near this is the spring which is called the Spring of the Sun from its behaviour. Its waters change in temperature oddly in accordance with the times of day. At sunrise it sends forth a warm stream, but as the day advances it grows cooler proportionally with the passage of the hours, until under the noonday heat it reaches its extreme degree of cold. Then again in the same proportion it grows warmer toward evening and as the night advances it continues to heat up until midnight when again the trend is reversed, and at daybreak once more the waters have returned to their original temperature.

The image of the god is encrusted with emeralds and other precious stones, and answers those who consult the oracle in a quite peculiar fashion. It is carried about upon a golden boat by eighty priests, and these, with the god on their shoulders, go without their own volition wherever the god directs their path. A multitude of girls and women follows them singing paeans as they go and praising the god in a traditional hymn.

51. When Alexander was conducted by the priests into the temple and had regarded the god for a while, the one who held the position of prophet, an elderly man, came to him and said, "Rejoice, son; take this form of address as from the god also." He replied, "I accept, father; for the future I shall be called thy son, but tell me if thou givest me the rule of the whole earth." The priest now entered the sacred enclosure and as the bearers now lifted the god and were moved according to certain prescribed sounds of the voice, the prophet cried that of a certainty the god had granted him his request, and Alexander spoke again: "The last, O spirit, of my questions now answer; have I punished all those who were the murderers of my father or have some escaped me?" The prophet shouted: "Silence! There is no mortal who can plot against the one who begot him. All the murderers of Philip, however, have been punished. The proof of his divine birth will reside in the greatness of his deeds; as formerly he has been undefeated, so now he will be unconquerable for all time." Alexander was delighted with these responses. He honoured the god with rich gifts and returned to Egypt.

52. He decided to found a great city in Egypt, and gave orders to the men left behind with this mission to build the city between the marsh and the sea. He laid out the site and traced the streets skilfully and ordered that the city should be called after him Alexandria. It was conveniently situated near the harbour of Pharos, and by selecting the right angle of the streets, Alexander made the city breathe with the etesian winds so that as these blow across a great expanse of sea, they cool the air of the town, and so he provided its inhabitants with a moderate climate and good health. Alexander also laid out the walls so that they were at once exceedingly large and marvellously strong. Lying between a great marsh and the sea, it affords by land only two approaches, both narrow and very easily blocked.

In shape, it is similar to a chlamys, and it is approximately bisected by an avenue remarkable for its size and beauty. From gate to gate it runs a distance of forty furlongs; it is a plethron in width, and is bordered throughout its length with rich facades of houses and temples. Alexander gave orders to build a palace notable for its size and massiveness. Not only Alexander, but those who after him ruled Egypt down to our own time, with few exceptions have enlarged this with lavish additions. The city in general has grown so much in later times that many reckon it to be the first city of the civilised world, and it is certainly far ahead of all the rest in elegance and extent and riches and luxury. The number of its inhabitants surpasses that of those in other cities. At the time when we were in Egypt, those who kept the census returns of the population said that its free residents were more than three hundred thousand, and that the king received from the revenues of the country more than six thousand talents.

However that may be, King Alexander charged certain of his Friends with the construction of Alexandria, settled all the affairs of Egypt, and returned with his army to Syria.

The battle of Alexander with Dareius at Arbela and the victory of Alexander (53-61).

53. By the time he heard of his arrival, Dareius had already assembled his forces from all directions and made everything ready for the battle. He had fashioned swords and lances much longer than his earlier types because it was thought that Alexander had had a great advantage in this respect in the battle in Cilicia. He had also constructed two hundred scythe-bearing chariots well designed to astonish and terrify the enemy. From each of these there projected out beyond the trace horses scythes three spans long, attached to the yoke, and presenting their cutting edges to the front. At the axle housings there were two more scythes pointing straight out with their cutting edges turned to the front like the others, but longer and broader. Curved blades were fitted to the ends of these.

All of the force the king adorned with shining armour and with brilliant commanders. As he marched out of Babylon, he had with him eight hundred thousand infantry and no less than two hundred thousand cavalry. He kept the Tigris on the right of his route and the Euphrates on the left, and proceeded through a rich country capable of furnishing ample fodder for the animals and food enough for so many soldiers. He had in mind to deploy for battle in the vicinity of Nineveh, since the plains there were well suited to his purpose and afforded ample manoeuvre room for the huge forces at his disposal. Pitching camp at a village named Arbela, he drilled his troops daily and made them well disciplined by continued training and practice. He was most concerned lest some confusion should arise in the battle from the numerous peoples assembled who differed in speech.

54. On the other hand, just as he had previously sent envoys to Alexander to treat for peace, offering to concede to him the land west of the Halys River, and also to give him twenty thousand talents of silver, but Alexander would not agree, so now again Dareius sent other envoys praising Alexander for his generous treatment of Dareius's mother and the other captives and inviting him to become a friend. He offered him all the territory west of the Euphrates, thirty thousand talents of silver, and the hand of one of his daughters. Alexander would become Dareius's son-in-law and occupy the place of a son, while sharing in the rule of the whole empire. Alexander brought together all his Friends into a council and laid before them the alternatives. He urged each to speak his own mind freely. None of the rest, however, dared to give an opinion in a matter of this importance, but Parmenion spoke up and said: If I were Alexander, I should accept what was offered and make a treaty." Alexander cut in and said: "So should I, if I were Parmenion."

He continued with proud words and refuted the arguments of the Persians, preferring glory to the gifts which were extended to him. Then he told the envoys that the earth could not preserve its plan and order if there were two suns nor could the inhabited world remain calm and free from war so long as two kings shared the rule. He bade them tell Dareius that, if he desired the supremacy, he should do battle with him to see which of them would have sole and universal rule. If, on the other hand, he despised glory and chose profit and luxury with a life of ease, then let him obey Alexander, but be king over all other rulers, since this privilege was granted him by Alexander's generosity.

Alexander dismissed the council and ordering his forces to resume their march, he advanced on the camp of the enemy. At this juncture the wife of Dareius died and Alexander gave her a sumptuous funeral.

55. Dareius heard Alexander's answer and gave up any hope of a diplomatic settlement. He continued drilling his troops each day and brought their battle discipline to a satisfactory state. He sent off one of his Friends, Mazaeus, with a picked body of men to guard the crossing of the river and to seize and hold the ford. Other troops he sent out to scorch the earth over which the enemy must come. He thought of using the bed of the Tigris as a defence against the advance of the Macedonians. Mazaeus, however, looked upon the river as uncrossable because of its depth and the swiftness of the current, and neglected to guard it. Instead he joined forces with those who were burning the countryside, and having wasted a great stretch of it, judged that it would be unusable by the enemy because of the lack of forage.

Alexander, nevertheless, when he came to the crossing of the Tigris River, learned of the ford from some of the local natives, and transferred his army to the east bank. This was accomplished not only with difficulty but even at substantial risk. The depth of the water at the ford was above a man's breast and the force of the current swept away many who were crossing and deprived them of their footing, and as the water struck their shields, it bore many off their course and brought them into extreme danger. But Alexander contrived a defence against the violence of the river. He ordered all to lock arms with each other and to construct a sort of bridge out of the compact union of their persons. Since the crossing had been hazardous and the Macedonians had had a narrow escape, Alexander rested the army that day, and on the following he deployed it and led it forward toward the enemy, then pitched camp not far from the Persians.

56. Casting over in his mind the number of the Persian forces and the decisive nature of the impending battle, since success or failure lay now entirely in the strength of their arms, Alexander lay awake throughout the night occupied with concern for the next day. About the morning watch he fell asleep, and slept so soundly that he could not be wakened when the sun rose. At first his Friends were delighted, thinking that the king would be all the keener for the battle for his thorough relaxation. As time passed, however, and sleep continued to possess him, Parmenion, the senior among the Friends, issued on his own responsibility the order to the troops to make ready for the battle, and since his sleep continued, the Friends came to Alexander and at last succeeded in wakening him. As all expressed astonishment at the matter and pressed him to tell the reason for his unconcern, Alexander said that Dareius had freed him from all anxiety by assembling all his forces into one place. Now in one day the decision would be reached on all issues, and they would be saved toils and dangers extending over a long period of time. Nevertheless, Alexander summoned his officers and encouraged them for the battle which they faced with suitable words, and then led out his army deployed for battle against the Persians, ordering the cavalry squadrons to ride ahead of the infantry phalanx.

57. On the right wing Alexander stationed the royal squadron under the command of Cleitus the Black (as he was called), and next to this the other Friends under the command of Parmenion's son Philotas, then in succession the other seven squadrons under the same commander. Behind these was stationed the infantry battalion of the Silver Shields, distinguished for the brilliance of their armour and the valour of the men; they were led by Nicanor, the son of Parmenion. Next to them was the battalion from Elimiotis, as it was called, under the command of Coenus; next he stationed the battalion of the Orestae and the Lyncestae, of which Perdiccas held the command. Meleager commanded the next battalion and Polyperchon the one after that, the people called Stymphaeans being under him. Philip the son of Balacrus held the next command and, after him, Craterus. As for the cavalry, the line of the squadrons which I have mentioned was continued with the combined Peloponnesian and Achaean horse, then cavalry from Phthiotis and Malis, then Locrians and Phocians, all under the command of Erigyius of Mitylenê. Next were posted the Thessalians who had Philip as commander; they were far superior to the rest in their righting qualities and in their horsemanship. Next to these he stationed the Cretan archers and the mercenaries from Achaia.

On both flanks he kept his wings back so that the enemy with their superior numbers could not envelop the shorter line of the Macedonians. Against the threat of the scythed chariots, he ordered the infantry of the phalanx to join shields as soon as these went into action against them and to beat the shields with their spears, creating such a din as to frighten the horses into bolting to the rear, or, if they persevered, to open gaps in the ranks such that they might ride through harmlessly. He himself took personal command of the right wing and advancing obliquely planned to settle the issue of the battle by his own actions.

58. Dareius based his formation for battle on the characteristics of his national contingents, and posting himself opposite Alexander gave the command to advance on the Macedonians. As the lines approached each other, the trumpeters on both sides sounded the attack and the troops charged each other with a loud shout. First the scythed chariots swung into action at full gallop and created great alarm and terror among the Macedonians, especially since Mazaeus in command of the cavalry made their attack more frightening by supporting it with his dense squadrons of horse. As the phalanx joined shields, however, all beat upon their shields with their spears as the king had commanded and a great din arose. As the horses shied off, most of the chariots were turned about and bore hard with irresistible impact against their own ranks. Others continued on against the Macedonian lines, but as the soldiers opened wide gaps in their ranks the chariots were channelled through these. In some instances the horses were killed by javelin casts and in others they rode through and escaped, but some of them, using the full force of their momentum and applying their steel blades actively, wrought death among the Macedonians in many and various forms. Such was the keenness and the force of the scythes ingeniously contrived to do harm that they severed the arms of many, shields and all, and in no small number of cases they cut through necks and sent heads tumbling to the ground with the eyes still open and the expression of the countenance unchanged, and in other cases they sliced through ribs with mortal gashes and inflicted a quick death.

59. As the main bodies now neared each other and, employing bows and slings and throwing javelins, expended their missiles, they turned to hand to hand fighting. The cavalry first joined battle, and as the Macedonians were on the right wing, Dareius, who commanded his own left, led his kinsman cavalry against them. These were men chosen for courage and for loyalty, the whole thousand included in one squadron. Knowing that the king was watching their behaviour, they cheerfully faced all of the missiles which were cast in his direction. With them were engaged the Apple Bearers, brave and numerous, and in addition to these Mardi and Cossaei, who were admired for their strength and daring, as well as all the household troops belonging to the palace and the best fighters among the Indians. They all raised a loud battle cry and, attacking, engaged the enemy valiantly and pressed hard upon the Macedonians because of their superior numbers.

Mazaeus was in command of the Persian right wing with the best of the cavalry under him and killed not a few of his opponents at the first onslaught, but sent off two thousand Cadusii and a thousand picked Scythian horsemen with orders to ride around the enemy's flank and to continue on to their camp and capture the baggage. This they did promptly, and as they burst into the camp of the Macedonians, some of the captives seized weapons and aided the Scythians in seizing the baggage. There was shouting and confusion throughout the whole camp area at this unexpected event. Most of the female captives rushed off to welcome the Persians, but the mother of Dareius, Sisyngambris, did not heed when the women called upon her, but remained placidly where she was, since she neither trusted the uncertain turns of Fortune nor would sully her gratitude toward Alexander. Finally, after the Scythians had rounded up much of the baggage, they rode off to Mazaeus to report their success. During this time, also, part of the cavalry of Dareius in superior numbers continued their pressure on the opposing Macedonians and forced them to give ground.

60. This was a second success for the Persians, and Alexander saw that it was time for him to offset the discomfiture of his forces by his own intervention with the royal squadron and the rest of the elite horse guards, and rode hard against Dareius. The Persian king received their attack and fighting from a chariot hurled javelins against his opponents, and many supported him. As the kings approached each other, Alexander flung a javelin at Dareius and missed him, but struck the driver standing beside him and knocked him to the ground. A shout went up at this from the Persians around Dareius, and those at a greater distance thought that the king had fallen. They were the first to take to flight, and they were followed by those next to them, and steadily, little by little, the solid ranks of Dareius's guard disintegrated. As both flanks became exposed, the king himself was alarmed and retreated. The flight thus became general. Dust raised by the Persian cavalry rose to a height, and as Alexander's squadrons followed on their heels, because of their numbers and the thickness of the dust, it was impossible to tell in what direction Dareius was fleeing. The air was rilled with the groans of the fallen, the din of the cavalry, and the constant sound of lashing of whips.

At this time Mazaeus, the commander of the Persian right wing, with the most and the best of the cavalry, was pressing hard on those opposing him, but Parmenion with the Thessalian cavalry and the rest of his forces put up a stout resistance. For a time, fighting brilliantly, he even seemed to have the upper hand thanks to the fighting qualities of the Thessalians, but the weight and numbers of Mazaeus's command brought the Macedonian cavalry into difficulties. A great slaughter took place, and despairing of withstanding the Persian power,

Parmenion sent off some of his horsemen to Alexander, begging him to come to their support quickly. They carried out their orders with dispatch, but finding that Alexander was already in full pursuit at a great distance from the battlefield they returned without accomplishing their mission. Nevertheless Parmenion handled the Thessalian squadrons with the utmost skill and finally, killing many of the enemy, routed the Persians who were by now much disheartened by the withdrawal of Dareius.

61. Dareius was a clever strategist. He took advantage of the great cloud of dust and did not withdraw to the rear like the other barbarians, but swinging in the opposite direction and covering his movement by the dust, got away safely himself and brought all his troops into villages which lay behind the Macedonian position. Finally all the Persians had fled, and as the Macedonians kept slaughtering the stragglers, before long the whole region in which the battle had taken place was covered with dead. On the Persian side in the battle fell, cavalry and infantry together, more than ninety thousand. About five hundred of the Macedonians were killed and there were very many wounded. Of the most prominent group of commanders, Hephaestion was wounded with a spear thrust in the arm; he had commanded the bodyguards. Perdiccas and Coenus, of the general's group, were also wounded, so also Menidas and others of the higher commanders.

That was the outcome of the battle near Arbela.

The battle of Antipater with the Lacedaemonians and the victory of Antipater (62-63).

62. When Aristophon was archon at Athens, [330/29] the consular office at Rome was assumed by Gaius Domitius and Aulus Cornelius. In this year word was brought to Greece about the battle near Arbela, and many of the cities became alarmed at the growth of Macedonian power and decided that they should strike for their freedom while the Persian cause was still alive. They expected that Dareius would help them and send them much money so that they could gather great armies of mercenaries, while Alexander would not be able to divide his forces. If, on the other hand, they watched idly while the Persians were utterly defeated, the Greeks would be isolated and never again be able to think of recovering their freedom.

There was also an upheaval in Thrace at just this time which seemed to offer the Greeks an opportunity for freeing themselves. Memnon, who had been designated governor-general there, had a military force and was a man of spirit. He stirred up the tribesmen, revolted against Alexander, quickly possessed a large army, and was openly bent on war. Antipater was forced to mobilise his entire army and to advance through Macedonia into Thrace to settle with him.

While Antipater was occupied with this, the Lacedaemonians thought that the time had come to undertake a war and issued an appeal to the Greeks to unite in defence of their freedom. The Athenians had been favoured beyond all the other Greeks by Alexander and did not move. Most of the Peloponnesians, however, and some of the northern Greeks reached an agreement and signed an undertaking to go to war. According to the capacity of the individual cities they enlisted the best of their youth and enrolled as soldiers not less than twenty thousand infantry and about two thousand cavalry. The Lacedaemonians had the command and led out their entire levy for the decisive battle, their king Agis having the position of commander in chief.

63. When Antipater learned of this Greek mobilisation, he ended the Thracian campaign on what terms he could and marched down into the Peloponnesus with his entire army. He added soldiers from those of the Greeks who were still loyal and built up his force until it numbered not less than forty thousand. When it came to a general engagement, Agis was struck down fighting, but the Lacedaemonians fought furiously and maintained their position for a long time; when their Greek allies were forced out of position they themselves fell back on Sparta. More than five thousand three hundred of the Lacedaemonians and their allies were killed in the battle, and three thousand five hundred of Antipater's troops.

An interesting event occurred in connection with Agis's death. He had fought gloriously and fell with many frontal wounds. As he was being carried by his soldiers back to Sparta, he found himself surrounded by the enemy. Despairing of his own life, he ordered the rest to make their escape with all speed and to save themselves for the service of their country, but he himself armed and rising to his knees defended himself, killed some of the enemy and was himself slain by a javelin cast; he had reigned nine years. (This is the end of the first half of the seventeenth book.)

Now that we have run through the events in Europe, we may in turn pass on to what occurred in Asia.

The capture of Arbela by Alexander and the seizure of great wealth (64. 1-3).

The refreshment of the army in Babylon and the rewards given to those who had distinguished themselves in service (64. 3-6).

64. After his defeat in the battle near Arbela, Dareius directed his course to the upper satrapies, seeking by putting distance between himself and Alexander to gain a respite and time enough to organise an army. He made his way first to Ecbatana in Media and paused there, picking up the stragglers from the battle and rearming those who had lost their weapons. He sent around to the neighbouring tribes demanding soldiers, and he posted couriers to the satraps and generals in Bactria and the upper satrapies, calling upon them to preserve their loyalty to him.

After the battle, Alexander buried his dead and entered Arbela, finding there abundant stores of food, no little barbaric dress and treasure, and three thousand talents of silver. Judging that the air of the region would be polluted by the multitude of un-buried corpses, he continued his advance immediately and arrived with his whole army at Babylon. Here the people received him gladly, and furnishing them billets feasted the Macedonians lavishly. Alexander refreshed his army from its previous labours and remained more than thirty days in the city because food was plentiful and the population friendly.

At this time he designated Agathon of Pydna to guard the citadel, assigning to him seven hundred Macedonian soldiers. He appointed Apollodorus of Amphipolis and Menes of Pella as military governors of Babylon and the other satrapies as far as Cilicia, giving them one thousand talents of silver with instructions to enlist as many soldiers as possible. He assigned Armenia as a province to Mithrines, who had surrendered to him the citadel of Sardes. From the money which was captured he distributed to each of the cavalrymen six minas, to each of the allied cavalrymen five, and to the Macedonians of the phalanx two, and he gave to all the mercenaries two months' pay.

The arrival of the mercenaries and allies dispatched to him (65. 1).

The organisation and equipment of his army (65. 2-4).

How Alexander occupied Susa and its treasures (65. 5-66).

65. After the king had marched out of Babylon and while he was still on the road, there came to him, sent by Antipater, five hundred Macedonian cavalry and six thousand infantry, six hundred Thracian cavalry and three thousand five hundred Trallians, and from the Peloponnese four thousand infantry and little less than a thousand cavalry. From Macedonia also came fifty sons of the king's Friends sent by their fathers to serve as bodyguards. The king welcomed all of these, continued his march, and on the sixth day crossed over into the province of Sittacene.

This was a rich country abounding in provisions of all sorts, and he lingered here for a number of days, at once anxious to rest his army from the fatigue of their long marches and concerned to review the organization of his army. He wanted to advance some officers and to strengthen the forces by the number and the ability of the commanders. This he effected. He scrutinised closely the reports of good conduct and promoted many from a high military command to an even higher responsibility, so that by giving all the commanders greater prestige he bound them to himself by strong ties of affection. He also examined the situation of the individual soldiers and introduced many improvements by considering what was useful. He brought the whole force up to an outstanding devotion to its commander and obedience to his commands, and to a high degree of effectiveness, looking toward the battles to come.

From there he entered Susiané without opposition and took over the fabulous palace of the kings. The satrap Abuleutes surrendered the city to him voluntarily, and some have written that he did this in compliance with orders given by Dareius to his trusted officials. The king of Persia hoped by this policy, it is suggested, that Alexander would be kept busy with dazzling distractions and the acquisition of brilliant cities and huge treasures, while he, Dareius, won time by his flight to prepare for a renewed warfare.

66. Alexander entered the city and found the treasure in the palace to include more than forty thousand talents of gold and silver bullion, which the kings had accumulated unused over a long period of time as a protection against the vicissitudes of Fortune. In addition there were nine thousand talents of minted gold in the form of darics.

A curious thing happened to the king when he was shown the precious objects. He seated himself upon the royal throne, which was larger than the proportions of his body. When one of the pages saw that his feet were a long way from reaching the footstool which belonged to the throne, he picked up Dareius's table and placed it under the dangling legs. This fitted, and the king was pleased by the aptness of the boy, but a eunuch standing by was troubled in his heart at this reminder of the changes of Fortune and wept. Alexander noticed him and asked, "What wrong have you seen that you are crying?" The eunuch replied, "Now I am your slave as formerly I was the slave of Dareius. I am by nature devoted to my masters and I was grieved at seeing what was most held in honour by your predecessor now become an ignoble piece of furniture."

This answer reminded the king how great a change had come over the Persian kingdom. He saw that he had committed an act of arrogance quite the reverse of his gentleness to the captives, and calling the page who had placed the table ordered him to remove it. Then Philotas, who was present, said, "But this was not insolence, for the action was not commanded by you; it occurred through the providence and design of a good spirit." So the king took this remark for an omen, and ordered the table to be left standing at the foot of the throne.

How he mastered the passes and took possession of the so-called Susian Gates (67-68).

67. After this Alexander left Dareius's mother, his daughters, and his son in Susa, providing them with persons to teach them the Greek language, and marching on with his army on the fourth day reached the Tigris River. This flows down from the mountains of the Uxii and passes at first for a thousand furlongs through rough country broken by great gorges, but then traverses a level plain and becomes ever quieter, and after six hundred furlongs empties into the Persian sea. This he crossed, and entered the country of the Uxii, which was rich, watered by numerous streams, and productive of many fruits of all kinds. At the season when the ripe fruit is dried, the merchants who sail on the Tigris are able to bring down to Babylonia all sorts of confections good for the pleasures of the table.

Alexander found the passages guarded by Madetes, a cousin of Dareius, with a substantial force, and he saw at once the difficulty of the place. The sheer cliffs offered no passage, but an Uxian native who knew the country offered to lead soldiers by a narrow and hazardous path to a position above the enemy. Alexander accepted the proposal and sent off with him a body of troops, while he himself expedited the move as far as possible and attacked the defenders in waves. The assault was pressed vigorously and the Persians were preoccupied with the struggle when to their astonishment above their heads appeared the flying column of Macedonians. The Persians were frightened and took to their heels. Thus Alexander won the pass and soon after took all the cities in Uxiane.

68. Thereafter Alexander marched on in the direction of Persis and on the fifth day came to the so-called Susian Rocks. Here the passage was held by Ariobarzanes with a force of twenty-five thousand infantry and three hundred cavalry. The king first thought to force his way through and advanced to the pass through narrow defiles in rough country, but without opposition. The Persians allowed him to proceed along the pass for some distance, but when he was about half-way through the hard part, they suddenly attacked him and rolled down from above huge boulders, which falling suddenly upon the massed ranks of the Macedonians killed many of them. Many of the enemy threw javelins down from the cliffs into the crowd, and did not miss their mark. Still others coming to close quarters flung stones at the Macedonians who pressed on. The Persians had a tremendous advantage because of the difficulty of the country, killed many and injured not a few.

Alexander was quite helpless to avert the sufferings of his men and seeing that no one of the enemy was killed or even wounded, while of his own force many were slain and practically all the attacking force were disabled, he recalled the soldiers from the battle with a trumpet signal. Withdrawing from the pass for a distance of three hundred furlongs, he pitched camp and from the natives sought to learn whether there was any other route through the hills. All insisted that there was no other way through, although it was possible to go around them at the cost of several days' travel. It seemed to Alexander, however, discreditable to abandon his dead and unseemly to ask for them, since this carried with it the acknowledgement of defeat, so he ordered all his captives to be brought up. Among these came hopefully a man who was bilingual, and knew the Persian language.

He said that he was a Lycian, had been brought there as a captive, and had pastured goats in these mountains for a number of years. He had come to know the country well and could lead a force of men over a path concealed by bushes and bring them to the rear of the Persians guarding the pass. The king promised that he would load him with gifts, and under his direction Alexander did make his way over the mountain at night struggling through deep snow. The route crossed a very broken country, seamed by deep ravines and many gorges. Coming into sight of the enemy outposts, he cut down their first line and captured those who were stationed in the second position, then routed the third line and won the pass, and killed most of the troops of Ariobarzanes.

How he showed kindness to the Greeks who had been mutilated, and took and sacked Persepolis (69-71).

69. Now he set out on the road to Persepolis, and while he was on the road received a letter from the governor of the city, whose name was Tiridates. It stated that if he arrived ahead of those who planned to defend the city for Dareius, he would become master of it, for Tiridates would betray it to him. Accordingly Alexander led his army on by forced marches; he bridged the Araxes River and so brought his men to the other bank.

At this point in his advance the king was confronted by a strange and dreadful sight, one to provoke indignation against the perpetrators and sympathetic pity for the unfortunate victims. He was met by Greeks bearing branches of supplication. They had been carried away from their homes by previous kings of Persia and were about eight hundred in number, most of them elderly. All had been mutilated, some lacking hands, some feet, and some ears and noses. They were persons who had acquired skills or crafts and had made good progress in their instruction; then their other extremities had been amputated and they were left only those which were vital to their profession. All the soldiers, seeing their venerable years and the losses which their bodies had suffered, pitied the lot of the wretches. Alexander most of all was affected by them and unable to restrain his tears.

They all cried with one voice and besought Alexander to help them in their misfortunes. The king-called their leaders to come forward and, greeting them with a respect in keeping with his own greatness of spirit, promised to make it a matter of utmost concern that they should be restored to their homes. They gathered to debate the matter, and decided that it would be better for them to remain where they were rather than to return home. If they were brought back safely, they would be scattered in small groups, and would find their abuse at the hands of Fortune an object of reproach as they lived on in their cities. If, however, they continued living together, as companions in misfortune, they would find a solace for their mutilation in the similar mutilation of the others. So they again appeared before the king, told him of their decision, and asked him to give them help appropriate to this proposal. Alexander applauded their decision and gave each of them three thousand drachmae, five men's robes and the same number for women, two yoke of oxen, fifty sheep, and fifty bushels of wheat. He made them also exempt from all royal taxes and charged his administrative officials to see that they were harmed by no one.

Thus Alexander mitigated the lot of these unfortunate persons by such benefactions in keeping with his natural kindness.

70. Persepolis was the capital of the Persian kingdom. Alexander described it to the Macedonians as the most hateful of the cities of Asia, and gave it over to his soldiers to plunder, all but the palaces. It was the richest city under the sun and the private houses had been furnished with every sort of wealth over the years. The Macedonians raced into it slaughtering all the men whom they met and plundering the residences; many of the houses belonged to the common people and were abundantly supplied with furniture and wearing apparel of every kind. Here much silver was carried off and no little gold, and many rich dresses gay with sea purple or with gold embroidery became the prize of the victors. The enormous palaces, famed throughout the whole civilised world, fell victim to insult and utter destruction.

The Macedonians gave themselves up to this orgy of plunder for a whole day and still could not satisfy their boundless greed for more. Such was their exceeding lust for loot withal that they fought with each other and killed many of their fellows who had appropriated a greater portion of it. The richest of the finds some cut through with their swords so that each might have his own part. Some cut *off* the hands of those who were grasping at disputed property, being driven mad by their passions. They dragged off women, clothes and all, converting their captivity into slavery.

As Persepolis had exceeded all other cities in prosperity, so in the same measure it now exceeded all others in misery.

71. Alexander ascended to the citadel terrace and took possession of the treasure there. This had been accumulated from the state revenues, beginning with Cyrus, the first king of the Persians, down to that time, and the vaults were packed full of silver and gold. The total was found to be one hundred and twenty thousand talents, when the gold was estimated in terms of silver. Alexander wanted to take some money with him to meet the costs of the war, and to deposit the rest in Susa and keep it under guard in that city. Accordingly he sent for a vast number of mules from Babylon and Mesopotamia, as well as from Susa itself, both pack and harness animals as well as three thousand pack camels. By these means Alexander transported everything to the desired places. He felt bitter enmity to the inhabitants. He did not trust them, and he meant to destroy Persepolis utterly.

I think that it is not inappropriate to speak briefly about the palace area of the city because of the richness of its buildings. The citadel is a noteworthy one, and is surrounded by a triple wall. The first part of this is built over an elaborate foundation. It is sixteen cubits in height and is topped by battlements. The second wall is in all other respects like the first but of twice the height. The third circuit is rectangular in plan, and is sixty cubits in height, built of a stone hard and naturally durable. Each of the sides contains a gate with bronze doors, beside each of which stand bronze poles twenty cubits high; these were intended to catch the eye of the beholder, but the gates were for security.

At the eastern side of the terrace at a distance of four plethra is the so-called royal hill in which were the graves of the kings. This was a smooth rock hollowed out into many chambers in which were the sepulchres of the dead kings. These have no other access but receive the sarcophagi of the dead which are lifted by certain mechanical hoists. Scattered about the royal terrace were residences of the kings and members of the royal family as well as quarters for the great nobles, all luxuriously furnished, and buildings suitably made for guarding the royal treasure.

How he set fire to the palace in a revel (72).

72. Alexander held games in honour of his victories. He performed costly sacrifices to the gods and entertained his friends bountifully. While they were feasting and the drinking was far advanced, as they began to be drunken a madness took possession of the minds of the intoxicated guests. At this point one of the women present, Thais by name and Attic by origin, said that for Alexander it would be the finest of all his feats in Asia if he joined them in a triumphal procession, set fire to the palaces, and permitted women's hands in a minute to extinguish the famed accomplishments of the Persians. This was said to men who were still young and giddy with wine, and so, as would be expected, someone shouted out to form the comus and to light torches, and urged all to take vengeance for the destruction of the Greek temples. Others took up the cry and said that this was a deed worthy of Alexander alone. When the king had caught fire at their words, all leaped up from their couches and passed the word along to form a victory procession in honour of Dionysus.

Promptly many torches were gathered. Female musicians were present at the banquet, so the king led them all out for the comus to the sound of voices and flutes and pipes, Thaïs the courtesan leading the whole performance. She was the first, after the king, to hurl her blazing torch into the palace. As the others all did the same, immediately the entire palace area was consumed, so great was the conflagration. It was most remarkable that the impious act of Xerxes, king of the Persians, against the acropolis at Athens should have been repaid in kind after many years by one woman, a citizen of the land which had suffered it, and in sport.

The murder of Dareius by Bessus (73. 1-4).

73. When all this was over, Alexander visited the cities of Persis, capturing some by storm and winning over others by his own fair dealing. Then he set out after Dareius. The Persian king had planned to bring together the armed forces of Bactria and the other satrapies, but Alexander was too quick for him. Dareius directed his flight toward the city of Bactra with thirty thousand Persians and Greek mercenaries, but in the course of this retirement he was seized and murdered by Bessus, the satrap of Bactria. Just after his death, Alexander rode up in hot pursuit with his cavalry, and, finding him dead, gave him a royal funeral. Some, however, have written that Alexander found him still breathing and commiserated with him on his disasters. Dareius urged him to avenge his death, and Alexander, agreeing, set out after Bessus, but the satrap had a long start and got away into Bactria, so Alexander suspended the chase and returned.

That was the situation in Asia.

In Europe the Lacedaemonians were forced by their defeat in a decisive battle to make overtures to Antipater. He referred his reply to the council of the Hellenic League. When the delegates came together in Corinth, there was a long discussion on both sides, and they decided to pass the issue on without a decision to Alexander. Antipater took as hostages fifty of the most notable of the Spartiates, and the Lacedaemonians sent envoys to Asia asking forgiveness for their mistakes.

74. After this year was over, Cephisophon became archon at Athens, [329/28] and Gaius Valerius and Marcus Clodius consuls in Rome. In this year, now that Dareius was dead, Bessus with Nabarnes and Barxaës and many others of the Iranian nobles got to Bactria, eluding the hands of Alexander. Bessus had been appointed satrap of this region by Dareius and being known to everyone because of his administration, now called upon the population to defend their freedom. He pointed out that the nature of their country would assist them very much, since the region was hard for an enemy to penetrate and furnished enough men for them to establish their independence. He proclaimed that he would take personal command of the war and designated himself king, with the approval of the people. Then he set to work enrolling soldiers, manufacturing an adequate stock of weapons, and busily making everything ready for the approaching time of need.

Alexander, for his part, was aware that the Macedonians regarded Dareius's death as the end of the campaign and were impatient to go home. He called them all to a meeting and, addressing them with effective arguments, made them willing to follow him in the part of the war which remained, but he assembled the allied troops from the Greek cities and praising them for their services released them from their military duty. He gave to each of the cavalry a talent and to each of the infantry ten minas. Besides this he paid them their wages up to date and added more to cover the period of their march back until they should return to their homes. To those who would remain with him in the royal army, he gave a bonus of three talents each. He treated the soldiers with such lavishness in part because of his native generosity and in part because he had come into possession of very much money in the course of his pursuit of Dareius. He had received from the royal treasurers the sum of eight thousand talents. Apart from this, what was distributed to the soldiers, including clothing and goblets, came to thirteen thousand talents, while what was stolen or taken as plunder was thought to be even more still.

The expedition of Alexander into Hyrcania and an account of its marvellous plants (75).

75. Alexander started out for Hyrcania and on the third day encamped near a city called Hecatontapylus. This was a wealthy city with a profusion of everything contributing to pleasure, so he rested his army there for some days. Then, advancing one hundred and fifty furlongs, he encamped near a huge rock; under its base there was a marvellous cave from which flowed a great river known as the Stiboeites. This tumbles out with a rapid current for a distance of three furlongs, and then divides into two courses on either side of a breast-shaped "rock," beneath which there is a vast cavern. Into this the river plunges with a great roar, foaming from its clash against the rock. After flowing underground a distance of three hundred furlongs, it again breaks its way to the surface.

Alexander entered Hyrcania with his army and took possession of all the cities there as far as the so-called Caspian Sea, which some name the Hyrcanian. In this they say are spawned many large serpents and fish of all sorts quite different in colour from ours. He passed through Hyrcania and came to the Fortunate Villages, as they are called, and truly such they are, for their land produces crops far more generously than elsewhere. They say that each vine produces a metretes of wine, while there are some fig trees which produce ten medimni of dried figs. The grain which is overlooked at the harvest and falls to the ground germinates without being sown and brings to maturity an abundant harvest. There is a tree known to the natives like an oak in appearance, from the leaves of which honey drips; this some collect and take their pleasure from it abundantly. There is a winged animal in this country which they call anthredon, smaller than the bee but very useful. It roams the mountains gathering nectar from every kind of flower. Dwelling in hollow rocks and lightning-blasted trees it forms combs of wax and fashions a liquor of surpassing sweetness, not far inferior to our honey.

How Alexander took the field against the Mardi and defeated them (76).

76. Thus Alexander acquired Hyrcania and the tribes which were its neighbours, and many of the Iranian commanders who had fled with Dareius came to him and gave themselves up. He received them kindly and gained wide repute for fair dealing; for instance, the Greeks who had served with Dareius, one thousand five hundred in number, and accomplished soldiers, also promptly turned themselves over to Alexander, and receiving a full pardon for their previous hostility were assigned to units of his army on the same pay scale as the rest.

Alexander followed the coastline to the west and entered the country of the people known as Mardians. They prided themselves on their fighting ability and thinking little of Alexander's growth in power sent him no petition or mark of honour, but held the passes with eight thousand soldiers and confidently awaited the Macedonian approach. The king attacked them and joining battle killed most of them and drove the rest into the fastnesses of the mountains.

As he was wasting the countryside with fire and the pages who led the royal horses were at a little distance from the king, some of the natives made a sudden rush and carried off the best one of them [Bucephalus]. This animal had come to Alexander as a gift from Demaratus of Corinth and had carried the king in all of his battles in Asia. So long as he was not caparisoned, he would permit only the groom to mount him, but when he had received the royal trappings, he would no longer allow even him, but for Alexander alone stood quietly and even lowered his body to assist in the mounting. Because of the superior qualities of this animal the king was infuriated at his loss and ordered that every tree in the land be felled, while he proclaimed to the natives through interpreters that if the horse were not returned, they should see the country laid waste to its furthest limit and its inhabitants slaughtered to a man. As he began immediately to carry out these threats, the natives were terrified and returned the horse and sent with it their costliest gifts. They sent also fifty men to beg forgiveness. Alexander took the most important of these as hostages.

How Thallestris queen of the Amazons had relations with Alexander (77. 1-3).

How the king, thinking himself invincible, imitated the luxury of the Persians (77. 4-7).

77. When Alexander returned to Hyrcania, there came to him the queen of the Amazons named Thallestris, who ruled all the country between the rivers Phasis and Thermodon. She was remarkable for beauty and for bodily strength, and was admired by her countrywomen for bravery. She had left the bulk of her army on the frontier of Hyrcania and had arrived with an escort of three hundred Amazons in full armour. The king marvelled at the unexpected arrival and the dignity of the women. When he asked Thallestris why she had come, she replied that it was for the purpose of getting a child. He had shown himself the greatest of all men in his achievements, and she was superior to all women in strength and courage, so that presumably the offspring of such outstanding parents would surpass all other mortals in excellence. At this the king was delighted and granted her request and consorted with her for thirteen days, after which he honoured her with fine gifts and sent her home.

It seemed to Alexander that he had accomplished his objective and now held his kingdom without contest, and he began to imitate the Persian luxury and the extravagant display of the kings of Asia. First he installed ushers of Asiatic race in his court, and then he ordered the most distinguished persons to act as his guards; among these was Dareius's brother Oxathres. Then he put on the Persian diadem and dressed himself in the white robe and the Persian sash and everything else except the trousers and the long-sleeved upper garment. He distributed to his companions cloaks with purple borders and dressed the horses in Persian harness. In addition to all this, he added concubines to his retinue in the manner of Dareius, in number not less than the days of the year and outstanding in beauty as selected from all the women of Asia. Each night these paraded about the couch of the king so that he might select the one with whom he would lie that night. Alexander, as a matter of fact, employed these customs rather sparingly and kept for the most part to his accustomed routine, not wishing to offend the Macedonians.

The campaign of Alexander against the Areii who had revolted and the capture of the "Rock" (78).

78. Many, it is true, did reproach him for these things, but he silenced them with gifts. At this juncture he learned that the satrap of Areia, Satibarzanes, had put to death the soldiers who were left with him, had made common cause with Bessus and with him had decided to attack the Macedonians, so Alexander set out against the man. This Satibarzanes had brought his forces into Chortacana, a notable city of that region and one of great natural strength, but as the king approached, he became alarmed at the size of the latter's forces and at the fighting reputation of the Macedonians. He himself with two thousand horsemen rode off to the protection of Bessus, asking him to send help with all speed, but told his other followers to take refuge in a mountain called . . ., which afforded difficult terrain and a secure refuge for those who did not dare to meet their enemies face to face. After they had done so, and had secured themselves upon a steep and high "rock," the king with his accustomed spirit invested the place, attacked them vigorously, and compelled them to surrender. In the course of thirty days thereafter, he brought into submission all the cities of the satrapy. Then he left Hyrcania and marched to the capital of Dranginê, where he paused and rested his army.

The conspiracy against the king and the punishment of the conspirators, the most distinguished among them being Parmenion and Philotas (79-80).

79. At this same time, Alexander stumbled into a base action which was quite foreign to his goodness of nature. One of the king's Friends named Dimnus found fault with him for some reason, and in a rash fit of anger formed a plot against him. He had a beloved named Nicomachus and persuaded him to take part in it. Being very young, the boy disclosed the plan to his brother Cebalinus, who, however, was terrified lest one of the conspirators should get ahead of the rest in revealing the plot to the king, and decided himself to be the informer.

He went to the court, met Philotas and talked with him, and urged him to tell the whole story to the king as quickly as he could. It may be that Philotas was actually a party to the plot; he may merely have been slow to act. At all events, he heard Cebalinus with indifference, and although he visited Alexander and took part in a long conversation on a variety of subjects, said no word about what had just been told him. When he returned to Cebalinus, he said that he had not found a suitable occasion to mention it, but would surely see the king alone the next day and tell him everything. Philotas did the same thing on the next day also, and Cebalinus, to insure himself against someone else betraying the plot and putting him in danger, dropped Philotas and accosted one of the royal pages, telling him all that had happened and begging him to report it to the king immediately.

The page brought Cebalinus into the armoury and hid him there, went on in to the king as he was bathing and told him the story, adding that he had Cebalinus concealed in the vicinity. The king's reaction was sharp. He arrested Dimnus at once and learned everything from him; then he sent for Cebalinus and Philotas. The whole story was investigated and the fact established. Dimnus stabbed himself on the spot, but Philotas, while acknowledging his carelessness, nevertheless denied that he had had any part in the plot and agreed to leave judgement concerning him to the Macedonians.

80. After many arguments had been heard, the Macedonians condemned Philotas and the other accused persons to death. Among these was Parmenion, he who seemed to be the first of Alexander's Friends; he was not with the army, but it was thought that he had contrived the conspiracy by means of his son Philotas. Philotas, then, was first tortured and confessed to the plot, and then was killed in the Macedonian manner with the other condemned persons.

This was the occasion for bringing up the case of Alexander the Lyncestian. He was charged with the crime of plotting against the king and had been kept for three years under guard. He had been delayed a hearing because of his relationship to Antigonus, but now he was brought before the court of the Macedonians and was put to death, lacking words to defend himself.

Alexander dispatched riders on racing camels, who travelled faster than the report of Philotas's punishment and murdered his father Parmenion. He had been appointed governor of Media and was in charge of the royal treasures in Ecbatana, amounting to one hundred and eighty thousand talents. Alexander selected from among the Macedonians those who made remarks hostile to him and those who were distressed at the death of Parmenion, as well as those who wrote in letters sent home to Macedonia to their relatives anything contrary to the king's interests. These he assembled into one unit which he called the Disciplinary Company, so that the rest of the Macedonians might not be corrupted by their improper remarks and criticism.

81. After his hands were free of this affair and he had settled things in Dranginê, Alexander marched with his army against a people who used to be called Arimaspians but are now known as Benefactors for the following reason. That Cyrus who had transferred the rule from the Medes to the Persians was once engaged in a campaign in the desert and running out of provisions was brought into extreme danger, so that for lack of food the soldiers were constrained to eat each other, when the Arimaspians appeared bringing thirty thousand wagons laden with provisions. Saved from utter despair, then, Cyrus gave them exemption from taxation and other marks of honour, and abolishing their former appellation, named them Benefactors. So now, when Alexander led his army into their country, they received him kindly and he honoured the tribe with suitable gifts.

Their neighbours, the so-called Cedrosians, did the same, and them too he rewarded with appropriate favours. He gave the administration of these two peoples to Tiridates. While he was thus occupied reports were brought to him that Satibarzanes had returned from Bactria with a large force of cavalry to Areia, and had caused the population to revolt from Alexander. At this news, the king dispatched against him a portion of his army under the command of Erigyius and Stasanor, while he himself conquered Arachosia and in a few days made it subject to him.

The campaign of Alexander into the territory of the Paropanisadae and his adventures there (82).

82. When this year was over, Euthycritus became archon at Athens [328/7] and at Rome Lucius Platius and Lucius Papirius became consuls. The one hundred and thirteenth Olympic Games were held. In this year Alexander marched against the so-called Paropanisadae, whose country lies in the extreme north; it is snow-covered and not easily approached by other tribes because of the extreme cold. The most of it is a plain and woodless, and divided up among many villages. These contain houses with roofs of tile drawn up at the top into a peaked vault. In the middle of each roof an aperture is left through which smoke escapes, and since the building is enclosed all around the people find ample protection against the weather. Because of the depth of the snow, they spend the most of the year indoors, having their own supplies at hand. They heap up soil about vines and fruit trees, and leave it so for the winter season, removing the earth again at the time of budding. The landscape nowhere shows any verdure or cultivation; all is white and dazzling because of the snow and the ice which form in it. No bird, therefore, alights there nor does any animal pass, and all parts of the country are unvisited and inaccessible.

The king, nevertheless, in spite of all those obstacles confronting the army, exercised the customary boldness and hardihood of the Macedonians and surmounted the difficulties of the region. Many of the soldiers and of the camp followers became exhausted and were left behind. Some too because of the glare of the snow and the hard brilliance of the reflected light lost their sight. Nothing could be seen clearly from a distance. It was only as the villages were revealed by their smoke that the Macedonians discovered where the dwellings were, even when they were standing right on top of them. By this method the villages were taken and the soldiers recovered from their hardships amidst a plenty of provisions. Before long the king made himself master of all the population.

The single combat that took place in the territory of the Areii and their annexation (83. 1-6).

The death of Bessus, the murderer of Dareius (83. 7-9).

83. Now in his advance Alexander encamped near the Caucasus, which some call Mt. Paropanisum. In sixteen days he marched across this range from side to side, and founded a city in the pass which leads down to Media, calling it Alexandria. In the midst of the Caucasus there is a "rock" ten furlongs in perimeter and four furlongs in height, in which the cave of Prometheus was pointed out by the natives, as well as the nesting place of the eagle in the story and the marks of the chains.

Alexander founded other cities also at the distance of a day's march from Alexandria. Here he settled seven thousand natives, three thousand of the camp followers, and volunteers from among the mercenaries. Then he marched his forces into Bactria, since news came that Bessus had assumed the diadem and was enrolling an army.

Such was the state of Alexander's affairs.

The generals who had been sent back to Areia found that the rebels had gathered substantial forces under the command of Satibarzanes, who was distinguished both for generalship and for personal bravery, and they encamped near them. There was constant skirmishing for a time, and numerous small engagements; then it came to a general battle. The Iranians were holding their own when their general Satibarzanes raised his hands and removed his helmet so that all could see who he was, and challenged any of the Macedonian generals who wished to fight with him alone. Erigyius accepted and a contest of heroic nature ensued, which resulted in Erigyius's victory. Disheartened at the death of their commander, the Iranians sought their safety in surrender, and gave themselves up to Alexander.

Bessus proclaimed himself king, sacrificed to the gods, and invited his friends to a banquet. In the course of the drinking, he fell into an argument with one of them, Bagodaras by name. As the quarrel increased, Bessus lost his temper and proposed to put Bagodaras to death, but was persuaded by his friends to think better of it. Bagodaras, however, saved from this danger, escaped by night to Alexander. His safe reception and the gifts promised by Alexander attracted Bessus's leading generals. They banded together, seized Bessus, and carried him off to Alexander. The king gave them substantial gifts, and turned Bessus over to Dareius's brother and his other relatives for punishment. They inflicted upon him every humiliation and abuse, and cutting his body up into little pieces they scattered them abroad.

How, after plundering the stronghold of Massaca, he cut down all the mercenaries although they fought magnificently (84).

84. A truce was concluded on these terms, and the queen, impressed by

Alexander's generosity, sent him valuable gifts and promised to follow his orders ill everything.

The mercenaries straightway under the terms of the truce left the city and encamped without interference at a distance of eighty furlongs, without an inkling of what would happen. Alexander, nevertheless, nursed an implacable hostility toward them; he held his forces in readiness, followed them, and falling upon them suddenly wrought a great slaughter. At first they kept shouting that this attack was in contravention of the treaty and they called to witness the gods against whom he had transgressed. Alexander shouted back that he had granted them the right to leave the city but not that of being friends of the Macedonians forever.

Not daunted at the greatness of their danger, the mercenaries joined ranks and, forming a full circle, placed their children and women in the centre so that they might effectively face those who were attacking from all directions. Filled with desperate courage and fighting stoutly with native toughness and the experience of previous contests, they were opposed by Macedonians anxious not to show themselves inferior to barbarians in fighting ability, so that the battle was a scene of horror. They fought hand to hand, and as the contestants engaged each other every form of death and wounds was to be seen. The Macedonians thrust with their long spears through the light shields of the mercenaries and pressed the iron points on into their lungs, while they in turn flung their javelins into the close ranks of their enemies and could not miss the mark, so near was the target.

As many were wounded and not a few killed, the women caught up the weapons of the fallen and fought beside their men, since the acuteness of the danger and the fierceness of the action forced them to be brave beyond their nature. Some of them, clad in armour, sheltered behind the same shields as their husbands, while others rushed in without armour, grasped the opposing shields, and hindered their use by the enemy. Finally, fighting women and all, they were overborne by numbers and cut down, winning a glorious death in preference to basely saving their lives at any cost. Alexander removed the feeble and unarmed together with the surviving women to another place, and put the cavalry in charge of them.

How he took by assault the Rock called Aornus, which had always proved impregnable (85).

85. After he had taken a number of other cities by storm and had slaughtered their defenders, he came to the "rock" called Aornus. Here the surviving natives had taken refuge because of its great strength. It is said that Heracles of old thought to lay siege to this "rock" but refrained because of the occurrence of certain sharp earthquake shocks and other divine signs, and this made Alexander even more eager to capture the stronghold when he heard it, and so to rival the god's reputation.

The circumference of the "rock" was one hundred furlongs, and its height sixteen. Its surface was even and circular on all sides. Its southern side was washed by the Indus River, the largest of those in India, and on the other sides it was surrounded by deep gorges and sheer cliffs. Alexander surveyed these difficulties and decided that its forcible capture was impossible, but then there came to him an old man with two sons. He lived in extreme poverty and had for a long time supported himself in the region, occupying a cave in which three

151

beds had been cut out of the rock. Here the old man camped with his sons, and had come to know the country intimately. When he appeared before the king, he told his story and offered to guide the king through the hills and bring him to a point where he would be above the people who occupied the rock.

Alexander promised him rich gifts. Using the old man as a guide, he first occupied the path which led up to the rock; since there was no other egress, he had thus enclosed the defenders in a hopeless siege. Then he put many hands to work filling up the chasm at the foot of the rock, drew near to it, and mounted a vigorous attack, assaulting continuously for seven days and seven nights with relays of troops. At first the defenders had the advantage because of holding the higher ground, and they killed many of those who attacked rashly. As the embankment was finished, however, and the dart-throwing catapults and other engines were emplaced, and the king also made it evident that he would not break off the siege, the Indians were alarmed, and Alexander, craftily anticipating what would happen, removed the guard which had been left in the path, allowing those who wished to withdraw from the rock. In fear of the Macedonian fighting qualities and the king's determination, the Indians left the rock under cover of darkness.

How he won over to his side Taxiles, king of the Indians, and in a great engagement defeated Porus, took him prisoner and gave him back his throne because of his gallant conduct (86-89).

86. So Alexander employed the false alarms of war to outgeneral the Indians and to gain possession of the "rock" without further fighting. He gave the promised reward to his guide and marched off with his army.

About this time, a certain Indian named Aphrices with twenty thousand troops and fifteen elephants was encamped in the vicinity. Some of his followers killed him and cut off his head and brought it to Alexander, and saved their own lives by this favour. The king took them into his service, and rounded up the elephants, which were wandering about the countryside.

Alexander now advanced to the Indus River and found his thirty-oared boats in readiness and fully equipped, and the stream spanned by a floating bridge. He rested his army for thirty days and offered splendid sacrifices to the gods, then moved his army across and experienced a startling fright and relief. Taxiles, the king, had died, and his son Mophis had succeeded to the throne. He had sent word to Alexander earlier when he was in Sogdiana, promising to join him in a campaign against his enemies among the Indians, and now he stated through his messengers that he turned his kingdom over to him. When Alexander was still forty furlongs off, Mophis deployed his force as if for war and marched forward, his elephants gaily caparisoned, surrounded by his Friends. Alexander saw a great army in warlike array approaching and concluded at once that the Indian's promises were made in order to deceive him, so that the Macedonians might be attacked before they had time to prepare themselves. He ordered the trumpeters to sound the call to arms, and when the soldiers had found their battle stations, marched against the Indians. Mophis saw the excited activity of the Macedonians and guessed the reason. He left his army and accompanied only by a few horsemen galloped forward, corrected the misapprehension of the Macedonians, and gave himself and his army over to the king. Alexander, much relieved, restored his kingdom to him and thereafter held him as a friend and ally. He also changed his name to Taxiles.

That is what happened in that year.

87. In the archonship of Chromes at Athens, [326/5] the Romans elected as consuls Publius Cornelius and Aulus Postumius. In this year Alexander repaired his army in the land of Taxiles and then marched against Porus, the king of the neighbouring Indians. He had more than fifty thousand infantry, about three thousand cavalry, more than a thousand chariots of war, and one hundred and thirty elephants. He had enlisted the support of a second king of the neighbouring regions, whose name was Embisarus; he had an army little smaller than that of Porus.

When Alexander received word that this king was four hundred furlongs away, he decided to attack Porus before the arrival of his ally. As he approached the Indians, Porus learned of his advance and deployed his forces promptly. He stationed his cavalry upon both flanks, and arranged his elephants, arrayed so as to strike terror in an opponent, in a single line at equal intervals along his front. Between these beasts he placed the rest of his infantry, with the mission of helping them and preventing their being attacked with javelins from the sides. His whole array looked very much like a city, for the elephants resembled towers, and the soldiers between them curtain walls. Alexander viewed the enemy's dispositions and arranged his own troops appropriately.

88. The fighting began, and practically all of the Indians' chariots were put out of action by Alexander's cavalry. Then the elephants came into play, trained to make good use of their height and strength. Some of the Macedonians were trodden under foot, armour and all, by the beasts and died, their bones crushed. Others were caught up by the elephants' trunks and, lifted on high, were dashed back down to the ground again, dying a fearful death. Many soldiers were pierced through by the tusks and died instantly, run through the whole body. Nevertheless the Macedonians faced the frightening experience manfully. They used their long spears to good effect against the Indians stationed beside the elephants, and kept the battle even. Then, as javelins began to find their marks in the sides of the great beasts and they felt the pain of the wounds, the Indian riders were no longer able to control their movements. The elephants veered and, no longer manageable, turned upon their own ranks and trampled friendly troops.

As his formations grew more confused, Porus observed what was happening. He was mounted on the largest of the elephants and gathered about him forty others which were not yet out of hand, then attacked the enemy with their combined weight and inflicted many losses. He was himself outstanding in bodily strength beyond any of his followers, being five cubits in height and with a breadth of chest double that of his mightiest soldiers. His javelins were flung with such force that they were little inferior to the darts of the catapults. The Macedonians who opposed him were amazed at his fighting ability, but Alexander called up the bowmen and other light armed troops and ordered them to concentrate their fire upon Porus. This was done promptly. Many weapons flew toward the Indian at the same time and none missed its mark because of his great size. He continued to fight heroically until, fainting from loss of blood from his many wounds, he collapsed upon his elephant and fell to the ground. The word went about that the king was killed, and the rest of the Indians fled.

89. Many were slain in their flight, but then Alexander, satisfied with his brilliant victory, ordered the trumpets to sound the recall. Of the Indians, there fell in the battle more than twelve thousand, among whom were the two sons of Porus and his best generals and officers. Above nine thousand men were taken alive, together with eighty elephants. Porus himself was still breathing, and was turned over to the Indians for medical attention. On the Macedonian side, the losses were two hundred and eighty cavalry and more than seven hundred infantry. The king buried the dead, rewarded those who had distinguished themselves in accordance with their deserts, and sacrificed to Helius who had given him the eastern regions to conquer.

There were mountains not far away where grew thriving firs in quantity, together with no little cedar and pine and an ample supply of other woods suitable for shipbuilding, and Alexander constructed a large number of ships. He intended to reach the borders of India and to subdue all of its inhabitants, and then to sail downstream to the Ocean. He founded two cities, one beyond the river where he had crossed and the other on the spot where he had defeated Porus. These were built quickly because there was a plentiful supply of labour. When Porus had recovered, Alexander appointed him, in recognition of his valour, king over the country where he formerly ruled. The Macedonian army rested for thirty days in the midst of a vast plenty of provisions.

An account of the marvellous serpents in the country and of the fruits which grow there (90).

90. Odd phenomena were observed in these mountains. In addition to the wood for shipbuilding, the region contained a large number of snakes remarkable for their size; they reached a length of sixteen cubits. There were also many varieties of monkey, differing in size, which had themselves taught the Indians the method of their capture. They imitate every action that they see, but cannot well be taken by force because of their strength and cleverness. The hunters, however, in the sight of the beasts, smear their eyes with honey, or fasten sandals about their ankles, or hang mirrors about their necks. Then they go away, having attached fastenings to the shoes, having substituted birdlime for honey, and having fastened slip nooses to the mirrors. So when the animals try to imitate what they had seen, they are rendered helpless, their eyes stuck together, their feet bound fast, and their bodies held immovable. That is the way in which they become easy to catch. Sasibisares, the king who had not moved in time to help Porus in the battle, was frightened, and Alexander forced him to accept his orders. Then Alexander resumed his march to the east, crossed the river, and continued on through a region of remarkable fertility. It possessed strange kinds of trees which reached a height of seventy cubits, were so thick that they could scarcely be embraced by four men, and cast a shadow of three plethra.

This country possessed a multitude of snakes, small and variously coloured. Some of them looked like bronze rods, others had thick, shaggy crests, and their bites brought sudden death. The person bitten suffered fearful pains and was covered with a bloody sweat. The Macedonians, who were much affected by the bites, slung their hammocks from trees and remained awake most of the night. Later, however, they learned from the natives the use of a medicinal root and were freed from these fears.

How he won over to his side many of the neighbouring tribes and defeated others (91. 1-4). How he subdued the country that was subject to Sopeithes (91- 4).

Concerning the good government of the cities in this country (91. 4-6).

91. As he continued his march, word came to Alexander that King Porus (a cousin of the Porus who had been defeated) had left his kingdom and fled to the people of Gandara. This annoyed Alexander, and he sent Hephaestion with an army into his country and ordered that the kingdom should be transferred to the friendly Porus.

He campaigned against the people known as the Adrestians, and got possession of their cities, partly by force and partly by agreement. Then he came into the country of the Cathaeans, among whom it was the custom for wives to be cremated together with their husbands. This law had been put into effect there because of a woman who had killed her husband with poison. Here he captured their greatest and strongest city after much fighting and burned it. He was in process of besieging another notable city when the Indians came to him with suppliant branches and he spared them further attack.

Next he undertook a campaign against the cities under the rule of Sopeithes. These are exceedingly well-governed. All the functions of this state are directed toward the acquiring of good repute, and beauty is valued there more than anything. From birth, their children are subjected to a process of selection. Those who are well formed and designed by nature to have a fine appearance and bodily strength are reared, while those who are bodily deficient are destroyed as not worth bringing up. So they plan their marriages without regard to dower or any other financial consideration, but consider only beauty and physical excellence. In consequence, most of the inhabitants of these cities enjoy a higher reputation than those elsewhere.

Their king Sopeithes was strikingly handsome and tall beyond the rest, being over four cubits in height. He came out of his capital city and gave over himself and his kingdom to Alexander, but received it back through the kindness of the conqueror. Sopeithes with great goodwill feasted the whole army bountifully for several days.

Concerning the excellence of the dogs presented to Alexander (92).

92. To Alexander he presented many impressive gifts, among them one hundred and fifty dogs remarkable for their size and courage and other good qualities. People said that they had a strain of tiger blood. He wanted Alexander to test their mettle in action, and he brought into a ring a full grown lion and two of the poorest of the dogs. He set these on the lion, and when they were having a hard time of it he released two others to assist them. The four were getting the upper hand over the lion when Sopeithes sent in a man with a scimitar who hacked at the right leg of one of the dogs. At this Alexander shouted out indignantly and the guards rushed up and seized the arm of the Indian, but Sopeithes said that he would give him three other dogs for that one, and the handler, taking a firm grip on the leg, severed it slowly. The dog, in the meanwhile, uttered neither yelp nor whimper, but continued with his teeth clamped shut until, fainting with loss of blood, he died on top of the lion.

Concerning the story told by the king of the Indians (93. 1-3).

How, when Alexander desired to cross the Ganges River and march against the people called Gandaridae, the Macedonians mutinied (93. 4-94).

93. While all this was going on, Hephaestion returned with his army from his mission, having conquered a big piece of India. Alexander commended him for his successes, then invaded the kingdom of Phegeus where the inhabitants cheerfully accepted the appearance of the Macedonians. Phegeus himself met the king with many gifts and Alexander confirmed him in his rule. Alexander and the army were feasted bountifully for two days, and then advanced to the Hyphasis River, the width of which was seven furlongs, the depth six fathoms, and the current violent. This was difficult to cross.

He questioned Phegeus about the country beyond the Indus River, and learned that there was a desert to traverse for twelve days, and then the river called Ganges, which was thirty-two furlongs in width and the deepest of all the Indian rivers. Beyond this in turn dwelt the peoples of the Tabraesians and the Gandaridae, whose king was Xandrames. He had twenty thousand cavalry, two hundred thousand infantry, two thousand chariots, and four thousand elephants equipped for war. Alexander doubted this information and sent for Porus, and asked him what was the truth of these reports. Porus assured the king that all the rest of the account was quite correct, but that the king of the Gandaridae was an utterly common and undistinguished character, and was supposed to be the son of a barber. His father had been handsome and was greatly loved by the queen; when she had murdered her husband, the kingdom fell to him.

Alexander saw that the campaign against the Gandaridae would not be easy, but he was not discouraged. He had confidence in the fighting qualities of his Macedonians, as well as in the oracles which he had received, and expected that he would be victorious. He remembered that the Pythia had called him "unconquerable," and Ammon had given him the rule of the whole world.

94. Alexander observed that his soldiers were exhausted with their constant campaigns. They had spent almost eight years among toils and dangers, and it was necessary to raise their spirits by an effective appeal if they were to undertake the expedition against the Gandaridae. There had been many losses among the soldiers, and no relief from fighting was in sight. The hooves of the. horses had been worn thin by steady marching. The arms and armour were wearing out, and Greek clothing was quite gone. They had to clothe themselves in foreign materials, recutting the garments of the Indians. This was the season also, as luck would have it, of the heavy rains. These had been going on for seventy days, to the accompaniment of continuous thunder and lightning.

All this he accounted adverse to his project, and he saw only one hope of gaining his wish, if he might gain the soldiers' great goodwill through gratitude. Accordingly he allowed them to ravage the enemy's country, which was full of every good thing. During these days when the army was busy foraging, he called together the wives of the soldiers and their children; to the wives he undertook to give a monthly ration, to the children he distributed a service bonus in proportion to the military records of their fathers. When the soldiers returned laden with wealth from their expedition, he brought them together to a meeting. He delivered a carefully prepared speech about the expedition against the Gandaridae but the Macedonians did not accept it, and he gave up the undertaking.

How, after marking the furthest point reached by his army, the king visited the remaining regions of the Indians (95).

95. Thinking how best to mark the limits of his campaign at this point, he first erected altars of the twelve gods each fifty cubits high and then traced the circuit of a camp thrice the size of the existing one. Here he dug a ditch fifty feet wide and forty feet deep, and throwing up the earth on the inside, constructed out of it a substantial wall. He directed the infantry to construct huts each containing two beds five cubits long, and the cavalry, in addition to this, to build two mangers twice the normal size. In the same way, everything else which would be left behind was exaggerated in size. His idea in this was to make a camp of heroic proportions and to leave to the natives evidence of men of huge stature, displaying the strength of giants.

After all this had been done, Alexander marched back with all his army to the Acesines River by the same route by which he had come. There he found the ships built which he had ordered. He fitted these out and built others. At this juncture there arrived from Greece allied and mercenary troops under their own commanders, more than thirty thousand infantry and a little less than six thousand cavalry. They brought with them elegant suits of armour for twenty-five thousand foot soldiers, and a hundred talents of medical supplies. These he distributed to the soldiers. Now the naval flotilla was ready; he had prepared two hundred open galleys and eight hundred service ships. He gave names to the two cities which had been founded on either side of the river, calling one of them Nicaea in celebration of his victory in war, and the other Bucephala in honour of his horse, who had died in the battle against Porus.

How he sailed down the Indus River to the southern Ocean, and almost died of an arrow wound (96-99).

96. He himself embarked with his Friends, and sailed down the river toward the southern Ocean. The bulk of his army marched along the bank of the river, under the command of Craterus and Hephaestion.

When they came to the junction of the Acesines and the Hydaspes, he disembarked his soldiers and led them against the people called Sibians. They say that these are the descendants of the soldiers who came with Heracles to the rock of Aornus and were unsuccessful in its siege, and then were settled in this spot by him. Alexander encamped beside a very fine city, and the leading notables of the citizens came out to see him. They were brought before the king, renewed their ties of kinship, and undertook to help him enthusiastically in every way, as being his relatives. They also brought him magnificent gifts. Alexander accepted their goodwill, declared their cities to be free, and marched on against the next tribes.

He found that the Agalasseis, as they were called, were drawn up in battle formation. Their strength was forty thousand infantry and three thousand cavalry. He engaged them and, conquering, cut down most of them. Those who escaped into the neighbouring cities he besieged, captured, and sold as slaves. Other groups of natives had collected also. He took by storm a large city in which twenty thousand persons had taken refuge. The Indians barricaded the streets and fought stoutly from the houses, and he lost not a few Macedonians in pressing his victory home. This made him angry. He set fire to the city and burned up most of the inhabitants with it. The remaining natives to the number of three thousand had fled to the citadel, whence they appealed for mercy with suppliant branches. Alexander pardoned them.

97. Again he embarked with his Friends upon the ships and continued his voyage down the river until he came to the confluence of the rivers named above with the Indus. As these mighty streams flowed together, many dangerous eddies were created and these, making the ships collide with each other, caused much damage. The current was swift and violent and overcame the skill of the helmsmen. Two of the galleys were sunk and not a few of the other vessels ran aground. The flagship was swept into a great cataract and the king was brought into extreme danger. With death staring him in the face, Alexander flung off his clothing and leaping into the water naked saved himself as best he could. His Friends swam with him, concerned to help the king to safety now that his ship was foundering. Aboard the ship itself there was wild confusion. The crew struggled against the might of the water but the river was superior to all human skill and power. Nevertheless, Alexander and the ships with him got safely ashore with difficulty. Thus narrowly escaping, he sacrificed to the gods as having come through mortal danger, reflecting that he, like Achilles, had done battle with a river.

98. Next Alexander undertook a campaign against the Sydracae and the people known as Mallians, populous and warlike tribes. He found them mobilized in force, eighty thousand infantry, ten thousand cavalry, and seven hundred chariots. Before the arrival of Alexander they had been at war with each other; but as he approached, they patched up their quarrel and made peace, giving and receiving ten thousand young women to establish a friendly relationship through marriage. Even so they did not come out to fight together but fell into a dispute over the command and retired into the neighbouring cities.

Alexander neared the first city and thought to take it by storm, but one of the seers, named Demophon, came to him and reported that there had been revealed to him by numerous portents a great danger which would come to the king from a wound in the course of the operation. He begged Alexander to leave that city alone for the present and to turn his mind to other activities. The king scolded him for dampening the enthusiasm of the soldiers, and then, disposing his army for the attack, led the way in person to the city, eager to reduce it by force. The engines of war were slow to come up, but he broke open a postern gate and was the first to burst into the city. He struck down many defenders and, driving the others before him, pursued them to the citadel.

The Macedonians were still busy fighting along the wall. Alexander seized a ladder, leaned it against the walls of the citadel, and clambered up holding a light shield above his head. So quick was he to act that he reached the top of the wall before the defenders could forestall him. The Indians did not dare to come within his reach, but flung javelins and shot arrows at him from a distance. He was staggering under the weight of their blows when the Macedonians raised two ladders and swarmed up in a mass, but both broke and the soldiers tumbled back upon the ground.

99. Thus the king was left alone, and boldly took a step which was as little expected as it is worthy of mention. It seemed to him out of keeping with his tradition of success to descend from the wall to his troops without accomplishing anything. In stead, he leapt down with his armour alone inside the city. As the Indians thronged about him, he withstood their attack undismayed. He protected himself on the right by a tree which grew close by the wall and on the left by the wall itself and kept the Indians off, displaying such courage as you would expect from a king who had his record of achievement. He was eager to make this, if it were the last feat of his life, a supremely glorious one. He took many blows upon the helmet, not a few upon the shield. At length he was struck by an arrow below the breast and fell upon one knee, overborne by the blow. Straightway the Indian who had shot him, thinking that he was helpless, ran up and struck at him; Alexander thrust his sword up into the man's side, inflicting a mortal wound. The Indian fell, and the king caught hold of a branch close by and getting on his feet, defied the Indians to come forward and fight with him.

At this point Peucestes, one of the guards, who had mounted another ladder, was the first to cover the king with his shield. After him a good many appeared together, which frightened the natives and saved Alexander. The city was taken by storm. In a fury at the injury to their king, the Macedonians killed all whom they met and filled the city with corpses.

For many days the king lay helpless under his treatment, and the Greeks who had been settled in Bactria and Sogdiana, who had long borne unhappily their sojourn among peoples of another race and now received word that the king had died of his wounds, revolted against the Macedonians. They formed a band of three thousand men and underwent great hardship on their homeward route. Later they were massacred by the Macedonians after Alexander's death.

Concerning the single combat that issued from a challenge (100-101).

100. Alexander recovered from his wound, sacrificed to the gods, and held a great banquet for his Friends. In the course of the drinking a curious event occurred which is worth mention. Among the king's companions there was a Macedonian named Coragus, strong in body, who had distinguished him self many times in battle. His temper was sharpened by the drink, and he challenged to single combat Dioxippus the Athenian, an athlete who had won a crown in the foremost games. As you would expect, the guests at the banquet egged them on and Dioxippus accepted. The king set a day for the contest, and when the time came, many myriads of men gathered to see the spectacle. The Macedonians and Alexander backed Coragus because he was one of them, while the Greeks favoured Dioxippus. The two advanced to the field of honour, the Macedonian clad in his expensive armour but the Athenian naked, his body oiled, carrying a well-balanced club.

Both men were fine to look upon with their magnificent physiques and their ardour for combat. Everyone looked forward, as it were, to a battle of gods. By his carriage and the brilliance of his arms, the Macedonian inspired terror as if he were Ares, while Dioxippus excelled in sheer strength and condition; still more because of his club he bore a certain resemblance to Heracles.

As they approached each other, the Macedonian flung his javelin from a proper distance, but the other inclined his body slightly and avoided its impact. Then the Macedonian poised his long lance and charged, but the Greek, when he came within reach, struck the spear with his club and shattered it. After these two defeats, Coragus was reduced to continuing the battle with his sword, but as he reached for it, the other leaped upon him and seized his sword hand with his left, while with his right hand the Greek upset the Macedonian's balance and made him lose his footing. As he fell to the earth, Dioxippus placed his foot upon his neck and, holding his club aloft, looked to the spectators.

101. The crowd was in an uproar because of the stunning quickness and superiority of the man's skill, and the king signed to let Coragus go, then broke up the gathering and left. He was plainly annoyed at the defeat of the Macedonian. Dioxippus released his fallen opponent, and left the field winner of a resounding victory and bedecked with ribands by his compatriots, as having brought a common glory to all Greeks. Fortune, however, did not allow him to boast of his victory for long.

The king continued more and more hostile to him, and Alexander's friends and all the other Macedonians about the court, jealous of the accomplishment, persuaded one of the butlers to secrete a golden cup under his pillow; then in the course of the next symposium they accused him of theft, and pretending to find the cup, placed Dioxippus in a shameful and embarrassing position. He saw that the Macedonians were in league against him and left the banquet. After a little he came to his own quarters, wrote Alexander a letter about the trick that had been played on him, gave this to his servants to take to the king, and then took his own life. He had been ill-advised to undertake the single combat, but he was much more foolish to make an end of himself in this way. Hence many of those who reviled him, mocking his folly, said that it was a hard fate to have great strength of body but little sense.

The king read the letter and was very angry at the man's death. He often mourned his good qualities, and the man whom he had neglected when he was alive, he regretted when he was dead. After it was no longer of use, he discovered the excellence of Dioxippus by contrast with the vileness of his accusers.

Concerning the Indians whom he conquered on both banks of the river as far as the Ocean (102-103).

102. Alexander gave orders to the army to march beside the river and escort the ships, while he resumed his river voyage in the direction of the ocean and sailed down to the country of the people called Sambastae. These, in numbers of men and in good qualities, were inferior to none of the Indian peoples. They lived in cities governed in a democratic manner, and learning of the coming of the Macedonians assembled sixty thousand infantry, six thousand cavalry, and five hundred armoured chariots.

When the fleet put in to them, they were amazed at the strange and unanticipated manner of its arrival and trembled at the great reputation of the Macedonians. Besides, their own older men advised them not to risk a fight, so they sent out fifty of their leading citizens as envoys, begging Alexander to treat them kindly. The king praised them and agreed to a peace, and was showered with large gifts and heroic honours by them.

Next Alexander received the submission of those who dwelt on either side of the river; they were called Sodrae and Massani. Here he built a city Alexandria by the river, and selected for it ten thousand inhabitants. Next he came to the country of King Musicanus; getting him into his hands he killed him and made the country subject. Then he invaded the kingdom of Porticanus, took two cities by storm, allowed the soldiers to plunder the houses, and then set them on fire. Porticanus himself escaped to a stronghold, but Alexander captured it and slew him, still fighting. Then he proceeded to take all of the other cities of his kingdom and destroyed them, and spread the terror of his name throughout the whole region.

Next he ravaged the kingdom of Sambus. He enslaved the population of most of the cities and, after destroying the cities, killed more than eighty thousand of the natives. He inflicted a similar disaster upon the tribe of the Brahmins, as they are called; the survivors came supplicating him with branches in their hands, and punishing the most guilty he forgave the rest. King Sambus fled with thirty elephants into the country beyond the Indus and escaped.

103. The last city of the Brahmins, called Harmatelia, was proud of the valour of its inhabitants and of the strength of its location. Thither he sent a small force of mobile troops with orders to engage the enemy and retire if they came out against them. These were five hundred in number, and were despised when they attacked the walls. Some three thousand soldiers issued out of the city, whereupon Alexander's task force pretended to be frightened and fled. Presently the king launched an unexpected attack against the pursuing natives and charging them furiously killed some of the natives, and captured others.

A number of the king's forces were wounded, and these met a new and serious danger. The Brahmins had smeared their weapons with a drug of mortal effect; that was their source of confidence when they joined the issue of battle. The power of the drug was derived from certain snakes which were caught and killed and left in the sun. The heat melted the substance of the flesh and drops of moisture formed; in this moisture the poison of the animals was secreted. When a man was wounded, the body became numb immediately and then sharp pains followed, and convulsions and shivering shook the whole frame. The skin became cold and livid and bile appeared in the vomit, while a black froth was exuded from the wound and gangrene set in. As this spread quickly and overran to the vital parts of the body, it brought a horrible death to the victim. The same result occurred to those who had received large wounds and to those whose wounds were small, or even a mere scratch.

So the wounded were dying in this fashion, and for the rest Alexander was not so much concerned, but he was deeply distressed for Ptolemy, the future king, who was much beloved by him. An interesting and quite extraordinary event occurred in the case of Ptolemy, which some attributed to divine Providence. He was loved by all because of his character and his kindnesses to all, and he obtained a succour appropriate to his good deeds. The king saw a vision in his sleep. It seemed to him that a snake appeared carrying a plant in its mouth, and showed him its nature and efficacy and the place where it grew. When Alexander awoke, he sought out the plant, and grinding it up plastered it on Ptolemy's body. He also prepared an infusion of the plant and gave Ptolemy a drink of it. This restored him to health.

Now that the value of the remedy had been demonstrated, all the other wounded received the same therapy and became well. Then Alexander prepared to attack and capture the city of Harmatelia, which was large and strongly fortified, but the inhabitants came to him with suppliant branches and handed themselves over. He spared them any punishment.

Concerning the marvels and practices found among the inhabitants and about the men who live a brutish existence (104-106. 3).

104. Now he resumed his voyage down the river and sailed out into the Ocean with his Friends. There he discovered two islands and on them performed rich sacrifices. He threw many large cups of gold into the sea following the libations which he poured from them. He erected altars to Tethys and Oceanus and judged that his projected campaign was at an end. Setting sail from there, he proceeded back up the river to Patala, a fine city. It had a government organized very much like that of Sparta. Two kings descended from two houses inherited their office from their fathers. They had charge of all arrangements concerning war, while the council of elders was the principal administrative body.

Alexander burned such of his boats as were damaged. The rest of the fleet he turned over to Nearchus and others of his Friends with orders to coast along through the Ocean and, having observed everything, to meet him at the mouth of the Euphrates River. He set his army in motion and traversed much territory and defeated his opponents, while those who submitted were received kindly. He brought over without fighting the so-called Abritae and the tribesmen of Cedrosia. Then he marched through a long stretch of waterless and largely desert country as far as the frontiers of Oreitis. There he divided his force into three divisions and named as commander of the first, Ptolemy, and of the second, Leonnatus. He ordered Ptolemy to plunder the district by the sea and Leonnatus to lay waste the interior. He himself devastated the upper country and the hills. At one and the same time much country was wasted, so that every spot was filled with fire and devastation and great slaughter. The soldiers soon became possessed of much booty, and the number of persons killed reached many myriads. By the destruction of these tribes, all their neighbours were terrified and submitted to the king.

Alexander wanted to found a city by the sea. He found a sheltered harbour with suitable terrain near by, and established there a city called Alexandria.

105. He advanced into the country of the Oreitae through the passes and quickly brought it all into submission. These Oreitae have the same customs as the Indians in other respects, but have one practice which is strange and quite unbelievable. The bodies of the dead are carried out by their relatives, who strip themselves naked and carry spears. They place the bodies in the thickets which exist in the country and remove the clothing from them, leaving them to be the prey of wild beasts. They divide up the clothing of the dead, sacrifice to the heroes of the nether world, and give a banquet to their friends.

Next Alexander advanced into Cedrosia, marching near the sea, and encountered a people unfriendly and utterly brutish. Those who dwelt here let the nails of their fingers and toes grow from birth to old age. They also let their hair remain matted like felt. Their colour is burned black by the heat of the sun, and they clothe themselves in the skins of beasts. They subsist by eating the flesh of stranded whales. They build up the walls of their houses from . . . and construct roofs with whale's ribs, which furnish them rafters eighteen cubits in length. In the place of tiles, they covered their roofs with the scales of these beasts.

Alexander passed through this territory with difficulty because of the shortage of provisions and entered a region which was desert, and lacking in everything which could be used to sustain life. Many died of hunger. The army of the Macedonians was disheartened, and Alexander sank into no ordinary grief and anxiety. It seemed a dreadful thing that they who had excelled all in fighting ability and in equipment for war should perish ingloriously from lack of food in a desert country. He determined, therefore, to send out swift messengers into Parthyaea and Dranginê and Areia and the other areas bordering on the desert, ordering these to bring quickly to the gates of Carmania racing camels and other animals trained to carry burdens, loading them with food and other necessities. These messengers hurried to the satraps of these provinces and caused supplies to be transported in large quantities to the specified place. Alexander lost many of his soldiers, nevertheless, first because of shortages that were not relieved, and then at a later stage of this march, when some of the Oreitae attacked Leonnatus's division and inflicted severe losses, after which they escaped to their own territory.

How the naval expedition through the Ocean rejoined Alexander as he was encamped by the sea and gave an account of their voyage (106. 4-7).

106. So with great difficulty Alexander passed through the desert and came into a well-populated country provided with everything needful. Here he rested his army, and for seven days proceeded with his troops in festive dress. He himself led a Dionysiac comus, feasting and drinking as he travelled.

After this celebration was over, Alexander learned that many of his officials who had used their powers arbitrarily and selfishly had committed serious offences, and he punished a number of his satraps and generals. As the word spread of his righteous indignation against his offending subordinates, many of the generals recalled acts of insolence or illegality which they had performed and became alarmed. Some who had mercenary troops revolted against the king's authority, and others got together sums of money and fled. As news of this was brought to the king, he wrote to all his generals and satraps in Asia, ordering them, as soon as they had read his letter, to disband all their mercenaries instantly.

At this juncture the king was resting in a seaside city called Salmus and was holding a dramatic contest in the theatre, when into the harbour there sailed the fleet which had been ordered to return by way of the Ocean and to explore the coastal waters. The officers came immediately into the theatre, greeted Alexander, and reported what they had done. The Macedonians were delighted at their arrival and welcomed their safe return with loud applause, so that the whole theatre was filled with the wildest rejoicing.

The mariners told how they had encountered astonishing ebbing and flowing in the Ocean. In the former case, many large and unsuspected islands appeared along the coast, but in the latter all such places were flooded over as a copious and strong current bore in towards the land, while the surface of the water was white with much foam. But their most remarkable experience was an encounter with a large school of incredibly big whales. The sailors had been terrified and despaired of their lives, thinking that they would be dashed to pieces immediately ships and all, but when they all shouted in unison, beating upon their shields to make a great din, and the trumpets were blown loudly in addition, the beasts were alarmed by the strange noise and plunged into the depths of the sea.

How again setting sail they skirted a long expanse of coastline (107. 1).

107. After this recital, the king ordered the officers of the fleet to sail on to the Euphrates, while he continued on a great distance with the army, and came to the frontier of Susianê. Here the Indian Caranus, who had advanced far in philosophy and was highly regarded by Alexander, put a remarkable end to his life. He had lived for seventy-three years without ever having experienced an illness, and now decided to remove himself from life, since he had received the utmost limit of happiness both from nature and from Fortune. He had been taken ill and each day becoming more exhausted he asked the king to erect for him a huge pyre and, after he had ascended it, to order the attendants to ignite it.

At first Alexander tried to dissuade him from this plan, but when he was unsuccessful, he agreed to do what was asked. After the project had become generally known, the pyre was erected, and everybody came to see the remarkable sight. True to his own creed, Caranus cheerfully mounted the pyre and perished, consumed along with it. Some of those who were present thought him mad, others vainglorious about his ability to bear pain, while others simply marvelled at his fortitude and contempt for death.

The king gave Caranus a magnificent funeral and then proceeded to Susa, where he married Stateira, the elder daughter of Dareius, and gave her younger sister Drypetis as wife to Hephaestion. He prevailed upon the most prominent of his Friends to take wives also, and gave them in marriage the noblest Persian ladies.

How he selected thirty thousand young Persians, trained them in military exercises and formed them into a counterpart of his Macedonian phalanx (108. 1-3).

How Harpalus, who was accused of luxurious living and excessive expenditures, fled from Babylon and sought the protection of the people of Athens (108. 4-7).

How he fled from Attica and was killed; he had deposited seven hundred talents of his money with the Athenians and placed four thousand talents and eight thousand mercenaries on Taenarum in Laconia (108. 7-8).

108. Now there came to Susa at this time a body of thirty thousand Persians, all very young and selected for their bodily grace and strength. They had been enrolled in compliance with the king's orders and had been under supervisors and teachers of the arts of war for as long as necessary. They were splendidly equipped with the full Macedonian armament and encamped before the city, where they were warmly commended by the king after demonstrating their skill and discipline in the use of their weapons. The Macedonians had not only mutinied when ordered to cross the Ganges River but were frequently unruly when called into an assembly and ridiculed Alexander's pretence that Amnion was his father. For these reasons Alexander had formed this unit from a single age-group of the Persians which was capable of serving as a counter-balance to the Macedonian phalanx.

These were the concerns of Alexander.

Harpalus had been given the custody of the treasury in Babylon and of the revenues which accrued to it, but as soon as the king had carried his campaign into India, he assumed that Alexander would never come back, and gave himself up to comfortable living. Although he had been charged as satrap with the administration of a great country, he first occupied himself with the abuse of women and illegitimate amours with the natives and squandered much of the treasure under his control on incontinent pleasure. He fetched all the long way from the Red Sea a great quantity of fish and introduced an extravagant way of life, so that he came under general criticism. Later, moreover, he sent and brought from Athens the most dazzling courtesan of the day, whose name was Pythonicê. As long as she lived he gave her gifts worthy of a queen, and when she died, he gave her a magnificent funeral and erected over her grave a costly monument of the Attic type.

After that, he brought out a second Attic courtesan named Glycera and kept her in exceeding luxury, providing her with a way of life which was fantastically expensive. At the same time, with an eye on the uncertainties of fortune, he established himself a place of refuge by benefactions to the Athenians.

When Alexander did come back from India and put to death many of the satraps who had been charged with neglect of duty, Harpalus became alarmed at the punishment which might befall him. He packed up five thousand talents of silver, enrolled six thousand mercenaries, departed from Asia and sailed across to Attica. When no one there accepted him, he shipped his troops off to Taenarum in Laconia, and keeping some of the money with him threw himself on the mercy of the Athenians. Antipater and Olympias demanded his surrender, and although he had distributed large sums of money to those persons who spoke in his favour, he was compelled to slip away and repaired to Taenarum and his mercenaries. Subsequently he sailed over to Crete, where he was murdered by Thibron, one of his Friends. At Athens, an accounting was undertaken of the funds of Harpalus, and Demosthenes and certain other statesmen were convicted of having accepted money from this source.

How Alexander, having paid the debts of his veteran Macedonians, which cost him ten thousand talents, returned them to their homes (109- 1-2).

How the Macedonians revolted and he punished their ringleaders (109. 2-3).

109. While the Olympic Games were being celebrated, Alexander had it proclaimed in Olympia that all exiles should return to their cities, except those who had been charged with sacrilege or murder. He selected the oldest of his soldiers who were Macedonians and released them from service; there were ten thousand of these. He learned that many of them were in debt, and in a single day he paid their obligations, which were little short of ten thousand talents.

The Macedonians who remained with him were becoming insubordinate, and when he called them to an assembly, they interrupted him by shouting. In a fury, he denounced them without regard to his own personal risk; then, having cowed the throng, he leaped down from the platform, seized the ringleaders of the tumult with his own hands, and handed them over to his attendants for punishment. This made the soldiers' hostility even more acute, so that the king appointed generals from specially selected Persians and advanced them into positions of responsibility. At this, the Macedonians were repentant. Weeping, they urgently petitioned Alexander to forgive them, and with difficulty persuaded him to take them back into favour.

How Peucestes brought to Alexander ten thousand bowmen and slingers whom he had recruited from among the Persians (110. 2).

How the king reorganised his army by intermingling Persians with Macedonians (110. 1).

How he paid expenses and educational fees for all the soldiers' children, ten thousand in number (110.3).

110. In the archonship of Anticles at Athens, [325/4] the Romans installed as consuls Lucius Cornelius and Quintus Popillius. In this year Alexander secured replacements from the Persians equal to the number of these soldiers whom he had released, and assigned a thousand of them to the bodyguards stationed at the court. In all respects he showed the same confidence in them as in the Macedonians. At this time Peucestes arrived with twenty thousand Persian bowmen and slingers. Alexander placed these in units with his other soldiers, and by the novelty of this innovation created a force blended and adjusted to his own idea.

Since there were by now sons of the Macedonians born of captive women, he determined the exact number of these. There were about ten thousand, and he set aside for them revenues sufficient to provide them with an upbringing proper for freeborn children, and set over them teachers to give them their proper training.

After this he marched with his army from Susa, crossed the Tigris, and encamped in the villages called Carae. Thence for four days he marched through Sittacenê and came to the place called Sambana. There he remained seven days and, proceeding with the army, came on the third day to the Celones, as they are called. There dwells here down to our time a settlement of Boeotians who were moved in the time of Xerxes's campaign, but still have not forgotten their ancestral customs. They are bilingual and speak like the natives in the one language, while in the other they preserve most of the Greek vocabulary, and they maintain some Greek practices.

After a stay of some days he resumed his march at length and diverging from the main road for the purpose of sight-seeing he entered the region called Bagistane, a magnificent country covered with fruit trees and rich in everything which makes for good living. Next he came to a land which could support enormous herds of horses, where of old they say that there were one hundred and sixty thousand horses grazing, but at the time of Alexander's visit there were counted only sixty thousand. After a stay of thirty days he resumed the march and on the seventh day came to Ecbatana of Media. They say that its circuit is two hundred and fifty stades. It contains the palace which is the capital of all Media and storehouses filled with great wealth.

Here he refreshed his army for some time and staged a dramatic festival, accompanied by constant drinking parties among his friends. In the course of these, Hephaestion drank very much, fell ill, and died. The king was intensely grieved at this and entrusted his body to Perdiccas to conduct to Babylon, where he proposed to celebrate a magnificent funeral for him.

How Leosthenes made preparations for starting a war against the Macedonians (111. 1-3).

How Alexander campaigned against the Cossaeans (111. 4-6).

111. During this period Greece was the scene of disturbances and revolutionary movements from which arose the war called Lamian. The reason was this. The king had ordered all his satraps to dissolve their armies of mercenaries, and as they obeyed his instructions, all Asia was overrun with soldiers released from service and supporting themselves by plunder. Presently they began assembling from all directions at Taenarum in Laconia, whither came also such of the Persian satraps and generals as had survived, bringing their funds and their soldiers, so that they constituted a joint force. Ultimately they chose as supreme commander the Athenian Leosthenes, who was a man of unusually brilliant mind, and thoroughly opposed to the cause of Alexander. He conferred secretly with the council at Athens and was granted fifty talents to pay the troops and a stock of weapons sufficient to meet pressing needs. He sent off an embassy to the Aetolians, who were unfriendly to the king, looking to the establishment of an alliance with them, and otherwise made every preparation for war.

So Leosthenes was occupied with such matters, being in no doubt about the seriousness of the proposed conflict, but Alexander launched a campaign with a mobile force against the Cossaeans, for they would not submit to him. This is a people outstanding in valour which occupied the mountains of Media; and relying upon the ruggedness of their country and their ability in war, they had never accepted a foreign master, but had remained un-conquered throughout the whole period of the Persian kingdom, and now they were too proudly self-confident to be terrified of the Macedonian arms. The king, nevertheless, seized the routes of access into their country before they were aware of it, laid waste most of Cossaea, was superior in every engagement, and both slew many of the Cossaeans and captured many times more.

So the Cossaeans were utterly defeated, and, distressed at the number of their captives, were constrained to buy their recovery at the price of national submission. They placed themselves in Alexander's hands and were granted peace on condition that they should do his bidding. In forty day's at most, he had conquered this people. He founded strong cities at strategic points and rested his army.

How, as the king was on his way to Babylon, the Chaldaeans prophesied to Alexander that he would die if he entered Babylon (112. 1-3). How the king at first was frightened and passed Babylon by, but later, persuaded by the Greek philosophers, entered the city (112. 4-6).

112. After the conclusion of his war with the Cossaeans, Alexander set his army in motion and marched towards Babylon in easy stages, interrupting the march frequently and resting the army. While he was still three hundred furlongs from the city, the scholars called Chaldaeans, who have gained a great reputation in astrology and are accustomed to predict future events by a method based on age-long observations, chose from their number the eldest and most experienced. By the configuration of the stars they had learned of the coming death of the king

167

in Babylon, and they instructed their representatives to report to the king the danger which threatened. They told their envoys also to urge upon the king that he must under no circumstances make his entry into the city; that he could escape the danger if he re-erected the tomb of Belus which had been demolished by the Persians, but he must abandon his intended route and pass the city by.

The leader of the Chaldaean envoys, whose name was Belephantes, was not bold enough to address the king directly but secured a private audience with Nearchus, one of Alexander's Friends, and told him everything in detail, requesting him to make it known to the king. When Alexander, accordingly, learned from Nearchus about the Chaldaeans' prophecy, he was alarmed and more and more disturbed, the more he reflected upon the ability and high reputation of these people. After some hesitation, he sent most of his Friends into Babylon, but altered his own route so as to avoid the city and set up his headquarters in a camp at a distance of two hundred furlongs.

This act caused general astonishment and many of the Greeks came to see him. notably among the philosophers Anaxarchus. When they discovered the reason for his action, they plied him with arguments drawn from philosophy and changed him to the degree that he came to despise all prophetic arts, and especially that which was held in high regard by the Chaldaeans. It was as if the king had been wounded in his soul and then healed by the words of the philosophers, so that he now entered Babylon with his army. As on the previous occasion, the population received the troops hospitably, and all turned their attention to relaxation and pleasure, since everything necessary was available in profusion.

These were the events of this year.

Concerning the multitude of embassies that arrived there (113).

113. When Agesias was archon at Athens, [324/3] the Romans installed as consuls Gaius Publius and Papirius, and the one hundred and fourteenth celebration of the Olympic Games took place, in which Micinas of Rhodes won the foot race. Now from practically all the inhabited world came envoys on various missions, some congratulating Alexander on his victories, some bringing him crowns, others concluding treaties of friendship and alliance, many bringing handsome presents, and some prepared to defend themselves against accusations. Apart from the tribes and cities as well as the local rulers of Asia, many of their counterparts in Europe and Libya put in an appearance; from Libya, Carthaginians and Libyphoenicians and all those who inhabit the coast as far as the Pillars of Heracles; from Europe, the Greek cities and the Macedonians also sent embassies, as well as the Illyrians and most of those who dwell about the Adriatic Sea, the Thracian peoples and even those of their neighbours the Gauls, whose people became known then first in the Greek world.

Alexander drew up a list of the embassies and arranged a schedule of those to whom first he would give his reply and then the others in sequence. First he heard those who came on matters concerning religion; second, those who brought gifts; next, those who had disputes with their neighbours; fourth, those who had problems concerning themselves alone; and fifth, those who wished to present arguments against receiving back their exiles. He dealt with the Eleians first, then with the Ammomans and the Delphians and the Corinthians, as well as with the Epidaurians and the rest, receiving their petitions in the order of importance of the sanctuaries. In all cases he made every effort to deliver replies which would be gratifying, and sent everyone away content so far as he was able.

Concerning the funeral of Hephaestion and the large sum expended on it (114-115).

114. When the embassies had been dismissed, Alexander threw himself into preparations for the burial of Hephaestion. He showed such zeal about the funeral that it not only surpassed all those previously celebrated on earth but also left no possibility for anything greater in later ages. He had loved Hephaestion most of the group of Friends who were thought to have been high in his affections, and after his death showed him superlative honour. In his lifetime, he had preferred him to all, although Craterus had a rival claim to his love; so, for example, that when one of the companions said that Craterus was loved no less than Hephaestion, Alexander had answered that Craterus was king-loving, but Hephaestion was Alexander-loving. At their first meeting with Dareius's mother, when she from ignorance had bowed to Hephaestion supposing him to be the king and was distressed when this was called to her attention, Alexander had said: "Never mind, mother. For actually he too is Alexander."

As a matter of fact, Hephaestion enjoyed so much power and freedom of speech based on this friendship that when Olympias was estranged from him because of jealousy and wrote sharp criticisms and threats against him in her letters, he felt strong enough to answer her reproachfully and ended his letter as follows: "Stop quarrelling with us and do not be angry or menacing. If you persist, we shall not be much disturbed. You know that Alexander means more to us than anything."

As part of the preparations for the funeral, the king ordered the cities of the region to contribute to its splendour in accordance with their ability, and he proclaimed to all the peoples of Asia that they should sedulously quench what the Persians call the sacred fire, until such time as the funeral should be ended. This was the custom of the Persians when their kings died, and people thought that the order was an ill omen, and that heaven was foretelling the king's own death. There were also at this time other strange signs pointing to the same event, as we shall relate shortly, after we have finished the account of the funeral.

115. Each of the generals and Friends tried to meet the king's desires and made likenesses of Hephaestion in ivory and gold and other materials which men hold in high regard. Alexander collected artisans and an army of workmen and tore down the city wall to a distance often furlongs. He collected the baked tiles and levelled off the place which was to receive the pyre, and then constructed this square in shape, each side being a furlong in length. He divided up the area into thirty compartments and laying out the roofs upon the trunks of palm trees wrought the whole structure into a square shape. Then he decorated all the exterior walls. Upon the foundation course were golden prows of quinqueremes in close order, two hundred and forty in all. Upon the catheads each carried two kneeling archers four cubits in height, and (on the deck) armed male figures five cubits high, while the intervening spaces were occupied by red banners fashioned out of felt. Above these, on the second level, stood torches fifteen cubits high with golden wreaths about their handles. At their flaming ends perched eagles with outspread wings looking downward, while about their bases were serpents looking up at the eagles. On the third level were carved a multitude of wild animals being pursued by hunters. The fourth level carried a centauromachy rendered in gold, while the fifth showed lions and bulls alternating, also in gold. The next higher level was covered with Macedonian and Persian arms, testifying to the prowess of the one people and to the defeats of the other. On top of all stood Sirens, hollowed out and able to conceal within them persons who sang a lament in mourning for the dead. The total height of the pyre was more than one hundred and thirty cubits.

All of the generals and the soldiers and the envoys and even the natives rivalled one another in contributing to the magnificence of the funeral, so, it is said, that the total expense came to over twelve thousand talents. In keeping with this magnificence and the other special marks of honour at the funeral, Alexander ended by decreeing that all should sacrifice to Hephaestion as god coadjutor. As a matter of fact, it happened just at this time that Philip, one of the Friends, came bearing a response from Ammon that Hephaestion should be worshipped as a god. Alexander was delighted that the god had ratified his own opinion, was himself the first to perform the sacrifice, and entertained everybody handsomely. The sacrifice consisted of ten thousand victims of all sorts.

Concerning the omens that appeared to Alexander and concerning his death (116-118).

116. After the funeral, the king turned to amusements and festivals, but just when it seemed that he was at the peak of his power and good fortune, Fate cut off the time allowed him by nature to remain alive. Straightway heaven also began to foretell his death, and many strange portents and signs occurred.

Once when the king was being rubbed with oil and the royal robe and diadem were lying on a chair, one of the natives who was kept in bonds was spontaneously freed from his fetters, escaped his guards' notice, and passed through the doors of the palace with no one hindering. He went to the royal chair, put on the royal dress and bound his head with the diadem, then seated himself upon the chair and remained quiet. As soon as the king learned of this, he was terrified at the odd event, but walked to the chair and without showing his agitation asked the man quietly who he was and what he meant by doing this. When he made no reply whatsoever, Alexander referred the portent to the seers for interpretation and put the man to death in accordance with their judgement, hoping that the trouble which was forecast by his act might light upon the man's own head. He picked up the clothing and sacrificed to the gods who avert evil, but continued to be seriously troubled. He recalled the prediction of the Chaldaeans and was angry with the philosophers who had persuaded him to enter Babylon. He was impressed anew with the skill of the Chaldaeans and their insight, and generally railed at those who used specious reasoning to argue away the power of Fate.

A little while later heaven sent him a second portent about his kingship. He had conceived the desire to see the great swamp of Babylonia and set sail with his friends in a number of skiffs. For some days his boat became separated from the others and he was lost and alone, fearing that he might never get out alive. As his craft was proceeding through a narrow channel where the reeds grew thickly and overhung the water, his diadem was caught and lifted from his head by one of them and then dropped into the swamp. One of the oarsmen swam after it and, wishing to return it safely, placed it on his head and so swam back to the boat.

After three days and nights of wandering, Alexander found his way to safety just as he had again put on his diadem when this seemed beyond hope. Again he turned to the soothsayers for the meaning of all this.

117. They bade him sacrifice to the gods on a grand scale and with all speed, but he was then called away by Medius, the Thessalian, one of his Friends, to take part in a comus. There he drank much unmixed wine in commemoration of the death of Heracles, and finally, filling a huge beaker, downed it at a gulp. Instantly he shrieked aloud as if smitten by a violent blow and was conducted by his Friends, who led him by the hand back to his apartments. His chamberlains put him to bed and attended him closely, but the pain increased and the physicians were summoned. No one was able to do anything helpful and Alexander continued in great discomfort and acute suffering. When he, at length, despaired of life, he took off his ring and handed it to Perdiccas. His Friends asked: "To whom do you leave the kingdom?" and he replied: "To the strongest." He added, and these were his last words, that all of his leading Friends would stage a vast contest in honour of his funeral. This was how he died after a reign of twelve years and seven months. He accomplished greater deeds than any, not only of the kings who had lived before him but also of those who were to come later down to our time.

Since some historians disagree about the death of Alexander, and state that this occurred in consequence of a draught of poison, it seems necessary for us to mention their account also.

118. They say that Antipater, who had been left by Alexander as viceroy in Europe, was at variance with the king's mother Olympias. At first he did not take her seriously because Alexander did not heed her complaints against him, but later, as their enmity kept growing and the king showed an anxiety to gratify his mother in everything out of piety, Antipater gave many indications of his disaffection. This was bad enough, but the murder of Parmenion and Philotas struck terror into Antipater as into all of Alexander's Friends, so by the hand of his own son, who was the king's wine-pourer, he administered poison to the king. After Alexander's death, Antipater held the supreme authority in Europe and then his son Casander took over the kingdom, so that many historians did not dare write about the drug. Casander, however, is plainly disclosed by his own actions as a bitter enemy to Alexander's policies. He murdered Olympias and threw out her body without burial, and with great enthusiasm restored Thebes, which had been destroyed by Alexander.

After the king's death Sisyngambris, Dareius's mother, mourned his passing and her own bereavement, and coming to the limit of her life she refrained from food and died on the fifth day, abandoning life painfully but not ingloriously.

Having reached the death of Alexander as we proposed to do at the beginning of the book, we shall try to narrate the actions of the Successors in the books which follow.

BOOK XVIII

The disturbance and contention in the armies after the death
of Alexander (1-2).

1. Pythagoras of Samos [323] and some others of the ancient philosophers declared that the souls of men are immortal, and also that, in accordance with this doctrine, souls foreknow the future at that moment in death when they are departing from the bodies. It seems that the poet Homer agreed with them, for he introduced Hector at the time of his decease foretelling to Achilles the death that was soon to come upon him. Likewise it is reported that even in more recent times what we have described above has happened in the case of many men as they were coming to the end of life, and in particular on the occasion of the death of Alexander of Macedon. When he was quitting life in Babylon and at his last breath was asked by his friends to whom he was leaving the kingdom, he said, "To the best man; for I foresee that a great combat of my friends will be my funeral games." [323] AThis actually happened; for after the death of Alexander the foremost of his friends quarrelled about the primacy and joined in many great combats.

This Book, which contains an account of the deeds accomplished by these friends, will make the philosopher's saying clear to the interested reader. The preceding Book included all the acts of Alexander up to his death; this one, containing the deeds of those who succeeded to his kingdom, ends with the year before the tyranny of Agathocles and includes seven years.

2. When Cephisodorus was archon at Athens, the Romans elected Lucius Frurius and Decius Junius consuls. During this term the throne was vacant, since Alexander the king had died without issue, and great contention arose over the leadership. The phalanx of the infantry was supporting Arrhidaeus, son of Philip, for the kingship, although he was afflicted with an incurable mental illness. [323] The most influential of the Friends and of the Bodyguard, however, taking counsel together and joining to themselves the corps of horsemen known as the Companions, at first decided to take up arms against the phalanx and sent to the infantry envoys chosen from men of rank, of whom the most prominent was Meleager, demanding submission to their orders. Meleager, however, when he came to the men of the phalanx, made no mention of his mission but, on the contrary, praised them for the resolution that they had taken and sharpened their anger against their opponents. As a result the Macedonians made Meleager their leader and advanced under arms against those who disagreed with them; but when the Bodyguard had withdrawn from Babylon and was making ready for war, the men most inclined toward conciliation persuaded the parties to come to an agreement. Straightway they made Arrhidaeus, son of Philip, their king and changed his name to Philip; Perdiccas, to whom the king had given his ring as he died, they made regent of the kingdom; and they decided that the most important of the Friends and of the Bodyguard should take over the satrapies and obey the king and Perdiccas.

How Perdiccas assumed the regency; and the division of the
satrapies (3-4).

3. After Perdiccas had assumed the supreme command and had taken counsel with the chief men, [323] he gave Egypt to Ptolemy, son of Lagus, Syria to Laomedon of Mitylenê, Cilicia to Philotas, and Media Maior to Pithon. To Eumenes he gave Paphlagonia and Cappadocia and all the lands bordering on these, which Alexander did not invade, having been prevented from doing so by the urgency of his affairs when he was finishing the war with Darius; to Antigonus he gave Pamphylia, Lycia, and what is called Great Phrygia; then to Asander, Caria; to Menander, Lydia; and to Leonnatus, Hellespontine Phrygia. These satrapies, then, were distributed in that way. In Europe, Thrace and the neighbouring tribes near the Pontic sea were given to Lysimachus, and Macedonia and the adjacent peoples were assigned to Antipater. Perdiccas, however, decided not to disturb the remaining satrapies in Asia but to permit them to remain under the same rulers; likewise he determined that Taxiles and Porus should be masters of their own kingdoms as Alexander himself had arranged. To Pithon he gave the satrapy next to Taxiles and the other kings; and the satrapy that lies along the Caucasus, called that of the Paropanisadae, he assigned to Oxyartes the Bactrian, whose daughter Roxanê Alexander had married. He gave Arachosia and Cedrosia to Sibyrtius, Aria and Dranginê to Stasanor of Soli, Bactrianê and Sogdianê to Philip, Parthia and Hyrcania to Phratapherenes, Persia to Peucestes, Carmania to Tlepolemus, Media to Atropates, Babylonia to Archon, and Mesopotamia to Arcesilaüs. He placed Seleucus in command of the cavalry of the Companions, a most distinguished office; for Hephaestion commanded them first, Perdiccas after him, and third the above-named Seleucus. The transportation of the body of the deceased king and the preparation of the vehicle that was to carry the body to Ammon they assigned to Arrhidaeus.

Revolt of the Greeks in the upper satrapies,1 and the dispatch of Pithon as general against them (4).

4. It happened that Craterus, who was one of the most prominent men, had previously been sent away by Alexander to Cilicia with those men who had been discharged from the army, ten thousand in number. At the same time he had received written instructions which the king had given him for execution; nevertheless, after the death of Alexander, it seemed best to the successors not to carry out these plans. For when Perdiccas found in the memoranda of the king orders for the completion of the pyre of Hephaestion, which required a great deal of money, and also for the other designs of Alexander, which were many and great and called for an unprecedented outlay, he decided that it was inexpedient to carry them out. But that he might not appear to be arbitrarily detracting anything from the glory of Alexander, he laid these matters before the common assembly of the Macedonians for consideration.

The following were the largest and most remarkable items of the memoranda. It was proposed to build a thousand warships, larger than triremes, in Phoenicia, Syria, Cilicia, and Cyprus for the campaign against the Carthaginians and the others who live along the coast of Libya and Iberia and the adjoining coastal region as far as Sicily; to make a road along the coast of Libya as far as the Pillars of Heracles and, as needed by so great an expedition, to construct ports and shipyards at suitable places; to erect six most costly temples, each at an expense of fifteen hundred talents; and, finally, to establish cities and to transplant populations from Asia to Europe and in the opposite direction from Europe to Asia, in order to bring the largest continents to common unity and to friendly kinship by means of intermarriages and family ties. The temples mentioned above were to be built at Delos, Delphi, and Dodona, and in Macedonia a temple to Zeus at Dium, to Artemis Tauropolus at Amphipolis, and to Athena at Cyrnus. Likewise at Ilium in honour of this goddess there was to be built a temple that could never be surpassed by any other. Cp. Strabo, 13. 1.26. A tomb for his father Philip was to be constructed to match the greatest of the pyramids of Egypt, buildings which some persons count among the seven greatest works of man. When these memoranda had been read, the Macedonians, although they applauded the name of Alexander, nevertheless saw that the projects were extravagant and impracticable and decided to carry out none of those that have been mentioned.

Perdiccas first put to death those soldiers who were fomenters of discord and most at enmity with himself, thirty in number. After that he also punished Meleager, who had been a traitor on the occasion of the contention and his mission, using as a pretext a private quarrel and a charge that Meleager was plotting against him. Then, since the Greeks who had been settled in the upper satrapies had revolted and raised an army of considerable size, he sent one of the nobles, Pithon, to fight it out with them.

Description of the situation in Asia, and of the satrapies therein (5-6).

5. Considering the events that are to be narrated, I think it proper first to set forth the causes of the revolt, the situation of Asia as a whole, and the size and characteristics of the satrapies; for by placing before my readers' eyes the topography in general and the distances I shall best make the narrative easy for them to follow.

Now from the Cilician Taurus a continuous range of mountains extends through the whole of Asia as far as the Caucasus and the Eastern Ocean. This range is divided by crests of varying heights, and each part has its proper name. Asia is thus separated into two parts, one sloping to the north, the other to the south. Corresponding to these slopes, the rivers flow in opposite directions. Of those on one side, some enter the Caspian Sea, some the Pontus Euxinus, and some the Northern Ocean. Of the rivers that lie opposite to these, some empty into the ocean that faces India, some into the ocean that is adjacent to this continent, and some flow into what is called the Red Sea. The satrapies likewise are divided, some sloping toward the north, the others toward the south. The first of those that face the north lie along the Tanais River: Sogdianê and Bactrianê; and next to these are Aria, Parthia, and Hyrcania, by which the Hyrcanian Sea, a detached body of water, is surrounded. Next is Media, which embraces many regions with distinctive names and is the greatest of all the satrapies. Armenia, Lycaonia, and Cappadocia, all having a very wintry climate, are next. Bordering on them in a straight line are both Great Phrygia and Hellespontine Phrygia; Lydia and Caria are to the side; above Phrygia and beside it is Pisidia, with Lycia next to it. In the coastal regions of these satrapies are established the cities of the Greeks; to give their names is not necessary for our present purposes. The satrapies that face the north are situated in the way described.

6. Of those satrapies that face the south, the first one along the Caucasus is India, a great and populous kingdom, inhabited by many Indian nations, of which the greatest is that of the Gandaridae, against whom Alexander did not make a campaign because of the multitude of their elephants. The river Ganges, which is the deepest of the region and has a width of thirty stades, separates this land from the neighbouring part of India. Adjacent to this is the rest of India, which Alexander conquered, irrigated by water from the rivers and most conspicuous for its prosperity. Here were the dominions of Porus and Taxiles, together with many other kingdoms, and through it flows the Indus River, from which the country received its name. Next to the Indian satrapy Arachosia was marked off, and Cedrosia and Carmania, and Persia next to them, in which are Susianê and Sittacinê. Next comes Babylonia extending to the Arabian Desert. On the other side, in the direction from which we make the march inland, is Mesopotamia encompassed by two rivers, the Euphrates and the Tigris, to which it owes its name. Next to Mesopotamia are Upper Syria, as it is called, and the countries adjacent thereto along the sea: Cilicia, Pamphylia, and Coelê Syria, which encloses Phoenicia. Along the frontiers of Coelê Syria and along the desert that lies next to it, through which the Nile makes its way and divides Syria and Egypt, the best satrapy of all and one that has great revenues, was set up, Egypt. All these countries are very hot, since the air in the south is different from that which extends to the north. The satrapies, then, that were conquered by Alexander, are situated as described, and were distributed to the most noteworthy men.

How Pithon conquered the Greeks who had rebelled (7).

7. The Greeks who had been settled by Alexander in the upper satrapies, as they were called, although they longed for the Greek customs and manner of life and were cast away in the most distant part of the kingdom, yet submitted while the king was alive through fear; but when he was dead they rose in revolt. After they had taken counsel together and elected Philon the Aenianian as general, they raised a considerable force. They had more than twenty thousand foot soldiers and three thousand horse, all of whom had many times been tried in the contests of war and were distinguished for their courage. When Perdiccas heard of the revolt of the Greeks, he drew by lot from the Macedonians three thousand infantry and eight hundred horsemen. As commander of the whole he selected Pithon, who had been of the Bodyguard of Alexander, a man full of spirit and able to command, and assigned to him the troops that had been drawn. After giving him letters for the satraps, in which it was written that they should furnish Pithon ten thousand footmen and eight thousand horsemen, he sent him against the rebels. Pithon, who was a man of great ambition, gladly accepted the expedition, intending to win the Greeks over through kindness, and, after making his army great through an alliance with them, to work in his own interests and become the ruler of the upper satrapies. Perdiccas, suspecting his design, gave him definite orders to kill all the rebels when he had subdued them, and to distribute the spoils to the soldiers.

Pithon, setting out with the troops that had been given to him and receiving the auxiliaries from the satraps, came upon the rebels with all his forces. Through the agency of a certain Aenianian he corrupted Letodorus, who had been made a commander of three thousand among the rebels, and won a complete victory. For when the battle was begun and the victory was doubtful, the traitor left his allies without warning and withdrew to a certain hill, taking his three thousand men. The rest, believing that these were bent on flight, were thrown into confusion, turned about, and fled. Pithon, being victorious in the battle, sent a herald to the conquered, ordering them to lay down their arms and to return to their several colonies after receiving pledges. When oaths to this effect had been sworn and the Greeks were interspersed among the Macedonians, Pithon was greatly pleased, seeing that the affair was progressing according to his intentions; but the Macedonians, remembering the orders of Perdiccas and having no regard for the oaths that had been sworn, broke faith with the Greeks. Setting upon them unexpectedly and catching them off their guard, they shot them all down with javelins and seized their possessions as plunder. Pithon then, cheated of his hopes, came back with the Macedonians to Perdiccas. This was the state of affairs in Asia.

How the Athenians began what is known as the Lamian War against Antipater (8-9).

8. In Europe the Rhodians drove out their Macedonian garrison and freed their city, and the Athenians began what is called the Lamian War against Antipater. It is necessary to set forth the causes of this war in order that the events that took place in it may be made clearer. A short time before his death, Alexander decided to restore all the exiles in the Greek cities, partly for the sake of gaining fame, and partly wishing to secure many devoted personal followers in each city to counter the revolutionary movements and seditions of the Greeks. Therefore, the Olympic games being at hand, he sent Nicanor of Stageira to Greece, giving him a decree about the restoration, which he ordered him to have proclaimed by the victorious herald to the crowds at the festival. Nicanor carried out his instructions, and the herald received and read the following message: "King Alexander to the exiles from the Greek cities. We have not been the cause of your exile, but, save for those of you who are under a curse, we shall be the cause of your return to your own native cities. We have written to Antipater about this to the end that if any cities are not willing to restore you, he may constrain them." When the herald had announced this, the crowd showed its approval with loud applause; for those at the festival welcomed the favour of the king with cries of joy, and repaid his good deed with praises. All the exiles had come together at the festival, being more than twenty thousand in number.

Now people in general welcomed the restoration of the exiles as a good thing, but the Aetolians and the Athenians took offence at the action and were angry. The reason for this was that the Aetolians had exiled the Oeniadae from their native city and expected the punishment appropriate to their wrong-doing; for the king himself had threatened that no sons of the Oeniadae, but he himself, would punish them. Likewise the Athenians, who had distributed Samos in allotments to their citizens, were by no means willing to abandon that island. Being no match, however, for the forces of the king, they remained quiet for the time being, waiting for a favourable opportunity, which Fortune quickly gave them.

How Leosthenes, having been made general and having assembled an army, defeated Antipater in battle and shut him up in Lamia (9-12).

9. When Alexander died a short time thereafter and left no sons as successors to the kingdom, the Athenians ventured to assert their liberty and to claim the leadership of the Greeks. As a resource for the war they had the sum of money left by Harpalus, the story of which we told in full in the preceding Book, and likewise the mercenaries who, some eight thousand in number, had been dismissed from service by the satraps and were waiting near Taenarum in the

Peloponnesus. They therefore gave secret instructions about these to Leosthenes the Athenian, ordering him at first to enrol them as if acting on his own responsibility without authority from the city, in order that Antipater, regarding Leosthenes with contempt, might be less energetic in his preparations, and the Athenians, on the other hand, might gain leisure and time for preparing some of the things necessary for the war. Accordingly Leosthenes had very quietly hired the troops mentioned above and, contrary to general belief, had secured a considerable number of men ready for action; for these men, who had campaigned throughout Asia for a long time and had taken part in many great conflicts, had become masters of warfare.

Now these things were being done while the death of Alexander was not yet certainly known; but when some came from Babylon who had been eyewitnesses of the king's death, then the popular government openly disclosed its intention of war and sent Leosthenes part of the money of Harpalus and many suits of armour, bidding him no longer act in secret but do openly whatever was advantageous. After Leosthenes had distributed their pay to the mercenaries and had fully armed those who lacked armour, he went to Aetolia to arrange for common action. When the Aetolians listened to him gladly and gave him seven thousand soldiers, he sent to the Locrians and the Phocians and the other neighbouring peoples and urged them to assert their freedom and rid Greece of the Macedonian despotism.

10. In the Assembly at Athens, while the men of property 'were advising that no action be taken and the demagogues were rousing the people and urging them to prosecute the war vigorously, those who preferred war and were accustomed to make their living from paid military service were far superior in numbers. These were the men of whom Philip once said that war was peace and peace was war for them. Straightway, then, the orators gave shape to the wishes of the commons by writing a decree to the effect that the people should assume responsibility for the common freedom of the Greeks and liberate the cities that were subject to garrisons: that they should prepare forty quadriremes and two hundred triremes; that all Athenians up to the age of forty should be enrolled; that three tribes should guard Attica, and that the other seven should be ready for campaigns beyond the frontiers; that envoys should be sent to visit the Greek cities and tell them that formerly the Athenian people, convinced that all Greece was the common fatherland of the Greeks, had fought by sea against those barbarians who had invaded Greece to enslave her, and that now too Athens believed it necessary to risk lives and money and ships in defence of the common safety of the Greeks.

When this decree had been ratified more promptly than was wise, those of the Greeks who were superior in understanding said that the Athenian people had counselled well for glory but had missed what was expedient; for they had left, the mark before the proper time and, with no necessity compelling them, were venturing to meet forces that were great and undefeated, and moreover, although they enjoyed a reputation for excelling in judgement, they had learned nothing even from the well-known misfortunes of the Thebans. Nevertheless, as the ambassadors made the circuit of the cities and roused them for war with their accustomed eloquence, most of the Greeks joined the alliance, some by national groups and some by cities.

11. Of the rest of the Greeks, some were well disposed toward the

Macedonians, others remained neutral. The Aetolians in full force were the first to join the alliance, as has been said, and after them all the Thessalians except those from Pelinnaeum, the Oetaeans except the inhabitants of Heraclea, the Achaeans of Phthiotis except the people of Thebae, the Melians except those of Lamia, then in succession all the Dorians, the Locrians, and the Phocians, also the Aenianians, the Alyzaeans, and the Dolopians, and in addition the Athamanians, the Leucadians, and those of the Molossians who were subject to Aryptaeus. The last named, after making a hollow alliance, later treacherously co-operated with the Macedonians. A few of the Illyrians and of the Thracians joined the alliance because of their hatred of the Macedonians. Next, the Carystians from Euboea undertook a share in the war, and finally, of the peoples of the Peloponnesus, the Argives, the Sicyonians, the Eleans, the Messenians, and those who dwell on Acte. Now those of the Greeks who joined the alliance were as I have listed them.

Athens sent citizen soldiers to Leosthenes as reinforcements, five thousand foot and five hundred horse, and also two thousand mercenaries. These were to go through Boeotia, but it happened that the Boeotians were hostile to the Athenians for some such reason as the following. After Alexander had razed Thebes, he had given the land to the neighbouring Boeotians. They, having portioned out the property of the unfortunate people, were receiving a large income from the land. Therefore, since they knew that the Athenians, if they were successful in the war, would restore both fatherland and fields to the Thebans, they were inclined toward the Macedonians. While the Boeotians were in camp near Plataea, Leosthenes, taking part of his own forces, came into Boeotia. Drawing up his own men along with the Athenians against the inhabitants, he defeated the latter in battle and, after erecting a trophy, hurried back to Thermopylae. For there, where he had spent some time in occupying the passes in advance of the enemy, he intended to meet the Macedonian forces.

12. When Antipater, who had been left by Alexander as general of Europe, heard of the death of the king in Babylon and of the distribution of the satrapies, he sent into Cilicia to Craterus, asking him to come to his aid as soon as possible (for the latter, having been previously dispatched to Cilicia, was going to bring back to Macedonia the Macedonians who had been mustered out of service, being more than ten thousand in number). He also sent to Philotas, who had received Hellespontine Phrygia as his satrapy, asking him likewise for aid and promising to give him one of his own daughters in marriage. As soon, however, as he learned of the movement concerted against him by the Greeks, he left Sippas as general of Macedonia, giving him a sufficient army and bidding him enlist as many men as possible, while he himself, taking thirteen thousand Macedonians and six hundred horsemen (for Macedonia was short of citizen soldiers because of the number of those who had been sent to Asia as replacements for the army), set out from Macedonia to Thessaly, accompanied by the entire fleet which Alexander had sent to convoy a sum of money from the royal treasury to Macedonia, being in all one hundred and ten triremes. At first the Thessalians were allies of Antipater and sent out to him many good horsemen; but later, won over by the Athenians, they rode off to Leosthenes and, arrayed with the Athenians, fought for the liberty of the Greeks. Now that this great force had been added to the Athenians, the Greeks, who far outnumbered the Macedonians, were successful. Antipater was defeated in battle, and subsequently, since he neither dared to engage in battle nor was able to return in safety to Macedonia, he took refuge in Lamia. He kept his troops in this city and strengthened its walls, besides preparing arms, engines, and food, while anxiously waiting for his allies from Asia.

The death of the general Leosthenes, and the funeral oration in his honour (13).

13. Leosthenes, when he had come near Lamia with all his forces, fortified a camp with a deep ditch and a palisade. At first he would draw up his forces, approach the city, and challenge the Macedonians to battle; then, as the latter did not dare risk an encounter, he made daily attacks on the walls with relays of soldiers. As the Macedonians defended themselves stoutly, many of the Greeks who pushed on rashly were killed; for the besieged, since there was a considerable force in the city and an abundance of all sorts of missiles, and the wall, moreover, had been constructed at great expense, easily had the better of the fighting. Leosthenes, giving up hope of capturing the city by storm, shut off all the supplies that were going into it, thinking that he would easily reduce by hunger the forces besieged in the city. He also built a wall and dug a deep, wide ditch, thereby cutting off all escape for the beleaguered troops.

After this the Aetolians all returned to Aetolia, having asked Leosthenes for permission to go home for the present because of some national business. Antipater and his men, however, were nearly exhausted and the city was in danger of being taken because of the anticipated famine, when chance gave the Macedonians an unexpected turn of good fortune. For when Antipater made an attack on the men who were digging the moat and a struggle ensued, Leosthenes, coming to aid his men, was struck on the head by a stone and at once fell and was carried to camp in a swoon. On the third day he died and was buried with the honours of a hero because of the glory he had gained in war. The Athenian people caused the funeral oration to be delivered by Hypereides, foremost of the orators in eloquence and in hostility toward the Macedonians; for at that time Demosthenes, the chief of the orators of Athens, was in exile, convicted of having taken some of the money of Harpalus. In place of Leosthenes, Antiphilus was made general, a man outstanding in military genius and courage.

Such was the situation in Europe.

How the satrapies were taken over by those to whom they had been assigned (14).

The cavalry battle of the Greeks against Leonnatus, and the victory of the Greeks (14-15).

14. In Asia, of those who had shared in the division of the satrapies, Ptolemy took over Egypt without difficulty and was treating the inhabitants with kindness. Finding eight thousand talents in the treasury, he began to collect mercenaries and to form an army. A multitude of friends also gathered about him on account of his fairness. With Antipater he carried on a diplomatic correspondence that led to a treaty of co-operation, since he well knew that Perdiccas would attempt to wrest from him the satrapy of Egypt.

Lysimachus, when he entered the Thracian region and found that the king of that country, Seuthes, had taken the field with twenty thousand infantry and eight thousand cavalry, was not frightened by the size of the army, and although he had in all no more than four thousand foot soldiers and only two thousand horsemen, he joined battle with the barbarians. In truth he was superior to them in the quality of his troops though inferior in numbers, and the battle was a stubborn one. After losing many of his own men but killing many times that number, he returned to his camp with but a doubtful claim to victory. Therefore for the moment the forces of both sides withdrew from the locality and busied themselves with greater preparations for the final conflict.

As for Leonnatus, when Hecataeus came to him as envoy and begged him to aid Antipater and the Macedonians with all speed, he promised to give military aid. He crossed over, therefore, into Europe and went on to Macedonia, where he enlisted many additional Macedonian soldiers. When he had gathered together in all more than twenty thousand infantry and fifteen hundred cavalry, he led them through Thessaly against the enemy.

How Antipater took over the army of Leonnatus after the latter had been slain in battle (15).

How Cleitus, the Macedonian admiral, defeated the Greeks in two naval battles (15).

15. The Greeks, [322] giving up the siege and burning their camp, sent away to the town of Melitia the camp followers, who were useless in a pitched battle, and the baggage train, while they themselves went forward with light equipment and ready for battle in order to engage the forces of Leonnatus before Antipater joined him and both armies came together in one place. They had in all twenty-two thousand foot soldiers, for all the Aetolians had previously departed to their own country and not a few of the other Greeks had at that time scattered to their native states. More than thirty-five hundred horsemen took part in the campaign, two thousand being Thessalians exceptional for their courage. In these especially the Greeks trusted for victory. Now when a fierce cavalry battle had gone on for some time and the Thessalians, thanks to their valour, were gaining the upper hand, Leonnatus, after fighting brilliantly even when cut off in a swampy place, was worsted at every point. Stricken with many wounds and at the point of death, he was taken up by his followers and carried, already dead, to the baggage train. The cavalry battle having been gloriously won by the Greeks under the command of Menon the Thessalian, the Macedonian phalanx, for fear of the cavalry, at once withdrew from the plain to the difficult terrain above and gained safety for themselves by the strength of the position. When the Thessalian cavalry, which continued to attack, was unable to accomplish anything because of the rough ground, the Greeks, who had set up a trophy and gained control of the dead, left the field of battle.

On the next day, however, when Antipater came up with his troops and joined the defeated, all the Macedonians united in a single camp, and Antipater took command of the whole. He decided to avoid fighting for the present and, in view of the fact that the enemy were superior in cavalry, determined not to retreat through the plain. Instead, by going through the rough country and seizing in advance any points of vantage, he made good his retreat from the region. Antiphilus, the Greek commander, having defeated the Macedonians in a glorious battle, played a waiting game, remaining in Thessaly and watching for the enemy to move.

The affairs of the Greeks were thus in thriving condition, but since the Macedonians had command of the sea, the Athenians made ready other ships in addition to those which they already had, so that there were in all one hundred and seventy. Cleitus was in command of the Macedonian fleet, which numbered two hundred and forty. Engaging with the Athenian admiral Evetion he defeated him in two naval battles and destroyed a large number of the ships of the enemy near the islands that are called the Echinades.

How Perdiccas, after defeating King Ariarathes in a great engagement, took the king and many others captive (16).

How Craterus, going to the aid of Antipater, defeated the Greeks and ended the Lamian War (16-17).

16. While these things were going on, Perdiccas, taking with him King Philip and the royal army, campaigned against Ariarathes, the ruler of Cappadocia. His failure to take orders from the Macedonians had been overlooked by Alexander, owing to the struggle with Darius and its distractions, and he had enjoyed a very long respite as king of Cappadocia. As a result he had amassed a great sum of money from the revenues and had formed a large body of native troops and mercenaries. He was thus ready to enter the lists against Perdiccas in defence of his kingdom with thirty thousand infantry and fifteen thousand cavalry. Perdiccas joined battle with him, and, defeating him in the conflict, slew men to the number of four thousand and took captive more than five thousand, among them Ariarathes himself. [322] Now the king and all his relatives Perdiccas tortured and impaled; but to the conquered people he granted immunity, and after putting in order the affairs of Cappadocia, he gave the satrapy to Eumenes of Cardia, just as it had originally been assigned.

About the same time Craterus also departed from Cilicia and arrived in Macedonia to reinforce Antipater and to make good the defeats that the Macedonians had suffered. He brought with him six thousand foot soldiers from those who had crossed into Asia with Alexander and four thousand from those who had been enlisted on the march, one thousand Persian bowmen and slingers, and fifteen hundred horsemen. Entering Thessaly and freely yielding the chief command to Antipater, he shared a camp with him beside the Peneius River. Including those who had been under Leonnatus, there were gathered together in all more than forty thousand heavy armed infantry, three thousand bowmen and slingers, and five thousand cavalry.

17. The Greeks who were encamped against them at this time were far inferior in numbers; for many of them, despising the enemy because of their former good fortune, had gone away to their own cities to look after their private affairs. Since many soldiers were absent from duty for this reason, there remained in camp only twenty-five thousand foot soldiers and thirty-five hundred cavalry. They placed their chief hope of victory in the latter, because the men were brave and the ground was level.

At last Antipater began to draw up his forces each day and challenge the Greeks to battle. For a while these waited for their men to return from their cities, but since time was pressing, they were forced to come out and stake all. They drew up their line, placing the cavalry in front of the phalanx of infantry, since they were eager to decide the battle by means of this arm. When the cavalry had met in battle and the Thessalian horsemen were getting the advantage because of their valour, Antipater led out his own phalanx and, rushing upon the infantry of the enemy, began to make great slaughter. The

Greeks, since they were not able to withstand the weight and number of the enemy, immediately withdrew to the rough ground, carefully keeping their ranks. Thus they occupied the higher ground and easily repulsed the Macedonians thanks to their possession of the superior position. Although the Greek cavalry had gained the advantage, as soon as the horsemen learned of the withdrawal of the infantry, they at once retired toward them. Then, after such a combat as I have described, the battle was broken off, as the scales of victory swung in favour of the Macedonians. More than five hundred of the Greeks were killed in the battle, and one hundred and thirty of the Macedonians.

On the next day Menon and Antiphilus, the leaders of the Greeks, came together and took counsel whether they should wait for the allies from the cities and then, when they were in position to fight on equal terms, seek a final decision, or, yielding to the present situation, should send envoys to seek a truce. They decided to dispatch heralds to treat for peace. These carried out their orders, but Antipater answered that the cities must negotiate separately, for he would by no means make a mass settlement. Since the Greeks refused to agree to peace terms city by city, Antipater and Craterus began to lay siege to the cities in Thessaly and to take them by storm, since the Greeks could not send aid to them. When the cities were thus badly frightened and each on its own account began to send envoys about a settlement, Antipater came to terms with all of them, granting them peace on easy terms. This resulted in a movement among the cities to secure their safety separately, and all quickly obtained terms of peace; but those who were most hostile to the Macedonians, the Aetolians and the Athenians, deserted by their allies, took counsel about the war with their own generals.

The dealings of Antipater with the Athenians and the other Greeks (18).

18. Antipater, after he had destroyed the alliance of the Greeks by this device, led all his forces against the Athenians. The people, bereft of the aid of their allies, were in great perplexity. All turned to Demades and shouted that he must be sent as envoy to Antipater to sue for peace; but, although he was called on by name to give advice, he did not respond. He had been convicted three times of introducing illegal decrees, and for this reason he had been deprived of his rights as a citizen and was prevented by the laws from advising; yet, on being restored to full rights by the people, he was at once sent as envoy along with Phocion and some others. When Antipater had heard what they had to say, he made answer that he would end the war against the Athenians on no other condition than that they surrender all their interests to his discretion; for, after they had shut Antipater up in Lamia, they had made that same reply to him when he had sent envoys about peace. The people, not being in position to fight, were forced to grant to Antipater such discretion and complete authority over the city. He dealt humanely with them and permitted them to retain their city and their possessions and everything else; but he changed the government from a democracy, ordering that political power should depend on a census of wealth, and that those possessing more than two thousand drachmas should be in control of the government and of the elections. He removed from the body of citizens all who possessed less than this amount on the ground that they were disturbers of the peace and warmongers, offering to those who wished it a place for settlement in Thrace. These men, more than twelve thousand in number, were removed from their fatherland; but those who possessed the stated rating, being about nine thousand, were designated as masters of both city and territory and conducted the government according to the constitution of Solon. All were permitted to keep their property un-curtailed. They were, however, forced to receive a garrison with Menyllus as its commander, its purpose being to prevent anyone from undertaking changes in the government. The decision in regard to Samos was referred to the kings. The Athenians, being thus humanely treated beyond their hopes, secured peace; and, since henceforth they conducted their public affairs without disturbance and enjoyed the produce of the land unmolested, they quickly made great progress in wealth.

When Antipater had returned to Macedonia, he presented Craterus with suitable honours and gifts, giving him also his eldest daughter Phila in marriage, and helped him to prepare for his return to Asia. He likewise showed moderation in dealing with the other Greek cities, both reducing their citizen bodies and wisely reforming them, for which he received eulogies and crowns. Perdiccas, restoring their city and territory to the Samians, brought them back to their fatherland after they had been exiles for forty-three years.

Concerning the achievements of Ptolemy in the war about Cyrenê (19-21).

19. Now that we have narrated all the actions in the course of the Lamian War, we shall turn to the war that took place in Cyrenê, so that the course of our history may not deviate too much from the chronological sequence. It is necessary to go back a little in time in order to make clearer the several series of events. When Harpalus had fled from Asia and sailed to Crete with the mercenaries, as we have shown in the preceding Book, Thibron, who was regarded as one of his friends, treacherously murdered him and gained control of the money and the soldiers, who numbered seven thousand. He also took possession of the ships, embarked the soldiers on them, and sailed to the land of the Cyrenians. He had taken with him the exiles from Cyrenê and was using them as instructors in his project because of their knowledge of the locality. When the Cyrenians opposed him and a battle took place, Thibron was victorious, killing many and taking captive no small number. By gaining control of the harbour and besieging and frightening the Cyrenians, he forced them to come to terms, and to agree to give him five hundred talents of silver and to contribute half of their chariots to aid his campaign. He sent envoys, moreover, to the other cities, asking them to make an alliance on the ground that he was going to subdue the neighbouring parts of Libya. He also treated as spoil the property of the traders that had been captured in the port and gave it to his soldiers as plunder, calling forth their zeal for the war.

20. Although the affairs of Thibron were thus prospering, Fortune by a sudden shift humbled him through the following circumstances. One of his leaders, a Cretan by birth, whose name was Mnasicles, a man of experience in warfare, quarrelled with him, having complained about the distribution of the booty; and being contentious by nature and bold, he deserted to the Cyrenians. Moreover, he made many complaints against Thibron, charging him with cruelty and faithlessness, and persuaded the Cyrenians to break the treaty and make a bid for liberty. So when sixty talents only had been paid, and the rest of the money was not being given, Thibron denounced the rebels, seized any Cyrenians who were in the port, some eighty in number, and then, leading his forces directly against the city, laid siege to it. As he was unable to accomplish anything, he returned to the port. Since the people of Barca and of Hesperis were allied with Thibron, the Cyrenians, leaving part of their forces in Cyrenê, took the field with part and plundered the land of their neighbours. When these called on Thibron to give them aid, he led all his soldiers against the alliance. At this the Cretan, concluding that the harbour was deserted, persuaded those who were left in Cyrenê to attack it. When they obeyed him, he at once made an attack on the port, leading the way himself; and, easily gaining control of it thanks to the absence of Thibron, he restored to the merchants what was left of the cargoes and zealously guarded the port.

At first Thibron was disheartened, since he had lost an advantageous position and the equipment of his soldiers; but afterwards, when he had recovered his spirits and captured by siege the city called Tauchira, his hopes again rose. It chanced, however, that in a short time he again encountered great misfortunes. The crews of his ships, having been deprived of their harbour and running short of food, were accustomed each day to go out into the country and gather supplies there; but the Libyans ambushed them as they were wandering about the country, killed many, and took no small number captive. Those who escaped the danger fled to the ships and sailed away for the allied cities, but when a great storm overtook them, most of the ships were swallowed by the sea; of the rest, some were cast ashore in Cyprus, others in Egypt.

21. Nevertheless Thibron, although he had encountered such a misfortune, did not give up the campaign. Selecting those of his friends who were fitted for the task, he sent them to the Peloponnesus to hire those of the mercenaries who were waiting about near Taenarum; for many of the discharged mercenaries were still roaming about seeking paymasters; and at that time there were more than twenty-five hundred of them at Taenarum. His messengers engaged these and set out upon the voyage to Cyrenê. But before their arrival the Cyrenians, encouraged by their successes, joined battle and defeated Thibron, killing many of his soldiers. When, on account of these failures, Thibron was now ready to abandon the operations against Cyrenê, he unexpectedly regained courage; for as soon as the soldiers from Taenarum put into port and a large force was added to his strength, he became confident in spirit. As the Cyrenians saw the tide of war again rising, they summoned the allied forces from the neighbouring Libyans and from the Carthaginians, and having collected in all thirty thousand men including their citizen soldiers, they made ready to reach a final decision in battle. When a great battle had taken place, Thibron, having won the victory with great slaughter of the enemy, was overjoyed, believing that he would at once capture the adjacent cities; but the Cyrenians, whose commanders had all been killed in the battle, elected the Cretan Mnasieles general along with others. Thibron, elated by the victory, laid siege to the port of the Cyrenians and made daily assaults on Cyrenê. As the war continued a long time, the Cyrenians, who were in want of food, quarrelled among themselves; and the commons, gaining the upper hand, drove out the rich, who, bereft of their fatherland, fled, some to Thibron, others to Egypt. The latter, after persuading Ptolemy to restore them, returned bringing with them a considerable force, both infantry and naval, with Ophelias as general. The exiles who were with Thibron, hearing of the approach of these men and attempting to go over to them secretly at night, were detected and cut down to a man. The democratic leaders of Cyrenê, becoming alarmed at the return of the exiles, made terms with Thibron and prepared to fight against Ophelias in common with him; but Ophelias, after defeating and capturing Thibron and also gaining control of the cities, delivered both the cities and the country over to Ptolemy the king. Thus the Cyrenians and the surrounding cities lost their freedom and were annexed to the kingdom of Ptolemy.

How Perdiccas invaded Pisidia and enslaved the Larandians, and, besieging the Isaurians, forced them to kill themselves and burn their city (22).

22. Now when Perdiccas and King Philip had defeated Ariarathes and delivered his satrapy to Eumenes, they departed from Cappadocia. Having arrived in Pisidia, they determined to lay waste two cities, that of the Larandians and that of the Isaurians; for while Alexander was still alive these cities had put to death Balacrus the son of Nicanor, who had been appointed general and satrap. Now the city of the Larandians they took by assault, and after killing the men of fighting age and enslaving the rest of the population, razed it to the ground. The city of the Isaurians, however, was strongly fortified and large and moreover was filled with stout warriors; so when they had besieged it vigorously for two days and had lost many of their own men, they withdrew; for the inhabitants, who were well provided with missiles and other things needed for withstanding a siege and were enduring the dreadful ordeal with desperate courage in their hearts, were readily giving their lives to preserve their freedom. On the third day, when many had been slain and the walls had few defenders because of the lack of men, the citizens performed a heroic and memorable deed. Seeing that the punishment that hung over them could not be averted, and not having a force that would be adequate to stave the enemy off, they determined not to surrender the city and place their fate in the hands of the enemy, since in that way their punishment combined with outrage was certain; but at night all with one accord, seeking the noble kind of death, shut up their children, wives, and parents in their houses, and set the houses on fire, choosing by means of the fire a common death and burial. As the blaze suddenly flared aloft, the Isaurians cast into the fire their goods and everything that could be of use to the victors; Perdiccas and his officers, astounded at what was taking place, stationed their troops about the city and made a strong effort to break into the city on all sides. When now the inhabitants defended themselves from the walls and struck down many of the Macedonians, Perdiccas was even more astonished and sought the reason why men who had given their homes and all else to the flames should be so intent upon defending the walls. Finally Perdiccas and the Macedonians withdrew from the city, and the Isaurians, throwing themselves into the fire, found burial in their homes along with their families. When the night was over, Perdiccas gave the city to his soldiers for booty. They, when they had put out the fire, found an abundance of silver and gold, as was natural in a city that had been prosperous for a great many years.

23. After the destruction of the cities there came two women to marry Perdiccas, Nicaea, the daughter of Antipater, for whose hand Perdiccas himself had sued, and Cleopatra, who was Alexander's own sister, daughter of Philip son of Amyntas. Perdiccas had formerly planned to work in harmony with Antipater, and for this reason he had pressed his suit when his position was not yet firmly established; but when he had gained control of the royal armies and the guardianship of the kings, he changed his calculations. For since he was now

reaching out for the kingship, he was bent upon marrying Cleopatra, believing that he could use her to persuade the Macedonians to help him gain the supreme power. But not wishing as yet to reveal his design, he married Nicaea for the time, so that he might not render Antipater hostile to his own undertakings. Presently, however, Antigonus learned his intentions, and since Antigonus was a friend of Antipater and, moreover, the most energetic of the commanders, Perdiccas decided to put him out of the way. So, by bringing false slanders and unjust charges against him, he clearly revealed his intention of destroying him. Antigonus, however, who excelled in keenness and daring, outwardly let it be known that he wished to defend himself against these charges, but secretly he made arrangements for flight and, with his personal friends and his son Demetrius, boarded the Athenian ships undetected at night. And having been brought to Europe in these, he travelled on to join forces with Antipater.

The invasion of Aetolia by Antipater and Craterus (24-25).

24. At this time Antipater and Craterus had taken the field against the Aetolians with thirty thousand infantry and twenty-five hundred cavalry; for of those who had taken part in the Lamian War, the Aetolians alone were left unconquered. Although such great forces were sent against them, they were in no panic-stricken mood, but gathering together all who were in the full vigour of manhood to the number of ten thousand, they retired to the mountainous and rough places, in which they placed the children, the women, and the old, together with the greater part of their wealth. The cities that could not be defended they abandoned, but those that were particularly strong they secured, each with a considerable garrison, and boldly awaited the approach of the enemy.

25. Antipater and Craterus, coming into Aetolia and finding that the cities which were easy to capture were deserted, moved against the men who had withdrawn into the difficult regions. At first, then, the Macedonians, violently attacking positions that were strongly fortified and in broken terrain, lost many of their soldiers; for the hardihood of the Aetolians joined with the strength of their positions easily turned back men who rushed headlong into dangers beyond reach of succour. Afterward, however, when Craterus had built shelters and was forcing the enemy to stay through the winter and to hold out in regions that were covered with snow and lacking in food, the Anatolians were brought into the greatest dangers; for they had either to come down from their mountains and fight against forces numbering many times their own and against famous generals, or to remain and be utterly destroyed by want and cold. When they were already giving up hope of salvation, relief from their troubles appeared of its own accord, just as if one of the gods had been moved to pity by their high courage. For Antigonus, he who had fled from Asia, joined Antipater and told him the whole plot of Perdiccas, and that Perdiccas, after marrying Cleopatra, would come at once with his army to Macedonia as king and deprive Antipater of the supreme command. Craterus and Antipater, dumbfounded by the unexpected news, met in council with their commanders. When the situation had been presented for deliberation, it was unanimously decided to make peace with the Aetolians on whatever terms were possible, to transport the armies with all speed to Asia, to assign the command of Asia to Craterus and that of Europe to Antipater, and also to send an embassy to Ptolemy to discuss concerted action, since he was utterly hostile to Perdiccas but friendly to them, and he in common with them was an object of the plot. Therefore they at once made a treaty with the Aetolians, firmly resolved to conquer them later and to move them all, men, women, and children, to the most distant desert of Asia. When they had recorded a decree embodying these plans, they made preparations for the campaign.

Perdiccas, gathering his friends and generals, referred to them for consideration the question whether it was better to march against Macedonia or first to take the field against Ptolemy. When all favoured defeating Ptolemy first in order that there might be no obstacle in the way of their Macedonian campaign, he sent Eumenes off with a considerable army, ordering him to watch over the region of the Hellespont and prevent a crossing; and he himself, taking the army from Pisidia, proceeded against Egypt.

Such, then, were the events of this year.

The transfer of the body of Alexander from Babylon to Alexandria, and description of the magnificent funeral chariot (26-28).

26. When Philocles was archon in Athens, Gaius Sulpicius and Gaius Aelius were elected consuls in Rome. In this year Arrhidaeus, who had been placed in charge of bringing home the body of Alexander, having completed the vehicle on which the royal body was to be carried, was making preparations for the journey. Since the structure that had been made ready, being worthy of the glory of Alexander, not only surpassed all others in cost; it had been constructed at the expense of many talents, but was also famous for the excellence of its workmanship, I believe that it is well to describe it.

First they prepared a coffin of the proper size for the body, made of hammered gold, and the space about the body they filled with spices such as could make the body sweet smelling and incorruptible. Upon this chest there had been placed a cover of gold, matching it to a nicety, and fitting about its upper rim. Over this was laid a magnificent purple robe embroidered with gold, beside which they placed the arms of the deceased, wishing the design of the whole to be in harmony with his accomplishments. Then they set up next to it the covered carriage that was to carry it. At the top of the carriage was built a vault of gold, eight cubits wide and twelve long, covered with overlapping scales set with precious stones. Beneath the roof all along the work was a rectangular cornice of gold, from which projected heads of goat-stags in high relief. Gold rings two palms broad were suspended from these, and through the rings there ran a festive garland beautifully decorated in bright colours of all kinds. At the ends there were tassels of network suspending large bells, so that any who were approaching heard the sound from a great distance. On each corner of the vault on each side was a golden figure of Victory holding a trophy. The colonnade that supported the vault was of gold with Ionic capitals. Within the colonnade was a golden net, made of cords the thickness of a finger, which carried four long painted: tablets, their ends adjoining, each equal in length to a side of the colonnade.

27. On the first of these tablets was a chariot ornamented with work in relief, and sitting in it was Alexander holding a very splendid sceptre in his hands. About the king were groups of armed attendants, one of Macedonians, a second of Persians of the bodyguard, and armed soldiers in front of them. The second tablet showed the elephants arrayed for war who followed the bodyguard. They carried Indian mahouts in front with Macedonians fully armed in their regular equipment behind them. The third tablet showed troops of cavalry as if in formation for battle; and the fourth, ships made ready for naval combat. Beside the entrance to the chamber there were golden lions with eyes turned toward those who would enter. There was a golden acanthus stretching little by little up the centre of each column from below to the capital. Above the chamber in the middle of the top under the open sky there was a purple banner blazoned with a golden olive wreath of great size, and when the sun cast upon it its rays, it sent forth such a bright and vibrant gleam that from a great distance it appeared like a flash of lightning.

The body of the chariot beneath the covered chamber had two axles upon which turned four Persian wheels, the naves and spokes of which were gilded, but the part that bore upon the ground was of iron. The projecting parts of the axle were made of gold in the form of lion heads, each holding a spear in its teeth. Along the middle of their length the axles had a bearing ingeniously fitted to the middle of the chamber in such a way that, thanks to it, the chamber could remain undisturbed by shocks from rough places. There were four poles, and to each of them were fastened four teams with four mules harnessed in each team, so that in all there were sixty-four mules, selected for their strength and size. Each of them was crowned with a gilded crown, each had a golden bell hanging by either cheek, and about their necks were collars set with precious stones.

28. In this way the carriage was constructed and ornamented, and it appeared more magnificent when seen than when described. Because of its widespread fame it drew together many spectators; for from every city into which it came the whole people went forth to meet it and again escorted it on its way out, not becoming sated with the pleasure of beholding it. To correspond to this magnificence, it was accompanied by a crowd of road menders and mechanics, and also by soldiers sent to escort it.

When Arrhidaeus had spent nearly two years in making ready this work, he brought the body of the king from Babylon to Egypt. Ptolemy, moreover, doing honour to Alexander, went to meet it with an army as far as Syria, and, receiving the body, deemed it worthy of the greatest consideration. He decided for the present not to send it to Ammon, but to entomb it in the city that had been founded by Alexander himself, which lacked little of being the most renowned of the cities of the inhabited earth. There he prepared a precinct worthy of the glory of Alexander in size and construction. Entombing him in this and honouring him with sacrifices such as are paid to demigods and with magnificent games, he won fair requital not only from men but also from the gods. For men, because of his graciousness and nobility of heart, came together eagerly from all sides to Alexandria and gladly enrolled for the campaign, although the army of the kings was about to fight against that of Ptolemy; and, even though the risks were manifest and great, yet all of them willingly took upon themselves at their personal risk the preservation of Ptolemy's safety. The gods also saved him unexpectedly from the greatest dangers on account of his courage and his honest treatment of all his friends.

How Eumenes, defeating Craterus in an engagement, killed him and Neoptolemus in the battle (29-32).

29. For Perdiccas, viewing with suspicion Ptolemy's increase in power, decided that he himself and the kings would make a campaign against Egypt with most of the army, but Eumenes he sent to the Hellespont to prevent

Antipater and Craterus from crossing into Asia, giving him a suitable force. He also sent with him enough of the commanders of note, of whom the most prominent were his brother Alcetas and Neoptolemus; and he ordered them to obey Eumenes in all things because of his skill as general and his firm loyalty. Eumenes, with the forces that had been given him, went to the Hellespont; and there, having already prepared a large body of cavalry from his own satrapy, he marshalled his army, which had previously been deficient in that branch.

When Craterus and Antipater had brought their forces across from Europe, Neoptolemus, who was jealous of Eumenes and had a considerable number of Macedonians in his following, secretly entered into negotiations with Antipater, came to an agreement with him, and plotted against Eumenes. On being discovered and forced to fight, he himself was in danger of being killed, and he lost almost all his forces; for Eumenes, after he had won the victory and had killed many, won over the remaining soldiers and increased his own power, not only by the victory but also by having acquired a large number of stout Macedonians. Neoptolemus, who had saved himself from the battle with three hundred horsemen, rode off with them to Antipater. A council of war was held, and it was decided to divide the forces into two parts. Antipater was to take one part and set out for Cilicia to fight against Perdiccas, and Craterus with the other part was to attack Eumenes and, after defeating him, to join Antipater. In this way, when they had combined their forces and had added Ptolemy to the alliance, they might be able to overmatch the royal armies.

30. As soon as Eumenes heard that the enemy was advancing upon him, he collected his forces, particularly his cavalry, from all sides. Since he could not equal the Macedonian phalanx with his foot soldiers, he made ready a noteworthy corps of horsemen, by means of whom he hoped to defeat those opposed to him. When the forces were near each other, Craterus summoned the whole army to an assembly and spurred them to battle with suitable words, saying that, if the soldiers were victorious in the battle, he would give them all the baggage of the enemy to plunder. Now that all had become eager for battle, he drew up the army, taking command of the right wing himself, and giving the command of the left to Neoptolemus. He had in all twenty thousand foot soldiers, chiefly Macedonians famed for their courage, on whom in particular he placed his hopes of victory, and more than two thousand horsemen as auxiliaries. Eumenes had twenty thousand foot soldiers, men of every race, and five thousand cavalry, by whom he had resolved to decide the encounter.

After both leaders had disposed their cavalry on the wings and had ridden far in advance of the line of infantry, Craterus was the first to charge upon the enemy with his picked troops, and he fought admirably; but his horse stumbled, and he fell to the ground, where he was trampled under foot and ended his life ingloriously, unrecognised in the confusion and dense array of the charge. By his death the enemy were so encouraged that they rushed upon the mass from every side, and great slaughter ensued. The right wing, crushed in this way, was compelled to flee to the phalanx of the foot soldiers, overwhelmingly defeated.

31. On the left wing, however, where Neoptolemus was arrayed against Eumenes himself, there occurred a great display of ambitious rivalry as the leaders rushed full at each other. For as soon as they recognized one another by their horses and other insignia, they engaged each other in close combat; and they made the victory depend upon the duel between themselves. After the opening exchange of sword strokes they engaged in a strange and most extraordinary duel; for, carried away by their anger and their mutual hatred, they let the reins fall from their left hands and grappled each other. As a result of this, their horses were carried out from under them by their own momentum, and the men themselves fell to the ground. Although it was difficult for either of them to get up because of the suddenness and force of the fall, especially as their armour hampered their bodies, Eumenes rose up first and forestalled Neoptolemus by striking him in the back of the knee. Since the gash proved to be severe and his legs gave way, the stricken man lay disabled, prevented by his wound from rising to his feet. Yet his courage overcame the weakness of his body, and, resting on his knees, he wounded his opponent with three blows on the arm and the thighs. As none of these blows was fatal and the wounds were still fresh, Eumenes struck Neoptolemus in the neck with a second blow and slew him.

32. Meanwhile the rest of the cavalry had joined battle and were making great slaughter. So, while some fell and others were wounded, the battle at first was even, but afterwards, when they became aware of the death of Neoptolemus and of the rout of the other wing, all made off and fled for refuge to the phalanx of their infantry as to a strong fortress. Eumenes, satisfied with his advantage and master of the bodies of both generals, recalled his soldiers with the sound of the trumpet. After he had set up a trophy and buried the dead, he sent to the phalanx of the vanquished, inviting them to unite with him and giving permission to them severally to withdraw to whatever places they wished. When the Macedonians had accepted the terms of surrender and had pledged their faith by oaths, they received permission to go for food to certain villages that lay near. They deceived Eumenes; for when they had recovered their strength and collected supplies, they set out at night and went off secretly to join Antipater. Eumenes attempted to punish the faithlessness of these men who had broken their oath and to follow at the heels of the phalanx; but, owing to the hardihood of those who were retreating and to the weakness caused by his wounds, he was unable to accomplish anything and gave up the pursuit. So by winning a notable victory and by slaying two mighty leaders, Eumenes gained great glory.

How Perdiccas invaded Egypt and was destroyed by his friends (33-36).

33. As soon as Antipater had received and enrolled those who escaped from the rout, he went on to Cilicia, making haste to go to the aid of Ptolemy. Perdiccas, on learning of the victory of Eumenes, became much more confident in regard to the Egyptian campaign; and when he approached the Nile, he camped not far from the city of Pelusium. When he undertook to clear out an old canal, and the river broke out violently and destroyed his work, many of his friends deserted him and went over to Ptolemy. Perdiccas, indeed, was a man of blood, one who usurped the authority of the other commanders and, in general, wished to rule all by force; but Ptolemy, on the contrary, was generous and fair and granted to all the commanders the right to speak frankly. What is more, he had secured all the most important points in Egypt with garrisons of considerable size, which had been well equipped with every kind of missile as well as with everything else. This explains why he had, as a rule, the advantage in his undertakings, since he had many persons who were well disposed to him and ready to undergo danger gladly for his sake. Still Perdiccas, in an effort to correct his deficiencies, called the commanders together, and by gifts to some, by great promises to others, and by friendly intercourse with all, won them over to his service and inspired them to meet the coming dangers. After warning them to be ready to break camp, he set out with his army at evening, disclosing to no one the point to which he intended to go. After marching all night at top speed he made camp beside the Nile near a certain fortified post that is called the Fort of Camels. As day was dawning, he began to send the army across, the elephants in the van, then following them the shield-bearers and the ladder-carriers, and the others whom he expected to use in the attack on the fort. Last of all came the bravest of the cavalry, whom he planned to send against the troops of Ptolemy if they happened to appear.

34. When they were halfway over, Ptolemy and his troops did appear, coming at a run to the defence of the post. Although these got the start of the attackers, threw themselves into the fort, and made their arrival known by blasts of the trumpet and by shouts, the troops of Perdiccas were not frightened, but boldly assaulted the fortifications. At once the shield-bearers set up the scaling ladders and began to mount them, while the elephant-borne troops were tearing the palisades to pieces and throwing down the parapets. Ptolemy, however, who had the best soldiers near himself and wished to encourage the other commanders and friends to face the dangers, taking his long spear and posting himself on the top of the outwork, put out the eyes of the leading elephant, since he occupied a higher position, and wounded its Indian mahout. Then, with utter contempt of the danger, striking and disabling those who were coming up the ladders, he sent them rolling down, in their armour, into the river. Following his example, his friends fought boldly and made the beast next in line entirely useless by shooting down the Indian who was directing it. The battle for the wall lasted a long time, as the troops of Perdiccas, attacking in relays, bent every effort to take the stronghold by storm, while many heroic conflicts were occasioned by the personal prowess of Ptolemy and by his exhortations to his friends to display both their loyalty and their courage. Many men were killed on both sides, such was the surpassing rivalry of the commanders, the soldiers of Ptolemy having the advantage of the higher ground and those of Perdiccas being superior in number. Finally, when both sides had spent the whole day in the engagement, Perdiccas gave up the siege and went back to his own camp.

Breaking camp at night, he marched secretly and came to the place that lies opposite Memphis, where it happens that the Nile is divided and makes an island large enough to hold with safety a camp of a very large army. To this island he began to transfer his men, the soldiers crossing with difficulty because of the depth of the river; for the water, which came up to the chins of those who were crossing, buffeted their bodies, especially as they were impeded by their equipment.

35. Perdiccas, seeing the difficulty caused by the current, in an effort to break the downward rush of the river, placed the elephants in line on the left, thus mitigating the strength of the current, and placed on the right side the horsemen, through whose agency he kept catching the men who were being carried away by the river and bringing them safe to the other side. A peculiar and surprising thing took place during the crossing of this army, namely, that after the first men had crossed in safety, those who tried to cross afterwards fell into great danger. For although there was no visible cause, the river became much deeper, and, their bodies being totally submerged, they would one and all become completely helpless. When they sought the cause of this rise, the truth could not be found by reasoning. Some said that that somewhere upstream a canal that had been closed had been opened and, joining with the river, had made the ford deeper; others said that rain falling in the regions above had increased the volume of the Nile. It was, however, neither of these things, but what happened was that the first crossing of the ford had been freer from danger because the sand at the crossing had been undisturbed, but in the course of the other crossings by the horses and elephants which had gone over before and then by the infantry, the sand, trodden by their feet and set in motion by the current, was carried down stream, and the place of crossing being hollowed out in this way, the ford became deeper in the middle of the river.

Since the rest of his army was unable to cross the river for this reason, Perdiccas was in great difficulty; and, as those who had crossed were not strong enough to fight the enemy and those on the nearer bank were not able to go to the aid of their fellows, he ordered all to come back again. When all were thus forced to cross the stream, those who knew how to swim well and were strongest of body succeeded in swimming ac ross the Nile with great distress, after throwing away a good deal of their equipment; but of the rest, because of their lack of skill some were swallowed by the river, and others were cast up on the shore toward the enemy, but most of them, carried along for some time, were devoured by the animals in the river.

How Pithon was chosen guardian of the kings and
Arrhidaeus with him, and Antipater afterwards (36-39).

36. Since more than two thousand men were lost, among them some of the prominent commanders, the rank and file of the army became ill disposed toward Perdiccas. Ptolemy, however, burned the bodies of those who were cast up on his side of the river and, having bestowed on them a proper funeral, sent the bones to the relatives and friends of the dead.

These things having been done, the Macedonians with Perdiccas became much more exasperated with him, but they turned with favour toward Ptolemy. When night had come, the encampment was filled with lamentations and mourning, so many men having been senselessly lost without a blow from an enemy, and of these no fewer than a thousand having become food for beasts. Therefore many of the commanders joined together and accused Perdiccas, and all the phalanx of the infantry, now alienated from him, made clear their own hostility with threatening shouts. Consequently about a hundred of the commanders were the first to revolt from him, of whom the most illustrious was Pithon, who had suppressed the rebellious Greeks, a man second to none of the Companions of Alexander in courage and reputation; next, some also of the cavalry conspired together and went to the tent of Perdiccas, where they fell on him in a body and stabbed him to death.

On the next day when there was an assembly of the soldiers, Ptolemy came, greeted the Macedonians, and spoke in defence of his own attitude; and as their supplies had run short, he provided at his own expense grain in abundance for the armies and filled the camp with the other needful things. Although he gained great applause and was in position to assume the guardianship of the kings through the favour of the rank and file, he did not grasp at this, but rather, since he owed a debt of gratitude to Pithon and Arrhidaeus, he used his influence to give them the supreme command. For the Macedonians, when the question of the primacy was raised in the assembly and Ptolemy advocated this course, without a dissenting voice enthusiastically elected as guardians of the kings and regents Pithon and that Arrhidaeus who had conveyed the body of Alexander. So Perdiccas, after he had ruled for three years, lost both his command and his life in the manner described.

37. Immediately after the death of Perdiccas there came men announcing that, in a battle fought near Cappadocia, Eumenes had been victorious and Craterus and Neoptolemus had been defeated and killed. If this had become known two days before the death of Perdiccas, no one would have dared raise a hand against him because of his great good fortune. Now, however, the Macedonians, on learning the news about Eumenes, passed sentence of death upon him and upon fifty of the chief men of his following, among whom was Alcetas, the brother of Perdiccas. They also slew the most faithful of Perdiccas' friends and his sister Atalante, the wife of Attalus, the man who had received command of the fleet.

After the murder of Perdiccas, Attalus, who had the command of the fleet, was waiting at Pelusium; but when he learned of the murder of his wife and of Perdiccas, he set sail and came to Tyre with the fleet. The commandant of the garrison of that city, Archelaüs, who was a Macedonian by race, welcomed Attalus and surrendered the city to him and also the funds that had been given him by Perdiccas for safe-keeping and had now been honourably repaid, being in amount eight hundred talents. Attalus remained in Tyre, receiving those of the friends of Perdiccas who escaped in safety from the camp before Memphis.

38. After the departure of Antipater for Asia, the Aetolians, in accordance with their compact with Perdiccas, made a campaign into Thessaly for the purpose of diverting Antipater. They had twelve thousand foot soldiers and four hundred horsemen, and their general was Alexander, an Aetolian. On the march they besieged the city of the Amphissian Locrians, overran their country, and captured some: of the neighbouring towns. They defeated Antipater's general Polycles in battle, killing him and no small number of his soldiers. Some of those who were taken captive they sold, others they released on receiving ransoms. Invading Thessaly next, they persuaded most of the Thessalians to join them in the war against Antipater, and a force was quickly gathered, numbering in all twenty-five thousand infantry and fifteen hundred cavalry. While they were gaining the cities, however, the Acarnanians, who were hostile to the Aetolians, invaded Aetolia, where they began to plunder the land and to besiege the cities. When the Aetolians learned that their own country was in danger, they left the other troops in Thessaly, putting Menon of Pharsalus in command, while they themselves with the citizen soldiers went swiftly into Aetolia and, by striking fear into the Acarnanians, freed their native cities from danger. While, however, they were engaged in these matters, Polyperchon, who had been left in Macedonia as general, came into Thessaly with a considerable army and, by defeating the enemy in a battle in which he killed the general Menon and cut most of his army to pieces, recovered Thessaly.

How Antipater, being set up as supreme commander, divided the satrapies anew at Triparadeisus in Syria (39).

39. In Asia Arrhidaeus and Pithon, the guardians of the kings, setting out from the Nile with the kings and the army, came to Triparadeisus in upper Syria. There Eurydicê, the queen, was interfering in many matters and working against the efforts of the guardians. Pithon and his colleague were distressed by this, and when they saw that the Macedonians were paying more and more attention to her commands, they summoned a meeting of the assembly and resigned the guardianship; whereupon the Macedonians elected Antipater guardian with full power. When Antipater arrived at Triparadeisus a few days later, he found Eurydicê stirring up discord and turning the Macedonians away from him. There was great disorder in the army; but a general assembly was called together, and Antipater put an end to the tumult by addressing the crowd, and by thoroughly frightening Eurydicê he persuaded her to keep quiet.

Thereafter he distributed the satrapies anew. To Ptolemy he assigned what was already his, for it was impossible to displace him, since he seemed to be holding Egypt by virtue of his own prowess as if it were a prize of war. He gave Syria to Laomedon of Mitylenê and Cilicia to Philoxenus. Of the upper satrapies Mesopotamia and Arbelitis were given to Amphimachus, Babylonia to Seleucus, Susianê to Antigenes because he had been foremost in making the attack on Perdiccas, Persia to Peucestes, Carmania to Tlepolemus, Media to Pithon, Parthia to Philip, Aria and Drangene to Stasander of Cyprus, Bactrianê and Sogdianê to Stasanor of Soli, who was from that same island. He added Paropanisadae to the domain of Oxyartes, father of Alexander's wife Roxanê, and the part of India bordering on Paropanisadae to Pithon son of Agenor. Of the two neighbouring kingdoms, the one along the Indus River was assigned to Porus and that along the Hydaspes to Taxiles, for it was not possible to remove these kings without employing a royal army and an outstanding general. Of the satrapies that face the north, Cappadocia was assigned to Nicanor, Great Phrygia and Lycia to Antigonus as before, Caria to Asander, Lydia to Cleitus, and Hellespontine Phrygia to Arrhidaeus. As general of the royal army he appointed Antigonus, assigning him the task of finishing the war against Eumenes and Alcetas; but he attached his own son Cassander to Antigonus as chiliarch so that the latter might not be able to pursue his own ambitions undetected. Antipater himself with the kings and his own army went on into Macedonia in order to restore the kings to their native land.

How Antigonus, having been made general by Antipater, defeated Eumenes (40-41).

40. Antigonus, who had been designated general [320] of Asia for the purpose of finishing the war with Eumenes, collected his troops from their winter quarters. After making preparations for the battle, he set out against Eumenes, who was still in Cappadocia. Now one of Eumenes' distinguished commanders named Perdiccas had deserted him and was encamped at a distance of three days' march with the soldiers who had joined him in the mutiny, three thousand infantry and five hundred cavalry. Eumenes, accordingly, sent against him Phoenix of Tenedos with four thousand picked foot-soldiers and a thousand horsemen. After a forced night march Phoenix fell unexpectedly on the deserters at about the second watch of the night, and catching them asleep, took Perdiccas alive and secured control of his troops. Eumenes put to death the leaders who had been most responsible for the desertion, but by distributing the common soldiers among the other troops and treating them with kindness, he secured them as loyal supporters.

Thereafter Antigonus sent messages to a certain Apollonides, who commanded the cavalry in the army of Eumenes, and by great promises secretly persuaded him to become a traitor and to desert during the battle. While Eumenes was encamped in a plain of Cappadocia well suited for cavalry fighting, Antigonus fell upon him with all his men and took the foothills that commanded the plain. Antigonus at that time had more than ten thousand foot soldiers, half of whom were Macedonians admirable for their hardihood, two thousand mounted troops, and thirty elephants; while Eumenes commanded not less than twenty thousand infantry and five thousand cavalry. When the battle became hot and Apollonides with his cavalry unexpectedly deserted his own side, Antigonus won the day and slew about eight thousand of the enemy. He also became master of the entire supply train, so that Eumenes' soldiers were both dismayed by the, defeat and despondent at the loss of their supplies.

41. After this Eumenes undertook to escape into Armenia and to bring over to his alliance some of the inhabitants of that land; but as he was being overtaken and saw that his soldiers were going over to Antigonus, he occupied a stronghold called Nora. This fortress was very small with a circuit of not more than two stades, but of wonderful strength, for its buildings had been constructed close together on the top of a lofty crag, and it had been marvellously fortified, partly by nature, partly by the work of men's hands. Furthermore, it contained a stock of grain, firewood, and salt, ample to supply for many years all the needs of those who took refuge there. Eumenes was accompanied in his flight by those of his friends who were exceptionally loyal and had determined to die along with him if it came to the worst straits. In all, counting both cavalry and infantry, there were about six hundred souls.

Now that Antigonus had taken over the army that had been with Eumenes, had become master of Eumenes' satrapies together with their revenues, and had seized a great sum of money besides, he aspired to greater things; for there was no longer any commander in all Asia who had an army strong enough to compete with him for supremacy. Therefore, although maintaining for the time being a pretence of being well disposed toward Antipater, he had decided that, as soon as he had made his own position secure, he would no longer take orders either from the kings or from Antipater. Accordingly he first surrounded those who had fled to the stronghold with double walls, ditches, and amazing palisades; but then he parleyed with Eumenes, renewed the former friendship, and tried to persuade him to cast his lot with him. Eumenes, however, being well aware that Fortune changes quickly, insisted upon greater concessions than his existing circumstances justified; in fact, he thought that he ought to be given back the satrapies that had been originally assigned to him and be cleared of all the charges, but Antigonus referred these matters to Antipater, and then, after placing a sufficient guard about the fortress, he set out to meet those commanders of the enemy who survived and had troops, namely Alcetas, who was brother of Perdiccas, and Attalus, who commanded the whole fleet.

About Eumenes, and the strange changes of fortune that befell him (42).

42. Eumenes later sent envoys to Antipater to discuss the terms of surrender. Their leader was Hieronymus, who has written the history of the Successors. Eumenes himself, who had experienced many and various changes in the circumstances of his life, was not cast down in spirit, since he knew well that Fortune makes sudden changes in both directions. He saw, on the one hand, that the kings of the Macedonians held an empty pretence of royalty, and on the other, that many men of lofty ambitions were succeeding to the positions of command, and that each of them wished to act in his own interests. He hoped, therefore, as truly happened, that many would have need of him because of his judgement and his experience in warfare, and even more because of his unusual steadfastness to any pledge.

Seeing that the horses, unable to exercise themselves because of the rough and confined space, would become unfit for use in mounted battle, Eumenes devised a certain strange and extraordinary exercise for them. Attaching their heads by ropes to beams or pegs and lifting them two or three double palms, he forced them to rest their weight upon their hind feet with their forefeet just clearing the ground. At once each horse, in an effort to find footing for its forefeet, began to struggle with its whole body and with its legs, all its members sharing in the exertion. At such activity sweat poured freely from the body and thus kept the animals in top condition through their excessive labours. He gave the same rations to all the soldiers, sharing in their simple food himself; and by his unchanging affability he gained great goodwill for himself and secured harmony among all his fellow refugees. Such was the situation of Eumenes and of those who had fled to the rock with him.

How Ptolemy added Phoenicia and Coelê Syria to his domains (43).

43. As for Egypt, Ptolemy, after he had unexpectedly rid himself of Perdiccas and the royal forces, was holding that land as if it were a prize of war. Seeing that Phoenicia and Coelê Syria, as it was called, were conveniently situated for an offensive against Egypt, he set about in earnest to become master of those regions. Accordingly he dispatched an adequate army with Nicanor as general, a man selected from among his friends. The latter marched into Syria, took the satrap Laomedon captive, and subdued the whole land. After he had likewise secured the allegiance of the cities of Phoenicia and placed garrisons in them, he returned to Egypt, having made a short and effective campaign.

How Antigonus defeated Alcetas in a noteworthy engagement (44-47).

44. When Apollodorus was archon at Athens, [319] the Romans elected Quintus Popillius and Quintus Poplius to the consulship. During their term Antigonus, who had defeated Eumenes, decided to make war against Alcetas and Attalus; for these two remained from the friends and household of Perdiccas, noteworthy generals with soldiers enough to make a bid for power. Therefore Antigonus set out with all his forces from Cappadocia and pushed on toward Pisidia, where Alcetas and his army were staying. Making a forced march that strained the endurance of his men to the utmost, he traversed two thousand five hundred stades in seven days and the same number of nights, reaching Cretopolis, as it is called. He escaped the notice of the enemy because of the rapidity of his march, and drawing close to them while they were still ignorant of his coming, he stole a march on them by occupying certain rugged ridges. As soon as Alcetas learned that the enemy was at hand, he drew up his phalanx at top speed and with a mounted force attacked the troops that were holding the ridge, trying with all his might to get the best of them by force and hurl them from the hill. A stubborn battle was waged and many fell on both sides; then Antigonus led six thousand horsemen in a violent charge against the phalanx of the enemy in order to cut Alcetas' line of retreat to it. When this manoeuvre had been successfully completed, the forces on the ridge, who were far superior in number and also had an advantage from the difficulty of the terrain, routed the attackers. Alcetas, whose retreat to the infantry had been cut off and who was caught in a trap by the superior numbers of the enemy, faced imminent destruction. Therefore now that survival itself was difficult, he abandoned many of his men and hardly escaped to the phalanx of the footmen.

45. Antigonus, however, led his elephants and his whole army down from a higher position and struck panic into his opponents, who were far inferior to him in number; for they were in all sixteen thousand foot and nine hundred horse, while Antigonus, in addition to the elephants, had more than forty thousand foot soldiers and above seven thousand horsemen. The elephants were now attacking the army of Alcetas from the front, and at the same time the horsemen because of superior numbers were pouring about them on all sides, while a force of infantry, which far outnumbered them and also surpassed them in valour, was holding a position above them. At this, tumult and panic began to grip Alcetas' soldiers; and because of the great rapidity and force of the attack, he was unable to draw up the phalanx properly. The rout was complete. Attalus, Docimus, Polemon, and many of the more important officers were taken captive; but Alcetas, accompanied by his own guards and attendants, escaped with his Pisidian allies to a city of Pisidia called Termessus. Antigonus obtained the surrender of all the rest by negotiation and enrolled them in his own ranks; by his kind treatment of them he brought no small addition to his forces. The Pisidians, however, who numbered six thousand and were of outstanding prowess, bade Alcetas be of good courage, promising that they would in no way fail him; for they were exceedingly well disposed to him for the following reasons.

46. Since Alcetas had had no supporters in Asia after the death of Perdiccas, he had decided to show kindness to the Pisidians, thinking that he would thus secure as allies men who were warlike and who possessed a country difficult to invade and well supplied with strongholds. For this reason during the campaigns he honoured them exceedingly above all the allies and distributed to them spoils from the hostile territory, assigning them half the booty. By employing the most friendly language in his conversation with them, by each day inviting the most important of them in turn to his table at banquets, and finally by honouring many of them with gifts of considerable value, he secured them as loyal supporters. Therefore even at this time Alcetas placed his hopes upon them, and they did not disappoint his hopes. For when Antigonus encamped near Termessus with all his army and demanded Alcetas, and even when the older men advised that he be surrendered, the younger, forming a compact group in opposition to their parents, voted to meet every danger in the interest of his safety.

The older men at first tried to persuade the younger not to permit their native land to become the spoil of war for the sake of a single Macedonian; but when they saw that the young men's determination was not to be shaken, after taking counsel in secret, they sent an embassy to Antigonus by night, promising to surrender Alcetas either alive or dead. They asked him to attack the city for a number of days and, drawing the defenders forward by light skirmishing, to withdraw as if in flight. They said that, when this had happened and the young men were engaged in the battle at a distance from the city, they would seize a suitable occasion for their own undertaking. Antigonus, prevailed on by them, shifted his camp a long way from the city, and by skirmishing with the young men kept drawing them into battle outside the city. When the older men saw that Alcetas had been left alone, selecting the most trustworthy of the slaves and those of the citizens in the prime of life who were not working in his behalf, they made their attempt while the young men were still away. They could not, it is true, take him alive, for he laid hands on himself first in order not to come into the power of his enemies while still living; but his body, laid on a bier and covered with a coarse cloak, they carried out through the gates and delivered to Antigonus without attracting the attention of the skirmishers.

47. By thus delivering their state from danger by their own devices, they averted the war, but they could not escape the disaffection of the younger men; for as soon as these on their return from the fighting heard what had happened, they became enraged at their kinsfolk on account of their own excessive devotion to Alcetas. At first they gained possession of part of the town and voted to set the buildings on fire and then, rushing from the town under arms and keeping to the mountains, to plunder the country that was subject to Antigonus; later, however, they changed their minds and refrained from burning the city, but they devoted themselves to brigandage and guerrilla warfare, ravaging much of the hostile territory. As for Antigonus, he took the body of Alcetas and maltreated it for three days; then, as the corpse began to decay, he threw it out unburied and departed from Pisidia. The young men of Termessus, still preserving their goodwill for the victim, recovered the body and honoured it with splendid obsequies. Thus kindness in its very nature possesses the peculiar power of a love charm in behalf of benefactors, preserving unchanged men's goodwill toward them. Be that as it may, Antigonus set out from Pisidia and marched toward Phrygia with all his forces. When he had come to Cretopolis, Aristodemus of Miletus met him with the news that Antipater had died, and that the supreme command and the guardianship of the kings had fallen to Polyperchon the Macedonian. Being delighted at what had happened, he was carried away by hope and made up his mind to maintain a firm grip upon the government of Asia and to yield the rule of that continent to no one.

This was the situation in regard to Antigonus.

The death of Antipater, and the taking over of the royal army by Polyperchon (48-49).

48. As to Macedonia, after Antipater had been stricken by a rather serious illness, which old age was tending to make fatal, the Athenians sent Demades as envoy to Antipater, a man who had the reputation of serving the city well in relation to Macedonia. They requested Antipater that he, as had been agreed from the beginning, remove the garrison from Munychia. Antipater at first had been well disposed to Demades, but after the death of Perdiccas certain letters were found in the royal archives in which Demades invited Perdiccas to cross over swiftly into Europe against Antipater. At this Antipater was alienated from him and kept his enmity hidden. Therefore when Demades in accordance with the instructions given him by the people demanded the fulfilment of the promise and indulged rather freely in threats about the garrison, Antipater gave him no answer but delivered Demades himself and his son Demeas, who had accompanied his father as an envoy, to those ministers who were in charge of punishments. They were taken away to a common prison and put to death for the reasons mentioned above.

Antipater, who was already at the point of death, appointed as guardian of the kings and supreme commander, Polyperchon, who was almost the oldest of those who had campaigned with Alexander and was held in honour by the Macedonians. Antipater also made his own son Cassander chiliarch and second in authority. The position and rank of chiliarch had first been brought to fame and honour by the Persian kings, and afterwards under Alexander it gained great power and glory at the time when he became an admirer of this and all other Persian customs. For this reason Antipater, following the same course, appointed his son Cassander, since he was young, to the office of chiliarch.

49. Cassander, however, did not approve of the arrangement made by his father, regarding it as outrageous that one not related by blood should succeed to the command of his father, and this while there was a son who was capable of directing public affairs and who had already given sufficient proof of his ability and courage. First going with his friends into the country where he had plenty of opportunity and leisure, he talked to them about the supreme command; then, taking them apart one by one, he kept urging them privately to join him in establishing his dominion, and having won them by great promises, he made them ready for the joint enterprise. He also sent envoys in secret to Ptolemy, renewing their friendship and urging him to join the alliance and to send a fleet as soon as possible from Phoenicia to the Hellespont. In like manner he sent messengers to the other commanders and cities to urge them to ally themselves with him. He himself, however, by making arrangements for a hunt to last many days, avoided suspicion of complicity in the revolt. After Polyperchon had assumed the guardianship of the kings and had consulted with his friends, with their approval he summoned Olympias, asking her to assume the care of Alexander's son, who was still a child, and to live in Macedonia with regal dignity. It so happened that some time before this Olympias had fled to Epirus as an exile because of her quarrel with Antipater.

This was the state of affairs in Macedonia.

How Antigonus, encouraged by the death of Antipater and by his own accomplishments, became a competitor for the throne (50-52).

50. In Asia, as soon as the death of Antipater was noised abroad, there was a first stirring of revolution, since each of those in power undertook to work for his own ends. Antigonus, who was foremost of these, had already won a victory over Eumenes in Cappadocia and had taken over his army, and he had also completely defeated Alcetas and Attalus in Pisidia and had annexed their troops. Moreover, he had been chosen supreme commander of Asia by Antipater, and at the same time he had been appointed general of a great army, for which reasons he was filled with pride and haughtiness. Already hopefully aspiring to the supreme power, he decided to take orders neither from the kings nor from their guardians; for he took it for granted that he himself, since he had a better army, would gain possession of the treasures of all Asia, there being no one able to stand against him. For at that time he had sixty thousand foot-soldiers, ten thousand horsemen, and thirty elephants; and in addition to these he expected to make ready other forces also if there should be need, since Asia could provide pay without end for the mercenaries he might muster. With these plans in mind he summoned Hieronymus the historian, a friend and; fellow citizen of Eumenes of Cardia, who had taken refuge in the stronghold called Nora. After endeavouring to attach

Hieronymus to himself by great gifts, he sent him as an envoy to Eumenes, urging the latter to forget the battle that had been fought against him in Cappadocia, to become his friend and ally, to receive gifts many times the value of what he had formerly possessed and a greater satrapy, and in general to be the first of Antigonus' friends and his partner in the whole undertaking. Antigonus also at once called a council of his friends and, after he had made them acquainted with his design for gaining imperial power, assigned satrapies to some of the more important friends and military commands to others; and by holding up great expectations to all of them, he filled them with enthusiasm for his undertakings. Indeed he had in mind to go through Asia, remove the existing satraps, and reorganise the positions of command in favour of his friends.

51. While Antigonus was engaged in these matters, Arrhidaeus, the satrap of Hellespontine Phrygia, discovering his plan, decided to provide for the safety of his own satrapy and also to secure the most considerable cities by means of garrisons. As the city of the Cyziceni was strategically most important and very large, he set out against it with an infantry force consisting of more than ten thousand mercenaries, a thousand Macedonians, and five hundred Persian bowmen and slingers. He had also eight hundred horsemen, all kinds of missiles, catapults both for bolts and for stones, and all the other equipment proper for storming a city. After falling suddenly upon the city and intercepting a great multitude in the outlying territory, he applied himself to the siege and, by terrifying those who were in the city, tried to force them to receive a garrison. Since the attack had been unexpected, most of the Cyziceni had been cut off in the country; and with only a few people left in the city, they were completely unprepared for the siege. Deciding, nevertheless, to maintain their freedom, they openly sent envoys to confer with Arrhidaeus about raising the siege, saying that the city would do anything for him except receive a garrison; but secretly, after assembling the young men and selecting the slaves who were suitable for the purpose, they armed them and manned the wall with defenders. When Arrhidaeus insisted that the city admit a garrison, the envoys said that they wished to consult the people in regard to this. As the satrap agreed, they obtained a truce, and during that day and the following night they improved their preparations for withstanding the siege. Arrhidaeus, outwitted, missed his opportunity and was balked of his expected success; for since the Cyziceni possessed a city that was strong and very easy to defend from attacks by land thanks to its being a peninsula, and since they controlled the sea, they easily warded off the enemy. Moreover, they sent for soldiers from Byzantium and for missiles and whatever else was of use for withstanding the attack. When the people of Byzantium supplied all this quickly and willingly, the Cyziceni became confident and set themselves courageously against the danger. They also launched ships of war at once and, coasting along the shore, recovered and brought back those who were in the country. Soon they had plenty of soldiers, and after killing many of the besieging force, they rid themselves of the siege. Thus Arrhidaeus, outgeneralled by the Cyziceni, returned to his own satrapy without accomplishing anything.

52. Antigonus happened to be tarrying in Celaenae when he learned that Cyzicus was being besieged. Deciding to get possession of the endangered city in view of his forthcoming undertakings, he selected the best from all his army, twenty thousand infantry and three thousand cavalry. Taking these he set out in haste to aid the Cyziceni. He was a little too late, but he made his goodwill toward the city manifest, even though failing to gain his entire object. He sent envoys to Arrhidaeus, bringing against him these charges: first, that he had dared to besiege a Greek city that was an ally and not guilty of any offence; and second, that he clearly intended rebellion and was converting his satrapy into a private domain. Finally, he ordered him to retire from his satrapy and, retaining a single city as a residence, to remain quiet. Arrhidaeus, however, after listening to the envoys and censuring the arrogance of their words, refused to retire from his satrapy, and said that in occupying the cities with garrisons he was making the first move in his war to a finish with Antigonus. In accordance with this decision, after making the cities secure, he sent away a part of his army and a general in command of it. He ordered the latter to get in touch with Eumenes, relieve the fortress from siege, and when he had freed Eumenes from danger, make him an ally. Antigonus, who was anxious to retaliate upon Arrhidaeus, sent a force to carry on the war against him, but he himself with a sufficient army set out for Lydia, from which province he wished to expel the satrap, Cleitus. The latter, foreseeing the attack, secured the more important cities with garrisons, but he himself went by ship to Macedonia to reveal to the kings and to Polyperchon the bold revolt of Antigonus and to beg for aid. Antigonus took Ephesus at the first assault with the aid of certain confederates within the city. After this, when Aeschylus of Rhodes sailed to Ephesus conveying from Cilicia in four ships six hundred talents of silver that were being sent to Macedonia for the kings, Antigonus laid hands on it, saying that he needed it to pay his mercenaries. By doing this he made it clear that he had begun to act for his own ends and was opposing the kings. Then after storming Syme, he advanced against the cities in order, taking some of them by force and winning others by persuasion.

How Eumenes unexpectedly gained in power and took over both the guardianship of the kings and the command of the Macedonian army (53).

53. Now that we have finished the activities of Antigonus, we shall turn our narrative to the fortunes of Eumenes. This man experienced great and incredible reversals of fortune, continually having a share in good and evil beyond expectation. For example, in the period preceding these events, when he was fighting for Perdiccas and the kings, he had received as his satrapy Cappadocia and the adjacent regions, in which as master of great armies and much wealth his good fortune became famous. For he defeated in a pitched battle Craterus and Neoptolemus, famous generals in command of the invincible forces of the Macedonians, and killed them on the field. Although he won the reputation of being irresistible, he experienced such a change of fortune that he was defeated by Antigonus in a great battle and compelled to take refuge with a few friends in a certain very small fortress. Shut up there and surrounded by the enemy with a double wall, he had no one to give him aid in his own misfortune. When the siege had lasted a year and hope of safety had been abandoned, there suddenly appeared an unexpected deliverance from his plight; for Antigonus, who was besieging him and bent on destroying him, changed his plan, invited him to share in his own undertakings, and after receiving an oath-bound pledge, freed him from the siege. Thus unexpectedly saved after a considerable time, he stayed for the present in Cappadocia, where he gathered together his former friends and those who had once served under him and were now wandering about the country. Since he was highly esteemed, he quickly found many men to share in his expectations and to enlist for the campaign with him. In the end, within a few days, in addition to the five hundred friends who had been besieged in the fortress with him, he had more than two thousand soldiers who followed him of their own free will. With the aid of Fortune he gained so great an increase in power that he took over the royal armies and championed the kings against those who had boldly tried to end their rule; but we shall relate these events in more detail a little later in their proper place.

The rise of Cassander and his war against Polyperchon, the guardian of the kings, and his cooperation with Antigonus (54-57).

54. Now that we have said enough about affairs throughout Asia, we shall turn our attention to what had taken place at the same time in Europe. Although Cassander had failed to gain the ruling position in Macedonia, he was not dismayed; but he determined to maintain his claim to it, holding it disgraceful that his father's office should be administered by others. Since he perceived that the favour of the Macedonians inclined to Polyperchon, he had further private conversations with the friends in whom he most trusted and sent them to the Hellespont without arousing suspicion; and he himself, by spending several days at leisure in the country and organising a hunt, created the general opinion that he would not try to gain the office. When everything necessary for his departure was ready, however, he set out from Macedonia unobserved. He came to the Chersonese and departing thence arrived at the Hellespont. Sailing across into Asia to Antigonus he begged him to aid him, saying that Ptolemy also had promised to be an ally. Antigonus eagerly received him and promised to co-operate with him actively in every way and to give him at once a force of infantry and a fleet. In doing this he pretended to be aiding him because of his own friendship for Antipater, but in truth it was because he wished Polyperchon to be surrounded by many great distractions, so that he himself might proceed against Asia without danger and secure the supreme power for himself.

55. Meanwhile in Macedonia, Polyperchon, the guardian of the kings, after Cassander had slipped away, foresaw the serious character of the war that was to be fought with him, and since he had made up his mind to do nothing without the advice of his friends, he called together all the commanders and the most important of the other Macedonians. It was clear that Cassander, reinforced by Antigonus, would hold the Greek cities against them, since some of the cities were guarded by his father's garrisons and others, dominated by Antipater's friends and mercenaries, were ruled by oligarchies, and since Cassander would also gain as allies both Ptolemy the ruler of Egypt, and Antigonus, who had already openly rebelled against the kings, and each of them possessed great armies and abundant wealth and was master of many nations and cities of consequence. After the question how to fight against these had been laid before them and many shrewd suggestions had been made about the war, it was decided to free the cities throughout Greece and to overthrow the oligarchies established in them by Antipater; for in this way they would best decrease the influence of Cassander and also win for themselves great glory and many considerable allies. At once, therefore, they called together the envoys who were present from the cities, and after bidding them be of good cheer, they promised to re-establish democratic governments in the cities. As soon as they had drafted the decree that had been adopted, they gave it to the envoys, in order that they might quickly return to their native cities and report to their assemblies the goodwill that the kings and the generals entertained for the Greeks. The edict was in such terms as these:

56. "Inasmuch as it has fallen to the lot of our ancestors to perform many acts of kindness to the Greeks, we wish to maintain their policy and to make evident to all the goodwill which we continue to have for that people. Formerly, indeed, when Alexander departed from among men and the kingship descended upon us, since we believed it necessary to restore all to peace and to the forms of government that Philip our sire established, we sent letters to all the cities in regard to these matters, but whereas it happened that, while we were far away, certain of the Greeks, being ill advised, waged war against the Macedonians and were defeated by our generals, and many bitter things befell the cities, know ye that the generals have been responsible for these hardships, but that we, holding fast to the original policy, are preparing peace for you and such governments as you enjoyed under Philip and Alexander, and that we permit you to act in all other matters according to the decrees formerly issued by them. Moreover, we restore those who have been driven out or exiled from the cities by our generals from the time when Alexander crossed into Asia; and we decree that those who are restored by us, in full possession of their property, undisturbed by faction, and enjoying complete amnesty, shall exercise their rights as citizens in their native states; and if any measures have been passed to their disadvantage, let such measures be void, except as concerning those who had been exiled for blood guilt or impiety in accordance with the law. Not to be restored are the men of Megalopolis who were exiled for treason along with Polyaenetus, nor those of Amphissa, Tricca, Pharcadon, or Heraclea; but let the cities receive back the others before the thirtieth day of Xanthicus. If in any case Philip or Alexander published regulations that are inconsistent with each other, let the cities concerned present themselves before us so that, after bringing the provisions into harmony, they may follow a course of action advantageous both to us and to themselves. The Athenians shall possess everything as at the time of Philip and Alexander, save that Oropus shall belong to its own people as at present. Samos we grant to Athens, since Philip our sire also gave it to them. Let all the Greeks pass a decree that no one shall engage either in war or in public activity in opposition to us, and that if anyone disobeys, he and his family shall be exiled and his goods shall be confiscated. We have commanded Polyperchon to take in hand these and other matters. Do you obey him, as we also have written to you formerly; for if anyone fails to carry out any of these injunctions, we shall not overlook him."

57. When this edict had been published and dispatched to all the cities, Polyperchon wrote to Argos and the other cities, ordering them to exile those who had been leaders of the governments in the time of Antipater, even to condemn certain of them to death and to confiscate their property, in order that these men, completely stripped of power, might be unable to co-operate with Cassander in any way. He also wrote to Olympias, the mother of Alexander, who was staying in Epirus because of her quarrel with Cassander, asking her to return to Macedonia as soon as possible, to take charge of the son of Alexander, and to assume responsibility for him until he should become of age and receive his father's kingdom. He also sent to Eumenes, writing a letter in the name of the kings, urging him not to put an end to his enmity toward Antigonus, but turning from him to the kings, either to cross over to Macedonia, if he wished, and become a guardian of the kings in co-operation with himself, or if he preferred, to remain in Asia and after receiving an army and money fight it out with Antigonus, who had already clearly shown that he was a rebel against the kings. He said that the kings were restoring to him the satrapy that Antigonus had taken away and all the prerogatives that he had ever possessed in Asia. Finally he set forth that it was especially fitting for Eumenes to be careful and solicitous for the royal house in conformity with his former public services in its interest. If he needed greater military power, Polyperchon promised that he himself and the kings would come from Macedonia with the entire royal army. This is what happened in that year.

How Eumenes took over the Silver Shields in Cilicia, retired to the upper satrapies, and made ready for himself a considerable army (58-59).

58. When Archippus was archon of Athens, [318] the Romans elected Quintus Aelius and Lucius Papirius consuls. While these held office Eumenes, just after he had made good his retreat from the fortress, received the letters that had been dispatched by Polyperchon. They contained, apart from what has been told above, the statement that the kings were giving him a gift of five hundred talents as recompense for the losses that he had experienced, and that to effect this they had written to the generals and treasurers in Cilicia directing them to give him the five hundred talents and whatever additional money he requested for raising mercenaries and for other pressing needs. The letter also added that they were writing to the commanders of the three thousand Macedonian Silver Shields ordering them to place themselves at the disposal of Eumenes and in general to co-operate wholeheartedly with him, since he had been appointed supreme commander of all Asia. There also came to him a letter from Olympias in which she begged and besought him to aid the kings and herself, saying that he alone was left, the most faithful of her friends and the one able to remedy the isolation of the royal house. Olympias asked him to advise her whether he thought it better for her to remain in Epirus and place no trust in those who were from time to time supposed to be guardians of the kings, but were in truth trying to transfer the kingdom to themselves, or to return to Macedonia. Eumenes at once replied to Olympias, advising her to remain in Epirus for the present until the war should come to some decision. As for himself, since he had always observed the most unwavering loyalty toward the kings, he decided not to take orders from Antigonus, who was trying to appropriate the kingship for himself; but since the son of Alexander was in need of help because of his orphaned state and the greediness of the commanders, he believed that it was incumbent upon himself to run every risk for the safety of the kings.

59. Immediately, therefore, Eumenes bade his men break camp and departed from Cappadocia with about five hundred horsemen and more than two thousand foot soldiers. Indeed, he did not have time to wait for the laggards among those who had promised to join him, for a considerable army was drawing near, sent from Antigonus under the general Menander to prevent Eumenes from staying in Cappadocia now that he had become an enemy of Antigonus. In fact, when this army arrived three days later, although it had missed its opportunity, it undertook to follow those who had gone with Eumenes; but since it was not able to come up with them, it returned to Cappadocia. Eumenes himself quickly passed over the Taurus by forced marches and entered Cilicia. Antigenes and Teutamus, the leaders of the Silver Shields, in obedience to the letters of the kings came from a considerable distance to meet Eumenes and his friends. After bidding him welcome and congratulating him on his unexpected escape from very great dangers, they promised to co-operate willingly with him in everything. The Macedonian Silver Shields, about three thousand in number, likewise met him with friendship and zeal. All wondered at the incredible fickleness of Fortune, when they considered that a little while before the kings and the Macedonians had condemned Eumenes and his friends to death, but now, forgetting their own decision, they not only had let him off scot-free of punishment, but also had entrusted to him the supreme command over the entire kingdom. It was with good reason that these emotions were shared by all who then beheld the reversals in Eumenes' fortunes; for who, taking thought of the inconstancies of human life, would not be astonished at the alternating ebb and flow of fortune? Or who, putting his trust in the predominance he enjoys when Fortune favours him, would adopt a bearing too high for mortal weakness? For human life, as if some god were at the helm, moves in a cycle through good and evil alternately for all time. It is not strange, then, that some one unforeseen event has taken place, but rather that all that happens is not unexpected. This is also a good reason for admitting the claim of history, for in the inconstancy and irregularity of events history furnishes a corrective for both the arrogance of the fortunate and the despair of the destitute.

About the shrewdness and generalship of Eumenes, and about his deeds up to his death (60-63).

60. Eumenes, who at this time also kept these things in mind, prudently made his own position secure, for he foresaw that Fortune would change again. He perceived that he himself was a foreigner and had no claim to the royal power, that the Macedonians who were now subject to him had previously decreed his death, and that those who occupied the military commands were filled with arrogance and were aiming at great affairs. He therefore understood that he would soon be despised and at the same time envied, and that his life would eventually be in danger; for no one will willingly carry out orders given by those whom he regards as his inferiors, or be patient when he has over him as masters those who ought themselves to be subject to others. Reasoning about these matters with himself, when the five hundred talents for refitting and organization were offered him in accordance with the kings' letters, he at first refused to accept them, saying that he had no need of such a gift as he had no desire to attain any position of command. Even now, he said, it was not of his own will that he had yielded with respect to his present office, but he had been compelled by the kings to undertake this great task. In any case, owing to his continuous military service, he was no longer able to endure the hardships and journeyings, especially since no magistracy was in prospect for one who was an alien and hence was excluded from the power that belonged of right to the Macedonians. He declared, however, that in his sleep he had seen a strange vision, which he considered it necessary to disclose to all, for he thought it would contribute much to harmony and the general good. He said that in his sleep he had seemed to see Alexander the king, alive and clad in his kingly garb, presiding over a council, giving orders to the commanders, and actively administering all the affairs of the monarchy. "Therefore," he said, "I think that we must make ready a golden throne from the royal treasure, and that after the diadem, the sceptre, the crown, and the rest of the insignia have been placed on it, all the commanders must at daybreak offer incense to Alexander before it, hold the meetings of the council in its presence, and receive their orders in the name of the king just as if he were alive and at the head of his own kingdom."

61. As all agreed to his proposal, everything needed was quickly made ready, for the royal treasure was rich in gold. Straightway then, when a magnificent tent had been set up, the throne was erected, upon which were placed the diadem, the sceptre, and the armour that Alexander had been wont to use. Then when an altar with a fire upon it had been put in place, all the commanders would make sacrifice from a golden casket, presenting frankincense and the most costly of the other kinds of incense and making obeisance to Alexander as to a god. After this those who exercised command would sit in the many chairs that had been placed about and take counsel together, deliberating upon the matters that from time to time required their attention. Eumenes, by placing himself on an equality with the other commanders in all the matters that were discussed and by seeking their favour through the most friendly intercourse, wore down the envy with which he had been regarded and secured for himself a great deal of goodwill among the commanders. As their reverence for the king grew stronger, they were all filled with happy expectations, just as if some god were leading them, and by conducting himself toward the Macedonian Silver Shields in a similar way, Eumenes gained great favour among them as a man worthy of the solicitude of the kings.

Eumenes selected the most able of his friends, gave them ample funds, and sent them out to engage mercenaries, establishing a notable rate of pay. Some of them went at once into Pisidia, Lycia, and the adjacent regions, where they zealously enrolled troops. Others travelled through Cilicia, others through Coelê Syria and Phoenicia, and some through the cities in Cyprus. Since the news of this levy spread widely and the pay offered was worthy of consideration, many reported of their own free will even from the cities of Greece and were enrolled for the campaign. In a short time more than ten thousand foot soldiers and two thousand horsemen were gathered together, not including the Silver Shields and those who had accompanied Eumenes.

62. At Eumenes' unexpected and sudden rise to power, Ptolemy, who had sailed to Zephyrium in Cilicia with a fleet, kept sending to the commanders of the Silver Shields, exhorting them not to pay any attention to Eumenes, whom all the Macedonians had condemned to death. Likewise he sent to those who had been placed in command of the garrisons in Cyinda, protesting solemnly against their giving any of the money to Eumenes, and promised to guarantee their safety. No one paid any attention to him because the kings and Polyperchon their guardian and also Olympias, the mother of Alexander, had written to them that they should serve Eumenes in every way, since he was the commander-in-chief of the kingdom. Antigonus in particular was displeased with the advancement of Eumenes and the magnitude of the power that was being concentrated in him; for he assumed that Eumenes was being made ready by Polyperchon as the strongest antagonist of himself now that he had become a rebel against the monarchy. Deciding, therefore, to organise a plot against Eumenes, he selected Philotas, one of his friends, and gave him a letter that he had written to the Silver Shields and to the other Macedonians with Eumenes. With him he also sent thirty other Macedonians, meddlesome and talkative persons, whom he instructed to meet separately with Antigenes and Teutamus, the commanders of the Silver Shields, and through them to organise some plot against Eumenes by promising great gifts and greater satrapies. Antigonus also told them to get in touch with their acquaintances and fellow citizens among the Silver Shields and secure their support for the plot against Eumenes by corrupting them with bribes. Now although they were unable to persuade any others, Teutamus, the leader of the Silver Shields, was bribed and undertook to persuade his fellow commander, Antigenes, to share in the enterprise. Antigenes, however, who was a man of great shrewdness and trustworthiness, not only argued against this, but he even won back the man who had been bribed; for he showed him that it was to his advantage that Eumenes rather than Antigonus should remain alive. The latter, indeed, if he became more powerful, would take away their satrapies and set up some of his friends in their places; Eumenes, however, since he was a foreigner, would never dare to advance his own interests, but, remaining a general, would treat them as friends and, if they co-operated with him, would protect their satrapies for them and perhaps give them others also. So those who were contriving plots against Eumenes met with failure in the way described.

63. When, however, Philotas gave the commanders the letter that had been addressed to all in common, the Silver Shields and the other Macedonians came together privately without Eumenes and ordered the letter to be read. In it Antigonus had written an accusation against Eumenes and had exhorted the Macedonians to seize Eumenes quickly and put him to death. If they should not do this, he said that he would come with his whole army to wage war against them, and that upon those who refused to obey he would inflict suitable punishment. At the reading of this letter the commanders and all the Macedonians found themselves in great perplexity, for it was necessary for them either to side with the kings and receive punishment from Antigonus, or to obey Antigonus and be chastised by Polyperchon and the kings. While the troops were in this confused state, Eumenes entered and, after reading the letter, urged the Macedonians to follow the decrees of the kings and not listen to one who had become a rebel. He discussed many matters pertinent to the subject and not only freed himself from the imminent danger but also gained greater favour with the crowd than before. Thus once more Eumenes, after falling into unforeseen danger, unexpectedly made his own power greater. Therefore he ordered the soldiers to break camp and led them to Phoenicia, desiring to gather ships from all the cities and assemble a considerable fleet, so that Polyperchon, by the addition of the Phoenician ships, might have control of the sea and be able to transport the Macedonian armies safely to Asia against Antigonus whenever he wished. Accordingly he remained in Phoenicia preparing the naval force.

What happened in Attica in regard to Cassander and Nicanor, commander of the garrison at Munychia (64-65, 68-69).

64. Meanwhile Nicanor, the commander of Munychia, on hearing that

Cassander had gone from Macedonia to Antigonus and that Polyperchon was expected to come shortly into Attica with his army, asked the Athenians to continue to favour Cassander. No one approved, but all thought that it was necessary to get rid even of the garrison as soon as possible. Nicanor therefore at first deceived the Assembly and persuaded them to wait for a few days, saying that Cassander would do what was for the advantage of the city; but then, while the Athenians remained inactive for a short time, he secretly introduced soldiers into Munychia by night, a few at a time, so that there was a force there strong enough to maintain the guard and fight against any who undertook to besiege the garrison. The Athenians, when they found out that Nicanor was not acting honourably with them, sent an embassy to the kings and to Polyperchon, asking them to send aid in accordance with the edict that had been issued concerning the autonomy of the Greeks; and they themselves, holding frequent meetings of the Assembly, considered what ought to be done about the war with Nicanor. While they were still engaged in this discussion, Nicanor, who had hired many mercenaries, made a secret sally by night and took the walls of the Piraeus and the harbour boom. The Athenians, who not only had failed to recapture Munychia but also had lost the Piraeus, were angry. They therefore selected as envoys some of the prominent citizens who were friends of Nicanor, Phocion the son of Phocus, Conon the son of Timotheüs, and Clearchus the son of Nausicles, and sent them to Nicanor to complain about what he had done and also to request him to restore their autonomy according to the edict that had been issued. Nicanor, however, answered that they should direct their mission to Cassander, since as a garrison commander appointed by Cassander he himself had no power of independent action.

65. At this time a letter came to Nicanor from Olympias, in which she ordered him to restore Munychia and the Piraeus to the Athenians. Since Nicanor had heard that the kings and Polyperchon were going to bring Olympias back to Macedonia, entrust to her the upbringing of the boy, and re-establish her in the state and honour that she had enjoyed during the lifetime of Alexander, he was frightened and promised to make the restoration, but he avoided the fulfilment of the promise by constantly making excuses. The Athenians, who had had great respect for Olympias in former times and now regarded the honours that had been decreed for her as actually in effect, were filled with joy, hoping that through her favour the recovery of their autonomy might be accomplished without risk. While the promise was still unfulfilled, however, Alexander the son of Polyperchon arrived in Attica with an army. The Athenians, indeed, believed that he had come to give back Munychia and the Piraeus to the people; this, however, was not the truth, but on the contrary he had come from interested motives to take both of them himself for use in the war. Now certain Athenians who had been friends of Antipater, of whom Phocion was one, fearing the punishment due them in accordance with the laws, went to Alexander and, by showing him what was to his own advantage, persuaded him to hold the forts for himself and not deliver them to the Athenians until after the defeat of Cassander. Alexander, who had pitched his camp near the Piraeus, did not admit the Athenians to his parley with Nicanor; but by conferring with him in private and negotiating secretly, he made it evident that he did not intend to deal fairly with the Athenians. The people, coming together in an assembly, removed from office the existing magistrates, filling the offices with men from the extreme democrats [318]; and they condemned those who had held office under the oligarchy, decreeing the death penalty for some of them, exile and confiscation of property for others, among whom was Phocion, who had held supreme authority under Antipater.

The death of Phocion, called the Good (66-67).

66. These men, on being driven from the city, fled to Alexander the son of Polyperchon and strove to secure safety for themselves through his good offices. They were well received by him and given letters to his father, Polyperchon, urging that Phocion and his friends should suffer no ill, since they had favoured his interests and now promised to co-operate with him in every way. The Athenian people also sent an embassy to Polyperchon laying charges against Phocion and praying Polyperchon to restore to them Munychia and their autonomy. Now Polyperchon was eager to occupy the Piraeus with a garrison because the port could be of great service to him in meeting the needs of the wars; but since he was ashamed of acting contrary to the edict that he himself had issued, believing that he would be held faithless among the Greeks if he broke his word to the most famous city, he changed his purpose. When he had heard the embassies, he gave a favourable answer in friendly terms to the one sent by the people, but he arrested Phocion and his companions and sent them bound to Athens, granting the people the authority either to put them to death or to dismiss the charges as they pleased.

When an assembly was called together in Athens and the case of Phocion and his fellows was brought forward, many of those who had been exiles in the days of Antipater and many of those who had been political opponents of the prisoners demanded the death penalty. The whole basis for the accusation was that after the Lamian War these men had been responsible for the enslavement of the fatherland and the overthrow of the democratic constitution and laws. When opportunity was given the defendants for their defence, Phocion began to deliver a plea in his own behalf, but the mob by its tumult rejected his defence, so that the defendants were left in utter helplessness. When the tumult subsided, Phocion tried again to defend himself, but the crowd shouted him down and prevented the voice of the accused from being fully heard; for the many supporters of democracy, who had been expelled from their citizenship and then, beyond their hopes, had been restored, were bitter against those who had deprived Athens of its independence.

67. As Phocion attempted to overcome the opposition and fought for his life in desperate circumstances, those who were near heard the justice of his plea, but those who were at a greater distance heard nothing because of the great uproar caused by the rioters and only beheld his gestures, which because of his great danger were impassioned and varied. Finally, abandoning hope of safety, Phocion shouted in a loud voice, begging them to condemn him to death but to spare the others. As the fury and violence of the mob remained unalterable, certain of Phocion's friends kept coming forward to add their pleas to his. The mob would listen to their opening words, but when, as they went on, they made it clear that they were speaking for the defence, they would be driven away by the tumult and by the jeers that greeted them. Finally by the universal voice of the people the accused were condemned and led off to the prison on the way to death. They were accompanied by many good men, mourning and sympathising with them at their great misfortune. For that men who were second to none in reputation and birth and had done many acts of human kindness during life should obtain neither a chance to defend themselves nor a fair trial turned many to arresting thoughts and fear, Fortune being not only unstable but impartial to all alike. Many of the popular party, men who were bitter in their opposition to Phocion, kept reviling him mercilessly and cruelly charging him with their misfortunes. For when hatred, that in prosperity finds no utterance, after a change of Fortune breaks out in adversity, it loses all human semblance in its rage against its object. So when, by taking the draught of hemlock according to the ancient custom, these men had ended their lives, they were all thrown unburied beyond the boundaries of Attica. In this manner died Phocion and those who had been falsely accused with him.

68. Cassander, after receiving from Antigonus thirty-five warships and four thousand soldiers, sailed into the Piraeus. Welcomed by Nicanor, the garrison commander, he took over the Piraeus and the harbour booms, while Munychia was retained by Nicanor himself, who had enough soldiers of his own to man the fortress. Polyperchon and the kings happened to be staying in Phocis, but when Polyperchon learned of Cassander's arrival in the Piraeus, he moved into Attica and camped near the Piraeus. He had with him twenty thousand Macedonian infantry and about four thousand of the other allies, a thousand cavalry, and sixty-five elephants. It was his intention to besiege Cassander; but since he was short of supplies and supposed that the siege would be long, he was forced to leave in Attica under the command of his son Alexander the part of the army that could be supplied with food, while he himself with the larger part of the forces moved into the Peloponnesus to enforce obedience to the kings upon the people of Megalopolis, who were in sympathy with Cassander and were governed by the oligarchy that had been established by Antipater.

How Polyperchon besieged the people of Megalopolis, and, after many losses and successes, withdrew without accomplishing anything (69-72).

69. While Polyperchon was busy with these affairs, Cassander with the fleet secured the allegiance of the people of Aegina and closely invested the Salaminians, who were hostile to him. Since he made continuous onslaughts day after day and was well supplied with both missiles and men, he reduced the Salaminians to the most desperate straits. The city was already in danger of being taken by storm when Polyperchon sent a considerable force of infantry and ships to attack the besiegers. At this Cassander was alarmed, abandoned the siege, and sailed back to the Piraeus. Polyperchon, in his anxiety to settle affairs in the Peloponnesus to his own advantage, went there and discussed with delegates, whom he had gathered from the cities, the question of their alliance with himself. He also sent envoys to the cities, ordering that those who through Antipater's influence had been made magistrates in the oligarchical governments should be put to death and that the people should be given back their autonomy. Many in fact obeyed him, there were massacres throughout the cities, and some were driven into exile; the friends of Antipater were destroyed, and the governments, recovering the freedom of action that came with autonomy, began to form alliances with Polyperchon. Since the Megalopolitans alone held to their friendship with Cassander, Polyperchon decided to attack their city.

70. When the Megalopolitans learned the intention of Polyperchon, they voted to bring all their property into the city from the country. On taking a census of citizens, foreigners, and slaves, they found that there were fifteen thousand men capable of performing military service. Some of these they at once attached to military formations, others they assigned to work gangs, and others they detailed to the care of the city wall. At one and the same time one group of men was digging a deep moat about the city, and another was bringing from the country timber for a palisade; some were repairing the weakened portions of the wall, while others were engaged in making weapons and in preparing engines for hurling bolts, and the whole city was deep in activity, owing both to the spirit of the population and to the danger that was foreseen. Indeed, word had spread abroad concerning the magnitude of the royal army and the multitude of the accompanying elephants, which were reputed to possess a fighting spirit and a momentum of body that were irresistible.

When all had been hastily made ready, Polyperchon arrived with his entire army and took up his position near the city, building two camps, one for the Macedonians, the other for the allies. Having constructed wooden towers higher than the walls, he brought them up to the city in those places that were convenient for the purpose, supplied them with missiles of many kinds and men to hurl these, and drove back those who were arrayed against him on the battlements. Meantime his sappers drove mines under the wall and then, by burning the mine props, caused the ruin of three very large towers and as many intervening sections of the wall. At this great and unexpected collapse the crowd of Macedonians shouted with joy, but those in the city were stunned by the seriousness of the event. Immediately the Macedonians began to pour through the breach into the city, while the Megalopolitans divided themselves, some of them opposing the enemy and, aided by the difficulty of the passage through the breach, putting up a stout fight, the rest cutting off the area inside the breach with a palisade and throwing up a second wall, applying themselves day and night without intermission to the task. Since this work was soon finished owing to the multitude of workmen and the ample supply of all the needed material, the Megalopolitans quickly made good the loss they had suffered by the breaching of the wall. Moreover, against those of the enemy who were fighting from the wooden towers they used bolt-shooting catapults, slingers, and bowmen, and mortally wounded many.

71. When many were falling or being disabled on each side and night had closed in about them, Polyperchon recalled his troops by a trumpet signal and returned to his own camp. On the next day he cleared the area of the breach, making it passable for the elephants, whose might he planned to use in capturing the city. The Megalopolitans, however, under the leadership of Damis, who had been in Asia with Alexander and knew by experience the nature and the use of these animals, got the better of him completely. Indeed, by pitting his native wit against the brute force of the elephants, Damis rendered their physical strength useless. He studded many great frames with sharp nails and buried them in shallow trenches, concealing the projecting points; over them he left a way into the city, placing none of the troops directly in the face of it, but posting on the flanks a great many javelin throwers, bowmen, and catapults. As Polyperchon was clearing the debris from the whole extent of the breach and making an attack through it with all the elephants in a body, a most unexpected thing befell them. There being no resistance in front, the Indian mahouts did their part in urging them to rush into the city all together; but the animals, as they charged violently, encountered the spike-studded frames. Wounded in their feet by the spikes, their own weight causing the points to penetrate, they could neither go forward any farther nor turn back because it hurt them to move. At the same time some of the mahouts were killed by the missiles of all kinds that poured upon them from the flanks, and others were disabled by wounds and so lost such use of the elephants as the situation permitted. The elephants, suffering great pain because of the cloud of missiles and the nature of the wounds caused by the spikes, wheeled about through their friends and trod down many of them. Finally the elephant that was the most valiant and formidable collapsed; of the rest, some became completely useless, and others brought death to many of their own side.

How Cleitus, the admiral of Polyperchon, defeated Nicanor, the admiral of Cassander, in a naval battle and How Antigonus gained the supremacy on the sea by brilliantly defeating Cleitus in a naval battle (72).

72. After this piece of good fortune the Megalopolitans were more confident, but Polyperchon repented of the siege; and as he himself could not wait there for a long time, he left a part of the army for the siege, while he himself went off about other more necessary business. He sent Cleitus the admiral out with the whole fleet, ordering him to lie in wait in the region of the Hellespont and block the forces that were being brought across from Asia into Europe. Cleitus was also to pick up Arrhidaeus, who had fled with his soldiers to the city of the Cianoi since he was an enemy of Antigonus. After Cleitus had sailed to the Hellespont, had won the allegiance of the cities of the Propontis, and had received the army of Arrhidaeus, Nicanor, the commander of Munychia, reached that region, Cassander having sent him with his entire fleet. Nicanor had also taken over the ships of Antigonus so that he had in all more than a hundred. A naval battle took place not far from Byzantium in which Cleitus was victorious, sinking seventeen ships of the enemy and capturing not less than forty together with their crews, but the rest escaped to the harbour of Chalcedon.

After such a victory Cleitus believed that the enemy would no longer dare fight at sea owing to the severity of their defeat, but Antigonus, after learning of the losses that the fleet had suffered, unexpectedly made good by his own keen wit and generalship the setback that he had encountered. Gathering auxiliary vessels from Byzantium by night, he employed them in transporting bowmen, slingers, and a sufficient number of other light-armed troops to the other shore. Before dawn they fell upon those who had disembarked from the ships of the enemy and were encamped on the land, spreading panic in the forces of Cleitus. At once these were all thrown into a tumult of fear, and when they leaped into the ships, there was great confusion because of the baggage and the large number of prisoners. At this point Antigonus, who had made his warships ready and had placed in them as marines many of his bravest infantry, sent them into the fight, urging them to fall on the enemy with confidence, since the victory would depend entirely upon them. During the night Nicanor had put to sea, and, as dawn appeared, his men fell suddenly upon the confused enemy and at once put them to flight at the first attack, destroying some of the ships by ramming them with the beaks, sweeping off the oars of others, and gaining possession of certain of them without danger when they surrendered with their crews. They finally captured all the ships together with their crews save for the one that carried the commander. Cleitus fled to the shore and abandoned his ship, endeavouring to make his way through Macedonia to safety, but he fell into the hands of certain soldiers of Lysimachus and was put to death.

How Eumenes, although he had been surrounded near Babylon by Seleucus and was in extreme danger, was saved by his own shrewdness (73).

73. As for Antigonus, by inflicting so disastrous a blow upon the enemy, he gained a great reputation for military genius. He now set out to gain command of the sea and to place his control of Asia beyond dispute. For this end he selected from his entire army twenty thousand lightly equipped infantry and four thousand cavalry and set out for Cilicia, hoping to destroy Eumenes before the latter should gather stronger forces. After Eumenes had news of Antigonus' move, he thought to recover for the kings Phoenicia, which had been unjustly occupied by Ptolemy; but being forestalled by events, he moved from Phoenicia and marched with his army through Coelê Syria with the design of making contact with what are called the upper satrapies. Near the Tigris, however, the inhabitants fell on him by night, causing him the loss of some soldiers. Likewise in Babylonia when Seleucus attacked him near the Euphrates he was in danger of losing his whole army; for a canal was breached and his entire camp inundated, but by a piece of strategy of his own he escaped to a mound, diverted the canal to its old course, and saved himself and his army. Thus unexpectedly slipping through the hands of Seleucus, he won through into Persia with his army, which consisted of fifteen thousand infantry and thirty-three hundred cavalry. After letting the army recover from its hardships, he sent word to the satraps and generals in the upper satrapies, requesting soldiers and money.

The affairs of Asia progressed to such a point during this year.

How Polyperchon, although despised and humiliated by the Greeks, continued to fight against Cassander (74-75).

74. In Europe, as Polyperchon had come to be regarded with contempt because of his failure at the siege of Megalopolis, most of the Greek cities deserted the kings and went over to Cassander. When the Athenians were unable to get rid of the garrison by the aid of either Polyperchon or Olympias, one of those citizens who were accepted leaders risked the statement in the Assembly that it was for the advantage of the city to come to terms with Cassander. At first a clamour was raised, some opposing and some supporting his proposal, but when they had considered more carefully what was the expedient course, it was unanimously determined to send an embassy to Cassander and to arrange affairs with him as best they could. After several conferences peace was made on the following terms: the Athenians were to retain their city and territory, their revenues, their fleet, and everything else, and to be friends and allies of Cassander; Munychia was to remain temporarily under the control of Cassander until the war against the kings should be concluded; the government was to be in the hands of those possessing at least ten minae; and whatever single Athenian citizen Cassander should designate was to be overseer of the city. Demetrius of Phalerum was chosen, who, when he became overseer, ruled the city peacefully and with goodwill toward the citizens.

75. Afterwards Nicanor sailed into the Piraeus with his fleet ornamented with the beaks of the ships taken at his victory. At first Cassander regarded him with great approval because of his success, but later, when he saw that he was filled with arrogance and puffed up, and that he was, moreover, garrisoning Munychia with his own men, he decided that he was planning treachery and had him assassinated. He also made a campaign into Macedonia, where he found many of the inhabitants coming over to him. The Greek cities, too, felt an impulse to join the alliance of Cassander; for Polyperchon seemed to lack both energy and wisdom in representing the kings and his allies, but Cassander, who treated all fairly and was active in carrying out his affairs, was winning many supporters of his leadership.

Since Agathocles became tyrant of Syracuse in the following year, we shall bring this book to an end at this point as was proposed at the beginning. We shall begin the next Book with the tyranny of Agathocles and include in it the events that deserve commemoration in our account.

BOOK XIX

From what beginnings Agathocles rose in making himself tyrant of Syracuse (1-9).

1. An old saying has been handed down that it is not men of average ability but those of outstanding superiority who destroy democracies. [317] For this reason some cities, suspecting those of their public men who are the strongest, take away from them their outward show of power. It seems that the step to the enslavement of the fatherland is a short one for men who continue in positions of power, and that it is difficult for those to abstain from monarchy who through eminence have acquired hopes of ruling; for it is natural that men who thirst for greatness should seek their own aggrandisement and cherish desires that know no bounds. The Athenians, for example, exiled the foremost of their citizens for this reason, having established by law what was known among them as ostracism; and this they did, not to inflict punishment for any injustice previously committed, but in order that those citizens who were strong enough to disregard the laws might not get an opportunity to do wrong at the expense of their fatherland. Indeed, they used to recite as an oracle that saying of Solon in which, while foretelling the tyranny of Peisistratus, he inserts this couplet:

> Destruction cometh upon a city from its great men; and through
> ignorance the people fall into slavery to a tyrant. Bk. 9. 21. 2;
> Diogenes Laertius.

More than anywhere else this tendency toward the rule of one man prevailed in Sicily before the Romans became rulers of that island; for the cities, deceived by demagogic wiles, went so far in making the weak strong that these became despots over those whom they had deceived. The most extraordinary instance of all is that of Agathocles who became tyrant of the Syracusans, a man who had the lowest beginnings, but who plunged not only Syracuse but also the whole of Sicily and Libya into the gravest misfortunes. Although, compelled by lack of means and slender fortune, he turned his hand to the potter's trade, he rose to such a peak of power and cruelty that he enslaved the greatest and fairest of all islands, for a time possessed the larger part of Libya and parts of Italy, and filled the cities of Sicily with outrage and slaughter. No one of the tyrants before him brought any such achievements to completion nor yet displayed such cruelty toward those who had become his subjects. For example, he used to punish a private individual by slaughtering all his kindred, and to exact reckoning from cities by murdering the people from youth up; and on account of a few who were charged with a crime, he would compel the many, who had done no evil at all, to suffer the same fate, condemning to death the entire population of cities.

Since this Book embraces all other events as well as the tyranny of Agathocles, we shall forgo preliminary statements about it and set forth the events that follow those already related, stating first the time covered by the account. In the preceding eighteen Books we have described to the best of our ability the events that have occurred in the known parts of the inhabited world from the earliest times down to the year before the tyranny of Agathocles, up to which time the years from the destruction of Troy are eight hundred and sixty-six; in this Book, beginning with that dynasty, we shall include events up to the

215

battle at Himera between Agathocles and the Carthaginians, embracing a period of seven years.

2. When Demogenes was archon in Athens, [317/6] the Romans elected to the consulship Lucius Plotius and Manius Fulvius, and Agathocles of Syracuse became tyrant of his city. In order to make clearer the series of events, we shall briefly take up the life of that dynast at an earlier point.

Carcinus of Rhegium, an exile from his native city, settled in Therma in Sicily, a city that had been brought under the rule of the Carthaginians. Having formed a union with a native woman and made her pregnant, he was constantly troubled in his sleep. Being thus made anxious about the begetting of the child, he instructed certain Carthaginian envoys who were setting out for Delphi to ask the god about his expected son. They duly carried out their commission, and an oracle was given forth that the child whom he had begotten would be the cause of great misfortunes to the Carthaginians and to all Sicily. Learning this and being frightened, Carcinus exposed the infant in a public place and set men to watch him that he might die. After some days had passed the child had not died, and those who had been set to watch him began to be negligent. At this time, then, the mother came secretly by night and took the child; and, although, fearing her husband, she did not bring him to her own home, she left him with her brother Heracleides and called him Agathocles, the name of her own father. The boy was brought up in the home of Heracleides and became much fairer in face and stronger in body than was to be expected at his age. When the child was seven years old, Carcinus was invited by Heracleides to some festival and, seeing Agathocles playing with some children of his own age, wondered at his beauty and strength. On the woman's remarking that the child who had been exposed would have been of the same age if he had been brought up, he said that he regretted what he had done and began to weep incessantly. Then she, seeing that the desire of the man was in harmony with her own past act, disclosed the entire truth. Gladly hearing her words, he accepted his son, but in fear of the Carthaginians removed to Syracuse with his whole household. Since he was poor he taught Agathocles the trade of pottery while he was still a boy.

At this time Timoleon the Corinthian, after having defeated the Carthagians in the battle at the Crimissus River, conferred Syracusan citizenship on all who wished. Carcinus was enrolled as a citizen together with Agathocles, and died after living only a short time longer. The mother dedicated a stone image of her son in a certain precinct, and a swarm of bees settled upon it and built their honeycomb about its hips. When this prodigy was reported to those who devoted themselves to such matters, all of them declared that at the prime of his life the boy would attain great fame; and this prophecy was fulfilled.

3. A certain Damas, who was counted among the notable men of Syracuse, fell in love with Agathocles and since in the beginning he supplied him lavishly with everything, was the cause of his accumulating a suitable property; and thereafter, when Damas had been elected general against Aeragas and one of his chiliarchs died, he appointed Agathocles in his place. Even before his military service Agathocles had been much respected on account of the great size of his armour, for in military reviews he was in the habit of wearing equipment so heavy that no one of the others was able to use it handily because of the weight of the armour. When he became a chiliarch, he gained even more fame since he was venturesome and daring in battle and bold and ready in haranguing the people. When Damas died of illness and left his property to his wife, Agathocles married her and was counted among the richest men.

Thereafter when the people of Croton were being besieged by the Bruttii, the Syracusans sent a strong force to their aid [235]. Antandrus, the brother of Agathocles, was one of the generals of this army, but the commanders of the whole were Heracleides and Sostratus, men who had spent the greater part of their lives in plots, murders, and great impieties; their careers in detail are contained in the Book before this one. Agathocles also took part in that campaign with them, having been recognized for his ability by the people and assigned to the rank of chiliarch. Although he had distinguished himself at first in the battles with the barbarians, he was deprived of the award for his deeds of valour by Sostratus and his friends because of jealousy. Agathocles was deeply offended at them and denounced before the people their resolve to establish an autocratic government. As the people of Syracuse paid no attention to the charges, the cabal of Sostratus did gain control of their native city after the return from Croton.

4. Since Agathocles was hostile to them, he remained at first in Italy with those who made common cause with him. Undertaking to establish himself in Croton, he was driven out and with a few others escaped to Tarentum. While among the Tarentines he was enrolled in the ranks of the mercenaries, and because he took part in many hazardous actions he was suspected of revolutionary designs. When he for this reason was released from this army also, he gathered together the exiles from all parts of Italy and went to the aid of Rhegium, which was then being attacked by Heracleides and Sostratus. Then when the cabal in Syracuse was brought to an end and the party of Sostratus was expelled, Agathocles returned to his own city. Many citizens of repute had been exiled along with the cabal on the ground that they had been members of the oligarchy of the Six Hundred Noblest, and now war arose between these exiles and those who were supporting the democracy. As the Carthaginians became allies of the exiles with Sostratus, there were constant engagements and pitched battles between strong forces, in which Agathocles, sometimes as a private soldier, sometimes appointed to a command, was credited with being energetic and ingenious, for in each emergency he contrived some helpful device. One instance of the kind is well worth mentioning. Once when the Syracusans were in camp near Gela, he stole into the city at night with a thousand men, but Sostratus with a large force in battle array appeared suddenly, routed those who had made their way in, and struck down about three hundred of them. When the remainder tried to escape through a certain narrow passage and had abandoned hope of safety, Agathocles unexpectedly saved them from the danger. Fighting most brilliantly of all, he had received seven wounds, and because of the quantity of blood he had lost, he was weak in body; but when the enemy were upon them, he ordered the trumpeters to go out to the walls on each side and sound the signal for battle. When they quickly carried out the order, those who had sallied out from Gela to give aid were not able to learn the truth because of the darkness, but supposing that the remaining force of the Syracusans had broken in on both sides, they abandoned further pursuit, divided their forces into two parts, and went quickly to meet the danger, running toward the sound made by the trumpeters. In this situation Agathocles and his men gained a respite from fighting and came safe to their fortified camp in complete security. Thus on this occasion, by outwitting the enemy in this way, he not only saved his own companions by a miracle but also seven hundred of the allies.

5. Thereafter, at the time when Acestorides the Corinthian had been elected general in Syracuse, Agathocles was reputed to have made an attempt at tyranny, but he escaped from this danger by his own shrewdness. For Acestorides, who was wary of factional strife and therefore was not willing to destroy him openly, ordered him to leave the city and sent out men to kill him on the road during the night. But Agathocles, who had shrewdly guessed the intention of the general, selected from his slaves the one who was most like himself in stature and face, and by equipping him with his own armour, horse, and even his own clothing, he deceived those who had been dispatched to kill him. As for himself, he put on rags and by avoiding the roads completed the journey. They, supposing from the armour and the other indications that it was Agathocles and not observing more closely because of the darkness, accomplished a murder indeed, but failed to carry out the task that had been assigned to them.

Afterwards the Syracusans received back those who had been expelled with Sostratus and made peace with the Carthaginians; but Agathocles as an exile gathered together an army of his own in the interior. After he had become an object of dread not only to his own fellow citizens but also to the Carthaginians, he was persuaded to return to his own city; and at the shrine of Demeter, to which he was taken by the citizens, he swore that he would undertake nothing against the democracy. And it was by pretending to be a supporter of democracy and by winning the favour of the people in artful ways that he secured his own election as general and protector of the peace until such time as real harmony might be established among the exiles who had returned to the city. For it happened that the political clubs of those who were holding meetings were divided into many factions and that important differences of opinion existed among them; but the chief group opposed to Agathocles was the society of the Six Hundred, which had directed the city in the time of the oligarchy; for the Syracusans who sit were first in reputation and in property had been enrolled in this society.

6. Agathocles, who was greedy for power, had many advantages for the accomplishment of his design. Not only as general was he in command of the army, but moreover, when news came that some rebels were assembling an army in the interior near Erbita, without rousing suspicion he obtained authority to enrol as soldiers what men he chose. Thus by feigning a campaign against Erbita he enrolled in the army the men of Morgantina and the other cities of the interior who had previously served with him against the Carthaginians. All these were very firmly attached to Agathocles, having received many benefits from him during the campaigns, but they were unceasingly hostile to the Six Hundred, who had been members of the oligarchy in Syracuse, and hated the populace in general because they were forced to carry out its orders. These soldiers numbered about three thousand, being both by inclination and by deliberate choice most suitable tools for the overthrow of the democracy. To them he added those of the citizens who because of poverty and envy were hostile to the pretensions of the powerful. As soon as he had everything ready, he ordered the soldiers to report at daybreak at the Timoleontium; and he himself summoned Peisarchus and Diocles, who were regarded as the leaders of the society of the Six Hundred, as if he wished to consult them on some matter of common interest. When they had come bringing with them some forty of their friends,

Agathocles, pretending that he himself was being plotted against, arrested all of them, accused them before the soldiers, saying that he was being seized by the Six Hundred because of his sympathy for the common people, and bewailed his fate. When, however, the mob was aroused and with a shout urged him not to delay but to inflict the just penalty on the wrongdoers out of hand, he gave orders to the trumpeters to give the signal for battle and to the soldiers to kill the guilty persons and to plunder the property of the Six Hundred and their supporters. All rushed out to take part in the plunder, and the city was filled with confusion and great calamity; for the members of the aristocratic class, not knowing the destruction that had been ordained for them, were dashing out of their homes into the streets in their eagerness to learn the cause of the tumult, and the soldiers, made savage both by greed and by anger, kept killing these men who, in their ignorance of the situation, were presenting their bodies bare of any arms that would protect them.

7. The narrow passages were severally occupied by soldiers, and the victims were murdered, some in the streets, some in their houses. Many, too, against whom there had been no charge whatever, were slain when they sought to learn the cause of the massacre. For the armed mob having seized power did not distinguish between friend and foe, but the man from whom it had concluded most profit was to be gained, him it regarded as an enemy. Therefore one could see the whole city filled with outrage, slaughter, and all manner of lawlessness. For some men because of long-existing hatred abstained from no form of insult against the objects of their enmity now that they had the opportunity to accomplish whatever seemed to gratify their rage; others, thinking by the slaughter of the wealthy to redress their own poverty, left no means untried for their destruction. Some broke down the doors of houses, others mounted to the housetops on ladders, still others struggled against men who were defending themselves from the roofs; not even to those who fled into the temples did their prayers to the gods bring safety, but reverence due the gods was overthrown by men. In time of peace and in their own city Greeks dared commit these crimes against Greeks, relatives against kinsfolk, respecting neither common humanity nor solemn compacts nor gods, crimes such that there is no one, I do not say no friend but not even any deadly enemy if he but have a spark of compassion in his soul, who would not pity the fate of the victims.

8. All the gates of the city were closed, and more than four thousand persons were slain on that day whose only crime was to be of gentler birth than the others. Of those who fled, some who rushed for the gates were arrested, while others who cast themselves from the walls escaped to the neighbouring cities; some, however, who in panic cast themselves down before they looked, crashed headlong to their doom. The number of those who were driven from their native city was more than six thousand, most of whom fled to the people of Acragas where they were accorded proper care. The party of Agathocles spent the day in the murder of their fellow citizens, nor did they abstain from outrage and crime against women, but they thought that those who had escaped death would be sufficiently punished by the violation of their kindred. For it was reasonable to suppose that the husbands and fathers would suffer something worse than death when they thought of the violence done their wives and the shame inflicted upon their unmarried daughters. We must keep our account of these events free from the artificially tragic tone that is habitual with historians, chiefly because of our

pity for the victims, but also because no one of our readers has a desire to hear all the details when his own understanding can readily supply them. For men who by day in the streets and throughout the market place were bold to butcher those who had done no harm need no writer to set forth what they did at night when by themselves in the homes, and how they conducted themselves toward orphaned maidens and toward women who were bereft of any to defend them and had fallen into the absolute power of their direst enemies. As for Agathocles, when two days had passed, since he was now sated with the slaughter of his fellow citizens, after gathering together the prisoners, he let Deinocrates go because of their former friendship, but of the others he killed those who were most bitterly hostile and exiled the rest.

9. Next he called together the Assembly and accused the Six Hundred and the oligarchy that they had brought into existence, saying that he had cleansed the state of those men who were trying to become her masters; and he proclaimed that he was restoring liberty undefiled to the people, and that he wished to be relieved at last of his burdens and become a private citizen on terms of equality with all. As he said this, he tore off his military cloak and, assuming civil garb, set out to leave, showing that he himself was one of the many, but in doing this he was merely playing the part of a democrat with full knowledge that the majority of the members of the Assembly had had a share in his unholy acts and for this reason would not be willing to vote the generalship to anyone else. At any rate, those who had plundered the property of the victims instantly cried out, begging him not to leave them but to accept the general administration of the state. At first he maintained silence; then, as the mob pressed more insistently upon him, he said that he accepted the generalship, but that he would not rule jointly with others, for he would not consent as one member of a board to be held legally accountable for acts illegally committed by the others. Since the majority agreed that he should rule alone, he was elected general with absolute power [317], and thereafter he openly exercised authority and governed the city. Of the Syracusans who were uncorrupted, some were forced to endure in patience because of their fears, and others, outmatched by the mob, did not venture to make an unavailing display of their hostility. On the other hand, many of those who were poor and involved in debt welcomed the revolution, for Agathocles promised in the Assembly both to abolish debts and to distribute land to the poor. When he had finished with these matters, he made an end of further slaughter and punishment. With a complete change of humour he showed himself affable to the common people and won no slight popularity by aiding many, by encouraging no small number with promises, and by currying favour from all by philanthropic words. Although he possessed such power, he neither assumed a diadem, nor employed a bodyguard, nor affected a haughty demeanour, as is the custom of almost all tyrants. He kept a careful watch over the public revenues and over the preparation of armour and weapons, and he had warships constructed in addition to those already at hand. He also gained control of most of the regions and cities of the interior.

This, then, was the situation in Sicily.

How the exiles from Croton took the field against their native city and were all slain (10).

10. In Italy the Romans were now in the ninth year of their war with the Samnites. Although in the previous period they had fought with large forces, at this time they accomplished nothing great or worthy of mention by the incursions that they were making upon the hostile territory; yet they did not cease attacking the strongholds and plundering the country. In Apulia also they plundered all Daunia and won back the Canusians, from whom they took hostages. They added two new tribes to those already existing: Falerna and Oufentina. While this was going on, the people of Croton made peace with the Bruttii, but they were still waging war against those of their own citizens who had been exiled by the democracy because of their alliance with Heracleides and Sostratus, about which we have told in detail in the preceding Book. This war was now in its second year, Paron and Menedemus, both outstanding men, having been elected generals. The exiles, setting out from Thurii and taking with them three hundred mercenaries, tried to enter their native city by night, were driven off by the people of Croton, and encamped on the boundaries of the land of the Bruttii. Soon afterwards, however, they were attacked by the army of citizens, which far outnumbered them, and all were slaughtered in the fight.

Now that we have finished the affairs of Sicily and Italy, we turn to the remaining parts of Europe.

The return of Olympias and her son to the kingdom (11).

The capture and death of Eurydicê and of King Philip (11).

11. In Macedonia, when Eurydicê, who had assumed the administration of the regency, heard that Olympias was making preparations for a return, she sent a courier into the Peloponnesus to Cassander, begging him to come to her aid as soon as possible; and, by plying the most active of the Macedonians with gifts and great promises, she was trying to make them personally loyal to herself. But Polyperchon, with Aeacides of Epirus as his ally, collected an army and restored Olympias and the son of Alexander to the throne. So, as soon as he heard that Eurydicê was at Euia in Macedonia with her army, he hastened against her with the intention of deciding the campaign in a single battle. When, however, the armies were drawn up facing each other, the Macedonians, out of respect for the position of Olympias and remembering the benefits that they had received from Alexander, changed their allegiance. King Philip with his court was captured at once, while Eurydicê was taken as she was making her way to Amphipolis with Polycles, one of her counsellors. After Olympias had thus captured the royal persons and had seized the kingdom without a fight, she did not carry her good fortune as a human being should, but first she placed Eurydicê and her husband Philip under guard and began to maltreat them. Indeed she walled them up in a small space and supplied them with what was necessary through a single narrow opening. After she had for many days unlawfully treated the unfortunate captives, since she was thereby losing favour with the Macedonians because of their pity for the sufferers, she ordered certain Thracians to stab Philip to death, who had been king for six years and four months; but she judged that Eurydicê, who was expressing herself without restraint and declaring that the kingdom belonged to herself rather than to Olympias, was worthy of greater punishment. She therefore sent to her a sword, a noose, and some hemlock, and ordered her to employ whichever of these she pleased as a means of death, neither displaying any respect whatever for the former dignity of the victim whom she was unlawfully treating, nor moved to pity for the fate that is common to all. Accordingly, when she herself met with a similar reversal, she experienced a death that was worthy of her cruelty. Eurydicê, indeed, in the presence of the attendant prayed that like gifts might fall to the lot of Olympias. She next laid out the body of her husband, cleansing its wounds as well as circumstances permitted, then ended her life by hanging herself with her girdle, neither weeping for her own fate nor humbled by the weight of her misfortunes. After these two had been made away with, Olympias killed Nicanor, Cassander's brother, and overturned the tomb of Iollas, avenging, as she said, the death of Alexander. She also selected the hundred most prominent Macedonians from among the friends of Cassander and slaughtered them all. By glutting her rage with such atrocities, she soon caused many of the Macedonians to hate her ruthlessness; for all of them remembered the words of Antipater, who, as if uttering a prophecy on his death bed, advised them never to permit a woman to hold first place in the kingdom.

This situation, then, in the internal affairs of Macedonia gave clear indication of the impending revolution.

How Eumenes went into the upper satrapies with the Silver Shields and collected the satraps and their armies in Persia (12-15).

12. In Asia Eumenes with the Macedonian Silver Shields and their commander Antigenes wintered in the villages of Babylonia known as the villages of the Carians. He sent embassies to Seleucus and Pithon asking them to aid the kings and to join him in the struggle against Antigonus. Of these men, Pithon had been appointed satrap of Media and the other had been named satrap of Babylonia at the time when the second distribution of satrapies was made at Triparadeisus. Seleucus said that he was willing to be of service to the kings, but that nevertheless he would never consent to carrying out the orders of Eumenes, whom the Macedonians in assembly had condemned to death. After much discussion in respect to this policy, they sent an ambassador from themselves to Antigenes and the Silver Shields, asking them to remove Eumenes from his command. Since the Macedonians paid no heed to this message, Eumenes, after praising their loyalty, set out with the army and pitched camp on reaching the Tigris River at a distance of three hundred stades from Babylon. It was his purpose to direct his course to Susa, where he intended to summon the armies from the upper satrapies and to make use of the royal treasure for his urgent needs. He was forced, however, to cross the river because the country behind him had been plundered, whereas that on the other side was untouched and able to furnish abundant food for his army. When he, accordingly, had gathered boats from all sides for the crossing, Seleucus and Pithon sailed down with two triremes and a good many punts, for these craft still survived from those that had been built by Alexander near Babylon.

13. Directing these craft to the landing place, Seleucus and Pithon again tried to persuade the Macedonians to remove Eumenes from his command and to cease preferring against their own interests a man who was a foreigner and who had killed very many Macedonians. When Antigenes and his men were in no way persuaded, Seleucus sailed off to a certain ancient canal and cleared its intake, which had been filled up in the course of time. Since the Macedonian camp was surrounded by water and the neighbouring land on all sides was now inundated, there was danger that the entire encamped army would be destroyed by the flood. On that day the Macedonians remained inactive, not knowing how to deal with the situation; but on the next they brought up the punts, about three hundred in number, and carried the best part of the army across, no one hindering them at the landing; for Seleucus had cavalry only and that too far inferior in number to its opponents. When night was overtaking them, Eumenes, since he was anxious about the baggage, got the Macedonians back across the river; and under the guidance of one of the inhabitants of the region he began to excavate a certain place through which it was easy to turn the canal and make the neighbouring land passable. Seleucus saw this, and since he wished to get them out of his satrapy as soon as possible, he sent envoys to propose a truce, conceding to Eumenes his passage across the river, but at the same time he also sent dispatch carriers into Mesopotamia to Antigonus, asking him to come with his army as soon as possible before the satraps should arrive with their forces. Eumenes, however, after crossing the Tigris and arriving in Susianê, divided his army into three parts because of the dearth of food. Marching through the country in separate columns, he was completely without grain, but he distributed to his soldiers rice, sesame, and dates, since the land produced such fruits as these in plenty. He had already sent to the commanders of the upper satrapies the letter from the kings in which it was written that they should obey Eumenes in every way; and at this time he again sent couriers bidding the satraps all to assemble in Susianê each with his own army, but it happened that at this very time they had themselves mobilised their forces and had assembled for other reasons, with which it is necessary to deal first.

14. Pithon had been appointed satrap of Media, but when he became general of all the upper satrapies, he put to death Philotas, the former general of Parthia, and set up his own brother Eudamus in his place. At this all the other satraps joined forces, fearing that they might suffer a similar fate since Pithon was seditious and had included great undertakings in his plans. They got the better of him in a battle, killed many of his supporters, and drove him out of Parthia. At first he withdrew to Media, but after a little he went on to Babylon, where he invited Seleucus to aid him and to share in his expectations. So, since the upper satraps had for this reason concentrated their armies in a single place, the couriers from Eumenes found the forces ready. The most eminent of the commanders and the one who by common consent had assumed command of all the forces was Peucestes, who had been a Bodyguard of Alexander and had been promoted by the king because of his courage. He had held the satrapy of Persia for many years and had gained great favour with the inhabitants. They say that for this reason Alexander permitted him alone of the Macedonians to wear the Persian raiment, wishing to please the Persians and believing that through Peucestes he could keep the nation in all respects obedient. At this time Peucestes had ten thousand Persian archers and slingers, three thousand men of every origin equipped for service in the Macedonian array, six hundred Greek and Thracian cavalry, and more than four hundred Persian horsemen. Tlepolemus the Macedonian, who had been appointed satrap of Carmania, had one thousand five hundred foot soldiers and seven hundred mounted men. Sibyrtius, the commander of Arachosia, brought a thousand foot and six hundred and ten horse. Androbazus had been dispatched from Paropanisadae, of which satrapy Oxyartes was governor, with twelve hundred infantry and four hundred cavalry. Stasander, the satrap of Aria and Danginê, who brought also the troops from Bactianê, had fifteen hundred infantry and a thousand horse. From India came Eudamus with five hundred horsemen, three hundred footmen, and one hundred and twenty elephants. These beasts he had secured after the death of Alexander by treacherously slaying King Porus. In all there were assembled with the satraps more than eighteen thousand seven hundred infantry and four thousand six hundred cavalry.

15. When the satraps had come into Susianê and had joined Eumenes, they called together a general assembly in which there was found to be a good deal of rivalry for the chief command. Peucestes thought that because of the number of soldiers who followed him on the campaign and because of his high rank under Alexander he ought to have the supreme command; but Antigenes, who was general of the Silver Shields, said that the right to make the selection ought to be granted to his Macedonians, since they had conquered Asia with Alexander and had been unconquered because of their valour. Eumenes, however, fearing that through their rivalry with each other they would become an easy prey for Antigonus, advised that they should not set up a single commander, but that all the satraps and generals who had been selected by the mass of the army should gather in the royal tent each day and take counsel together about what was to the common advantage. For a tent had been set up for Alexander although he was dead, and in the tent a throne, before which they were accustomed to make offerings and then to sit as a council in regard to matters that demanded attention. Since all approved his proposal as made in the general interest, he called a council each day like that of some city ruling itself on democratic principles. Later, when they arrived at Susa, Eumenes received from those in charge of the treasury a sum of money sufficient for his needs; for it was to him alone that the kings in their letter had ordered the treasurers to give whatever sum he should ask. After paying the Macedonians for six months, he gave two hundred talents to Eudamus, who had brought down the elephants from India, saying that this was for the cost of maintaining the animals, but really trying to win the favour of the man by this gift; for he would tip the scales decisively in favour of any one of the rivals to whom he might attach himself, since the employment of the beasts strikes terror. Each of the other satraps provided for the support of the troops who had followed him from the territory under his command.

While Eumenes remained in Susianê refreshing his forces, Antigonus, who had wintered in Mesopotamia, at first had planned to follow Eumenes close on his heels before his strength should be increased; but on hearing that the satraps and their armies had joined the Macedonians, he checked his speed and began to refresh his forces and to enrol additional soldiers, for he perceived that the war called for large armies and for no ordinary preparation.

How Attalus and Polemon, together with those who took part with them in the attack on the guard, were taken and killed (16).

16. While these things were happening, Attalus, Polemon, and Docimus, together with Antipater and Philotas, the commanders who had been captured along with the army of Alcetas, were being kept under guard in a certain exceedingly strong fortress; but when they heard that Antigonus was leading his expedition into the upper satrapies, believing that they had a favourable opportunity, they persuaded certain of their custodians to release them, and then, gaining possession of arms, they set upon the guard at about midnight. They themselves numbered only eight and were guarded by four hundred soldiers, but they excelled in daring and dexterity, thanks to their service with Alexander.

They laid violent hands upon Xenopeithes, the captain of the garrison, and threw him from the wall at a point where the cliff was six hundred feet high; and then, after slaughtering some of the remaining guards and casting the others down, they set fire to the buildings. From those who had been standing aside to observe the outcome they increased their number to fifty. Since the stronghold held a large amount of grain and other provisions, they took counsel together whether they ought to remain and take advantage of the strength of the position, awaiting the aid to be expected from Eumenes, or should flee as quickly as possible and move about the country while waiting for a change in the situation. There was a considerable argument, for Docimus advised flight while Attalus declared that he would not be able to endure hardship because of the bad physical condition that had been caused by his imprisonment. While they were disputing with each other, troops had already assembled from sir the adjacent fortresses, more than five hundred foot soldiers and four hundred horsemen; and in addition, others had come from the native peoples, men of every kind to a number exceeding three thousand, who had selected a commander from their own ranks and encamped about the stronghold. When they had unexpectedly been shut in again, Docimus, who had learned that a certain way of descent was unguarded, sent an ambassador to Antigonus' wife Stratonicê, who was in the neighbourhood. When he and one companion escaped by arrangement with her, he was accorded no confidence but was handed over to a guard; and the man who had gone out with him became a guide for the enemy, conducted a considerable number of them into the stronghold, and occupied one of the peaks. Although the followers of Attalus were far outnumbered, their courage enabled them to hold their ground, and keeping up the fight day after day they resisted stubbornly; only after they had been besieged for a year and four months were they taken by assault.

How Antigonus pursued Eumenes and was defeated at the Coprates River (17-18).

17. When Democleides was archon at Athens [316/7], the Romans elected Gaius Junius and Quintus Aemilius consuls. This was the one hundred and sixteenth celebration of the Olympic Games, at which Deinomenes the Laconian won the footrace. At this time Antigonus set out from Mesopotamia and came into Babylonia, where he made an agreement for common action with Seleucus and Pithon. He received soldiers from them also, made a pontoon bridge over the Tigris River, took his army across, and set out against the enemy. When Eumenes learned what had taken place, he ordered Xenophilus, who was guarding the citadel of Susa, not to give any of the money to Antigonus nor to have any conference with him. Eumenes himself with his forces set out for the Tigris River, which is a day's march from Susa at the place where it flows out of the mountainous country that is occupied by the unconquered tribesmen called the Uxii. Its width in many places is three stades, and in some places even four; and in the middle of the stream the depth is about the height of an elephant. After flowing along for some seven hundred stades from the mountains, it empties into the Red Sea, and it contains abundant salt-water fishes as well as sharks, which appear just about the time of the rising of the Dog Star. Keeping this river in front of them as a protection and holding the bank from its source to the sea with pickets, they awaited the onset of the enemy. Since this guard because of its length required no small number of soldiers, Eumenes and Antigenes requested Peucestes to summon ten thousand bowmen from Persia. At first he paid no heed to them, since he still bore a grudge for not having received the generalship; but later, reasoning with himself, he admitted that should Antigonus be victorious the result would be that he himself would lose his satrapy and also be in danger of his life. In his anxiety, therefore, about himself, and thinking also that he would be more likely to gain the command if he had as many soldiers as possible, he brought up ten thousand bowmen as they requested. Although some of the Persians were distant a thirty days' journey, they all received the order on that very day, thanks to the skilful arrangement of the posts of the guard, a matter that it is not well to pass over in silence. Persia is cut by many narrow valleys and has many lookout posts that are high and close together, on which those of the inhabitants who had the loudest voices had been stationed. Since these posts were separated from each other by the distance at which a man's voice can be heard, those who received the order passed it on in the same way to the next, and then these in turn to others until the message had been delivered at the border of the satrapy.

18. While Eumenes and Peucestes were engaged in these matters, Antigonus advanced with his army and came to Susa, the capital. He appointed Seleucus satrap of that country, gave him troops, and ordered him to lay siege to the citadel, since the treasurer, Xenophilus, refused to accept his orders. He himself with his army broke camp and set out against the enemy although the road was very hot and very dangerous for a foreign army to traverse. For this reason they were forced to march at night and make camp near the river before sunrise. Nevertheless, he was not able to escape altogether untouched by the hardships characteristic of the country; although he did everything in his power, he lost a large number of men because of the extreme heat, for it was in fact the season when the Dog Star rises. When he reached the Coprates River, he began to make preparations for crossing. This river, running from a certain mountainous region, enters the Pasitigris, which was at a distance of about eighty stades from Eumenes' camp. It is about four plethra in width, but since it is swift in current, it required boats or a bridge. Seizing a few punts, he sent some of the infantry across in them, ordering them to dig a moat and build a palisade in front of it, and to receive the rest of the army. But as soon as Eumenes heard from scouts of the enemy's move, he crossed the pontoon bridge over the Tigris with four thousand foot soldiers and thirteen hundred horsemen and surprised the soldiers of Antigonus who had crossed - more than three thousand foot soldiers, four hundred cavalry, and not less than six thousand of those soldiers who were in the habit of crossing in scattered groups in search of forage. Falling suddenly upon them while they were in disorder, Eumenes routed the rest of them at once, and those of the Macedonians who resisted he overcame by his onset and by weight of numbers and compelled them all to flee to the river. They all rushed to the boats, but these were submerged by the great number of the men who embarked, and most of those who ventured to swim were carried away by the current and drowned, only a few getting safely over. Those who did not know how to swim, preferring captivity to death in the river, were taken prisoners to the number of four thousand. Antigonus, although he saw that great number being destroyed, could not go to their aid on account of his lack of boats.

How he set out into Media and lost many of his troops in the passes (19-20).

19. Believing that the crossing was impossible, Antigonus set out toward the city of Badacê, which is situated on the bank of the Eulaeus River. Since the march was scorching hot because of the intensity of the sun's rays, many soldiers perished, and the army became discouraged. Nevertheless, after staying in the above mentioned city for a few days and letting the army recover from its sufferings, he decided that the best course was to march to Ecbatana in Media and with that as a base to gain control of the upper satrapies. There were two roads leading into Media, each having a disadvantage: the road leading to Colon was a good royal highway, but it was hot and long, extending for almost forty days' march; while the other, which passed through the Cossaean tribes, was difficult and narrow, skirting precipices and passing through enemy territory, and moreover lacking in supplies, but it was short and cool. It is not easy for an army to follow this route without having gained the consent of the tribesmen who inhabited the mountain ranges. These men, who have been independent from ancient times, live in caves, eating acorns and mushrooms, and also the smoked flesh of wild beasts. Since Antigonus regarded it as beneath his dignity to use persuasion on these people or to make them presents when he had so great an army following him, he selected the finest of the peltasts and divided the bowmen, the slingers, and the other light-armed troops into two bodies, one of which he gave to Nearchus, ordering him to go on ahead and occupy in advance the places that were narrow and difficult. After arranging the other group along the entire line of march, he himself advanced with the phalanx, putting Pithon in command of the rear guard. Now Nearchus' detachment going on ahead occupied a few of the lookouts; but since they were too late in the case of most of them and those the most important, they lost many men and barely made their way through with the barbarians pressing hard upon them. As for the troops led by Antigonus, whenever they came to these difficult passes, they fell into dangers in which no aid could reach them. For the natives, who were familiar with the region and had occupied the heights in advance, kept rolling great rocks in quick succession upon the marching troops; and at the same time, sending arrows thick and fast, they wounded men who were able neither to turn aside the missiles nor to avoid them because of the difficulties of the terrain. Since the road was precipitous and nearly impassable, the elephants, the cavalry, and even the heavy armed soldiers found themselves forced at the same time to face death and to toil hard, without being able to help themselves. Caught in such toils, Antigonus regretted that he had not heeded Pithon when he advised him to purchase the right of passage with money; nevertheless, after losing many men and endangering the entire undertaking, he came with difficulty on the ninth day safe into the settled part of Media.

20. The soldiers of Antigonus, however, because of the continuous misfortunes and their own extreme misery, became so critical of him that they let fall hostile remarks; for in forty days they had met with three great disasters. Nevertheless, by mingling with the soldiers on friendly terms and by making ready an abundant supply of all provisions, he restored the army from its miserable state. He sent Pithon out, ordering him to go through all Media and gather as many horsemen and war horses as he could, and also a quantity of baggage animals. As that land always abounds in four-footed beasts, Pithon readily accomplished his mission and returned bringing two thousand horsemen, more than a thousand horses with their trappings, a sufficient number of beasts of burden to equip the entire army, and in addition to this, five hundred talents of the royal treasure. Antigonus organized the horsemen in troops, and by giving horses to men who had lost their own and by distributing most of the pack animals as presents, he regained the goodwill of the soldiers.

Antigonus' battle against Eumenes and the satraps in Paraetacenê (21-31).

21. When the satraps and generals with Eumenes learned that the enemy was encamped in Media, they disagreed among themselves; for Eumenes, Antigenes, who commanded the Silver Shields, and all those who had made the march up from the sea, believed that they should go back to the coast; but those who had come down from the satrapies, anxious about their own private affairs, asserted that it was essential to maintain control of the upper country. As the disagreement became more violent, Eumenes, seeing that if the army should be divided neither part would be capable of fighting by itself, deferred to the wishes of the satraps who had come from the interior. Leaving the Pasitigris, accordingly, they proceeded to Persepolis, the capital of Persia, a march of twenty-four days. The first part of the road as far as the so-called Ladder was through an enclosed valley, torrid and lacking in provisions, but the rest was over high land, blessed with a very healthful climate and full of the fruits appropriate to the season. For there were glens heavily overgrown and shady, cultivated trees of various kinds in parks, also natural converging glades full of trees of every sort and streams of water, so that travellers lingered with delight in places pleasantly inviting repose. Also there was an abundance of cattle of every kind, which Peucestes gathered together from the inhabitants and distributed without stint to the soldiers, seeking their goodwill. But those who inhabited this country were the most warlike of the Persians, every man being a bowman and a slinger, and in density of population, too, this country far surpassed the other satrapies.

22. When they had arrived in Persepolis, the capital, Peucestes, who was general of this land, performed a magnificent sacrifice to the gods and to Alexander and Philip; and, after gathering from almost the whole of Persia a multitude of sacrificial animals and of whatever else was needed for festivities and religious gatherings, he gave a feast to the army. With the company of those participating he filled four circles, one within the other, with the largest circle inclosing the others. The circuit of the outer ring was of ten stades and was filled with the mercenaries and the mass of the allies; the circuit of the second was of eight stades, and in it were the Macedonian Silver Shields and those of the Companions who had fought under Alexander; the circuit of the next was of four stades and its area was filled with reclining men; the commanders of lower rank, the friends and generals who were unassigned, and the cavalry; lastly in the inner circle with a perimeter of two stades each of the generals and hipparchs and also each of the Persians who was most highly honoured occupied his own couch. In the middle of these there were altars for the gods and for Alexander and Philip. The couches were formed of heaps of leaves covered by hangings and rugs of every kind, since Persia furnished in plenty everything needed for luxury and enjoyment; and the circles were sufficiently separated from each other so that the banqueters should not be crowded and that all the provisions should be near at hand.

23. While all were being duly served, the crowd applauded the generosity of Peucestes, and it was clear that he had made a great advance in popularity. But Eumenes, seeing this and reasoning that Peucestes was playing up to the crowd in furtherance of his desire for the chief command, had fabricated a false letter, through which he made the soldiers confident of the outcome of the battles and, by lowering the pomp and circumstance of Peucestes, improved his own standing and increased his prospects of success in the eyes of the crowd. The purport of what he had written was that Olympias, associating Alexander's son with herself, had recovered firm control of the kingdom of Macedonia after slaying Cassander, and that Polyperchon had crossed into Asia against Antigonus with the strongest part of the royal army and the elephants and was already advancing in the neighbourhood of Cappadocia. The letter, written in the Syrian writing, was sent from Orontes, who held the satrapy of Armenia and who was a friend of Peucestes. Since the letter was believed because of the previous friendship between the satraps, Eumenes ordered it to be carried around and shown to the commanders and also to most of the other soldiers. The sentiment of the entire encampment was changed and all began to turn their attention to Eumenes' prospects in the belief that he would be able by help of the kings both to promote whomever he wished and to exact punishment from those who wronged him. After the feast Eumenes, in his desire to overawe those who did not obey him or who craved a command, brought to trial Sibyrtius, who was satrap of Arachosia and a very close friend of Peucestes. Without Sibyrtius' knowledge, Eumenes sent some horsemen into Arachosia, and by ordering the seizure of his baggage, he brought him into such danger that, if he had not escaped secretly, he would have been condemned to death by the assembly.

24. After Eumenes had frightened the others in this manner and had surrounded himself with pomp and circumstance, he changed once more and, having won Peucestes over with kind words and great promises, rendered him loyal toward himself and eager to join in the struggle in behalf of the kings. Desiring to exact from the other satraps and generals hostages, as it were, to prevent their deserting him, he pretended to be in need of money and called on each of them to lend all the money he could to the kings. By taking four hundred talents from those leaders from whom he considered it expedient, he converted men whom he had formerly suspected of plotting against him or of intending to abandon him into most faithful guards of his person and partners in the contest.

While Eumenes was making these strategic moves with an eye to the future, there came men from Media with information that Antigonus and his army had broken camp and set out for Persia. When he heard this, he also set out, having made up his mind to meet the enemy and risk the issue. On the second day of the journey he performed a sacrifice to the gods and entertained the army sumptuously; the large majority he had indeed encouraged to loyalty, but he himself during the drinking bout was led on by those of the invited guests who were eagerly engaged in drinking, and he became ill. For this reason he delayed the march for some days, since he was overcome by his ailment; and the army was disheartened, for the enemy were expected to engage them shortly and the ablest of their generals was handicapped by his illness. Nevertheless, when the attack had passed its crisis and he had recovered a little, Eumenes advanced with the army, which Peucestes and Antigenes were leading, while he himself, carried in a litter, followed the rearguard so that he might not be disturbed by the confusion and the congestion of the road.

25. When the armies were a day's march from each other, they both sent scouts, and after learning the size and the intentions of the enemy, they both made ready for the fray; but they separated without a battle; for each had drawn up his army with a river and a ravine in front of him, and because of the difficulty of the terrain they were not able to come to blows. The armies, encamped at a distance of three stades from each other for four days, continued to skirmish and to plunder the country, for they were entirely without supplies; but on the fifth day Antigonus sent envoys to the satraps and the Macedonians, urging them not to obey Eumenes but to put trust in himself. He said that he would allow the satraps to keep their own satrapies, that to some of the Macedonians he would give a large gift of land, would send back others to their homes with honours and gifts, and would assign to appropriate posts those who wished to serve in his army. When, however, the Macedonians paid no heed to these offers and even threatened the envoys, Eumenes came forward and praised them and told them a tale, one of the traditional time-worn stories, it is true, but one not unsuited to the situation. He said that a lion, having fallen in love with a maiden, spoke to the girl's father about marriage. The father said that he was ready to give her to him, but that he was afraid of the lion's claws and teeth, fearing that after he had married her he might lose his temper about something and turn on the maiden in the manner of a beast. When, however, the lion had pulled out his claws and his teeth, the father, perceiving that the lion had thrown away everything which had made him formidable, killed him easily by beating him with a club. "It is this same sort of thing," he added, "that Antigonus is doing now; he will only keep his promises until he becomes master of the army, and in that very moment will execute its leaders." While the crowd was shouting approval and saying "Right," he dismissed the assembly.

26. That night, however, there appeared certain deserters from Antigonus' army with the report that Antigonus had given his soldiers orders to break camp at about the second watch. Eumenes, on considering the matter, concluded rightly that the enemy intended to withdraw into Gabene, as this place, distant about three days' march, was un-plundered and filled with grain, fodder, and in general with that which could amply supply the provisions for a great army. Furthermore, the terrain itself supplemented these advantages, since it had rivers and ravines that were hard to cross. Being anxious, therefore, to occupy this place before the enemy, he imitated him. He caused certain mercenaries, whose consent he had won by money, to go away as if they were deserting, ordering them to say that Eumenes had decided to attack the camp during that night. He himself, however, sent the baggage on ahead and ordered the soldiers to break camp after having taken a very hasty meal. When all this had been swiftly accomplished, Antigonus, who had heard from the deserters that the enemy had decided to fight during the night, postponed his departure and drew up his forces for the battle. While he was distracted by these operations and concentrating on the coming battle, he failed to notice that Eumenes had got the start of him and was marching at top speed for Gabene. For some time Antigonus kept his army under arms; but when he learned from his scouts that his opponent had departed, although he knew that he had been outgeneralled, none the less he held to his original purpose. So, ordering his soldiers to break camp, he led them on a forced march that resembled a pursuit. Eumenes, however, had a start of two watches; therefore Antigonus, knowing that it was not easy to overtake with his whole army a force that was so far ahead, devised a stratagem as follows. He gave the rest of the army to Pithon and ordered him to follow at leisure, but he himself with the cavalry pursued at top speed; and overtaking the rearguard of the enemy at daybreak just as it was coming down from some hilly country, he took position on the ridges, where he was visible to the enemy. When Eumenes from a considerable distance beheld cavalry of the enemy and supposed that the entire army was near, he halted the march and drew up his army on the assumption there would be an engagement immediately. Thus in the manner described the generals of the two armies each outwitted the other as if they were taking part in a preliminary contest of skill and showing that each placed his hope of victory in himself. In any case, Antigonus by this device prevented the enemy from going forward while securing for himself a respite in which to bring up his army, and then when the army arrived, he drew it all up for battle and marched down in awe-inspiring array against the enemy.

27. Including the reinforcements brought by Pithon and Seleucus, Antigonus had in all more than twenty-eight thousand foot soldiers, eight thousand five hundred horsemen, and sixty-five elephants. The generals employed different formations in drawing up the armies, vying with each other in regard to their competence in tactical skill as well. On his left wing Eumenes stationed Eudamus, who had brought the elephants from India, with his squadron of one hundred and fifty horsemen, and as an advance guard for them two troops of selected mounted lancers with a strength of fifty horsemen. He placed them in contact with the higher land of the base of the hill, and next to them he put Stasander, the general, who had his own cavalry to the number of nine hundred and fifty. After them he stationed Amphimachus, the satrap of Mesopotamia, whom six hundred horsemen followed, and in contact with these were the six hundred horsemen from Arachosia, whose leader formerly had been Sibyrtius, but, because of the latter's flight, Cephalon had assumed command of them. Next were five hundred from Paropanisadae and an equal number of Thracians from the colonies of the upper country. In front of all these he drew up forty-five elephants in a curved line with a suitable number of bowmen and slingers in the spaces between the animals. When Eumenes had made the left wing strong in this way, he placed the phalanx beside it. The outer end of this consisted of the mercenaries, who numbered more than six thousand; next were about five thousand men who had been equipped in the Macedonian fashion although they were of all races.

28. After them he drew up the Macedonian Silver Shields, more than three thousand in number, undefeated troops, the fame of whose exploits caused much fear among the enemy, and finally the men from the hypaspists, more than three thousand, with Antigenes and Teutamus leading both them and the Silver Shields. In front of the whole phalanx he placed forty elephants, filling the spaces between them with light armed soldiers. On the right wing he stationed cavalry: next to the phalanx, eight hundred from Carmania led by the satrap Tlepolemus, then the nine hundred called the Companions and the squadron of Peucestes and Antigenes, which contained three hundred horsemen arranged in a single unit. At the outer end of the wing was Eumenes' squadron with the same number of horsemen, and as an advance-guard for them two troops of Eumenes' slaves, each composed of fifty mounted men, while at an angle beyond the end of the wing and guarding it were four troops, in which there were two hundred selected horsemen. In addition to these, three hundred men selected from all the cavalry commands for swiftness and strength were stationed by Eumenes behind his own squadron. Along the whole of the wing he drew up forty elephants. The entire army of Eumenes consisted of thirty-five thousand foot soldiers, sixty-one

hundred horsemen, and one hundred and fourteen elephants.

29. As Antigonus looked down from a high position, he saw the battle line of his enemy and disposed his own army accordingly. Seeing that the right wing of the enemy had been strengthened with the elephants and the strongest of the cavalry, he arrayed against it the lightest of his horsemen, who, drawn up in open order, were to avoid a frontal action but maintain a battle of wheeling tactics and in this way thwart that part of the enemies' forces in which they had the greatest confidence. On this wing he stationed the mounted archers and lancers from Media and Parthia, a thousand in number, men well trained in the execution of the wheeling movement; and next he placed the twenty-two hundred Tarentines who had come up with him from the sea, men selected for their skill in ambushing, and very well disposed to himself, the thousand cavalry from Phrygia and Lydia, the fifteen hundred with Pithon, the four hundred lancers with Lysanias, and in addition to all these, the cavalry who are called the "two-horse men," and the eight hundred cavalry from the colonists established in the upper country. The left wing was made up of these cavalrymen, all of whom were under the command of Pithon. Of the infantry, more than nine thousand mercenaries were placed first, next to them three thousand Lycians and Pamphylians, then more than eight thousand mixed troops in Macedonian equipment, and finally nearly eight thousand Macedonians, whom Antipater had given him at the time when he was appointed regent of the kingdom. The first of the horsemen on the right wing adjacent to the phalanx were five hundred mercenaries of mixed origin, then a thousand Thracians, five hundred from the allies, and next to them the thousand known as the Companions with Antigonus' son Demetrius as commander, now about to fight in company with his father for the first time. At the outer end of the wing was the squadron of three hundred horsemen with whom Antigonus himself was entering the battle. As an advance guard for these there were three troops from his own slaves, and parallel to them were as many units reinforced by a hundred Tarentines. Along the whole wing he drew up the strongest thirty of the elephants, making a curved line, and he filled the intervals between them with selected light armed men. Most of the other elephants he placed before the phalanx, but a few were with the cavalry on the left wing. When he had drawn up the army in this fashion, he advanced down the hill against the enemy keeping an oblique front, for he thrust forward the right wing, in which he had most confidence, and held the left back, having determined to avoid battle with the one and to decide the contest with the other.

30. When the armies were close to each other and the signal had been raised in each of them, the troops shouted the battle-cry alternately several times and the trumpeters gave the signal for battle. First Pithon's cavalry, who had no stability or any advance-guard worth mentioning yet were superior to those arrayed against them in numbers and in mobility, began trying to make use of their own advantages. They did not consider it safe to make a frontal attack against elephants, yet by riding out around the wing and making an attack on the flanks, they kept inflicting wounds with repeated flights of arrows, suffering no harm themselves because of their mobility but causing great damage to the beasts, which because of their weight could neither pursue nor retire when the occasion demanded. When Eumenes, however, observed that the wing was hard pressed by the multitude of mounted archers, he summoned the most lightly equipped of his cavalry from Eudamus, who had the left wing. Leading the whole squadron in a flanking movement, he made an attack upon his opponents with light armed soldiers and the most lightly equipped of the cavalry. Since the elephants also followed, he easily routed the forces of Pithon, and pursued them to the foothills. At the same time that this was going on, it so happened that the infantry for a considerable time had been engaged in a battle of phalanxes, but finally, after many had fallen on both sides, Eumenes' men were victorious because of the valour of the Macedonian Silver Shields. These warriors were already well on in years, but because of the great number of battles they had fought they were outstanding in hardihood and skill, so that no one confronting them was able to withstand their might. Therefore, although there were then only three thousand of them, they had become, so to speak, the spearhead of the whole army.

Although Antigonus saw that his own left wing had been put to flight and that the entire phalanx had been defeated, he did not heed those who advised him to retire to the mountains and furnish a rallying point for those who escaped from the rout, while keeping the part of the army under his immediate command an unbroken unit; but rather, by cleverly taking advantage of the opportunities offered by the situation, he both saved the fugitives and gained the victory. For as soon as Eumenes' Silver Shields and the remaining body of his infantry had routed those who opposed them, they pursued them as far as the nearer hills; but Antigonus, now that a break was thus caused in the line of his enemy, charged through with a detachment of cavalry, striking on the flank the troops who had been stationed with Eudamus on the left wing. Because the attack was unexpected, he quickly put to flight those who faced him, destroying many of them; then he sent out the swiftest of his mounted men and by means of them he assembled those of his soldiers who were fleeing and once more formed them into a line along the foothills. As soon as Eumenes learned of the defeat of his own soldiers he recalled the pursuers by a trumpet signal, for he was eager to aid Eudamus.

31. Although it was already lamp-lighting time, both rallied their fleeing troops and began to put their entire forces in battle order once more, such zeal for victory filled not only the generals but also the mass of the contestants. Since the night was clear and lighted by a full moon and the armies were forming parallel to each other at a distance of about four plethra, the clatter of arms and the snorting of the horses seemed close at hand to all the contestants. As they were moving from column into line, being distant about thirty stades from those who had fallen in the battle, the hour of midnight overtook them, and both armies were so exhausted by marching, by their suffering in the battle, and by lack of food, that they were forced to give up the battle and go into camp. Eumenes undertook to march back to the dead, desiring to control the disposal of the bodies and to put his claim to victory beyond dispute. When, however, the soldiers would not listen to him, insisting with shouts that they return to their own baggage train, which was some distance away, he was forced to yield to the majority; for he was not able to punish the soldiers severely when there were many who disputed his right to command, and he saw that the time was not suitable for chastising those who disobeyed. On the other hand, Antigonus, who firmly held the command without need of courting popular favour, forced his army to make camp by the bodies; and since he gained control of their burial, he claimed the victory, declaring that to possess the fallen is to be victorious in battle. In this battle three thousand seven hundred foot and fifty-four horse from the army of Antigonus were slain and more than four thousand men were wounded; five hundred and forty of Eumenes' infantry and very few of his cavalry fell, and the wounded were more than nine hundred.

The withdrawal of Antigonus and his army into Media for winter quarters (32-34).

32. When after leaving the battle Antigonus saw that his men were disheartened, he decided to move as far as possible from the enemy with the utmost speed. Wishing to have the army unencumbered for the retirement, he sent the wounded men and the heaviest part of the baggage ahead to one of the neighbouring cities. He began to bury the dead at dawn and detained the herald who had come from the enemy to treat for the recovery of the bodies; and he ordered his men to eat dinner at once. When the day had passed he sent the herald back, assigning the removal of the bodies to the next morning, but he himself at the beginning of the first watch broke camp with the whole army, and by making forced marches withdrew a long distance from the enemy and gained an un-plundered country in which to refresh his soldiers. He went, indeed, as far as Gamarga in Media, a land that was subject to Pithon and that was able to supply great armies abundantly with everything needed for their support. When Eumenes learned through scouts of the departure of Antigonus, he refrained from following him because his own soldiers also had lacked food and had suffered great hardship; but he attended to the taking up of the dead and saw to it that they received a magnificent burial. Then an event took place that was amazing and very different from Greek custom.

33. Ceteus, the general of the soldiers who had come from India, was killed in the battle after fighting brilliantly, but he left two wives who had accompanied him in the army, one of them a bride, the other married to him some years before, but both of them loving him deeply. It is an ancient custom among the Indians that the men who marry and the maidens who are married do not do so as a result of the decision of their parents but by mutual persuasion. Formerly, since the wooing was done by persons who were too young, it often happened that, the choice turning out badly, both would quickly regret their act, and that many wives were first seduced, then through wantonness gave their love to other men, and finally, not being able without disgrace to leave the mates whom they had first selected, would kill their husbands by poison. The country, indeed, furnished no few means for this, since it produced many and varied deadly poisons, some of which when merely spread upon the food or the wine cups cause death. But when this evil be- sir came fashionable and many were murdered in this way, the Indians, although they punished those guilty of the crime, since they were not able to deter the others from wrongdoing, established a law that wives, except such as were pregnant or had children, should be cremated along with their deceased husbands, and that one who was not willing to obey this law should not only be a widow for life but also be entirely debarred from sacrifices and other religious observances as unclean. When these laws had been established, the lawlessness of the women changed into the opposite, for as each one because of the great loss of caste willingly met death, they not only cared for the safety of their husbands as if it were their own, but they even vied with each other as for a very great honour.

34. Such rivalry appeared on this occasion. Although the law ordered only one of Ceteus' wives to be cremated with him, both of them appeared at his funeral, contending for the right of dying with him as for a prize of valour. When the generals undertook to decide the matter, the younger wife claimed that the other was pregnant and for that reason could not take advantage of the law; and the elder asserted that more justly should the one who had the precedence in years have precedence also in honour, for in all other matters those who are older are regarded as having great precedence over the younger in respect and in honour. The generals, ascertaining from those skilled in midwifery that the elder was pregnant, decided for the younger. When this happened, the one who had lost the decision departed weeping, rending the wreath that was about her head and tearing her hair, just as if some great disaster had been announced to her; but the other, rejoicing in her victory, went off to the pyre crowned with fillets that her maidservants bound upon her head, and magnificently dressed as if for a wedding she was escorted by her kinsfolk, who sang a hymn in honour of her virtue. As she drew near the pyre, she stripped off her ornaments and gave them to her servants and friends, leaving keepsakes, as one might say, to those who loved her. These were the ornaments: upon her hands a number of rings set with precious stones of various colours, about her head no small number of golden stars interspersed with stones of every kind, and about her neck numerous necklaces, some of them smaller, the others each a little larger in a constant progression. Finally, after taking leave of the household, she was assisted to mount the pyre by her brother, and while the multitude that had gathered for the spectacle watched with amazement, she ended her life in heroic fashion. For the entire army under arms marched three times about the pyre before it was lighted, and she herself, reclining beside her husband and letting no ignoble cry escape her during the onset of the fire, stirred some of those who beheld her to pity, others to extravagant praise. Nevertheless some of the Greeks denounced the custom as barbarous and cruel.

When Eumenes had completed the burial of the dead, he moved the army from among the Paraetaceni into Gabene, which was un-plundered and. capable of supplying everything in abundance for the armies. It happened that this country was a twenty-five days' march from Antigonus if one went through inhabited country, but if one went through waterless desert, a march of nine days. In these regions and at this distance from each other Eumenes and Antigonus passed the winter and at the same time refreshed their men [317/16].

Cassander's invasion of Macedonia and his siege of Olympias in Pydna (35-36).

35. In Europe when Cassander, who was besieging Tegea in the Peloponnesus, learned of the return of Olympias to Macedonia and of the murder of Eurydicê and King Philip, and moreover what had befallen the tomb of his brother Iollas, he came to terms with the people of Tegea and set out for Macedonia with his army, leaving his allies in complete confusion; for Polyperchon's son Alexander with an army was waiting to attack the cities of the Peloponnesus. The Aetolians, who wished to please Olympias and Polyperchon, had occupied the pass at Thermopylae and barred Cassander from the passage. Cassander decided against forcing his way through this region, which was difficult to attack, but he secured boats and barges from Euboea and Locris and transported his army to Thessaly. Hearing that Polyperchon and his army were in position in Perrhaebia, he dispatched his general Callas with an army, ordering him to carry on the war with Polyperchon. Deinias, however, in order to occupy the passes, went to meet the soldiers who had been sent out by Olympias and gained control of the defiles ahead of them. Olympias, on learning that Cassander and a large army were near Macedonia, designated Aristonoüs general, ordering him to fight Cassander, and she herself went to Pydna accompanied by the following: Alexander's son, his mother Roxanê, and Thessalonicê, daughter of Philip son of Amyntas; also Deidameia, daughter of Aeacides king of the Epirotes and sister of that Pyrrhus who later fought against the Romans, the daughters of Attalus, and finally the kinsfolk of Olympias' other more important friends. Thus there were gathered about her a large number of persons, but persons for the most part useless in war; and there was not a sufficient supply of food for people who were about to endure a very long siege. Although the risk involved in all these circumstances was clear, none the less she decided to remain there, hoping that many Greeks and Macedonians would come to her aid by sea. She had with her some of the Ambracian horse and most of the soldiers who were accustomed to serve about the court, also those of Polyperchon's elephants that remained, for Cassander had gained possession of the rest of the elephants in his previous expedition into Macedonia.

36. Cassander, going through the passes of Perrhaebia and arriving near Pydna, surrounded the city from sea to sea with a stockade and requisitioned ships, missile weapons of all sorts, and engines of war from those who wished to become his allies, with the intention of laying siege to Olympias by land and sea [317/6]. Being informed that Aeacides king of the Epirotes was about to come to the aid of Olympias with an army, he sent out Atarrhias as general, giving him an army and ordering him to meet the Epirotes. Atarrhias carried out his orders quickly and by occupying the passes from Epirus succeeded in holding Aeacides inactive. Indeed, most of the Epirotes set out for Macedonia against their will and were mutinying in the camp; and Aeacides, who wished at all costs to aid Olympias, by releasing from the army those who were disaffected and taking those who wished to share the fortunes of war with him, although he showed his zeal for a fight to a finish, was not a match for his opponents because few of his army remained. Those of the Epirotes who went back to their native land rebelled against their absent king, condemned him to exile by a public decree, and made an alliance with Cassander. This was something that had never happened in Epirus from the time when Neoptolemus the son of Achilles was king of the land; for sons had always succeeded to their fathers' authority and had died on the throne up to this time. Cassander received Epirus in his alliance and sent Lyciscus to it as regent and general, at which the people throughout Macedonia who had previously held apart from the alliance abandoned the fortunes of Olympias in despair and joined themselves to Cassander. Her only hope of aid was from Polyperchon, and this was also unexpectedly crushed; for when Callas, who had been sent by Cassander as general, drew near Polyperchon in Perrhaebia and camped there, he corrupted most of Polyperchon's soldiers by bribes so that there remained only a few and these the most faithful. Thus Olympias' hopes were humbled in a brief time.

How Eumenes outgeneralled Antigonus when the latter was going through the desert (37-38).

37. In Asia Antigonus, who was wintering in Gadamala in Media, seeing that his force was weaker than that of the enemy, was anxious to get the better of them by attacking them without warning. It happened that the enemy were occupying winter quarters which were divided in many parts, so that some of the detachments were six days' march distant from others. So Antigonus disapproved of the idea of marching through the inhabited country because the route was long and easily observed by the enemy, and decided that to venture the journey through the waterless desert although difficult, would be most suitable for the attack that he had planned; for not only was it possible to go quickly by that route, but it was also easy to escape attention and fall unexpectedly upon an army that, because ignorant of his movements, would be scattered among villages and at its ease. Having formed this plan he ordered the soldiers to be ready to break camp and to prepare ten days' supply of food that would not require cooking. He himself, after spreading the report that he was going to lead the army against Armenia, suddenly and contrary to the assumption of all set out across the desert, it being about the time of the winter solstice. He gave orders to build the fires in the camps by day, but to extinguish them completely at night, so that no one seeing them from the higher ground might take word to the enemy of what was happening; for almost the entire desert was a plain, but it was surrounded by high hills from which it was easy to see the gleam of fire from a great distance. After the army had been marching five days with great suffering, the soldiers because of the cold and to satisfy their urgent needs burned fires in the camps both by day and by night. On seeing this, certain of those who lived near the desert sent men to report it on the same day to Eumenes and Peucestes, giving them dromedaries, for this animal can travel continuously for almost fifteen hundred stades.

38. When Peucestes learned that a camp had been seen in the middle of the route, he made up his mind to withdraw to the most distant part of the territory in which they were wintering, for he was afraid that they might be overtaken by the enemy before the allied force assembled from all directions. Seeing his lack of spirit, Eumenes urged him to take courage and to remain on the borders of the desert; for, he said, he had found a way through which he would delay Antigonus' arrival by three or four days. If this took place, he added, their own force would easily be assembled, and the enemy would be delivered over into their hands when utterly worn out and lacking everything. While all were wondering at this strange promise and were trying to learn what in the world it would be that could prevent the enemy from advancing, he ordered all the commanders to follow him with their own soldiers bringing fire in many jars. He then selected a place in the higher ground that faced toward the desert and was well situated to be clearly visible from every direction and by setting up markers laid out a space with a perimeter of seventy stades. Assigning an area to each of those who followed him, he ordered them at night to light fires about twenty cubits apart and to keep the flames bright in the first watch as if men were still awake and busy with the care of their bodies and the preparation of food, but dimmer in the second watch, and in the third watch to leave only a very few, so that to those who watched from a distance it would seem to be a genuine camp. The soldiers carried out the directions. The flames were seen by some of those who pastured flocks on the hills opposite and who were friendly toward Pithon, the satrap of Media. Believing that this truly was a camp, they hurried down into the plain and carried the news to Antigonus and Pithon. These were astonished at this unexpected news and halted the march while they took counsel how they should use this information, for it was dangerous to lead an army that had been undergoing hardship and was in need of everything against hostile forces that were already assembled and were well provided with everything. Believing that there had been treachery and that the enemy had assembled because they knew in advance what was to happen, they gave up the plan of going straight forward and, turning to the right, went to un-plundered parts of the inhabited country, since they wished to refresh the army after its hardships.

The march of Antigonus through the desert against the enemy and his attack on their elephants in the winter quarters (39).

39. When Eumenes had outgeneralled the enemy in the manner described, he called together from all sides those of his soldiers who had been widely scattered while wintering in the villages. After building a palisade as a protection and strengthening the encampment by a deep ditch, he received those of the allies who came down from time to time, and he filled the camp with all the necessary supplies. Antigonus, having got across the desert, learned from the inhabitants that, although almost all the rest of Eumenes' army had assembled, the elephants were slow in leaving their winter quarters and were near at hand, cut off from all assistance. He sent cavalry against them, two thousand Median lancers and two hundred Tarentines, and all his light infantry, for he hoped that, by attacking the elephants when they were isolated, he could easily gain control of them and deprive the enemy of the strongest element in his army. Eumenes, however, guessing what was on foot, sent to the rescue fifteen hundred of the strongest cavalry and three thousand light infantry. Since the soldiers of Antigonus arrived first, the commanders of the elephants arranged them in a square and advanced, placing the baggage train in the centre and in the rear the cavalry that accompanied the elephants, consisting of a force of not more than four hundred men. As the enemy fell upon them with all its weight and pressed ever more heavily, the cavalry was routed, overwhelmed by numbers; but those who were in charge of the elephants resisted at first and held firm even though they were receiving wounds from all directions and were not able to injure the enemy in return in any way; and then, when they were now becoming exhausted, the troops sent by Eumenes suddenly appeared and rescued them from their danger. A few days later, when the armies were encamped opposite each other at a distance of forty stades, each general drew up his army for battle, expecting to decide the issue.

How after a pitched battle Antigonus gained control of all the forces of his opponents (40-43).

40. Antigonus placed his cavalry on the wings, giving the command of the left to Pithon and that of the right to his own son Demetrius, beside whom he himself planned to fight. He stationed the foot soldiers in the centre and extended the elephants across the whole front, filling the spaces between them with light armed troops. The total number of his army was twenty-two thousand foot, nine thousand horse including the additional troops enlisted in Media, and sixty-five elephants.

When Eumenes learned that Antigonus had taken his place on the right with his best cavalry, he drew up his army against him, stationing his best troops on the left wing. In fact, he placed there most of the satraps with the selected bodies of cavalry that accompanied them in battle, and he himself intended to take part in the fight along with them. There was also present with them Mithridates, the son of Ariobarzanes and a descendant of one of the seven Persians who slew the Magian Smerdis, a man remarkable for courage and trained from childhood as a soldier.

In front of the whole wing he drew up in a curved line the sixty strongest of the elephants and screened the intervals with light troops. Of the foot soldiers he placed first the hypaspists, then the Silver Shields, and finally the mercenaries and those of the other soldiers who were armed in the Macedonian fashion. In front of the infantry he stationed elephants and an adequate force of his light troops. On the right wing he drew up the weaker of the cavalry and of the elephants, putting all of them under the command of Philip, whom he ordered to avoid battle and to observe the outcome on the other wing. In all there were in Eumenes' army at this time thirty-six thousand seven hundred foot soldiers, six thousand horsemen and one hundred and fourteen elephants.

41. A short, time before the battle Antigenes, the general of the Silver Shields, sent one of the Macedonian horsemen toward the hostile phalanx, ordering him to draw near to it and make proclamation. This man, riding up alone to within earshot opposite the place where the phalanx of Antigonus' Macedonians was stationed, shouted: "Wicked men, are you sinning against your fathers, who conquered the whole world under Philip and Alexander?" and added that in a little while they would see that these veterans were worthy both of the kings and of their own past battles. At this time the youngest of the Silver Shields were about sixty years old, most of the others about seventy, and some even older; but all of them were irresistible because of experience and strength, such was the skill and daring acquired through the unbroken series of their battles. When this proclamation had been delivered as we have said, there arose from the soldiers of Antigonus angry cries to the effect that they were being forced to fight against their kinsfolk and their elders, but from the ranks of Eumenes there came a cheer and a demand that he lead them against the enemy as soon as possible. When Eumenes saw their enthusiasm, he gave the sign by which he directed the trumpeters to sound the signal for combat and the whole army to raise the battle cry.

42. The first to join in battle were the elephants, and after them the main body of the cavalry. Since the plain was of great extent and entirely uncultivated because of the salt that permeated it, such a cloud of dust was raised by the cavalry that from a little distance one could not easily see what was happening. When Antigonus perceived this, he dispatched the Median cavalry and an adequate force of Tarentines against the baggage of the enemy; for he hoped, as indeed happened, that this manoeuvre might not be discovered because of the dust, and that by the capture of the baggage he might prevail over the enemy without labour. The detachment rode around the flank of their opponents and without being noticed attacked the baggage train, which was about five stades distant from the battle. They found that it was packed with a multitude of persons who were useless for fighting but had few defenders, and after quickly defeating those who resisted, they captured all the others. While this was taking place, Antigonus joined battle with those who were opposite him and by appearing with a large number of cavalry struck panic into Peucestes, satrap of Persia, who in retiring from the dust cloud with his own cavalry drew away fifteen hundred others as well. Eumenes, although he and a few troopers were left unsupported at the extremity of the wing, regarded it as shameful to yield to fortune and flee; preferring to die while still upholding with noble resolution the trust that had been given him by the kings, he forced his way toward Antigonus himself. A fierce cavalry battle ensued, in which Eumenes' men were superior in spirit but those of Antigonus had the advantage in number, and many were falling on both sides. It was at this time, while the elephants also were struggling against each other, that Eumenes' leading elephant fell after having been engaged with the strongest of those arrayed against it. Thereupon Eumenes, seeing that his forces were everywhere having the worst of it, led what remained of the cavalry out of the battle and went around to the other wing, where he assumed command of those troops whom he had assigned to Philip and had ordered to avoid fighting. This was the outcome of the cavalry engagement.

43. As for the infantry, the Silver Shields in close order fell heavily upon their adversaries, killing some of them in hand to hand fighting and forcing others to flee. They were not to be checked in their charge and engaged the entire opposing phalanx, showing themselves so superior in skill and strength that of their own men they lost not one, but of those who opposed them they slew over five thousand and routed the entire force of foot soldiers, whose numbers were many times their own. When Eumenes learned that his baggage train was taken but that the cavalry force of Peucestes was not far away, he tried to collect all his mounted men and renew the cavalry battle against Antigonus; for he hoped, if superior in battle, not only to save his own baggage, but also to capture that of the enemy. Since Peucestes, however, would not listen to him but on the contrary retired still farther to a certain river, and since night was now coming on, Eumenes was forced to yield to the situation. Antigonus divided his cavalry into two bodies with one of which he himself lay in wait for Eumenes, watching for his first move; but the other he gave to Pithon and ordered him to attack the Silver Shields now that they had been cut off from their cavalry support. When Pithon promptly carried out his orders, the Macedonians formed themselves into a square and withdrew safely to the river, where they accused Peucestes of being responsible for the defeat of the mounted forces. After Eumenes joined them at about the time for lighting lamps, they took counsel together what should be done. The satraps, indeed, said that it was necessary to retire to the upper satrapies as rapidly as possible, but Eumenes declared that they should stay and fight it out, for the phalanx of the enemy had been shattered and the cavalry forces on the two sides were equal. The Macedonians, however, refused to heed either party since their baggage had been taken, and their children, their wives, and many other relatives were in the hands of the enemy. The meeting accordingly broke up without having adopted any generally approved plan, whereupon the Macedonians secretly entered into negotiations with Antigonus, seized and surrendered Eumenes, recovered their baggage, and after receiving pledges were enrolled in Antigonus' army. In the same way the satraps and most of the other commanders and soldiers deserted their general, thinking only of their own safety.

How he killed Eumenes and such other generals as had been his enemies (44).

44. Now that Antigonus had unexpectedly mastered Eumenes and all the army that had been opposing him, he seized Antigenes, the commander of the Silver Shields, put him into a pit, and burned him alive. He slew Eudamus, who had brought the elephants from India, and Celbanus, as well as certain others of those who had always been hostile to him. Putting Eumenes under guard, he considered how best to dispose of him. He wished, indeed, to have at his side a man who was a good general and who would be under obligations to him, but he had little faith in Eumenes' promises because of the latter's loyalty to Olympias and the kings; in fact, on the previous occasion, after Eumenes had been spared by Antigonus at Nora in Phrygia, he had none the less supported the kings most whole-heartedly. When Antigonus saw also that the ardent desire of the Macedonians for the punishment of Eumenes was not to be turned aside, he put him to death; but because of his former friendship for him, he burned his body, and after placing his bones in an urn, he sent them to his relatives. Among the wounded there was also brought in as a captive the historian Hieronymus of Cardia, who hitherto always had been held in honour by Eumenes, but after Eumenes' death enjoyed the favour and confidence of Antigonus.

After Antigonus had taken his entire army into Media, he himself spent the winter [317/16] in a village that is near Ecbatana, where the capital of this country is situated, but he distributed the soldiers throughout the entire satrapy and particularly in the eparchy called Rhagae, which had received this name from a catastrophe that had occurred there in former times. Of all the lands in that part of the world, its cities had been the most numerous and the most prosperous, but it had experienced so violent an earthquake that both the cities and all their inhabitants vanished, and, in general, the land was altered and new rivers and marshy lakes appeared in place of the former ones.

The flood at Rhodes and the disasters that befell that city (45).

45. At this time occurred the third inundation of the city of Rhodes, which destroyed many of its inhabitants. Of these floods, the first did little damage to the population since the city was newly founded and therefore contained much open space; the second was greater and caused the death of more persons. The last befell at the beginning of spring, great rain storms suddenly bursting forth with hail of incredible size. Indeed, hail-stones fell weighing a mina and sometimes more, so that many of the houses collapsed because of the weight, and no small number of the inhabitants were killed. Since Rhodes is shaped like a theatre and since the streams of water were thus deflected chiefly into a single region, the lower parts of the city were straightway flooded; for, because it was thought that the rainy season of winter had passed, the drains had been neglected and the drainage openings through the city walls had become clogged. The water that suddenly gathered filled the whole region about the Market and the Temple of Dionysus; and then, as the flood was already advancing to the Temple of Asclepius, all were struck with fear and began to follow various plans for gaining safety. Some of them fled to the ships, others ran to the theatre; certain of those overtaken by the calamity in their extremity climbed upon the highest altars and the bases of statues. When the city and all its inhabitants were in danger of being utterly destroyed, relief of a sort came of itself; for, as the walls gave way over a long stretch, the water that had been confined poured out through this opening into the sea, and each man soon returned again to his former place. It was to the advantage of those who were endangered that the flood came by day, for most of the people escaped in time from their houses to the higher parts of the city; and also that the houses were not constructed of sun-dried brick but of stone and that for this reason those who took refuge upon the roofs were safe. Yet in this great disaster more than five hundred persons lost their lives, while some houses collapsed completely and others were badly shaken.

Such was the disaster which befell Rhodes.

The death of Pithon at the hands of Antigonus and the destruction of those who had been instigated by him to revolt in Media (46-48).

46. When Antigonus, who was wintering in Media, was informed that Pithon was winning the support of many of the soldiers in the winter quarters by promises and gifts and that he planned to revolt, he concealed his own intentions and, pretending not to believe those who were spreading the charges, he rebuked them, in the hearing of many, for trying to disrupt his friendship, and caused a report to be spread abroad that he was about to leave Pithon as general of the upper satrapies with an army sufficient for their safety. He even wrote to Pithon himself a letter asking him to come as soon as possible, so that he might discuss the necessary matters with him in person and then quickly make his journey to the sea. He devised this plan because he wished to prevent Pithon from suspecting the truth and to persuade him to come within reach on the assumption that he was about to be left behind as satrap; for it was no easy matter to arrest a man by force who had gained preferment for merit while serving under Alexander and who at that very time was satrap of Media and had curried favour with the entire army. Pithon, who was wintering in the most distant parts of Media, had already corrupted a large number who promised to join him in the revolt, but when his friends wrote to him about the plans of Antigonus and hinted at his own great prospects, he was deceived by empty expectations and came to Antigonus. The latter, when he had gained possession of his person and had accused him before the members of the council, easily won a conviction and had him executed at once. Then,gathering the army into one place,he appointed Orontobates, a Mede, satrap of Media, but he made Hippostratus general with an infantry force of thirty-five hundred mercenaries. . . . Antigonus himself moved to Ecbatana with his army. There he took possession of five thousand talents of uncoined silver and then led the army into Persia, the march to the capital, which is called Persepolis, lasting about twenty days.

47. While Antigonus was on the march, Pithon's friends who had shared in his conspiracy, of whom the most notable were Meleager and Menoetas, collected the scattered comrades of Eumenes and of Pithon to the number of eight hundred mounted men. At first they harried the territory of those Medes who refused to join the revolt, but afterwards, on learning that Hippostratus and Orontobates were encamped with no thought of danger, they set upon the camp by night. They almost took the outer works, but were overcome by numbers and withdrew after winning certain of the soldiers to join the revolt, Since these were without heavy equipment and were all mounted on horses, their raids were unexpected, and the country was filled with confusion. After some time, however, they were hemmed up in a narrow place that was surrounded by cliffs, where some of them were killed and the others were taken alive. Meleager and Ocranes the Mede, who were among the commanders, and some of the outstanding men were killed while resisting the attack.

This was the outcome of the revolt in Media.

48. As soon as Antigonus came into Persia, he was granted the dignity of kingship by the inhabitants as if he was the acknowledged lord of Asia, and he himself sitting in council with his friends considered the question of the satrapies. He permitted Tlepolemus to retain Carmania, and likewise Stasanor to retain Bactianê, for it was not easy to remove them by sending a message since they had conducted themselves well toward the inhabitants and had many supporters. He sent Evitus to Aria, but when Evitus died soon afterwards he put Evagoras in his place, a man admired for both courage and shrewdness. He permitted Oxyartes, the father of Roxanê, to keep the satrapy in Paropanisadae as before, for he too could not be removed without a long campaign and a strong army.

From Arachosia he summoned Sibyrtius, who was well disposed to him, permitted him to retain the satrapy, and assigned to him the most turbulent of the Silver Shields, ostensibly that they might be useful in the war, but in reality to insure their destruction; for he privately directed the satrap to send a few of them at a time on duties in which they were bound to be killed. Among them there were, as it happened, those who had betrayed Eumenes, so that punishment for their treachery to their general came upon them speedily. Unholy acts, in truth, are of advantage to princes because of their power, but to private individuals who have merely obeyed orders they are usually the cause of great evil.

Now Antigonus, perceiving that Peucestes was enjoying great favour among the Persians, first took his satrapy away from him. Then when the Persians were angry, and when Thespius, one of their leading men, even said frankly that the Persians would not obey anyone else, Antigonus had this man killed and set up Asclepiodorus as ruler of Persia, giving him a sufficient number of soldiers. As for Peucestes, Antigonus, after leading him on to hope for other things and filling him with vain expectations, removed him from the country. While Antigonus himself was journeying to Susa, he was met at the Pasitigris River by Xenophilus, the supervisor of the treasury at Susa, who had been sent by Seleucus with orders to carry out Antigonus' every command. Antigonus received him and pretended to honour him among his closest friends, taking care lest he change his mind and shut him out again. When he himself had occupied the citadel of Susa, he found in it the golden climbing vine [Herodotus 7,27] and a great number of other objects of art, weighing all told fifteen thousand talents. There was collected for him, besides, a great amount of money from the crowns and the other gifts, and also from the spoils. This came to five thousand talents; and there was another equal amount in Media apart from the treasury in Susa, so that in all twenty-five thousand talents were gathered together.

Such was the state of the affairs of Antigonus.

The capture of Olympias by Cassander, and her death (49-51).

49. Now that we have completed the account of events in Asia, we shall turn our attention to Europe and set forth what took place there following the events previously described. Although Cassander had shut Olympias into Pydna in Macedonia, he was not able to assault the walls because of the winter storms, but by encamping about the city, throwing up a palisade from sea to sea, and blockading the port, he prevented any who might wish to aid the queen from doing so. As the supplies were rapidly exhausted, he created such famine among those within that they were completely incapacitated. In truth, they were brought to such extreme need that they gave each soldier five choenices of grain per month, sawed up wood and fed the sawdust to the imprisoned elephants, and slaughtered the pack animals and horses for food. While the situation of the city was so serious and while Olympias was still clinging to hopes of rescue from outside, the elephants died from lack of nourishment, the horsemen that were not in the ranks and did not receive any food whatever nearly all perished, and no small number of the soldiers also met the same fate. Some of the non-Greeks, their natural needs overcoming their scruples, found flesh to eat by collecting the bodies of the dead. Since the city was being quickly filled with corpses, those in charge of the queen's company, though they buried some of the bodies, threw others over the city wall. The sight of these was horrible, and their stench was unbearable, not merely to ladies who were of the queen's court and addicted to luxury, but also to those of the soldiers who were habituated to hardship.

50. As spring came on and their want increased from day to day, many of the soldiers gathered together and appealed to Olympias to let them go because of the lack of supplies. Since she could neither issue any food at all nor break the siege, she permitted them to withdraw. Cassander, after welcoming all the deserters and treating them in most friendly fashion, sent them to the various cities; for he hoped that when the Macedonians learned from them how weak Olympias was, they would despair of her cause, and he was not mistaken in his surmise about what would happen: those who had resolved to fight on the side of the besieged forces changed their minds and went over to Cassander; and the only men in Macedonia to preserve their loyalty were Aristonoüs and Monimus, of whom Aristonous was ruler of Amphipolis and Monimus of Pella. Olympias, when she saw that most of her friends had gone over to Cassander and that those who remained were not strong enough to come to her aid, attempted to launch a quinquereme and by this means to save herself and her friends. When, however, a deserter brought news of this attempt to the enemy and Cassander sailed up and took the ship, Olympias, recognizing that her situation was beyond hope, sent envoys to treat of terms. When Cassander gave his opinion that she must put all her interests into his hands, she with difficulty persuaded him to grant the single exception that he guarantee her personal safety. As soon as he had gained possession of the city, he sent men to take over Pella and Amphipolis. Now Monimus, the ruler of Pella, on hearing the fate of Olympias, surrendered his city; but Aristonoüs at first was minded to cling to his position, since he had many soldiers and had recently enjoyed a success. That is, a few days before this in a battle against Cassander's general Cratevas he had killed most of those who faced him, and when Cratevas himself with two thousand men had fled to Bedyndia in Bisaltia, he invested him, took him by siege, and dismissed him on terms after taking away his arms. Aristonoüs, encouraged by this and ignorant of the death of Eumenes, believing, moreover, that Alexander and Polyperchon would support him, refused to surrender Amphipolis. When Olympias wrote to him demanding his loyalty and ordering him to surrender, he perceived that it was necessary to do as ordered and delivered the city to Cassander, receiving pledges for his own safety.

51. Cassander, seeing that Aristonoüs was respected s because of the preferment he had received from Alexander, and being anxious to put out of the way any who were able to lead a revolt, caused his death through the agency of the kinsfolk of Cratevas. He also urged the relatives of those whom Olympias had slain to accuse the aforesaid woman in the general assembly of the Macedonians. They did as he had ordered; and, although Olympias was not present and had none to speak in her defence, the Macedonians condemned her to death. Cassander, however, sent some of his friends to Olympias advising her to escape secretly, promising to provide a ship for her and to carry her to Athens. He acted thus, not for the purpose of securing her safety, but in order that she, condemning herself to exile and meeting death on the voyage, might seem to have met a punishment that was deserved; for he was acting with caution both because of her rank and because of the fickleness of the Macedonians. As Olympias, however, refused to flee but on the contrary was ready to be judged before all the Macedonians, Cassander, fearing that the crowd might change its mind if it heard the queen defend herself and was reminded of all the benefits conferred on the entire nation by Alexander and Philip, sent to her two hundred soldiers who were best fitted for such a task, ordering them to slay her as soon as possible. They, accordingly, broke into the royal house, but when they beheld Olympias, overawed by her exalted rank, they withdrew with their task unfulfilled, but the relatives of her victims, wishing to curry favour with Cassander as well as to avenge their dead, murdered the queen, who uttered no ignoble or womanish plea.

Such was the end of Olympias, who had attained to the highest dignity of the women of her day, having been daughter of Neoptolemus, king of the Epirotes, sister of the Alexander who made a campaign into Italy, and also wife of Philip, who was the mightiest of all who down to this time had ruled in Europe, and mother of Alexander, whose deeds were the greatest and most glorious.

How Cassander married Thessalonice, the daughter of Philip son of Amyntas; and how he founded a city named for himself on Pallene (52).

How Polyperchon, giving up the cause of the kings as hopeless, fled to Aetolia (52).

How Antigonus built many ships and sent generals to Greece and to Pontus (chaps. 58-60).

52. As for Cassander, now that his affairs had succeeded according to his intentions, he began to embrace in his hopes the Macedonian kingdom. For this reason he married Thessalonicê, who was Philip's daughter and Alexander's half-sister, since he desired to establish a connection with the royal house. He also founded on Pallenê a city called Cassandreia after his own name, uniting with it as one city the cities of the peninsula, Potidaea, and a considerable number of the neighbouring towns. He also settled in this city those of the Olynthians who survived, not few in number. Since a great deal of land, and good land too, was included within the boundaries of Cassandreia, and since Cassander was very ambitious for the city's increase, it quickly made great progress and became the strongest of the cities of Macedonia. Cassander had determined to do away with Alexander's son and the son's mother, Roxanê, so that there might be no successor to the kingdom; but for the present, since he wished to observe what the common people would say about the slaying of Olympias and since he had no news of Antigonus' success, he placed Roxanê and the child in custody, transferring them to the citadel of Amphipolis, in command of which he placed Glaucias, one of his most trusted henchmen. Also he took away the pages who,

245

according to custom, were being brought up as companions of the boy, and he ordered that he should no longer have royal treatment but only such as was proper for any ordinary person of private station. After this, already conducting himself as a king in administering the affairs of the realm, he buried Eurydicê and Philip, the queen and king, and also Cynna, whom Alcetas had slain, in Aegae as was the royal custom. After honouring the dead with funeral games, he enrolled those of the Macedonians who were fit for military service, for he had decided to make a campaign into the Peloponnesus. While Cassander was engaged with these matters, Polyperchon was being besieged in Azorius in Perrhaebia, but on hearing of the death of Olympias he finally, despairing of success in Macedonia, escaped from the city with a few followers. Leaving Thessaly and taking over the troops led by Aeacides, he withdrew into Aetolia, believing that he could wait there with greatest safety and observe the changes in the situation; for as it chanced he was on friendly terms with: this people.

How Cassander restored the city of Thebes, which had been razed by Alexander (53).

About the misfortunes that had befallen Thebes in former times, and how often the city had been destroyed (53).

53. But Cassander, after assembling an adequate force, set out from Macedonia, desiring to drive Polyperchon's son Alexander from the Peloponnesus; for of those who opposed Cassander he alone was left with an army, and he had occupied strategically situated cities and districts. Cassander crossed Thessaly without loss, but when he found the pass at Thermopylae guarded by Aetolians, he with difficulty dislodged them and entered Boeotia. Summoning from all sides those of the Thebans who survived, he undertook to re-establish Thebes, for he assumed that this was a most excellent opportunity to set up once more a city that had been widely known both for its achievements and for the myths that had been handed down about it; and he supposed that by this benevolent act he would acquire undying fame. The fact is that this city has experienced many very great changes of fortune and has been destroyed on no few occasions; and it will not be out of place to recount here the chief events of its history. When, after the flood that occurred in the days of Deucalion, Cadmus built the Cadmeia, which was called after his name, there came together there with him a folk whom some call the Spartoi because they had been gathered together from all sides, and others the Thebagenes because they were originally from Thebes but had been driven out and scattered by the flood. Be that as it may, these people then settled in the city but later the Encheleans defeated them in war and drove them out, at which time Cadmus and his followers also were driven to Ulyria. Later Amphion and Zethus became masters of the site and then built the lower city for the first time, as the poet says:

First by them was established Thebes of the seven gates. [Od. 11,263]

Then the inhabitants of the place were exiled a second time, for Polydorus, son of Cadmus, came back and was dissatisfied with the situation because of the misfortunes that had befallen Amphion in connection with his children. Next, when Polydorus' own descendants were kings and the whole country had already received the name Boeotia from Boeotus, who was the son of Melanippê and Poseidon and had been ruler of the region, the Thebans for the third time suffered exile, for the Epigoni from Argos took the city by siege. The survivors of those driven out took refuge in Alalcomenia and on Mount Tilphosium, but after the Argives had departed they returned to their native city. After that, when the Thebans had gone to Asia for the Trojan War, those who were left behind were expelled along with the rest of the Boeotians by Pelasgians. Thereafter they met with many misfortunes, and only with difficulty in the fourth generation according to the prophecy of the ravens did they return to Boeotia and re-establish Thebes. From that time the city persisted for nearly eight hundred years, the Thebans at first becoming the leaders of their own people and later disputing for the leadership of the Greeks, until Alexander, son of Philip, captured the city by storm and destroyed it.

On the operations of Cassander in the Peloponnesus (54).

54. In the twentieth year thereafter Cassander in his desire for glory, after first obtaining the consent of the Boeotians, rebuilt the city for those of the Thebans who survived. Many of the Greek cities shared in the resettlement both because of their pity for the unfortunate and because of the glory of the city. The Athenians, for example, rebuilt the greater part of the wall, and of the other Greeks, not alone from Greece itself but from Sicily and Italy as well, some erected buildings to the extent of their ability, and others sent money for the pressing needs. In this way the Thebans recovered their city.

To return to Cassander, he set out with his army for the Peloponnesus, but on finding that Alexander, son of Polyperchon, had blocked the Isthmus with guards, he turned aside to Megara. There he constructed barges upon which he transported the elephants to Epidaurus, taking the rest of the army in boats. Coming to the city of the Argives, he forced it to abandon its alliance with Alexander and to join him, after which he won over the cities of Messenia except Ithome, and gained Hermionis through negotiation. As Alexander, however, did not come out to fight, he left at the end of the Isthmus toward Gerania two thousand soldiers commanded by Molyccus and returned to Macedonia.

The march of Antigonus and his army to the sea, and the flight of Seleucus into Egypt to Ptolemy (55).

55. When this year had passed, Praxibulus was archon at Athens [315/14] and in Rome Xautius Spurius and Marcus Poplius were consuls. While these held office Antigonus left Aspisas, a native, as satrap of Susianê, while he himself, having decided to convey all the money to the sea, prepared wagons and camels and, taking the treasure, set out for Babylonia with the army. In twenty-two days he arrived in Babylon, and Seleucus, the satrap of the country, honoured him with gifts suitable for a king and feasted the whole army. When Antigonus, however, demanded an accounting for the revenues, Seleucus answered that he was not bound to undergo a public investigation of his administration of this country which the Macedonians had given him in recognition of his services rendered while Alexander was alive. As the dispute grew more serious each day, Seleucus, reasoning from the fate of Pithon, feared that Antigonus would some day seize a pretext and undertake to destroy him; for Antigonus seemed eager to put out of the way all of his associates who were of high rank and were capable of claiming a share in the government. Therefore to avoid this, he escaped with fifty horsemen, intending to retire into Egypt to Ptolemy; for word had spread abroad of Ptolemy's kindness and of his cordiality and friendliness toward those who fled to him. When Antigonus learned of the flight, he was pleased, since it seemed that he himself had been spared the necessity of laying violent hands upon a man who had been his friend and had actively co-operated with him, and that Seleucus, by condemning himself to exile, had surrendered his satrapy without struggle or danger. Then the Chaldean astrologers came to him and foretold that if ever he let Seleucus escape from his hands, the consequence would be that all Asia would become subject to Seleucus, and that Antigonus himself would lose his life in a battle against him. At this, Antigonus repented his former course and sent men to pursue Seleucus, but they, after tracking him for a certain distance, returned with their mission unaccomplished. Although Antigonus was accustomed to despise prophecies of this kind on other occasions, he was not a little troubled at this time, being disturbed by the reputation of the men, for they are reputed to possess a great deal of experience and to make most exact observations of the stars. Indeed they declare that for many myriads of years the study of these matters has been pursued among them. It is also believed that they foretold to Alexander that, if he entered Babylon, he would die. Just as was the case with the prophecy about Alexander, it came to pass that this prophecy in regard to Seleucus was fulfilled according to the assertion of these men. Of this we shall speak in detail when we come to the proper period.

The alliance of Ptolemy, Seleucus, and Cassander, and Lysimachus also, for the war against Antigonus (56-57).

56. Seleucus, arriving safely in Egypt, met with nothing but kindness from Ptolemy. He bitterly accused Antigonus, saying that Antigonus had determined to remove from their satrapies all who were men of rank and in particular those who had served under Alexander; as examples of this he mentioned the slaying of Pithon, the removal of Peucestes from Persia, and his own experiences; for all of these men, who were guiltless of wrongdoing and had even performed great services out of friendship, had been patiently awaiting a reward for virtue. He reviewed also the magnitude of Antigonus' armed forces, his vast wealth, and his recent successes, and went on to intimate that in consequence he had become arrogant and had encompassed in his ambitious plans the entire kingdom of the Macedonians. When by such arguments he had induced Ptolemy to prepare for war, he sent certain of his friends to Europe, directing them to try by similar arguments to convert Cassander and Lysimachus into enemies of Antigonus. They quickly carried out their instructions, and the seed of a quarrel and of great wars began to grow. Antigonus, who had deduced by reasoning from probabilities what course of action Seleucus was following, sent envoys to Ptolemy, Lysimachus, and Cassander, urging them to maintain the existing friendship. He next established as satrap of Babylonia that Pithon who had come from India, and then, setting out with his army, he marched toward Cilicia. He arrived at Malus and, after the setting of Orion [November 316], divided the army for passing the winter. He also took the money at Cyinda, which amounted to ten thousand talents. Apart from this there fell to him from the annual revenue eleven thousand talents. As a result he was a formidable antagonist both because of the size of his armies and because of the amount of his wealth.

57. While Antigonus was going into upper Syria, envoys arrived from Ptolemy, Lysimachus, and Cassander. When they had been brought into the council, they demanded that Cappadocia and Lycia be given to Cassander, Hellespontine Phrygia to Lysimachus, all Syria to Ptolemy, and Babylonia to Seleucus, and that Antigonus should divide the treasures that he had captured after the battle with Eumenes, since they too had had a share in the war. They said that if he did none of these things, they would all join in waging war on him. Antigonus answered rather harshly and bade them make ready for war, with the result that the envoys went away with their mission unaccomplished. At this Ptolemy, Lysimachus, and Cassander, after making a mutual alliance, gathered their forces and prepared stocks of arms, missiles, and the other needful things. Now that Antigonus saw that many men of great repute had combined against him, and computed the extent of the war that was springing up, he summoned the nations, cities, and rulers to join his alliance. He sent Agesilaüs to the kings in Cyprus, Idomeneus and Moschion to Rhodes, and his own nephew Ptolemy with an army to Cappadocia to raise the siege of Amisus, to drive out all who had been sent by Cassander into Cappadocia, and finally to take a position on the Hellespont and lie in wait for Cassander if he should try to cross over from Europe. He sent Aristodemus of Miletus to the Peloponnesus with a thousand talents, instructing him to establish friendship with Alexander and Polyperchon and, after raising an adequate force of mercenaries, to carry on the war against Cassander. He himself established at intervals throughout all that part of Asia of which he was master a system of fire-signals and dispatch-carriers, by means of which he expected to have quick service in all his business.

58. After attending to these matters, Antigonus set out for Phoenicia, hastening to organise a naval force; for it so happened that his enemies then ruled the sea with many ships, but that he had, altogether, not even a few. Camping at Old Tyre in Phoenicia and intending to besiege Tyre, he called together the kings of the Phoenicians and the viceroys of Syria. He instructed the kings to assist him in building ships, since Ptolemy was holding in Egypt all the ships from Phoenicia with their crews. He ordered the viceroys to prepare quickly four and a half million measures of wheat . . ., for such was the annual consumption. He himself collected wood cutters, sawyers, and shipwrights from all sides, and carried wood to the sea from Lebanon. There were eight thousand men employed in cutting and sawing the timber and one thousand pair of draught animals in transporting it. This mountain range extends along the territory of Tripolis, Byblus, and Sidon, and is covered with cedar and cypress trees of wonderful beauty and size. He established three shipyards in Phoenicia, at Tripolis, Byblus, and Sidon, and a fourth in Cilicia, the timber for which was brought from Mount Taurus. There was also another in Rhodes, where the state agreed to make ships from imported timber. While Antigonus was busy with these matters and after he had established his camp near the sea, Seleucus arrived from Egypt with a hundred ships, which were royally equipped and which sailed excellently. As he sailed contemptuously along past the very camp, men from the allied cities and all who were co-operating with Antigonus were downhearted; for it was very clear that, since the enemy dominated the sea, they would plunder the lands of those who aided their opponents out of friendship for Antigonus. Antigonus, however, bade them be of good courage, affirming that in that very summer he would take the sea with five hundred vessels.

59. While Antigonus was thus engaged, Agesilaüs, the envoy whom he had sent to Cyprus, arrived with the information that Nicocreon and the most powerful of the other kings had made an alliance with Ptolemy, but that the kings of Cition, Lapithus, Marion, and Ceryneia had concluded a treaty of friendship with himself. On learning this, Antigonus left three thousand soldiers under

Andronicus to carry on the siege, but he himself set out with the army and took by storm Joppa and Gaza, cities that had refused obedience. The soldiers of Ptolemy whom he captured he distributed among his own ranks, but he placed in each city a garrison to force the inhabitants to obey him. He himself then went back to the camp at Old Tyre and made preparations for the siege.

At this time Ariston, to whose care the bones of Craterus had been entrusted by Eumenes, gave them for burial to Phila, who had formerly been the wife of Craterus, but now was married to Demetrius, the son of Antigonus. This woman seems to have been of exceptional sagacity; for example, she would quell the trouble-makers in the camp by dealing with each individual in a manner appropriate to his case, she would arrange marriages at her own expense for the sisters and daughters of the poor, and she would free from jeopardy many who had been trapped by false accusations. It is even said that her father Antipater, who is reputed to have been the wisest of the rulers of his own time, used to consult with Phila about the most important matters when she was still a child. The character of the woman will be more clearly revealed by my narrative as it progresses and by the events that brought change and a final crisis to the reign of Demetrius.

This was the situation of the affairs of Antigonus and of Phila, the wife of Demetrius.

60. Of the generals who had been sent out by Antigonus, Aristodemus sailed to Laconia and, on receiving permission from the Spartans to recruit mercenaries, enrolled eight thousand soldiers from the Peloponnesus. Meeting Alexander and Polyperchon, he established friendship between them and Antigonus. He appointed Polyperchon general of the Peloponnesus, and he persuaded Alexander to sail to Antigonus in Asia. The other general, Ptolemy, proceeded with his army to Cappadocia where he found Amisus under siege by Asclepiodorus, a general of Cassander. He delivered the city from danger and recovered the satrapy after dismissing Asclepiodorus and his men under a truce. Thereafter advancing through Bithynia and finding Zibytes, the king of the Bithynians, laying siege to the city of the Astacenians and the Chalcedonians, he forced him to abandon the siege. After making alliances with these cities and with Zibytes and also taking hostages from them, he proceeded toward Ionia and Lydia; for Antigonus had written ordering him to go quickly to the support of the coast, since Seleucus was about to make a naval expedition into that region. It so happened that, as he finally drew near to this area, Seleucus was laying siege to Erythrae, but when he heard that the hostile force was near, he sailed away with nothing accomplished.

How he established friendship with Alexander, the son of Polyperchon, and took Tyre by siege; and how Alexander shifted his allegiance to Cassander (61-64).

61. Antigonus, after Polyperchon's son Alexander had come to him, made a pact of friendship with him, and then, calling a general assembly of the soldiers and of the aliens who were dwelling there, laid charges against Cassander, bringing forward the murder of Olympias and the treatment of Roxanê and the king. Moreover, he said that Cassander had married Thessalonicê by force, and was clearly trying to establish his own claim to the Macedonian throne; and also that, although the Olynthians were very bitter enemies of the Macedonians, Cassander had re-established them in a city called by his own name and had rebuilt Thebes, which had been razed by the Macedonians. When the crowd showed that it shared his wrath, he introduced a decree according to the terms of which it was voted that Cassander was to be an enemy unless he destroyed these cities again, released the king and his mother Roxanê from imprisonment and restored them to the Macedonians, and, in general, yielded obedience to Antigonus the duly established general who had succeeded to the guardianship of the throne. It was also stated that all the Greeks were free, not subject to foreign garrisons, and autonomous. When the soldiers had voted in favour of these measures, Antigonus sent men in every direction to carry the decree, for he believed that through their hope of freedom he would gain the Greeks as eager participants with him in the war, and that the generals and satraps in the upper satrapies, who had suspected that he was determined to depose the kings who inherited from Alexander, would, if he publicly took upon himself the war in their behalf, all change their minds and promptly obey his orders. Having finished these matters, he gave Alexander five hundred talents and, after leading him to hope for great things to come, sent him back to the Peloponnesus. He himself, after summoning ships from Rhodes and equipping most of those that had been built, sailed against Tyre. Although he pressed the siege with vigour for a year and three months, controlling the sea and preventing food from being brought in [315], yet after he had reduced the besieged to extreme want, he permitted the soldiers who had come from Ptolemy to depart each with his own possessions; but when the city capitulated [314], he introduced into it a garrison to watch it closely.

62. While these things were going on, Ptolemy, who had heard what had been decreed by the Macedonians with Antigonus in regard to the freedom of the Greeks, published a similar decree himself, since he wished the Greeks to know that he was no less interested in their autonomy than was Antigonus. Each of them, indeed, perceiving that it was a matter of no little moment to gain the goodwill of the Greeks, rivalled the other in conferring favours upon this people. Ptolemy also brought into his alliance Asander, satrap of Caria, who was strong and had a considerable number of cities subject to him. To the kings on Cyprus, to whom he had previously sent three thousand soldiers, he now dispatched a strong army, for he was anxious to force those who were opposing him to carry out his commands. Myrmidon the Athenian, therefore, was sent with ten thousand men, and Polycleitus with a hundred ships, while Menelaüs, his own brother, was made commander of the whole force. When these had sailed to Cyprus and there had found Seleucus and his fleet, they met together and considered what they ought to do. They decided that Polycleitus with fifty ships should sail to the Peloponnesus and carry on the war against Aristodemus, Alexander, and Polyperchon; that Myrmidon and the mercenaries should go to Caria to aid Asander, who was being attacked by Ptolemy the general; and that Seleucus and Menelaüs, left in Cyprus with King Nicocreon and the other allies, should carry on the war against those who opposed them. After the forces had been divided in this way, Seleucus took Ceryneia and Lapithus, secured the support of Stasioecus, king of the Marienses, forced the ruler of the Amathusii to give a guaranty, and laid unremitting siege with all his forces to the city of the Citienses, which he had not been able to induce to join him. At about this time forty ships under the command of Themison came to Antigonus from the Hellespont, and likewise Dioscorides put in with eighty vessels from the Hellespont and Rhodes. The first to be finished of the ships that had been made in Phoenicia were also at hand fully equipped; including those captured at Tyre, they were one hundred and twenty, so that in all there were gathered together about Antigonus two hundred and forty fully equipped ships of war. Of these there were ninety with four orders of oarsmen, ten with five, three with nine, ten with ten, and thirty un-decked boats. Dividing this naval force, he sent fifty ships to the Peloponnesus, and ordered his nephew, Dioscorides, whom he had made commander of the rest, to make sis a circuit of the sea, guaranteeing the safety of the allies and winning the support of the islands that had not yet joined the alliance. Such was the state of Antigonus' affairs.

63. Now that we have related the events that took place in Asia, we shall in turn discuss the affairs of Europe. Apollonides, who had been appointed general over Argos by Cassander, made a raid into Arcadia by night and captured the city of the Stymphalians, but while he was engaged in this, those of the Argives who were hostile to Cassander sent for Alexander, Polyperchon's son, promising to hand the city over to him. Alexander, however, delayed, and Apollonides arrived back in Argos before him. Finding about five hundred of his antagonists gathered in the prytaneion, he prevented them from leaving the building and burned them alive. He exiled most of the others, but arrested and killed a few. When Cassander learned of Aristodemus' arrival in the Peloponnesus and of the multitude of mercenaries that he had collected there, his first effort was to turn Polyperchon from his alliance with Antigonus. When Polyperchon, however, would not listen to him, he brought his army through Thessaly into Boeotia. After aiding the Thebans in building their walls, he went on into the Peloponnesus. First he took Cenchreae and plundered the fields of the Corinthians. Then, after taking two fortresses by storm, he dismissed under a truce the garrisons that had been placed in them by Alexander. Next he attacked the: city of Orchomenus. Being admitted by the faction hostile to Alexander, he installed a garrison in the city, and when the friends of Alexander took refuge in the shrine of Artemis, he permitted the citizens to treat them as they wished. The people of Orchomenus, accordingly, dragged the suppliants away by force and slew them all, contrary to the universal custom of the Greeks.

How Polycleitus, the admiral of Ptolemy, defeated the generals of Antigonus both on land and on sea (64).

64. Cassander passed on into Messenia, but finding the city garrisoned by Polyperchon, he temporarily relinquished his plan of laying siege to it. Passing over into Arcadia, he left Damis as governor of Megalopolis, while he himself, after going into Argolis and presiding at the Nemean Games [315], returned to Macedonia. After he had gone, Alexander visited the cities of the Peloponnesus accompanied by Aristodemus and tried to drive out the garrisons that had been established by Cassander and to restore freedom to the cities. As soon as Cassander learned this, he sent Prepelaüs to Alexander, asking him to desert Antigonus and conclude with himself an alliance in due form. He said that if he did this, he would give him the command of all the Peloponnesus, make him general of an army, and honour him according to his deserts. Alexander, since he saw that the thing for which he had originally made war against Cassander was being granted to him, made the alliance and was appointed general of the Peloponnesus.

While all this was taking place, Polycleitus, who had been sent by Seleucus from Cyprus, sailed into Cenchreae, but when he heard of Alexander's change in allegiance and saw that there was no hostile force in existence, he sailed for Pamphylia. He sailed along the coast from Pamphylia to Aphrodisias in Cilicia; and, hearing that Theodotus, the admiral of Antigonus, was sailing from Patara in Lycia in Rhodian ships with Carian crews, and that Perilaüs was accompanying him with an army on land, thus securing the safety of the fleet in its voyage, he out-generalled both of them. Disembarking his soldiers, he concealed them in a suitable place where it was necessary for the enemy to pass, and he himself sailed near with all his ships, taking cover behind a promontory while awaiting the coming of the enemy. The army was first to fall into the ambush; Perilaüs was captured, some of the rest fell while fighting, and others were taken prisoners. When the Rhodian ships tried to go to the aid of their own forces, Polycleitus sailed up suddenly with his fleet drawn up for battle and easily routed the disorganised enemy. The result was that all the ships were captured and a considerable number of the men also, among them Theodotus himself, who was wounded and a few days later died. After Polycleitus had gained so great an advantage without danger, he sailed away to Cyprus and thence to Pelusium. Ptolemy praised him, honoured him with great gifts, and gave him much greater preferment as having been the author of an important victory. He released Perilaüs and some of the other captives when an envoy in their behalf came from Antigonus. He himself went to Ecregma, as it is called, where he conferred with Antigonus, returning again since Antigonus would not agree to his demands.

About the campaign of Agathocles against the Messenians, and the peace in which the Carthaginians were the mediators (65).

The revolt of Nuceria from the Romans (65).

65. Now that we have related the deeds of the European Greeks in Greece and Macedonia, we shall consider in due order the history of the western regions. Agathocles, the dynast of Syracuse, who was holding a fort of the Messenians, promised to surrender the position on receiving from them thirty talents; but when the Messenians gave him the money, he not only failed to keep his promise to those who had put faith in him, but he also undertook to capture Messenê itself. On learning that a certain section of the wall of the city was in ruins, he sent his cavalry by land from Syracuse while he himself sailed close to the city by night with light vessels. Since, however, the intended victims of the plot learned of it beforehand, this attack failed; but he sailed to Mylae and besieged the fort, which surrendered by capitulation. He then departed for Syracuse, but at the time of the harvest he made another expedition against Messenê. He camped near the city and made repeated attacks, but he was not able to inflict any considerable damage upon his enemies, for many of the exiles from Syracuse had taken refuge in the city, and these fought furiously both for the sake of their own safety and because of their hatred for the tyrant. At this time there came envoys from Carthage, who censured Agathocles for what he had done on the ground that he had violated the treaty. They also secured peace for the people of Messenê, and then, when they had forced the tyrant to restore the fort, they sailed back to Libya. Agathocles, however, went on to Abacaenon, an allied city, where he put to death those who appeared to be hostile to him, being more than forty in number.

While these things were taking place, the Romans in their war with the Samnites took Ferentum, a city of Apulia, by storm. The inhabitants of Nuceria, which is called Alfaterna, yielding to the persuasion of certain persons, abandoned their friendship for Rome and made an alliance with the Samnites.

The operations of the generals of Antigonus and of Cassander in Greece (66).

The capture in Caria of the army sent out by Cassander (chap. 68).

66. After this year had passed, Nicodorus was archon at Athens, [314] and at Rome Lucius Papirius was consul for the fourth time and Quintus Publius for the second. While these held office, Aristodemus, who had been made general by Antigonus, on learning of the defection of Polyperchon's son Alexander, presented his own side of the matter to the common assembly of the Aetolians and persuaded the majority to support the fortunes of Antigonus. He himself, however, with his mercenaries crossed from Aetolia to the Peloponnesus, where he found Alexander and the Eleans laying siege to Cyllene, and, arriving at a moment opportune for the endangered people, raised the siege. Leaving troops there to insure the safety of the stronghold, he advanced into Achaia and freed Patrae, which was subject to a garrison of Cassander's troops. After a successful siege of Aegium he became master of its garrison, but, although he wished to establish freedom for the people of Aegium according to the decree, he was blocked by the following incident: for while the soldiers were engaged in pillaging, many of the Aegienses were killed and very many of their buildings were destroyed. Thereafter, when Aristodemus had sailed to Aetolia, the Dymaeans, who were subject to a garrison sent by Cassander, cut off their city by a dividing wall in such a way that it was isolated and separated from the citadel. Then, after encouraging each other to assert their freedom, they invested the citadel and made unremitting attacks upon it. Alexander on learning of this came with his army, forced his way within the wall, and became master of the city, slaying some of the Dymaeans, imprisoning others, and sending many into exile. When Alexander had departed from the city, the survivors remained quiet for some time, stunned by the magnitude of the disaster and also bereft of allies. After a little while, however, they summoned from Aegium the mercenaries of Aristodemus and once more made an attack on the garrison. Taking the citadel, they freed the city' and when they had massacred most of those who had been left there, they likewise slew all those of their own citizens who maintained friendship with Alexander.

Cassander's campaign in Aetolia and the country about the Adriatic (67-68).

67. While this was taking place, Polyperchon's son Alexander, as he was setting out from Sicyon with his army, was killed by Alexion of Sicyon and certain others who pretended to be friends. His wife, Cratesipolis, however, succeeded to his power and held his army together, since she was most highly esteemed by the soldiers for her acts of kindness, for it was her habit to aid those who were in misfortune and to assist many of those who were without resources. She possessed, too, skill in practical matters and more daring than one would expect in a woman. Indeed, when the people of Sicyon scorned her because of her husband's death and assembled under arms in an effort to gain their freedom, she drew up her forces against them and defeated them with great slaughter, but arrested and crucified about thirty. When she had a firm hold on the city, she governed the Sicyonians, maintaining many soldiers, who were ready for any emergency.

Such, then, was the situation in the Peloponnesus.

When Cassander saw that the Aetolians were supporting Antigonus and were also engaged in a border war with the Acarnanians, he decided that it was to his advantage at a single stroke to make the Acarnanians his allies and to humble the Aetolians. For this reason, setting out from Macedonia with a large army, he moved into Aetolia and camped beside the river called the Campylus. When he had summoned the Acarnanians to a common assembly and had related to them in detail how they had been engaged in border warfare from ancient days, he advised them to move from their villages, which were small and unfortified, into a few cities so that they would no longer, because their homes were scattered, be powerless to aid each other and find difficulty in assembling to meet the unexpected raids of their enemies. The Acarnanians were persuaded, and most of them came to live together in Stratus, since this was their strongest and largest city, but the Oeniadae and some others gathered at Sauria, and the Derians and the rest settled at Agrinium. Cassander left Lyciscus in command with adequate troops, ordering him to aid the Acarnanians; but he himself moved upon Leucas with an army and secured the allegiance of the city through an embassy. Thereafter, directing his campaign to the Adriatic, he took Apollonia at the first assault. Advancing into Illyria and crossing the Hebrus River, he drew up his army against Glaucias, the king of the Illyrians. Being successful in the battle, he made a treaty with the king according to which Glaucias was not to wage war on Cassander's allies, then he himself, after securing the city of Epidamnus and establishing a garrison therein, returned to Macedonia.

68. When Cassander had departed from Aetolia, the Aetolians, gathering together to the number of three thousand, invested Agrinium and began a siege. The inhabitants of the place came to terms with them, agreeing to surrender the city and depart under safe conduct, but when, trusting in the treaty, they were leaving, the Aetolians violated the terms, pursued hotly after these men while they were anticipating no danger, and slaughtered all but a few of them. When Cassander had arrived in Macedonia and heard that war was being waged on all the cities in Caria that were allied to Ptolemy and Seleucus, he sent an army into Caria, for he both wished to aid his allies and at the same time was eager to force Antigonus into distracting undertakings so that he might not have leisure for crossing over into Europe. He also wrote to Demetrius of Phalerum and to Dionysius, who commanded the garrison on Munychia, bidding them dispatch twenty ships to Lemnos. They at once sent the boats with Aristotle in command of them. After the latter had sailed to Lemnos and had summoned Seleucus and a fleet, he undertook to persuade the Lemnians to revolt from Antigonus, but as they did not assent, he ravaged their land, invested the city, and began a siege. Afterwards, however, Seleucus sailed off to Cos, and Dioscurides, who had been made admiral by Antigonus, on learning of Seleucus' departure, swooped down upon Lemnos, drove Aristotle himself from the island, and captured most of his ships together with their crews.

Asander and Prepelaüs were in command of the expedition sent by Cassander into Caria, and, on being informed that Ptolemaeus, the general of Antigonus, had divided his army for wintering [314/13] and was himself engaged in burying his father, they dispatched Eupolemus to lie in wait for the enemy near Caprima in Caria, sending with him eight thousand foot soldiers and two hundred horse.

At this time Ptolemaeus, who had heard from some deserters of the plan of the enemy, gathered from the troops who were wintering near by eight thousand three hundred foot soldiers and six hundred horse. Falling unexpectedly upon the fortified camp of the enemy about midnight and catching them off guard and asleep, he captured Eupolemus himself alive and forced the soldiers to give themselves up.

This, then, is what befell the generals who were sent by Cassander into Asia.

Antigonus' preparations against Ptolemy (69).

69. When Antigonus perceived that Cassander was trying to win Asia for himself, he left his son Demetrius in Syria, ordering him to lie in wait for Ptolemy, whom he suspected of intending to advance from Egypt with an army against Syria, with Demetrius he left an infantry force consisting of ten thousand mercenaries, two thousand Macedonians, five hundred Lycians and Pamphylians, and four hundred Persian archers and slingers, a cavalry force of five thousand, and forty-three elephants. He assigned to him four counsellors: Nearchus of Crete, Pithon, son of Agenor, who had returned a few days before from Babylon, also Andronicus of Olynthus and Philip, men advanced in years who had accompanied Alexander on his whole campaign, for Demetrius was still youthful, being twenty-two years of age. Antigonus himself, taking' the rest of the army, first tried to cross the Taurus Range, where he encountered deep snow and lost large numbers of his soldiers. Turning back therefore into Cilicia and seizing another opportunity, he crossed the aforesaid range in greater safety, and, on reaching Celaenae in Phrygia, he divided his army for wintering [314/13]. Thereafter he summoned from Phoenicia his fleet under the command of Medius, who fell in with the ships of the Pydnaeans, thirty-six in number, defeated them in an engagement, and captured the vessels together with their crews.

This was the situation in Greece and in Asia.

How the Syracusan exiles, after persuading the people of Acragas to fight against Agathocles, sent for a general from Lacedaemon, Acrotatus (70).

70. In Sicily those of the Syracusan exiles who were tarrying in Acragas urged the rulers of that city not to watch complacently while Agathocles organized the cities, for it was better, they said, to fight it out of their own free will before the tyrant became strong than to await the increase of his power and then be forced to struggle against him when he had grown stronger. Since they seemed to speak the truth, the popular assembly of the Acragantines voted for the war, added the people of Gela and Messenê to the alliance, and sent some of the exiles to Lacedaemon, instructing them to try to bring back a general capable of taking charge of affairs, for they were suspicious of their own statesmen as being inclined toward tyranny, but, remembering the generalship of Timoleon the Corinthian, assumed that leaders from abroad would honestly devote themselves to the common cause. The envoys, when they arrived in Laconia, found that Acrotatus, the son of King Cleomenes, had given offence to many of the younger men and for this reason was eager for activity away from home. This was because, when the Lacedaemonians after the battle against Antipater relieved from ignominy those who had survived the defeat, he alone opposed the decree. He thus gave offence to many others and in particular to those who were subject to the penalties of the laws, indeed, these persons gathered together and gave him a beating, and they were constantly plotting against him. Being therefore anxious for a foreign command, he gladly accepted the invitation of the men from Acragas. Taking his departure from the state without the consent of the ephors, he set sail with a few ships as if to cross to Acragas. He was, however, carried by the winds into the Adriatic and landed in the territory of Apollonia. Finding that city besieged by Glaucias, the king of the Illyrians, he brought the siege to an end, persuading the king to make a treaty with the people of Apollonia. Thence he sailed to Tarentum, where he urged the people to join in freeing the Syracusans, and he persuaded them to vote to assist with twenty ships, for because of ties of kinship and on account of the dignity of his family, they ascribed to his words a high degree of sincerity and great importance.

How Acrotatus accepted the generalship and ruled as a tyrant; and how the Acragantines made peace with the dynast (71).

71. While the Tarentines were engaged in their preparations, Acrotatus immediately sailed to Acragas where he assumed the office of general. At first he buoyed up the common people with great expectations and caused all to anticipate a speedy overthrow of the tyrant; however, as time advanced, he accomplished nothing worthy either of his fatherland or of the distinction of his family, but on the contrary, being bloodthirsty and more cruel than the tyrants, he continually gave offence to the common people. Moreover, he abandoned his native manner of living and devoted himself so unrestrainedly to pleasure that he seemed to be a Persian and not a Spartan. When he had squandered the larger part of the revenue, partly by his public activity, partly by private peculation, he finally invited to dinner Sosistratus, who was the most distinguished of the exiles and had often commanded armies, and treacherously killed him, not having any charge whatever to bring against him and yet being eager to put out of the way a man who was accustomed to act and who was capable of keeping under surveillance those who misused positions of leadership. When this deed became known, the exiles at once began to join forces against Acrotatus, and all the rest were alienated from him. First they removed him from his generalship, and soon afterwards they attempted to stone him, whereupon, terrified by the popular uprising, he took flight by night and sailed secretly to Laconia. After his departure the Tarentines, who had sent their fleet to Sicily, recalled it, and the peoples of Acragas, Gela, and Messenê brought their war against Agathocles to an end, Hamilcar the Carthaginian acting as mediator in making the treaty. The chief points of the agreement were as follows: of the Greek towns in Sicily, Heraclea, Selinus, and Himera were to be subject to the Carthaginians as they had been before, and all the others were to be autonomous under the hegemony of Syracuse.

The Roman operations in Iapygia (72).

72. Afterwards, however, when Agathocles perceived that Sicily was clear of hostile armies, he began unhampered to subject the cities and strongholds to himself. Mastering many of them quickly, he made his power secure; in fact, he built up for himself a host of allies, ample revenues, and a considerable army. Indeed, without counting the allies and those of the Syracusans who had enlisted for military service, he had a picked mercenary force comprising ten thousand foot soldiers and thirty-five hundred horse. Moreover, he prepared a store of weapons and of missiles of all kinds, since he knew that the Carthaginians, who had censured Hamilcar for the terms of peace, would shortly wage war against him.

This was the situation of Sicilian affairs at this time. In Italy the Samnites, fighting bitterly against the Romans for supremacy in a struggle lasting many years, took by siege Plestice, which had a Roman garrison, and persuaded the people of Sora to slay the Romans who were among them and to make an alliance with themselves. Next, as the Romans were besieging Saticula, the Samnites suddenly appeared with a strong army intent on raising the siege. A great battle then took place in which many were slain on both sides, but eventually the Romans gained the upper hand. After the battle the Romans carried the siege of the city to completion and then advanced at will, subjecting the near-by towns and strongholds. Now that the struggle for the cities of Apulia had been joined, the Samnites enrolled all who were of age for military service and encamped near the enemy as if intending to decide the whole issue. When the Roman people learned this, they became anxious about what was impending and sent out a large army. As it was their custom in a dangerous crisis to appoint as military dictator one of their eminent men, they now elected Quintus Fabius and with him Quintus Aulius as master-of-horse. These, after assuming command of the army, took the field and fought against the Samnites at Laustolae, as it is called, losing many of their soldiers. As panic spread through the whole army, Aulius, in shame at the flight, stood alone against the mass of the enemy, not that he hoped to prevail, but he was maintaining his fatherland undefeated as far as he was concerned. Thus he, by not sharing with his fellow citizens in the disgrace of flight, gained a glorious death for himself alone, but the Romans, fearing that they might completely lose control throughout Apulia, sent a colony to Luceria, which was the most noteworthy of the cities of that region. Using it as a base, they continued the war against the Samnites, having made no mean provision for their future security, for not only were the Romans victorious in this war because of this city, but also in the wars that have subsequently taken place down to our own time they have continued to use Luceria as a base of operations against the neighbouring peoples.

The revolt of the Callantians from Lysimachus, and what befell those who were dispatched to their aid by Antigonus (73).

73. When the activities of this year had come to an end, Theophrastus obtained the archonship in Athens, [313] and Marcus Publius and Gaius Sulpicius became consuls in Rome. While these were in office, the people of Callantia, who lived on the left side of the Pontus and who were subject to a garrison that had been sent by Lysimachus, drove out this garrison and made an effort to gain autonomy. In like manner they freed the city of the Istrians and the other neighbouring cities, and formed an alliance with them binding them to fight together against the prince. They also brought into the alliance those of the Thracians and Scythians whose lands bordered upon their own, so that the whole was a union that had weight and could offer battle with strong forces. As soon, however, as Lysimachus learned what had taken place, he set out with his army against the rebels. After marching through Thrace and crossing the Haemus Mountains, he encamped near Odessus. Beginning a siege, he quickly frightened the inhabitants and took the city by capitulation. Next, after recovering the Istrians in a similar way, he set out against the Callantians. At this very time the Scythians and the Thracians arrived with large forces to aid their allies in accordance with the treaty. Lysimachus, meeting them and engaging them at once, terrified the Thracians and induced them to change sides, but the Scythians he defeated in a pitched battle, slaying many of them and pursuing the survivors beyond the frontiers. Then, encamping about the city of the Callantians, he laid siege to it, since he was very eager to chastise in every way those who were responsible for the revolt. While he was thus engaged, there came certain men bringing word that Antigonus had sent two expeditions to the support of the Callantians, one by land and one by sea, that the general Lycon with the fleet had sailed through into the Pontus, and that Pausanias with a considerable number of soldiers was in camp at a place called Hieron. Perturbed at this, Lysimachus left an adequate body of soldiers to carry on the siege; but with the strongest part of the army he himself pushed on, intent on making contact with the enemy. When, however, he reached the pass over the Haenius, he found Seuthes, the Thracian king, who had gone over to Antigonus, guarding the crossing with many soldiers. Engaging him in a battle that lasted a considerable time, Lysimachus lost not a few of his own men, but he destroyed a vast number of the enemy and overpowered the barbarians. He also came suddenly upon the forces of Pausanias, catching them after they had taken refuge in a place difficult of access. This he captured, and, after slaying Pausanias, he dismissed some of the soldiers on receiving ransom and enrolled others in his own army.

This was the situation of Lysimachus.

How Philip, who had been sent as general into Aetolia by Cassander, defeated at one time the peoples of Aetolia and Epirus (74).

74. Antigonus, after he had failed in this undertaking, dispatched Telesphorus into the Peloponnesus, giving him fifty ships and a suitable force of infantry, and he ordered him to free the cities, for he hoped by doing this to establish among the Greeks the belief that he truly was concerned for their independence, and at the same time he gave him a hint to note the activities of Cassander. As soon as Telesphorus had reached port in the Peloponnesus, he advanced upon the cities that were occupied by Alexander's garrisons and freed all of them except Sicyon and Corinth; for in these cities Polyperchon had his quarters, maintaining strong forces and trusting in these and in the strength of the positions. While this was being done, Philip, who had been sent by Cassander to the war against the Aetolians as commander, immediately on arriving in Acarnania with his army undertook to plunder Aetolia, but soon, hearing that Aeacides the Epirote had returned to his kingdom and had collected a strong army, he set out very quickly against him, for he was eager to bring this struggle to an end separately before the army of the Aetolians joined forces with the king. Although he found the Epirotes ready for battle, he attacked them at once, slaying many and taking captive no small number, among whom there chanced to be about fifty of those responsible for the return of the king; these he bound and sent to Cassander. As Aeacides and his men rallied from the fight and joined the Aetolians, Philip again advanced and overpowered them in battle, slaying many, among whom was King Aeacides himself, By gaining such victories in a few days Philip so terrified many of the Aetolians that they abandoned their unfortified cities and fled to the most inaccessible of their mountains with their children and their women.

Such was the outcome of the campaign in Greece.

Operations of Antigonus in Asia Minor, and of Cassander in Greece (75)

75. In Asia, Asander, the ruler of Caria, being hard pressed by the war, came to terms with Antigonus, agreeing to transfer to him all his soldiers, to relinquish the Greek cities and leave them autonomous, and to hold as a grant the satrapy that he had formerly had, remaining a steadfast friend of Antigonus. Having given his brother Agathon as a hostage for the fulfilment of these terms and then after a few days having repented of the agreement, he secretly removed his brother from custody and sent emissaries to Ptolemy and Seleucus, begging them to aid him as soon as possible. Antigonus, enraged at this, dispatched a force both by sea and by land to liberate the cities, appointing Medius admiral of the fleet and making Docimus general of the army. These men, coming to the city of the Milesians, encouraged the citizens to assert their freedom; and, after taking by siege the citadel, which was held by a garrison, they restored the independence of the government. While they were thus engaged, Antigonus besieged and took Tralles: then, proceeding to Caunus and summoning the fleet, he captured that city also except for its citadel. Investing this, he kept making continuous attacks on the side where it was most easily assailed. Ptolemaeus, who had been sent to Iasus with an adequate force, compelled that city to support Antigonus. In this way, then, these cities, which were in Caria, were made subject to Antigonus. A few days later, when ambassadors came to the latter from the Aetolians and the Boeotians, he made an alliance with them; but, when he entered into negotiations with Cassander about peace in the Hellespontine region, he accomplished nothing since they could in no way agree. For this reason Cassander gave up hope of settlement and decided to play a part once more in the affairs of Greece. Setting out for Oreüs, therefore, with thirty ships, he laid siege to the city. While he was vigorously attacking and was already at the point of taking the city by storm, reinforcements appeared for the people of Oreüs; Telesphorus from the Peloponnesus with twenty ships and a thousand soldiers, and Medius from Asia with a hundred ships. They saw the ships of Cassander blockading the harbour and threw fire into them, burning four and almost destroying them all; but when reinforcements for the defeated came from Athens, Cassander sailed out against the enemy, who were off their guard. When they met, he sank one ship and seized three with their crews.

Such were the activities in Greece and the Pontus.

How the Romans defeated the Samnites in battle, and a little later won back the Campanians who had revolted (76).

76. In Italy, the Samnites were advancing with a large army, destroying whatever cities in Campania were supporting their enemies; and the Roman consuls, coming up with an army, were trying to aid those of their allies who were in danger. They took the field against the enemy near Tarracina and at once relieved that city from its immediate fears; then a few days later, when both sides had drawn up their armies, a hard-fought battle took place and very many fell on both sides. Finally the Romans, pressing on with all their strength, got the better of their enemies and, pushing the pursuit for a long time, slew more than ten thousand. While this battle was still unknown to them, the Campanians, scorning the Romans, rose in rebellion, but the people at once sent an adequate force against them with the dictator Gaius Manius as commander and accompanying him, according to the national custom, Manius Fulvius as master-of-horse. When these were in position near Capua, the Campanians at first endeavoured to fight; but afterwards, hearing of the defeat of the Samnites and believing that all the forces would come against themselves, they made terms with the Romans. They surrendered those guilty of the uprising, who without awaiting the judgement of the trial that was instituted killed themselves. But the cities gained pardon and were reinstated in their former alliance.

How Antigonus sent Ptolemaeus as general with an army to liberate the Greeks, and about his operations in Greece (chaps. 77-78).

77. When this year had passed, Polemon was archon in Athens, and in Rome the consuls were Lucius Papirius for the fifth time and Gaius Iunius; and in this year the Olympic Games were celebrated for the one hundred and seventeenth time, Parmenion of Mitylenê winning the footrace. In this year Antigonus ordered his general Ptolemaeus into Greece to set the Greeks free and sent with him one hundred and fifty warships, placing Medius in command of them as admiral, and an army of five thousand foot and five hundred horse. Antigonus also made an alliance with the Rhodians and received from them for the liberation of the Greeks ten ships fully equipped for war. Ptolemaeus, putting in with the entire fleet at the harbour of Boeotia known as Bathys, received from the Boeotian League two thousand two hundred foot soldiers and one thousand three hundred horse. He also summoned his ships from Oreüs, fortified Salganeus, and gathered there his entire force; for he hoped to be admitted by the Chalcidians, who alone of the Euboeans were garrisoned by the enemy. Cassander, in his anxiety for Chalcis, gave up the siege of Oreüs, moved to Chalcis, and summoned his forces. When Antigonus heard that in Euboea the armed forces were watching each other, he recalled Medius to Asia with the fleet, and at once with his armies set out at top speed for the Hellespont as if intending to cross over into Macedonia, in order that, if Cassander remained in Euboea, he might himself occupy Macedonia while it was stripped of defenders, or that Cassander, going to the defence of his kingdom, might lose his supremacy in Greece. Cassander, perceiving Antigonus' plan, left Pleistarchus in command of the garrison in Chalcis and setting out himself with all his forces took Oropus by storm and brought the Thebans into his alliance. Then, after making a truce with the other Boeotians and leaving Eupolemus as general for Greece, he went into Macedonia, for he was apprehensive of the enemy's crossing. As for Antigonus, when he came to the Propontis, he sent an embassy to the Byzantines, asking them to enter the alliance, but there had arrived envoys from Lysimachus also who were urging them to do nothing against either Lysimachus or Cassander, and the Byzantines decided to remain neutral and to maintain peace and friendship toward both parties. Antigonus, because he had been foiled in these undertakings and also because the winter season was closing in upon him, distributed his soldiers among the cities for the winter [313/12].

78. While these things were going on, the Corcyraeans, who had gone to the aid of the people of Apollonia and Epidamnus, dismissed Cassander's soldiers under a truce; and of these cities they freed Apollonia, but Epidamnus they gave over to Glaucias, the king of the Illyrians. After Cassander had departed for Macedonia, Antigonus' general Ptolemaeus, striking fear into the garrison that was holding Chalcis, took the city' and he left the Chalcidians without a garrison in order to make it evident that Antigonus in very truth proposed to free the Greeks, for the city is well placed for any who wish to have a base from which to carry through a war for supremacy. However that may be, when Ptolemaeus had taken Oropus by siege, he gave it back to the Boeotians and made captive the troops of Cassander. Thereafter, having received the people of Eretria and Carystus into the alliance, he moved into Attica, where Demetrius of Phalerum was governing the city. At first the Athenians kept sending secretly to Antigonus, begging him to free the city, but then, taking courage when Ptolemaeus drew near the city, they forced Demetrius to make a truce and to send envoys to Antigonus about an alliance. Ptolemaeus, moving from Attica into Boeotia, took the Cadmea, drove out the garrison, and freed Thebes. After this he advanced into Phocis where he won over most of the cities and from all of these expelled the garrisons of Cassander. He also marched against Locris; and, since the Opuntians belonged to the party of Cassander, he began a siege and made continuous attacks.

The revolt and the capture of Cyrenê, also the campaign of Ptolemy into Cyprus and Syria (chap. 79).

79. In that same summer [313] the people of Cyrenê revolted from Ptolemy, invested the citadel, and seemed on the point of immediately casting out the garrison and, when envoys came from Alexandria and bade them cease from their sedition, they killed them and continued the attack on the citadel with greater vigour. Enraged at them, Ptolemy dispatched Agis as general with a land army and also sent a fleet to take part in the war, placing Epaenetus in command. Agis attacked the rebels with vigour and took the city by storm. Those who were guilty of the sedition he bound and sent to Alexandria and then, after depriving the others of their arms and arranging the affairs of the city in whatever way seemed best to himself, he returned to Egypt.

Ptolemy, now that the matter of Cyrenê had been disposed of according to his wishes, crossed over with an army from Egypt into Cyprus against those of the kings who refused to obey him. Finding that Pygmalion was negotiating with Antigonus, he put him to death, and he arrested Praxippus, king of Lapithia and ruler of Cerynia, whom he being ill disposed toward himself, and also Stasioecus, ruler of Marion, destroying the city and transporting the inhabitants to Paphos. After accomplishing these things, he appointed Nicocreon as general of Cyprus, giving him both the cities and the revenues of the kings who had been driven out; but he himself with his army, sailing toward Upper Syria, as it is called, captured and sacked Poseidium and Potami Caron. Sailing without delay to Cilicia, he took Malus and sold as booty those who were captured there. He also plundered the neighbouring territory and, after sating his army with spoil, sailed back to Cyprus. His playing up to the soldiers in this way was designed to evoke enthusiasm in face of the encounters that were approaching.

The battle of Demetrius against Ptolemy, and the victory of Ptolemy (80-86).

80. Now Antigonus' son Demetrius was staying on in Coelê Syria lying in wait for the Egyptian armies, but when he heard of the capture of the cities, he left Pithon as general in charge of the region, giving him the elephants and the heavy-armed units of the army, and he himself, taking the cavalry and the light-armed units, moved rapidly toward Cilicia to give aid to those who were in danger. Arriving after the opportunity had passed and finding that the enemy had sailed away, he went rapidly back to his camp, having lost most of his horses during the march; for in six days' march towards Malus he covered twenty-four stages, with the result that on account of the excessive hardship not one of his sutlers or of his grooms kept up the pace.

Ptolemy, since his undertakings had turned out as he wished, now sailed away to Egypt, but after a little while, spurred on by Seleucus because of his hostility toward Antigonus, he decided to make a campaign into Coelê Syria and take the field against the army of Demetrius. He therefore gathered together his forces from all sides and marched from Alexandria to Pelusium with eighteen thousand foot and four thousand horse. Of his army some were Macedonians and some were mercenaries, but a great number were Egyptians, of whom some carried the missiles and the other baggage but some were armed and serviceable for battle. Marching through the desert from Pelusium, he camped near the enemy at Old Gaza in Syria. Demetrius, who had likewise summoned his soldiers to Old Gaza from their winter quarters on all sides, awaited the approach of his opponents.

81. Although his friends were urging him not to take the field against so great a general and a superior force, Demetrius paid no heed to them but confidently prepared for the conflict even though he was very young and was about to engage in so great a battle apart from his father. When he had called together an assembly under arms and, anxious and agitated, had taken his position on a raised platform, the crowd shouted with a single voice, bidding him be of good courage and then, before the herald bade the shouting men cease their tumult, they all became silent. For, because he had just been placed in command, neither soldiers nor civilians had for him any ill will such as usually develops against generals of long standing when at a particular time many minor irritations are combined in a single mass grievance; for the multitude becomes exacting when it remains under the same authority, and every group that is not preferred welcomes change. Since his father was already an old man, the hopes of the kingdom, centring upon his succession, were bringing him the command and at the same time the goodwill of the multitude. Moreover, he was outstanding both in beauty and in stature, and also when clad in royal armour he had great distinction and struck men with awe, whereby he created great expectations in the multitude. Furthermore, there was in him a certain gentleness becoming to a youthful king, which won for him the devotion of all, so that even those outside the ranks ran together to hear him, feeling sympathetic anxiety on account of his youth and the critical struggle that impended. For he was about to fight a decisive battle not only against more numerous forces, but also against generals who were almost the greatest, Ptolemy and Seleucus. Indeed, these generals, who had taken part with Alexander in all his wars and had often led armies independently, were unconquered up to this time. At all events, Demetrius, after encouraging the crowd with words suitable to the occasion and promising to give gifts to them as they were deserved and to yield the booty to the soldiers, drew up his army for the battle.

82. On the left wing, where he himself was going to take part in the battle, he placed first the two hundred selected horsemen of his guard, among whom were all his other friends and, in particular, Pithon, who had campaigned with Alexander and had been made by Antigonus co-general and partner in the whole undertaking. As an advanced guard he drew up three troops of cavalry and the same number as guards on the flank, and in addition to these and stationed separately outside the wing, three troops of Tarentines; thus those that were drawn up about his person amounted to five hundred horsemen armed with the lance and one hundred Tarentines. Next he posted those of the cavalry who were called the Companions, eight hundred in number, and after them no less than fifteen hundred horsemen of all kinds. In front of the whole wing he stationed thirty of his elephants, and he filled the intervals between them with units of light-armed men, of whom a thousand were javelin-throwers and archers and five hundred were Persian slingers. In this fashion then he formed the left wing, with which he intended to decide the battle. Next to it he drew up the infantry phalanx composed of eleven thousand men, of whom two thousand were Macedonians, one thousand were Lycians and Pamphylians, and eight thousand were mercenaries. On the right wing he drew up the rest of his cavalry, fifteen hundred men commanded by Andronicus. This officer was ordered to hold his line back at an angle and avoid fighting, awaiting the outcome of the conflict fought by Demetrius. The thirteen other elephants he stationed in front of the phalanx of the infantry with the normal complement of light troops in the intervals. In this manner, then, Demetrius arrayed his army.

83. Ptolemy and Seleucus at first made strong the left part of their line, not knowing the intention of the enemy; but when they learned from scouts the formation he had adopted, they quickly reformed their army in such a way that their right wing should have the greatest strength and power and be matched against those arrayed with Demetrius on his left. They drew up on this wing the three thousand strongest of their cavalry, along with whom they themselves had decided to fight. In front of this position they placed the men who were to handle the spiked devices made of iron and connected by chains that they had prepared against the onset of the elephants; for when this contrivance had been stretched out, it was easy to prevent the beasts from moving forward. In front of this wing they also stationed their light-armed units, ordering the javelin-men and archers to shoot without ceasing at the elephants and at those who were mounted upon them. When they had made their right wing strong in this manner and had drawn up the rest of their army as circumstances permitted, they advanced upon them. When they had made their right wing strong in this manner and had drawn up the rest of their army as circumstances permitted, they advanced upon the enemy with a great shout.

Their opponents also advanced; and first there was a cavalry action on the extreme wings between the troops of the advance guards in which the men of Demetrius had much the better of it, but after a little, when Ptolemy and Seleucus had ridden around the wing and charged upon them more heavily with cavalry drawn up in depth, there was severe fighting because of the zeal of both sides. In the first charge, indeed, the fighting was with spears, most of which were shattered, and many of the antagonists were wounded; then, rallying again, the men rushed into battle at sword's point, and, as they were locked in close combat, many were slain on each side. The very commanders, endangering themselves in front of all, encouraged those under their command to withstand the danger stoutly; and the horsemen upon the wings, all of whom had been selected for bravery, vied with each other since as witnesses of their valour they had their generals, who were sharing the struggle with them.

84. After the cavalry battle had continued for a long time on equal terms, the elephants, urged on into the combat by their Indian mahouts, advanced for a certain distance in a way to inspire terror, just as if no one were going to withstand them. When, however, they came up to the barrier of spikes, the host of javelin-throwers and archers, who were sending their missiles unremittingly, began to wound severely the elephants themselves and those who were mounted upon them; and while the mahouts were forcing the beasts forward and were using their goads, some of the elephants were pierced by the cleverly devised spikes and. tormented by their wounds and by the concentrated efforts of the attackers, began to cause disorder. For on smooth and yielding ground these beasts display in direct onset a might that is irresistible, but on terrain that is rough and difficult their strength is completely useless because of the tenderness of their feet. Thus, too, on this occasion, since Ptolemy shrewdly foresaw what would result from the setting up of the spikes, he rendered the power of the elephants unavailing. The final outcome was that, after most of the mahouts had been shot down, all the elephants were captured. When this happened, most of Demetrius' horsemen were panic-stricken and rushed into flight; and he himself was left with a few and then, since no one heeded him when he begged them each to stand and not desert him, was forced to leave the field with the rest. Now as far as Gaza most of the cavalry who were following with him listened to orders and remained in formation, so that no one of those who were pursuing at random lightly risked attacking; for the plain was open and yielding, and favourable to men who wished to withdraw in formation. There followed also those of the infantry who preferred to leave their lines and, abandoning their heavy arms, save themselves by travelling light, but as Demetrius was passing Gaza at about sunset, some of the cavalry dropped out and entered the city since they wished to carry away their baggage. Then, when the gates were opened and a large number of pack animals were gathered together and when each man tried to lead out his own beasts first, there arose such confusion around the gates that when the troops of Ptolemy came up no one was able to close the gates in time. Hence the enemy dashed within the walls, and the city came into the possession of Ptolemy.

85. After the battle had ended in this fashion, Demetrius reached Azotus about the middle of the night, covering two hundred and seventy stades. Thence he sent a herald about the burial of the dead since he was very anxious at any cost to honour those who had perished with the funeral that was their due, for it happened that most of his friends had fallen, the most distinguished of whom were Pithon, who had shared the command on equal terms with himself, and Boeotus, who for a long time had lived with his father Antigonus and had shared in all his state secrets. In the battle there had fallen more than five hundred men, the majority of whom were cavalry and men of distinction, and more than eight thousand had been captured. Ptolemy and Seleucus permitted the recovery of the dead, and they returned to Demetrius without ransom the royal baggage, which had been captured, and those of the prisoners who had been accustomed to be in attendance at the court; for, they said, it was not about these that they were at variance with Antigonus but because, although he and they had made war in common, first against Perdiccas and later against Eumenes, he had not turned over to his companions their share of the captured territory, and again because, after making a compact of friendship with Seleucus, he had nevertheless taken away from him his satrapy of Babylonia contrary to all right. Ptolemy sent the captured soldiers off into Egypt, ordering them to be distributed among the nomes, but he himself, after giving a magnificent burial to all those of his own men who had died in the battle, went with his forces against the cities of Phoenicia, besieging some of them and winning others by persuasion. Demetrius, since he did not have a sufficiently strong army, sent a messenger to his father, asking him to aid him as quickly as possible. He himself, moving to Tripolis in Phoenicia, summoned the soldiers from Cilicia and also those of his other men who were guarding cities or strongholds far removed from the enemy.

86. Ptolemy, after he had gained control of the open country, first won Sidon to his side, and then, camping near Tyre, he summoned Andronicus, the commander of the garrison, to surrender the city, and he promised to give him gifts and abundant honours. Andronicus, however, said that he would in no wise betray the trust that had been placed in him by Antigonus and Demetrius, and he vilely insulted Ptolemy. Later, when his soldiers mutinied and he was expelled from the city and fell into the hands of Ptolemy, he expected to receive punishment both for the insults and for his unwillingness to surrender Tyre, but in truth Ptolemy bore no malice; on the contrary, he gave him gifts and kept him in his court, making him one of his friends and advancing him in honour. For indeed, that prince was exceptionally gentle and forgiving and inclined toward deeds of kindness. It was this very thing that most increased his power and made many men desire to share his friendship. For example, when Seleucus had been driven from Babylonia, he received him with friendship; and he used to share his own prosperity with him and with his other friends. Therefore on this occasion also, when Seleucus asked him to give him soldiers for an expedition into Babylonia, he readily consented and in addition, he promised to aid him in every way until he should regain the satrapy that had formerly been his.

Such was the situation of affairs in Asia.

The desertion of Antigonus by his general Telesphorus (87).

How Antigonus took Coelê Syria without a battle, and how he dispatched an army into Arabia (chaps. 93-100).

87. In Europe, Antigonus' admiral Telesphorus, who was tarrying near Corinth, when he saw Ptolemaeus preferred to himself and entrusted with all affairs throughout Greece, charged Antigonus with this, sold what ships he had, enlisted such of the soldiers as volunteered to join his cause, and organized an enterprise of his own. Entering Elis as if still preserving his friendship for Antigonus, he fortified the citadel and enslaved the city. He even plundered the sacred precinct at Olympia and, after collecting more than five hundred talents of silver, began hiring mercenaries. In this manner then, Telesphorus, because he was jealous of the advancement of Ptolemaeus, betrayed the friendship of Antigonus. Ptolemaeus, the general of Antigonus, had been placed in charge of affairs throughout Greece and he, on hearing of the revolt of Telesphorus, the capture of the city of the Eleans, and the plundering of the wealth of Olympia, moved into the Peloponnesus with an army. When he had come into Elis and levelled the citadel that had been fortified, he gave the Eleans back their freedom and restored the treasure to the god. Then by winning Telesphorus' consent he recovered Cyllene, which the latter had garrisoned, and restored it to the Eleans.

The operations of Cassander in Epirus and on the Adriatic (88-89).

88. While this was happening, the Epirotes, their king Aeacides being dead, gave the kingship to Alcetas, who had been banished by his father Arymbus and who was hostile to Cassander. For this reason, Lyciscus, who had been placed as general over Acarnania by Cassander, entered Epirus with an army, hoping to remove Alcetas easily from his throne while the affairs of the kingdom were still in disorder. While Lyciscus was in camp before Cassopia, Alcetas sent his sons Alexander and Teucer to the cities, ordering them to levy as many soldiers as possible and he himself, taking the field with what force he had, came near the enemy and awaited the return of his sons. However, since the forces of Lyciscus were at hand and were far superior in number, the Epirotes were frightened and went over to the enemy; and Alcetas, deserted, fled for refuge to Eurymenae, a city of Epirus. While he was being besieged there, Alexander came up bringing reinforcements to his father. A violent battle took place in which many of the soldiers were slain, among whom were certain others of the followers of Lyciscus and in particular the general Micythus and Lysander, an Athenian who had been put in charge of Leucas by Cassander. Afterwards, when Deinias brought reinforcements to the defeated army, there was another battle, in which Alexander and Teucer were defeated and fled with their father to a certain stronghold, while Lyciscus took Eurymenae, plundered it, and destroyed it.

89. At this time Cassander, who had heard of the defeat of his forces but did not know of the victory that had followed, moved into Epirus in haste to assist Lyciscus. On finding that the latter had gained the upper hand, he made terms and established friendship with Alcetas; and then, taking a part of his army, he moved to the Adriatic to lay siege to Apollonia because the people of that city had driven out his garrison and gone over to the Illyrians. Those in the city, however, were not frightened, but summoned aid from their other allies and drew up their army before the walls. In a battle, which was hard fought and long, the people of Apollonia, who were superior in number, forced their opponents to flee; and Cassander, who had lost many soldiers, since he did not have an adequate army with him and saw that the winter was at hand [312/11], returned into Macedonia. After his departure, the Leucadians, receiving help from the Corcyraeans, drove out Cassander 's garrison. For some time the Epirotes continued to be ruled by Alcctas, but then, since he was treating the common people too harshly, they murdered him and two of his sons, Esioneus and Nisus, who were children.

How Seleucus received a small force from Ptolemy, gained control of Babylon, and recovered the satrapy that he had formerly possessed (90-92)

90. In Asia, after the defeat of Demetrius at Gaza in Syria, Seleucus, receiving from Ptolemy no more than eight hundred foot soldiers and about two hundred horse, set out for Babylon. He was so puffed up with great expectations that, even if he had had no army whatever, he would have made the expedition into the interior with his friends and his own slaves, for he assumed that the Babylonians, on account of the goodwill that had previously existed, would promptly join him, and that Antigonus, by withdrawing to a great distance with his army, had given him a suitable opportunity for his own enterprises. While such was his own enthusiasm, those of his friends who accompanied him were no little disheartened when they saw that the men who were making the campaign with them were very few and that the enemy against whom they were going-possessed large armies ready for service, magnificent resources, and a host of allies. When Seleucus saw that they were terror-stricken, he encouraged them, saying that men who had campaigned with Alexander and had been advanced by him because of their prowess ought not to rely solely on armed force and wealth when confronting difficult situations, but upon experience and skill, the means whereby Alexander himself had accomplished his great and universally admired deeds. He added that they ought also to believe the oracles of the gods which had foretold that the end of his campaign would be worthy of his purpose; for, when he had consulted the oracle in Branchidae, the god had greeted him as King Seleucus, and Alexander standing beside him in a dream had given him a clear sign of the future leadership that was destined to fall to him in the course of time. Moreover, he pointed out that everything that is good and admired among men is gained through toil and danger. He also sought the favour of his fellow soldiers and put himself on an equality with them all in such a way that each man respected him and willingly accepted the risk of the daring venture.

91. When in his advance he entered Mesopotamia, he persuaded some of the Macedonians who were settled at Carae to join his forces, and compelled the rest. When he pushed into Babylonia, most of the inhabitants came to meet him, and, declaring themselves on his side, promised to aid him as he saw fit, for, when he had been for four years satrap of that country, he had shown himself generous to all, winning the goodwill of the common people and long in advance securing men who would assist him if an opportunity should ever be given him to make a bid for supreme power. He was joined also by Polyarchus, who had been placed in command of a certain district, with more than a thousand soldiers. When those who remained loyal to Antigonus saw that the impulse of the people could not be checked, they took refuge together in the citadel, of which Diphilus had been appointed commander. But Seleucus, by laying siege to the citadel and taking it by storm, recovered the persons of all those of his friends and slaves who had been placed there under guard by the order of Antigonus after Seleucus' own departure from Babylon into Egypt. When he had finished this, he enlisted soldiers, and, having bought up horses, he distributed them to those who were able to handle them. Associating with all on friendly terms and raising high hopes in all, he kept his fellow adventurers ready and eager under every condition. In this way, then, Seleucus regained Babylonia.

92. But when Nicanor, the general in Media, gathered against him from Media and Persia and the neighbouring lands more than ten thousand foot soldiers and about seven thousand horse, Seleucus set out at full speed to oppose the enemy. He himself had in all more than three thousand foot and four hundred horse. He crossed the Tigris River; and, on hearing that the enemy were a few days' march distant, he hid his soldiers in the adjacent marshes, intending to make his attack a surprise. When Nicanor arrived at the Tigris River and did not find the enemy, he camped at one of the royal stations, believing that they had fled to a greater distance than was the case. When night was come and the army of Nicanor was keeping a perfunctory and negligent guard, Scleucus fell on them suddenly, causing great confusion and panic, for it happened that when the

Persians had joined battle, their satrap Evager fell together with some of the other leaders. When this occurred, most of the soldiers went over to Seleucus, in part because they were frightened at the danger but in part because they were offended by the conduct of Antigonus. Nicanor, who was left with only a few men and feared lest he be delivered over to the enemy, took flight with his friends through the desert. Seleucus, now that he had gained control of a large army and was comporting himself in a way gracious to all, easily won over Susianê, Media, and some of the adjacent lands, and he wrote to Ptolemy and his other friends about his achievements, already possessing a king's stature and a reputation worthy of royal power.

93. Meanwhile Ptolemy remained in Coelê Syria after having conquered Antigonus' son Demetrius in a great battle. On hearing that Demetrius had returned from Cilicia and was encamped in Upper Syria, he chose from the friends who were with him Cilles the Macedonian; and, giving him an adequate army, he ordered him to drive Demetrius completely out of Syria or to entrap and crush him. While Cilles was on the way, Demetrius, hearing from spies that he was carelessly encamped at Myus, left his baggage behind and with his soldiers in light equipment made a forced march' then, falling suddenly upon the enemy during the early morning watch, he captured the army without a battle and took the general himself prisoner. By achieving such a success he believed that he had wiped out the defeat. Nevertheless, assuming that Ptolemy would march against him with all his army, he went into camp, using as the outworks of his defence swamps and marshes. He also wrote to his father about the success that had been gained, urging him either to send an army as soon as possible or to cross over into Syria himself. Antigonus chanced to be in Celaenae in Phrygia; and, on receiving the letter, he rejoiced greatly that his son, young as he was, seemed to have got out of his difficulties by himself and to have shown himself worthy to be a king. He himself with his army set out from Phrygia, crossed the Taurus, and within a few days joined Demetrius. Ptolemy, however, on hearing of the arrival of Antigonus, called together his leaders and friends and took counsel with them whether it was better to remain and reach a final decision in Syria or to withdraw to Egypt and carry on the war from there as he had formerly done against Perdiccas. Now all advised him not to risk a battle against an army that was many times stronger and had a larger number of elephants as well as against an unconquered general for, they said, it would be much easier for him to settle the war in Egypt where he had plenty of supplies and could trust to the difficulty of the terrain. Deciding, therefore, to leave Syria, he razed the most noteworthy of the cities that he had captured: Ake in Phoenician Syria, and Ioppe, Samaria, and Gaza in Syria, then he himself, taking the army and what of the booty it was possible to drive or carry, returned into Egypt.

About the customs observed by the Arabian tribes (94).

94. Now that Antigonus without a fight had gained possession of all Syria and Phoenicia, he desired to make a campaign against the land of the Arabs who are called Nabataeans. Deciding that this people was hostile to his interests, he selected one of his friends, Athenaeus, gave him four thousand light foot-soldiers and six hundred horsemen fitted for speed, and ordered him to set upon the barbarians suddenly and cut off all their cattle as booty.

For the sake of those who do not know, it will be useful to state in some detail the customs of these Arabs, by following which, it is believed, they preserve their liberty. They live in the open air, claiming as native land a wilderness that has neither rivers nor abundant springs from which it is possible for a hostile army to obtain water. It is their custom neither to plant grain, set out any fruit-bearing tree, use wine, nor construct any house, and if anyone is found acting contrary to this, death is his penalty. They follow this custom because they believe that those who possess these things are, in order to retain the use of them, easily compelled by the powerful to do their bidding. Some of them raise camels, others sheep, pasturing them in the desert. While there are many Arabian tribes who use the desert as pasture, the Nabataeans far surpass the others in wealth although they are not much more than ten thousand in number, for not a few of them are accustomed to bring down to the sea frankincense and myrrh and the most valuable kinds of spices, which they procure from those who convey them from what is called Arabia Eudaemon. They are exceptionally fond of freedom; and, whenever a strong force of enemies comes near, they take refuge in the desert, using this as a fortress; for it lacks water and cannot be crossed by others, but to them alone, since they have prepared subterranean reservoirs lined with stucco, it furnishes safety. As the earth in some places is clayey and in others is of soft stone, they make great excavations in it, the mouths of which they make very small, but by constantly increasing the width as they dig deeper, they finally make them of such size that each side has a length of one plethrum. After filling these reservoirs with rain water, they close the openings, making them even with the rest of the ground, and they leave signs that are known to themselves but are unrecognisable by others. They water their cattle every other day, so that, if they flee through waterless places, they may not need a continuous supply of water. They themselves use as food flesh and milk and those of the plants that grow from the ground which are suitable for this purpose, for among them there grow the pepper and plenty of the so-called wild honey from trees, which they drink mixed with water. There are also other tribes of Arabs, some of whom even till the soil, mingling with the tribute-paying peoples, and have the same customs as the Syrians, except that they do not dwell in houses.

95. It appears that such are the customs of the Arabs. When the time draws near for the national gathering at which those who dwell round about are accustomed to meet, some to sell goods and others to purchase things that are needful to them, they travel to this meeting, leaving on a certain rock their possessions and their old men, also their women and their children. This place is exceedingly strong but unwalled, and it is distant two days' journey from the settled country.

After waiting for this season, Athenaeus set out for the rock with his army in light marching order. Covering the twenty-two hundred stades from the district of Idumaea in three days and the same number of nights, he escaped the attention of the Arabs and seized the rock at about midnight. Of those that were caught there, some he slew at once, some he took as prisoners, and others who were wounded he left behind; and of the frankincense and myrrh he gathered together the larger part, and about five hundred talents of silver. Delaying no longer than the early morning watch, he at once departed at top speed, expecting to be pursued by the barbarians. When he and his men had marched without pause for two hundred stades, they made camp, being tired and keeping a careless watch as if they believed that the enemy could not come before two or three days. When the Arabs heard from those who had seen the expedition, they at once gathered together and, leaving the place of assembly, came to the rock, then, being informed by the wounded of what had taken place, they pursued the Greeks at top speed. While the men of Athenaeus were encamped with little thought of the enemy and because of their weariness were deep in sleep, some, of their prisoners escaped secretly, and the Nabataeans, learning from them the condition of the enemy, attacked the camp at about the third watch, being no less than eight thousand in number. Most of the hostile troops they slaughtered where they lay, the rest they slew with their javelins as they awoke and sprang to arms. In the end all the foot-soldiers were slain, but of the horsemen about fifty escaped, and of these the larger part were wounded.

And so Athenaeus, after being successful at first, later because of his own folly failed in this manner; for carelessness and indifference are, in general, wont to follow success. For this reason some rightly believe that it is easier to meet disaster with skill than very great success with discretion, for disaster, because of the fear of what is to follow, forces men to be careful, but success, because of the previous good fortune, tempts men to be careless about everything.

96. When the Nabataeans had manfully punished the enemy they themselves returned to the rock with the property that they had recovered, but to Antigonus they wrote a letter in Syrian characters in which they accused Athenaeus and vindicated themselves. Antigonus replied to them, agreeing that they had been justified in defending themselves, but he found fault with Athenaeus, saying that he had made the attack contrary to the instructions that had been given. He did this, hiding his own intentions and desiring to delude the barbarians into a sense of security so that, by making an unexpected attack, he might accomplish his desire, for it was not easy without some deception to get the better of men who zealously pursued a nomadic life and possessed the desert as an inaccessible refuge. The Arabs were highly pleased because they seemed to have been relieved of great fears; yet they did not altogether trust the words of Antigonus, but, regarding their prospects as uncertain, they placed watchmen upon the hills from which it was easy to see from a distance the passes into Arabia, and they themselves, after having arranged their affairs in proper fashion, anxiously awaited the issue. Antigonus, when he had treated the barbarians as friends for some time and believed that they had been thoroughly deceived and thus had given him his opportunity against themselves, selected from his whole force four thousand foot-soldiers, who were lightly armed and well fitted by nature for rapid marching, and more than four thousand mounted men. He ordered them to carry several days' supply of food that would not require cooking, and, after placing his son Demetrius in command, lie sent them off during the first watch, ordering him to punish the Arabs in whatever way he could.

97. Demetrius, therefore, advanced for three days through regions with no roads, striving not to be observed by the barbarians, but the lookouts, having seen that a hostile force had entered, informed the Nabataeans by means of prearranged fire signals. The barbarians, having thus learned at once that the Greeks had come, sent their property to the rock and posted there a garrison that was strong enough since there was a single artificial approach, and they themselves divided their flocks and drove them into the desert, some into one place and some into another. Demetrius, on arriving at the rock and finding that the flocks had been removed, made repeated assaults upon the stronghold. Those within resisted stoutly, and easily had the upper hand because of the height of the place, and so on this day,after he had continued the struggle until evening, he recalled his soldiers by a trumpet call.

On the next day, however, when he had advanced upon the rock, one of the barbarians called to him, saying: "King Demetrius, with what desire or under what compulsion do you war against us who live in the desert and in a land that has neither water nor grain nor wine nor any other thing whatever of those that pertain to the necessities of life among you. For we, since we are in no way willing to be slaves, have all taken refuge in a land that lacks all the things that are valued among other peoples and have chosen to live a life in the desert and one altogether like that of wild beasts, harming you not at all. We therefore beg both you and your father to do us no injury but, after receiving gifts from us, to withdraw your army and henceforth regard the Nabataeans as your friends. For neither can you, if you wish, remain here many days since you lack water and all the other necessary supplies, nor can you force us to live a different life; but you will have a few captives, disheartened slaves who would not consent to live among strange ways." When words such as these had been spoken, Demetrius withdrew his army and ordered the Arabs to send an embassy about these matters. They sent their oldest men, who, repeating arguments similar to those previously uttered, persuaded him to receive as gifts the most precious of their products and to make terms with them.

About what is called the Bituminous Sea (98-99).

98. Demetrius received hostages and the gifts that had been agreed upon and departed from the rock. After marching for three hundred stades, he camped near the Dead Sea, the nature of which ought not to be passed over without remark. It lies along the middle of the satrapy of Idumaea, extending in length about five hundred stades and in width about sixty. Its water is very bitter and of exceedingly foul odour, so that it can support neither fish nor any of the other creatures usually found in water. Although great rivers whose waters are of exceptional sweetness flow into it, it prevails over these by reason of its foulness, and from its centre each year it sends forth a mass of solid asphalt, sometimes more than three plethra in area, sometimes a little less than one plethrum. When this happens the barbarians who live near habitually call the larger mass a bull and the smaller one a calf. When the asphalt is floating on the sea, its surface seems to those who see it from a distance just like an island. It appears that the ejection of the asphalt is indicated twenty days in advance, for on every side about the sea for a distance of many stades the odour of the asphalt spreads with a noisome exhalation, and all the silver, gold, and bronze in the region lose their proper colours. These, however, are restored as soon as all the asphalt has been ejected; but the neighbouring region is very torrid and ill smelling, which makes the inhabitants sickly in body and exceedingly short lived. Yet the land is good for raising palm trees in whatever part it is crossed by serviceable rivers or is supplied with springs that can irrigate it. In a certain valley in this region there grows what is called balsam, from which there is a great income since nowhere else in the inhabited world is this plant found, and its use as a drug is very important to physicians.

99. When the asphalt has been ejected, the people who live about, the sea on both sides carry it off like plunder of war since they are hostile to each other, making the collection without boats in a peculiar fashion. They make ready large bundles of reeds and cast them into the sea. On these not more than three men take their places, two of whom row with oars, which are lashed on, but one carries a bow and repels any who sail against them from the other shore or who venture to interfere with them. When they have come near the asphalt they jump upon it with axes and, just as if it were soft stone, they cut out pieces and load them on the raft, after which they sail back. If the raft comes to pieces and one of them who does not know how to swim falls off, he does not sink as he would in other waters, but stays afloat as well as do those who do know. For this liquid by its nature supports heavy bodies that have the power of growth or of breathing, except for solid ones that seem to have a density like that of silver, gold, lead, and the like; and even these sink much more slowly than do these same bodies if they are east into other lakes. The barbarians who enjoy this source of income take the asphalt to Egypt and sell it for the embalming of the dead, for unless this is mixed with the other aromatic ingredients, the preservation of the bodies cannot be permanent.

How Antigonus sent his son Demetrius with the army into Babylonia (100).

100. Antigonus, when Demetrius returned and made a detailed report of what he had done, rebuked him for the treaty with the Nabataeans, saving that he had made the barbarians much bolder by leaving them unpunished, since it would seem to them that they had gained pardon not through his kindness but through his inability to overcome them, but he praised him for examining the lake and apparently having found a source of revenue for the kingdom. In charge of this he placed Hieronymus, the writer of the history, and instructed him to prepare boats, collect all the asphalt, and bring it together in a certain place. The result was not in accord with the expectations of Antigonus, for the Arabs, collecting to the number of six thousand and sailing up on their rafts of reeds against those on the boats, killed almost all of them with their arrows. As a result, Antigonus gave up this source of revenue because of the defeat he had suffered and because his mind was engaged with other and weightier matters. For there came to him at this time a dispatch-bearer with a letter from Nicanor, the general of Media and the upper satrapies. In this letter was written an account of Seleucus' march inland and of the disasters that had been suffered in connection with him. Therefore Antigonus, worried about the upper satrapies, sent his son Demetrius with five thousand Macedonian and ten thousand mercenary foot-soldiers and four thousand horse; and he ordered him to go up as far as Babylon and then, after recovering the satrapy, to come down to the sea at full speed.

So Demetrius, having set out from Damascus in Syria, carried out his father's orders with zeal. Patrocles, who had been established as general of Babylonia by Seleucus, hearing that the enemy was on the frontiers of Mesopotamia, did not dare await their arrival since he had few men at hand, but he gave orders to the civilians to leave the city, bidding some of them cross the Euphrates and take refuge in the desert and some of them pass over the Tigris and go into Susianê to Euteles and to the Red Sea; and he himself with what soldiers he had, using river courses and canals as defences, kept moving about in the satrapy, watching the enemy and at the same time sending word into Media to Seleucus about what was taking place from time to time and urging him to send aid as soon as possible. When Demetrius on his arrival at Babylon found the city abandoned, he began to besiege the citadels. He took one of these and delivered it to his own soldiers for plundering, the other he besieged for a few days and then, since the capture required time, left Archelaus, one of his friends, as general for the siege, giving him five thousand infantry and one thousand cavalry, while he himself, the time being close at hand at which he had been ordered to return, made the march down to the sea with the rest of his army.

About the operations of the Romans and the Samnites (101).

101. While this was taking place, in Italy the Romans were carrying on their war with the Samnites, and there were repeated raids through the country, sieges of cities, and encampments of armies in the field, for the two most war-like of the peoples of Italy were struggling as rivals for the supremacy and meeting in conflicts of every sort. Now the Roman consuls with part of the army had taken a position in the face of the encampments of the enemy and were awaiting an opportune time for battle while at the same time furnishing protection to the allied cities. With the rest of the army Quintus Fabius, who had been chosen dictator, captured the city of the Fregellani and made prisoners the chief men among those who were hostile to the Romans. These to the number of more than two hundred he took to Rome, and, bringing them into the Forum, he beat them with rods and beheaded them according to the ancestral custom. Soon afterwards, entering the hostile territory, he took by siege Calatia and the citadel of Nola, and he sold a large amount of spoil but allotted much of the land to his soldiers. The people, since matters were progressing according to their will, sent a colony to the island that is called Pontia.

How Agathocles deceived the Messenians and became ruler of their city (102). How he slew those of the Messenians, Tauromenians, and Centoripians who opposed him (102-103).

102. In Sicily, where peace had just been established between Agathocles and the Sicilians except the Messenians, the exiles of Syracuse gathered in Messenê since they saw that this was the only city remaining of those that were hostile to the dynast; but Agathocles, who was eager to break up their group, sent Pasiphilus with an army to Messenê as general, telling him in secret instructions what he should do. Pasiphilus, entering the region unexpectedly and gaining possession of many prisoners and much other booty, urged the Messenians to choose friendship with him and not be forced to seek terms in common with his bitterest foes. The Messenians, gaining hope of a bloodless termination of the war, expelled the Syracusan exiles and welcomed Agathocles when he came near with his army. At first he treated them in a friendly manner and persuaded them to receive back the exiles who were in his army, men who had been legally banished by the Messenians. Then he brought together from Tauromenium and Messenê those who had previously been opposed to his rule and put them all to death, being no less than six hundred in number, for his intention was to wage war on the Carthaginians, and he was getting rid of all opposition throughout Sicily. When the Messenians had driven out of the city those non-citizens who were most favourably disposed to them and best able to protect them from the tyrant, and saw that those of their own citizens who were opposed to the dynast had been put to death, and when, moreover, they had been forced to receive back men who had been convicted of crime, they regretted what they had done; but they were forced to submit, since they were completely cowed by the superior power of those who had become their masters. Agathocles first set out for

Acragas, intending to organise that city also in his own interest; when, however, the Carthaginians sailed in with sixty ships, he abandoned that purpose, but he entered the territory subject to the Carthaginians and plundered it, taking some of the fortified places by force and winning others by negotiation.

103. While this was taking place, Deinocrates, the leader of the Syracusan exiles, sent a message to the Carthaginians, asking them to send aid before Agathocles should bring all Sicily under his sway, and he himself, since he had a strong army after receiving those exiles who had been driven out of Messenê, dispatched one of his friends, Nymphodorus, with part of the soldiers to the city of the Centoripini. Although this city was garrisoned by Agathocles, some of its chief men had promised to betray it on condition that the people be given autonomy. When Nymphodorus broke into the city by night, the commanders of the garrison, perceiving what had taken place, slew both the man himself and those who pressed fiercely on within the walls. Seizing upon this opportunity, Agathocles brought accusations against the Centoripini and slaughtered all who were thought to have been guilty of the sedition. While the dynast was thus engaged, the Carthaginians sailed into the great harbour of Syracuse with fifty light boats. They were able to do nothing more, but falling upon two merchant ships from Athens, they sank the ships themselves and cut off the hands of the crews. They had clearly treated with cruelty men who had done them no harm at all, and the gods quickly gave them a sign of this, for immediately, when some of the ships were separated from the fleet in the vicinity of Brettia, they were captured by the generals of Agathocles, and those of the Phoenicians who were taken alive suffered a fate similar to that which they had inflicted upon their captives.

How Agathocles defeated Deinocrates and the exiles at Galaria (104).

104. The exiles who were with Deinocrates, having more than three, thousand foot-soldiers and not less than two thousand mounted men, occupied the place called Galeria, the citizens of their own free will inviting them, and they exiled the followers of Agathocles, but they themselves encamped before the city. When, however, Agathocles quickly dispatched against them Pasiphilus and Demophilus with five thousand soldiers, a battle was fought with the exiles, who were led by Deinocrates and Philonides, each in command of a wing. For some time the conflict was evenly balanced, both of the armies fighting with zest, but when one of the generals, Philonides, fell and his part of the army was put to flight, Deinocrates also was forced to withdraw. Pasiphilus killed many of his opponents during the flight and, after gaining possession of Galeria, punished those guilty of the uprising. Agathocles, on hearing that the Carthaginians had seized the hill called Ecnomus in the territory of Gela, decided to fight them to a finish with his whole army. When he had set out against them and had drawn near, he challenged them to battle since he was elated by his previous victory, but the barbarians not venturing to meet him in battle, he assumed that he now completely dominated the open country without a fight and went off to Syracuse, where he decorated the chief temples with the spoils.

These are the events of this year that we have been able to discover.

The death of Roxanê and of King Alexander (105).

The operations of the Romans in Italy (105).

105. When Simonides was archon in Athens, [311] the Romans elected to the consulship Marcus Valerius and Publius Decius. While these held office, Cassander, Ptolemy, and Lysimachus came to terms with Antigonus and made a treaty. In this it was provided that Cassander be general of Europe until Alexander, the son of Roxanê, should come of age, that Lysimachus rule Thrace, and that Ptolemy rule Egypt and the cities adjacent thereto in Libya and Arabia, that Antigonus have first place in all Asia; and that the Greeks be autonomous. However, they did not abide by these agreements but each of them, putting forward plausible excuses, kept seeking to increase his own power. Now Cassander perceived that Alexander, the son of Roxanê, was growing up and that word was being spread throughout Macedonia by certain men that it was fitting to release the boy from custody and give him his father's kingdom; and, fearing for himself, he instructed Glaucias, who was in command of the guard over the child, to murder Roxanê and the king and conceal their bodies, but to disclose to no one else what had been done. When Glaucias had carried out the instructions, Cassander, Lysimachus, and Ptolemy, and Antigonus as well, were relieved of their anticipated danger from the king, for henceforth, there being no longer anyone to inherit the realm, each of those who had rule over nations or cities entertained hopes of royal power and held the territory that had been placed under his authority as if it were a kingdom won by the spear.

This was the situation in Asia and in Greece and Macedonia.

In Italy the Romans with strong forces of foot and horse took the field against Pollitium, a city of the Marrucini. They also sent some of their citizens as a colony and settled the place called Interamna.

About the shipwreck that befell the Carthaginians (106).

106. In Sicily, where Agathocles was constantly increasing in power and collecting stronger forces, the Carthaginians, since they heard that the dynast was organising the cities of the island for his own ends and that with his armed forces he surpassed their own soldiers, decided to wage the war with more energy. Accordingly they at once made ready one hundred and thirty triremes, chose as general Hamilcar [son of Gisco], one of their most distinguished men, gave him two thousand citizen soldiers among whom were many of the nobles, ten thousand men from Libya, a thousand mercenaries and two hundred zeugippae from Etruria, a thousand Baliaric slingers, and also a large sum of money and the proper provision of missiles, food, and the other things necessary for war. After the whole fleet had sailed from Carthage and was at sea, a storm fell suddenly upon it, sank sixty triremes, and completely destroyed two hundred of the ships that were carrying supplies. The rest of the fleet, after encountering severe storms, with difficulty reached Sicily in safety. Not a few of the Carthaginian nobles were lost, for whom the city instituted public mourning, for it is their custom whenever any major disaster has befallen the city, to cover the walls with black sackcloth. Hamilcar, the general, gathered together the men who had survived the storm, enrolled mercenaries, and enlisted those troops of the Sicilian allies who were fit for service. He also took over the forces that were already in Sicily and, having attended to all things expedient for war, mustered his armies in the open country, about forty thousand foot-soldiers and nearly live thousand mounted men. Since he had quickly rectified the misfortune that he had suffered and won the reputation of being a good general, he revived the shattered spirits of his allies and presented no ordinary problem to his enemies.

How the Carthaginians defeated Agathocles in a battle at Himera and shut him up in Syracuse (107-110).

107. As Agathocles saw that the forces of the Carthaginians were superior to his own, he surmised that not a few of the strongholds would go over to the Phoenicians, and also those of the cities that were offended with him. He was particularly concerned for the city of the Geloans since he learned that all the forces of the enemy were in their land. At about this time he also suffered a considerable naval loss, for at the straits twenty of his ships with their crews fell into the hands of the Carthaginians. Deciding nevertheless to make the city of Gela secure with a garrison, he did not venture to lead an army in openly lest the result be that the Geloans, who were looking for an excuse, forestall him and he lose the city, which provided him with great resources. He therefore sent in his soldiers a few at a time as if for particular needs until his troops far surpassed those of the city in number. Soon he himself also arrived and charged the Geloans with treason and desertion, either because they were actually planning to do something of this sort, or because he was persuaded by false charges made by exiles, or again because he wished to gain possession of wealth; and he slew more than four thousand of the Geloans and confiscated their property. He also ordered all the other Geloans to turn over to him their money and their uncoined silver and gold, threatening to punish those who disobeyed. Since all quickly carried out the command because of fear, he gathered together a large amount of money and caused a dreadful panic among all who were subject to him. Being thought to have treated the Geloans more cruelly than was proper, he heaped together in the ditches outside the walls those who had been slain, and, leaving behind in the city an adequate garrison, he took the field against the enemy.

108. The Carthaginians held the hill Ecnomus, which men say had been a stronghold of Phalaris. Here it is reported that the tyrant had constructed the bronze bull that has become famous, the device being heated by a fire beneath for the torment of those subjected to the ordeal, and so the place has been called Ecnomus [lawless] because of the impiety practised upon his victims. On the other side Agathoeles held another of the strongholds that had belonged to Phalaris, the one which was called Phalarium after him. In the space between the encamped armies was a river [Himeras], which each of them used as a defence against the enemy, and sayings from earlier times were current that near this place a great number of men were destined to perish in battle. Since, however, it was not clear to which of the two sides the misfortune would happen, the armies were filled with superstitious fear and shrank from battle. Therefore for a long time neither dared to cross the river in force, until an unexpected cause brought them into general battle. The raids made by the Libyans through the enemy's country aroused Agathocles into doing the same, and while the Greeks were engaged in plundering and were driving away some beasts of burden taken from the Carthaginian camp, soldiers issued from that encampment to pursue them. Agathocles, foreseeing what was about to happen, placed beside the river an ambush of men selected for courage. These, as the Carthaginians crossed the river in their pursuit of those who were driving the beasts, sprang suddenly from the ambush, fell upon the disordered soldiers, and easily drove them back. While the barbarians were being slaughtered and were fleeing to their own camp, Agathocles, thinking that the time had come to fight to a finish, led his whole army against the camp of the enemy. Falling on them unexpectedly and quickly filling up a part of the moat, he overthrew the palisade and forced an entrance into the camp. The Carthaginians, who had been thrown into a panic by the unexpected attack and could find no opportunity for forming their lines, faced the enemy and fought against them at random. Both sides fought fiercely for the moat, and the whole place round about was quickly covered with dead, for the most notable of the Carthaginians rushed up to give aid when they saw the camp being taken, and the forces of Agathocles, encouraged by the advantage gained and believing that they would end the whole war by a single battle, pressed hard upon the barbarians.

109. But when Hamilcar saw that his men were being overpowered and that the Greeks in constantly increasing numbers were making their way into the camp, he brought up his slingers, who came from the Baliaric Islands and numbered at least a thousand. By hurling a shower of great stones, they wounded many and even killed not a few of those who were attacking, and they shattered the defensive armour of most of them. For these men, who are accustomed to sling stones weighing a mina, contribute a great deal toward victory in battle, since from childhood they practise constantly with the sling. In this way they drove the Greeks from the camp and defeated them. Agathocles continued to attack at other points, and indeed the camp was already being-taken by storm when unexpected reinforcements from Libya arrived by water for the Carthaginians. Thus again gaining heart, those from the camp fought against the Greeks in front, and the reinforcements surrounded them on all sides. Since the Greeks were now receiving wounds from an unexpected quarter, the battle quickly reversed itself; and some of them fled into the Himeras River, others into the camp. The withdrawal was for a distance of forty stades; and since it was almost entirely over level country, they were hotly pursued by the barbarian cavalry, numbering not less than five thousand. As a result the space between was filled with dead; and the river itself contributed greatly to the destruction of the Greeks. Since it was the season of the Dog Star and since the pursuit took place in the middle of the day, most of the fugitives became very thirsty because of the heat and the distress caused by the flight and drank greedily, and that too although the stream was salt. Therefore no fewer men than those killed in the pursuit itself were found dead beside the river without a wound. In this battle about five hundred of the barbarians fell, but of the Greeks no less than seven thousand.

110. Agathocles, having met with such a disaster, collected those who had survived the rout and after burning his camp withdrew into Gela. After lie had given it out that he had decided to set out quickly for Syracuse, three hundred of the Libyan cavalry fell in with some of the soldiers of Agathocles in the open country. Since these said that Agathocles had departed for Syracuse, the Libyans entered Gela as friends, but they were cheated of their expectations and shot down. Agathocles, however, shut himself up in Gela, not because he was unable to go safely to Syracuse, but because he wished to divert the Carthaginians to the siege of Gela in order that the Syracusans might quite fearlessly gather in their crops as the season demanded. Hamilcar at first attempted to besiege Gela, but discovering that there were troops in the city defending it and that Agathocles had ample supplies of all kinds, he gave up the attempt, instead, by visiting the fortresses and cities, he won them over and treated all the people with kindness, seeking to win the goodwill of the Sicilians. The people of Camarina and Leontini, also those of Catana and Tauromenium, at once sent embassies and went over to the Carthaginian, and within a few days Messenê and Abacaenum and very many of the other cities vied with each other in deserting to Hamilcar, for such was the desire that came upon the common people after the defeat because of their hatred of the tyrant. Agathocles conducted what survived of his army to Syracuse, repaired the ruined parts of the walls, and carried off the grain from the countryside, intending to leave an adequate garrison for the city, but with the strongest part of his army to cross to Libya and transfer the war from the island to the continent.

But we, following the plan laid down at the beginning, will make Agathocles' expedition into Libya the beginning of the following book.

BOOK XX

1. One might justly censure those who in their histories insert over-long orations or employ frequent speeches; for not only do they rend asunder the continuity of the narrative by the ill-timed insertion of speeches, but also they interrupt the interest of those who are eagerly pressing on toward a full knowledge of the events. Yet surely there is opportunity for those who wish to display rhetorical prowess to compose by themselves public discourses and speeches for ambassadors, likewise orations of praise and blame and the like; for by recognising the classification of literary types and by elaborating each of the two by itself, they might reasonably expect to gain a reputation in both fields of activity. As it is, some writers by excessive use of rhetorical passages have made the whole art of history into an appendage of oratory. Not only does that which is poorly composed give offence, but also that which seems to have hit the mark in other respects yet has gone far astray from the themes and occasions that belong to its peculiar type. Therefore, even of those who read such works, some skip over the orations although they appear to be entirely successful, and others, wearied in spirit by the historian's wordiness and lack of taste, abandon the reading entirely; and this attitude is not without reason, for the genius of history is simple and self-consistent and as a whole is like a living organism. If it is mangled, it is stripped of its living charm; but if it retains its necessary unity, it is duly preserved and, by the harmony of the whole composition, renders the reading pleasant and clear.

2. Nevertheless, in disapproving rhetorical speeches, we do not ban them wholly from historical works; for, since history needs to be adorned with variety, in certain places it is necessary to call to our aid even such passages, and of this opportunity I should not wish to deprive myself, so that, whenever the situation requires either a public address from an ambassador or a statesman, or some such thing from the other characters, whoever does not boldly enter the contest of words would himself be blameworthy. For one would find no small number of reasons for which on many occasions the aid of rhetoric will necessarily be enlisted; for when many things have been said well and to the point, one should not in contempt pass over what is worthy of memory and possesses a utility not alien to history, nor when the subject matter is great and glorious should one allow the language to appear inferior to the deeds; and there are times when, an event turning out contrary to expectation, we shall be forced to use words suitable to the subject in order to explain the seeming paradox.

Let this suffice on this subject; we must now write about the events that belong to my theme, first setting forth the chronological scheme of our narrative. In the preceding Books we have written of the deeds of both the Greeks and the barbarians from the earliest times down to the year before Agathocles' Libyan campaign; the years from the sack of Troy to that event total eight hundred and eighty-three. In this Book, adding what comes next in the account, we shall begin with Agathocles' crossing into Libya, and end with the year in which the kings, after reaching an agreement with each other, began joint operations against Antigonus, son of Philip, embracing a period of nine years.

How Agathocles crossed.into Libya, defeated the
Carthaginians in a battle, and became master of many cities
(3-18).

3. When Hieromnemon was archon in Athens, [310] the Romans elected to the consulship Gaius Julius and Quintus Aemilius; and in Sicily Agathocles, who had been defeated by the Carthaginians in the battle at the Himeras River and had lost the largest and strongest part of his army, took refuge in Syracuse. When he saw that all his allies had changed sides and that the barbarians were masters of almost all Sicily except Syracuse and were far superior in both land and sea forces, he carried out an undertaking that was unexpected and most reckless. For when all had concluded that he would not even try to take the field against the Carthaginians, he determined to leave an adequate garrison for the city, to select those of the soldiers who were fit, and with these to cross over into Libya. For he hoped that, if he did this, those in Carthage, who had been living luxuriously in long-continued peace and were therefore without experience in the dangers of battle, would easily be defeated by men who had been trained in the school of danger; that the Libyan allies of the Carthaginians, who had for a long time resented their exactions, would grasp an opportunity for revolt; most important of all, that by appearing unexpectedly, he would plunder a land which had not been ravaged and which, because of the prosperity of the Carthaginians, abounded in wealth of every kind; and in general, that he would divert the barbarians from his native city and from all Sicily and transfer the whole war to Libya. And this last, indeed, was accomplished.

4. Disclosing this intention to none of his friends, he set up his brother Antander as curator of the city with an adequate garrison; and he himself selected and enrolled those of the soldiers who were fit for service, bidding the infantry be ready with their arms, and giving special orders to the cavalry that, in addition to their full armour, they should have with them saddle-pads and bridles, in order that, when he got possession of horses, he might have men ready to mount them, equipped with what was needed for the service; for in the earlier defeat the greater part of the foot-soldiers had been killed, but almost all the horsemen had survived uninjured, whose horses he was not able to transport to Libya. In order that the Syracusans might not attempt a revolution after he had left them, he separated relatives from each other, particularly brothers from brothers and fathers from sons, leaving the one group in the city and taking the others across with him; for it was clear that those who remained in Syracuse, even if they were most ill disposed toward the tyrant, because of their affection for their relatives would do nothing unbecoming against Agathocles. Since he was in need of money he exacted the property of the orphans from those who were their guardians, saying that he would guard it much better than they and return it more faithfully to the children when they became of age; and he also borrowed from the merchants, took some of the dedications in the temples, and stripped the women of their jewels. Then, seeing that the majority of the very wealthy were vexed by his measures and were very hostile to him, he summoned an assembly in which, deploring both the past disaster and the expected hardships, he said that he himself would endure the siege easily because he was accustomed to every manner of hardship, but that he pitied the citizens if they should be shut in and forced to endure a siege. He therefore ordered those to save themselves and their own possessions who were unwilling to endure whatever fortune might see fit that they should suffer. When those who were wealthiest and most bitter against the tyrant, had set out from the city, sending after them some of his mercenaries, he killed the men themselves and confiscated their property. When, through a single unholy act, he had gained an abundance of wealth and had cleared the city of those who were opposed to him, he freed those of their slaves who were fit for military service.

5. When everything was ready, Agathocles manned sixty ships and awaited a suitable time for the voyage. Since his purpose was unknown, some supposed that he was making an expedition into Italy, and others that he was going to plunder the part of Sicily that was under Carthaginian control; but all despaired of the safety of those who were about to sail away and condemned the prince for his mad folly. Since the enemy was blockading the port with triremes many times more numerous than his own, Agathocles at first for some days was compelled to detain his soldiers in the ships since they could not sail out; but later, when some grain ships were putting in to the city, the Carthaginians with their whole fleet made for these ships, and Agathocles, who already despaired of his enterprise, as he saw the mouth of the harbour freed of the blockading ships, sailed out, his men rowing at top speed. Then when the Carthaginians, who were already close to the cargo vessels, saw the enemy sailing with their ships in close order, assuming at first that Agathocles was hastening to the rescue of the grain ships, they turned and made their fleet ready for battle; but when they saw the ships sailing straight past and getting a long start of them, they began to pursue. Thereupon, while these were contending with each other, the ships that were bringing grain, unexpectedly escaping the danger, brought about a great abundance of provisions in Syracuse, when a scarcity of food was already gripping the city; and Agathocles, who was already at the point of being overtaken and surrounded, gained unhoped-for safety as night closed in. On the next day there occurred such an eclipse of the sun that utter darkness set in and the stars were seen everywhere [15/8/310]; wherefore Agathocles' men, believing that the prodigy portended misfortune for them, fell into even greater anxiety about the future.

6. After they had sailed for six days and the same number of nights, just as day was breaking, the fleet of the Carthaginians was unexpectedly seen not far away. At this both fleets were filled with zeal and vied with each other in rowing, the Carthaginians believing that as soon as they destroyed the Greek ships they would have Syracuse in their hands and at the same time free their fatherland from great dangers; and the Greeks foreseeing that, if they did not get to land first, punishment was in store for themselves and the perils of slavery for those who had been left at home. When Libya came into sight, the men on board began to cheer and the rivalry became very keen; the ships of the barbarians sailed faster since their crews had undergone very long-training, but those of the Greeks had sufficient lead. The distance was covered very quickly, and when the ships drew near the land they rushed side by side for the beach like men in a race; indeed, since they were within range, the first of the Carthaginian ships were sending missiles at the last of those of Agathocles. Consequently, when they had fought for a short time with bows and slings and the barbarians had come to close quarters with a few of the Greek ships, Agathocles got the upper hand since he had his complement of soldiers. At this the Carthaginians withdrew and lay offshore a little beyond bowshot; but Agathocles, having disembarked his soldiers at the place called Latomiae and constructed a palisade from sea to sea, beached his ships.

7. When he had thus carried through a perilous enterprise, Agathocles ventured upon another even more hazardous. For after surrounding himself with those among the leaders who were ready to follow his proposal and after making sacrifice to Demeter and Corê, he summoned an assembly; next he came forward to speak, crowned and clad in a splendid himation, and when he had made prefatory remarks of a nature appropriate to the undertaking, he declared that to Demeter and Corê, the goddesses who protected Sicily, he had at the very moment when they were pursued by the Carthaginians vowed to offer all the ships as a burnt offering. Therefore it was well, since they had succeeded in gaining safety, that they should pay the vow. In place of these ships he promised to restore many times the number if they would but fight boldly; and in truth, he added, the goddesses by omens from the victims had foretold victory in the entire war. While he was saying this, one of his attendants brought forward a lighted torch. When he had taken this and had given orders to distribute torches likewise to all the ship captains, he invoked the goddesses and himself first set out to the trireme of the commander. Standing by the stern, he bade the others also to follow his example. Then as all the captains threw in the fire and the flames quickly blazed high, the trumpeters sounded the signal for battle and the army raised the war-cry, while all together prayed for a safe return home. This Agathocles did primarily to compel his soldiers in the midst of dangers to have no thought at all of flight; for it was clear that, if the retreat to the ships was cut off, in victory alone would they have hope of safety. Moreover, since he had a small army, he reasoned that if he guarded the ships he would be compelled to divide his forces and so be by no means strong enough to meet the enemy in battle, and if he left the ships without defenders, he would put them into the hands of the Carthaginians.

8. Nevertheless, when all the ships were aflame and the fire was spreading widely, terror laid hold upon the Sicilians. Carried away at first by the wiles of Agathocles and by the rapidity of his undertakings, which gave no time for reflection, all acquiesced in what was being done; but when time made possible detailed consideration, they were plunged into regret, and as they considered the vastness of the sea that separated them from home, they abandoned hope of safety. Agathocles, however, in an effort to rid his soldiers of their despondency, led his army against the place called Megalepolis, a city of the Carthaginians. The intervening country through which it was necessary for them to march was divided into gardens and plantations of every kind, since many streams of water were led in small channels and irrigated every part. There were also country houses one after another, constructed in luxurious fashion and covered with stucco, which gave evidence of the wealth of the people who possessed them. The farm buildings were filled with everything that was needful for enjoyment, seeing that the inhabitants in a long period of peace had stored up an abundant variety of products. Part of the land was planted with vines, and part yielded olives and was also planted thickly with other varieties of fruit-bearing trees. On each side herds of cattle and flocks of sheep pastured on the plain, and the neighbouring meadows were filled with grazing horses. In general there was a manifold prosperity in the region, since the leading Carthaginians had laid out there their private estates and with their wealth had beautified them for their enjoyment. Therefore the Sicilians, amazed at the beauty of the land and at its prosperity, were, buoyed up by expectation, for they beheld prizes commensurate with their dangers ready at hand for the victors; and Agathocles, seeing that the soldiers were recovering from their discouragement and had become eager for battle, attacked the city walls by direct assault. Since the onset was unforeseen and the inhabitants, because they did not know what was happening and because they had had no experience in the wars, resisted only a short time, he took the city by storm; and giving it over to his soldiers for pillage, he at a single stroke loaded his army with booty and filled it with confidence. Then, setting out immediately for White Tunis, as it is called, he subdued this city, which lies about two thousand stades from Carthage. The soldiers wished to garrison both of the captured cities and deposit the booty in them; but Agathocles, meditating actions conforming to those that had already been accomplished and telling the crowd that it was advantageous to leave behind them no places of refuge until they should have been victorious in battle, destroyed the cities and camped in the open.

9. When the Carthaginians who lay at anchor off the station where the Sicilian fleet was beached saw the ships burning, they were delighted, thinking that it was through fear of themselves that the enemy had been forced to destroy his ships; but when they saw that the army of their opponents was moving into the country, as they reckoned up the consequences, they concluded that the destruction of the fleet was their own misfortune. Therefore they spread hides over the prows of their ships as they were in the habit of doing whenever it seemed that any public misfortune had befallen the city of Carthage; and, after taking the bronze beaks of the ships of Agathocles on board their own triremes, they sent to Carthage messengers to report exactly what had happened. Before these had explained the situation, the country folk who had seen the landing of Agathocles, reported it quickly to the Carthaginians. Panic-stricken at the unexpected event, they supposed that their own forces in Sicily, both army and navy, had been destroyed; for Agathocles, they believed, would never have ventured to leave Syracuse stripped of defenders unless he had been victorious, nor to transport an army across the straits while the enemy controlled the sea. Therefore panic and great confusion seized upon the city; the crowds rushed to the market place, and the council of elders consulted what should be done. In fact there was no army at hand that could take the field against the enemy; the mass of the citizens, who had had no experience in warfare, were already in despair; and the enemy was thought to be near the walls. Accordingly, some proposed to send envoys to Agathocles to sue for peace, these same men serving also as spies to observe the situation of the enemy; but some urged that they should delay until they had learned precisely what had taken place. However, while such confusion prevailed in the city, the messengers sent by the commander of the fleet sailed in and made clear the true explanation of what had happened.

10. Now that all had regained their courage, the council reprimanded all the commanders of the fleet because, although controlling the sea, they had allowed a hostile army to set foot on Libya; and it appointed as generals of the armies Hanno and Bormilcar, men who had an inherited feud. The councillors thought, indeed, that because of the private mistrust and enmity of the generals the safety of the city as a whole would be secured; but they completely missed the truth.

For Bormilcar, who had long had his heart set on tyranny but had lacked authority and a proper occasion for his attempt, now gained an excellent starting point by getting the command as general. The basic cause in this matter was the Carthaginians' severity in inflicting punishments. In their wars they advance their leading men to commands, taking it for granted that these should be first to brave danger for the whole state; but when they gain peace, they plague these same men with suits, bring false charges against them through envy, and load them down with penalties. Therefore some of those who are placed in positions of command, fearing the trials in the courts, desert their posts, but others attempt to become tyrants; and this is what Bormilcar, one of the two generals, did on this occasion; about him we shall speak a little later.

To resume, the generals of the Carthaginians, seeing that the situation was not at all consistent with delay, did not await soldiers from the country and from the allied cities; but they led the citizen soldiers themselves into the field, in number not less than forty thousand foot-soldiers, one thousand horsemen, and two thousand chariots. Occupying a slight elevation not far from the enemy, they drew up their army for battle. Hanno had command of the right wing, those enrolled in the Sacred Band fighting beside him; and Bormilcar, commanding the left, made his phalanx deep since the terrain prevented him from extending it on a broader front. The chariots and the cavalry they stationed in front of the phalanx, having determined to strike with these first and test the temper of the Greeks.

11. After Agathocles had viewed the array of the barbarians, he entrusted the right wing to his son Archagathus, giving him twenty-five hundred foot-soldiers; next he drew up the Syracusans, who were thirty-five hundred in number, then three thousand Greek mercenaries, and finally three thousand Samnites, Etruscans, and Celts. He himself with his bodyguard fought in front of the left wing, opposing with one thousand hoplites the Sacred Band of the Carthaginians. The five hundred archers and slingers he divided between the wings. There was hardly enough equipment for the soldiers; and when he saw the men of the crews unarmed he had the shield covers stretched with sticks, thus making them similar in appearance to the round shields, and distributed them to these men, of no use at all for real service but when seen from a distance capable of creating the impression of arms in the minds of men who did not know the truth. Seeing that his soldiers were frightened by the great numbers of barbarian cavalry and infantry, he let loose into the army in many places owls, which he had long since prepared as a means of relieving the discouragement of the common soldiers. The owls, flying through the phalanx and settling on the shields and helmets, encouraged the soldiers, each man regarding this as an omen because the bird is held sacred to Athena. Such things as this, although they might seem to some an inane device, have often been responsible for great successes, and so it happened on this occasion also; for when courage inspired the common soldiers and word was passed along that the deity was clearly foretelling victory for them, they awaited the battle with greater steadfastness.

12. Indeed, when the chariots charged against them, they shot down some, and allowed others to pass through, but most of them they forced to turn back against the line of their own infantry. In the same way they withstood also the charge of the cavalry; and by bringing down many of them, they made them flee to the rear. While they were distinguishing themselves in these preliminary contests, the infantry force of the barbarians had all come to close quarters. A gallant battle developed, and Hanno, who had fighting under him the Sacred Band of selected men and was intent upon gaining the victory by himself, pressed heavily upon the Greeks and slew many of them. Even when all kinds of missiles were hurled against him, he would not yield but pushed on though suffering many wounds until he died from exhaustion. When he had fallen, the Carthaginians who were drawn up in that part of the line were disheartened, but Agathocles and his men were elated and became much bolder than before. When Bormilcar, the other general, heard of this from certain persons, thinking the gods had given him the opportunity for gaining a position from which to make a bid for the tyranny, he reasoned thus with himself: If the army of Agathocles should be destroyed, he himself would not be able to make his attempt at supremacy since the citizens would be strong; but if the former should win the victory and quench the pride of the Carthaginians, the already defeated people would be easy for him to manage, and he could defeat Agathocles readily whenever he wished. When he had reached this conclusion, he withdrew with the men of the front rank, presenting to the enemy an inexplicable retirement but making known to his own men the death of Hanno and ordering them to withdraw in formation to the high ground; for this, he said, was to their advantage. As the enemy pressed on and the whole retreat was becoming like a rout, the Libyans of the next ranks, believing that the front rank was being defeated by sheer force, broke into flight; those, however, who were leading the Sacred Band after the death of its general Hanno, at first resisted stoutly and, stepping over the bodies of their own men as they fell, withstood every danger, but when they perceived that the greater part of the army had turned to flight and that the enemy was surrounding them in the rear, they were forced to withdraw and so, when rout spread throughout the entire army of the Carthaginians, the barbarians kept fleeing toward Carthage; but Agathocles, after pursuing them to a certain point, turned back and plundered the camp of the enemy.

13. There fell in this battle Greeks to the number of two hundred, and of Carthaginians not more than a thousand, but as some have written, upwards of six thousand. In the camp of the Carthaginians were found, along with other goods, many wagons, in which were being transported more than twenty thousand pairs of manacles; for the Carthaginians, having expected to master the Greeks easily, had passed the word along among themselves to take alive as many as possible and, after shackling them, to throw them into slave pens. I think, the divinity of set purpose in the case of men who are arrogant in their calculations, changes the outcome of their confident expectations into its contrary. Now Agathocles, having surprisingly defeated the Carthaginians, was holding them shut up within their walls; but fortune, alternating victories with defeats, humbled the victors equally with the vanquished. For in Sicily the Carthaginians, who had defeated Agathocles in a great battle, were besieging Syracuse, but in Libya Agathocles, having gained the upper hand in a battle of such importance, had brought the Carthaginians under siege; and what was most amazing, on the island the tyrant, though his armaments were unscathed, had proved inferior to the barbarians, but on the continent with a portion of his once defeated army he got the better of those who had been victorious.

14. Therefore the Carthaginians, believing that the misfortune had come to them from the gods, betook themselves to every manner of supplication of the divine powers; and, because they believed that Heracles, who was worshipped in their mother city, was exceedingly angry with them, they sent a large sum of money and many of the most expensive offerings to Tyre. Since they had come as colonists from that city, it had been their custom in the earlier period to send to the god a tenth of all that was paid into the public revenue; but later, when they had acquired great wealth and were receiving more considerable revenues, they sent very little indeed, holding the divinity of little account. Turning to repentance because of this misfortune, they bethought them of all the gods of Tyre. They even sent from their temples in supplication the golden shrines with their images, believing that they would better appease the wrath of the god if the offerings were sent for the sake of winning forgiveness. They also alleged that Cronus had turned against them inasmuch as in former times they had been accustomed to sacrifice to this god the noblest of their sons, but more recently, secretly buying and nurturing children, they had sent these to the sacrifice; and when an investigation was made, some of those who had been sacrificed were discovered to have been supposititious. When they had given thought to these things and saw their enemy encamped before their walls, they were filled with superstitious dread, for they believed that they had neglected the honours of the gods that had been established by their fathers. In their zeal to make amends for their omission, they selected two hundred of the noblest children and sacrificed them publicly; and others who were under suspicion sacrificed themselves voluntarily, in number not less than three hundred. There was in their city a bronze image of Cronus, extending its hands, palms up and sloping toward the ground, so that each of the children when placed thereon rolled down and fell into a sort of gaping pit filled with fire. It is probable that it was from this that Euripides has drawn the mythical story found in his works about the sacrifice in Tauris, in which he presents Iphigeneia being asked by Orestes:

But what tomb shall receive me when I die?

A sacred fire within, and earth's broad rift.

Also the story passed down among the Greeks from ancient myth that Cronus did away with his own children appears to have been kept in mind among the Carthaginians through this observance.

15. However this may be, after such a reversal in Libya, the Carthaginians sent messengers into Sicily to Hamilcar, begging him to send aid as soon as possible; and they dispatched to him the captured bronze beaks of Agathocles' ships. Hamilcar ordered those who had sailed across to keep silent about the defeat that had been sustained, but to spread abroad to the soldiers word that Agathocles had utterly lost his fleet and his whole army. Hamilcar himself, dispatching into Syracuse as envoys some of those who had come from Carthage and sending with them the beaks, demanded the surrender of the city; for, he said, the army of the Syracusans had been cut to pieces by the Carthaginians and their ships had been burned, and the production of the beaks offered proof to those who disbelieved. When the inhabitants of the city heard the reported misfortune of Agathocles, the common people believed; the magistrates, however, being in doubt, watched closely that there might be no disorder, but they sent the envoys away at once; and the relatives and friends of the exiles and any others who were displeased with the actions of the magistrates they cast out of the city, in number not less than eight thousand. Thereupon, when so great a multitude was suddenly forced to leave its native place, the city was filled with running to and fro and with uproar and the lamentation of women; for there was no household that did not have its share of mourning at that time. Those who were of the party of the tyrant lamented at the misfortune of Agathocles and his sons; and some of the private citizens wept for the men believed to have been lost in Libya, and others for those who were being driven from hearth and ancestral gods, who could neither remain nor yet go outside the walls since the barbarians were besieging the city, and who, in addition to the aforesaid evils, which were great enough, were being compelled to drag along with them in their flight infant children and women. When the exiles took refuge with Hamilcar, he offered them safety; and, making ready his army, he led it against Syracuse, expecting to take the city both because it was bereft of defenders and because of the disaster that had been reported to those who had been left there.

16. After Hamilcar had sent an embassy in advance and had offered safety to Antander and those with him if they surrendered the city, those of the leaders who were held in highest esteem came together in council. After prolonged discussion Antander thought it necessary to surrender the city, since he was unmanly by nature and of a disposition the direct opposite of the boldness and energy of his brother; but Erymnon the Aetolian, who had been set up by Agathocles as co-ruler with his brother, expressing the contrary opinion persuaded all of them to hold out until they should hear the truth. When Hamilcar learned the decision of those in the city, he constructed engines of all kinds, having determined to attack. Agathocles, who had built two thirty-oared ships after the battle, sent one of them to Syracuse, placing on board his strongest oarsmen and Nearchus, one of his trusted friends, who was to report the victory to his own people. Having had a fair voyage, they approached Syracuse during the night of the fifth day. and wearing wreaths and singing paeans as they sailed they reached the city at daybreak. The picket ships of the Carthaginians caught sight of them and pursued them vigorously, and since the pursued had no great start, there arose a contest in rowing. While they were vying with each other, the folk of the city and the besiegers, seeing what was happening, both ran to the port, and each group, sharing in the anxiety of its own men, encouraged them with shouts. When the dispatch boat was already at the point of being taken, the barbarians raised a shout of triumph, and the inhabitants of the city, since they could give no aid, prayed the gods for the safety of those who were sailing in. When, not far from the shore, the ram of one of the pursuers was already bearing down to deliver its blow, the pursued ship succeeded in getting inside of the range of missiles and, the Syracusans having come to its aid, escaped from the danger. When Hamilcar saw that the inhabitants of the city, because of their anxiety and because of the surprising nature of the message they now anticipated, had run together to the port, surmising that some portion of the wall was unguarded, he advanced his strongest soldiers with scaling ladders. These, finding that the guard-posts had been abandoned, ascended without being discovered; but, when they had almost taken the wall between two towers, the guard, making its rounds according to custom, discovered them. In the fighting that ensued the men of the city ran together and arrived in advance of those who were coming to reinforce the men who had scaled the wall, of whom they killed some and hurled others down from the battlements. Hamilcar, greatly distressed at this, withdrew his army from the city and sent to those in Carthage a relief expedition of five thousand men.

17. Meanwhile Agathocles, who had control of the open country, was taking the strongholds about Carthage by storm; and he prevailed on some of the cities to come over to him because of fear, others because of their hatred for the Carthaginians. After fortifying a camp near Tunis and leaving there an adequate garrison, he moved against the cities situated along the sea. Taking by storm the first, Neapolis, he treated the captured people humanely; then, marching against Hadrumetum, he began a siege of that city, but received Aelymas, the king of the Libyans, into alliance. On hearing of these moves the Carthaginians brought their entire army against Tunis and captured the encampment of Agathocles; then, after bringing siege engines up to the city, they made unremitting attacks. Agathocles, when some had reported to him the reverses suffered by his men, left the larger part of his army for the siege, but with his retinue and a few of the soldiers went secretly to a place in the mountains whence he could be seen both by the people of Hadrumetum and by the Carthaginians who were besieging Tunis. By instructing his soldiers to light fires at night over a great area, he caused the Carthaginians to believe that he was coming against them with a large army, while the besieged thought that another strong force was at hand as an ally for their enemy. Both of them, deceived by the deceptive stratagem, suffered an unexpected defeat: those who were besieging Tunis fled to Carthage abandoning their siege engines, and the people of Hadrumetum surrendered their home-land because of their fright. After receiving this city on terms, Agathocles took Thapsus by force; and of the other cities of the region some he took by storm and some he won by persuasion. When he had gained control of all the cities, which were more than two hundred in number, he had in mind to lead his army into the inland regions of Libya.

18. After Agathocles had set out and had marched for a good many days, the Carthaginians, advancing with the force that had been brought across from Sicily and their other army, again undertook the siege of Tunis; and they recaptured many of the positions that were in the hands of the enemy. But Agathocles, since dispatch bearers had come to him from Tunis and disclosed what the Phoenicians had done, at once turned back. When he was at a distance of about two hundred stades from the enemy, he pitched camp and forbade his soldiers to light fires. Then, making a night march, he fell at dawn upon those who were foraging in the country and those who were wandering outside their camp in disorder, and by killing over two thousand and taking captive no small number he greatly strengthened himself for the future. For the Carthaginians, now that their reinforcements from Sicily had arrived and that their Libyan allies were fighting along with them, seemed to be superior to Agathocles; but as soon as he gained this success, the confidence of the barbarians again waned. In fact, he defeated in battle Aelymas, the king of the Libyans, who had deserted him, and slew the king and many of the barbarians.

This was the situation of affairs in Sicily and Libya.

How Cassander went to the aid of Audoleon; and how he
made an alliance with Ptolemaeus, Antigonus' general, who
had become a rebel (19).

How Ptolemy took some of the cities of Cilicia, and how
Antigonus' son Demetrius recovered them (19).

19. In Macedonia, Cassander, going to the aid of Audoleon, king of the

Paeonians, who was fighting against the Autariatae, freed the king from danger, but the Autariatae with the children and women who were following them, numbering in all twenty thousand, he settled beside the mountain called Orbelus. While he was thus engaged, in the Peloponnesus Ptolemaeus, the general of Antigonus, who had been entrusted with an army but had taken offence at the prince because, as he said, he was not being honoured according to his deserts, revolted from Antigonus and made an alliance with Cassander. Having left as governor of the satrapy along the Hellespont one of his most faithful friends, Phoenix, Ptolemaeus sent soldiers to him, bidding him garrison the strongholds and the cities and not to obey Antigonus.

Since the agreements common to the leaders provided for the liberation of the Greek cities, Ptolemy, the ruler of Egypt, charged Antigonus with having occupied some of the cities with garrisons, and prepared to go to war. Sending his army and Leonides as its commander, Ptolemy subdued the cities in Cilicia Trachea which were subject to Antigonus; and he sent also to the cities that were controlled by Cassander and Lysimachus, asking them to cooperate with him and prevent Antigonus from becoming too powerful. Antigonus sent Philip, the younger of his sons, to the Hellespont to fight it out with Phoenix and the rebels; and to Cilicia he sent Demetrius, who, carrying on the campaign with vigour, defeated the generals of Ptolemy and recovered the cities.

How Polyperchon attempted to bring Heracles, the son of Barsinê, back to his ancestral kingdom; and how Ptolemy made away with Nicocreon, the king of Paphos (20-21).

20. Meanwhile Polyperchon, who was biding his time in the Peloponnesus, and who was nursing grievances against Cassander and had long craved the leadership of the Macedonians, summoned from Pergamon Barsinê's son Heracles, who was the son of Alexander but was being reared in Pergamon, being about seventeen years of age. Moreover, Polyperchon, sending to his own friends in many places and to those who were at odds with Cassander, kept urging them to restore the youth to h is ancestral throne. He also wrote to the governing body of the Aetolians, begging them to grant a safe conduct and to join forces with him and promising to repay the favour many times over if they would aid in placing the youth on his ancestral throne. Since the affair proceeded as he wished, the Aetolians being in hearty agreement and many others hurrying to aid in the restoration of the king, in all there were assembled more than twenty thousand infantry and at least one thousand horsemen. Meanwhile Polyperchon, intent on the preparations for the war, was gathering money; and sending to those of the Macedonians who were friendly, he kept urging them to join in the undertaking.

21. Ptolemy, however, who was master of the cities of Cyprus, on learning from certain persons that Nicocles, the king of Paphos, had secretly and privately formed an alliance with Antigonus, dispatched two of his friends, Argaeus and Callicrates, ordering them to slay Nicocles; for he was taking all precautions lest any others also should hasten to shift allegiance when they saw that those were left unpunished who had previously rebelled. These two men, accordingly, after sailing to the island and obtaining soldiers from Menelaüs the general, surrounded the house of Nicocles, informed him of the king's wishes and ordered him to take his own life. At first he tried to defend himself against the charges, but then, since no one heeded him, he slew himself. Axiothea, the wife of

Nicocles, on learning of her husband's death, slew her daughters, who were unwed, in order that no enemy might possess them; and she urged the wives of Nicocles' brothers to choose death along with her, although Ptolemy had given no instructions in regard to the women but had agreed to their safety. When the palace had thus been filled full of death and unforeseen disaster, the brothers of Nicocles, after fastening the doors, set fire to the building and slew themselves. Thus the house of the kings of Paphos, after meeting such tragic suffering, was brought to its end in the way described.

Now that we have followed to its end the tale of what took place in Cyprus, we shall turn the course of our narrative toward the events which follow.

Concerning the actions of the kings in the Bosporus, and of the Romans and Samnites in Italy (22-26).

22. At about this same time in the region of the Pontus, after the death of Parysades, who was king of the Cimmerian Bosporus, his sons Eumelus, Satyrus, and Prytanis were engaged in a struggle against each other for the primacy. Of these, Satyrus, since he was the eldest, had received the government from his father, who had been king for thirty-eight years; but Eumelus, after concluding a treaty of friendship with some of the barbarians who lived near by and collecting a strong army, set up a rival claim to the throne. On learning this, Satyrus set out against him with a strong army: and, after he had crossed the river Thates and drawn near the enemy, he surrounded his camp with the wagons in which he carried his abundant supplies, and drew up his army for battle, taking his own place in the centre of the phalanx as is the Scythian custom. Enrolled in his army were not more than two thousand Greek mercenaries and an equal number of Thracians, but all the rest were Scythian allies, more than twenty thousand foot-soldiers and not less than ten thousand horse. Eumelus, however, had as ally Aripharnes, the king of the Siraces, with twenty thousand horse and twenty-two thousand foot. In a stubborn battle-that took place, Satyrus with picked cavalry about him charged against Aripharnes, who had stationed himself in the middle of the line; and after many had fallen on both sides, he finally forced back and routed the king of the barbarians. At first he pushed on, slaying the enemy as he over took them; but after a little, hearing that his brother Eumelus was gaining the upper hand on the right wing and that his own mercenaries had been turned to flight, he gave up the pursuit. Going to the aid of those who had been worsted and for the second time becoming the author of victory, he routed the entire army of the enemy, so that it became clear to all that, by reason both of his birth and of his valour, it was proper that he should succeed to the throne of his fathers.

23. Aripharnes and Eumelus, however, after having been defeated in the battle, escaped to the capital city. This was situated on the Thates River, which made the city rather difficult of access since the river encircled it and was of considerable depth. The city was surrounded also by great cliffs and thick woods, and had only two entrances, both artificial, of which one was within the royal castle itself and was strengthened with high towers and outworks, and the other was on the opposite side in swampy land, fortified by wooden palisades, and it rested upon piles at intervals and supported houses above the water. Since the strength of the position was so great, Satyrus at first plundered the country of the enemy and fired the villages, from which he collected prisoners and much booty. Afterwards, however, he attempted to make his way by force through the approaches. At the outworks and towers he lost many of his soldiers and

withdrew, but he forced a passage through the swamp and captured the wooden barricades. After destroying these and crossing the river, he began to cut down the woods through which it was necessary to advance to reach the palace. While this was being energetically carried on, King Aripharnes, alarmed lest his citadel should be taken by storm, fought against him with great boldness since he believed that in victory alone lay hope of safety. He stationed archers on both sides of the passage, by whose aid he easily inflicted mortal wounds on the men who were cutting down the woods, for because of the density of the trees they could neither see the missiles in time nor strike back at the archers. The men of Satyrus for three days went on cutting down the woods and making a roadway, bearing up amid hardship; on the fourth day they drew near to the wall but they were overcome by the great number of missiles and by the confined space, and sustained great losses. Indeed, Meniscus, the leader of the mercenaries, a man excelling in sagacity and boldness, after pushing forward through the passage to the wall and fighting brilliantly together with his men, was forced to withdraw when a much stronger force came out against him. Seeing him in danger, Satyrus quickly came to his aid; but, while withstanding the onrush of the enemy, he was wounded with a spear through the upper arm. Grievously-disabled because of the wound, he returned to the camp and when night came on he died, having reigned only nine months after the death of his father Parysades. But Meniscus, the leader of the mercenaries, giving up the siege, led the army back to the city Gargaza, whence he conveyed the king's body by way of the river to Panticapaeum to his brother, Prytanis.

24. Prytanis, after celebrating a magnificent funeral and placing the body in the royal tombs, came quickly to Gargaza and took over both the army and the royal power. When Eumelus sent envoys to discuss a partition of the kingdom, he did not heed him but he left a garrison in Gargaza and returned to Panticapaeum in order to secure the royal prerogatives for himself. During this time Eumelus with the co-operation of the barbarians captured Gargaza and several of the other cities and villages. When Prytanis took the field against him, Eumelus defeated his brother in battle; and, after shutting him up in the isthmus near the Maeotic Lake, he forced him to accept terms according to which he gave over his army and agreed to vacate his place as king. However, when Prytanis entered Panticapaeum, which had always been the capital of those who had ruled in Bosporus, he tried to recover his kingdom; but he was overpowered and fled to the so-called Gardens, where he was slain. After his brothers' death Eumelus, wishing to establish his power securely, slew the friends of Satyrus and Prytanis, and likewise their wives and children. The only one to escape him was Parysades, the son of Satyrus, who was very young; he, riding out of the city on horseback, took refuge with Agarus, the king of the Scythians. Since the citizens were angry at the slaughter of their kinsmen, Eumelus summoned the people to an assembly in which he defended himself in this matter and restored the constitution of their fathers. He even granted to them the immunity from taxation that those who lived in Panticapaeum had enjoyed under his ancestors. He promised also to free all of them from special levies, and he discussed many other measures as he sought the favour of the people. When all had been promptly restored to their former goodwill by his benevolence, from that time on he continued to be king, ruling in a constitutional way over his subjects and by his excellence winning no little admiration.

25. For Eumelus continued to show kindness to the people of Byzantium and to those of Sinope and to most of the other Greeks who lived on the Pontus; and when the people of Callantia were besieged by Lysimachus and were hard pressed by lack of food, he took under his care a thousand who had left their homes because of the famine. Not only did he grant them a safe place of refuge, but he gave them a city in which to live and allotted to them the region called Psoancaëticê. In the interests of those who sailed on the Pontus he waged war against the barbarians who were accustomed to engage in piracy, the Heniochians, the Taurians, and the Achaeans; and he cleared the sea of pirates, with the result that, not only throughout his own kingdom but even throughout almost all the inhabited world, since the merchants carried abroad the news of his nobility, he received that highest reward of well-doing praise. He also gained possession of much of the adjacent region inhabited by the barbarians and made his kingdom far more famous. In sum, he undertook to subdue all the nations around the Pontus, and possibly he would have accomplished his purpose if his life had not been suddenly cut off. For, after he had been king for five years and an equal number of months, he died, suffering a very strange mishap. As he was returning home from Sindicê and was hurrying for a sacrifice, riding to his palace in a four-horse carriage which had four wheels and a canopy, it happened that the horses were frightened and ran away with him. Since the driver was unable to manage the reins, the king, fearing lest he be carried to the ravines, tried to jump out: but his sword caught in the wheel. and he was dragged along by the motion of the carriage and died on the spot.

26. About the death of the brothers, Eumelus and Satyrus, prophecies have been handed down, rather silly yet accepted among the people of the land. They say that the god had told Satyrus to be on his guard against the mouse lest it sometime cause his death. For this reason he permitted neither slave nor freeman of those assigned to his service to have this name; and he also feared domestic and field mice and was always ordering his slaves to kill them and block up their holes. Although he did everything possible by which he thought to ward off his doom, he died, struck in the upper arm through the "mouse." [*musculus*] In the case of Eumelus the warning was that he should be on guard against the house that is on the move. Therefore he never afterward entered a house freely unless his servants had previously examined the roof and the foundations. When he died because of the canopy that was carried on the four-horse chariot, all agreed that the prophecy had been fulfilled.

Concerning the events that took place in the Bosporus, let this suffice us.

In Italy the Roman consuls with an army invaded the hostile territory and defeated the Samnites in battle at the place called Talium. When the defeated had occupied the place named the Holy Mount, the Romans for the moment withdrew to their own camp since night was coming on; but on the next day a second battle was waged in which many of the Samnites were killed and more than twenty-two hundred were taken prisoners. After such successes had been won by the Romans, it came to pass that their consuls from then on dominated the open country with impunity and overcame the cities which did not submit. Taking Cataracta and Ceraunilia by siege, they imposed garrisons upon them, but some of the other cities they won over by persuasion.

The campaign of Ptolemy against Cilicia and the adjacent coast (27).

27. When Demetrius of Phalerum was archon in Athens, [309] in Rome Quintus Fabius received the consulship for the second time and Gaius Marcius for the first. While these were in office, Ptolemy, the king of Egypt, hearing that his own generals had lost the cities of Cilicia, sailed with an army to Phaselis and took this city. Then, crossing into Lycia, he took by storm Xanthus, which was garrisoned by Antigonus. Next he sailed to Caunus and won the city; and violently attacking the citadels, which were held by garrisons, he stormed the Heracleum, but he gained possession of the Persicum when its soldiers delivered it to him. Thereafter he sailed to Cos and sent for Ptolemaeus, who, although he was the nephew of Antigonus and had been entrusted by him with an army, had deserted his uncle and was offering cooperation to Ptolemy. When Ptolemaeus had sailed from Chalcis and had come to Cos, Ptolemy at first received him graciously: then, on discovering that he had become presumptuous and was trying to win over the leaders to himself by conversing with them and giving them gifts, fearing lest he should devise some plot, he forestalled this by arresting him and compelled him to drink hemlock. As for the soldiers who had followed Ptolemaeus, after Ptolemy had won their favour through promises, he distributed them among the men of his own army.

Assassination of Heracles by Polyperchon (28).

28. Meanwhile Polyperchon, who had collected a strong army, brought back to his father's kingdom Heracles, the son of Alexander and Barsinê; but when he was in camp at the place called Stymphaeum, Cassander arrived with his army. As the camps were not far distant from each other and the Macedonians regarded the restoration of the king without disfavour, Cassander, since he feared lest the Macedonians, being by nature prone to change sides easily, should sometime desert to Heracles, sent an embassy to Polyperehon. As for the king, Cassander tried to show Polyperehon that if the restoration should take place he would do what was ordered by others; but, he said, if Polypevchon joined with him and slew the stripling, he would at once recover what had formerly been granted him throughout Macedonia, and then, after receiving an army, he would be appointed general in the Peloponnesus and would be partner in everything in Cassander's realm, being honoured above all. Finally he won Polyperehon over by many great promises, made a secret compact with him, and induced him to murder the king. When Polyperehon had slain the youth and was openly co-operating with Cassander, he recovered the grants in Macedonia and also, according to the agreement, received four thousand Macedonian foot-soldiers and five hundred Thessalian horse. Enrolling also those of the others who wished, he attempted to lead them through Boeotia into the Peloponnesus: but, when he was prevented by Boeotians and Peloponnesians, he turned aside, advanced into Locris. and there passed the winter.

Capture of Hamilcar, the general of the Carthaginians, by the Syracusans (29-30).

29. While these events were taking place, Lysimachus founded a city in the Chersonesus, calling it Lysimachea after himself. Cleomenes, the king of the Lacedaemonians, died after having ruled sixty years and ten months; and Areus, grandson of Cleomenes and son of Acrotatus, succeeded to the throne and ruled for forty-four years.

At about this time Hamilcar, the general of the armies in Sicily, after gaining possession of the remaining outposts, advanced with his army against Syracuse, intending to take that city also by storm. He prevented the importation of grain since he had controlled the sea for a long time; and after destroying the crops on the land he now undertook to capture the region about the Olympieum, which lies before the city. Immediately on his arrival, however, he also decided to attack the walls, since the soothsayer had said to him at the inspection of the victims that on the next day he would certainly dine in Syracuse. The people of the city, learning the intention of their enemy, sent out at night about three thousand of their infantry and about four hundred of their cavalry, ordering them to occupy Euryelus. These quickly carried out the orders; but the Carthaginians advanced during the night, believing that they would not be seen by the enemy. Now Hamilcar was in the foremost place with those who were regularly arrayed about him, and he was followed by Deinocrates, who had received command of the cavalry. The main body of the foot-soldiers was divided into two phalanxes, one composed of the barbarians and one of the Greek allies. Outside the ranks a mixed crowd of rabble also followed along for the sake of booty, men who are. of no use whatever to an army, but are the source of tumult and irrational confusion, from which the most extreme dangers often arise. On this occasion, since the roads were narrow and rough, the baggage train and some of the camp-followers kept jostling each other as they competed for the right of way; and, since the crowd was pressed into a narrow space and for this reason some became involved in brawls and many tried to help each side, great confusion and tumult prevailed in the army.

At this point the Syracusans who had occupied Euryelus, perceiving that the enemy were advancing in confusion whereas they themselves occupied higher positions, charged upon their opponents. Some of them stood on the heights and sent missiles at those who were coming up, some by occupying advantageous positions blocked the barbarians from the passage, and others forced the fleeing soldiers to cast themselves down the cliffs; for on account of the darkness and the lack of information the enemy supposed that the Syracusans had arrived with a large force for the attack. The Carthaginians, being at a disadvantage partly because of the confusion in their own ranks and partly because of the sudden appearance of the enemy, and in particular at a loss because of their ignorance of the locality and their cramped position, were driven into flight. But since there was no broad passage through the place, some of them were trodden down by their own horsemen, who were numerous, and others fought among themselves as if enemies, ignorance prevailing because of the darkness. Hamilcar at first withstood the enemy stoutly and exhorted those drawn up near him to join with him in the fighting; but afterwards the soldiers abandoned him on account of the confusion and panic, and he, left alone, was pounced upon by the Syracusans.

30. One might with reason note the inconsistency of Fortune and the strange manner in which human events turn out contrary to expectation. For Agathocles, who was outstanding in courage and who had had a large army fighting in his support, not only was defeated decisively by the barbarians at the Himeras River, but he even lost the strongest and largest part of his army; whereas the garrison troops left behind in Syracuse, with only a small part of those who had previously been defeated, not only got the better of the Carthaginian army that had besieged them, but even captured alive Hamilcar, the most famous of their citizens. What was most amazing, one hundred and twenty thousand foot-soldiers and five thousand horsemen were defeated in battle by a small number of the enemy who enlisted deception and terrain on their side; so that the saying is true that many are the empty alarms of war.

After the rout the Carthaginians, scattered some here some there, were with difficulty gathered on the next day; and the Syracusans, returning to the city with much plunder, delivered Hamilcar over to those who wished to take vengeance upon him. They recalled also the word of the soothsayer who had said that Hamilcar would enter Syracuse and dine there on the next day, the divinity having presented the truth in disguise. The kinsmen of the slain, after leading Hamilcar through the city in bonds and inflicting terrible tortures upon him, put him to death with the utmost indignities. Then the rulers of the city cut off his head and dispatched men to carry it into Libya to Agathocles and report to him the successes that had been gained.

How the people of Acragas attempted to liberate the Sicilians (31).

31. When the Carthaginian army after the disaster had taken place learned the cause of its misfortune, it was with difficulty relieved from its fears. There being no established commander, the barbarians separated from the Greeks. Then the exiles along with the other Greeks elected Deinocrates general, and the Carthaginians gave the command to those who had been second in rank to Hamilcar.

About this time the Acragantines, seeing that the situation in Sicily was most favourable for an attempt, made a bid for the leadership of the whole island; for they believed that the Carthaginians would scarcely sustain the war against Agathocles; that Deinocrates was easy to conquer since he had collected an army of exiles; that the people of Syracuse, pinched by famine, would not even try to compete for the primacy; and, what was most important, that if they took the field to secure the independence of the cities, all would gladly answer the summons both through hatred for the barbarians and through the desire for self-government that is implanted in all men. They therefore elected Xenodicus [Xenodocus] as general, gave him an army suitable for the undertaking, and sent him forth to the war. He at once set out against Gela, was admitted at night by certain personal friends, and became master of the city together with its strong army and its wealth. The people of Gela, having been thus freed, joined in his campaign very eagerly and unanimously, and set about freeing the cities. As news of the undertaking of the Acragantines spread throughout the whole island, an impulse toward liberty made itself manifest in the cities. And first the people of Enna sent to the Acragantines and delivered their city over to them; and when they had freed Enna, the Acragantines went on to Erbessus, although a garrison stationed there was keeping watch over the city. After a bitter battle had taken place in which the citizens aided the Acragantines, the garrison was captured and, although many of the barbarians fell, at least five hundred of them laid down their arms and surrendered.

How they captured twenty ships of the Syracusans (32).

32. While the Acragantines were thus engaged, some of the soldiers who had been left in Syracuse by Agathocles, after seizing Echetla, plundered Leontini and Camarina. Since the cities were suffering from the plundering of their fields and the destruction of all their crops, Xenodicus entered the region and freed the peoples of Leontini and Camarina from the war; and after taking Echetla, a walled town, by siege, he re-established democracy for its citizens and struck fear into the Syracusans; and. in general, as he advanced he liberated the strongholds and the cities from Carthaginian domination.

Meantime the Syracusans, hard pressed by famine and hearing that grain ships were about to make the voyage to Syracuse, manned twenty triremes and, watching the barbarians who were accustomed to lie at anchor off the harbour to catch them off guard, sailed out unseen and coasted along to Megara. where they waited for the approach of the traders. Afterwards, however, when the Carthaginians sailed out against them with thirty ships, they first tried to fight at sea, but were quickly driven to land and leapt from their ships at a certain shrine of Hera. Then a battle took place for the ships; and the Carthaginians, throwing grappling irons into the triremes and with great force dragging them off from the shore, captured ten of them, but the others were saved by men who came to the rescue from the city.

And this was the condition of affairs in Sicily.

About the revolt that took place in Libya, and the peril of Agathocles (33-34).

33. In Libya, when those who were carrying the head of Hamilcar had come into port, Agathocles took the head and, riding near the hostile camp to within hearing distance, showed it to the enemy and related to them the defeat of their expedition. The Carthaginians, deeply grieved and prostrating themselves on the ground in barbarian fashion, regarded the death of the king as their own misfortune, and they fell into deep despair in regard to the whole war. Agathocles, who was already elated by his successes in Libya, when such strokes of fortune were now added, was borne aloft by soaring hopes, thinking himself freed from all dangers. Fortune notwithstanding did not permit success to remain long on the same side but brought the greatest danger to the prince from his own soldiers. For Lyciscus, one of those who had been placed in command, invited to dinner by Agathocles, became drunk and insulted the prince. Now Agathocles, who valued the man for his services in the war, turned aside with a joke what had been said in bitterness: but his son, Archagathus, becoming angry, censured and threatened Lyciscus. When the drinking was concluded and the men were going away to their quarters, Lyciscus taunted Archagathus on the score of his adultery with his stepmother; for he was supposed to possess Aleia, for this was the woman's name, without his father's knowledge. Archagathus, driven into an overpowering rage, seized a spear from one of the guard and thrust Lyciscus through his ribs. Now he died at once and was carried away to his own tent by those whose task it was; but at daybreak the friends of the murdered man came together, and many of the other soldiers hastened to join them, and all were indignant at what had happened and filled the camp with uproar. Many, too, of those who had been placed in command, as they also were subject to accusation and feared for themselves, turned the crisis to their own advantage and kindled no inconsiderable sedition. When the whole army was full of indignation, the troops severally donned full armour to punish the murderer; and finally the mob made up its mind that Archagathus should be put to death, and that, if Agathocles did not surrender his son, he himself should pay the penalty in his place. They also kept demanding the pay that was due them, and they elected generals to lead the army; and finally some of them seized the walls of Tunis and surrounded the princes with guards on every side.

34. The Carthaginians, on learning of the discord among the enemy, sent men to them urging them to change sides, and promised to give them greater pay and noteworthy bonuses, and indeed many of the leaders did agree to take the army over to them; but Agathocles, seeing that his safety was in the balance and fearing that, if he should be delivered to the enemy, he would end his life amid insults, decided that it was better, if he had to suffer, to die at the hands of his own men. Therefore, putting aside the purple and donning the humble garb of a private citizen, he came out into the middle of the crowd. Silence fell because his action was unexpected, and when a crowd had run together, he delivered a speech suitable to the critical situation. After recalling his earlier achievements, he said that he was ready to die if that should seem best for his fellow soldiers; for never had he, constrained by cowardice, consented to endure any indignity through love of life. Declaring that they themselves were witnesses of this, he bared his sword as if to slay himself. When he was on the point of striking the blow, the army shouted bidding him stop, and from every side came voices clearing him from the charges, and when the crowd kept pressing him to resume his royal garb, he put on the dress of his rank, weeping and thanking the people, the crowd meanwhile acclaiming his restoration with a clash of arms. While the Carthaginians were waiting intently, expecting that the Greeks would very soon come over to them, Agathocles, not missing the opportunity, led his army against them. The barbarians, believing that their opponents were deserting to them, had no idea at all of what had actually taken place; and when Agathocles had drawn near the enemy, he suddenly ordered the signal for battle to be given, fell upon them, and created great havoc. The Carthaginians, stunned by the sudden reversal, lost many of their soldiers and fled into their camp. Thus Agathocles, after having fallen into the most extreme danger on account of his son, through his own excellence not only found a way out of his difficulties, but even defeated the enemy. Those, however, who were chiefly responsible for the sedition and any of the others who were hostile to the prince, more than two hundred in number, found the courage to desert to the Carthaginians.

Now that we have completed the account of events in Libya and in Sicily, I we shall relate what took place in Italy.

35. When the Etruscans had taken the field against the city Sutrium, a Roman colony, the consuls, coming out to its aid with a strong army, defeated them in battle and drove them into their camp; but the Samnites at this time, when the Roman army was far distant, were plundering with impunity those Iapyges who supported the Etonians. The consuls, therefore, were forced to divide their armies; Kabius remained in Etruria, but Marcius. setting out against the Samnites, took the city Allifae by storm and freed from danger those of the allies who were being besieged. Fabius, however, while the Etruscans in great numbers were gathering against Sutrium, marched without the knowledge of the enemy through the country of their neighbours into upper Etruria, which had not been plundered for a long time. Falling upon it unexpectedly, he ravaged a large part of the country; and in a victory over those of the inhabitants who came against him, he slew many of them and took no small number of them alive as prisoners. Thereafter, defeating the Etruscans in a second battle near the place called

Perusia and destroying many of them, he overawed the nation since he was the first of the Romans to have invaded that region with an army. He also made truces with the peoples of Arretium and Crotona, likewise with those of Perusia; and, taking by siege the city called Castola, he forced the Etruscans to raise the siege of Sutrium.

About the acts of Appius Claudius during his censorship (36).

36. In Rome in this year censors were elected, and one of them Appius Claudius, who had his colleague, Lucius Flautius, under his influence, changed many of the laws of the fathers; for since he was following a course of action pleasing to the people, he considered the Senate of no importance. In the first place he built the Appian Aqueduct, as it is called, from a distance of eighty stades to Rome, and spent a large sum of public money for this construction without a decree of the Senate. Next he paved with solid stone the greater part of the Appian Way, which was named for him, from Rome to Capua, the distance being more than a thousand stades. Since he dug through elevated places and levelled with noteworthy fills the ravines and valleys, he expended the entire revenue of the state but left behind a deathless monument to himself, having been ambitious in the public interest. He also mixed the Senate, enrolling not merely those who were of noble birth and superior rank as was the custom, but also including many sons of freedmen. For this reason those were incensed with him who boasted of their nobility. He also gave each citizen the right to be enrolled in whatever tribe he wished, and to be placed in the census class he preferred. In short, seeing hatred toward himself treasured up by the most distinguished men, he avoided giving offence to any of the other citizens, securing as a counterpoise against the hostility of the nobles the goodwill of the many. At the inspection of the equestrian order he deprived no man of his horse, and in drawing up the album of the Senate he removed no one of the unworthy Senators, which it was the custom of the censors to do. Then the consuls, because of their hatred for him and their desire to please the most distinguished men, called together the Senate, not as it had been listed by him but as it had been entered in the album by the preceding censors; and the people in opposition to the nobles and in support of Appius, wishing also to establish firmly the promotion of their own class. elected to the more distinguished of the aedileships the son of a freedman, Gnaeus Flavius, who was the first Roman whose father had been a slave to gain that office. When Appius had completed his term of office, as a precaution against the ill will of the Senate, he professed to be blind and remained in his house.

Delivery of Corinth and Sicyon to Ptolemy (37).

Assassination of Cleopatra in Sardis (37).

37. When Charinus was archon at Athens, [308] the Romans gave the consulship to Publius Decius and Quintus Fabius; and in Elis the Olympian Games were celebrated for the one hundred and eighteenth time, at which celebration Apollonides of Tegea won the foot race. At this time, while Ptolemy was sailing from Myndus with a strong fleet through the islands, he liberated Andros as he passed by and drove out the garrison. Moving on to the Isthmus, he took Sicyon and Corinth from Cratesipolis. Since the causes that explain her becoming ruler of famous cities were made clear in the preceding Book, we shall refrain from again discussing the same subject. Now Ptolemy planned to free the other Greek cities also, thinking that the goodwill of the Greeks would be a great gain for him in his own undertakings; but when the Peloponnesians, having agreed to contribute food and money, contributed nothing of what had been promised, the prince in anger made peace with Cassander, by the terms of which peace each prince was to remain master of the cities that he was holding; and after securing Sicyon and Corinth with a garrison, Ptolemy departed for Egypt.

Meanwhile Cleopatra quarrelled with Antigonus and, inclining to cast, her lot with Ptolemy, she started from Sardis in order to cross over to him. She was the sister of Alexander the conqueror of Persia and daughter of Philip, son of Amyntas, and had been the wife of the Alexander who made an expedition into Italy. Because of the distinction of her descent Cassander and Lysimachus, as well as Antigonus and Ptolemy and in general all the leaders who were most important after Alexander's death, sought her hand; for each of them, hoping that the Macedonians would follow the lead of this marriage, was seeking alliance with the royal house in order thus to gain supreme power for himself. The governor of Sardis, who had orders from Antigonus to watch Cleopatra, prevented her departure; but later, as commanded by the prince, he treacherously brought about her death through the agency of certain women. Antigonus, not wishing the murder to be laid at his door, punished some of the women for having plotted against her, and took care that the funeral should be conducted in royal fashion. Thus Cleopatra, after having been the prize in a contest among the most eminent leaders, met this fate before her marriage was brought to pass.

Now that we have related the events of Asia and of Greece, we shall turn our narrative to the other parts of the inhabited world.

How Agathocles defeated the Carthaginians in battle; and how, after summoning Ophelias, the tyrant of Cyrenê, to co-operate with him, he assassinated him and took over the army that was with him (38-42).

38. In Libya, when the Carthaginians had sent out an army to win over the Nomads who had deserted, Agathocles left his son Archagathus before Tunis with part of the army, but he himself, selecting the strongest men, eight thousand foot, eight hundred horse, and fifty Libyan chariots, followed after the enemy at full speed. When the Carthaginians had come to the tribe of Nomads called the Zuphones, they won over many of the inhabitants and brought back some of the deserters to their former alliance, but on learning that the enemy were at hand, they camped on a certain hill, which was surrounded by streams that were deep and difficult to cross. These they used as protection against the unexpected attacks of their opponents, but they directed the fittest of the Nomads to follow the Greeks closely and by harassing them to prevent them from advancing. When these did as they had been directed, Agathocles sent against them his slingers and bowmen, but he himself with the rest of his army advanced against the camp of the enemy. The Carthaginians on discovering his intention led their army out from their camp, drew it up, and took their positions ready for battle. When they saw that Agathocles was already crossing the river, they attacked in formation, and at the stream, which was difficult to ford, they slew many of their opponents. However, as Agathocles pressed forward, the Greeks were superior in valour, but the barbarians had the advantage of numbers. Then when the armies had been fighting gallantly for some time, the Nomads on both sides withdrew from the battle and awaited the outcome of the struggle, intending to plunder the baggage train of those who were defeated. Agathocles, who had his best men about him, first forced back those opposite to him, and by their rout he caused the rest of the barbarians to flee. Of the cavalry only the Greeks who, led by Clinon. were assisting the Carthaginians withstood Agathocles' heavy armed men as they advanced. Although they struggled brilliantly, most of these Greeks were slain while fighting gallantly, and those who survived were saved by mere chance.

39. Agathocles, giving up the pursuit of the cavalry, attacked the barbarians who had taken refuge in the camp; and, since he had to force his way over terrain steep and difficult of access, he suffered losses no less great than those he inflicted on the Carthaginians. Nevertheless, he did not slacken his zeal, but rather, made confident by his victory, pressed on, expecting to take the camp by storm. At this the Nomads who were awaiting the outcome of the battle, not being able to fall on the baggage train of the Carthaginians since both armies were fighting near the camp, made an attack on the encampment of the Greeks, knowing that Agathocles had been drawn off to a great distance. Since the camp was without defenders capable of warding them off, they easily launched an attack, killing the few who resisted them and gaining possession of a large number of prisoners and of booty as well. On hearing this Agathocles led his army back quickly and recovered some of the spoil, but most of it the Nomads kept in their possession, and as night came on they withdrew to a distance. The prince, after setting up a trophy, divided the booty among the soldiers so that no one might complain about his losses; but the captured Greeks, who had been fighting for the Carthaginians, he put into a certain fortress. Now these men, dreading punishment from the prince, attacked those in the fortress at night and, although defeated in the battle, occupied a strong position, being in number not less than a thousand, of whom above five hundred were Syracusans. However, when Agathocles heard what had happened, he came with his army, induced them to leave their position under a truce, and slaughtered all those who had made the attack.

40. After he had finished this battle, Agathocles, examining in mind every device for bringing the Carthaginians into subjection, sent Orthon the Syracusan as an envoy into Cyrcne to Ophelias. The latter was one of the companions who had made the campaign with Alexander; now, master of the cities of Cyrenê and of a strong army, he was ambitious for a greater realm. So it was to a man in this state of mind that there came the envoy from Agathocles inviting him to join him in subduing the Carthaginians. In return for this service Orthon promised Ophelias that Agathocles would permit him to exercise dominion over Libya. For, he said, Sicily was enough for Agathocles, if only it should be possible for him, relieved of danger from Carthage, to rule over all the island without fear. Moreover, Italy was close at his hand for increasing his realm if he should decide to reach after greater things. For Libya, separated by a wide and dangerous sea, did not suit him at all, into which land he had even now come through no desire but because of necessity. Ophelias, now that to his long-considered judgement was added this actual hope, gladly consented and sent to the Athenians an envoy to confer about an alliance, for Ophelias had married Euthydicê, the daughter of a Miltiades who traced that name back to him who had commanded the victorious troops at Marathon. On account of this marriage and the other marks of favour which he had habitually displayed toward their city, a good many of the Athenians eagerly enlisted for the campaign. No small number also of the other Greeks were quick to join in the undertaking since they hoped to portion out for colonization the most fertile part of Libya and to plunder the wealth of Carthage. For conditions throughout Greece on account of the continuous wars and the mutual rivalries of the princes had become unstable and straitened, and they expected not only to gain many advantages, but also to rid themselves of their present evils.

41. So Ophelias, when everything for his campaign had been prepared magnificently, set out with his army, having more than ten thousand foot-soldiers, six hundred horsemen, a hundred chariots, and more than three hundred charioteers and men to fight beside them. There followed also of those who are termed non-combatants not less than ten thousand; and many of these brought their children and wives and other possessions, so that the army was like a colonising expedition. When they had marched for eighteen days and had traversed three thousand stades, they encamped at Automala; thence as they advanced there was a mountain, precipitous on both sides but with a deep ravine in the centre, from which extended a smooth rock that rose up to a lofty peak. At the base of this rock was a large cave thickly covered with ivy and bryony, in which according to myth had been born Lamia, a queen of surpassing beauty, but on account of the savagery of her heart they say that the time that has elapsed since has transformed her face to a bestial aspect. For when all the children born to her had died, weighed down in her misfortune and envying the happiness of all other women in their children, she ordered that the new-born babies be snatched from their mothers' arms and straightway slain. Wherefore among us even down to the present generation, the story of this woman remains among the children and her name is most terrifying to them. Whenever she drank freely, she gave to all the opportunity to do what they pleased unobserved. Therefore, since she did not trouble herself about what was taking place at such times, the people of the land assumed that she could not see, and for that reason some tell in the myth that she threw her eyes into a flask, metaphorically turning the carelessness that is most complete amid wine into the aforesaid measure, since it was a measure of wine that took away her sight. One might also present Euripides as a witness that she was born in Libya, for he says:

> Who does not know the name of Lamia, Libyan in race, a name of
> greatest reproach among mortals?

42. Now Ophelias with his army was advancing with great difficulty through a waterless land filled with savage creatures; for not only did he lack water, but since dry food also gave out, he was in danger of losing his entire army. Fanged monsters of all kinds infest the desert near the Syrtis, and the bite of most of these is fatal; therefore it was a great disaster into which they were fallen since they were not helped by remedies supplied by physicians and friends. For some of the serpents, since they had a skin very like in appearance to the ground that was beneath them, made their own forms invisible; and many of the men, treading upon these in ignorance, received bites that were fatal. Finally, after suffering great hardships on the march for more than two months, they with difficulty completed the journey to Agathocles and encamped, keeping the two forces a short distance apart.

The Carthaginians, on hearing of their presence, were panic stricken, seeing that so great a force had arrived against them; but Agathocles, going to meet

Ophelias and generously furnishing all needed supplies, begged him to relieve his army from its distress. He himself remained for some days and carefully observed all that was being done in the camp of the new arrivals. When the larger part of the soldiers had scattered to find fodder and food, and when he saw that Ophelias had no suspicion of what he himself had planned, he summoned an assembly of his own soldiers and, after accusing the man who had come to join the alliance as if he were plotting against himself and thus rousing the anger of his men, straightway led his army in full array against the Cyrenêans. Then Ophelias, stunned by this unexpected action, attempted to defend himself; but, pressed for time, the forces that he had remaining in camp not being adequate, he died fighting. Agathocles forced the rest of the army to lay down its arms, and by winning them all over with generous promises, he became master of the whole army. Thus Ophelias, who had cherished great hopes and had rashly entrusted himself to another, met an end so inglorious.

How the Carthaginians put down Bormilcar, who had attempted to become tyrant (43-44).

43. In Carthage Bormilcar, who had long planned to make an attempt, at tyranny, was seeking a proper occasion for his private schemes. Time and again when circumstances put him in a position to carry out what he had planned, some little cause intervened to thwart him. For those who are about to undertake lawless and important enterprises are superstitious and always choose delay rather than action, and postponement rather than accomplishment. This happened also on this occasion and in regard to this man; for he sent out the most distinguished of the citizens to the campaign against the Nomads so that he might have no man of consequence to oppose him, but he did not venture to make an open bid for the tyranny, being held back by caution. It happened that at the time when Agathocles attacked Ophelias, Bormilcar made his effort to gain the tyranny, each of the two being ignorant of what the enemy was doing. Agathocles did not know of the attempt at tyranny and of the confusion in the city when he might easily have become master of Carthage, for when Bormilcar was discovered in the act he would have preferred to co-operate with Agathocles rather than pay the penalty in his own person to the citizens. Again, the Carthaginians had not heard of Agathocles' attack, for they might easily have overpowered him with the aid of the army of Ophelias, but I suppose that not without reason did such ignorance prevail on both sides, although the actions were on a large scale and those who had undertaken deeds of such daring were near each other. For Agathocles, when about to kill a man who was his friend, paid attention to nothing that was happening among his enemies; and Bormilcar, when depriving his fatherland of its liberty, did not concern himself at all with events in the camp of the enemy, since he had as a fixed purpose in his mind to conquer at the time, not his enemies, but his fellow citizens.

At this point one might censure the art of history, when he observes that in life many different actions are consummated at the same time, but that it is necessary for those who record them to interrupt the narrative and to parcel out different times to simultaneous events contrary to nature, with the result that, although the actual experience of the events contains the truth, yet the written record, deprived of such power, while presenting copies of the events, falls far short of arranging them as they really were.

*How, when Agathocles sent the booty to Sicily, some of the
ships were wrecked (44).*

*How the Romans went to the aid of the Marsi, who were
being attacked by the Samnites; and how they took Caprium
in Etruria after a siege (44).*

44. Be that as it may, when Bormilcar had reviewed the soldiers in what was
called the New City, which is a short distance from Old Carthage, he dismissed
the rest, but holding those who were his confederates in the plot, five hundred
citizens and about a thousand mercenaries, he declared himself tyrant. Dividing
his soldiers into five bands, he attacked, slaughtering those who opposed him in
the streets. Since an extraordinary tumult broke out everywhere in the city, the
Carthaginians at first supposed that the enemy had made his way in and that the
city was being betrayed; when, however, the true situation became known, the
young men ran together, formed companies, and advanced against the tyrant.
Bormilcar, killing those in the streets, moved swiftly into the market place; and
finding there many of the citizens unarmed, he slaughtered them. The
Carthaginians, however, after occupying the buildings about the market place,
which were tall, hurled missiles thick and fast, and the participants in the
uprising began to be struck down since the whole place was within range.
Therefore, since they were suffering severely, they closed ranks and forced their
way out through the narrow streets into the New City, being continuously struck
with missiles from whatever houses they chanced at any time to be near. After
these had occupied a certain elevation, the Carthaginians, now that all the
citizens had assembled in arms, drew up their forces against those who had taken
part in the uprising. Finally, sending as envoys such of the oldest men as were
qualified and offering amnesty, they came to terms. Against the rest they invoked
no penalty on account of the dangers that surrounded the city, but they cruelly
tortured Bormilcar himself and put him to death, paying no heed to the oaths
which had been given. In this way, then, the Carthaginians, after having been in
the gravest danger, preserved the constitution of their fathers.

Agathocles, loading cargo vessels with his spoil and embarking on them
those of the men who had come from Cyrenê who were useless for war, sent
them to Syracuse, but storms arose, and some of the ships were destroyed, some
were driven to the Pithecusan Islands off the coast of Italy, and a few came safe
to Syracuse.

In Italy the Roman consuls, going to the aid of the Marsi, against whom the
Samnites were making war, were victorious in the battle and slew many of the
enemy. Then, crossing the territory of the Umbrians, they invaded Etruria, which
was hostile, and took by siege the fortress called Caerium. When the people of
the region sent envoys to ask a truce, the consuls made a truce for forty years
with the Tarquinians but with all the other Etruscans for one year.

*The naval expedition of Demetrius Poliorcetes into the
Peiraeus, and his capture of Munychia (45).*

45. When that year had come to an end, Anaxicrates was archon in Athens
[307] and in Rome Appius Claudius and Lucius Volumnius became consuls.
While these held office, Demetrius, the son of Antigonus, having received from
his father strong land and sea forces, also a suitable supply of missiles and of the
other things requisite for carrying on a siege, set sail from Ephesus. He had

instructions to free all the cities throughout Greece, but first of all Athens, which was held by a garrison of Cassander. Sailing into the Peiraeus with his forces, he at once made an attack on all sides and issued a proclamation. Dionysius, who had been placed in command of the garrison on Munychia, and Demetrius of Phalerum, who had been made military governor of the city by Cassander, resisted him from the walls with many soldiers. Some of Antigonus' men, attacking with violence and effecting an entrance along the coast, admitted many of their fellow soldiers within the wall. The result was that in this way the Peiraeus was taken; and, of those within it, Dionysius the commander fled to Munychia and Demetrius of Phalerum withdrew into the city. On the next day, when he had been sent with others as envoys by the people to Demetrius and had discussed the independence of the city and his own security, he obtained a safe-conduct for himself and, giving up the direction of Athens, fled to Thebes and later into Egypt to Ptolemy. So this man, after he had been director of the city for ten years, was driven from his fatherland in the way described. The Athenian people, having recovered their freedom, decreed honours to those responsible for their liberation.

Demetrius, however, bringing up ballistae and the other engines of war and missiles, assaulted Munychia both by land and by sea. When those within defended themselves stoutly from the walls, it turned out that Dionysius had the advantage of the difficult terrain and the greater height of his position, for Munychia was strong both by nature and by the fortifications which had been constructed, but that Demetrius was many times superior in the number of his soldiers and had a great advantage in his equipment. Finally, after the attack had continued unremittingly for two days, the defenders, severely wounded by the catapults and the ballistae and not having any men to relieve them, had the worst of it; and the men of Demetrius, who were fighting in relays and were continually relieved, after the wall had been cleared by the ballistae, broke into Munychia, forced the garrison to lay down its arms, and took the commander Dionysius alive.

Liberation of the Athenians and the Megarians (46).

46. After gaining these successes in a few days and razing Munychia completely, Demetrius restored to the people their freedom and established friendship and an alliance with them. The Athenians, Stratocles writing the decree, voted to set up golden statues of Antigonus and Demetrius in a chariot near the statues of Harmodius and Aristogeiton, to give them both honorary crowns at a cost of two hundred talents, to consecrate an altar to them and call it the altar of the Saviours, to add to the ten tribes two more, Demetrias and Antigonis, to hold annual games in their honour with a procession and a sacrifice, and to weave their portraits in the peplos of Athena. Thus the common people, deprived of power in the Lamian War by Antipater, fifteen years afterwards unexpectedly recovered the constitution of the fathers. Although Megara was held by a garrison, Demetrius took it by siege, restored their autonomy to its people, and received noteworthy honours from those whom he had served.

When an embassy had come to Antigonus from Athens and had delivered to him the decree concerning the honours conferred upon him and discussed with him the problem of grain and of timber for ships, he gave to them one hundred and fifty thousand medimni of grain and timber sufficient for one hundred ships;

he also withdrew his garrison from Imbros and gave the city back to the Athenians. He wrote to his son Demetrius ordering him to call together counsellors from the allied cities who should consider in common what was advantageous for Greece, and to sail himself with his army to Cyprus and finish the war with the generals of Ptolemy as soon as possible. Demetrius, promptly doing all according to his father's orders, moved toward Caria and summoned the Rhodians for the war against Ptolemy. They did not obey, preferring to maintain a common peace with all, and this was the beginning of the hostility between that people and Antigonus.

Voyage of Demetrius to Cyprus, his battle against the general Menelaüs, and the siege of Salamis (47-48).

47. Demetrius, after coasting along to Cilicia and there assembling additional ships and soldiers, sailed to Cyprus with fifteen thousand foot-soldiers and four hundred horsemen, more than one hundred and ten swift triremes, fifty-three heavier transports, and freighters of every kind sufficient for the strength of his cavalry and infantry. First he went into camp on the coast of Carpasia [Cyprus], and after beaching his ships, strengthened his encampment with a palisade and a deep moat; then, making raids on the peoples who lived near by, he took by storm Urania and Carpasia; then leaving an adequate guard for the ships, he moved with his forces against Salamis. Menelaüs, who had been made general of the island by Ptolemy, had gathered his soldiers from the outposts and was waiting in Salamis; but when the enemy was at a distance of forty stades, he came out with twelve thousand foot and about eight hundred horse. In a battle of short duration which occurred, the forces of Menelaüs were overwhelmed and routed; and Demetrius, pursuing the enemy into the city, took prisoners numbering not much less than three thousand and killed about a thousand. At first he freed the captives of all charges and distributed them among the units of his own soldiers; but when they ran off to Menelaüs because their baggage had been left behind in Egypt with Ptolemy, recognising that they would not change sides, he forced them to embark on his ships and sent them off to Antigonus in Syria. At this time Antigonus was tarrying in upper Syria, founding a city on the Orontes River, which he called Antigonia after himself. He laid it out on a lavish scale, making its perimeter seventy stades; for the location was naturally well adapted for watching over Babylon and the upper satrapies, and again for keeping an eye upon lower Syria and the satrapies near Egypt. It happened, however, that the city did not survive very long, for Seleucus dismantled it and transported it to the city which he founded and called Seleucea after himself. We shall make these matters clear in detail when we come to the proper time. As to affairs in Cyprus, Menelaüs, after having been defeated in the battle, had missiles and engines brought to the walls, assigned positions on the battlements to his soldiers, and made ready for the fight; and since he saw that Demetrius was also making preparations for siege, he sent messengers into Egypt to Ptolemy to inform him about the defeat and to ask him to send aid as his interests on the island were in danger.

48. Since Demetrius saw that the city of the Salaminians was not to be despised and that a large force was in the city defending it, he determined to prepare siege engines of very great size, catapults for shooting bolts and ballistae of all kinds, and the other equipment that would strike terror. He sent for skilled workmen from Asia, and for iron, likewise for a large amount of wood and for the proper complement of other supplies. When everything was quickly made ready for him, he constructed a device called the "helepolis," [city-taker] which had a length of forty-five cubits on each side and a height of ninety cubits. It was divided into nine storeys, and the whole was mounted on four solid wheels each eight cubits high. He also constructed very large battering rams and two penthouses to carry them. On the lower levels of the helepolis he mounted all sorts of ballistae, the largest of them capable of hurling missiles weighing three talents; on the middle levels he placed the largest catapults, and on the highest his lightest catapults and a large number of ballistae; and he also stationed on the helepolis more than two hundred men to operate these engines in the proper manner.

Bringing the engines up to the city and hurling a shower of missiles, he cleared the battlements with the ballistae and shattered the walls with the rams. Since those within resisted boldly and opposed his engines of war with other devices, for some days the battle was doubtful, both sides suffering hardships and severe wounds; and when finally the wall was falling and the city was in danger of being taken by storm, the assault was interrupted by the coming of night. Menelaüs, seeing clearly that the city would be taken unless he tried something new, gathered a large amount of dry wood, at about midnight threw this upon the siege engines of the enemy, and at the same time all shot down fire-bearing arrows from the walls and set on fire the largest of the siege engines. As the flames suddenly blazed high, Demetrius tried to come to the rescue; but the flames got the start of him, with the result that the engines were completely destroyed and many of those who manned them were lost. Demetrius, although disappointed in his expectations, did not stop but pushed the siege persistently by both land and sea, believing that he would overcome the enemy in time.

Demetrius' naval battle against Ptolemy and victory of Demetrius (49-52).

49. When Ptolemy heard of the defeat of his men, he sailed from Egypt with considerable land and sea forces. Reaching Cyprus at Paphos, he received ships from the cities and coasted along to Citium, which was distant from Salamis two hundred stades. He had in all one hundred and forty ships of war, of which the largest were quinqueremes and the smallest quadriremes; more than two hundred transports followed, which carried at least ten thousand foot-soldiers. Ptolemy sent certain men to Menelaüs by land, directing him, if possible, to send him quickly the ships from Salamis, which numbered sixty; for he hoped that, if he received these as reinforcement, he would easily be superior in the naval engagement since he would have two hundred ships in the battle. Learning of his intention, Demetrius left a part of his forces for the siege; and, manning all his ships and embarking upon them the best of his soldiers, he equipped them with missiles and ballistae and mounted on the prows a sufficient number of catapults for throwing bolts three spans in length. After making the fleet ready in every way for a naval battle, he sailed around the city and, anchoring at the mouth of the harbour just out of range, spent the night, preventing the ships from the city from joining the others, and at the same time watching for the coming of the enemy and occupying a position ready for battle. When Ptolemy sailed up toward Salamis, the service vessels following at a distance, his fleet was awe-inspiring to behold because of the multitude of its ships.

50. When Demetrius observed Ptolemy's approach, he left the admiral

Antisthenes with ten of the quinqueremes to prevent the ships in the city from going forth for the battle, since the harbour had a narrow exit; and he ordered the cavalry to patrol the shore so that, if any wreck should occur, they might rescue those who should swim across to the land. He himself drew up the fleet and moved against the enemy with one hundred and eight ships in all, including those that had been provided with crews from the captured towns. The largest of the ships were sevens and most of them were quinqueremes. The left wing was composed of seven Phoenician sevens and thirty Athenian quadriremes, Medius the admiral having the command. Sailing behind these he placed ten sixes and as many quinqueremes, for he had decided to make strong this wing where he himself was going to fight the decisive battle. In the middle of the line he stationed the lightest of his ships, which Themison of Samos and Marsyas, who compiled the history of Macedonia, commanded. The right wing was commanded by Hegesippus of Halicarnassus and Pleistias of Cos, who was the chief pilot of the whole fleet.

At first, while it was still night, Ptolemy made for Salamis at top speed, believing that he could gain an entrance before the enemy was ready; but as day broke, the fleet of the enemy in battle array was visible at no great distance, and Ptolemy also prepared for the battle. Ordering the supply ships to follow at a distance and effecting a suitable formation of the other ships, he himself took command of the left wing with the largest of his warships fighting under him. After the fleet had been disposed in this way, both sides prayed to the gods as was the custom, the signalmen leading and the crews joining in the response.

51. The princes, since they were about to fight for their lives and their all, were in much anxiety. When Demetrius was about three stades distant from the enemy, he raised the battle signal that had been agreed upon, a gilded shield, and this sign was made known to all by being repeated in relays. Since Ptolemy also gave a similar signal, the distance between the fleets was rapidly reduced. When the trumpets gave the signal for battle and both forces raised the battle cry, all the ships rushed to the encounter in a terrifying manner; using their bows and their ballistae at first, then their javelins in a shower, the men wounded those who were within range; then when the ships had come close together and the encounter was about to take place with violence, the soldiers on the decks crouched down and the oarsmen, spurred on by the signalmen, bent more desperately to their oars. As the ships drove together with force and violence, in some cases they swept off each other's oars so that the ships became useless for flight or pursuit, and the men who were on board, though eager for a fight, were prevented from joining in the battle; but where the ships had met prow to prow with their rams, they drew back for another charge, and the soldiers on board shot at each other with effect since the mark was close at hand for each party. Some of the men, when their captains had delivered a broadside blow and the rams had become firmly fixed, leaped aboard the ships of the enemy, receiving and giving severe wounds: for certain of them, after grasping the rail of a ship that was drawing near, missed their footing, fell into the sea, and at once were killed with spears by those who stood above them; and others, making good their intent, slew some of the enemy and, forcing others along the narrow deck, drove them into the sea. As a whole the fighting was varied and full of surprises: many times those who were weaker got the upper hand because of the height of their ships, and those who were stronger were foiled by inferiority of position and by the irregularity with which things happen in fighting of this kind. For in contests on land, valour is made clearly evident, since it is able to gain the upper hand when nothing external and fortuitous interferes; but in naval battles there are many causes of various kinds that, contrary to reason, defeat those who would properly gain the victory through prowess.

52. Demetrius fought most brilliantly of all, having taken his stand on the stern of his seven. A crowd of men rushed upon him, but by hurling his javelins at some of them and by striking others at close range with his spear, he slew them; and although many missiles of all sorts were aimed at him, he avoided some that he saw in time and received others upon his defensive armour. Of the three men who protected him with shields, one fell struck by a lance and the other two were severely wounded. Finally Demetrius drove back the forces confronting him, created a rout in the right wing, and forthwith forced even the ships next to the wing to flee. Ptolemy, who had with himself the heaviest, of his ships and the strongest men, easily routed those stationed opposite him, sinking some of the ships and capturing others with their crews. Turning back from that victorious action, he expected easily to subdue the others also; but when he saw that the right wing of his forces had been shattered and all those next to that wing driven into flight, and further, that Demetrius was pressing on with full force, he sailed back to Citium.

Demetrius, after winning the victory, gave the transports to Neon and Burichus, ordering them to pursue and pick up those who were swimming in the sea; and he himself, decking his own ships with bow and stern ornaments and towing the captured craft, sailed to his camp and his home port. At the time of the naval battle Menelaüs, the general in Salamis, had manned his sixty ships and sent them as a reinforcement to Ptolemy, placing Menoetius in command. When a battle occurred at the harbour mouth with the ships on guard there, and when the ships from the city pressed forward vigorously, Demetrius' ten ships fled to the camp of the army; and Menoetius, after sailing out and arriving a little too late, returned to Salamis.

In the naval battle, whose outcome was as stated more than a hundred of the supply ships were taken, upon which were almost eight thousand soldiers, and of the warships forty were captured with their crews and about eighty were disabled, which the victors towed, full of sea water, to the camp before the city. Twenty of Demetrius' ships were disabled, but all of these, after receiving proper care, continued to perform the services for which they were suited.

Capture of all Cyprus and of the army of Ptolemy (53).

How, because Antigonus and Demetrius assumed the diadem
after this victory, the other dynasts, jealous of them,
proclaimed themselves kings (53).

53. Thereafter Ptolemy gave up the fight in Cyprus and returned to Egypt. Demetrius, after he had taken over all the cities of the island and their garrisons, enrolled the men in companies; and when they were organized they came to sixteen thousand foot and about six hundred horse. He at once sent messengers to his father to inform him of the successes, embarking them on his largest ship. When Antigonus heard of the victory that had been gained, elated by the magnitude of his good fortune, he assumed the diadem and from that time on he used the style of king; and he permitted Demetrius also to assume this same title

and rank. Ptolemy, however, not at all humbled in spirit by his defeat, also assumed the diadem and always signed himself king. In a similar fashion in rivalry with them the rest of the princes also called themselves kings: Seleucus, who had recently gained the upper satrapies, and Lysimachus and Cassander, who still retained the territories originally allotted to them.

Now that we have said enough about these matters, we shall relate in their turn the events that took place in Libya and in Sicily.

How Agathocles, having besieged and taken Utica, transported part of his troops across into Sicily (54-55).

54. When Agathocles heard that the princes whom we have just mentioned had assumed the diadem, since he thought that neither in power nor in territory nor in deeds was he inferior to them, he called himself king. He decided not to take a diadem; for he habitually wore a chaplet, which at the lime when he seized the tyranny was his because of some priesthood and which he did not give up while he was struggling to gain the supreme power, but some say that he originally had made it his habit to wear this because he did not have a good head of hair. However this may be, in his desire to do something worthy of this title, he made a campaign against the people of Utica, who had deserted him. Making a sudden attack upon their city and taking prisoner those of the citizens who were caught in the open country to the number of three hundred, he at first offered a free pardon and requested the surrender of the city; but when those in the city did not heed his offer, he constructed a siege engine, hung the prisoners upon it, and brought it up to the walls. The Uticans pitied the unfortunate men; yet, holding the liberty of all of more account than the safety of these, they assigned posts on the walls to the soldiers and bravely awaited the assault. Then Agathocles, placing upon the engine his catapults, slingers, and bowmen, and fighting from this, began the assault, applying, as it were, branding-irons to the souls of those within the city. Those standing on the walls at first hesitated to use their missiles since the targets presented to them were their own fellow-countrymen, of whom some were indeed the most distinguished of their citizens; but when the enemy pressed on more heavily, they were forced to defend themselves against those who manned the engine. As a result there came unparalleled suffering and despiteful treatment of fortune to the men of Utica, placed as they were in dire straits from which there was no escape; for since the Greeks had set up before them as shields the men of Utica who had been captured, it was necessary either to spare these and idly watch the fatherland fall into the hands of the enemy or, in protecting the city, to slaughter mercilessly a large number of unfortunate fellow citizens, and this, indeed, is what took place; for as they resisted the enemy and employed missiles of every kind, they shot down some of the men who were stationed on the engine, and they also mangled some of their fellow citizens who were hanging there, and others they nailed to the engine with their bolts at whatever places on the body the missiles chanced to strike, so that the wanton violence and the punishment almost amounted to crucifixion. And this fate befell some at the hands of kinsmen and friends, if so it chanced, since necessity is not curiously concerned for what is holy among men.

55. But when Agathocles saw that they were cold bloodedly intent on fighting, he put his army in position to attack from every side and, forcing an entrance at a point where the wall had been poorly constructed, broke into the city. As some of the Uticans fled into their houses, others into temples,

Agathocles, enraged as he was against them, filled the city with slaughter. Some he killed in hand-to-hand fighting; those who were captured he hanged, and those who had fled to temples and altars of the gods he cheated of their hopes. When he had sacked the movable property, he left a garrison in possession of the city, and led his army into position against the place called Hippu Acra, which was made naturally strong by the marsh that lay before it. After laying siege to this with vigour and getting the better of its people in a naval battle, he took it by storm. When he had conquered the cities in this way, he became master both of most of the places along the sea and of the peoples dwelling in the interior except the Nomads, of whom some arrived at terms of friendship with him and some awaited the final issue. For four stocks have divided Libya: the Phoenicians, who at that time occupied Carthage; the Libyphoenicians, who have many cities along the sea and intermarry with the Carthaginians, and who received this name as a result of the interwoven ties of kinship. Of the inhabitants the race that was most numerous and oldest was called Libyan, and they hated the Carthaginians with a special bitterness because of the weight of their overlordship: and last were the Nomads, who pastured their herds over a large part of Libya as far as the desert.

Now that Agathocles was superior to the Carthaginians by reason of his Libyan allies and his own armies, but was much troubled about the situation in Sicily, he constructed light ships and penteconters and placed upon them two thousand soldiers. Leaving his son Agatharchus in command of affairs in Libya, he put out with his ships and made the voyage to Sicily.

How the people of Acragas took the field against Agathocles' generals and were defeated (56).

How Agathocles won over to himself Heraclea, Therma, and Cephaloedium, but reduced the country and city of the Apolloniates to utter slavery (56).

56. While this was happening, Xenodocus, the general of the Acragantines, having freed many of the cities and roused in the Sicilians great hopes of autonomy throughout the whole island, led his army against the generals of Agathocles. It consisted of more than ten thousand foot-soldiers and nearly a thousand horsemen. Leptines and Demophilus, assembling from Syracuse and the fortresses as many men as they could, took up a position opposite him with eighty-two hundred foot-soldiers and twelve hundred horse. In a bitter fight that ensued, Xenodocus was defeated and fled to Acragas, losing not less than fifteen hundred of his soldiers. The people of Acragas after meeting with this reverse put an end to their own most noble enterprise and, at the same time, to their allies' hopes of freedom. Shortly after this battle had taken place, Agathocles put in at Selinus in Sicily and forced the people of Heraclea, who had made their city free, to submit to him once more. Having crossed to the other side of the island, he attached to himself by a treaty the people of Therma, granting safe conduct to the Carthaginian garrison. Then, after taking Cephaloedium and leaving Leptines as its governor, he himself marched through the interior and attempted to slip by night into Centoripa, where some of the citizens were to admit him. When their plan was discovered, however, and the guard came to the defence, he was thrown out of the city, losing more than five hundred of his soldiers. Thereupon, men from Apollonia having invited him and promised to betray their fatherland, he came to that city. As the traitors had become known and had been punished, he attacked the city but without effect for the first day, and on the next, after suffering heavily and losing a large number of men, he barely succeeded in taking it. After slaughtering most of the Apolloniates, he plundered their possessions.

How in Sicily Agathocles defeated the Carthaginians in a naval battle and the people of Acragas in a battle on land (57-63).

57. While Agathocles was engaged on these matters, Deinocrates, the leader of the exiles, taking over the policy of the Acragantines and proclaiming himself champion of the common liberty, caused many to flock to him from all sides; for some eagerly gave ear to his appeals because of the desire for independence inborn in all men, and others because of their fear of Agathocles. When Deinocrates had collected almost twenty thousand foot-soldiers and fifteen hundred mounted men, all of them men who had had uninterrupted experience of exile and hardship, he camped in the open, challenging the tyrant to battle. However, when Agathocles, who was far inferior in strength, avoided battle, he steadily followed on his heels, having secured his victory without a struggle.

From this time on the fortunes of Agathocles, not only in Sicily but also in Libya, suffered a change for the worse. Archagathus, who had been left by him as general, after the departure of his father at first gained some advantage by sending into the inland regions a part of the army under the command of Eumachus. This leader, after taking the rather large city of Tocae, won over many of the Nomads who dwelt near by. Then, capturing another city called Phellinê, he forced the submission of those who used the adjacent country as pasture, men called the Asphodelodes, who are similar to the Ethiopians in colour. The third city that he took was Meschela, which was very large and had been founded long ago by the Greeks who were returning from Troy, about whom we have already spoken in the third Book. Next he took the place called Hippu Acra, which has the same name as that captured by storm by Agathocles, and finally the free city called Acris, which he gave to his soldiers for plundering after he had enslaved the people.

58. After sating his army with booty, he returned to Archagathus; and since he had gained a name for good service, he again led an army into the inland regions of Libya. Passing by the cities that he had previously mastered, he gained an entrance into the city called Miltinê, having appeared before it without warning; but when the barbarians gathered together against him and overpowered him in the streets, he was, to his great surprise, driven out and lost many of his men. Departing thence [307], he marched through a high mountain range that extended for about two hundred stades and was full of wildcats, in which, accordingly, no birds whatever nested either among the trees or the ravines because of the rapacity of the aforementioned beasts. Crossing this range, he came out into a country containing a large number of apes and to three cities called from these beasts Pithecusae [ape-cities], if the name is translated into the Greek language. In these cities many of the customs were very different from those current among us. For the apes lived in the same houses as the men, being regarded among them as gods, just as the dogs are among the Egyptians, and from the provisions laid up in the storerooms the beasts took their food without hindrance whenever they wished. Parents usually gave their children names taken from the apes, just as we do from the gods. For any who killed this animal, as if he had committed the greatest sacrilege, death was established as the penalty. For this reason, among some there was current a proverbial saying about those slain with impunity that they were paying the penalty for a monkey's blood. However this may be, Eumachus, after taking one of these cities by storm, destroyed it, but the other two he won over by persuasion. When, however, he heard that the neighbouring barbarians were collecting great forces against him, he pushed on more vigorously, having decided to go back to the regions by the sea.

59. Up to this time all the campaign in Libya had been satisfactory to Archagathus. But after this the senate in Carthage took good counsel about the war and the senators decided to form three armies and send them forth from the city, one against the cities of the coast, one into the midland regions, and one into the interior. They thought that if they did this they would in the first place relieve the city of the siege and at the same time of the scarcity of food; for since many people from all parts had taken refuge in Carthage, there had resulted a general scarcity, the supply of provisions being already exhausted, but there was no danger from the siege since the city was inaccessible because of the protection afforded by the walls and the sea. In the second place, they assumed that the allies would continue more loyal if there were more armies in the field aiding them, and what was most important, they hoped that the enemy would be forced to divide his forces and to withdraw to a distance from Carthage. All of these aims were accomplished according to their purpose; for when thirty thousand soldiers had been sent out from the city, the men who were left behind as a garrison not only had enough to maintain themselves, but out of their abundance they enjoyed everything in profusion; and the allies, who hitherto, because of their fear of the enemy, were compelled to make terms with him, again gained courage and hastened to return to the formerly existing friendship.

60. When Archagathus saw that all Libya was being occupied in sections by hostile armies, he himself also divided his army; part he sent into the coastal region, and of the rest of his forces he gave part to Aeschrion and sent him forth, and part he led himself, leaving an adequate garrison in Tunis. When so many armies were wandering everywhere in the country and when a decisive crisis in the campaign was expected, all anxiously awaited the final outcome. Now Hanno, who commanded the army of the midland region, laid an ambush for Aeschrion and fell on him suddenly, slaying more than four thousand foot-soldiers and about two hundred mounted troops, among whom was the general himself; of the others some were captured and some escaped in safety to Archagathus, who was about five hundred stades distant. As for Himilco, who had been appointed to conduct the campaign into the interior, at first he rested in a certain city lying in wait for Eumachus, who was dragging along his army heavily loaded with the spoils from the captured cities. Then when the Greeks drew up their forces and challenged him to battle, Himilco left part of his army under arms in the city, giving them orders that, when he retired in pretended flight, they should burst out upon the pursuers. He himself, leading out half of his soldiers and joining battle a little distance in front of the encampment, at once took to flight as if panic-stricken. Eumachus' men, elated by their victory and giving no thought at all to their formation, followed, and in confusion pressed hard upon those who were withdrawing; but when suddenly from another part of the city there poured forth the army all ready for battle and when a great host shouted at a single command, they became panic-stricken. Accordingly, when the barbarians fell upon an enemy who had been thrown into disorder and frightened by the sudden onslaught, the immediate result was the rout of the Greeks. Since the Carthaginians cut off the enemy's return to his camp, Eumachus was forced to withdraw to the nearby hill, which was ill supplied with water. When the Phoenicians invested the place, the Greeks, who had become weak from thirst and were being overpowered by the enemy, were almost all killed. In fact, of eight thousand foot-soldiers only thirty were saved, and of eight hundred horsemen forty escaped from the battle.

61. After meeting with so great a disaster Archagathus returned to Tunis. He summoned from all sides the survivors of the soldiers who had been sent out; and he sent messengers to Sicily to report to his father what had happened and to urge him to come to his aid with all possible speed. In addition to the preceding disasters, another loss befell the Greeks; for all their allies except a few deserted them, and the armies of the enemy gathered together and, pitching camp near by, lay in wait for them. Himilco occupied the passes and shut off his opponents, who were at a distance of a hundred stades, from the routes leading from the region; and on the other side Atarbas camped at a distance of forty stades from Tunis. Therefore, since the enemy controlled not only the sea but also the land, the Greeks both suffered from famine and were beset by fear on every side.

While all were in deep despair, Agathocles, when he learned of the reverses in Libya, made ready seventeen warships intending to go to the aid of Archagathus. Although affairs in Sicily had also shifted to his disadvantage because of the increase in the strength of the exiles who followed Deinocrates, he entrusted the war on the island to Leptines as general; and he himself, manning his ships, watched for a chance to set sail, since the Carthaginians were blockading the harbour with thirty ships. Now at this very time eighteen ships arrived from Etruria as a reinforcement for him, slipping into the harbour at night without the knowledge of the Carthaginians. Gaining this resource, Agathocles outgeneralled his enemies; ordering the allies to remain until he should have sailed out and drawn the Carthaginians into the chase, he himself, just as he had planned, put to sea from the harbour at top speed with his seventeen ships. The ships on guard pursued, but Agathocles, on seeing the Etruscans appearing from the harbour, suddenly turned his ships, took position for ramming, and pitted his ships against the barbarians. The Carthaginians, terror-stricken by the surprise and because their own triremes were cut off between the enemy fleets, fled. Thereupon the Greeks captured five ships with their crews; and the commander of the Carthaginians, when his flagship was on the point of being captured, killed himself, preferring death to the anticipated captivity. But in truth he was shown by the event to have judged unwisely; for his ship caught a favouring wind, raised its jury mast and fled from the battle.

62. Agathocles, who had no hope of ever getting the better of the Carthaginians on the sea, unexpectedly defeated them in a naval battle, and thereafter he ruled the sea and gave security to his merchants. For this reason the people of Syracuse, goods being brought to them from all sides, in place of scarcity of provisions soon enjoyed an abundance of everything. The tyrant, encouraged by the success that had been won, dispatched Leptines to plunder the country of the enemy and, in particular, that of Acragas. For Xenodocus, vilified by his political opponents because of the defeat he had suffered, was at strife with them. Agathocles therefore ordered Leptines to try to entice the man out to a battle; for, he said, it would be easy to defeat him since his army was seditious and had already been overcome. Indeed this was accomplished; for when Leptines entered the territory of Acragas and began plundering the land, Xenodocus at first kept quiet, not believing himself strong enough for battle; but when he was reproached by the citizens for cowardice, he led out his army, which in number fell little short of that of his opponents but in morale was far inferior since the citizen army had been formed amid indulgence and a sheltered way of life and the other had been trained in military service in the field and in constant campaigns. Therefore when battle was joined, Leptines quickly routed the men of Acragas and pursued them into the city; and there fell in the battle on the side of the vanquished about five hundred foot soldiers and more than fifty horsemen. Then the people of Acragas, vexed over their disasters, brought charges against Xenodocus, saying that because of him they had twice been defeated; but he, fearing the impending investigation and trial, departed to Gela.

63. Agathocles, having within a few days defeated his enemies both on land and on sea, sacrificed to the gods and gave lavish entertainments for his friends. In his drinking bouts he used to put off the pomp of tyranny and to show himself more humble than the ordinary citizens; and by seeking through a policy of this sort the goodwill of the multitude and at the same time giving men licence to speak against him in their cups he used to discover exactly the opinion of each, since through wine the truth is brought to light without concealment. Being by nature also a buffoon and a mimic, not even in the meetings of the assembly did he abstain from jeering at those who were present and from portraying certain of them, so that the common people would often break out into laughter as if they were watching one of the impersonators or conjurors. With a crowd serving as his bodyguard he used to enter the assembly unattended, unlike Dionysius the tyrant. For the latter was so distrustful of one and all that as a rule he let his hair and beard grow long so that he need not submit the most vital parts of his body to the steel of the barber; and if ever it became necessary for him to have his head trimmed, he singed off the locks, declaring that the only safety of a tyrant was distrust. Now Agathocles at the drinking bout, taking a great golden cup, said that he had not given up the potters' craft until in his pursuit of art he had produced in pottery beakers of such workmanship as this. For he did not deny his trade but on the contrary used to boast of it, claiming that it was by his own ability that in place of the most lowly position in life he had secured the most exalted one. Once when he was besieging a certain not inglorious city and people from the wall shouted, "Potter and furnace-man, when will you pay your soldiers?" he said in answer, "When I have taken this city." None the less, however, when through the jesting at drinking bouts he had discovered which of those who were flushed with wine were hostile to his tyranny he invited them individually on another occasion to a banquet, and also those of the other Syracusans who had become particularly presumptuous, in number about five hundred; and surrounding them with suitable men from his mercenaries he slaughtered them all. For he was taking very careful precautions lest, while he was absent in Libya, they should overthrow the tyranny and recall Deinocrates and the exiles. After he had made his rule secure in this way, he sailed from Syracuse.

Agathocles' crossing to Libya for the second time and his defeat (64).

64. When he arrived in Libya he found the army discouraged and in great want: deciding, therefore, that it was best to fight a battle, he encouraged the soldiers for the fray and, after leading forth the army in battle array, challenged the barbarians to combat. As infantry he had all the surviving Greeks, six thousand in number, at least as many Celts, Samnites, and Etruscans, and almost ten thousand Libyans, who, as it turned out, only sat and looked on, being always ready to change with changing conditions. In addition to these there followed him fifteen hundred horsemen and more than six thousand Libyan chariots. The Carthaginians, since they were encamped in high and inaccessible positions, decided not to risk a battle against men who had no thought of safety; but they hoped that, by remaining in their camp where they were plentifully supplied with everything, they would defeat their enemy by famine and the passage of time. Agathocles, since he could not lure them down to the plain and since his own situation forced him to do something daring and chance the result, led his army against the encampment of the barbarians. Then when the Carthaginians came out against him, even though they were far superior in number and had the advantage of the rough terrain, Agathocles held out for some time although hard pressed on every side; but afterwards, when his mercenaries and the others began to give way, he was forced to withdraw toward his camp. The barbarians, as they pressed forward stoutly, passed by the Libyans without molesting them in order to elicit their goodwill; but recognizing the Greeks and the mercenaries by their weapons, they continued to slay them until they had driven them into their own camp.

Now on this occasion about three thousand of Agathocles' men were killed; but on the following night it so happened that each army was visited by a strange and totally unexpected mishap.

The confusion that arose in the camps of both armies (65-70).

65. While the Carthaginians after their victory were sacrificing the fairest of their captives as thank-offerings to the gods by night, and while a great blaze enveloped the men who were being offered as victims, a sudden blast of wind struck them, with the result that the sacred hut, which was near the altar, caught fire, and from this the hut of the general caught and then the huts of the leaders, which were in line with it, so that great consternation and fear sprang up throughout the whole camp. Some were trapped by the conflagration while trying to put out the fire and others while carrying out their armour and the most valued of their possessions; for, since the huts were made of reeds and straw and the fire was forcibly fanned by the breeze, the aid brought by the soldiers came too late. Thus when almost the entire camp was in flames, many, caught in the passages which were narrow, were burned alive and suffered due punishment on the spot for their cruelty to the captives, the impious act itself having brought about a punishment to match it; and as for those who dashed from the camp amid tumult and shouting, another greater danger awaited them.

66. As many as five thousand of the Libyans who had been taken into Agathocles' army had deserted the Greeks and were going over by night to the barbarians. When those who had been sent out as scouts saw these men coming toward the Carthaginian camp, believing that the whole army of the Greeks was advancing ready for battle, they quickly reported the approaching force to their fellow soldiers. When the report had been spread through the whole force, there arose tumult and dread of the enemy's attack. Each man placed his hope of safety in flight; and since no order had been given by the commanders nor was there any formation, the fugitives kept running into each other. When some of them failed to recognize their friends because of the darkness and others because of fright, they fought against them as if they were enemies. A general slaughter took place; and while the misunderstanding still prevailed, some were slain in hand to hand fighting and others, who had sped away unarmed and were fleeing through the rough country, fell from cliffs, distraught in mind by the sudden panic. Finally after more than five thousand had perished, the rest of the multitude came safe to Carthage. Those in the city, who had also been deceived at that time by the report of their own people, supposed that they had been conquered in a battle and that the largest part of the army had been destroyed. Therefore in great anxiety they opened the city gates and with tumult and excitement received their soldiers, fearing lest with the last of them the enemy should burst in. When day broke, however, they learned the truth and were with difficulty freed from their expectation of disaster.

67. At this same time, however, Agathocles by reason of deceit and mistaken expectation met with similar disaster. For the Libyans who had deserted did not dare go on after the burning of the camp and the tumult that had arisen, but turned back again; and some of the Greeks, seeing them advancing and believing that the army of the Carthaginians had come, reported to Agathocles that the enemy's forces were near at hand. The dynast gave the order to take up arms, and the soldiers rushed from the camp with great tumult. Since at the same time the fire in the Carthaginian camp blazed high and the shouting of the Carthaginians became audible, the Greeks believed that the barbarians were in very truth advancing against them with their whole army. Since their consternation prevented deliberation, panic fell upon the camp and all began to flee. Then as the Libyans mingled with them and the darkness fostered and increased their uncertainty, those who happened to meet fought each other as if they were enemies. They were scattered about everywhere throughout the whole night and were in the grip of panic fear, with the result that more than four thousand were killed. When the truth was at long last discovered, those who survived returned to their camp. Thus both armies met with disaster in the way described, being tricked, according to the proverb, by the empty alarms of war.

68. Since after this misfortune the Libyans all deserted him and the army which remained was not strong enough to wage battle against the Carthaginians, Agathocles decided to leave Libya. He did not believe that he would be able to transport his soldiers since he had not prepared any transports and the Carthaginians would never permit it while they controlled the sea. He did not expect that the barbarians would agree to a truce because they were far superior in their armies and were determined by the destruction of those who had first come across to prevent others from attacking Libya. He decided, therefore, to make the return voyage with a few in secret, and he took on board with him the younger of his sons, Heracleides; for he was on his guard against Archagathus, lest at some time this son, who was on intimate terms with his step-mother and was bold by nature, should form a conspiracy against himself. Archagathus, however, suspecting his purpose watched for the sailing with care, being determined to reveal the plot to such of the leaders as would prevent the attempt; for he thought it monstrous that, although he had shared willingly in the battles, fighting in behalf of his father and brother, yet he alone should be deprived of a safe return and left behind as a victim to the enemy. He therefore disclosed to some of the leaders that Agathocles was about to sail-away in secret by night. These coming quickly together not only prevented this, but also revealed Agathocles' knavery to the rank and file; and the soldiers, becoming furious at this, seized the tyrant, bound him, and put him in custody.

69. Consequently, when discipline disappeared in the camp, there was tumult and confusion, and as night came on word was spread abroad that the enemy was near. When fright and panic fear fell upon them, each man armed himself and rushed forth from the encampment, no man giving orders. At this very time those who were guarding the tyrant, being no less frightened than the others and imagining that they were being summoned by somebody, nastily brought out Agathocles bound with chains. When the common soldiers saw him they were moved to pity and all shouted to let him go. When released, he embarked on the transport with a few followers and secretly sailed away, although this was in the winter at the season of the setting of the Pleiades [Nov. 307]. This man, then, concerned about his own safety, abandoned his sons, whom the soldiers at once slew when they learned of his escape; and the soldiers selected generals from their own number and made peace with the Carthaginians on these terms: they were to give back the cities which they held and to receive three hundred talents, and those who chose to serve with the Carthaginians were to receive pay at the regular rates, and the others, when transported to Sicily, were to receive Solus as a dwelling-place. Now, most of the soldiers abided by the terms and received what had been agreed upon; but all those who continued to occupy the cities because they still clung to hopes of Agathocles were attacked and taken by storm. Their leaders the Carthaginians crucified; the others they bound with fetters and forced them by their own labour to bring back again into cultivation the country they had laid waste during the war.

In this way, then, the Carthaginians recovered their liberty in the fourth year of the war.

70. One might well draw attention both to the almost incredible elements in Agathocles' expedition to Libya [307] and to the punishment that befell his children as if by divine providence. For although in Sicily he had been defeated and had lost the largest part of his army, in Libya with a small portion of his forces he defeated those who had previously been victorious. After he had lost all the cities in Sicily, he was besieged at Syracuse; but in Libya, after becoming master of all the other cities, he confined the Carthaginians by a siege, Fortune, as if of set purpose, displaying her peculiar power when a situation has become hopeless. After he had come to such a position of superiority and had murdered Ophelias although he was a friend and a guest, the divine power clearly showed that it established through his impious acts against Ophelias a portent of that which later befell him; for in the same month and on the same day on which he murdered Ophelias and took his army, he caused the death of his own sons and lost his own army. What is most peculiar of all, the god like a good lawgiver exacted a double punishment from him; for when he had unjustly slain one friend, he was deprived of two sons, those who had been with Ophelias laying violent hands upon the young men. Let these things, then, be said as our answer to those who scorn such matters.

Agathocles' flight to Sicily (71) and the slaughter of the Sicilians by Agathocles (71-72).

71. When with all speed Agathocles had crossed from Libya into Sicily, he summoned a part of his army and went to the city of Segesta, which was an ally. Because he was in need of money, he forced the well-to-do to deliver to him the greater part of their property, the city at that time having a population of about ten thousand. Since many were angry at this and were holding meetings, he charged the people of Segesta with conspiring against him and visited the city with terrible disasters. For instance, the poorest of the people he brought to a place outside the city beside the river Scamander and slaughtered them; but those who were believed to have more property he examined under torture and compelled each to tell him how much wealth he had; and some of them he broke on the wheel, others he placed bound in the catapults and shot forth, and by applying knucklebones with violence to some, he caused them severe pain. He also invented another torture similar to the bull of Phalaris: that is, he prepared a brazen bed that had the form of a human body and was surrounded on every side by bars; on this he fixed those who were being tortured and roasted them alive, the contrivance being superior to the bull in this respect, that those who were perishing in anguish were visible. As for the wealthy women, he tortured some of them by crushing their ankles with iron pincers, he cut off the breasts of others, and by placing bricks on the lower part of the backs of those who were pregnant, he forced the expulsion of the foetus by the pressure. While the tyrant in this way was seeking all the wealth, great panic prevailed throughout the city, some burning themselves up along with their houses, and others gaining release from life by hanging. Thus Segesta, encountering a single day of disaster, suffered the loss of all her men from youth upward. Agathocles then took the maidens and children across to Italy and sold them to the Bruttians, leaving not even the name of the city; but he changed the name to Dicaeopolis and gave it as dwelling to the deserters.

72. On hearing of the murder of his sons Agathocles became enraged at all those who had been left behind in Libya, and sent some of his friends into Syracuse to Antander his brother, ordering him to put to death all the relatives of those who had taken part in the campaign against Carthage. As Antander promptly carried out the order, there occurred the most elaborately devised massacre that had taken place up to this time; for not only did they drag out to death the brothers, fathers, and sons who were in the prime of manhood, but also the grandfathers, and even the fathers of these if such survived, men who lingered on in extreme old age and were already bereft of all their senses by lapse of time, as well as infant children borne in arms who had no consciousness whatever of the fate that was bearing down upon them. They also led away any women who were related by marriage or kinship, and in sum, every person whose punishment would bring grief to those who had been left in Libya. When a crowd, large and composed of all kinds of people, had been driven to the sea for punishment and when the executioners had taken their places beside them, weeping and prayers and wailing arose mingled together, as some of them were mercilessly slaughtered and others were stunned by the misfortunes of their neighbours and because of their own imminent fate were no better in spirit than those who were being put to death before them. What was most cruel of all, when many had been slain and their bodies had been cast out along the shore, neither kinsmen nor friend dared pay the last rites to any, fearing lest he should seem to inform on himself as one who enjoyed intimacy with those who were dead. And because of the multitude of those who had been slain beside its waves, the sea, stained with blood over a great expanse, proclaimed afar the unequalled savagery of this outrage.

Expedition of King Antigonus against Egypt with great forces (73-76).

73. When this year had passed, Coroebus became archon in Athens, [306] and in Rome Quintus Marcius and Publius Cornelius succeeded to the consulship. While these held office King Antigonus, the younger of whose sons, Phoenix, [Philip] had died, buried this son with royal honours; and, after-summoning Demetrius from Cyprus, he collected his forces in Antigonia. He had decided to make a campaign against Egypt. So he himself took command of the land army and advanced through Coelê Syria with more than eighty thousand foot soldiers, about eight thousand horsemen, and eighty-three elephants. Giving the fleet to Demetrius, he ordered him to follow along the coast in contact with the army as it advanced. In all there had been made ready a hundred and fifty warships and a hundred transports in which a large stock of ordnance was being conveyed. When the pilots thought it necessary to heed the setting of the Pleiades, which was expected to take place after eight days, Antigonus censured them as men afraid of danger; but he himself, since he was encamped at Gaza and was eager to forestall the preparations of Ptolemy, ordered his soldiers to provide themselves with ten days' rations, and loaded on the camels, which had been gathered together by the Arabs, one hundred and thirty thousand measures of grain and a good stock of fodder for the beasts; and, carrying his ordnance in wagons, he advanced through the wilderness with great hardship because many places in the region were swampy, particularly near the spot called Barathra.

74. As for Demetrius, after setting sail from Gaza about midnight, since the weather at first was calm for several days, he had his transports towed by the swifter ships; then the setting of the Pleiades overtook them and a north wind arose, so that many of the quadriremes were driven dangerously by the storm to Raphia, a city which affords no anchorage and is surrounded by shoals. Of the ships that were carrying his ordnance, some were overwhelmed by the storm and destroyed, and others ran back to Gaza; but pressing on with the strongest of the ships he held his course as far as Casium. This place is not very distant from the Nile, but it has no harbour and in the stormy season it is impossible to make a landing here. They were therefore compelled to cast their anchors and ride the waves at a distance of about two stades from the land, where they were at once encompassed by many dangers; for since the surf was breaking rather heavily, there was danger that the ships would founder with their crews, and since the shore was harbourless and in enemy hands, the ships could neither approach without danger, nor could the men swim ashore, and what was worst of all, the water for drinking had given out and they were reduced to such straits that, if the storm had continued for a single day more, all would have perished of thirst. When all were in despair and already expecting death, the wind fell, and the army of Antigonus came up and camped near the fleet. They therefore left the ships and recuperated in the camp while waiting for those vessels that had become separated. In this exposure to the waves three of the quinqueremes were lost, but some of the men from these swam to the shore. Then Antigonus led his army nearer to the Nile and camped at a distance of two stades from the river.

75. Ptolemy, who had occupied in advance the most strategic points with trustworthy garrisons, sent men in small boats, ordering them to approach the landing-place and proclaim that he would pay a premium to any who deserted Antigonus, two minae to each of the ordinary soldiers and one talent to each man who had been assigned to a position of command. When proclamations to that effect had been made, an urge to change sides fell upon the mercenaries of Antigonus, and it transpired that many even of their officers were inclined for one reason or another to desire a change. When many were going over to Ptolemy, Antigonus, stationing bowmen, slingers, and many of his catapults on the edge of the river, drove back those who were drawing near in their punts; and he captured some of the deserters and tortured them frightfully, wishing to intimidate any who were contemplating such an attempt as this. After adding to his force the ships that were late in arriving, he sailed to the place called Pseudostomon [False-Mouth], believing that he would be able to disembark some of the soldiers there. When he found at that place a strong garrison and was held in check by bolts and other missiles of every kind, he sailed away as night was closing in. Then giving orders to the pilots to follow the ship of the general, keeping their eyes fixed on its light, he sailed to the mouth of the Nile called Phatniticum; but when day came, since many of the ships had missed the course, he was forced to wait for these and to send out the swiftest of those that had followed him to search for them.

76. Since this caused considerable delay, Ptolemy, hearing of the arrival of the enemy, came quickly to reinforce his men and after drawing up his army, stationed it along the shore; but Demetrius, having failed to make this landing also and hearing that the adjacent coast was naturally fortified by swamps and marshes, retraced his course with his whole fleet. Then a strong north wind burst upon them and the billows rose high; and three of his quadriremes and in the same way some of the transports were cast violently upon the land by the waves and came into the possession of Ptolemy; but the other ships, whose crews had kept them from the shore by main force, reached the camp of Antigonus in safety. Since Ptolemy, however, had already occupied every landing-place along the river with strong guards, since many river boats had been made ready for him, and since all of these were equipped with ordnance of every kind and with men to use it, Antigonus was in no little difficulty; for his naval force was of no use to him since the Pelusiac mouth of the Nile had been occupied in advance by the enemy, and his land forces found their advance thwarted since they were checked by the width of the river, and what was of greatest importance, as many days had passed, food for the men and fodder for the beasts were falling short. Since, then, his forces for these reasons were disheartened, Antigonus called together the army and its leaders and laid before them the question whether it was better to remain and continue the war or to return for the present to Syria and later make a campaign with more complete preparation and at the time at which the Nile was supposed to be lowest. When all inclined toward the quickest possible withdrawal, he commanded the soldiers to break camp and speedily returned to Syria, the whole fleet coasting along beside him. After the departure of the enemy Ptolemy rejoiced greatly; and, when he had made a thank-offering to the gods, he entertained his friends lavishly. He also wrote to Seleucus, Lysimachus, and Cassander about his successes and about the large number of men who had deserted to him; and he himself, having finished the second struggle for Egypt and convinced that the country was his as a prize of war, returned to Alexandria.

Desertion of Pasiphilus, a general, from Agathocles (77).

77. While these events were taking place, Dionysius, the tyrant of Heraclea Pontica, died after having ruled for thirty-two years; and his sons, Oxathras and Clearchus, succeeding to his tyranny, ruled for seventeen years.

In Sicily Agathocles visited the cities that were subject to him, making them secure with garrisons and exacting money from them; for he was taking extreme precautions lest, because of the misfortunes that had befallen him, the Sicilian Greeks should make an effort to gain their independence. Indeed at that very time Pasiphilus the general, having heard of the murder of Agathocles' sons and of his reverses in Libya, regarded the tyrant with contempt; and, deserting to Deinocrates and establishing friendship with him, he both kept a firm grip on the cities which had been entrusted to him and by alluring the minds of his soldiers with hopes alienated them from the tyrant. Agathocles, now that his hopes were being curtailed in every quarter, was so cast down in spirit that he sent an embassy to Deinocrates and invited him to make a treaty on these terms: that, on the one hand, Agathocles should withdraw from his position as tyrant and restore Syracuse to its citizens, and Deinocrates should no longer be an exile, and that, on the other hand, there should be given to Agathocles two designated fortresses, Therma and Cephaloedium, together with their territories.

78. One might with good reason express wonder at this point that Agathocles, who had shown himself resolute in every other situation and had never lost confidence in himself when his prospects were at their lowest, at this time became a coward and without a fight abandoned to his enemies the tyranny for the sake of which he had previously fought many great battles, and what was the most unaccountable of all, that while he was master of Syracuse and of the other cities and had possession of ships and wealth and an army commensurate with these, he lost all power of calculating chances, recalling not one of the experiences of the tyrant Dionysius. For instance, when that tyrant had been driven into a situation that was confessedly desperate and when, because of the greatness of the impending dangers, he had given up hope of retaining his throne and was about to ride out from Syracuse into voluntary exile, Heloris, the eldest of his friends, opposing his impulse, said, "Dionysius, tyranny is a good winding-sheet;" and similarly his brother-in-law, Megacles, spoke his mind to Dionysius, saying that the man who was being expelled from a tyranny ought, to make his exit dragged by the leg and not to depart of his own free choice. Encouraged by these exhortations, Dionysius firmly faced all the emergencies that seemed formidable, and not only made his dominion greater, but when he himself had grown old amid its blessings, he left to his sons the greatest empire of Europe.

How the Carthaginians made peace with Agathocles (79).

79. Agathocles, however, buoyed up by no such consideration and failing to test his mortal hopes by experience, was on the point of abandoning his empire, great as it was, on these terms. [306] As it happened, the treaty never went into effect, ratified indeed by the policy of Agathocles, but not accepted because of the ambition of Deinocrates. The latter, having set his heart upon sole rule, was hostile to the democracy in Syracuse and was well pleased with the position of leadership that he himself then had; for he commanded more than twenty thousand foot soldiers, three thousand horsemen, and many great cities, so that, although he was called general of the exiles, he really possessed the authority of a king, his power being absolute. If he should return to Syracuse, it would inevitably be his lot to be a private citizen and be numbered as one of the many, since independence loves equality; and in the elections he might be defeated by any chance demagogue, since the crowd is opposed to the supremacy of men who are outspoken. Thus Agathocles might justly be said to have deserted his post as tyrant, and Deinocrates might be regarded as responsible for the later successes of the dynast. For Deinocrates, when Agathocles kept sending embassies to discuss the terms of peace and begging him to grant the two fortresses in which he might end his days, always trumped up specious excuses by which he cut off any hope of a treaty, now insisting that Agathocles should leave Sicily, and now demanding his children as hostages. When Agathocles discovered his purpose, he sent to the exiles and accused Deinocrates of hindering them from gaining their independence, and to the Carthaginians he sent envoys and made peace with them on terms such that the Phoenicians should regain all the cities which had formerly been subject to them, and in return for them he received from the Carthaginians gold to the value of three hundred talents of silver (or, as Timaeus says, one hundred and fifty), and two hundred thousand measures of grain.

And affairs in Sicily were in this condition.

80. In Italy the Samnites took Sora and Calatia, cities that were allied to the Romans, and enslaved the inhabitants; and the consuls with strong armies invaded Iapygia and camped near Silvium. This city was garrisoned by the Samnites, and the Romans began a siege which lasted a considerable number of days. Capturing the city by storm, they took prisoner more than five thousand persons and collected a considerable amount of booty besides. When they had finished with this, they invaded the country of the Samnites, cutting down the trees and destroying every district. For the Romans, who had for many years been fighting the Samnites for the primacy, hoped that if they deprived the enemy of their property in the country, it would force them to submit to the stronger. For this reason they devoted five months to the ruining of the enemy's land; and they burned nearly all the farm-buildings and laid waste the land, destroying everything that could produce cultivated fruit. Thereafter they declared war on the Anagnitae, who were acting unjustly, and taking Frusino they distributed the land.

How Demetrius, after laying siege to Rhodes, abandoned the siege (81-88, 91-99).

81. When this year had passed, Euxenippus became archon in Athens, [305] and in Rome Lucius Postumius and Tiberius Minucius were consuls. While these held office war arose between the Rhodians and Antigonus for some such reasons as these. The city of the Rhodians, which was strong in sea power and was the best governed city of the Greeks, was a prize eagerly sought after by the dynasts and kings, each of them striving to add her to his alliance. Seeing far in advance what was advantageous and establishing friendship with each of the dynasts separately, Rhodes took no part in their wars with each other. As a result she was honoured by each of them with regal gifts and, while enjoying peace for a long time, made great steps forward. In fact she advanced to such strength that in behalf of the Greeks she by herself undertook her war against the pirates and purged the seas of these evil-doers; and Alexander, the most powerful of men known to memory, honouring Rhodes above all cities, both deposited there the testament disposing of his whole realm and in other ways showed admiration for her and promoted her to a commanding position. At any rate, the Rhodians, having established pacts of friendship with all the rulers, carefully avoided giving legitimate grounds for complaint; but in displaying goodwill they inclined chiefly toward Ptolemy, for it happened that most of their revenues were due to the merchants who sailed to Egypt, and that in general the city drew its food supply from that kingdom.

82. Because Antigonus knew this and was intent on separating the Rhodians from their connection with Ptolemy, he first sent out envoys to them at the time when he was fighting with Ptolemy for Cyprus and asked them to ally themselves with him and to dispatch ships in company with Demetrius; and when they did not consent, he dispatched one of his generals with ships, ordering him to bring to land any merchants sailing to Egypt from Rhodes and to seize their cargoes. When this general was driven off by the Rhodians, Antigonus, declaring that they were authors of an unjust war, threatened to lay siege to the city with strong forces. The Rhodians, however, first voted great, honours for him; and, sending envoys, they begged him not to force the city to rush into the war against Ptolemy contrary to their treaties. Then, when the king-answered rather harshly and sent, his son Demetrius with an army and siege equipment, they were so frightened by the superior power of the king that at first they sent to Demetrius, saying that they would join Antigonus in the war with Ptolemy, but when Demetrius demanded as hostages a hundred of the noblest citizens and ordered also that his fleet should be received in their harbours, concluding that he was plotting against the city, they made ready for war. Demetrius, gathering all his forces in the harbour at Loryma [Caria], made his fleet ready for the attack on Rhodes. He had two hundred warships of all sizes and more than one hundred and seventy auxiliary vessels; on these were transported not quite forty thousand soldiers besides the cavalry and the pirates who were his allies. There was also an ample supply of ordnance of all sorts and a large provision of all the things necessary for a siege. In addition there accompanied him almost a thousand privately owned ships, which belonged to those who were engaged in trade; for since the land of the Rhodians had been un-plundered for many years, there had gathered together from all quarters a host of those who were accustomed to consider the misfortunes of men at war a means of enriching themselves.

83. So Demetrius, having drawn up his fleet as if for a naval battle in a way to inspire panic, sent forward his warships, which had on their prows the catapults for bolts three spans in length; and he had the transports for men and horses follow, towed by the ships that used oarsmen; and last of all came . also the cargo-ships of the pirates and of the merchants and traders, which as we have already said, were exceedingly numerous, so that the whole space between the island and the opposite shore was seen to be filled with his vessels, which brought great fear and panic to those who were watching from the city. For the soldiers of the Rhodians, occupying their several positions on the walls, were awaiting the approach of the hostile fleet, and the old men and women were looking on from their homes, since the city is shaped like a theatre; and all, being terror-stricken at the magnitude of the fleet and the gleam of the shining armour, were not a little anxious about the final outcome. Then Demetrius sailed to the island; and after disembarking his army, he took position near the city, setting up his camp out of range of missiles. He at once sent out fit and proper men from the pirates and others to plunder the island both by land and by sea. He also cut down the trees in the region near by and destroyed the farm buildings, and with this material he fortified the camp, surrounding it with a triple palisade and with great, close-set stockades, so that the loss suffered by the enemy became a protection for his own men. After this, using the whole army and the crews, he in a few days closed with a mole the space between the city and the exit, and made a port large enough for his ships.

84. For a time the Rhodians kept sending envoys and asking him to do nothing irreparable against the city; but as no one paid any heed to these, they gave up hope of a truce and sent envoys to Ptolemy, Lysimachus, and Cassander, begging them to give aid and saying that the city was fighting the war on their behalf. As to the metics and aliens who dwelt in the city, to those who wished they gave permission to join them in the fighting, and the others who were of no service they sent forth from the city, partly as a precaution against scarcity of supplies, and partly that there might be no one to become dissatisfied with the situation and try to betray the city. When they made a count of those who were able to fight, they found that there were about six thousand citizens and as many as a thousand metics and aliens. They voted also to buy from their masters any slaves who proved themselves brave men in the battle, and to emancipate and enfranchise them. They also wrote another decree, that the bodies of those who fell in the war should be given public burial and, further, that their parents and children should be maintained, receiving their support from the public treasury, that their unmarried daughters should be given dowries at the public cost, and that their sons on reaching manhood should be crowned in the theatre at the Dionysia and given a full suit of armour. When by these measures they had roused the spirits of all to endure the battles with courage, they also made what preparation was possible in regard to other matters. Since the whole people was of one mind, the rich contributed money, the craftsmen gave their skilled services for the preparation of the arms, and every man was active, each striving in a spirit of rivalry to surpass the others. Consequently, some were busy with the catapults and ballistae, others with the preparation of other equipment, some were repairing any ruined portions of the walls, and very many were carrying stones to the walls and stacking them. They even sent out three of their swiftest ships against the enemy and the merchant ships which brought provisions to him. These ships on appearing unexpectedly sank many vessels belonging to merchants who had sailed for the purpose of plundering the land for their own profit, and even hauled not a few of the ships up on the beach and burned them. As for the prisoners, those who could pay a ransom they took into the city, for the Rhodians had made an agreement with Demetrius that each should pay the other a thousand drachmae as ransom for a free man and five hundred for a slave.

85. Demetrius, who had an ample supply of everything required for setting up his engines of war, began to prepare two penthouses, one for the ballistae, the other for the catapults, each of them firmly mounted on two cargo vessels fastened together, and two towers of four storeys, exceeding in height the towers of the harbour, each of them mounted upon two ships of the same size and fastened there in such a way that as the towers advanced the support on each side upheld an equal weight. He also prepared a floating boom of squared logs studded with spikes, in order that as this was floated forward it might prevent the enemy from sailing up and ramming the ships that were carrying the engines of war. In the interval while these were receiving their finishing touches, he collected the strongest of the light craft, fortified them with planks, provided them with ports that could be closed, and placed upon them those of the catapults for bolts three palms long which had the longest range and the men to work them properly, and also Cretan archers; then, sending the boats within range, he shot down the men of the city who were building higher the walls along the harbour.

When the Rhodians saw that the entire attack of Demetrius was aimed against the harbour, they themselves also took measures for its security. They placed two machines on the mole and three upon freighters near the boom of the small harbour; in these they mounted a large number of catapults and ballistae of all sizes, in order that if the enemy should disembark soldiers on the mole or should advance his machines, he might be thwarted in his design by this means. They also placed on such cargo ships as were at anchor in the harbour platforms suitable for the catapults that were to be mounted on them.

86. After both sides had made their preparations in this way, Demetrius at first endeavoured to bring his engines of war against the harbour, but he was prevented when too rough a sea arose; later on, however, taking advantage of calm weather at night, he sailed in secretly, and after seizing the end of the mole of the great harbour he at once fortified the place, cutting it off with walls of planks and stones, and landed there four hundred soldiers and a supply of ordnance of all kinds. This point was five plethra distant from the city walls. Then at daybreak he brought his engines into the harbour with the sound of trumpets and with shouts; and with the lighter catapults, which had a long range, he drove back those who were constructing the wall along the harbour, and with the ballistae he shook or destroyed the engines of the enemy and the wall across the mole, for it was weak and low at this time. Since those from the city also fought stoutly, during that whole day both sides continued to inflict and suffer severe losses; and when night was already closing in, Demetrius by means of towboats drew his engines back out of range. The Rhodians, however, filled light boats with dry pitchy wood and placed fire in them; at first they went in pursuit and, drawing near to the engines of the enemy, lighted the wood, but afterwards, repelled by the floating boom and by the missiles, they were forced to withdraw. As the fire gained force a few put it out and sailed back with their boats, but most of them plunged into the sea as their boats were consumed. On the following day Demetrius made a similar attack by sea, but he also gave orders to assail the city at the same time by land from all sides with shouts and sound of trumpet in order to throw the Rhodians into an agony of terror because of the many distractions.

87. After carrying on this kind of siege warfare for eight days, Demetrius shattered the engines of war upon the mole by means of his heavy ballistae and weakened the curtain of the cross-wall together with the towers themselves. Some of his soldiers also occupied a part of the fortifications along the harbour; the Rhodians rallying their forces joined battle against these, and now that they outnumbered the enemy, they killed some and forced the rest to withdraw. The men of the city were aided by the ruggedness of the shore along the wall, for many large rocks lay close together beside the structure outside of the wall. Of the ships which had conveyed these soldiers no small number ran aground in their ignorance: and the Rhodians at once, after stripping off the beaks, threw dry pitchy wood into the ships and burned them. While the Rhodians were so occupied, the soldiers of Demetrius sailing up on every side placed ladders against the walls and pressed on more strongly, and the troops who were attacking from the land also joined in the struggle from every side and raised the battle cry in unison. Then indeed, since many had recklessly risked their lives, and a good number had mounted the walls, a mighty battle arose, those on the outside trying to force their way in and those in the city coming to the defence with one accord. Finally, as the Rhodians contended furiously, some of the men who had mounted were thrown down and others were wounded and captured, among whom were some of their most distinguished leaders. Since such losses had befallen those who fought from the outside, Demetrius withdrew his engines of war to his own harbour and repaired the ships and engines that had been damaged; and the Rhodians buried those of their citizens who had perished, dedicated to the gods the arms of the enemy and the beaks of the ships, and rebuilt the parts of the wall that had been overthrown by the ballistae.

88. After Demetrius had spent seven days on the repair of his engines and ships and had made all his preparations for the siege, he again attacked the harbour; for his whole effort centred upon capturing this and shutting off the people of the city from their grain supplies. When he was within range, with the fire-arrows, of which he had many, he made an attack on the ships of the Rhodians that lay at anchor, with his ballistae he shook the walls, and with his catapults he cut down any who showed themselves. Then when the attack had become continuous and terrifying, the Rhodian ship-captains, after a fierce struggle to save their ships, put out the fire-arrows, and the magistrates, since the harbour was in danger of being taken, summoned the noblest citizens to undergo the perils of war for the sake of the common safety. When many responded with alacrity, they manned the three staunchest ships with picked men, whom they instructed to try to sink with their rams the ships that carried the engines of the enemy. These men, accordingly, pushed forward although missiles in large numbers were speeding against them; and at first they broke through the iron studded boom, and then by delivering repeated blows with their rams upon the ships and filling them with water, they overthrew two of the engines; but when the third was drawn back with ropes by the men of Demetrius, the Rhodians, encouraged by their successes, pressed on into the battle more boldly than was prudent, and so, when many large ships crowded around them and the sides of their own ships had been shattered in many places by the rams, the admiral Execestus, the trierarch, and some others were disabled by wounds and captured; and as the rest of its crew jumped into the sea and swam to their own fellows, one of the ships came into the possession of Demetrius; but the other ships escaped from the battle. When the naval battle had turned out in this way, Demetrius constructed another machine three times the size of the former in height and width; but while he was bringing this up to the harbour, a violent storm from the south sprang up, which swept over the ships that were anchored and overthrew the engine. At this very time the Rhodians, shrewdly availing themselves of the situation, opened a gate and sallied out upon those who had occupied the mole. A severe battle ensued lasting for a long time; and since Demetrius could not send reinforcements because of the storm, and the Rhodians, on the other hand, were fighting in relays, the king's men were forced to lay down their arms and surrender, in number about four hundred. After the Rhodians had gained these advantages there sailed in as allies for the city one hundred and fifty soldiers from the Cnossians and more than five hundred from Ptolemy, some of whom were Rhodians serving as mercenaries in the king's army.

This was the state of the siege of Rhodes.

89. In Sicily Agathocles, since he had been unable to make terms with Deinocrates and the exiles, took the field against them with what forces he had, believing that it was necessary for him to fight a battle with them and stake everything on the result. Not more than five thousand foot soldiers followed him and horsemen to the number of eight hundred. Deinocrates and the exiles, when they saw the move made by the enemy, gladly came out to meet him in battle, being many times as strong; for their foot soldiers came to more than twenty-five thousand and their cavalry to not less than three thousand. When the armies had encamped opposite each other near the place called Torgium, and then were drawn up against each other in battle array, for a short time there was a stubborn battle because of the eagerness of both sides; but then some of those who were at odds with Deinocrates, more than two thousand in number, went over to the tyrant and were responsible for the defeat of the exiles. For those who were with Agathocles gained much more confidence, and those who were fighting on the side of Deinocrates were dismayed and, overestimating the number of the deserters, broke into flight. Then Agathocles, after pursuing them for a certain distance and refraining from slaughter, sent envoys to the defeated and asked them to put an end to the quarrel and return to their native cities; for, he said, they had found by experience that the exiles would never be able to prevail in a battle with him, seeing that even on this occasion, although they were many times more numerous, they had been defeated. Of the exiles, all the horsemen survived the flight and came safe into Ambicae; but as for the foot soldiers, although some escaped when night came on, most of them after occupying a hill made terms with Agathocles, for they had lost hope of victory by fighting and longed for their relatives and friends and for their fatherland and its comforts. Now when they had received pledges of good faith and had come down from the hill-fort, such as it was, Agathocles took their arms; and then, stationing his army about them, he shot them all down, their number being about seven thousand, as Timaeus says, but as some have written, about four thousand. Indeed, this tyrant always scorned faith and his oaths; and he maintained his own power, not by the strength of his armed forces but by the weakness of his subjects, fearing his allies more than his enemies.

How the Romans defeated the Samnites in two battles (90).

90. When he had destroyed in this manner the army that had been arrayed against him, Agathocles received any exiles who survived and, making terms with Deinocrates, appointed him general over part of his army and continued to entrust the most important matters to him. In this connection one might well wonder why Agathocles, who was suspicious of everyone and never completely trusted anybody, continued his friendship toward Deinocrates alone until death. Deinocrates, after betraying his allies, seized and slew Pasiphilus in Gela and handed the strongholds and the cities to Agathocles, spending two years in the delivery of the enemy.

In Italy the Romans defeated the Paeligni and took their land, and to some of those who seemed well disposed toward Rome, they granted citizenship. Thereafter, since the Samnites were plundering Falernitis, the consuls took the field against them, and in the battle that followed the Romans were victorious. They took twenty standards and made prisoners of more than two thousand soldiers. The consuls at once took the city of Bola, but Gellius Gaius, the leader of the Samnites, appeared with six thousand soldiers. A hard fought battle took place in which Gellius himself was made prisoner, and of the other Samnites most were cut down but some were captured alive. The consuls, taking advantage of such victories, recovered those allied cities that had been captured: Sora, Harpina, and Serennia.

91. When that year had passed, Pherecles became archon in Athens [304] and in Rome Publius Sempronius and Publius Sulpicius received the consulship; and in Elis the Olympian Games were celebrated for the one hundred and nineteenth time, at which celebration Andromenes of Corinth won the footrace. While these held office, Demetrius, who was besieging Rhodes, failing in his assaults by sea, decided to make his attacks by land. Having provided therefore a large quantity of material of all kinds, he built an engine called the helepolis, which far surpassed in size those which had been constructed before it. Each side of the square platform he made almost fifty cubits in length, framed together from squared timber and fastened with iron; the space within he divided by bars set about a cubit from each other so that there might be standing space for those who were to push the machine forward. The whole structure was movable, mounted on eight great solid wheels; the width of their rims was two cubits and these were overlaid with heavy iron plates. To permit motion to the side, pivots had been constructed, by means of which the whole device was easily moved in any direction. From each corner there extended upward beams equal in length and little short of a hundred cubits long, inclining toward each other in such a way that, the whole structure being nine storeys high, the first storey had an area of forty-three hundred square feet and the topmost storey of nine hundred. The three exposed sides of the machine he covered externally with iron plates nailed on so that it should receive no injury from fire carriers. On each storey there were ports on the front, in size and shape fitted to the individual characteristics of the missiles that were to be shot forth. These ports had shutters, which were lifted by a mechanical device and which secured the safety of the men on the platforms who were busy serving the artillery; for the shutters were of hides stitched together and were filled with wool so that they would yield to the blows of the stories from the ballistae. Each of the storeys had two wide stairways, one of which they used for bringing up what was needed and the other for descending, in order that all might be taken care of without confusion. Those who were to move the machine were selected from the whole army, three thousand four hundred men excelling in strength; some of them were enclosed within the machine while others were stationed in its rear, and they pushed it forward, the skilful design aiding greatly in its motion. He also constructed penthouses, some to protect the men who were filling the moat, others to carry rams, and covered passages through which those who were going to their labours might go and return safely. Using the crews of the ships, he cleared a space four stades wide through which he planned to advance the siege engines he had prepared, wide enough so that it covered a front of six curtains and seven towers. The number of craftsmen and labourers collected was not much less than thirty thousand.

92. As everything, therefore, because of the many hands was finished sooner than was expected, Demetrius was regarded with alarm by the Rhodians; for not only did the size of the siege engines and the number of the army which had been gathered stun them, but also the king's energy and ingenuity in conducting sieges. For, being exceedingly ready in invention and devising many things beyond the art of the master builders, he was called Poliorcetes [stormer of cities]; and he displayed such superiority and force in his attacks that it seemed that no wall was strong enough to furnish safety from him for the besieged. Both in stature and in beauty he displayed the dignity of a hero, so that even those strangers who had come from a distance, when they beheld his comeliness arrayed in royal splendour, marvelled at him and followed him as he went abroad in order to gaze at him. Furthermore, he was haughty in spirit and proud and looked down not only upon common men but also upon those of royal estate; and what was most peculiar to him, in time of peace he devoted his time to winebibbing and to drinking bouts accompanied by dancing and revels, and in general he emulated the conduct said by mythology to have been that of Dionysus among men; but in his wars he was active and sober, so that beyond all others who practised this profession he devoted both body and mind to the task. For it was in his time that the greatest weapons were perfected and engines of alt kinds far surpassing those that had existed among others; and this man launched the greatest ships after this siege and after the death of his father.

93. When the Rhodians saw the progress of the enemy's siege works, they built a second wall inside parallel to the one that was on the point of failing under the attacks. They used stones obtained by tearing down the theatre's outer wall and the adjacent houses, and also some of the temples, vowing to the gods that they would build finer ones when the city had been saved. They also sent out nine of their ships, giving the commanders orders to sail in every direction and, appearing unexpectedly, to sink some of the ships they intercepted and bring others to the city. After these had sailed out and had been divided into three groups, Damophilus, who had ships of the kind called by the Rhodians "guard-ships," sailed to Carpathos; and finding there many of Demetrius' ships, he sank some, shattering them with his rams, and some he beached and burnt after selecting the most useful men from their crews, and not a few of those that were transporting the grain from the island, he brought back to Rhodes. Menedemus, who commanded three light un-decked ships, sailed to Patara in Lycia; and finding at anchor there a ship whose crew was on shore, he set the hull on fire; and he took many of the freighters that were carrying provisions to the army and dispatched them to Rhodes. He also captured a quadrireme that was a sailing from Cilicia and had on board royal robes and the rest of the outfit that Demetrius' wife Phila had with great pains made ready and sent off for her husband. The clothing Damophilus sent to Egypt since the garments were purple and proper for a king to wear; but the ship he hauled up on land, and he sold the sailors, both those from the quadrireme and those from the other captured ships. Amyntas, who was in command of the three remaining ships, made for islands where he fell in with many freighters carrying to the enemy materials useful for the engines of war; he sank some of these and some he brought to the city. On these ships were also captured eleven famous engineers, man of outstanding skill in making missiles and catapults.

Thereafter, when an assembly had been convened, some advised that the statues of Antigonus and Demetrius should be pulled down, saying that it was absurd to honour equally their besiegers and their benefactors. At this the people were angry and censured these men as erring, and they altered none of the honours awarded to Antigonus, having made a wise decision with a view both to fame and to self interest. For the magnanimity and the soundness of this action in a democracy won plaudits from all others and repentance from the besiegers; for while the latter were setting free the cities throughout Greece, which had displayed no goodwill at all toward their benefactors, they were manifestly trying to enslave the city that in practice showed itself most constant in repaying favours; and as protection against the sudden shift of fortune if the war should result in the capture of Rhodes, the Rhodians retained as a means of gaining mercy the memory of the friendship that they had preserved. These things, then, were done prudently by the Rhodians.

94. When Demetrius had undermined the wall by using his sappers, one of the deserters informed the besieged that those who were working underground were almost within the walls. Therefore the Rhodians by digging a deep trench parallel to the wall which was expected to collapse and by quickly undertaking mining operations themselves, made contact with their opponents underground and prevented them from advancing farther. Now the mines were closely watched by both sides, and some of Demetrius' men tried to bribe Athenagoras. who had been given command of the guard by the Rhodians. This man was a Milesian by descent, sent by Ptolemy as commander of the mercenaries. Promising to turn traitor he set a day on which one of the ranking leaders should be sent from Demetrius to go by night through the mine up into the city in order to inspect the position where the soldiers would assemble, but after leading Demetrius on to great hopes, he disclosed the matter to the council; and when the king sent one of his friends, Alexander the Macedonian, the Rhodians captured him as he came up through the mine. They crowned Athenagoras with a golden crown and gave him a gift of five talents of silver, their object being to stimulate loyalty to the city on the part of the other men who were mercenaries and foreigners.

95. Demetrius, when his engines of war were completed and all the space before the walls was cleared, stationed the helepolis in the centre, and assigned positions to the penthouses, eight in number, which were to protect the sappers. He placed four of these on each side of the helepolis and connected with each of them one covered passage so that the men who were going in and out might accomplish their assigned tasks in safety; and he brought up also two enormous penthouses in which battering rams were mounted. For each shed held a ram with a length of one hundred and twenty cubits, sheathed with iron and striking a blow like that of a ship's ram; and the ram was moved with ease, being mounted on wheels and receiving its motive power in battle from not less than a thousand men. When he was ready to advance the engines against the walls, he placed on each storey of the helepolis ballistae and catapults of appropriate size, stationed his fleet in position to attack the harbours and the adjacent areas, and distributed his infantry along such parts of the wall as could be attacked. Then, when all at a single command and signal had raised the battle cry together, he launched attacks on the city from every side. While he was shaking the walls with the rams and the ballistae, Cnidian envoys arrived, asking him to withhold his attack and promising to persuade the Rhodians to accept the most feasible of his demands. The king broke off the attack, and the envoys carried on negotiations back and forth at great length; but in the end they were not able to reach any agreement, and the siege was actively resumed. Demetrius also overthrew the strongest of the towers, which was built of squared stones, and shattered the entire curtain, so that the forces in the city were not able to maintain a thoroughfare on the battlements at this point.

96. At this same period King Ptolemy dispatched to the Rhodians a large number of supply ships in which were three hundred thousand measures of grain and legumes. While these ships were on their way to the city, Demetrius attempted to dispatch ships to bring them to his own camp, but a wind favourable to the Egyptians sprang up, and they were carried along with full sails and brought into the friendly harbours, but those sent out by Demetrius returned with their mission unaccomplished. Cassander also sent to the Rhodians ten thousand measures of barley, and Lysimachus sent them forty thousand measures of wheat and the same amount of barley. Consequently, when those in the city obtained such large supplies, the besieged, who were already disheartened, regained their courage. Deciding that it would be advantageous to attack the siege engines of the enemy, they made ready a large supply of fire-bearing missiles and placed all their ballistae and catapults upon the wall. When night had fallen, at about the second watch, they suddenly began to strike the helepolis with an unremitting shower of the fire missiles, and by using other missiles of all kinds, they shot down any who rushed to the spot. Since the attack was unforeseen, Demetrius, alarmed for the siege works that had been constructed, hurried to the rescue. The night was moonless; and the fire missiles shone bright as they hurtled violently through the air; but the catapults and ballistae, since their missiles were invisible, destroyed many who were not able to see the impending stroke. It also happened that some of the iron plates of the helepolis were dislodged, and where the place was laid bare the fire missiles rained upon the exposed wood of the structure. Therefore Demetrius, fearing that the fire would spread and the whole machine be ruined, came quickly to the rescue, and with the water that had been placed in readiness on the platforms he tried to put out the spreading fire. He finally assembled by a trumpet signal the men who were assigned to move the apparatus and by their efforts dragged the machine beyond range.

97. Then when day had dawned he ordered the camp followers to collect the missiles that had been hurled by the Rhodians, since he wished to estimate from these the armament of the forces within the city. Quickly carrying out his orders, they counted more than eight hundred fire missiles of various sizes and not less than fifteen hundred catapult bolts. Since so many missiles had been hurled in a short time at night, he marvelled at the resources possessed by the city and at their prodigality in the use of these weapons.

Next Demetrius repaired such of his works as had been damaged, and devoted himself to the burial of the dead and the care of the wounded. Meanwhile the people of the city, having gained a respite from the violent attacks of the siege engines, constructed a third crescent-shaped wall and included in its circuit every part of the wall that was in a dangerous condition; but none the less they dug a deep moat around the fallen portion of the wall so that the king should not be able to break into the city easily by an assault, with a heavily armed force. They also sent out some of their fastest ships, installing Amyntas as commander; he, sailing to Peraea in Asia, suddenly confronted some pirates who had been sent out by Demetrius. These had three deck-less ships and were supposed to be the strongest of the pirates who were fighting as allies of the king. In the brief naval battle that ensued, the Rhodians overpowered the foe and took the ships with their crews, among whom was Timocles, the chief pirate. They also encountered some of the merchants and, seizing a fair number of light craft loaded with grain, they sent these and the un-decked ships of the pirates to harbour in Rhodes by night, escaping the notice of the enemy. Demetrius, after he had repaired such of his equipment as was damaged, brought his siege engines up to the wall. By using all his missiles without stint, he drove back those who were stationed on the battlements, and striking with his rams a continuous portion of the wall, he overthrew two curtains; but as the city's forces fought obstinately for the tower that was between them, there were bitter and continuous encounters, one after another, with the result that their leader Ananias was killed fighting desperately and many of the soldiers were slain also.

98. While these events were taking place, King-Ptolemy sent to the Rhodians grain and other supplies in no less quantity than those formerly sent, and fifteen hundred soldiers, whose leader was Antigonus, the Macedonian. At this very time there came to Demetrius more than fifty envoys from the Athenians and the other Greek cities, all of them asking the king to come to terms with the Rhodians. A truce, therefore, was made; but although many arguments of all sorts were presented to the city and to Demetrius, they could in no way agree; and so the envoys returned without accomplishing their aim.

Demetrius, having determined to attack the city at night through the breach in the wall, selected the strongest of his fighting men and of the rest those fitted for his purpose to the number of fifteen hundred. These, then, he ordered to advance to the wall in silence during the second watch; as for himself, when he had made his preparations, he gave orders to those stationed on each side that when he gave the signal they should raise the battle cry and make attacks both by land and sea. When they all carried out the order, those who had advanced against breaches in the walls, after dispatching the advance guards at the moat, charged past into the city and occupied the region of the theatre; but the magistrates of the Rhodians, learning what had happened and seeing that the whole city had been thrown into confusion, sent orders to those at the harbour and the walls to remain at their own posts and oppose the enemy outside if he should attack; and they themselves, with their contingent of selected men and the soldiers who had recently sailed in from Alexandria, attacked the troops who had got within the walls. When day returned and Demetrius raised the ensign, those who were attacking the port and those who had been stationed about the wall on all sides shouted the battle cry, giving encouragement to the men who had occupied part of the region of the theatre; but in the city the throng of children and women were in fear and tears, thinking that their native city was being taken by storm. Nevertheless, fighting began between those who had made their way within the wall and the Rhodians, and many fell on both sides. At first neither side withdrew from its position; but afterwards, as the Rhodians constantly added to their numbers and were prompt to face danger, as is the way with men fighting for their native land and their most precious things, and on the other hand the king's men were in distress, Alcimus and Mantias, their commanders, expired after receiving many wounds, most of the others were killed in hand-to-hand fighting or were captured, and only a few escaped to the king and survived. Many also of the Rhodians were slain, among whom was the president Damoteles, who had won great acclaim for his valour.

99. When Demetrius realized that Fortune had snatched from his hand the capture of the city, he made new preparations for the siege. When his father thereafter wrote to him to come to terms with the Rhodians as best he could, he awaited a favourable opportunity that would provide a specious excuse for the settlement. Since Ptolemy had written to the Rhodians, first saying that he would send them a great quantity of grain and three thousand soldiers, but then advising them, if it should be possible, to make equitable terms with Antigonus, everyone inclined toward peace. At just this time the Aetolian League sent envoys to urge a settlement, and the Rhodians came to terms with Demetrius on these conditions: that the city should be autonomous and un-garrisoned and should enjoy its own revenue; that the Rhodians should be allies of Antigonus unless he should be at war with Ptolemy; and that they should give as hostages a hundred of their citizens whom Demetrius should select, those holding office being exempt.

How Demetrius sailed from Rhodes to Greece and freed most of the cities (100, 102-103).

100. In this way, then, the Rhodians, after they had been besieged for a year, brought the war to an end. Those who had proved themselves brave men in the battles they honoured with the prizes that were their due, and they granted freedom and citizenship to such slaves as had shown themselves courageous. They also set up statues of King Cassander and King Lysimachus, who though they held second place in general opinion, yet had made great contributions to the salvation of the city. In the case of Ptolemy, since they wanted to surpass his record by repaying his kindness with a greater one, they sent a sacred mission into Libya to ask the oracle at Ammon if it, advised the Rhodians to honour Ptolemy as a god. Since the oracle approved, they dedicated in the city a square precinct, building on each of its sides a portico a stade long, and this they called the Ptolemaeum. They also rebuilt the theatre, the fallen portions of the walls, and the buildings that had been destroyed in the other quarters in a manner more beautiful than before.

Now that Demetrius, in accordance with injunctions of his father, had made peace with the Rhodians, he sailed out with his whole force; and after passing through the islands, he put in at Aulis in Boeotia. Since he was intent on freeing the Greeks (for Cassander and Polyperchon having up to this time enjoyed impunity were engaged in plundering the greater part of Greece), he first freed the city of the Chalcidians, which was garrisoned by Boeotians, and by striking fear into the Boeotians, he forced them to renounce their friendship with Cassander; and after this he made an alliance with the Aetolians and began bis preparations for carrying on war against Polyperchon and Cassander.

While these events were taking place, Eumelus, the king of Bosporus, died in the sixth year of his reign, and his son Spartaeus succeeded to the throne and reigned for twenty years.

How Agathocles unjustly exacted money from the
Liparaeans and lost the ships in which the money was (101).

How the Romans reduced the tribe of the Aecli and made
peace with the Samnites (101).

101. Now that we have carefully passed in review the happenings in Greece and Asia, we shall turn our narrative toward the other parts of the inhabited world.

In Sicily, although the inhabitants of the Liparaean Islands were at peace with him, Agathocles sailed against them without warning and exacted from men who had done him no prior injury whatever, fifty talents of silver. To many, indeed, what I am about to relate seemed the work of a god, since his crime received its brand from the divinity. When the Liparaeans begged him to grant them time for what was lacking in the payment and said that they had never turned the sacred offerings to profane uses, Agathocles forced them to give him the dedications in the Prytaneum, of which some bore inscriptions to Aeolus and some to Hephaestus; and taking these he at once sailed away. A wind came up and the eleven of his ships that were carrying the money were sunk, and so it seemed to many that the god who was said in that region to be master of the winds at once on his first voyage exacted punishment from him, and that at the end Hephaestus punished him in his own country in a way that matched the tyrant's impious actions and the god's own name by burning him alive on hot coals; for it belonged to the same character and the same justice to refrain from touching those who were saving their own parents on Aetna, and with his proper power to search after those who had been guilty of impiety toward his shrine.

However, as regards the disaster that befell Agathocles, when we come to the proper time, the action itself will confirm what we now have said; but we must now tell of events in the adjacent parts of Italy.

The Romans and the Samnites interchanged envoys and made peace after having fought for twenty-two years and six months; and one of the consuls, Publius Sempronius, invading the country of the Aecli with an army, captured forty cities in a total of fifty days, and after forcing the entire tribe to submit to Rome, returned home and celebrated a triumph with great applause. The Roman people made alliances with the Marsi, the Paligni. and the Marrucini.

102. When the year had come to its end, Leostratus was archon in Athens, [303] and in Rome the consuls were Servius Cornelius and Lucius Genucius. While these held office Demetrius proposed to carry on his war with Cassander and to free the Greeks; and first he planned to establish order in the affairs of Greece, for he believed that the freeing of the Greeks would bring him great honour, and at the same time he thought it necessary to wipe out Prepelaüs and the other leaders before attacking Cassander, and then to go on against Macedonia itself if Cassander did not march against him. Now the city of Sicyon was garrisoned by King Ptolemy's soldiers, commanded by a very distinguished general, Philip. Attacking this city suddenly by night, Demetrius broke his way inside the walls. Then the garrison fled to the acropolis, but Demetrius took possession of the city and occupied the region between the houses and the acropolis. While he hesitated to bring up his siege engines, the garrison in panic surrendered the acropolis on terms and the men themselves sailed off to Egypt. After Demetrius had moved the people of Sicyon into their acropolis, he destroyed the part of the city adjacent to the harbour, since its site was quite insecure; then, after he had assisted the common people of the city in building their houses and had re-established free government for them, he received divine honours from those whom he had benefited; for they called the city Demetrias, and they voted to celebrate sacrifices and public festivals and also games in his honour every year and to grant him the other honours of a founder. Time, however, whose continuity has been broken by changes of conditions, has invalidated these honours: but the people of Sicyon, having thus obtained a much better location, continue to live there down to our times. For the enclosed area of the acropolis is level and of ample size, and it is surrounded on all sides by cliffs difficult to scale, so that on no side can engines of war be brought near; moreover, it has plenty of water by the aid of which they developed rich gardens, so that the king in his design seems to have made excellent provision both for comfort in time of peace and for safety in time of war.

103. After Demetrius had settled the affairs of the people of Sicyon, he set out with his whole army for Corinth, which was held by Prepelaüs, a general of Cassander. At first, after he had been admitted at night by certain citizens through a postern gate. Demetrius gained possession of the city and its harbours. The garrison, however, fled, some to the place called Sisyphium [on Acrocorinth], some to Acrocorinth; but he brought up engines of war to the fortifications and took Sisyphium by storm after suffering heavy losses. Then, when the men there fled to those who had occupied Acrocorinth, he intimidated them also and forced them to surrender the citadel; for this king-was exceedingly irresistible in his assaults, being particularly skilled in the construction of siege equipment. Be that as it may, when once he had freed the Corinthians he brought a garrison into Acrocorinth, since the citizens wished the city to be protected by the king until the war with Cassander should be brought to an end. Prepelaüs, ignominiously driven out of Corinth, withdrew to Cassander, but Demetrius, advancing into Achaia, took Bura by storm and restored autonomy to its citizens; then, capturing Scyrus in a few days, he cast out its garrison. After this, making a campaign against Arcadian Orchomenus, he ordered the garrison commander, Strombichus, to surrender the city. When he paid no attention to the orders but even poured much abuse upon him from the wall in an insulting manner, the king brought up engines of war, overthrew the walls, and took the city by storm. As for Strombichus, who had been made garrison-commander by Polyperchon, and at least eighty of the others who were hostile to him, Demetrius crucified them in front of the city, but having captured at least two thousand of the other mercenaries, he incorporated them with his own men. After the capture of this city, those who commanded the forts in the vicinity, assuming that it was impossible to escape the might of the king, surrendered the strongholds to him. In like fashion those also who guarded the cities withdrew of their own accord, since Cassander, Prepelaüs, and Polyperchon failed to come to their aid but Demetrius was approaching with a great army and with overwhelming engines of war.

This was the situation of Demetrius.

What Cleonymus did in Italy (104-105).

104. In Italy the people of Tarentum were waging war with the Lucanians and the Romans; and they sent envoys to Sparta asking for assistance and for Cleonymus as general. When the Lacedaemonians willingly granted them the leader whom they requested and the Tarentines sent money and ships,

Cleonymus enrolled five thousand mercenaries at Taenarum in Laconia and sailed at once to Tarentum. After collecting there other mercenaries no less in number than those previously enrolled, he also enlisted more than twenty thousand citizens as foot-soldiers and two thousand as mounted troops. He won the support also of most of the Greeks in Italy and of the tribe of the Messapians. Then, since he had a strong army under his command, the Lucanians in alarm established friendship with the Tarentines; and when the people of Metapontum did not come over to him, he persuaded the Lucanians to invade the territory of the Metapontines and, by making a simultaneous attack himself, intimidated them. Then,entering their city as a friend, he exacted more than six hundred talents of silver; and he took two hundred maidens of the best families as hostages, not so much as a guarantee of the city's faith as to satisfy his own lust. Indeed, having discarded the Spartan garb, he lived in continued luxury and made slaves of those who had trusted in him; for although he had so strong an army and such ample supplies, he did nothing worthy of Sparta. He planned to invade Sicily as if to overthrow the tyranny of Agathocles and restore their independence to the Siciliots; but postponing this campaign for the present, he sailed to Corcyra, and after getting possession of the city exacted a great sum of money and installed a garrison, intending to use this place as a base and to await a chance to take part in the affairs in Greece.

105. But soon, when envoys did come to him both from Demetrius Poliorcetes and from Cassander proposing alliances, he joined with neither of them; but when he learned that the Tarentines and some of the others were in revolt, he left an adequate garrison in Corcyra, and with the rest of his army sailed at top speed to Italy in order to punish those who defied his commands. Putting in to land in the district that was defended by the barbarians, he took the city, sold its people into slavery, and plundered the countryside. He likewise took by siege the city called Triopium, capturing about three thousand prisoners. At this very time the barbarians throughout the region came together and attacked his camp by night, and in the battle that took place they slew more than two hundred of Cleonymus' men and made prisoners about a thousand. A storm rising at the time of the battle destroyed twenty of the ships that lay at anchor near his encampment. Having met with two such disasters, Cleonymus sailed away to Corcyra with his army.

For what reasons Cassander and Lysimachus, and likewise Seleucus and Ptolemy, combined and made war on Antigonus (106).

106. When this year had passed, Nicocles was archon in Athens, [302] and in Rome Marcus Livius and Marcus Aemilius received the consulship. While these held office, Cassander, the king of the Macedonians, on seeing that the power of the Greeks was increasing and that the whole war was directed against Macedonia, became much alarmed about the future. He therefore sent envoys into Asia to Antigonus, asking him to come to terms with him. When Antigonus replied that he recognized only one basis for a settlement, Cassander's surrender of whatever he possessed, Cassander was alarmed and summoned Lysimachus from Thrace to take concerted action in regard to their highest interests; for it was his invariable custom when facing the most alarming situations to call on Lysimachus for assistance, both because of his personal character and because his kingdom lay next to Macedonia. When these kings had taken counsel together about their common interest, they sent envoys to Ptolemy, the king of Egypt, and to Seleucus, who was ruler of the upper satrapies, revealing the arrogance of Antigonus' answer and showing that the danger arising from the war was common to all. For they said, if Antigonus should gain control of Macedonia, he would at once take their kingdoms from the others also; indeed he had given proof many times that he was grasping and regarded any command as a possession not to be shared. It would therefore, they said, be advantageous for all to make plans in common and jointly undertake a war against Antigonus. Now Ptolemy and Seleucus, believing that the statements were true, eagerly agreed and arranged with Cassander to assist one another with strong forces.

Campaign of Cassander into Thessaly against. Demetrius, and of Lysimachus into Asia (107).

Revolt of the generals Docimus and Phoenix from Antigonus (107).

107. Cassander, however, thought it best not to await the attack of his enemies but to get the start of them by opening the campaign himself and seizing what he could use to advantage. Therefore Cassander gave to Lysimachus a part of his army and sent with it Prepelaüs as general, while he himself moved with the rest of the army into Thessaly to carry on the war with Demetrius and the Greeks. Lysimachus with his army crossed from Europe to Asia, and since the inhabitants of Lampsacus and Parium came over to him willingly, he left them free, but when he took Sigeum by force, he installed a garrison there. Next, giving his general Prepelaüs six thousand foot-soldiers and a thousand horse, he sent him to win over the cities throughout Aeolis and Ionia; as for himself, he first attempted to invest Abydus and set about preparing missiles and engines and the other equipment: but when there arrived by sea to assist the besieged a large body of soldiers sent by Demetrius, a force sufficient to secure the safety of the city, he gave up this attempt and won over Hellespontine Phrygia, and also laid siege to the city of Synnada, which possessed a great royal treasure. It was at this very time that he even persuaded Docimus, the general of Antigonus, to make common cause with him, and by his aid he took Synnada and also some of the strongholds that held the royal wealth. Prepelaüs, the general who had been sent by Lysirnachus to Aeolis and Ionia, mastered Adramyttium as he passed by, and then, laying siege to Ephesus and frightening its inhabitants, he took the city. The hundred Rhodian hostages whom he found there he sent back to their native land; and he left the Ephesians free but burned all the ships in the harbour, since the enemy controlled the sea and the whole outcome of the war was uncertain. After this he secured the adherence of the people of Teos and of Colophon, but since reinforcements came by sea to Erythrae and Clazomenae, he could not capture these cities; however, he plundered their territory and then set out for Sardis. There, by persuading Antigonus' general Phoenix to desert the king, he gained control of the city except the acropolis; for Philip, one of the friends of Antigonus, who was guarding the citadel, held firm his loyalty toward the man who had placed trust in him.

The affairs of Lysimachus were in this position.

How Antigonus, taking the field against Lysimachus, was far superior to him in military might (108-109).

108. Antigonus, who had made preparations to celebrate great games and a festival in Antigonia, had collected from all sides the most famous athletes and artists to compete for great prizes and fees. When he heard of the crossing of Lysimachus and the desertion of his own generals, he abandoned the games but distributed to the athletes and artists not less than two hundred talents as compensation. He himself taking his army set out from Syria and made a rapid march against the enemy. Arriving at Tarsus in Cilicia, he paid the army for three months from the money he had brought down from Cyinda. Apart from this fund, he was carrying three thousand talents with the army in order that he might have this provision whenever he had need of money. Then, crossing the Taurus Range, he marched toward Cappadocia; and, advancing upon those who had deserted him in upper Phrygia and Lycaonia, he restored them again to the former alliance. At this very time Lysimachus, on hearing of the presence of the enemy, held a council considering how he ought to meet the approaching dangers. They decided not to join in battle until Seleucus should come down from the upper satrapies, but to occupy strong positions and, after making their encampment safe with-palisade and ditch, to await the onslaught of the enemy. They therefore carried out their decision with vigour; but Antigonus, when he came near the enemy, drew up his army and challenged them to battle. When no one dared to issue forth, he himself occupied certain places through which it was necessary that the provisions for his opponents should be transported; and Lysimachus, fearing that if their food supply should be cut off, they would then be at the mercy of the enemy, broke camp at night, made a forced march of four hundred stades, and camped near Dorylaeum; for the stronghold had an ample store of grain and other supplies, and a river ran by it that could give protection to those who camped beside it. Pitching camp, they strengthened their encampment with a deep ditch and a triple stockade.

How he summoned his son Demetrius from Greece (109, 111).

109. When Antigonus learned of the departure of the enemy he at once pursued them; and, after he had approached their encampment, since they did not come out for battle, he began to surround their camp with a trench, and he sent for catapults and missiles, intending to storm it. When shots were exchanged about the excavation and Lysimachus' men tried to drive away with missiles those who were working, in every case Antigonus had the better of it. Then as time passed and the work was already nearing completion, since food was growing scarce for the besieged, Lysimachus, after waiting for a stormy night, set out from the camp and departed through the higher land to go into winter quarters. When at daybreak Antigonus saw the departure of the enemy, he himself marched parallel with them through the plains. Great rainstorms occurred, with the result that, as the country had deep soil and became very muddy, he lost a considerable number of his pack animals and a few of his men, and in general the whole army was in serious difficulty. Therefore the king, both because he wished to restore his soldiers after their sufferings and because he saw that the winter season was at hand, gave up the pursuit; and selecting the places best suited for wintering, he divided his army into sections. When he learned that Seleucus was coming down from the upper satrapies with a great force, he sent some of his friends into Greece to Demetrius, bidding him come to him with his army as soon as possible; for, since all the kings had united against him, he was taking every precaution not to be forced to decide the whole war in battle before the army in Europe came to join him. Similarly Lysimachus also divided his army in order to go into winter quarters in the plain called that of Salonia. He obtained ample supplies from Heraclea, having made a marriage alliance with the Heracleotes; for he had married Amestris, the daughter of Oxyartes and niece of King Darius. She had been wife of Craterus, given him by Alexander, and at the time in question was ruler of the city.

Such was the situation in Asia.

110. In Greece Demetrius, who was tarrying in Athens, was eager to be initiated and to participate in the mysteries at Eleusis. Since it was a considerable time before the legally established day on which the Athenians were accustomed to celebrate the mysteries, he persuaded the people because of his benefactions to change the custom of their fathers, and so, giving himself over unarmed to the priests, he was initiated before the regular day and departed from Athens. First he gathered together his fleet and his land army in Chalcis of Euboea; then, learning that Cassander had already occupied the passes in advance, he gave up the attempt to advance into Thessaly by land, but sailed along the coast with the army into the port of Larisa [Cremaste]. Disembarking the army, he captured the city at once; and taking the acropolis, he imprisoned the garrison and put them under guard, but he restored their autonomy to the people of Larisa. Thereafter he won over Antrones and Pteleum, and when Cassander would have transported the people of Dium and Orchomenus into Thebes, he prevented the transplanting of the cities. When Cassander saw that Demetrius' undertakings were prospering, he first protected Pherae and Thebes with stronger garrisons; and then, after collecting his whole army into one place, he encamped over against Demetrius. He had in all twenty-nine thousand foot-soldiers and two thousand horsemen. Demetrius was followed by fifteen hundred horsemen, not less than eight thousand Macedonian foot-soldiers, mercenaries to the number of fifteen thousand, twenty-five thousand from the cities throughout Greece, and at least eight thousand of the light armed troops and of the freebooters of all sorts who had gathered for the fighting and the plundering; so that there were in all about fifty-six thousand foot-soldiers. For many days the camps were pitched opposite each other, and the battle lines were drawn up on both sides, but neither came forward into battle since each was awaiting the decision of the whole matter that would take place in Asia. Demetrius, however, when the people of Pherae called upon him, entering their city with part of his army and taking the citadel, dismissed the soldiers of Cassander on terms and restored their liberty to the people of Pherae.

111. While affairs in Thessaly were in this state, there came to Demetrius the messengers sent by Antigonus, accurately detailing the orders of his father and bidding him take his army across into Asia as swiftly as possible. Since he regarded obedience to his father's orders as obligatory, the king came to terms with Cassander, making the condition that the agreements should be valid only if they were acceptable to his father; for although he very well knew that his father would not accept them since he had definitely made up his mind to bring to an end by force of arms the war which had set in, yet Demetrius wished to make his withdrawal from Greece appear respectable and not like a flight. Indeed, it was written among other conditions in the agreement that the Greek cities were to be free, not only those of Greece but also those of Asia. Then Demetrius, after preparing ships for the transportation of the soldiers and the equipment, set sail with his whole fleet and, going through the islands, put in at Ephesus. Disembarking his army and camping near the walls, he forced the city to return to its former status; then he dismissed on terms the garrison that had been introduced by Prepelaüs, the general of Lysimachus, and after stationing his own garrison on the acropolis, he went on to the Hellespont. He also recovered Lampsacus and Parium, likewise some of the other cities that had changed sides: and when he arrived at the entrance of the Pontus, he constructed a camp beside the shrine of the Chalcedonians and left to guard the region three thousand foot-soldiers and thirty warships. Then he sent the rest of the army into winter quarters, dividing it, among the cities.

At about this time Mithridates [II of Cius], who was subject to Antigonus but appeared to be shifting his allegiance to Cassander, was slain at Cius in Mysia after having ruled that city and Myrlea for thirty-five years; and Mithridates [III], inheriting the kingdom, added many new subjects and was king of Cappadocia and Paphlagonia for thirty-six years.

112. In these same days Cassander, after the departure of Demetrius, took possession of the cities of Thessaly and sent Pleistarchus with an army into Asia to aid Lysimachus. Those sent with him were twelve thousand foot-soldiers and five hundred horsemen. When Pleistarchus came to the entrance of the Pontus, he found that the region had already been taken over by the enemy and, abandoning the crossing, he turned aside to Odessus, which lies between Apollonia and Callantia, directly opposite to Heraclea on the opposite shore, where a part of the army of Lysimachus was quartered. Since he did not have ships enough for transporting his soldiers, he divided his army into three contingents. Now the first force sent out came safe to Heraclea, but the second was captured by the guard-ships at the entrance to the Pontus. When Pleistarchus himself set sail with the third group, so great a tempest rose that most of the vessels and the men on them were lost; and indeed the large warship that carried the general sank, and of the not less than five hundred men who sailed in her, only thirty-three were saved. Among these was Pleistarchus who, holding to a piece of wreckage, was cast ashore half dead. He was carried to Heraclea and after recovering from the misfortune went to Lysimachus at winter quarters, having lost the larger part of his army.

How Ptolemy subdued the cities of Coelê Syria; and how Seleucus made an expedition from the upper satrapies as far as Cappadocia (113).

Dispersion of all the armies for wintering (113).

113. During these same days King Ptolemy, setting out from Egypt with an army of considerable size, subjugated all the cities of Coelê Syria; but while he was besieging Sidon certain men came to him with the false report that a battle had taken place between the kings in which Lysimachus and Seleucus had been defeated, that they had withdrawn to Heraclea, and that Antigonus, after winning the victory, was advancing with an army against Syria. Consequently Ptolemy, deceived by them and believing that their report was true, made a four-month's truce with the Sidonians, secured with garrisons the cities that he had captured, and went back to Egypt with his army. At the same time as this was taking place, some of the soldiers of Lysimachus, having left their winter quarters as deserters, went over to Antigonus, namely two thousand Autariatae and about eight hundred Lycians and Pamphylians. Now Antigonus, receiving these men in kindly fashion, not only gave them the pay which they said was due them from Lysimachus but also honoured them with gifts. At this time Seleucus also arrived, having crossed over from the upper satrapies into Cappadocia with a large army, and after making huts for the soldiers he went into winter quarters near by. He had foot-soldiers to the number of about twenty thousand, about twelve thousand horsemen including Iris mounted archers, four hundred and eighty elephants, and more than a hundred scythed chariots.

In this way, then, the forces of the kings were being-gathered together, since they all had determined to decide the war by force of arms during the coming summer. But, as we proposed in the beginning, we shall make the war that these kings waged against each other for supreme rule the beginning of the following book.

BOOK XXI FRAGMENTS

1. 4a. All vice should be shunned by men of intelligence, but especially greed, for this vice, because of the expectation of profit, prompts many to injustice and becomes the cause of very great evils to mankind. Hence, since it is a very *metropolis* of unjust acts, it-brings many great misfortunes not only on private citizens but even on the greatest kings.

King Antigonus, who rose from private station to high power and became the mightiest king of his day, was not content with the gifts of Fortune, but undertook to bring unjustly into his own hands the kingdoms of all the others; thus he lost his own dominion and was deprived of life as well.

Ptolemy, Seleucus, and Lysimaehus united against King Antigonus; not so much prompted by goodwill towards one another as compelled by the fears each had for himself, they moved readily to make common cause in the supreme struggle.

In the battle, the elephants of Antigonus and Lysimaehus fought as if nature had matched them equally in courage and strength.

[After this certain Chaldaeans approached Antigonus and prophesied that if he should let Seleucus out of his grasp, it would come to pass that all Asia would be made subject to Seleucus, and that Antigonus himself would die in battle against him. . . . This stirred him deeply . . . for he was impressed by the reputation that the men enjoyed. . . . They are in fact reputed to have prophesied to Alexander that if he entered Babylon, he would die. And just as in the case of Alexander, it came about that the prophecy concerning Seleucus was fulfilled according to the pronouncements of these men. Of this prophecy we shall speak in detail when we come to the proper period.]

Antigonus, king of Asia, made war against a coalition of four kings, Ptolemy, son of Lagus, king of Egypt, Seleucus, king of Babylonia, Lysimaehus, king of Thrace, and Cassander, son of Antipater, king of Macedonia. When he engaged them in battle, he was pierced by many missiles, and his body was carried from the field and was buried with royal honours. His son Demetrius, however, joining his mother Stratonicê, who had remained in Cilicia with all their valuables, sailed to Salamis in Cyprus, since it was in his possession.

As for Seleucus, after the partition of the kingdom of Antigonus, he took his army and went to Phoenicia, where, in accordance with the terms of the agreement, he endeavoured to appropriate Coelê Syria, but Ptolemy had already occupied the cities of that region, and was denouncing Seleucus because, although he and Ptolemy were friends, Seleucus had accepted the assignment to his own share of a district that was already subject to Ptolemy; in addition, he accused the kings of giving him no part of the conquered territory, even though he had been a partner in the war against Antigonus. To these charges Seleucus replied that it was only just that those who were victorious on the battlefield should dispose of the spoils; but in the matter of Coelê Syria, for friendship's sake he would not for the present interfere, but would consider later how best to deal with friends who chose to encroach.

[It so happened, however, that the city did not long abide, for Seleucus tore it down and transferred its population to the city that he had founded and called

Seleuceia after himself. As for these matters, we shall set them forth exactly and in detail when we come to the proper period.]

If anyone, is eager to know about the colonies sent out to this region from Greece, there are painstaking accounts of the matter by Strabo the geographer, Phlegon, and Diodorus of Sicily.

2. When Corcyra was being besieged on land and sea by Cassander, king of Macedonia, and was on the point of capture, it was delivered by Agathocles, king of Sicily, who set fire to the entire Macedonian fleet.

The utmost spirit of rivalry was not lacking on either side, for the Macedonians were bent on saving their ships, while the Siceliotes wished not only to be regarded as victors over the Carthaginians and the barbarians of Italy, but also to show themselves in the Greek arena as more than a match for the Macedonians, whose spears had subjugated both Asia and Europe.

Had Agathocles, after landing his army, attacked the enemy, who were near at hand, he would easily have crushed the Macedonians; but since he was ignorant of the message that had been received and of the consternation of the men, he was satisfied, after landing his forces, to set up a trophy, and thus to prove the truth of the proverb, "Many are the futilities of warfare." For misapprehension and deceit often accomplish as much as armed action.

3. When, on his return from Corcyra, Agathocles rejoined the army that he had left behind, and learned that in his absence the Ligurians and Etruscans had mutinously demanded their pay from his son Agatharchus, he put them all to death, to the number of at least two thousand. This action alienated the Bruttians, whereupon Agathocles attempted to capture the city which is called Ethae. When the barbarians, however, assembled a large force and made an unexpected attack by night upon him, he lost four thousand men, and in consequence returned to Syracuse.

4. Agathocles brought together his naval forces , and sailed across to Italy. Planning to move on Croton, since he wished to besiege the city, he sent a messenger to Menedemus, the tyrant of Croton, his friend, bidding him not to be alarmed falsely and saying that he was escorting his daughter Lanassa with royal honours to Epirus for her marriage [to Pyrrhus]; and by this ruse he caught the Crotoniates off their guard. He then invested the city and encircled it with walls from sea to sea, and by means of a stone-thrower and by tunnelling brought down in ruins the largest of the buildings. When the Crotoniates saw this they were frightened, and opening the gate, received Agathocles and his army, who rushed into the city, plundered the houses, and slew the male inhabitants. With the neighbouring barbarians, both the Iapygians and the Peucetians, Agathocles made an alliance and supplied them with pirate ships, receiving in return a share of their booty. Then, leaving a garrison in Croton, he sailed back to Syracuse.

5. Diyllus, the Athenian historian, compiled a universal history in twenty-six books and Psaon of Plataea wrote a continuation of this work in thirty books.

6. In the war with the Etruscans, Gauls, Samnites, and the other allies [295], the Romans slew one hundred thousand men in the consulship of Fabius, according to Duris.

Something similar is told by Duris, Diodorus, and Dio: that when the Samnites, Etruscans, and the other nations were at war with the Romans, Decius, the Roman consul, colleague of Torquatus, in like manner devoted himself to death, and on that day one hundred thousand of the enemy were slain.

7. Because of envy, Antipater [son of Cassander & Thessaloncê] murdered his own mother.

Alexander, the brother of Antipater, was assassinated by King Demetrius, whom he had summoned to aid him. He likewise assassinated Antipater the matricide, the brother of Alexander, not wishing to have a partner in rule.

8. Agathocles assembled an army and crossed over ₍c₎ into Italy with thirty thousand infantry and three thousand cavalry. The navy he entrusted to Stilpo with orders to ravage the territory of the Bruttians; but while Stilpo was plundering the estates along the shore, he encountered a storm and lost most of his ships. Agathocles laid siege to Hipponium . . . and by means of stone-throwers they overpowered the city and captured it. This terrified the Bruttians, who sent an embassy to treat for terms. Agathocles, having obtained six hundred hostages from them and having left an occupying force, returned to Syracuse. The Bruttians, however, instead of abiding by their oath, marched out in full force against the soldiers who had been left behind, crushed them, recovered the hostages, and so freed themselves from the domination of Agathocles.

9. King Demetrius, after arresting all who habitually defamed him in the public assemblies and contentiously opposed him in all things, let them go. unharmed, remarking that pardon is better than punishment.

10. Most leaders of armies, when confronted with serious reverses, follow the urgings of the mob rather than risk its opposition.

11. The Thracians captured Agathocles [son of Lysimachus], the king's son, but sent him home with gifts, partly to prepare for themselves a refuge against the surprises of Fortune, partly in the hope of recovering through this act of humanity that part of their territory which Lysimachus had seized. For they no longer hoped to be able to prevail in the war, since almost all the most powerful kings were now in agreement, and were in military alliance one with another.

12. When the army of Lysimachus was hard pressed for food, [292] and his friends kept advising him to save himself as best he could and not to hope for safety in the encampment, he replied to them that it was not honourable to provide a disgraceful safety for himself by abandoning his army and his friends.

Dromichaetes, the king of the Thracians, having given King Lysimachus every mark of welcome, having kissed him, and even called him "Father," then brought him and his children to a city called Helis.

After the capture of the army of Lysimachus, the Thracians assembling in haste shouted that the captured king should be brought into their midst for punishment. It was but right, they cried, that the multitude who had shared the hazard of battle should debate and decide what was to be done with the prisoners. Dromichaetes spoke against punishing the king and pointed out to the soldiers the advantages of preserving his life. Were he to be executed, he said, other kings, possibly more to be feared than their predecessor, would assume the authority of Lysimachus. If, on the other hand, his life were spared, he would owe a debt of gratitude to the Thracians, and with no hazard to themselves they would recover the forts that had formerly been Thracian. When the multitude had given its approval to this policy, Dromichaetes searched out from among the prisoners the friends of Lysimachus and those who were accustomed to be in constant attendance upon him, and led them to the captive monarch. Then, having offered sacrifice, he invited Lysimachus and his friends to the banquet, together with the most suitable Thracians. He prepared two sets of couches, using for the company of Lysimachus the royal drapery that formed part of the spoils, but for himself and his friends cheap beds of straw. In like manner, he had two different meals prepared, and set before his foreign guests a prodigal array of all kinds of viands, served on a silver table, while before the Thracians was placed a modestly prepared dish of herbs and meat, their meal being set out upon a cheap board. Finally, for his guests he poured out wine in gold and silver cups, but for his fellow-countrymen, as was the custom of the Getae, in cups of horn or wood. After they had been drinking some time, he filled the largest of the drinking-horns, and addressing Lysimachus as "Father," asked him which banquet seemed more fit for kings, the Macedonian or the Thracian. Lysimachus replied: "The Macedonian." "Why then," he asked, "forsaking such ways, a splendid manner of life, and a more glorious kingdom as well, did you desire to come among men who are barbarous and lead a bestial existence, and to a wintry land deficient in cultivated grains and fruit,? Why did you force a way against nature to bring an army into such a place as this, where no foreign force can survive in the open?" In reply Lysimachus said that in regard to this campaign he had acted blindly; but for the future he would endeavour to aid him as a friend, and not to fall short in returning kindness for kindness. Dromichaetes received these words graciously, obtained the return of the districts that Lysimachus had seized, placed a diadem on his head, and sent him on his way.

13. This Xermodigestus, as Diodorus writes, ranking as the most trusted friend, I think, of Audoleon, king of the Paeonians, reveals the treasures to Lysimachus, or to some other king of Thrace ('tis difficult for me, without books as I am, to relate all, like a god; you to whom I speak know [*Il.* 12.176]). He revealed to the crowned head of Thrace the treasures hidden beneath the river Sargentius, which he himself, aided only by captives, had buried, turning aside the river bed, and burying the treasure beneath, then letting in the stream, and slaying the captives.

14. King Demetrius laid siege to Thebes when it revolted a second time, demolished the walls with siege engines, and took the city by storm, but put to death only the ten men who were responsible for the revolt.

King Demetrius, having gained possession of the other cities also, dealt generously with the Boeotians; for he dismissed the charges against all except the fourteen men who were chiefly responsible for the revolt.

In many cases one should decline to fight to the bitter end, indulging ones wrath. For sometimes it is expedient to come to terms, to pay a price for security, and in general to rate forgiveness above revenge.

15. Agathocles sent his son Agathocles to King Demetrius to arrange a treaty of friendship and alliance. The king welcomed the young man warmly, dressed him in princely robes, and gave him magnificent gifts. He sent back with him Oxythemis, one of his friends, ostensibly to receive pledges of the alliance, in reality to spy out Sicily.

16. [But as for the death of Agathocles, when we come to its place in the narrative, what actually occurred will confirm what has just been said.]

King Agathocles, who had remained on terms of peace with the Carthaginians for a long time, had now made extensive naval preparations; for he intended to transport an army once again to Libya and with his ships to prevent the Phoenicians from importing grain from Sardinia and Sicily. Indeed, in the preceding war with Libya, it was by control of the sea that the Carthaginians had brought their country safely out of danger. King Agathocles now had, fully equipped, two hundred ships, quadriremes and sexremes. Nevertheless, he did not carry out his project for the following reasons. There was a certain Menon, a Segestan by birth, who was taken captive on the seizure of his native city [307], and became the king's slave because of the beauty of his person. For a while he pretended to be content, being reckoned among the king's favourites and friends; but the disaster to his city and the outrage to his person produced a rankling enmity to the king, and he seized an opportunity to take his revenge. Now the king, being now well advanced in years, had entrusted the command of his forces in the field to Archagathus. He was the son of the Archagathus who was killed in Libya, and thus the grandson of King Agathocles; in manliness and fortitude he far surpassed ordinary expectations. . . . While he was encamped near Etna, the king, wishing to promote his son Agathocles as successor to the throne, first of all presented the young man at Syracuse, and declared that he would leave him heir to his power; he then sent him to the camp. To Archagathus he wrote a letter, ordering him to hand over to Agathocles both the land and naval forces. When Archagathus thus perceived that another was to fall heir to the kingdom, he resolved to lay a plot for both men. He sent word to Menon the Segestan, and persuaded him to poison the king. He himself offered sacrifice on a certain island, and when the younger Agathocles put in there, invited him to the feast, plied him with drink, and murdered him during the night. The body was thrown into the sea, and was washed ashore by the waves, where certain men recognized it and carried it to Syracuse.

Now it was the king's habit after dinner always to clean his teeth with a quill. Having finished his wine, therefore, he asked Menon for the quill, and Menon gave him one that he had smeared with a putrefactive drug. The king, unaware of this, applied it rather vigorously and so brought it into contact with the gums all about his teeth. The first effect was a continuous pain, which grew daily more excruciating, and this was followed by an incurable gangrene everywhere near the teeth. As he lay dying [289], he summoned the populace, denounced Archagathus for his impiety, aroused the masses to avenge him, and declared that he restored to the people their self-government. Then, when the king was already at the point of death, Oxythemis, the envoy of King Demetrius, placed him on the pyre and burned him, still alive, but because of the characteristic ravages of his affliction unable to utter a sound. Agathocles had committed numerous and most varied acts of slaughter during his reign, and since to his cruelty towards his own people he added impiety towards the gods, the manner of his death was appropriate to his lawless life. He lived for seventy-two years and ruled for twenty-eight, according to Timaeus of Syracuse, Callias, another Syracusan, the author of twenty-two books, and Antander, the brother of Agathocles, who was himself a historian. The Syracusans, upon the recovery of their popular government, confiscated the property of Agathocles and pulled down the statues that he had set up. Menon, who had plotted against the king, stayed with Archagathus, having fled from Syracuse. He was puffed up, however, by the credit that he enjoyed as over-thrower of the kingdom; he assassinated Archagathus, gained control of the camp, and, having won over the masses by expressions of goodwill, determined to wage war on Syracuse and to claim for himself the chief power.

In manliness and fortitude Agatharchus was much in advance of his years, for he was extremely young.

17. This historian [Timaeus of Tauromenium], who had so sharply rebuked earlier historians for their errors, showed very high regard for the truth in the rest of his writings, but the greater part of his history of Agathocles consists of lying propaganda against the ruler because of personal enmity. For since he was banished from Sicily by Agathocles and could not strike back while the monarch lived, after his death he defamed him in his history for all time. For, in general, to the bad qualities that this king did in fact possess the historian adds others of his own invention. He strips him of his successes, leaving him his failures, not only those for which the king was himself responsible, but even those due to ill luck, which he transfers to the score of one who was not at all at fault. Though it is generally agreed that the king was a shrewd strategist, and that he was energetic and confident where courage in battle was called for, yet Timaeus throughout his history incessantly calls him a poltroon and coward. Yet who does not know that of all men who ever came to power, none acquired a greater kingdom with fewer resources? Reared from childhood as an artisan because of scant means and humble parentage, he later, thanks to his own ability, not only became master of nearly all Sicily, but even reduced by arms much of Italy and Libya. One may well marvel at the nonchalance of the historian, who throughout his work praises the people of Syracuse for their courage, but says that he who mastered them surpasses all men in cowardice. The evidence of these contradictions shows clearly that he deserted the honest standard of historical candour to gratify his personal animosity and contentiousness. Consequently we cannot fairly accept the last five books of this writer's history, in which he covers the deeds of Agathocles.

Likewise Callias of Syracuse might justly and fittingly be held liable to censure. For ever since he was taken up by Agathocles and for a great price in gifts sold into bondage Madam History, the mouthpiece of truth, he has never ceased singing dishonest praises of his paymaster. Thus, although Agathocles' acts of impiety to the gods and of lawlessness to men were not few, yet the historian says that he far surpassed other men in piety and humanity. In general, just as Agathocles robbed the citizens of their goods and gave to the historian, contrary to all justice, what was not his to give, so this remarkable chronicler employed his pen to endow the monarch with all the virtues. It was quite easy, no doubt, in this exchange of favours for the writer not to let his praises fall short of the bribery coming from the royal family.

18. The people of Syracuse dispatched Hicetas [289] as general with an army to conduct the war against Menon. For a while he carried on the war, so long as the enemy avoided action and refused to face them in battle, but when the Carthaginians, with their vastly superior forces, began to aid Menon, the Syracusans were compelled to give four hundred hostages to the Phoenicians, to make an end of hostilities, and to restore the exiles. Then, because the mercenaries were not allowed to vote in the elections, the city was filled with civil strife. Both the Syracusans and the mercenaries had recourse to arms, and it was only with difficulty that the Elders, after long negotiations and many appeals to both factions, ended the disturbance on the condition that within a set time the mercenaries should sell their possessions and leave Sicily. After these terms had

been ratified, the mercenaries left Syracuse in accordance with the agreement; and when they reached the Strait, they were welcomed by the people of Messana as friends and allies. When they had been hospitably received into the homes of the citizens, they slew their hosts in the night, married their wives, and took possession of the city. They named this city Mamertina after Ares, since in their language [Osean] he is called Mamertos.

When the mercenaries had left Syracuse in accordance with the agreement, they were welcomed by the people of Messana as friends and allies, but when they had been hospitably received by the citizens into their own homes, they slew their hosts in the night, married the wives of the men they had so wronged, and took possession of the city.

Those who are not eligible for the tribunate may not participate in a vote sanctioned by a tribune.

19. [The sequel of our narrative and the sudden change in circumstances, which brought on the final crisis of the kingdom of Demetrius, will reveal more clearly the character of the woman [Phila].]

While Demetrius was held under guard in After Pella [Apameia], Lysimachus sent ambassadors to Seleucus [285+] with the request that he should on no account release Demetrius from his power, since he was a man of restless ambition and had plotted against all the kings; he offered to give Seleucus two thousand talents to do away with him. But the king rebuked the ambassadors for urging him not only to set at naught his solemn pledge but also to incur that pollution in respect of a man allied to him by marriage. To his son Antiochus, who was in Media, he wrote, advising him how to deal with Demetrius. For he had previously decided to release him and restore him with great pomp to his throne, but wanted to give his son joint credit for this kindness, since Antiochus had married Stratonicê, the daughter of Demetrius, and had begot children by her.

21. One should be most formidable to one's enemies, but to one's friends be most steadfastly cordial.

Since on that occasion through ignorance of what was to your advantage you gave heed to flattering words, now that you have seen in actuality the misfortunes that pervade the country, be better instructed.

For it is but human to go astray now and again in the course of one's life, but to err repeatedly in the same circumstances marks a man as totally disordered in his calculations. For the more numerous the failures we have met with, the greater is the punishment that we deserve to get.

Some of our citizens have gone so far in their greed for gain as to wish to raise their own estates to greatness at the expense of their country's misfortunes.

How can men who have treated unjustly those who aid their fellow men find such aid for themselves?

We should grant pardon for the mistakes of the past, and henceforth live in peace.

We should not punish without exception those who have made mistakes, but only those who do not learn better by the mistakes they have made.

Among mortals fair dealing is better than anger, and an act of kindness better than punishment.

It is right and suitable to wipe out enmity and replace it with friendship. For when a man gets into straits, he is wont to turn first to his friends for aid.

When an alien soldier gets into straits, he is wont to turn first to plundering his friends.

The greed that is innate in kings will not hold aloof from such a city.

The greed that is innate in mankind will not altogether abstain from such an enterprise.

For the pomp of pride and the raiment of tyranny should be kept at home, and when one enters a city of freemen, one should obey its laws.

When a man has inherited the blood and dominion of another, he will want to succeed to his good name also. For it is shameful to bear the name of Pyrrhus, son of Achilles, and to show oneself in conduct a Thersites. (rebuke addressed to Philip of Macedon by the orator Demades.)

The greater the reputation that a man possesses, the greater will be his gratitude to those who are the authors of his good fortune. Hence a man will not desire to obtain dishonestly and dishonourably the things that he can get with honour and goodwill.

It is therefore well, gentlemen, to find in other men's mistakes the experience you need for your own safety.

One should never prefer the foreign to that which is kindred, nor yet the hatred of enemies to the loyalty of comrades-in-arms.

BOOK XXII FRAGMENTS

1. It is traditional with the people of Epirus not only to fight for their own country but also to face danger in defence of their friends and allies.

Decius, the Roman tribune, appointed to guard Rhegium because of King Pyrrhus, slaughtered the men of the city and appropriated their wives and property. These soldiers were Campanians, and acted just as the Mamertines did, after they slaughtered the men of Messana. Then because his distribution of the property of the victims was unjust, Decius was driven out of Rhegium and was sent into exile by his own Campanians. The Mamertines also gave assistance . . . with the money that was plundered, and made him general. On a certain occasion, being afflicted with a disease of the eye, he summoned the leading physician; and he, to avenge the outrage to his fatherland, anointed Decius' eyes with a salve made from the blister-beetle, thus deprived him of his sight, and then fled from Messana.

A garrison was sent to Rhegium by the Romans. Decius the tribune, a Campanian by race and a man of unusual greed and daring, imitated the lawless conduct of the Mamertines. For although the Mamertines had been received as friends by the people of Messana, they seized control of the city, slaughtered the men, each at his own hearth, married the wives of their own hosts, and possessed themselves of the property of their victims. So Decius and his Campanians, though they had been sent by Rome to guard the inhabitants of Rhegium, emulated the savagery of the Mamertines; for they slaughtered the citizens, divided up their property, and occupied the city as a prize of war. Decius, who had been appointed commander of the garrison, converted into money the property of the hapless populace, and because he made an unfair distribution of the spoils, was driven out of Rhegium and sent into exile by the Campanians, his partners in guilt. The transgressors did not, however, escape punishment, but Decius, when he had a severe attack of ophthalmia, called in the best of the physicians, who, taking revenge for his country, anointed him amply with blister-beetle salve, and having robbed Decius of his sight fled from Messana.

2. Throughout Sicily there were tyrants, Hicetas in Syracuse, Phintias in Acragas, Tyndarion in Tauromenium, and others in the lesser cities. A war arose between Phintias and Hicetas, and when they met in battle near the Hyblaeus, Hicetas was victorious; in their raids against one another, they pillaged the estates and made the district a wasteland. Hicetas was so elated by his victory that he joined battle with the Carthaginians, but was defeated and lost many men near the river Terias. Phintias founded a city, which he named Phintias, settling in it the inhabitants of Gela, who were driven from their homes. This city, Phintias, is by the sea. He tore down the walls and houses of Gela, and transferred its people to Phintias, where he had built a wall, a notable marketplace, and temples of the gods.

Hence, since he had shown himself a bloodthirsty murderer, all the cities subject to him came to loathe him and drove out their garrisons, the first to revolt being the people of Agyrium.

Since Phintias ruled the cities by main force and put to death many of the wealthy men, his lawlessness won him the hatred of his subjects; consequently, since all were at the point of revolt, he was soon humbled, changed his ways, and by a more humane rule held his subjects under control.

3. Ptolemy [Keraunos], the king of the Macedonians, being quite young and inexperienced in the business of war, and being by nature rash and impetuous, exercised no prudence or foresight. For instance, when his friends advised him to wait for the troops which were tardy in arriving, he paid no attention.

King Ptolemy was slain and the whole Macedonian army was cut to pieces and destroyed by the Gauls.

4. During this period the Gauls attacked Macedonia and harried it [279-76], since there were many claimants to the kingship, who possessed themselves of it briefly and were driven out. One of these was Meleager, a brother of Ptolemy, son of Lagus, who ruled for only a few days and was then expelled. Similarly, Antipater [Etesias] ruled for forty-five days. After them came Sosthenes, then Ptolemy [son of Lysimachus?], as well as Alexander, and Pyrrhus of Epirus. All together they ruled for three years, according to Diodorus.

5. Apollodorus, [278] who aimed at a tyranny, and thought to render the conspiracy secure, invited a young lad, one of his friends, to a sacrifice, slew him as an offering to the gods, gave the conspirators his vitals to eat, and when he had mixed the blood with wine, bade them drink it.

This same Apollodorus, having recruited some Gauls, furnished them too with arms, and, when he had conferred gifts upon them, found them loyal guardsmen and convenient tools, because of their cruelty, to execute his punishments. By confiscating the property of the well-to-do he amassed great wealth. Then, by an increase in the pay of his soldiers, and by sharing his riches with the poor, he made himself master of a formidable force. Turning then to cruelty and greed he began to exact money from the citizens at large, and by inflicting the penalty of torture upon many men and more than a few women he forced everyone to hand over gold and silver. His guide and tutor in tyranny was Calliphon the Sicel, who had lived at the court of many of the Sicilian tyrants.

6. A "Cadmean victory" is a proverbial expression. It signifies that the victors suffer misfortune, while the defeated are not endangered because of the magnitude of their dominion.

King Pyrrhus had lost many of the Epirotes who had crossed over with him, and when one of his friends asked how he had fared in the battle, he replied:

> If I win a victory in one more battle with the Romans, I shall not
> have left a single soldier of those who crossed over with me.

In very truth, all his victories were, as the proverb has it, Cadmean; for the enemy, though defeated, were in no way humbled, since their dominion was so great, whereas the victor had suffered the damage and disaster that commonly go with defeat.

Cineas, whom Pyrrhus sent as ambassador to treat for terms with the Romans [280?], was a persuasive diplomat, and, in addition, offered valuable presents to the appropriate persons. They did not accept these presents, but all gave him the selfsame answer, that since he was at this time an enemy, such a gift was quite unfitting; if, however, he should bring about a peace and become a friend of the Roman people, they would gladly accept his gift, which would then be above reproach.

7. Phintias, the founder of the city of Phintias and tyrant of Acragas, had a dream that revealed the manner of his death: he was hunting a wild boar, when the swine rushed at him, struck his side with its tusks, pierced him through, and killed him.

Hicetas had ruled Syracuse for nine years when he was thrust from power by Thoenon, the son of Mameus.

When Thoenon and Sostratus had succeeded Hicetas, they once again invited King Pyrrhus to come to Sicily.

The Mamertines, who had treacherously murdered the men of Messana. having made an alliance with the Carthaginians, decided to join them in trying to prevent Pyrrhus from crossing over into Sicily, but Tyndarion, the tyrant of Tauromenia, inclined in favour of Pyrrhus and was ready to receive his forces into the city.

The Carthaginians, having made an alliance with the Romans [279], took five hundred men on board their own ships and sailed across to Rhegium; they made assaults, and though they desisted from the siege, set fire to the timber that had been brought together for ship-building, and they continued to guard the Strait, watching against any attempt by Pyrrhus to cross.

Thoenon controlled the Island [Ortrygia], while Sostratus ruled Syracuse. They had ten thousand soldiers, and carried on war with each other. But both, becoming exhausted in the war, sent ambassadors to Pyrrhus.

8. Pyrrhus waged war in Italy for two years and four months. While he was making ready to set sail, the Carthaginians were besieging Syracuse both by land and by sea; they blockaded the Great Harbour with a hundred ships, and on land they carried on operations close to the walls with fifty thousand men. Thus they held the Syracusans pent up while they overran their territory and laid it waste. Consequently the Syracusans, being exhausted by the war, pinned their hopes on Pyrrhus because of his wife Lanassa, the daughter of Agathocles, who had borne Pyrrhus a son, Alexander; therefore they daily dispatched envoys to him, one group after the other. He embarked his men, his elephants, and his other equipment of war aboard his ships, set sail from Tarentum, and put in at Locri on the tenth day. From there he sailed to the Narrows, and crossing to Sicily, put in at Tauromenium. Thence after adding Tyndarion, the dynast of Tauromenia, to his alliance and after obtaining soldiers from him, he sailed to Catana. There, having been welcomed by the inhabitants with great state and crowned with golden crowns, he disembarked his infantry. As they made their way to Syracuse, the fleet accompanied them in battle array. When they approached Syracuse, the Carthaginians, who had sent away thirty ships on some necessary missions, did not venture to do battle with the ships that remained. Thus Pyrrhus sailed unchallenged into Syracuse, and accepted delivery of the Island from Thoenon, and of the rest of the city from the citizens and Sosistratus. This Sosistratus had made himself master of Acragas and of many other cities, and had an army of more than ten thousand men. Pyrrhus effected a reconciliation between Thoenon and Sosistratus and the Syracusans and restored harmony, thinking to gain great popularity by virtue of the peace. The king took over the missiles, engines of war, and such equipment as was in the city; the ships that he took over in Syracuse were: one hundred and twenty decked vessels, twenty without decks, and the royal "niner": the total, including the ships he had brought with him, now amounted to a fleet of more than two hundred. While he was busy with these matters envoys arrived from Leontini, sent by Heracleides the ruler, who said that he would hand over to the king the city and its forts, together with four thousand infantry and five hundred cavalry. Many other embassies also came to Syracuse, offering to hand over their cities and saying that they would co-operate with Pyrrhus. He received them all courteously, and then sent them back to their several countries, hoping now to win even Libya.

The harbour of Corinth is called Lechaeum.

9. Brennus, the king of the Gauls, accompanied by one hundred and fifty thousand infantry, armed with long shields, and ten thousand cavalry, together with a horde of camp followers, large numbers of traders, and two thousand wagons, invaded Macedonia and engaged in battle. Having in this conflict lost many men . . . as lacking sufficient strength . . . when later he advanced into Greece and to the oracle at Delphi, which he wished to plunder. In the mighty battle fought there he lost tens of thousands of his comrades-in-arms, and Brennus himself was three times wounded. Weighed down and near to death, he assembled his host there and spoke to the Gauls. He advised them to kill him and all the wounded, to burn their wagons, and to return home unburdened; he advised them also to make Cichorius king. Then, after drinking deeply of undiluted wine, Brennus slew himself. After Cichorius had given him burial, he killed the wounded and those who were victims of cold and starvation, some twenty thousand in all; and so he began the journey homeward with the rest by the same route. In difficult terrain the Greeks would attack and cut off those in the rear, and carried off all their baggage. On the way to Thermopylae, food being scarce there, they abandoned twenty thousand more men. All the rest perished as they were going through the country of the Dardani, and not a single man was left to return home.

Brennus, the king of the Gauls, on entering a temple found no dedications of gold or silver, and when he came only upon images of stone and wood he laughed at them, to think that men, believing that gods have human form, should set up their images in wood and stone.

At the time of the Gallic invasion the inhabitants of Delphi, seeing that danger was at hand, asked the god if they should remove the treasures, the children, and the women from the shrine to the most strongly fortified of the neighbouring cities. The Pythia replied to the Delphians that the god commanded them to leave in place in the shrine the dedications and whatever else pertained to the adornment of the gods; for the god, and with him the White Maidens, would protect all. As there were in the sacred precinct two temples of extreme antiquity, one of Athena Pronaia and one of Artemis, they assumed that these goddesses were the "White Maidens" named in the oracle. [The "White Maiden" appeared as a blinding snow storm, during which the Greeks successfully attacked the Gauls.]

10. Pyrrhus, after settling matters in Syracuse and Leontini, set out with an army for Acragas. While he was on the way, men of Enna arrived, saying that they had expelled the Carthaginian garrison, which they had kept to prevent Phintias from becoming their ruler, and promising to hand over their city to Pyrrhus and become his allies. Pyrrhus, taking his army with him . . . he arrived at Acragas and took over from Sosistratus the city and the soldiers, eight thousand infantry and eight hundred horsemen, all picked men, no whit inferior to the men of Epirus. He also took over thirty cities that Sosistratus ruled. He then sent to Syracuse and brought siege engines and a great quantity of missiles.

He marched against the territory subject to the Carthaginians with an army of thirty thousand infantry, fifteen hundred cavalry and his elephants. He subdued first the city of Heracleia, which had a Carthaginian garrison. He then seized Azones. The people of Selinus then came over to the king, and then the people of Halicyae, of Segesta, and of many other cities. Although Eryx had a considerable garrison of Carthaginians and is by nature strong and not easily stormed, yet Pyrrhus determined to take it forcibly by siege. Hence he brought up his engines against the walls, and a mighty and violent siege took place and continued for a long time, until the king, desiring to win high renown and vying to rank with Heracles, personally led an assault on the walls; putting up an heroic fight, he slew the Carthaginians who stormed against him, and when the king's "Friends" also joined in the struggle, he took the city by storm. After stationing a garrison there, he set out for the city of Iaetia, a place of exceptional strength, favourably situated for an attack on Panormus. The people of Iaetia yielded of their own accord, whereupon he advanced at once to the city of Panormus, which has the finest harbour in all Sicily, whence, in fact, the city received this, its name. This place also he took by storm, and when he gained control of the fortress of Herctae, he had now overcome the whole empire of Carthage and become its master, except for Lilybaeum. This city had been founded by the Carthaginians after their city of Motya had been captured by the tyrant Dionysius [397] for they had gathered together all the survivors of Motya and settled them in Lilybaeum. While Pyrrhus was making ready to lay siege to this city, the Carthaginians brought over from Libya to Lilybaeum a considerable army, and having control of the seas, they transported a large amount of grain, and engines of war and missiles in incredible quantities. Since most of the city is surrounded by the sea, they walled off the land approaches, constructed towers at short intervals, and dug a great ditch. They then sent an embassy to the king to discuss a truce and peace, for they were ready to come to terms and even to pay a large sum of money. Though the king refused to accept money he was prevailed upon to concede Lilybaeum to the Carthaginians; but the king's "Friends" who were taking part in the meeting and the delegates from the cities called him aside and urged him under no circumstances to grant the barbarians a stepping-stone for an attack on Sicily, but rather to drive the Phoenicians out of the entire island and to make the sea the boundary of his domain. The king immediately encamped near the walls, and at first made constant attacks with relays of troops against them. The Carthaginians were able to defend themselves because of the number of their fighters and the abundance of their equipment. For the Carthaginians had collected so great a number of catapults, both dart-shooters and stone-throwers, that there was not room on the walls for all the equipment, and so, as missiles of all sorts were hurled against the attackers, and as many of his men fell, and many others received wounds, Pyrrhus was at a disadvantage. The king undertook to construct engines of war more powerful than those he had transported from Syracuse, and to unsettle the walls by mining operations. The Carthaginians kept up their resistance, since the ground was rocky, and after a siege of two months Pyrrhus despaired of capturing the city by force, and lifted the siege. Deciding to construct a large fleet and, when by this means he should have won mastery of the seas, to transport his forces to Libya, he now bent his efforts towards this.

11. Pyrrhus, having won a famous victory, dedicated the long shields of the Gauls and the most valuable of the other spoils in the shrine of Athena Itonis with the following inscription:

> These shields, taken from the brave Gauls, the Molossian Pyrrhus
> hung here as a gift to Athena Itonis, after he had destroyed the
> entire host of Antigonus. Small wonder: the sons of Aeacus are
> warriors now even as aforetime.

Being therefore conscious that they had committed acts of impiety so great, they expected, with good reason, to suffer punishment befitting their crimes.

12. After Pyrrhus had sacked Aegeae, the seat of the Macedonian royal family, he left his Gauls there. They, learning from certain informants that in accordance with a certain ancient custom much wealth was buried with the dead at royal funerals, dug up and broke into all the graves, divided up the treasure, and scattered the bones of the dead. Pyrrhus was much reviled because of this, but did not punish the barbarians since he needed them for his wars.

13. Since the Mamertines who inhabited Messana had increased in power . . . many forts . . . and they themselves, having put their army in light array, came in haste to the aid of the territory of Messana which was under attack. Hiero, after quitting enemy territory, took Mylae by storm and acquired fifteen hundred soldiers. Straightway moving to reduce the other strongholds also, he came to Ameselum, situated between Centuripa and Agyrium. Though Ameselum was well fortified and strongly manned, he captured and razed this fortress to the ground, but dismissed all charges against the men of the garrison, whom he enrolled in his own ranks. Part of the land he gave to the people of Centuripa, part to the people of Agyrium. After this, Hiero with a considerable army waged war against the Mamertines. Halaesa he brought over by surrender, and having been eagerly welcomed by the inhabitants of Abacaenum and Tyndaris, he became master of these cities and drove the Mamertines into a narrow area. For on the Sicilian sea he held the city of Tauromenium, near Messana, and on the Tyrrhenian sea he held Tyndaris. He invaded the territory of Messana, and encamped along the Loitanus River with ten thousand foot-soldiers and fifteen hundred cavalry. The Mamertines faced him with eight thousand foot-soldiers and forty (?) cavalry; their general was Ciôs. Now Ciôs assembled diviners to inspect the entrails, and after sacrificing, he questioned them about the battle. When they replied that the gods revealed through the victims that he would pass the night in the encampment of the enemy, he was overjoyed, thinking that he was to gain possession of the king's camp. Immediately he deployed his forces and attempted to cross the river. Hiero, who had in his army two hundred exiles from Messana, men noted for their courage and deeds of valour, added to them four hundred more picked soldiers, and ordered them to go around the nearby hill, named Thorax, and to fall upon the enemy from the rear. He himself deployed his forces and encountered the enemy in front. There was a cavalry engagement near the stream, and at the same time the infantry, who at the order of the king had occupied a certain mound near the river, gained the advantage of favourable terrain; yet for a while the battle was evenly balanced, but when those who had gone around the hill also charged the Mamertines unexpectedly and slew them with no difficulty, since they were fresh and the enemy were battle-worn, then the Mamertines, surrounded on all sides, took to flight, and the Syracusans, attacking in force, cut the whole army to pieces. The general of the Mamertines fought desperately, but after he had received many wounds and had fallen to the ground unconscious he was captured alive. He was carried still breathing to the encampment of the king, and was handed over to the physicians for treatment. Now when he thus, in accordance with the prophecy and the prediction of the soothsayers, had spent the night in the enemy's camp, and the king, moreover, was solicitous to restore Ciôs to health, certain men arrived bringing horses from the battle to the king, and Ciôs, recognizing his son's horse, supposed that the youth had been killed. In his excessive grief he burst the stitches of his wounds and by his own death set the price at which he rated the destruction of his son. As for the Mamertines, when the news was brought to them that Ciôs their general and all their soldiers as well had perished, they decided to come before the king as suppliants. Fortune did not, however, permit the utter collapse of the Mamertine cause. For Hannibal, the general of the Carthaginians, happened to be moored at the island of Lipara. When he heard the unexpected news, he came posthaste to the king, ostensibly to offer his congratulations, but in reality seeking to outmanoeuvre Hiero by deceit. The king trusted the Phoenician and remained inactive. Hannibal turned aside to Messana, and finding the Mamertines on the point of handing over the city, he dissuaded them, and on the pretext of lending aid, introduced into the city forty (?) soldiers. Thus the Mamertines, who because of their defeat had despaired of their cause, were restored to security in the manner just described. Hiero, outwitted by the Phoenician, abandoned the siege as hopeless and returned to Syracuse, having achieved a resounding success.

The Carthaginians and Hiero, after the former had been driven out of Messana, held a conference, and when they had arranged a treaty of alliance, they agreed on a joint attack on Messana.

BOOK XXIII FRAGMENTS

1. Sicily is the noblest of all islands, since it can contribute greatly to the growth of an empire.

Hanno, the son of Hannibal, went to Sicily, [264] and having gathered his forces at Lilybaeum, advanced to Solus; his land force he left encamped near the city, while he himself went on to Acragas and fortified its citadel, after having persuaded the citizens, who were already friendly to the Carthaginians, to become their allies. Upon his return to his own encampment, envoys came to him from Hiero to discuss their common interest; for they had formed an alliance to make war on the Romans unless these should quit Sicily with all speed. When both had brought their armies to Messana, Hiero pitched camp on the Chalcidian Mount, while the Carthaginians encamped with their land army at a place called Eunes, and with their naval force seized the headland called Pelorias; and they kept Messana under continuous siege. When the Roman people learned this, they sent one of the consuls, Appius Claudius by name, with a strong force, who went straightway to Rhegium. He dispatched envoys to Hiero and the Carthaginians to discuss the raising of the siege. He kept promising in addition . . . but to state publicly that he would not proceed against Hiero with war. Hiero replied that the Mamertines, who had laid waste Camarina and Gela and had seized Messana in so impious a manner, were besieged with just cause, and that the Romans, harping as they did on the word *fides,* certainly ought not to protect assassins who had shown the greatest contempt for good faith; but if, on behalf of men so utterly godless, they should enter upon a war of such magnitude, it would be clear to all mankind that they were using pity for the imperilled as a cloak for their own advantage, and that in reality they coveted Sicily.

2. The Phoenicians and Romans fought a naval battle; afterwards, in consideration of the magnitude of the war that lay before them, they sent envoys to the consul to discuss terms of friendship. There was much discussion, and both sides engaged in acrimonious debate: the Phoenicians said that they marvelled how the Romans could venture to cross over into Sicily, inasmuch as the Carthaginians had control of the seas; for it was obvious to all that if they did not maintain friendly relations, the Romans would not dare even to wash their hands in the sea. The Romans, for their part, advised the Carthaginians not to teach them to meddle with maritime affairs, since the Romans, so they asserted, were pupils who always outstripped their masters. For example, in ancient times, when they were using rectangular shields, the Etruscans, who fought with round shields of bronze and in phalanx formation, impelled them to adopt similar arms and were in consequence defeated. Then again, when other peoples were using shields such as the Romans now use, and were fighting by maniples, they had imitated both and had overcome those who introduced the excellent models. From the Greeks they had learned siegecraft and the use of engines of war for demolishing walls, and had then forced the cities of their teachers to do their bidding. So now, should the Carthaginians compel them to learn naval warfare, they would soon see that the pupils had become superior to their teachers.

At first the Romans had rectangular shields for war, but later, when they saw that the Etruscans had bronze shields, they copied them and thus conquered the Etruscans.

3. After the consul had crossed over to Messana, Hiero, thinking that the Carthaginians had treacherously permitted the crossing, fled to Syracuse. The Carthaginians, however, engaged in battle but were defeated, and the consul then laid siege to Echetla, but after the loss of many soldiers withdrew to Messana.

4. Both consuls went to Sicily, and laying siege to the city of Hadranum took it by storm. Then, while they were besieging the city of Centuripa and were encamped by the Brazen Gates, envoys arrived, first from the people of Halaesa; then, as fear fell upon the other cities as well, they too sent ambassadors to treat for peace and to deliver their cities to the Romans. These cities numbered sixty-seven. The Romans, after adding the forces of these cities to their own, advanced upon Syracuse, intending to besiege Hiero. Hiero, perceiving the discontent of the Syracusans, sent envoys to the consuls to discuss a settlement, and inasmuch as the Romans were eager to have as their foe the Carthaginians alone, they readily consented and concluded a fifteen-year peace: the Romans received one hundred and fifty thousand drachmas; Hiero, on condition of returning the captives of war, was to continue as ruler of the Syracusans and of the cities subject to him, Acrae, Leontini, Megara, Helorum, Neetum, and Tauromenium. While these things were taking place Hannibal arrived with a naval force at Xiphonia, intending to bring aid to the king, but when he learned what had been done, he departed.

Though the Romans kept Macella and the village of Hadranon under siege for many days, they went away without having accomplished their purpose.

5. The Segestans, though at first subject to the Carthaginians, turned to the Romans. The Halicyaeans acted in a similar fashion; but Ilarus and Tyrittus and Ascelus they took only after a siege. The Tyndarians, seeing themselves deserted, were alarmed and desired to surrender their city, too, but the Phoenicians, becoming suspicious of their intentions, took their leading men as hostages to Lilybaeum, and carried off their grain, wine, and the rest of their provisions.

6. Philemon the comic poet wrote ninety-seven plays and lived ninety-nine years.

7. Those who with the Romans were engaged in the siege of Acragas, digging trenches and constructing palisades, numbered one hundred thousand. After prolonged resistance the Phoenicians finally yielded the city of Acragas to the Romans.

8. During the siege of Acragas, Hanno the Elder transported from Libya to Sicily a large army, fifty thousand infantry, six thousand cavalry, and sixty elephants. Philinus of Acragas, the historian, has recorded this. Be that as it may, Hanno marched out from Lilybaeum with all his troops and had reached Heracleia when certain men arrived and declared that they would betray Herbessus to him. Hanno fought two battles, in which he lost three thousand infantry, two hundred cavalry, and had four thousand men taken prisoner; eight elephants were killed and thirty-three disabled by wounds.

Entella too was a city.

Hanno adopted a clever plan and by a single stratagem destroyed both the malcontents and the public foe.

9. After a siege of six months they became masters of Acragas in the manner described and carried off all the slaves, to the number of more than twenty-five thousand. The Romans also suffered losses, thirty thousand infantry and fifteen hundred (?) cavalry. The Carthaginians stripped Hanno of his civic rights, fined him six thousand pieces of gold, and in his stead sent Hamilcar to Sicily as commander. The Romans laid siege to Mytistratus and constructed many siege engines, but seven months later, having lost many men, they went away empty-handed. Hamilcar encountered the Romans at Thermae, and having engaged them in battle, was victorious and slew six thousand men, very nearly the whole army [260]. The fort of Mazarin also was taken by the Romans and the people enslaved. Hamilear the Carthaginian, with the aid of traitors, got possession of Camarina for the second time, and a few days later made himself master of Enna in the same way. Having fortified Drepanum and set up a city, he removed thither the Erycinians and demolished Eryx except for the area about the temple. The Romans, having put Mytistratus under siege for the third time [258], captured it, razed the city to the ground, and sold the surviving inhabitants as spoils of war. They then advanced to Camarina and he encamped beside it, but was unable to take it; but later, having sent to Hiero for engines of war, he captured the city, and sold into slavery most of the inhabitants. Immediately thereafter, with the help of traitors, he captured Enna too; of the garrison some were slain, others got away safely to their allies. Then he advanced to Sittana and took it by assault. Then, having established a garrison there, as in the other cities, he went on to Camicus, a fortress belonging to Acragas. This place too he took by treachery, and stationed a garrison there. By this time Herbessus, also, had been abandoned. Still the river Halycus . . . for others also . . . farthest.

10. Hannibal, the general of the Carthaginians, having been defeated in a naval battle [Mylae 269], and fearing that because of the defeat he might be punished by the senate, made use of the following artifice. He dispatched one of his friends to Carthage, and gave him such orders as seemed to him expedient. This man sailed home to the city, and when he had been brought before the senate said that Hannibal had ordered him to ask if it be the council's bidding that, with a fleet of two hundred ships, he should engage in battle the Roman fleet of one hundred and twenty ships. With shouts of approval they urged him to give battle. "Very well," he said, "that is just why Hannibal did fight, and we have been beaten. But since you commanded it, he is relieved of the blame." Hannibal, then, knowing that his fellow citizens were wont to persecute their generals after the event, thus forestalled the accusations that were in the offing.

Since in the previous battles they had been accused of being responsible for the losses incurred, they were eager to retrieve their damaged reputation by means of this naval engagement.

11. No one is so shattered in spirit by defeat [Cape Economus 256] as are the Carthaginians. They could, for example, easily have destroyed the naval force of the enemy as they were putting in to land, but did not even attempt to repel them. For while the Romans, with thirty ships, were approaching the shore and were neither in battle array nor in compact formation because of the violence of the wind, it would have been possible without any danger to capture the vessels, men and all, and certainly if they had gone down into the plain, and had engaged in battle on even terms and put into action every part of their army, they would easily have prevailed over the enemy. Instead, since they were intent on one thing only, the security afforded by the hill, and since they let slip some of their advantages through excessive caution and failed to recognize others because of their inexperience, they suffered a crushing defeat.

12. Since the Carthaginians were in a state of great despondency, the senate sent three of their most eminent citizens as ambassadors to Atilius, to discuss terms of peace. Of these, Hanno, the son of Hamilcar, was the man held in highest esteem, and after he had said what was appropriate to the occasion, he urged the consul to treat them with moderation and in a manner worthy of Rome. Atilius, however, since he was elated by his success and took no account of the vicissitudes of human fortune, dictated terms of such scope and nature that the peace framed by him was no better than slavery. Seeing the ambassadors were displeased at these terms, he said that on the contrary they should be grateful, for this reason, that inasmuch as they were unable to offer resistance either on land or sea in defence of their freedom, they should accept as a gift whatever concessions he might make. When Hanno and his companions continued to voice their opinions frankly to him, he threatened them insolently and ordered them to depart as quickly as possible, remarking that brave men ought either to conquer or to submit to those whose power is greater. Now in so acting the consul both failed to observe the custom of his country and to guard against divine retribution, and in a short time he met with the punishment that his arrogance deserved.

13. Now all men are more apt to be mindful of divinity in times of misfortune, and though often, in the midst of victories and success, they scorn the gods as myths and fabrications, yet in defeat they quickly revert to their natural piety. So, in particular, the Carthaginians, because of the greatness of the fears that now hung over them, sought out the sacrifices that had been omitted for many years, and multiplied the honours paid to the gods.

14. Xanthippus, the Spartan, kept advising the generals to advance against the enemy. He did this, he said, not so that by urging and spurring them on he might himself remain out of danger, but that they might know that he was confident of their ready victory if they would do so. As for himself, he added, he would lead the attack and would display his valour at the foremost point of danger.

During the battle Xanthippus, the Spartan, rode up and down, turning back any foot-soldiers who had taken flight. When someone remarked that it was easy for one on horseback to urge others into danger, he at once jumped down from his horse, handed it over to a servant, and going about on foot, begged his men not to bring defeat and destruction upon the whole army.

15. We consider it to be a proper part of history not to pass over without comment the policy, whether good or bad, of men in positions of leadership. For by the denunciation of their errors others who are drifting into a like mistake may be set straight, while by the praise of noble behaviour the minds of many are prompted to right action. Could anyone, in all justice, fail to censure the folly and arrogance of Atilius? By his inability to bear adroitly the heavy burden, as it were, of success, he robbed himself of the highest renown and involved his country in serious disasters. Though he could have made peace on terms advantageous to Rome, as well as humiliating and utterly shameful to Carthage, and could in addition have won for himself among all mankind enduring remembrance for clemency and humanity, he took no account of these things, but dealt so arrogantly with the defeated in their misfortunes and dictated terms so harsh that the gods were roused to just anger and the defeated enemy were driven by his excessive severity to turn and resist. In consequence there now occurred, thanks to him, so great a turn of the tide that the Carthaginians, who in consternation at their defeat had previously despaired of safety, now veered round and in an access of courage cut to pieces the army of their enemies, while Rome was altogether dealt so disastrous a blow that those who were reputed to be foremost in all the world in infantry warfare no longer ventured to engage the foe in battle at the first opportunity. In consequence the war turned out to be the longest on record, and the conflict resolved itself into a series of naval battles, in which the Romans and their allies lost a multitude of ships and no fewer than one hundred thousand men, including those who perished by shipwreck; as for the amount of money expended, it was as great as one might expect in view of the cost of manning a navy consisting of so many ships and of carrying on the war for fifteen years after this time. But indeed the man who was the cause of all this gained as his reward no

[**15.7.** After the Romans crossed over to Libya with a large army commanded by the consul Atilius, they were at first victorious over the Carthaginians, and captured many cities and forts and cut to pieces a large army. Later, however, after a Spartan general, Xanthippus, a mercenary soldier, had come from Greece, the Carthaginians defeated the Romans by main force and cut to pieces a large army. Thereafter there were naval battles and the Romans lost many ships and men, so that the number of those who perished was one hundred thousand.]

small portion of the disaster. In exchange for the esteem he already enjoyed he received dishonour and disgrace many times as great, and by his personal misfortunes he taught other men to observe moderation in the exercise of power; worst of all, since he had already deprived himself of the possibility of forgiveness and of the pity that is accorded to the fallen, he was forced to endure the insolence and arrogance of those whose ill-fortune he had treated with such disdain. Xanthippus, on the other hand, by his personal excellence not only rescued the Carthaginians from their desperate situation but reversed the course of the whole war. For he utterly humbled those whose might was altogether superior, while by the magnitude of his success he enabled those who by reason of their defeat were expecting destruction to look with scorn upon their enemies. As a result, when the fame of these achievements was spread abroad throughout almost all the world, all men marvelled, not without reason, at his ability; for it seemed incredible that by the addition of a single man to the Carthaginians so great a change in the whole situation had resulted that those who just now had been shut in and besieged should turn about and lay siege to their opponents, and that those whose bravery had given them the upper hand on land and sea should have taken refuge in a small city and be awaiting capture. Yet it is not at all surprising that the native intelligence and the practical experience of a general overcame seemingly insuperable difficulties. For intelligence makes all things accessible and possible, and in all matters skill overcomes brute force.

Just as the body is the servant of the soul, so great armies respond to the intelligent control of their leaders.

With an eye to what was expedient the senate, prevailing over all difficulties . . .

16. Learn the fate that befell Marcus Regulus, the Roman general, after his capture by the Sicels. They cut off his eyelids with a knife and left his eyes open. Then, having penned him in a very small and narrow hut, they goaded to madness a wild elephant, and incited it to draw him down under itself and mangle him. Thus the great general, as though driven by an avenging fury, breathed his last and died a most wretched death. Xanthippus the Spartan also died at the hands of the Sicels. For round about Lilybaeum, a city of the Sicels, there was the clash of war between Romans and Sicels, war that had continued for twenty-four years. The Sicels, having suffered defeat in battle many times, offered to put their city in subjection to the Romans. The Romans, however, would not listen even to this offer but ordered the Sicels to go forth empty-handed. Xanthippus the Spartan, who had come from Sparta with a hundred soldiers (or alone, or with fifty soldiers, according to various authorities), approached the Sicels while they were yet hemmed in, and after conversing with them at length through an interpreter finally gave them courage to oppose their enemies. He clashed in battle with the Romans and with the aid of the Sicels cut to pieces their whole army. Yet for his good service he received a recompense worthy of and appropriate to that perverse people, since the foul wretches set him in a leaking ship and sank him beneath the swirling waters of the Adriatic, in their envy of the hero and of his nobility. Diodorus the Sicel records this story and that of Regulus.

17. Philistus [of Syracuse d.356] was an historian.

18. The Romans crossed over to Libya [255] and engaged the Carthaginian fleet in battle; having been victorious and having captured twenty-four Carthaginian vessels, they took on board the Roman survivors of the battle on land, but while sailing across to Sicily ran into danger near Camarina and lost three hundred and forty warships, as well as cavalry transports and other vessels to the number of three hundred; bodies of men and beasts and pieces of wreckage lay strewn from Camarina as far as Pachynus. Hiero received the survivors hospitably, and having refreshed them with clothing, food, and other essentials, brought them safely to Messana. After the shipwreck of the Romans, Carthalo the Carthaginian laid siege to Acragas [254], captured and burned the city, and tore down its walls. The surviving inhabitants took refuge in the sanctuary of Olympian Zeus. The Romans constructed another fleet after the shipwreck, and proceeding to Cephaloedium with two hundred and fifty ships got possession of that place by treason. They went on to Drepana and put it under siege, but when Carthalo came to its aid they were driven off and went to Panormus. There they moored their ships in the harbour close to the walls, and after disembarking their men, invested the city with a palisade and a trench; for since the countryside is heavily wooded right up to the city gates, the earthworks and trenches were made to extend from sea to sea. Thereupon the Romans by making constant assaults and by employing engines of war broke down the city wall, and having gained possession of the outer city slew many; the rest fled for refuge to the old city, and sending envoys to the consuls asked for assurances that their lives would be spared. An agreement was made that those who paid two minas apiece should go free, and the Romans then took over the city; at this price fourteen thousand persons were brought under the agreement upon payment of the money, and were released. All the others, to the number of thirteen thousand, as well as the household goods, were sold by the Romans as booty. The inhabitants of Iaetia expelled their Punic garrison and handed over the city to the Romans. The people of Solus, Petra, Enattaros, and Tyndaris acted in like fashion. The consuls, having stationed a garrison in Panormus, then withdrew to Messana.

19. In the following year [253] the Romans again sailed to Libya, but being prevented by the Carthaginians from mooring their ships they turned about and went to Panormus. Having set sail thence for Rome they were overtaken by a storm and again suffered shipwreck, and lost one hundred and fifty warships and all their transports and booty besides. . . . The keeper of the gate at Thermae, having gone without the walls for the needs of nature, was captured by the Roman army; he sent word to the commander that if he would release him he would open the city gate for him during the night. The commander released him and having fixed a time sent a thousand men at night. They arrived and he opened the gate at the appointed time. The leaders, men of note, entered and ordered the gate-keeper to bolt the gate and to allow no one else to enter, since they wished to carry off the wealth of the city themselves. All of these men were cut down and suffered the death that their greed deserved.

20. On another occasion the Romans got possession of both Thermae and Lipara. Though the Romans also laid siege, with forty thousand men and a thousand cavalry, to the fortress of Hercte, they did not prevail against it.

21. Hasdrubal, the general of the Carthaginians, being berated by his own people for not fighting, marched with his whole army through the rough country about Selinus and arrived in Panormus. And when he had brought his men across the river, which lies near by, he encamped near the city walls, but ordered neither palisade nor trench because he thought it did not matter. On this occasion again the merchants brought in a great quantity of wine; the Celts became drunk, and were in complete disorder and shouting noisily when the consul Caecilius attacked them in force. He won a victory over them and captured sixty elephants, which he sent to Rome. The Romans were struck with wonder.

22. Hamilcar the Carthaginian, surnamed Barca, and Hannibal his son were by common consent considered the greatest generals of the Carthaginians, greater not only than their predecessors but than those of later ages as well, and by their personal achievements they very greatly increased the power of their native land.

BOOK XXIV FRAGMENTS

1. The Carthaginians, having razed to the ground the city of Selinus, removed its population to Lilybaeum. The Romans, with a fleet of two hundred and forty warships, sixty light vessels, and a large number of transports of all types, sailed into Panormus and thence to Lilybaeum, which they put under siege. On land they blockaded the city from sea to sea by means of a trench, and constructed catapults, battering rams, covered sheds, and penthouses. The entrance of the harbour they blocked with fifteen light vessels, which they had loaded with stones. The Roman host numbered one hundred and ten thousand, while the besieged had seven thousand infantry and seven hundred cavalry. In the course of the siege relief arrived from Carthage, four thousand men and supplies of food, and Adherbal and his men took heart again. The Romans, who had observed the force effecting an entrance, again blocked the mouth of the harbour with stones and jetties, and barred the channels with huge timbers and anchors; but when a strong wind arose, the sea grew turbulent and broke everything up. The Romans constructed an engine for hurling stones, but the Carthaginians built another wall on the inner side. The Romans then filled the moat, which was sixty cubits wide and forty deep. Joining battle at the seaward wall they placed men in ambush in front of the city, and when the defending forces had been drawn off into the battle on the seaward side the men who were lying in ambush with ladders ready climbed up and captured the first wall. When the Carthaginian general got news of this, he fell upon them, killed large numbers in a single place, and forced the others to flee. With the aid of a strong gale they set fire to all the Roman engines of war, their penthouses, stone-throwers, battering rams, and covered sheds. Perceiving, however, that their cavalry was of no service to them in the confined space, the Carthaginians dispatched them to Drepana; there they greatly assisted the Carthaginians. The Romans were rendered helpless by the burning of their engines, as well as by short rations and pestilence, for since they and their allies fed solely on flesh they were so infected that large numbers died in a few days. For this reason they were even ready to abandon the siege, but Hiero, the king of Syracuse, dispatched an abundant supply of grain, and gave them fresh courage to resume the siege.

On the accession to office of the new consuls, [249] the Romans gave the command to the consul Claudius, son of Appius. Upon assuming command of the army he again blocked the harbour, as his predecessors had done, and again the sea hurled all to bits. Claudius, however, in high self-confidence, equipped the best ships, two hundred and ten in number, and set off to Drepana to do battle with the Carthaginians. He was defeated with the loss of one hundred and seventeen ships and twenty thousand men. It would not be easy to discover a fierce fight at sea followed by a more glorious victory in this period, no comparable victory, I mean, for anyone, not merely for the Carthaginians. The surprising thing, however, is that though the Carthaginians were involved in so great a battle and . . . with ten ships . . . not only was no one killed but even the wounded were few. After this they sent Hannibal the trierarch to Panormus with thirty ships, and plundered and carried off to Drepana the stores of grain belonging to the Romans. Then, taking from Drepana whatever other provisions were of use, they went to Lilybaeum, and provided the besieged population with an abundance of good things of all sorts. Carthalo the general also arrived from Carthage with seventy warships and a like number of provision transports. When they also had set upon the Romans, he succeeded in sinking some ships and in dragging to the shore five of those lying at anchor. Then, hearing that the Roman fleet had set sail from Syracuse, he prevailed upon his fellow commanders and put to sea with one hundred and twenty ships, the best of the fleet. When the two fleets sighted one another off the coast of Gela the Romans took fright and put in at Phintias, where they left under shelter of land the ships laden with provisions and the remainder of their fleet; when the Carthaginians bore down, there was a sharp struggle. Finally the Carthaginians disabled fifty of the large freighters, sent to the bottom seventeen men-of-war, and stove in and rendered useless thirteen others. Afterwards, the Carthaginians, on reaching the Halycus River, gave their wounded men a period of rest. The consul, Iunius, knowing nothing of these events, put to sea from Messana with thirty-six warships and a considerable number of transports. Having rounded Cape Pachynus and anchored near Phintias, he was astounded to learn what had taken place. Later, when the Carthaginians advanced against them with their entire fleet, the consul, seized with fear, burned the thirteen ships that were useless, and attempted to sail back to Syracuse, thinking that Hiero would provide them safety. Being overtaken off the coast of Camarina he put in to land for refuge, at a place where the shores were rocky and the water shallow. When the wind increased in violence, the Carthaginians rounded Cape Pachynus and anchored in a relatively calm spot, whereas the Romans, placed in great peril, lost all their provision ships and likewise their warships, so that of one hundred and five of the latter only two were saved and most of the men perished. Iunius, with the two warships and the surviving men, made his way to the army encamped at Lilybaeum, whence he made a sally by night and gained Eryx; he also fortified Aegithallus (now called Acellum) and left eight hundred men there as a garrison. When Carthalo learned that Eryx and its environs had already been occupied, he brought over an army by sea at night, and by an attack on the garrison of Aegithallus got possession of that stronghold. In his success he slew some and forced others to seek refuge at Eryx. Three thousand men guarded the fortress. In the first naval battle thirty-five thousand Romans were lost, and the number of men taken captive was no less.

2. The Carthaginians [250] selected the men who were keenest to get money and most daring (some three hundred in all) for the attempt to burn the siege engines, since it is these qualities that provide the strongest motive to make men scorn all danger. In general it was the bravest who were killed in making assaults and in the storming of walls, since of their own accord they went headlong into perils that offered scant hope of succour.

3. When Claudius arrived in Sicily [249] he took command of the forces at Lilybaeum, and calling an assembly bitterly assailed the consuls who had just handed over the army to him, charging that they had been remiss in their handling of the war, drunkards who lived lives of licence and luxury, and that on the whole they had been the victims of a siege rather than the besiegers. Since he was naturally hot-blooded and mentally unstable, his conduct of affairs often verged on the lunatic. In the first place, he repeated the mistake of those whose leadership he had denounced, for he likewise reconstructed the jetties and barriers in the sea; his witlessness, however, outdid theirs in so far as the error of not being able to learn from experience is greater than that of being the first to try and fail. He was also a born martinet, and applied the traditional punishments unmercifully to soldiers who were Roman citizens and flogged the allies with rods. In general, the distinction of his clan and the reputation of his family had so spoiled him that he was supercilious and looked down on everyone.

4. Finding himself overtaken he fled for refuge to the shore, for he regarded the terrors of shipwreck more lightly than the risk of battle.

5. Even before he became general, [247] Hamilcar's nobility of spirit was apparent, and when he succeeded to the command he showed himself worthy of his country by his zeal for glory and scorn of danger. He was reputed to be a man of exceptional intelligence, and since he surpassed all his fellow citizens both in daring and in ability at arms, he was indeed:

Both a goodly prince and a brave warrior. [*Il.* 3.179]

6. Near Longon there was a fort, called Italium, belonging to Catana. Barca the Carthaginian, having attacked this . . .

7. He revealed to no one what had been planned; for he was of the opinion that when such stratagems are imparted to one's friends they either become known to the enemy through deserters or produce cowardice among the soldiers by their anticipation of great danger.

For the plans and stratagems of generals, when imparted to one's friends, become known to the enemy through deserters, and engendering cowardice in the soldiers fill them with anticipations of great danger.

8. Barca, after sailing in at night and disembarking his army, took the lead in person on the ascent to Eryx, a distance of thirty stades. He captured the city and slew all the . . . The survivors he removed to Drepana.

9. On every occasion and in every undertaking good discipline turns out to be productive of good results.

Although Hamilcar had given orders that the soldiers should not engage in plunder, Vodostor was disobedient and as a result lost many of his men. So true is it that on every occasion good discipline turns out to be productive of good results that now, though the foot-soldiers, let alone ruining the great success that had already been achieved, even risked complete destruction, the cavalry, though not more than two hundred in number, not only came through safe themselves but provided safety for the others as well.

Hamilcar sent to Eryx to arrange for taking up the dead for burial. The consul Fundanius bade the messengers, if they were sensible men, request a truce to recover, not the dead, but the living. After giving this arrogant reply the consul straightway suffered serious losses, so that it appeared to many that his boastfulness had met with due retribution from the gods.

When Fundanius sent heralds to arrange for the burial of the dead, Barca's reply was very different from that given on the earlier occasion. For stating that he was at war with the living, but had come to terms with the dead, he granted permission for their burial.

10. Hanno, being a man of great enterprise and eager to win renown, and, above all, having at his disposal an idle army, hoped by means of this expedition to train the army while providing its maintenance from the enemy's country, thus relieving the city of its expense, and at the same time to accomplish many things that would redound to the glory and advantage of the fatherland.

When Hanno had forced Hecatompylus to capitulate, the elders of the city approached him, bearing the olive-branches of supplication, and besought him to treat them humanely. Since the general was concerned to enjoy a good reputation, and preferred kindness to retribution, he took three thousand hostages but left the city and its estates untouched, and in consequence received crowns and other high honours from the grateful people. His soldiers, whom the inhabitants entertained splendidly and with great cordiality, feasted on the abundance of all things provided for their enjoyment.

11. The consul Lutatius, with three hundred warships and seven hundred transports and carriers, a thousand vessels in all, sailed to Sicily and cast anchor at the trading-station of the Erycinians. Likewise, Hanno himself, setting out from Carthage with two hundred and fifty warships, together with cargo ships, came to the island of Hiera. As he proceeded thence towards Eryx the Romans came out to meet him, and a battle ensued, hotly contested on both sides. In this battle the Carthaginians lost a hundred and seventeen ships, twenty of them with all men aboard (the Romans lost eighty ships, thirty of them completely, while fifty were partially destroyed), while the number of Carthaginians taken prisoner was, according to the account of Philinus, six thousand, but according to certain others, four thousand and forty. The rest of the ships, aided by a favouring wind, fled to Carthage.

Such heights of bravery were reached that even the generals on both sides distinguished themselves by their personal exploits and led the way amid hazards. Here the most surprising accidents on occasion befell the bravest men. For when their ships were sunk, some who were far superior in courage to their opponents were captured, not because they fell short in deeds of valour, but because they were overpowered by the irresistible force of necessity. For what does bravery profit a man when his ship goes down, and his person, robbed of its footing, is delivered by the sea into the hands of the enemy?

12. The mother of the young men was bitter at the death of her husband [Regulus], and believing that he had died of neglect she made her sons maltreat the prisoners. They were accordingly cooped up in an extremely narrow room, where for lack of space they were forced to make do by contorting their bodies like coiling serpents. Later, when they had been deprived of food for five days, Bodostor died of despair and privation. Hamilcar, however, being a man of exceptional spirit, held out and clung still to hope, desperate though he was. Although he repeatedly pled with the woman and recounted with tears the care he had lavished upon her husband, she was so far removed from any feelings of kindliness or considerations of humanity that for five days she shut the corpse in with him, and though she allowed him a little food her sole aim was to enable him thereby to endure his wretched state. When finally he despaired of winning pity by supplications, he cried aloud and called upon Zeus Xenios and the gods who watch over the affairs of men to witness that instead of a due return of kindness he was receiving punishment beyond human endurance. Yet he did not die, whether because some god took pity on him, or because chance brought him unexpected assistance. For when he was at the point of death as a result of the effluvia from the corpse and his general maltreatment, some of the household slaves recounted to certain persons what was going on. They were scandalised, and reported it to the tribunes. Since in any case the cruelty that had been revealed was shocking, the magistrates summoned the Atilii and very nearly brought them to trial on a capital charge, on the ground that they were bringing disgrace upon Rome; and they threatened to exact fitting punishment from them if they should not bestow all possible care upon the prisoners. The Atilii rebuked their mother sternly, cremated the body of Bodostor and sent the ashes to his kinsmen, and brought Hamilcar relief from his dire distress.

13. When the envoys of the Romans, together with Gesco, came to Barca and read the terms of the agreement, he remained silent up to a certain point.

But when he heard that they were to surrender arms and hand over the deserters, he could not restrain himself but ordered them to depart at once. He was prepared, he said, to die fighting rather than agree through cowardice to a shameful act; and he knew too that Fortune shifts her allegiance and comes over to the side of men who stand firm when all seems lost, and that the case of Atilius had provided a striking demonstration of such unexpected reversals.

14. After the Romans had been at war with the Carthaginians for twenty-four years and had held Lilybaeum under siege for ten years, they made peace.

BOOK XXV FRAGMENTS

1. Epicurus the philosopher, in his work entitled *Principal Doctrines,* declared that whereas the just life is unperturbed, the unjust is heavily burdened with perturbation. Thus in a single brief sentence he encompassed much true wisdom, which has, moreover, in general the power to correct the evil that is in man. For injustice, as it is a very *metropolis* of evils, brings the greatest misfortunes not only upon private citizens, but also collectively upon actual nations and peoples, and upon kings.

2. Though the Carthaginians had endured great struggles and perils over Sicily [241-37] and had been continuously at war with the Romans for twenty-four years, they experienced no disasters so great as those brought upon them by the war against the mercenaries whom they had wronged. For as a result of defrauding their foreign troops of the arrears of pay that were due, they very nearly lost their empire and even their own country. For the mercenaries thus cheated suddenly revolted, and thereby brought Carthage into the direst distress.

Those who had served in the Carthaginian forces were Iberians, Celts, Balearic Islanders, Libyans, Phoenicians, Ligurians, and mongrel Greek slaves; and they it was who revolted.

3. The Carthaginians sent a herald to the rebels to negotiate for the recovery of the dead bodies. Spondius and the other leaders, with intensified brutality, not only refused the request for burial but forbade them ever again to send a herald about any matter whatsoever, threatening that the same punishment would await anyone who came. They also decreed that henceforth all captives who were Carthaginians should incur the same penalty as these, while any who were allies of the Phoenicians should have their hands cut off and be sent back thus mutilated to Carthage. Hence, by such impiety and cruelty as I have described, Spondius and the other leaders succeeded in undermining Barca's strategy of leniency. For Hamilcar himself, though distressed by their cruelty, was in this way forced to abandon his kindness to prisoners and to impose a like penalty upon those who fell into his hands. Accordingly, by way of torture, he tossed to the elephants all who were taken prisoner, and it was a stern punishment as these trampled them to death.

The inhabitants of Hippo and Utica revolted and cast the men of the garrisons down from the walls to lie unburied; and when envoys arrived from Carthage to take up the bodies, they blocked the move to bury them.

4. And so it came about that the rebels, because of the scarcity of food, were as much in the position of men besieged as of besiegers.

In courage they were fully the equals of the enemy, but they were seriously handicapped by the inexperience of their leaders. Here again, therefore, it was possible to see in the light of actual experience how great an advantage a general's judgement has over a layman's inexperience or even a soldier's unreasoned routine.

5. For it was a higher power, apparently, that exacted from them this retribution for their impious deeds.

Hamilcar crucified Spondius, but when Matho took Hannibal prisoner, he nailed him to the same cross. Thus it seemed as if Fortune of set purpose was assigning success and defeat in turn to these offenders against humanity.

The two cities [Hippo & Utica] had no grounds for negotiating a settlement, because from the first onslaught they had left themselves no room for mercy or forgiveness. Such is the great advantage, even in wrongdoing, of moderation and the avoidance of practices that are beyond reason.

6. After their withdrawal from Sicily the mercenary forces of the Carthaginians rose in insurrection against them for the following reasons. They demanded excessive compensation for the horses that had died in Sicily and for the men who had been killed . . . and they carried on the war for four years and four months. They were slaughtered by the general, Hamilcar Barca, who had also fought valiantly in Sicily against the Romans.

7. [This island [Sardinia] gained such fame for the abundance of its crops that at a later time the Carthaginians, when they had grown powerful, coveted it and faced many struggles and perils for its possession. We shall write of these matters in connection with the period to which they belong.]

Hamilcar, surnamed Barca, performed many great services for his country, both in Sicily, in the war against the Romans, and in Libya, when the mercenaries and the Libyans rose in insurrection and held Carthage under siege. Since in both these wars his achievements were outstanding and his conduct of affairs prudent, he gained the well-deserved approbation of all his fellow citizens. Later on, however, after the conclusion of the Libyan War, he formed a political group of the lowest sort of men, and from this source, as well as from the spoils of war, amassed wealth; perceiving, moreover, that his successes were bringing him increased power, he gave himself over to demagoguery and to currying favour with the populace, and thus induced the people to put into his hands for an indefinite period the military command over all Iberia. [237]

9. Since the Celts were many times over more numerous, and because of their daring spirit and bold deeds had grown very arrogant, their attitude throughout the struggle was one of contempt, whereas Barca and his men sought to remedy their deficiency in numbers by bravery and experience. That their plans were soundly conceived was generally agreed, yet it was Fortune who beyond their hopes presided over the course of events and unexpectedly brought to a happy issue an undertaking that appeared impossible and fraught with peril.

10. When Hamilcar was placed in command at Carthage he soon enlarged the empire of his country and ranged by sea as far as the Pillars of Heracles, Gadeira [Gades], and the ocean. Now the city of Gadeira is a colony of the Phoenicians, and is situated at the farthest extremity of the inhabited world, on the very ocean, and it possesses a roadstead. Hamilcar made war on the Iberians and Tartessians, together with the Celts, led by Istolatius and his brother, and cut, to pieces their whole force, including the two brothers and other outstanding leaders; he took over and enrolled in his own army three thousand survivors. Indortes then raised an army of fifty thousand men, but before the fighting even began he was put to flight and took refuge on a certain hill; there he was besieged by Hamilcar, and although, under cover of night, he again fled, most of his force was cut to pieces and Indortes himself was captured alive. After putting out his eyes and maltreating his person Hamilcar had him crucified; but the rest of the prisoners, numbering more than ten thousand, he released. He won over many cities by diplomacy and many others by force of arms. Hasdrubal, the son-in-law of Hamilcar, having been sent by his father-in-law to Carthage to take part in the war with the Numidians who had revolted against the Carthaginians, cut down eight thousand men and captured two thousand alive; the rest of the Numidians were reduced to slavery, having formerly paid tribute. As for Hamilcar, after bringing many cities throughout Iberia under his dominion, he founded a very large city which, from its situation, he named Acra Leucê [White Citadel]. While Hamilcar was encamped before the city of Helice [Elche?] and had it under siege, he sent off the greater part of his army and the elephants into winter quarters at Acra Leucê, a city of his own foundation, and remained behind with the rest. The king of the Orissi, however, came to the aid of the beleaguered city, and by a feigned offer of friendship and alliance succeeded in routing Hamilcar. In the course of his flight Hamilcar contrived to save the lives of his sons and his friends by turning aside on another road; overtaken by the king, he plunged on horseback into a large river and perished in the flood under his steed, but his sons Hannibal and Hasdrubal made their way safely to Acra Leucê.

As for Hamilcar, therefore, although he died many years before our time, let him have from History by way of epitaph the praise that is properly his.

11. Hasdrubal, having learned that fair dealing is more effective than force, preferred peace to war.

The entire city was constantly agog for news, and since every rumour that spread brought a change of heart, anxiety was universal.

12. Hasdrubal, the son-in-law of Hamilcar, immediately upon learning of the disaster to his kinsman [229/8] broke camp and made for Acra Leucê; he had with him more than a hundred elephants. Acclaimed as general by the army and by the Carthaginians alike, he collected an army of fifty thousand seasoned infantry and six thousand cavalry, together with two hundred elephants. He made war first on the king of the Orissi and killed all who had been responsible for Hamilcar's rout. Their twelve cities, and all the cities of Iberia, fell into his hands. After his marriage to the daughter of an Iberian prince he was proclaimed general with unlimited power by the whole Iberian people. He thereupon founded a city on the sea coast, and called it New Carthage; later, desiring to outdo Hamilcar, he founded yet another city. He put into the field an army of sixty thousand infantry, eight thousand cavalry, and two hundred elephants. One of his household slaves plotted against him, and he was slain after he had held the command for nine years.

13. The Celts and Gauls, having assembled a force of two hundred thousand men, joined battle with the Romans and in the first combat were victorious. In a second attack they were again victorious, and even killed one of the Roman consuls. The Romans, who for their part had seven hundred thousand infantry and seventy thousand cavalry, after suffering these two defeats, won a decisive victory in the third engagement. They slew forty thousand men and took the rest captive, with the result that the chief prince of the enemy slashed his own throat and the prince next in rank to him was taken alive. After this exploit Aemilius, now become proconsul, overran the territory of the Gauls and Celts, captured many cities and fortified places, and sent back to Rome an abundance of booty.

14. Hiero, king of Syracuse, coming to the aid of the Romans, sent grain to them during the Celtic War, and was paid for it after the conclusion of the war.

15. Since after the assassination of Hasdrubal the Carthaginian there was no one in command, they chose as general Hannibal, the elder son of Hamilcar. The people of Zacantha [Saguntum], whose city was under siege by Hannibal, collected their sacred objects, the gold and silver that was in their houses, and the ornaments, earrings, and silver pieces of their women, and melting them down put copper and lead into the mixture; having thus rendered their gold useless they sallied forth and after an heroic struggle were all cut down, having themselves inflicted many casualties. The women of the city put their children to death and hanged themselves. The occupation of the city, therefore, brought Hannibal no gain. The Romans requested the surrender of Hannibal to be tried for his lawless acts, and when this was refused embarked on the "Hannibalic" War.

16. In the senate-chamber of the Carthaginians the eldest of the envoys sent by Rome showed to the senate the lap of his toga and said that he brought them both peace and war, and would leave there whichever the Carthaginians wished. When the suffete [king] of the Carthaginians bade him do whichever he wished, he replied,"I send on you war." [218] Straightway a majority of the Carthaginians cried aloud that they accepted it.

17. The men of Victomela [Victumulae?], having been forced to yield their city, hastened home to their wives and children to take pleasure in them for the last time. [218/7] For indeed, what pleasure is there for men who are doomed to die save only tears and the last parting embraces of family and kindred, whereby, as it seems, such hapless wretches do gain some ease from their misfortunes? Be that as it may, most of the men set their houses ablaze, were consumed in the flames together with all their household, and raised for themselves a tomb above their own hearths; others, again, with high courage killed their families first and then slew themselves, considering a self-inflicted death preferable to death with outrage at the hands of their enemies.

18. Antigonus [Doson], son of Demetrius, was appointed his [Philip V] guardian and ruled over the Macedonians for twelve years or, according to Diodorus, for nine.

Hannibal, as Diodorus, Dio, and Dionysius of Halicarnassus all record, was general of the Sicels and the son of Hamilcar. This Hamilcar had conquered the whole of Iberia but was killed when the Iberians treacherously set upon him. On this occasion he ordered his whole army to flee, and when his sons, Hannibal, aged fifteen, and Hasdrubal, aged twelve, clung to him and desired to share his death, he drove them off with whips and made them join the others in flight; then lifting the crest and helmet from his head he was recognized by the Iberians. Since all the Iberians, just as they were, rushed to attack him, the fugitives gained a respite and escaped. As soon as Hamilcar saw that the army was safe he turned about and strove against his own defeat by the Iberians, but when they pressed hard on every side he spurred his horse furiously and dashed into the waters of the Iber River. As he sped on someone struck him with a javelin; though he was drowned, still his corpse was not found by the Iberians, and that was his object, for it was swept away by the currents. Hannibal, the son of this heroic man, served under Hamilcar's son-in-law, and with him ravaged all Iberia to avenge his father's death.

Meanwhile the Ausonian Romans after many reverses had defeated the Sicels and had laid upon them the stern injunction that no one might retain even a sword. Hannibal, at the age of twenty-five, without the consent of the senate or of those in authority, brought together a hundred and more impetuous and spirited young men and lived by plundering Iberia, the while he constantly increased the size of his band. As its numbers passed beyond the hundreds and ran into the thousands and into the tens of thousands, and, though assembled thus without pay or bounties, when it became at last a great army of stalwart warriors, then straightway this was revealed to the Romans. One and all they arrayed themselves for war on land and sea, and seven hundred and seventy thousand strong they strove to destroy the Sicels root and branch. The Sicels besought Hannibal to desist, lest they perish utterly. He suffered such as were so inclined to talk and bluster, and without waiting for the aforesaid Romans to attack, one man alone of all the Sicels he moves on Italy and over the Alpine mountains makes his way. Where access was difficult he cut his way down rocky cliffs, and in six months had met the Roman forces. In various battles he slew large numbers of their men. He kept waiting and watching for his brother Hasdrubal, who, after crossing the Alps in fifteen days, was approaching Hannibal leading a mighty army. [208?] Having discovered this the Romans, attacking secretly, slew him, then brought the head and cast it at the feet of Hannibal. After he had duly mourned his beloved brother, Hannibal later arrayed his forces against the Romans at Cannae; the Roman generals were Paullus and Terentius. Cannae is a plain land of Apulia, where Diomedes founded the city of Argyrippa [Arpi], that is, in the Greek tongue, Argos Hippeion. This plain has belonged to the Daunians, thereafter to the Iapygians, then to the Sallentians, and now to the people whom all men call Calabrians; it was furthermore at the boundary between Calabrians and Lombards that the great battle between them broke forth. On the occasion of this fearsome battle there was a dreadful earthquake, which made mountains split asunder, and showers of great stones poured from heaven, but fighting hotly the warriors were unaware of anything. Finally, so many Romans fell in battle that when Hannibal, the general, sent to Sicily the rings of the commanders and other men of distinction, it was by pecks and bushels that they were measured. The noble and prominent ladies of Rome thronged weeping to the temples of the city and cleansed the statues with their hair; later, when the Roman land suffered a total dearth of males, they even consorted with slaves and barbarians, that their race might not be wiped out root and branch. At this time Rome, when absolutely all its men were lost, stood wide open for many days, and the elders sat before its gates, bewailing that most grievous calamity and asking those who passed by whether none at all was left alive. Though Rome was then gripped by such misfortunes, Hannibal neglected the chance to raze it to the ground, and showed himself too sluggish for such action by reason of victories and drinking and soft living, until the Romans again had an army of their own levied. Then he was thrice balked in his attacks on Rome, for suddenly out of a clear sky came hail most violent and a darkness that hindered his advance. At a later time Hannibal, now regarded with envy by the Sicels, ran short of food, and when they sent none, that once noble conqueror, himself now conquered by starvation, was put to flight by the Roman Scipio, and was the occasion for fearful destruction to the Sicels. He himself died by drinking poison in Bithynia, at a place called Libyssa, though he had thought to die in his own Libyan land. For Hannibal had a certain oracle, which ran somewhat like this:

> A Libyan sod shall cover the body of Hannibal.

BOOK XXVI FRAGMENTS

1. Neither the poet nor the historian nor indeed any craftsman in literary form can in all respects satisfy all his readers; for human nature, even though carried to the highest degree of perfection, cannot succeed in winning the approval of all men and the censure of none. Pheidias, for example, was admired above all others for the fabrication of ivory statues; Praxiteles in masterly fashion embodied the emotions in works of stone; Apelles and Parrhasius by their practised skill in blending colours brought the art of painting to its peak. Yet not one of these men attained such success in his work that he could display a product of his skill in all respects above censure. Who, for instance, among poets is more illustrious than Homer? Who among orators than Demosthenes? Who among men of upright life than Aristeides and Solon? Yet even their reputations and talents have been assailed by criticism and the demonstration of mistakes. For they were but human, and though they achieved pre-eminence in their professions, yet through human frailty they failed in many cases. Now there are certain paltry fellows, full of envy and wise in petty things, who dismiss all that is excellent in any achievement but fasten upon whatever admits of distortion or plausible censure. Thereby, through their denunciation of others, they aspire to enhance their own skill, failing to realise that infirmity of talent is not the result of external influences, but that, on the contrary, every talent is judged in and for itself. We may well marvel at the industry which such foolish minds expend upon trivialities in their attempts to win a good name for themselves by reviling others. It is the very nature of some people, I think, to be stupidly mischievous, just as it is the nature of frosts and snow to blast fine young crops. Indeed, just as the eye is dimmed by the dazzling whiteness of snow and loses its power of exact vision, so there are men who neither will nor can themselves achieve anything of note, and who therefore of set purpose disparage the accomplishments of others. Hence men of good understanding should award to those who by diligent efforts have won success the praise due to excellence, but should not carp at the human frailties of those whose success is small. So much, then, for those who make a practice of evil speaking.

2. Hannibal was a born fighter, and having been reared from boyhood in the practice of warfare and having spent many years in the field as the companion of great leaders, he was well versed in war and its struggles. Nature, moreover, had richly endowed him with sagacity, and since by long years of training in war he had acquired the ability to command, he now had high hopes of success.

3. As a countermeasure to the shrewd policy of Fabius the dictator Hannibal challenged him again and again to open combat, and by taunts of cowardice sought to compel him to accede to a decision by battle. When he remained unmoved, the Roman populace began to criticise the dictator, called him "Lackey," [pedagogue] and reproached him with cowardice. Fabius, however, bore these insults calmly and with self-possession.

Like a good athlete he [Fabius?] entered the contest only after long training, when he had gained much experience and strength.

Once Minucius had been worsted by Hannibal, everyone decided after the event that his total failure was the result of folly and inexperience, but that

Fabius, by his sagacity and his ability as a strategist, had shown throughout a prudent concern for safety.

4. Menodotus of Perinthus wrote a *Treatise on Greek History* in fifteen books; Sosylus of Elis wrote a *History of Hannibal* in seven books.

5. The Roman legion consists of five thousand men.

6. Men naturally rally to the banners of success, but join in attacks on the fortunes of the fallen.

Fortune is changeable by nature and will swiftly bring about a reversal of our situation.

7. Dorimachus [of Trichonium], the Aetolian general, perpetrated an impious deed, for he plundered the oracle of Dodona and set fire to the temple, except for the cella.

8. For since Rhodes had been laid low by a great earthquake, Hiero of Syracuse gave six talents of silver for the reconstruction of the city walls and, in addition to the money, gave a number of fine vases of silver; and he exempted their grain ships from the payment of duty.

9. What is now called Philippopolis in Thessaly was formerly called Phthiotic Thebes. [217]

10. When the question of revolt was brought forward [216] at a public assembly in Capua and the course of action to be taken was being debated, the Capuans allowed a certain Pancylus Paucus to express his opinion. Fear of Hannibal had driven him out of his mind, and he swore to his fellow citizens a peculiar oath. If, he said, there were still one chance in a hundred for the Romans, he would not go over to the Carthaginians; but since, in fact, the superiority of the enemy was manifest and danger now stood at their very gates, they must perforce yield to this superiority. In this way, all having agreed to join forces with the Carthaginians . . .

11. After the army of Hannibal had for some time greedily taken their fill of the riches of Campania, [216/7] their whole pattern of life was reversed. For constant luxury, soft couches, and perfumes and food of every sort, all in lavish abundance, relaxed their strength and their wonted ability to endure danger, and reduced both body and spirit to a soft and womanish condition. Human nature, in fact, accepts only with distaste the unaccustomed practice of hardships and meagre diet, whereas it takes eagerly to a life of ease and luxury.

12. The cities shifted and floundered as the weight of public opinion tipped the scales now this way, now that.

Even the goodwill of friends may be seen to change with changing circumstances.

The virtues of good men sometimes win them honour even among enemies.

Many women, unmarried girls, and freeborn boys accompanied the Capuan forces because of the shortage of food. [212?] War does, in fact, sometimes compel those who in times of peace live in high dignity to endure conditions from which their years should exempt them.

13. Wreaking widespread devastation as he went, Hannibal also took over the cities of Bruttium, and later captured Croton and was about to invest Rhegium. Having set out from the west and the Pillars of Heracles, he brought into subjection all the territory of the Romans except for Rome and Naples, and he carried the war as far as Croton.

14. After having denounced the Romans at length for their cruelty and dishonesty, and especially their arrogance, Hannibal singled out those who were the sons and kinsmen of senators, and in order to punish the senate, put them to death.

Because of his deep hostility to the Romans, Hannibal selected suitable prisoners and paired them off for single combat. He compelled brothers to fight against brothers, fathers against sons, kinsmen against kinsmen. Here, indeed, there is just cause to detest the savage cruelty of the Phoenician, and to admire the piety of the Romans and their steadfast endurance in so grievous a plight. For though they were subjected to fire and goads and were most cruelly scourged, not one of them consented to do violence to his kindred, but all in an access of noble devotion expired under torture, having kept themselves free from the mutual stain of parricide.

15. Upon the death at Syracuse of Gelo and Hiero [215], the rulers of Sicily, and the succession to the throne of Hieronymus, who was a lad in his teens, the kingdom was left without a capable leader. As a result the youth, keeping company with flatterers who courted him, was led astray into luxurious living, profligacy, and despotic cruelty. He committed outrages against women, put to death friends who spoke frankly, summarily confiscated many estates, and presented them to those who courted his favour. This behaviour brought in its train first the hatred of the populace, then a conspiracy, and finally the downfall that usually attends wicked rulers.

After the death of Hieronymus, the Syracusans, having met in assembly, voted to punish the whole family of the tyrant and to put them all to death, men and women alike, in order to uproot completely the tyrant stock.

16. Mago sent the body of Sempronius to Hannibal. Now when the soldiers saw the corpse, they raised a clamour and demanded that it should be hacked apart and flung piecemeal to the winds. Hannibal, however, declared that it was not seemly to vent one's anger upon a senseless corpse, and confronted as he was by evidence of the uncertainty of Fortune, and at the same time moved by admiration for the man's valour, he granted the dead hero a costly funeral. Then having gathered up the bones and bestowed them decently, he sent them to the Roman camp.

17. When the Roman senate heard that Capua had been completely invested with a double wall, they did not persist in a policy of unalterable hostility, even though the capture of the city now appeared (imminent?). On the contrary, influenced by ties of kinship, they decreed that all Campanians who changed sides before a fixed date should be granted immunity. The Campanians, however, rejected the senate's generous proposals, and deluding themselves as to the aid received from Hannibal repented only when repentance was of no avail.

18. [A man may well marvel at the ingenuity of the designer [Archimedes], in connection not only with this invention but with many other and greater ones as well, the fame of which has encompassed the entire inhabited world and of which we shall give a detailed and precise account when we come to the age of Archimedes.]

Archimedes, the famous and learned engineer and mathematician, a Syracusan by birth, was at this time an old man, in his seventy-fifth year [212].

He constructed many ingenious machines, and on one occasion by means of a triple pulley launched with his left hand alone a merchant ship having a capacity of fifty thousand medimni. During the time when Marcellus, the Roman general, was attacking Syracuse both by land and by sea, Archimedes first hauled up out of the water some of the enemy's barges by means of a mechanical device, and after raising them to the walls of Syracuse, sent them hurtling down, men and all, into the sea. Then, when Marcellus moved his barges a bit farther off, the old man made it possible for the Syracusans, one and all, to lift up stones the size of a wagon, and by hurling them one at a time to sink the barges. When Marcellus now moved the vessels off as far as an arrow can fly, the old man then devised an hexagonal mirror, and at an appropriate distance from it set small quadrangular mirrors of the same type, which could be adjusted by metal plates and small hinges. This contrivance he set to catch the full rays of the sun at noon, both summer and winter, and eventually, by the reflection of the sun's rays in this, a fearsome fiery heat was kindled in the barges, and from the distance of an arrow's flight he reduced them to ashes. Thus did the old man, by his contrivances, vanquish Marcellus. Again, he used to say, in the Doric speech of Syracuse: "Give me a place to stand and with a lever I will move the whole world." Now when Syracuse was, as Diodorus relates, suddenly betrayed to Marcellus, or according to Dio, sacked by the Romans while the citizens were celebrating a nocturnal festival of Artemis, this man was killed by one of the Romans, under the following circumstances. Engaged in sketching a mechanical diagram, he was bending over it when a Roman came upon him and began to drag him off' as a prisoner of war. Archimedes, wholly intent on his diagram and not realising who was tugging at him, said to the man: "Away from my diagram, fellow!" Then, when the man continued to drag him along, Archimedes turned and, recognissng him for a Roman, cried out: "Quick there, one of my machines, someone!" The Roman, alarmed, slew him on the spot, a weak old man, but one whose achievements were wondrous. As soon as Marcellus learned of this, he was grieved, and together with the noblemen of the city and all the Romans gave him splendid burial amid the tombs of his fathers. As for the murderer, he had him, I fancy, beheaded. Dio and Diodorus record the story.

19. Diodorus the historian, in his comparison of Antioch on the Orontes to Syracuse, says that Syracuse is a tetrapolis [Ortygia, Neapolis, Achradina, Tyche].

20. When, after the fall of Syracuse, [212] the inhabitants approached Marcellus as suppliants, he ordered that the persons of all who were freeborn were to be spared, but that all their property was to be taken as booty.

Being unable to procure food after the capture because of their poverty, [211] he Syracusans agreed to become slaves, so that when sold they might receive food from those who purchased them. Thus Fortune imposed upon the defeated Syracusans, over and above their other losses, a calamity so grievous that in place of proffered freedom they voluntarily chose slavery.

21. By his release of the hostages [209/8] Scipio [Africanus] demonstrated how time and time again the virtue of a single man has been able summarily to impose kings upon nations.

22. Indibeles the Celtiberian, [206] after winning forgiveness from Scipio, again kindled the flames of war when a suitable occasion presented itself. For indeed, those who benefit knaves, in addition to wasting their favours, fail to realise that ofttimes they are actually raising up enemies for themselves.

23. The Carthaginians, after bringing the Libyan War [Mercenary War] to an end, had avenged themselves on the Numidian tribe of the Micatani, women and children included, and crucified all whom they captured. As a result their descendants, mindful of the cruelty meted out to their fathers, were firmly established as the fiercest enemies of the Carthaginians.

24. He [Polybius] did not leave unrecorded the great ability of the man (I mean, of course, Hasdrubal), but on the contrary affirms it. For Hasdrubal was the son of Hamilcar, surnamed Barca, the most distinguished man of his time, inasmuch as in the Sicilian War Hamilcar was the only leader who repeatedly defeated the Romans, and after bringing to an end the Civil War, was the first to carry an army across to Spain. As the son of such a father, Hasdrubal proved himself not unworthy of his father's fame. It is generally agreed that next to his brother Hannibal he was the finest general in all Carthage; accordingly Hannibal left him in command of the armies in Spain. He engaged in many battles throughout Spain, constantly building up his forces after each reverse, and he stood firm in the face of frequent and manifold dangers. Indeed, even after he had been driven back into the interior, his outstanding personal qualities enabled him to bring together a large army, and contrary to all expectations he made his way into Italy.

If Hasdrubal had enjoyed the assistance of Fortune as well, it is generally agreed that the Romans could not have carried on the struggle simultaneously against both him and Hannibal. For this reason we should estimate his ability not on the basis of his achievements but of his aims and enterprise. For these qualities are subject to men's control, but the outcome of their actions lies in the hands of Fortune.

BOOK XXVII FRAGMENTS

1. Nabis, the tyrant of Sparta, put to death Pelops, the son of the late king Lycurgus, [207] who was at this time still a boy. This was a measure of precaution lest when he came of age the youth, emboldened by his noble birth, should some day restore his country's freedom. Nabis personally selected and put to death those Lacedaemonians who were most accomplished, and gathered from all sides hirelings of the basest stamp to defend his régime. As a result temple-robbers, thieves, pirates, and men under sentence of death streamed into Sparta from every direction. For since it was by impious deeds that Nabis had made himself tyrant, he supposed that only by such men could he be most securely guarded.

Nabis, the tyrant of Sparta, devised many forms of punishment for the citizens, in the belief that by degrading his country he would enhance his own position. Indeed, when a knave comes to power he is not, I think, likely to bear his good fortune as a mortal should.

2. As *pontifex maximus* he [P. Licinius Dives, 205] was obliged by reason of his religious duties not to absent himself from the vicinity of Rome.

2a. In like manner Scipio, according to the account of Diodorus, set before the Sicilian aristocrats the choice of joining him in the expedition to Libya or of handing over to his men their horses and slaves.

3. With a fleet of seven ships the Cretans began to engage in piracy, and plundered a number of vessels. This had a disheartening effect upon those who were engaged in commerce by sea, whereupon the Rhodians, reflecting that this lawlessness would affect them also, declared war on the Cretans.

4. Pleminius, whom Scipio had appointed as governor of Locri, tore down the treasure houses of Persephonê, for he was indeed an impious man, and he plundered and carried off their wealth. The Locrians, deeply outraged by this, appealed for protection to the pledged word of the Romans. Moreover, two of the military tribunes affected to be shocked at the offence. Their behaviour, however, was not motivated by any indignation at what was occurring; on the contrary, it was because they had failed to receive their share in the plunder that they now brought charges against Pleminius. Divine Providence speedily inflicted upon one and all the punishment that their wickedness deserved. For indeed this temple of Persephonê is said to be the most renowned in all Italy and to have been kept inviolate by the men of the land at all times. So, for example, when Pyrrhus brought over his forces from Sicily to Locri and, faced with his soldiers' demand for pay, was driven by lack of funds to lay hand on the treasures, it is said that such a tempest arose as he was putting out again to sea that he and all his fleet suffered shipwreck; Pyrrhus, smitten with fear and awe, thereupon made propitiation to the goddess, and delayed his departure until he had restored the treasures.

The tribunes, to resume, with a pretence of righteous indignation now stood forth as champions of the Locrians, and began to inveigh against Pleminius and threaten to bring him to justice. The railings growing apace, they finally came to blows, and the tribunes, having knocked him to the ground, bit off his ears and nose and split open his lips. Pleminius put the tribunes under arrest, subjected them to severe torture, and did away with them. The religious fears of the Roman senate were strongly-aroused by the pillaging of the temple; moreover, the political opponents of Scipio, having found a suitable occasion for discrediting him, charged that Pleminius had acted throughout in accordance with his wishes. The senate sent out an aedile and two tribunes of the people as commissioners, [204] with orders to bring Scipio post-haste back to Rome if they should find that the sacrilege had been committed with his approval; otherwise, they were to allow him to transport his armies to Libya. While the commissioners were yet on the way, Scipio summoned Pleminius, put him in chains, and busied himself with training his army. The tribunes of the people were amazed at this, and praised Scipio. As for Pleminius, he was taken back to Rome, placed in custody by the senate, and, while still in prison, died; the senate confiscated his property and, after making up from the public treasury any deficiency in what had been stolen from the temple, dedicated it to the goddess. It was also decreed that the Locrians should be free, and that any soldiers possessing property belonging to Phersis should, if they failed to restore it, be liable to death.

After these measures concerning the Pleminius affair had been voted as a gesture of goodwill towards the Locrians, the men who had stolen most of the votive offerings and who now perceived the retribution which had befallen the tribunes and Pleminius fell a prey to superstitious fears. Such is the punishment that one who is conscious of wrongdoing suffers in secret, even though he succeed in hiding his guilt from other mortals. So now these men, tortured in spirit, cast away their plunder in an effort to appease the gods.

5. A lie told in the proper circumstances is sometimes productive of great benefits.

6. When Syphax [king of the Masaesyli] and the others were brought before him in chains, Scipio promptly burst into tears at the sight, as he thought of the man's former prosperity and kingly state. After a short time, in keeping with his resolve to practise moderation even in the midst of success, he ordered Syphax to be loosed from his bonds, gave him back his tent, and allowed him to retain his retinue. While still holding him prisoner, though in free custody, he treated him with kindness and frequently invited him to his table.

Scipio, having taken King Syphax prisoner, released him from his bonds and treated him with kindness. The personal enmities of war should, he felt, be maintained up to the point of victory, but since a prisoner's lot had now befallen one of royal rank, he himself, being but human, should do nothing amiss. For there is, it would seem, a divine Nemesis that keeps watch over the life of man and swiftly reminds those whose presumption passes mortal bounds of their own weakness. Who then, with an eye to the fear and terror that Scipio inspired in the enemy, while his own heart was overcome by pity for the unfortunate, could fail to praise such a man? It is generally true, in fact, that men dreaded by their opponents in combat are apt to behave with moderation towards the defeated. So on this occasion Scipio soon won from Syphax gratitude for his considerate treatment.

7. Sophonba, who was the wife first of Masinissa, then of Syphax, and who finally, as a result of her captivity, was reunited with Masinissa, was comely in appearance, a woman of many varied moods, and one gifted with the ability to bind men to her service. As a partisan of the Carthaginian cause she daily urged and entreated her husband with great importunity to revolt from Rome, for she was, indeed, deeply devoted to her country. Now Syphax knew this and informed Scipio about the woman, urging him to be on his guard. Since this tallied with the advice of Laelius as well, Scipio ordered her brought before him, and when Masinissa attempted to intercede, rebuked him sharply. Warily, Masinissa then bade him send his men to fetch her, but went himself to her tent, handed his wife a deadly potion, and forced her to drink it.

8. By his compassion towards those who had blundered, Scipio rendered the alliance with Masinissa secure ever after.

9. Hannibal, having called together his allies, told them that it was now necessary for him to cross over into Libya, and offered any who might wish it his permission to accompany him. Some chose to cross with Hannibal; those, however, who were set on remaining in Italy he encircled with his army, and having first given his soldiers leave to take anyone they wished as a slave, he then slaughtered the rest, some twenty thousand men, as well as three thousand horses and innumerable pack animals.

10. Four thousand cavalry, men who after the defeat of Syphax had gone over to Masinissa, now deserted to Hannibal. In an access of anger, Hannibal encircled them with his army, shot them all down, and distributed their horses to his own soldiers.

11. Carthage being hard pressed for food, those citizens who were disgruntled and desired the abrogation of the treaty of peace incited the populace to attack the ships and bring into port the cargo of provisions. And though the senate forbade them to violate the agreement, no one paid heed: "Bellies," they said, "have no ears."

Wrongdoing bore the semblance of right.

12. Scipio sent envoys to the Carthaginians, and the mob all but put them to death. Men of wiser counsel, however, rescued them and sent them off with an escort of triremes. The leaders of the mob at Carthage urged the admiral [Hasdrubal] to attack the envoys at sea after the escorting triremes turned back, and to kill them all. The attack took place, but the envoys managed to escape to the shore, and made their way safely back to Scipio. The gods swiftly made manifest their power to the wilful sinners. For the Carthaginian envoys who had been sent to Rome were driven by a storm on their return voyage to the very place where the Romans lay at anchor; and when they had been brought before Scipio there was a general outcry to retaliate on the oath-breakers. Scipio, however, declared that they must not commit the very crimes of which they were accusing the Carthaginians. Accordingly the men were released and made their way in safety to Carthage, marvelling at the piety of the Romans.

The Carthaginians, having previously wronged the Romans, were on a certain occasion driven by a storm into the hands of Scipio. Though there was a general outcry to retaliate on the oath-breakers, Scipio declared that they must not commit the very crimes of which they were accusing the Carthaginians.

13. To persuade men to a noble course of action is, in my opinion, of all things the most difficult, whereas words designed to please have wondrous power to suggest a semblance of advantage, even though they lead to the ruin of those who adopt such counsel.

14. There is no honour in conquering the world by force of arms only to be overcome by anger directed against hapless wretches; nor yet in nursing a bitter hatred against the overweening if in prosperity we do the very things ourselves for which we blame others. Glory is the true portion of those who win success only when the conqueror bears his good fortune with moderation. When such men are mentioned everyone remarks that they are worthy of their laurels, but envy dogs those who forget their common mortality, and taints the glory of their success. It is no great thing to slay the suppliant at one's feet, no wondrous exploit to destroy the life of a defeated enemy. Not without reason do men win an ill repute when unmindful of the frailty of all things human they abolish the refuge that is the common privilege of all unfortunates.

15. An act of kindness avails men more than revenge, and gentle treatment of a fallen foe more than savage cruelty.

The more favourable the tide of fortune, the more one must beware of the Nemesis that watches over the life of man.

In the affairs of men nothing remains stable, neither the good nor the ill, since Fortune, as if of set purpose, keeps all things in constant change. It becomes us, therefore, to put aside our high conceits, and profit by the misfortunes of others to make our own lives secure; for the man who has used the fallen gently most richly deserves whatever consideration he himself meets in the vicissitudes of life. Undying praise commonly attends such men even from those not affected, and those who have actually received the favour cherish a feeling of gratitude such as it merits. Even a bitter enemy, in fact, if he find mercy, is transformed by the act of kindness, and straightway becomes a friend as he sees his own fault.

16. The intelligent man should see to it that his friendships are immortal, his enmities mortal. Thus most surely will it ensue that his friends will be legion, while those who are ill disposed will be fewer in number.

It is less essential that men who aspire to exercise authority should be superior to their fellows in other respects than that they should altogether surpass them in clemency and moderation. For whereas the fear engendered by conquest makes the conquerors an object of hatred, consideration for the defeated is productive of goodwill, and will be a stable bond of empire. It follows from this that the greater our concern for the future welfare of our country, the more we must beware of taking some harsh and irremediable action against those who have made voluntary submission to us. For everyone pities those who have succumbed to overwhelming misfortunes, even though there be no personal bond, and everyone hates those who make arrogant use of good fortune, even though they be allies. Each of us, I suppose, regards whatever is done as though it were done to him; he shares the resentment of the unfortunate, and begrudges the prosperity of the successful.

17. Whenever a city of the highest renown is thus pitilessly ravaged, then indeed do the current notions about these people spread even more readily throughout the world, since men are never so ready to agree in praising noble actions as to join with one accord in hating those who behave savagely towards a fallen foe.

The failure to carry with due moderation whatever good fortune the gods grant usually produces many ill consequences.

Any occasion whatsoever is sufficient to prompt a change for the worse when men are unable to carry their good fortune with due moderation. Be warned, then, and see to it that we do not force these men, made desperate, into a display of bravery. Why, even the most cowardly beasts, which turn and run if a way be open, put up an incredible struggle when cornered; in like manner the Carthaginians continue to give way as long as they retain some hopes of safety, but once driven to desperation will stand and face any possible danger in battle. If death lies in store for them whether they flee or fight, death with honour will seem to them preferable to death and disgrace.

Life is full of the unexpected. In times of misfortune, therefore, men should take risks and pursue their venture even at great peril; but when the stream of fortune flows smoothly, it is not well to put oneself in jeopardy.

No one who has won control over a foreign people willingly resigns to others the command of his army.

18. There is a vast difference, to my mind, between misfortune and misdoing, and we should deal with each of them in the way that is appropriate to it, as befits men of wise counsel. So, for example, a man who has blundered but yet has committed no great wrong may justly take refuge in the compassion that is extended to all unfortunates. On the other hand, the man who has sinned deeply and who has perpetrated deeds of violence and brutality that are, as they say, "unutterable," puts himself wholly beyond the reach of such human feelings. It is impossible that one who has proved cruel towards others should meet with compassion when he in turn blunders and falls, or that one who has done all in his power to abolish pity among men should find refuge in the moderation of others. To apply to each the law that he has set for others is no more than just.

One who in the name of the whole people has exacted vengeance from the common foe may, quite clearly, be considered a public benefactor. Just as those who destroy the more dangerous beasts win praise for contributing to the welfare of all, so now those who have curbed the savage cruelty of the Carthaginians and the bestial strain in humanity will by common consent gain the highest renown.

Everyone faces danger bravely when the hope of victory is well founded, but for one who knows in advance that he will be defeated safety lies only in flight and escape.

BOOK XXVIII FRAGMENTS

1. Philip [V] the king of the Macedonians, induced Dicaearchus of Aetolia, a hold adventurer, to engage in piracy, and gave him twenty ships. [204] He ordered him to levy tribute on the islands and to support the Cretans in their war against the Rhodians. Obedient to these commands Dicaearchus harried commercial shipping, and by marauding raids exacted money from the islands.

2. Philip, the king of the Macedonians, had by him a certain knavish fellow, Heracleides of Tarentum, who in private conversations with the king made many false and malicious charges against the friends whom Philip held in high esteem. Eventually Philip sank so low in impiety as to murder five leading members of the council. From that point on his situation deteriorated, and by embarking upon unnecessary wars he came near losing his kingdom at the hands of the Romans. For none of his friends any longer dared speak their minds or rebuke the king's folly for fear of his impetuous temper. He also led an expedition against the Dardanians, though they had done him no wrong, and after defeating them in pitched battle massacred more than ten thousand men.

3. Quite apart from his aggressive ambition, Philip, the king of the Macedonians, was so arrogant in prosperity that he had his friends put to death without benefit of trial, destroyed the tombs of earlier generations, and razed many temples to the ground. As for Antiochus [III], his project of pillaging the sanctuary of Zeus at Elymaïs brought him to appropriate disaster, and he perished with all his host. Both men, though convinced that their armies were irresistible, found themselves compelled by the outcome of a single battle to do the bidding of others. In consequence they ascribed to their own shortcomings the misfortunes that befell them, while for the generous treatment that they were accorded they were duly grateful to those who in the hour of victory practised such moderation. So it was that, as if following a design sketched in their own acts, they beheld the decline into which heaven was leading their kingdoms. The Romans, however, who both on this occasion and thereafter engaged only in just wars and were scrupulous in the observance of oaths and treaties, enjoyed, not without reason, the active support of the gods in all their undertakings.

4. Not only, we may note, do those who wickedly violate private contracts fall foul of the law and its penalties, but even among kings all who engage in acts of injustice meet with retribution from on high. Just as the law is the arbiter of men's deeds for the citizens of a democratic state, so is god the judge of men in positions of authority: to those who seek after virtue he grants rewards appropriate to their virtue, and for those who indulge in greed or any other vice he appoints prompt and fitting punishment.

5. Driven by the need to obtain provisions, Philip, the king of the Macedonians, went about plundering the territory of Attalus, even to the very gates of Pergamum. He razed to the ground the sanctuaries round about the city, and did extreme violence to the richly bedecked Nicephorium and to other temples admired for their sculptures. He was, in fact, enraged with Attalus and, because he failed to find him in that part of the country, vented his spleen on the temples.

6. Having sailed to Abydus to meet Philip, Marcus Aemilius announced to him the decisions of the senate respecting the allies. Philip replied that if the Romans abided by their agreements they would be acting rightly, but that, if they trampled them under foot, he would call the gods to witness their unjust aggression and would defend himself against them.

7. On his arrival at Athens, Philip of Macedon encamped at Cynosarges, and proceeded to set fire to the Academy, to pull down the tombs, and even to outrage the sanctuaries of the gods. By thus indulging his anger as if it were Athens rather than the gods that he was offending, he now not only incurred the utter hatred of mankind, that had long reviled him, but also brought down upon his head swift and fitting chastisement from the gods. For through his own lack of prudence he was thoroughly defeated, and it was only through the forbearance of the Romans that he met with lenient treatment.

8. Philip, observing that his men were disheartened, pointed out to them by way of encouragement that none of these ills attend a victorious army, while for those who perish in defeat it makes no difference whether their death-wounds are large or small.

As a general rule men of base character inculcate a similar baseness in their associates.

9. Philip, perceiving that most of the Macedonians were angry with him because of his friendship for Heracleides, had him placed in custody. A native of Tarentum, Heracleides was a man of surpassing wickedness, who had transformed Philip from a virtuous king into a harsh and godless tyrant, and had thereby incurred the deep hatred of all Macedonians and Greeks.

11. On the occasion of the Epirote embassy to Philip and Flamininus, [198] Flamininus held that Philip must completely evacuate Greece, which should thereafter be un-garrisoned and autonomous, and that he must offer satisfactory compensation for damage done to those who had suffered from his breaches of faith. Philip replied that he must have assured possession of what he had inherited from his father, but that he would withdraw the garrisons from whatever cities he had himself won over, and would submit the question of damages to arbitration.

To this Flamininus replied that there was no need of arbitration, that Philip himself must make terms with those whom he had wronged; furthermore he himself was under orders from the senate to liberate Greece, the whole of it, not merely a part. Philip retorted by asking: "What heavier condition would you have imposed if you had defeated me in war?", and with these words he departed in a rage.

12. While Antiochus, the king of Asia, was engaged in re-founding the city of Lysimacheia [Thrace], the commissioners sent by Flamininus arrived. Having been led before the council, they called upon Antiochus to retire from the cities previously subject to Ptolemy or to Philip, and said that in general they wondered what purpose he had in assembling military and naval forces, and with what intention he had crossed the strait to Europe if not to undertake war against the Romans. By way of rejoinder, Antiochus expressed surprise that the Romans claimed interests in Asia though he did not meddle in any matter that concerned Italy; in resettling the Lysimacheians he was wronging neither the Romans nor anyone else; and as for his relations with Ptolemy, he himself had in mind a plan for avoiding all disputes, for he would give him his daughter in marriage. After this exchange the Romans, though ill content, took their departure.

10. The mere name and reputation of Hannibal had made him a celebrity the whole world through, [195] and in every city each individual was eager for a sight of him.

13. Envoys were sent to Rome by Nabis and by Flamininus to conclude the treaty, [195/4] and when they had discussed with the senate the matters contained in their instructions, the senate agreed to ratify the agreement and to withdraw its garrisons and armies in Greece. When news of the settlement reached him, Flamininus summoned the leading men of all Greece, and convoking an assembly repeated to them Rome's good services to the Greeks. In defence of the settlement made with Nabis he pointed out that the Romans had done what was in their power, and that in accordance with the declared policy of the Roman people all the inhabitants of Greece were now free, un-garrisoned, and most important of all, governed by their own laws. In return he asked the Greeks to seek out such Italians as were held in slavery among them, and to repatriate them within thirty days. This was accomplished.

14. Ptolemy [V Epiphanes], the king of Egypt, was for a time regarded with approval. Aristomenes had been appointed his guardian and had been in all respects an able administrator. Now at the start Ptolemy revered him like a father and was wholly guided by his judgement. Later, however, corrupted by the flattery of his courtiers, he came to hate Aristomenes for his frankness of speech, and finally compelled him to end his life with a draught of hemlock. His ever-increasing brutality and his emulation, not of kingly authority, but of tyrannical licence, brought on him the hatred of the Egyptian people and nearly cost him his kingdom.

15. Once more the senate granted audience to embassies from Greece and greeted them with friendly words, [194/5] for they wanted the goodwill of the Greeks in case of war with Antiochus, which they considered imminent. The envoys of Philip were told that if he remained faithful, the senate would relieve him of the payments of indemnity and would release his son Demetrius. In the case of the envoys who had come from Antiochus a commission of ten senators was set up to hear of the matters with which they stated they had been charged by the king. The session having convened, Menippus, the leader of the embassy, stated that he had come with the aim of forming a pact of friendship and alliance between Antiochus and the Romans. He said, however, that the king wondered what possible reason the Romans had for ordering him not to meddle in certain European affairs, to renounce his claims to certain cities, and not to exact from some the tribute owing to him: such demands as these were unprecedented when a pact of friendship between equals was being negotiated; they were the demands of conquerors settling a war, yet the envoys sent to the king at Lysimacheia had presumed to dictate to him precise instructions on these matters; Antiochus had never been at war with the Romans, and if they wished to effect a treaty of friendship with him, the king stood ready and willing. Flamininus replied that two possible courses lay open, and that the senate allowed the king his choice of one: if he was willing to keep his hands off Europe, the Romans would not meddle with Asiatic affairs; if, however, he did not elect this policy, he must know that the Romans would go to the aid of their friends who were being enslaved. The ambassadors having then made answer that they would agree to no condition of this nature, whereby they would impair the authority of the throne, the senate on the following day announced to the Greeks that if Antiochus interfered at all in European affairs the Romans would bend every effort to liberate the Asiatic Greeks. After the ambassadors of the Greek states had applauded this statement, the king's envoys called upon the senate to reflect how great was the risk to which they exposed each of the two parties, and to take no immediate action, but rather to give the king time to consider, and themselves to engage in more careful consideration of the case.

BOOK XXIX FRAGMENTS

1. Delium was a sanctuary, not far distant from Chalcis. . . . [192] Because he had thus begun the war against Rome with an act of sacrilege the king was vilified by the Greeks . . . and Flamminus, who was then at Corinth, called upon all men and gods to bear him witness that the first act of aggression in the war had been committed by the king.

2. Antiochus established his winter quarters at Demetrias. [192/1] Being now more than fifty years old, he neglected to make preparations for the war, but having fallen in love with a beautiful maiden, whiled away the time in celebrating his marriage to her, and held brilliant assemblies and festivals. By this behaviour he not only ruined himself, body and mind, but also demoralised his army. Indeed, his soldiers, after passing the whole winter in ease and soft living, acquitted themselves poorly when confronted with scarcity, being unable to endure thirst or other hardships. In consequence, some would fall ill, and others, straggling on the march, became widely separated from their formations.

3. King Antiochus, learning that the cities of Thessaly had gone over to the Romans, [191] that his Asiatic forces were slow in arriving, and that the Aetolians were negligent and full of excuses, was deeply distressed. He was, in consequence, angry with those who, on the strength of the Aetolian alliance, had induced him to embark upon a war for which he was not prepared; for Hannibal, however, who had held the contrary opinion, he was now filled with admiration, and pinned all his hopes upon him. Whereas previously he had been disposed to regard him with suspicion, he now looked upon Hannibal as a most trustworthy friend and followed his advice in all matters.

4. As to the Aetolians, from whom an embassy had come to discuss terms of peace, the senate decided that they must either place themselves at the discretion of the Romans, or pay Rome at once a thousand talents of silver. The Aetolians, who because of the severity of the reply refused to accede to these demands, were thoroughly alarmed and found themselves in grave danger; for their zealous support of the king had plunged them into hopeless difficulties, and there was no way out of their troubles.

5. Humbled by his defeat Antiochus decided to withdraw from Europe and to concentrate on the defence of Asia. [190] He ordered the inhabitants of Lysimacheia to abandon their city one and all, and find residence in the cities of Asia. It was the universal opinion that this was a foolish plan, and that he had thereby abandoned to the enemy without a struggle a city most conveniently situated to prevent them from bringing their forces over from Europe into Asia. The sequel of events fully confirmed this judgement, since [L. Cornelius] Scipio, on finding the city deserted, gained a gratuitous success by occupying it.

6. In warfare a ready supply of money is indeed, as the familiar proverb has it, the sister of success, since he who is well provided with money never lacks men able to fight. So, for example, the Carthaginians recently brought the Romans to the brink of disaster, yet it was not with an army of citizens that they won their victories in those great engagements, but by the great number of their mercenary soldiers. An abundance of foreign troops is, in fact, very advantageous to the side that employs them, and very formidable to the enemy, inasmuch as the employers bring together at trifling cost men to do battle in their behalf, while citizen soldiers, even if victorious, are nevertheless promptly faced with a fresh crop of opponents. In the case of citizen armies, a single defeat spells complete disaster, but in the case of mercenaries, however many times they suffer defeat, none the less the employers maintain their forces intact as long as their money lasts. It is not, however, the custom of the Romans to employ mercenaries, nor have they sufficient resources.

As a general rule soldiers follow the example set by their commanders.

Antiochus, having swiftly reaped the reward of his own folly, learned at the cost of great misfortunes not to let success turn his head.

7. Antiochus, on learning that the Romans had crossed to Asia, sent Heracleides of Byzantium to the consul to sue for peace, offering to pay half the costs of the war, and also to give up the cities of Lampsacus, Smyrna, and Alexandria [Troas], which had, it was thought, been responsible for bringing on the conflict. Of the Greek cities in Asia these were, in fact, the first to dispatch embassies to the senate, invoking its aid in behalf of their independence.

8. Antiochus, in addition, offered Publius Scipio, the senior member of the senate, the return of his son without ransom (he had taken him prisoner during his stay on Euboea), and a large sum of money as well, if only he would give his support to the proposed peace. Scipio replied that he would be grateful to the king for the release of his son, but that there was no need of "a large sum of money" besides; in return for this kindness, however, he advised Antiochus not to engage the Romans in battle now that he had had a sample of their prowess. Antiochus, however, finding the Roman unjustifiably harsh, rejected his counter-proposal.

With an eye to the surprises of Fortune Antiochus deemed it advantageous to release Scipio's son, and accordingly decked him out in rich array and sent him back.

10. Antiochus, [189] abandoning the conflict in despair, dispatched an embassy to the consul, requesting pardon for his errors and the granting of peace on whatever terms possible. The consul, adhering to the traditional Roman policy of fair dealing, and moved by the appeals of his brother Publius, granted peace on the following terms: the king must withdraw, in favour of the Romans, from Europe and from the territory on this side Taurus and the cities and nations included therein; he must surrender his elephants and warships, and pay in full the expenses incurred in the war, which were assessed at 15,000 Euboean talents; and he must deliver up Hannibal the Carthaginian, Thoas the Aetolian, and certain others, together with twenty hostages to be designated by the Romans. In his desire for peace Antiochus accepted all the conditions and brought the fighting to a close.

9. At Rome, before the defeat of Antiochus, the envoys from Aetolia, on being brought before the senate, said not a word of their own shortcomings, but spoke at length of their services to Rome. A member of the senate thereupon arose and asked the envoys whether or not the Aetolians were willing to put

themselves in the hands of the Roman people. When the envoys made no reply, the senate, assuming that the Aetolians still had their hopes pinned on Antiochus, sent them empty-handed back to Greece.

11. After the defeat of Antiochus envoys presented themselves from all the cities and principalities of Asia, some suing for independence, others for a return for their good services to Rome in the common struggle against Antiochus. The senate intimated to one and all that they had good reason to hope, and announced the dispatch of ten legates to Asia, who together with the generals in the field were to settle all matters. The envoys returned to their homes, and the ten legates, after first meeting in consultation with Scipio and Aemilius, [188] decided and proclaimed that the territory this side Taurus, and the elephants, were to belong to Eumenes; Caria and Lycia they added to the domain of Rhodes; the cities that had previously paid tribute to Eumenes were to be subject to Eumenes, and any that still paid tribute to Antiochus were relieved of all obligations.

12. Gnaeus Manlius, the proconsul, when approached by envoys from the Galatians seeking an end to hostilities, replied that he would make a treaty of peace with them only when their kings appeared before him in person.

13. Manlius proceeded to Lycaonia and received from Antiochus the grain that was due and the annual payment of a thousand talents stipulated in the agreement.

14. Marcus Furius, [187] who while praetor violated the rights of the Ligurian allies, met with fitting punishment. For coming among the Cenomani, ostensibly as a friend, and without having grounds for complaint against them, he deprived them of their arms. The consul, however, learning of the incident, restored the arms and imposed a fine on Marcus.

15. Antiochus, pressed for funds and hearing that the temple of Bel in Elymaïs had a large store of silver and gold, derived from the dedications, resolved to pillage it. He proceeded to Elymaïs and after accusing the inhabitants of initiating hostilities, pillaged the temple; but though he amassed much wealth he speedily received meet punishment from the gods.

16. Philip upbraided the Thessalians [185] for reviling their former masters now that by the favour of Rome they had unexpectedly gained their freedom. They were not aware, he said, that the Macedonian sun had not yet altogether set. This sally led those who heard it to suspect that Philip intended to make war on Rome, and the commissioners, in a rage, decreed that Philip should be allowed to hold no city save those in Macedonia.

17. As regards Peloponnesian affairs, the Achaean League having convened in general assembly, the Roman envoys were introduced. They stated that the senate was displeased at the dismantling of the Lacedaemonian fortifications, an act that the Achaean League had carried out when it gained control of Sparta and enrolled the Lacedaemonians in the League. Next the envoys of Eumenes were introduced, who brought with them a gift of twenty talents, out of which the king thought payment should be made to the members of the Achaean assembly. The Achaeans, however, rejecting an offer of money as unbecoming, refused to accept the gift. Envoys also came from Seleucus [IV Philopator], seeking to renew the alliance that the Achaeans had had with King Antiochus. The assembly renewed the alliance and accepted his gift.

18. Philopoemen, the general of the Achaean League, was a man of outstanding attainments, intellectual, military, and moral alike, and his life-long political career was irreproachable throughout. Time and again he was preferred to the office of general, and for forty years he guided the affairs of state. More than anyone else he advanced the general welfare of the Achaean confederacy, for he not only made it his policy to treat the common man kindly, but also by force of character won the esteem of the Romans. Yet in the final scene of life he found Fortune unkind. After his death, however, as if by some divine Providence he obtained honours equal to those paid the gods, in compensation for the misfortunes that attended his demise. In addition to the decrees in his honour voted by the Achaeans jointly, his native city set up an altar, (instituted) an annual sacrifice to him, and appointed hymns and praises of his exploits to be sung by the young men of the city.

19. Hannibal, who stands first among all Carthaginians in strategic skill and in the magnitude of his achievements, never at any time experienced disaffection among his troops; on the contrary his wise foresight enabled him to maintain in concord and harmony elements that were by birth set widely apart and that were divided by the wide variety of tongues spoken. Likewise, though it is the common practice of alien troops to desert to the enemy on slight provocation, under his command no one ventured to do this. He always maintained a large army, yet never ran short of money or provisions. Most extraordinary of all, the aliens who served with him did not fall short of the citizens in their affection for him, but even far surpassed them. Naturally, therefore, his good control of his troops produced good results. Engaging in war the strongest military power in the world, he ravaged Italy for some seventeen years and remained undefeated in all his battles. So many and great were the actions in which he defeated the rulers of the world, that the casualties inflicted by him prevented anyone from being bold enough ever to face him in open battle. Many were the cities that he captured and put to the torch, and though the peoples of Italy were outstanding in numbers, he made them know a dearth of men. These world-renowned exploits he achieved at public expense, to be sure, yet with forces that were a miscellaneous collection of mercenaries and allies; and though his opponents, by virtue of sharing a common language, were hard to withstand, his personal shrewdness and his capacity as a general gave him success against them. All may read the lesson that the commander is to an army what the mind is to the body and is responsible for its success.

20. Scipio, while still a very young man, handled affairs in Spain surprisingly well and vanquished the Carthaginians; and he rescued his country, which was then in dire jeopardy. For that Hannibal, whom no one had ever defeated, he forced by artful planning, without battle or risk, to withdraw from Italy. And in the end, by the use of a bold strategy he overcame the hitherto unconquered Hannibal in pitched battle, and thus brought Carthage to her knees.

21. Because of his great achievements Scipio wielded more influence than seemed compatible with the dignity of the state. Once, for example, being charged with an offence punishable by a painful death, he said only, when it was his turn to speak, that it ill behooved Romans to cast a vote against the man to whom his very accusers owed their enjoyment of the right to speak freely. At these words the whole populace, shamed by the force of his remark, left the meeting at once, and his accuser, deserted and alone, returned home discredited. On another occasion, at a meeting of the senate, when funds were needed and the quaestor refused to open the treasury, Scipio took over the keys to do it himself, saying that it was thanks to him that the quaestors were in fact able to lock it. On still another occasion, when someone in the senate demanded from him an accounting of the monies he had received to maintain his troops, he acknowledged that he had the account but refused to render it, on the ground that he ought not to be subjected to scrutiny on the same basis as others. When his accuser pressed the demand, he sent to his brother, had the book brought into the senate chamber, and after tearing it to bits bade his accuser add up the reckoning from the pieces. Then, turning to the other senators, he asked why they demanded an account of the three thousand talents that had been expended, but did not demand an account of the ten thousand five hundred talents that they were receiving from Antiochus, and did not even consider how they came to be masters, almost in an instant, of Spain, Libya, and Asia too. He said no more, but the authority that went with his plain speaking silenced both his accuser and the rest of the senate.

28. The city of the Cemeletae, a nest of brigands and fugitives, accepted the challenge of Rome. They dispatched envoys to Fulvius, demanding in the name of each of the men who had been killed a cloak, a dagger, and a horse; failing this, they threatened war to the finish. Fulvius, on encountering the delegation, bade them spare their pains: he would himself proceed against their city and be there before their expedition could set out. Wishing to make good his word, he straightway broke camp and marched against the barbarians, following close on the heels of the envoys.

29. King Ptolemy, being asked by one of his courtiers why he neglected Coelê Syria though it was rightfully his, replied that he was giving good heed to the matter. When the friend continued and asked where he would find sufficient money for the campaign, the king pointed to his friends and said: "There, walking about, are my money-bags."

[22.] On the arrival at Rome of the Asiatic princes who had been sent as envoys, Attalus and his entourage received a warm welcome: they were met and escorted into the city in style, presented with rich gifts, and shown every courtesy. These princes were, indeed, steadfast friends of Rome, and since they were in all things submissive to the senate, and were, moreover, most generous and hospitable to such Romans as visited their kingdom, they were granted the finest possible reception. For their sake the senate gave audience to all the envoys, and showing the greatest concern to please Eumenes, returned them a favourable response, announcing that a senatorial commission would be sent out that would settle at all costs the conflict with Pharnaces.

23. Leocritus, the general of Pharnaces, by constant assaults at last forced the mercenaries in Tius to surrender the city and, under terms of a truce that assured them safe conduct, to leave under escort. These mercenaries, who were now quitting the city in accordance with the agreement, had in times past wronged

Pharnaces; and Leocritus, who had orders from Pharnaces to put them all to death, now violated the truce, and on their departure from Tius set upon them on the way and shot them down one and all with darts.

24. Seleucus, leading an army of considerable size, advanced as if intending to cross the Taurus in support of Pharnaces; but on taking note of the treaty that his father had made with the Romans, the terms of which forbade . . .

25. Those who perpetrated this crime and murdered Demetrius did not escape the avenging punishment of divine justice. On the contrary, the men who had fabricated the false accusations and brought them from Rome soon after fell foul of the king and were put to death. Philip himself for the remainder of his life was haunted by dreams and by terrors of a guilty conscience because of the impious crime against the noblest of sons. He survived less than two years, succumbing to the burden of an incurable sorrow. Perseus, finally, the chief contriver of all the villainy, was defeated by the Romans and fled to Samothrace, but his claim as a suppliant of the Most Pure Gods [of the Mysteries] was invalidated by the monstrous impiety that he had perpetrated against his brother.

26. Tiberius Gracchus, the praetor, prosecuted the war with vigour. Indeed, while still a young man he surpassed all his contemporaries in courage and intelligence, and since his abilities commanded admiration and showed great hopes for the future, he enjoyed a reputation that greatly distinguished him among his contemporaries.

27. Aemilius the consul, who also became *patronus,* was a man of noble birth and handsome appearance, and was, in addition, gifted with superior intelligence. As a result his country honoured him with all its high magistracies, while he, for his part, continued throughout his lifetime to win men's praise, and provided for his own good repute after death along with the welfare of his country.

30. The political aims of Perseus were the same as those of his father, but since he wished to keep this from the Romans he sent ambassadors to Rome to renew his father's treaty of alliance and friendship. The senate, though aware of nearly all that was happening, nevertheless renewed the alliance, thereby deceiving the deceiver on his own ground.

31. Our concerns are advanced less by fear and force of arms than by moderation towards the defeated. So, for example, when Thoas was handed over and the senate had him in their power, they behaved magnanimously and acquitted him on all charges.

32. Antiochus [IV], on first succeeding to the throne, embarked upon a quixotic mode of life foreign to other monarchs. To begin with, he would often slip out of the palace without informing his courtiers, and wander at random about the city with one or two companions. Next, he took pride on stooping to the company of common people, no matter where, and in drinking with visiting foreigners of the meanest stamp. In general, if he learned that any young men were forgathering at an early hour, he would suddenly appear at the party with a fife and other music, so that in their astonishment some of the commoners who were guests would take to their heels and others be struck dumb with fear. Finally, he would at times put off his royal garb, and wrapping himself in a toga, as he had seen candidates for office do at Rome, would accost the citizens, saluting and embracing them one by one, and ask them to give him their vote, now for the office of aedile, and again for that of tribune. Upon being elected, he would sit on an ivory chair, and in the Roman fashion listen to the opposing arguments in ordinary cases of contract. He did this with such close attention and zeal that all men of refinement were perplexed about him, some ascribing his behaviour to artless simplicity, others to folly, and some to madness.

33. The cancelling of debts in Aetolia was emulated in Thessaly, and factional strife and disorder broke out in every city. The senate assumed that Perseus was at the bottom of this turmoil, and reported to his envoys that while they would drop all the other charges against him, the expulsion of Abrupolis the Thracian from his kingdom was an act that, they insisted, Perseus must rectify.

34. Harpalus, the ambassador of Perseus, made no reply. The senate, after allowing Eumenes the honour of an ivory curule chair and granting him other kindly marks of favour, dispatched him on his way to Asia.

When, following the attempt upon Eumenes' life, the rumour reached Pergamum that he was dead, Attalus made short work of wooing the queen. Yet Eumenes on his return took no notice, greeted his brother warmly, and was as friendly as before.

BOOK XXX FRAGMENTS

7.1. When the Roman (envoys) reported [171] that they had outwitted Perseus without recourse to arms, some members of the senate made a move to praise them. The older men, however, were far from pleased with what had been done, and said it did not become Romans to ape the Phoenicians, nor to get the better of their enemies by knavery rather than by bravery.

1. On the same day the senate approved a declaration of war against Perseus, and though it gave an audience to his envoys, made no reply to their statements. In addition the senate ordered the consuls to make solemn proclamation before assemblies of the people, bidding the envoys and all other Macedonians depart from Rome that very day and from Italy within thirty days.

2.. Ptolemy, king of Egypt, [170/69] knowing that his ancestors had held Coelê Syria, made great preparations for war in support of his claim, hoping that since it had been detached in times past through an unjust war he might now justly recover it on the same terms. Antiochus, learning of this, dispatched envoys to Rome bidding them call the senate to witness that Ptolemy, without just cause, was bent on making war. Ptolemy, however, also sent off envoys to speak in his defence, and to inform the senate that Coelê Syria had belonged to his forebears and that its subjection to Antiochus was contrary to all justice. He also instructed them to renew friendly relations with the Romans and to try to bring about peace with Perseus.

3. Cotys, king of the Thracians, was a man who in matters of warfare moved with vigour and was superior in judgement, and who in other respects as well was responsible and deserving of friendship. He was abstinent and circumspect in the highest degree, and most important of all, was completely exempt from the besetting vices of the Thracian people.

4. After the siege of the small township of Chalestrum Perseus put all the inhabitants to death. About five hundred, however, having made good their escape under arms to a certain stronghold, requested an assurance of safe-conduct, and Perseus consented to spare their lives on condition that they laid down arms. They complied with the terms agreed on, but the Macedonians, whether of their own accord or under orders of the king, followed those who had received the assurance and put them all to death.

5. Charops of Epirus was the grandson and name sake of that Charops who, during the war against Philip, had sent to Flamininus a guide to show him unexpected paths across the mountains, whereby the Romans, making a surprise advance, won control of the pass. Thanks to that grandfather's friendship with the Romans, the younger Charops was educated in Rome and formed ties of hospitality with many prominent men. He was, however, an arrant knave and adventurer, and set out to traduce to the Romans the men of Epirus who were held in highest esteem, hurling false charges against them in the hope that once he had confounded all who were capable of opposing him he might be left master of all Epirus. It was in consequence of this that they now sent to Macedon, [170] offering to deliver Epirus to Perseus.

5a. Upon arrival of the consul Hostilius in Epirus from Rome, Theodotus and Philostratus, the chief partisans of Perseus, plotted to betray him to the king.

While they were still urgently summoning Perseus, Hostilius, whose suspicions had been aroused, departed by night, and Perseus, arriving too late, failed to capture him.

6. During the siege of Abdera, Eumenes, despairing of carrying the city by storm, sent secretly to a certain Python, a man of the highest esteem among the Abderites, who with two hundred of his own slaves and freedmen was defending the key position. By beguiling him with promises they gained entrance within the walls through his assistance and took the city. Python, the traitor, though moderately rewarded, had ever present to his mind's eye the vision of his country's devastation, and lived out the remainder of his days in despair and regret.

7. 2-3. Andronicus, [169] who assassinated the son of Seleucus and who was in turn put to death, willingly lent himself to an impious and terrible crime, only to share the same fate as his victim. For it is the practice of potentates to save themselves from danger at the expense of their friends.

8. Prudently and always alert to the needs of the moment, the senate took in hand a revision of its benevolences. For when Perseus, proving unexpectedly defiant, prolonged the war to a stalemate, many Greeks had high hopes. The senate, however, by constantly renewed acts of generosity towards the Greeks exerted a contrary influence, and on each occasion made a bid for the support of the masses. What man of affairs who aspires to leadership could fail to admire this? What intelligent historian would pass over without comment the sagacity of the senate? Indeed, one might reasonably conclude that Rome's mastery over most of mankind was achieved by means of just such refinements of policy. This justifies the observation that harmonious adaptation to all occasions, connivance at some things, the turning of a deaf ear to some reports, the timely restraint of some impulse of blind rage, or, laying aside considerations of national dignity and power, to pay court to inferiors while paving the way for some success later; that such adaptation indicates consummate excellence in the individual, superb realism in the deliberating body, and virtue and intelligence in the state. All this the Roman senate of those days did, and thereby left, as it were, models and patterns for all who strive for empire and have the imagination to see how necessary it is to deal with problems in the light of circumstances.

9. Perseus sent envoys to Gentius, [170/69] king of the Illyrians and their most powerful chieftain at this time, proposing that they take concerted action. When Gentius asserted that he was quite willing to fight against the Romans but lacked money, Perseus again sent to him, turning, however, a deaf ear to the subject of money. On receiving the same reply he sent a third time, and though well aware what was in Gentius' mind he affected not to be, and said that if their undertaking turned out as planned he would give him ample satisfaction.

Perseus, being still unwilling to advance money, again dispatched envoys to Gentius, saying not a word about an immediate gift of money but hinting at great things that he might expect upon the successful completion of their business. It is a nice problem whether we should consider such evasiveness stupidity or downright madness on the part of men who act thus. They set their hand to great enterprises and place their own lives in jeopardy, yet overlook the one thing that is really essential, even though they themselves see the point and have it in their power to meet the need. Assuredly Philip, the son of Amyntas, a real master of statecraft, never was sparing of money in such circumstances; on the contrary, by handing out more than was requested, he always found a ready and abundant supply of traitors and allies. Consequently, although he was at first among the least of the kings of Europe, he left at his death a power that enabled his successor, Alexander, to conquer most of the inhabited world. Perseus, however, though the possessor of great treasures, amassed over many years by his ancestors and by Perseus himself, was utterly unwilling to touch them, with the result that he stripped himself of allies and further enriched those who later conquered him. Yet it was evident to all that had he only chosen to be open-handed, his money would have persuaded many monarchs and peoples to become his allies. Actually we may be thankful that he did not do so, since, if he had, more Greeks would have been involved with him in the disaster of defeat, or else he would have become master of all and won for himself a position of proud authority and of well-nigh irresistible influence.

10. Perseus, [169] though Fortune had given him golden opportunity to wipe out the Roman army, stayed on near Dium in Macedonia; he was not far from the place of action, but he weakly neglected the most important issues. Indeed, it would have taken only a shout and a bugle call to make captives of the enemy's whole army, enclosed as it was among cliffs and gorges from which escape was difficult. Since he had been so heedless, the Macedonians encamped on the mountain ridges were also slack about guards and patrols.

While Perseus, at Dium, was busy with the care of his person, one of his bodyguards, bursting into the bath, announced that the enemy were upon them. The king was so distraught that as he sprang from his bath he smote his thigh furiously and exclaimed: "Ye gods above, do you then deliver us to the foe ignominiously, without time even to form our battle order?"

11. Perseus, thinking that all was completely lost, and utterly crushed in spirit, dispatched Nicon, his treasurer, with orders to cast into the sea the treasures and money that were at Phaeus, and sent his bodyguard Andronicus to Thessalonica, with orders to set fire to the dockyards instantly. Andronicus, showing himself wiser than his master, went to Thessalonica but did not carry out his orders, thinking . . . for the Romans to gain a complete triumph.

Perseus also pulled down the gilded statues at Dium, and taking with him the whole population, women and children included, removed to Pydna. No greater mistake is to be found among his acts.

12. The Romans turned and put their victors to flight. Sometimes, in fact, the courage born of desperation brings even an utterly hopeless situation to a conclusion that would have seemed impossible.

13. The people of Cydonia [Crete] carried out an action that was monstrous and utterly foreign to Greek custom. In time of peace and while enjoying the position of trusted friends, they seized the city of Apollonia, killed all the men and youths, and dividing among themselves the women and children, occupied the city.

14. Though Antiochus was in a position to slaughter the defeated Egyptians, he rode about calling to his men not to kill them, but to take them alive. Before long he reaped the fruits of his shrewdness, since this act of generosity contributed very greatly to his seizure of Pelusium, and later to the acquisition of all Egypt.

15. The ministers of the young Ptolemy, Eulaeus the eunuch and the Syrian

Lenaeus, resorted to every possible means and device, and piled up gold, silver, and all other kinds of wealth in the royal treasury. Small wonder, then, if, through the efforts of such men, such great spectacles were set up in so brief a space of time, nor yet that one who was a eunuch and had only recently laid aside comb and scent pots should exchange the service of Aphrodite for the contests of Ares, or that he who was born a slave in Coelê Syria, and from whose hands the abacus had just fallen, should have dared to take upon his shoulders the war for Syria, notwithstanding that Antiochus was second to none in the strength of his armies and his resources in general. What is more, the men who undertook these great tasks were completely without experience of warfare and battles, and they lacked even a single competent adviser or capable commander. They themselves, as might be expected, soon met with the punishment that their folly deserved, and they brought the kingdom to utter ruin as far as it was in their power to do so.

It is our aim in emphasising these and similar events to provide an accurate estimate of the causes of success and failure. We both apportion praise to those whose conduct of affairs is excellent, and denounce those whose management is faulty. We bring into clear view the principles, both good and bad, by which men live and act, and by rendering a proper account of each we direct the minds of our readers to the emulation of what is good; at the same time, to the best of our ability we make our history fruitful and useful to all men, since a bare narrative of naval battles, military engagements, and legislation too, is no better than so much fiction.

16. The regents of Ptolemy, having summoned the populace to an assembly, promised to bring the war to a speedy end. In this at least they were not in error, since they swiftly succeeded in putting an end both to the war and to themselves. Because of their inexperience, however, they entertained such high hopes of gaining not only Syria but even the whole realm of Antiochus, that they took with them the greater part of the treasures they had amassed, including the gold ware from the sideboard. They also packed up and took along from the palace a number of couches, mostly with silver feet, but a few actually with feet of gold, as well as a large quantity of clothes, women's jewellery, and precious stones. These things, they declared, they were taking along for those who would then promptly surrender cities or fortresses to them. The outcome, however, was very different, and the treasures they carried off were a ready means to their own destruction.

17. In keeping with our policy we could not pass over without comment the ignoble flight of Ptolemy. That he, though standing in no immediate danger and though separated by such a distance from his enemies, should at once and virtually without a struggle abandon his claim to a great and opulent throne, can only, it would seem, be regarded as indicating a thoroughly effeminate spirit. Now had Ptolemy been a man endowed by Nature with such a spirit, we might perhaps have found fault with her, but since Nature finds a sufficient rebuttal to the charge in his subsequent actions and has demonstrated that the king was second to none whether in firmness to resist or in energy to act, we are forced to assign the responsibility for his ignoble cowardice on this occasion to the eunuch and to Ptolemy's close association with him. For he, by rearing the lad from boyhood amid luxury and womanish pursuits, had been undermining his character.

18. Antiochus showed himself a true statesman, and a man worthy of the royal dignity, except in the stratagem that he employed at Pelusium.

Antiochus got possession of Pelusium by means of a questionable bit of strategy. For though all warfare is an exception to humane standards of law and justice, even so it has certain quasi-laws of its own: a truce, for example, may not be broken; heralds must not be put to death; a man who has placed himself under the protection of a superior opponent may not be visited with punishment or vengeance. These and similar matters . . . one might fairly say that Antiochus, in making the seizure after the truce, rather like a pettifogging lawyer held fast to the letter of the law but not to justice and honour, which are the bonds of social life. For on the grounds of kinship he should, as he said himself, have spared the lad, but on the contrary after winning his confidence he deceived him and sought to bring him to utter ruin.

19. Perseus, learning that a picked group of Gauls had crossed the Danube to join his forces, [168] was overjoyed and dispatched messengers to the district of Maedicê, urging them to proceed with all speed. The leader of the Gauls consented but demanded that his men be paid a fixed stipend, amounting in all to five hundred talents. Perseus agreed to pay this, but when through avarice he failed to carry out the agreement, the Gauls returned again to their own land.

20. Aemilius [Paullus] the Roman, on taking command of the army, called together his men and exhorted them to be of good cheer. He was about sixty years old, and because of his earlier exploits he was at this time held in the highest esteem at Rome. In this war also he originated many novel devices, things that would have eluded the invention of other men, and by his personal shrewdness and audacity he defeated the Macedonians.

21. Perseus, wishing to induce more of his men to join him in flight and sail with him [from Amphipolis], set before them treasure to the value of sixty talents and allowed whoever would to seize it. After he had put to sea and reached Galepsus, he announced to those who had taken the property that he was seeking certain objects made from the spoils captured by Alexander. Promising to make full compensation to those who restored these objects to him, he asked for their immediate return. The men all complied with a will, but when he had recovered the objects, he cheated the donors of their promised reward.

Perseus, after recovering the treasures that he had allowed his men to seize, defrauded the donors of their promised reward, thereby providing most palpable proof that avarice, in addition to the other ills that it brings in its train, also deprives men of their wits. Indeed, his failure to forget profit and the desire for gain, even when the outlook was desperate, can only be regarded as the conduct of a man completely out of his senses. It is not surprising, then, that the Macedonians were defeated by the Romans, but only that with such a leader they held out for four years.

Alexander and Perseus were not at all alike in temperament. The former, with a greatness of mind that matched his personal aspirations, won for himself an empire; the latter, however, who from petty meanness alienated the Celts, a pattern of conduct that he followed consistently, brought down an ancient and mighty kingdom.

When Darius, after the first battle, proposed to give up a portion of his empire and offered Alexander forty thousand talents and the hand of his daughter in marriage, he received the reply that the universe could not be governed by two suns nor the world by two masters.

22. After Perseus fled, Aemilius began to look for his younger son, Publius Africanus [the Younger]. He was by birth the son of Aemilius but by adoption the grandson of Scipio, the conqueror of Hannibal, and was now a mere lad of about seventeen; from early youth he was present at those great battles, and gained such experience of warfare that he became a man not inferior to his grandfather. None the less, when he was found (and brought safely) into the camp the consul's anxiety was dispelled, for his feeling for the boy was not merely that of a father for his son, but something like the passion of a lover.

23. The consul Aemilius, taking Perseus by the hand, seated him in the midst of his council, and with words appropriate to the occasion offered him consolation and reassurance. Then, addressing the members of the council, he exhorted them, especially the younger men, to mark well the present scene and, keeping the fate of Perseus before their eyes, never to boast of their achievements improperly, never to harbour arrogant designs towards anyone, nor, in general, to take their good fortune for granted at any time. Indeed, whenever a man's success was greatest, whether in private life or public affairs, then above all should he reflect on the reverses of fortune and be most mindful of his mortal nature. "Fools," he said, "differ from the wise in this respect, that the former are schooled by their own misfortunes, the latter by the misfortunes of others."

Having discoursed at length in this vein he made those present at the council so sympathetic and humble of mood that it seemed as if they, and not their opponents, had suffered defeat.

Aemilius, by his generous treatment of Perseus, admitting him to the mess and giving him a place in the council, demonstrated to all men that he was stern towards those who stood against him, but considerate of a defeated foe. Since there were others also who affected a similar attitude, Rome's worldwide rule brought her no odium so long as she had such men to direct her empire.

24. The Rhodian envoys agreed that they had come in order to mediate a settlement, since war, they declared, was harmful to everyone.

BOOK XXXI FRAGMENTS

1. Antiochus at first put up a fine front, [169/8] asserting that no thought of taking the throne of Egypt lay behind his extensive military preparations, and that his only motive was to assist the elder Ptolemy [VI] in securing the position that was his by right of inheritance. This was by no means true; on the contrary, he conceived that by presiding over a dispute between the youths and so making an investment in goodwill he should conquer Egypt without a blow. But when Fortune put his professions to the test and deprived him of the pretext he had alleged, he stood revealed as one of the many princes who count no point of honour more important than gain.

2. As the Romans approached, [168] Antiochus, after greeting them verbally from a distance, stretched out his hand in welcome. Popillius, however, who had in readiness the document in which the senate's decree was recorded, held it out and ordered Antiochus to read it. His purpose in acting thus, it was thought, was that he might avoid clasping the king's hand in friendship until it was evident from his decision whether he was, in fact, friend or foe. When the king, after reading the document, said that he would consult with his friends on these matters, Popillius, hearing this, acted in a manner that seemed offensive and arrogant in the extreme. Having a vine stock ready at hand, with the stick he drew a line about Antiochus, and directed him to give his answer in that circle. The king, astonished by what had taken place, and awed, too, by the majesty and might of Rome, found himself in a hopeless quandary, and on full consideration said that he would do all that the Romans proposed. Popillius and his colleagues then took his hand and greeted him cordially. Now the purport of the letter was that he must break off at once his war against Ptolemy. Pursuant to these instructions the king withdrew his forces from Egypt, panic-stricken by the superior might of Rome, the more so as he had just had news of the Macedonian collapse. Indeed, had he not known that this had taken place, never of his own free will would he have heeded the decree.

3. It is then apparently true, as certain of the sages of old have declared, that forgiveness is preferable to revenge. We all, in fact, approve those who use their power with moderation, and we are offended by men who are quick to punish those who fall into their hands. Thus, too, we see that the former class of men have ready against the surprises of Fortune a rich store of goodwill laid up in the hearts of those to whom they have been gracious; the latter, however, whenever the situation is reversed, not only receive like vengeance from those towards whom they have been unfeeling, but find too that they have deprived themselves of the pity generally accorded to the fallen. Nor would it, indeed, be just that a man who has denied all humanity to others should himself, when he in turn stumbles and falls, meet with consideration from those who have him in their power. Yet many men have the temerity to pride themselves on the severity with which they avenge themselves on their foes, though this pride is ill founded. For what is splendid or great in inflicting irremediable disaster upon men whose fall has placed them in our power? What do victories profit us if in prosperity we behave with such arrogance that we cancel the fair fame that we had earlier by showing ourselves unworthy of our good fortune? Surely the honour that is gained by noble deeds is rightly considered the highest reward of men who aspire to control events. This being so, it is astonishing that while nearly all men acknowledge the truth and the utility of the principle that at first they acclaimed, they do not when it comes to a test endorse their own verdict. The proper course, I suggest, for men of intelligence would be to bear in mind, especially at the supreme moment of triumph, that the tables may be turned; and so, although by their courage they conquer the foe, yet on grounds of prudence they will surrender to pity for the victims of fortune. This does much to augment the influence of any man, but particularly that of the representatives of empire. For then each one of those whose strength is lost, yielding voluntary allegiance, gives eager service and is in all things a loyal collaborator.

This principle the Romans have evidently taken much to heart. They are statesmanlike in their deliberations, and by conferring benefits on those whom they have defeated they seek to gain the undying gratitude of the recipients and the well-deserved praise of the rest of mankind.

4. Since the tide of Fortune was running strongly in their favour the Romans gave careful attention to the question how to act in view of their successes. (Many suppose that a right use of victory) is easier than to subdue one's adversaries by force of arms. In point of fact, this is not true, for men who are brave in battle are to be found in greater numbers than men who are humane in seasons of prosperity.

5. Just at this time envoys of the Rhodians arrived in Rome to clear themselves of the allegations that had been made against them; for it was believed that during the war with Perseus their sympathies had inclined towards the king and that they had been disloyal to their friendship with Rome. Failing completely to achieve the purposes of their embassy, the envoys lost heart, and gave vent to tears as they made their petitions. Introduced before the senate by Antonius, one of the tribunes, Philophron spoke first on behalf of the delegation, and then Astymedes. At great length they pled for mercy and forgiveness, and at last, after having, as the saying goes, sung their swan-song, they only just managed to elicit a reply. This did indeed relieve them of their worst fears, though in it they were bitterly upbraided for their alleged offences.

Envoys of the Rhodians now arrived in Rome to clear themselves of the allegations that had been made against them. For it was believed that in the war with Perseus their sympathies had inclined towards the king and that they had been disloyal to their friendship with Rome. When the envoys perceived the coolness with which they were received, they lost heart; and when a certain praetor, convoking an assembly, urged the people to make war on Rhodes, they feared utter destruction for their country and were so dismayed that they put on mourning, and in appealing to their friends no longer spoke as advocates or claimants, but besought them with tears not to adopt measures fatal to Rhodes. When they were introduced before the senate by one of the tribunes, the same who had pulled from the rostra the praetor who was urging to war, . . . made speeches. Only after many entreaties did they obtain an answer. This did indeed relieve them of their fear of total ruin, though they were subjected to bitter reproaches on the score of the particular charges.

These men presented their pleas and entreaties at great length, and at last, after having, as the saying goes, sung their swan-song, they only just managed to elicit a reply, which eased them of their fear.

They thought that they were now quit of the fears that had hung over them, and readily put up with all else, however distasteful. As a general rule, indeed, any enormity of anticipated suffering makes men think little of lesser misfortunes.

6. Hence it is that among the Romans the most distinguished men are to be seen vying with one another for glory, and it is by their efforts that virtually all matters of chief moment to the people are brought to a successful issue. In other states men are jealous of one another, but the Romans praise their fellow citizens. The result is that the Romans, by rivalling one another in promotion of the common weal, achieve the most glorious successes, while other men, striving for an undeserved fame and thwarting one another's projects, inflict damage upon their countries.

7.1. At about this same time envoys arrived in winter Rome from all quarters, [167/6] to offer congratulations on the victory that had been won. The senate received them all courteously, briefly gave each a fair reply, and sent them off home.

8. Earlier, when the Romans defeated Antiochus and Philip, [167] the greatest monarchs of that age, they so far abstained from exacting vengeance that they not only allowed them to keep their kingdoms but even accepted them as friends. So, too, on this present occasion, notwithstanding their repeated struggles with Perseus and the many grave dangers that they had had to face, having now at last subjugated the kingdom of Macedon, contrary to all expectations they set the captured cities free. Not only would no one else have anticipated this but not even the Macedonians themselves had any hope of being accorded such consideration, having on their conscience many serious offences that they had committed against Rome. Indeed, since their earlier errors had been forgiven, they supposed, as well they might, that no just argument for pity or pardon was still available to them for these later shortcomings.

The Roman senate, however, harboured no grudges but acted towards them with magnanimity, yet with due regard to the merits of the several cases. Perseus, for example, owed them an inherited debt of gratitude, and since in violation of his covenant he was the aggressor in an unjust war, they held him, after he became their prisoner, in "free custody," thereby exacting a punishment far less, certainly, than his crimes. The Macedonian people, whom they might in all justice have reduced to slavery, they set free, and they were so generous and so prompt in conferring this boon that they did not even wait for the defeated to petition them. Likewise with the Illyrians, to whom, once they had been subdued, they granted autonomy, less from any belief that the barbarians deserved their indulgence than from the conviction that it was fitting and proper for the Roman people to take the initiative in acts of beneficence and to avoid over-confidence in their day of power.

The senate resolved that the Macedonians and the Illyrians should be free, and that they should pay one-half the amount that they formerly paid their own kings in taxes.

Marcus Aemilius, consul of the Romans and a general of the highest ability, on taking Perseus prisoner placed him in "free custody," although Perseus had made war upon the Romans without just cause and in violation of his covenants. Moreover, to everyone's surprise he set free all the Macedonian and Illyrian cities that had been captured, despite the fact that the Romans had repeatedly faced grave dangers in the war against Perseus and, earlier still, had met and defeated Philip, his father, and Antiochus the Great, and had shown them such consideration as not only to permit them to retain their kingdoms but even to enjoy the friendship of Rome. Since in the sequel the Macedonians had behaved irresponsibly, they thought that they should have no title to mercy when, along with Perseus, they fell into the hands of the Romans. On the contrary the senate dealt with them in a forgiving and generous spirit, and instead of slavery bestowed freedom. In like manner they dealt with the Illyrians, whose king, Getion [Gentius], they had taken prisoner along with Perseus. Having thus nobly bestowed the gift of freedom upon them, the Romans ordered them to pay one-half as much as they had formerly paid their own kings in taxes.

They sent out ten commissioners from the senate to Macedonia, and five to the Illyrians, who met with Marcus Aemilius and agreed to dismantle the walls of Demetrias, the chief city of the Macedonians, to detach Amphilochia from Aetolia, and to bring together the prominent men of Macedon at a meeting: there they set them free and announced the removal of the garrisons. In addition, they cut off the revenues derived from the gold and silver mines, partly to keep the local inhabitants from being oppressed, and partly to prevent anyone from stirring up a revolution thereafter by using this wealth to get control of Macedon. The whole region they divided into four cantons: the first comprised the area between the Nestus River and the Strymon, the forts east of the Nestus (except those of Abdera, Maroneia, and Aenus), and, west of the Strymon, the whole of Bisaltica, together with Heracleia Sintica; the second, the area bounded on the east by the Strymon River, and on the west by the river called the Axius and the lands that border it; the third, the area enclosed on the west by the Peneus River, and on the north by Mt. Bernon, with the addition of some parts of Paeonia, including the notable cities of Edessa and Beroea; fourth and last, the area beyond Mt. Bernon, extending to Epirus and the districts of Illyria. Four cities were the capitals of the four cantons, Amphipolis of the first, Thessalonica of the second, Pella of the third, and Pelagonia of the fourth; here four governors were established and here the taxes were collected. Troops were stationed on the border regions of Macedonia because of the hostility of the neighbouring tribes.

Subsequently Aemilius, after arranging splendid games and revelries for the assembled multitude, sent off to Rome whatever treasure had been discovered, and when he himself arrived, along with his fellow generals, he was ordered by the senate to enter the city in triumph. Anicius first, and Octavius, the commander of the fleet, celebrated each his triumph for a single day, but the very wise Aemilius celebrated his for three days. On the first day the procession opened with twelve hundred wagons filled with embossed white shields, then another twelve hundred filled with bronze shields, and three hundred more laden with lances, pikes, bows, and javelins; as in war, trumpeters led the way. There were many other wagons as well, carrying arms of various sorts, and eight hundred panoplies mounted on poles. On the second day there were carried in procession a thousand talents of coined money, twenty-two hundred talents of silver, a great number of drinking-cups, five hundred wagons loaded with divers statues of gods and men, and a large number of golden shields and dedicatory plaques. On the third day the procession was made up of one hundred and twenty choice white oxen, talents of gold conveyed in two hundred and twenty carriers, a ten-talent bowl of gold set with jewels, gold-work of all sorts to the value of ten talents, two thousand elephant tusks three cubits in length, an ivory chariot enriched with gold and precious stones, a horse in battle array with cheek-pieces set with jewels and the rest of its gear adorned with gold, a golden couch spread with flowered coverlets, and a golden palanquin with crimson curtains. Then came Perseus, the hapless king of the Macedonians, with his two sons, a daughter, and two hundred and fifty of his officers, four hundred garlands presented by the various cities and monarchs, and last of all, in a dazzling chariot of ivory, Aemilius himself.

Aemilius remarked to those who were amazed at the care he devoted to the spectacle that to conduct games in proper fashion and to make suitable arrangements for a revelry call for the same qualities of mind that are needed to marshal one's forces with good strategy against an enemy.

9. Perseus, the last king of Macedonia, whose relations with the Romans were often amicable, but who also repeatedly fought against them with a not inconsiderable army, was finally defeated and taken captive by Aemilius, who for this victory celebrated a magnificent triumph. The misfortunes that Perseus encountered were so great that his sufferings seem like the inventions of fiction, yet even so he was not willing to be quit of life. For before the senate had decided on the penalty he should suffer, one of the urban praetors had him cast with his children into the prison at Alba [Fucens]. This prison is a deep underground dungeon, no larger than a nine-couch room, dark, and noisome from the large numbers committed to the place, who were men under condemnation on capital charges, for most of this category were incarcerated there at that period. With so many shut up in such close quarters, the poor wretches were reduced to the physical appearance of brutes, and since their food and everything pertaining to their other needs was all foully commingled, a stench so terrible assailed anyone who drew near that it could scarcely be endured. There for seven days Perseus remained, in such sorry plight that he begged succour even from men of the meanest stamp, whose food was the prison ration. They, indeed, affected by the magnitude of his misfortune, in which they shared, wept and generously gave him a portion of whatever they received. A sword with which to kill himself was thrown down to him, and a noose for hanging, with full freedom to use them as he might wish. Nothing, however, seems so sweet to those who have suffered misfortune as life itself, even when their sufferings would warrant death. And at last he would have died under these deprivations had not Marcus Aemilius, leader of the senate, to maintain both his own principles and his country's code of equity, indignantly admonished the senate, even if they had nothing to fear from men, at least to respect the Nemesis that dogs those who arrogantly abuse their power. As a result, Perseus was placed in more suitable custody, and, because of the senate's kindness, sustained himself by vain hopes, only to meet at last an end that matched his earlier misfortunes. For after clinging to life for two years, he offended the barbarians who were his guards, and was prevented from sleeping until he died of it.

10. While the kingdom of the Macedonians was at its height, Demetrius of Phalerum, in his treatise *On Fortune,* as if he were a true prophet of its future, aptly made this inspired pronouncement: "If," he said, "you were to consider, not some limitless expanse of time nor yet many generations, but merely these fifty years just past, you would perceive therein the inscrutability of Fortune. Fifty years ago, do you think that the Persians or the king of the Persians, the Macedonians or the king of the Macedonians, if some god had foretold the future, would ever have believed that at this moment not even the name of the Persians, who were then the masters of well-nigh the whole inhabited world, would still survive, and that the Macedonians, whose very name was formerly unknown, would indeed rule all? Nevertheless Fortune, who with her unforeseeable effect upon our lives disappoints our calculations by her shifts and demonstrates her power by marvellous and unexpected events, is now also, in my opinion, pointing much the same moral; that in seating the Macedonians on the throne of the Persians she has but lent them her riches to be used until such time as she changes her mind about them." The fulfilment came to pass in the period with which we are now concerned. Accordingly I judge it my duty to make some comment appropriate to this situation, and to recall the statement of Demetrius, an utterance of more than human inspiration. For a hundred and fifty years in advance he foretold what was to occur.

11. The two sons of Aemilius having suddenly died, to the great grief of the entire populace, their father called a public assembly, where, after giving a defence of his actions in the war, he concluded his address with the following remarks. He said, namely, that after seeing the sun rise as he was about to begin transporting his army from Italy to Greece, he had then made the voyage, and at the ninth hour, without a single loss, had put in at Corcyra; thence on the fourth day he had offered sacrifice to the god at Delphi; five days later had arrived in Macedonia and taken command of the forces; and within a total of fifteen days had forced the pass at Petra, given battle, and defeated Perseus. In sum, though it was then the fourth year of the king's defiance of the Romans, he, Aemilius, had subdued the whole of Macedon in the aforesaid number of days. Even at the time, he said, he marvelled at the unexpectedness of his victories, and when, shortly thereafter, he captured the king, his children, and the royal treasure, he marvelled even more at the favourable tide of fortune. When, further, the treasure and his soldiers were conveyed safely and swiftly across to Italy, he was utterly puzzled by the fact that the whole affair was being brought to an end so much more fortunately than he had expected. But when all men joined in rejoicing with him, and felicitated him on his good fortune, then above all did he look for some calamity from destiny, and therefore he implored the god that the reversal might not in any way affect the state, but rather, if it was certainly the divine pleasure to bring some hardship to pass, that the burden might fall on him. Accordingly, as soon as this misfortune touching his sons took place, while it was a matter of deep grief to him, yet with regard to the state and its concerns he was now reassured, inasmuch as Fortune had visited her recoil and her malice, not upon the citizen body, but on his own person. As he said this, the whole people marvelled at his greatness of soul, and their sympathy at his loss was increased many times over.

12. After the defeat of Perseus, [168/6] King Eumenes experienced great and unexpected reverses. For whereas he assumed that his dominion was securely established, now that the kingdom most hostile to him had been broken up, at this very time he ran into very grave dangers. Fortune is indeed given to overturning such institutions as seem to be securely established, and again, if ever she lends a helping hand to a man, she redresses the balance by shifting, and so mars his record of success.

13. The general of the barbarous Gauls, returning from his pursuit, gathered the prisoners together and perpetrated an act of utter inhumanity and arrogance.

Those of the prisoners who were most handsome in appearance and in the full bloom of life he crowned with garlands and offered in sacrifice to the gods, if indeed there be any god who accepts such offerings; all the rest he had shot down, and though many of them were acquaintances known to him through prior exchanges of hospitality, yet no one received pity on the score of friendship. It is really not surprising, however, that savages, in the flush of unexpected success, should celebrate their good fortune with inhuman behaviour.

14. Eumenes, having recruited a force of mercenary troops, not only gave all of them their pay, but honoured some with gifts and beguiled them all with promises, evoking their goodwill; in this he did not at all resemble Perseus. For Perseus, when twenty thousand Gauls arrived to join him in the war against Rome, alienated this great body of allies in order to husband his wealth. Eumenes, however, though not over rich, when enlisting foreign troops honoured with gifts all who were best able to render him service. Accordingly, the former, by adopting a policy, not of royal generosity, but of ignoble and plebeian meanness, saw the wealth he had guarded taken captive together with his whole kingdom, while the latter, by counting all things else second to victory, not only rescued his kingdom from great dangers but also subjugated the whole nation of the Gauls.

15. Prusias, king of Bithynia, [167] also came to congratulate the senate and the generals who had brought the conflict to a successful issue. This man's ignobility of spirit must not be allowed to go without comment. For when the virtue of good men is praised, many in later generations are guided to strive for a similar goal; and when the poltroonery of meaner men is held up to reproach, not a few who are taking the path of vice are turned aside. Accordingly the frank language of history should of set purpose be employed for the improvement of society.

Prusias was a man unworthy of the royal dignity, and throughout his entire life continually engaged in abject flattery of those above him. Once, for example, when visited by a Roman embassy, he laid aside the insignia of royalty, the diadem and the purple, and in imitation of newly emancipated freed-men at Rome went to meet the envoys with shaven head and wearing a white cap, a toga, and Roman shoes; having greeted them, he declared that he was a freedman of the Romans. A more ignoble remark it would be difficult to imagine.

Much else in his earlier behaviour was in the same vein, and now also, when he reached the entrance leading into the senate chamber, he stood in the doorway facing the senators, and lowering both hands kissed the threshold in obeisance and greeted the seated members with the words: "Hail, ye saviour gods," thereby achieving unsurpassable depths of unmanly fawning and effeminate behaviour. In keeping with this conduct was the speech that he delivered before the senate, in which he related things of such a nature that it is not fitting for us even to record them. The senate, offended by most of his remarks, and forming an unfavourable impression of Prusias, gave him the answer that his flattery deserved. For the Romans desire even the enemies whom they conquer to be men of high spirit and bravery.

15a. Dionysius, also called Petosarapis, one of the "Friends" of Ptolemy, attempted to win control of the state for himself, and thus brought the kingdom into great danger. Wielding, as he did, the greatest influence of anyone at court, and being without a peer among his fellow Egyptians on the field of battle, he scorned both the kings because of their youth and inexperience. Pretending that he had been urged by the elder to shed kindred blood, he spread word among the populace to the effect that a plot against the younger Ptolemy was being hatched by his brother. The populace assembled in haste at the stadium, and when they had all been aroused to such a pitch that they were preparing to kill the elder brother and entrust the kingdom to the younger, word of the disturbance having now been brought to the court, the king summoned his brother, and protesting his innocence with tears in his eyes, begged him not to give credence to one who was seeking to usurp the royal power, and who treated them both as too young to matter; in case, however, his brother still harboured any doubts and apprehensions, he urged him to accept at his own hand the diadem and the rule. The youth at once cleared his brother of any suspicion, and both of them, donning their royal robes, went out and appeared before the populace, making it manifest to one and all that they were in harmony. Dionysius, on failing in his attempt, placed himself out of reach, and at first, sending messages to those soldiers who were ripe for rebellion, he sought to persuade them to share his hopes; then, withdrawing to Eleusis, he welcomed all who decided in favour of revolution, and when a band of turbulent soldiers some four thousand strong had been assembled . . . The king marched out against them and was victorious, slaying some and putting others to flight; Dionysius himself was obliged to swim naked across the flowing river and to withdraw into the interior, where he tried to incite the masses to revolt. Being a man of action and finding himself popular with the Egyptians, he soon enlisted many who were willing to share his fortunes.

16. Certain of the enterprises and acts of Antiochus were kingly and altogether admirable, [166 or 5] while others again were so cheap and so tawdry as to bring upon him the utter scorn of all mankind. For example, in celebrating his festal games [at Daphne] he adopted, in the first place, a policy contrary to that of the other kings. They, while strengthening their kingdoms both in arms and in wealth, as far as possible tried to conceal their intentions because of the superiority of Rome. He, however, taking the opposite approach, brought together at his festival the most distinguished men from virtually the whole world, adorned all parts of his capital in magnificent fashion, and having assembled in one spot, and, as it were, put upon the stage his entire kingdom, left them ignorant of nothing that concerned him.

In putting on these lavish games and this stupendous festival Antiochus outdid all earlier rivals. Yet for him personally to manage the affair was a shabby business, worthy of contempt. He would, for example, ride at the side of the procession on a sorry nag, ordering these men to advance, those to halt, and assigning others to their posts, as occasion required; consequently, but for the diadem, no one who did not already know him would have believed that, this person was the king, lord of the whole domain, seeing that his appearance was not even that of an average subordinate. At the drinking parties, stationing himself at the entrance he would lead some of the guests in, seat others at their places, and assign to their posts the attendants who were serving food. Continuing in the same vein he would, on occasion, approach the banqueters, and sometimes sit down, sometimes recline beside them; then, laying aside his cup or tossing away his sop, he would leap to his feet and move on, and making the rounds of the whole party accept toasts even while he stood and jested with the entertainers. Indeed once, when the merrymaking was well advanced and the greater part of the guests had already departed, he made an entrance, all bundled up and carried in procession by the mimes. Placed on the ground by his fellow-actors, as soon as the symphony sounded his cue he leapt to his feet naked, and jesting with the mimes performed the kind of dances that usually provoke laughter and hoots of derision: to the great embarrassment of the company, who all left the party in haste. Each and every person, in fact, who attended the festival found that when he regarded the extravagance of the outlay and the general management and administration of the games and processions, he was astounded, and that he admired both the king and the kingdom; when, however, he focused his attention on the king himself and his unacceptable behaviour, he could not believe that it was possible for such excellence and such baseness to exist in one and the same character.

17. After the games had ended, the embassy of [Sempronius] Gracchus arrived to investigate the kingdom. The king held friendly conversations with them, with the result that they caught no hint of intrigue on his part, nor anything to indicate such enmity as might be expected to exist covertly after the rebuff that he had received in Egypt. His true policy was not, however, what it appeared to be; on the contrary he was deeply disaffected towards the Romans.

17a. Artaxes [Artaxias], the king of Armenia, [165] broke away from Antiochus, founded a city named after himself, and assembled a powerful army. Antiochus, whose strength at this period was unmatched by any of the other kings, marched against him, was victorious, and reduced him to submission.

17b. Still another uprising occurred in the Thebaïd, where an urge to revolt swept over the populace. King Ptolemy, moving against them in force, easily regained control of the rest of the Thebaïd. But the city known as Panonpolis stands upon an ancient mound and by reason of its inaccessibility was reputed to be secure; hence the most active of the rebels assembled there. Ptolemy, (observing?) the desperation of the Egyptians and the strength of the place, prepared to besiege it, and after undergoing every kind of hardship captured the city. Then, having punished the ringleaders, he returned to Alexandria.

7.2. At about this same time many embassies having arrived, the senate dealt first with that headed by Attalus. For the Romans were suspicious of Eumenes because of the correspondence that, had come to light, in which he had contracted an alliance with Perseus against Rome. Since charges had also been levelled at him by a good many of the envoys from Asia, in particular those sent out by King Prusias and by the Gauls, Attalus and his companions did all in their power to refute the charges, point by point, and not only cleared themselves of these calumnies but returned home laden with honours. The senate, however, did not entirely abate its suspicion of Eumenes, but appointed and sent, out Gaius to look into his affairs.

18. As King Ptolemy, now in exile, [164/3] was approaching Rome on foot, Demetrius [I Soter] the son of Seleucus recognised him, and shocked by his strange plight, gave a truly royal and magnificent example of his own character. For he prepared at once a royal costume and diadem, and in addition a valuable horse with trappings of gold, and with his family went out to meet Ptolemy. Encountering him at a distance of two hundred stades from the city and giving him a friendly salute, he urged him to adorn himself with the insignia of kingship, and make an entrance into Rome worthy of his rank, so that he might not be thought a person of no account whatever. Ptolemy appreciated his zeal, but was so far from accepting any part of the offer that he even asked Demetrius to remain behind in one of the towns along the way, and wanted Archias and the others to remain with him.

Ptolemy, the king of Egypt, having been driven from the kingdom by his own brother, repaired to Rome in the miserable garb of a commoner, accompanied by but one eunuch and three slaves. Discovering while still on the way the address of Demetrius the topographer, he sought him out and lodged with him, a man whom he had often entertained when he was resident in Alexandria; now, because rents at Rome were so high, he was living in a small and altogether shabby garret. In the light of this, who, pray, would put his faith in the things that the multitude consider good, or would regard as enviable those whose good fortune is more than average? Indeed, it would be hard to find a change in fortune sharper and greater than this, or a reversal so unexpected. For no cause or occasion worth mentioning, his high and kingly estate was brought down to the lowly fortune of a commoner, and he who commanded all those thousands of free men of a sudden had only three servants left him from the shipwreck of his personal fortune.

18a. Polybius and Diodorus, [168] the authors of the *Historical Libraries,* relate that he [Antiochus IV] not only opposed the god in Judea but also, inflamed by the fires of avarice, tried to despoil the temple of Artemis, which was very rich, in Elymaïs. But thwarted by the guardians of the temple, and by the neighbouring peoples, he was driven mad by certain apparitions and terrors, and finally died of disease; and they state that this happened to him because he attempted to violate the temple of Artemis.

20. After Antipater died under torture, they carried off Asclepiades, the prefect of the city, loudly protesting that Timotheus was the author of this tragedy and that it was he who had provoked the youth to take unjust and impious vengeance upon his brother. As the populace from this point on was little by little becoming aware of the utter knavery of their leaders and was beginning to regard the hapless victims with pity, Timotheus and his associates, alarmed, put an end to their torture of the rest of the accused and had them done away with in private.

17c. After the assassination of Timotheus the populace . . . and being disgusted at Alexandria with the king for his shameless treatment of his brother, stripped him of his royal retinue and sent to recall the elder Ptolemy from Cyprus.

19. The kings of Cappadocia say that they trace their ancestry back to Cyrus the Persian, and also assert that they are descendants of one of the seven Persians who did away with the Magus. Now as to their connection with Cyrus, they count as follows. Cambyses the father of Cyrus had a sister, of legitimate birth, Atossa. To her and Pharnaces, king of Cappadocia, was born a son, Gallus; his son was Smerdis, his Artamnes, and his Anaphas, a man of outstanding bravery and daring, who was one of the seven Persians. Such then is the pedigree they trace for their kinship with Cyrus and with Anaphas, to whom, they say, because of his valour the satrapy of Cappadocia was granted, with the understanding that no tribute would be paid to the Persians. After his death a son of the same name ruled. When he died, leaving two sons, Datames and Arimnaeus, Datames succeeded to the throne, a man who both in war and in the other spheres of royal duty won praise, and who, engaging the Persians in battle, fought brilliantly and died in battle. The kingdom passed to his son Ariamnes, whose sons were Ariarathes and Holophernes; Ariamnes ruled for fifty years and died without achieving anything worthy of note. The throne passed to Ariarathes (I), the elder of his sons, who is said to have loved his brother with a surpassing love, and promoted him to the most prominent positions: thus he was sent to aid the Persians in their war against the Egyptians, and returned home laden with honours, which [Artaxeres III] Ochus, the Persian king, bestowed for bravery; he died in his native land, leaving two sons, Ariarathes and Aryses. Now his brother, the king of Cappadocia, having no legitimate offspring of his own, adopted Ariarathes, the elder son of his brother. At about this time Alexander of Macedon defeated and overthrew the Persians, and then died; Perdiccas, who at this point held the supreme command, dispatched Eumenes [of Cardia] to be military governor of Cappadocia. Ariarathes (I) was defeated, and fell in battle, [322] and Cappadocia itself and the neighbouring regions fell to the Macedonians. Ariarathes (II), the son of the late king, regarding the situation as hopeless for the present, retired with a few followers to Armenia. Not long after, Eumenes and Perdiccas having died, and Antigonus and Seleucus being elsewhere engaged, he obtained an army from Ardoates, king of Armenia, slew Amyntas, the Macedonian general, expelled the Macedonians from the land in short order, and recovered his original domain. Of his three sons Ariamnes, the eldest, inherited the kingdom; he arranged a marital alliance with Antiochus (called Theos), whose daughter Stratonicê he married to his eldest son Ariarathes (III),, and being a man unusually devoted to his children, he placed the diadem upon his son's head, made him joint ruler, and shared with him on equal terms all the privileges of kingship. On his father's death, Ariarathes became sole ruler, and when he departed this life left the kingdom to his son Ariarathes (IV), who was then a mere infant. He in turn married a daughter of Antiochus (surnamed the Great), Antiochis by name, an utterly unscrupulous woman. Failing to have children, she palmed off on her unwitting husband two supposititious sons, Ariarathes and Holophernes. After a certain time, however, she ceased to be barren and unexpectedly bore two daughters and a single son, named Mithridates. Thereupon, after revealing the truth to her husband, she arranged for the elder of the supposititious sons to be sent off to Rome with a suitable stipend, and the younger to Ionia, in order to avoid any dispute with the legitimate son over the kingdom. He, they say, changed his name to Ariarathes (V) after he grew to manhood, received a Greek education, and won commendation as well for other merits. Now because he was such a filial son, his father made a point of taking a parental interest in return, and their regard for one another reached such a point that the father was bent on retiring from the throne altogether in favour of his son, while the son declared that it was impossible for him to accept this kind of favour while his parents yet. lived. When the fatal day came for his father, he inherited the kingdom, [163] and by his whole way of life, and especially by his devotion to philosophy, showed himself worthy of the highest praise; and thus it was that Cappadocia, so long unknown to the Greeks, offered at this time a place of sojourn to men of culture. This king also renewed with Rome the treaty of alliance and friendship. So much, then, for the descent from Cyrus of the dynasty which to this point ruled over Cappadocia.

Seven kings of Cappadocia, whose dynasty lasted one hundred and sixty years, began at about this time, as Diodorus writes.

21. Ariarathes, surnamed Philopator, on succeeding to his ancestral kingdom, first of all gave his father a magnificent burial. Then, when he had duly attended to the interests of his friends, of those in positions of authority, and of the other subordinate officials, he succeeded in winning great favour with the populace.

22. After Ariarathes had restored Mithrobuzanes to his ancestral domain, Artaxias, the king of Armenia, abating not a whit his original rapacity sent envoys to Ariarathes, urging him to make common cause with him, and proposing that they should each put to death the young man who was at his court, and divide Sophenê between them. Ariarathes, to whom such villainy was completely foreign, rebuked the envoys and wrote to Artaxias, urging him to abstain from such actions. When this result was achieved, Ariarathes in consequence enhanced his own reputation in no slight degree, while Mithrobuzanes, thanks to the admirable good faith and nobility of his sponsor, succeeded to the throne of his fathers.

19a. Ptolemaeus, the governor of Commagenê, [162] who even before had shown little respect for the Syrian kings, now asserted his independence, and because they were busy with their own affairs, established himself without interference in control of the country, being chiefly emboldened by its natural advantages for defence. Not satisfied with this gain, he raised an army and invaded Melitene, which belonged to Cappadocia and was subject to Ariarathes, and he won an initial success by occupying the points of vantage. When Ariarathes, however, marched against him with a strong force, he withdrew into his own province.

23. Envoys arrived in Rome both from the younger Ptolemy and from the elder. [161] An audience before the senate having been granted them, the senate, after hearing both sides out, decreed that the envoys of the elder Ptolemy must leave Italy within not more than five days, that their alliance with him was at an end, and that legates should be sent to the younger Ptolemy to inform him of the senate's goodwill and of their instructions to his brother.

24. Because certain young men paid a talent for a male favourite and three hundred Attic drachmas for a jar of Pontic pickled fish, Marcus Porcius Cato, a man held in high esteem, declared before an assembly of the people that they could very readily discern herein the turn for the worse in men's conduct and in the state, when favourites were sold at a higher price than farm lands, and a jar of pickled fish than teamsters.

25. Aemilius, the conqueror of Perseus, [160] who held the office of censor and excelled his fellow citizens in nearly every virtuous capacity, at this time died. As the report of his death spread abroad and the time of his funeral drew near, the entire city was so moved by grief that not only did the labouring men and the rest of the common people assemble with alacrity, but even the magistrates and the senate laid aside the affairs of state. Equally, too, from all the towns round about Rome, wherever they were able to arrive in time, the inhabitants almost to a man came down to Rome, eager both to witness the spectacle and to pay honour to the deceased.

Diodorus, in his account of the funeral of Lucius Aemilius, the conqueror of Perseus, states that it was conducted with the utmost splendour, and adds the following passage: "Those Romans who by reason of noble birth and the fame of their ancestors are pre-eminent are, when they die, portrayed in figures that are not only lifelike as to features but show their whole bodily appearance. For they

413

employ actors who through a man's whole life have carefully observed his carriage and the several peculiarities of his appearance. In like fashion each of the dead man's ancestors takes his place in the funeral procession, with such robes and insignia as enable the spectators to distinguish from the portrayal how far each had advanced in the *cursus honorum* and had had a part in the dignities of the state."

26. This same Aemilius in departing this life left behind him a reputation for character equal to that which he had enjoyed while living. For though he had brought to Rome, from Spain, more gold than any of his contemporaries, had had in his possession the fabulous treasures of Macedonia, and had had unlimited powers in the said cases, he so completely abstained from appropriating any of this money that after his death his sons, whom he had given in adoption, on receiving their inheritance were unable to pay off from the whole of his personal property the dowry of his widow, except by selling some of the real property as well. Hence it seemed to many that in freedom from avarice he had outdone even those who were the marvel of Greece in this respect, Aristeides and Epaminondas. For they had refused gifts whenever the offer was made in the interest of the donors, but he, with full power to take as much as he wanted, had coveted nothing. Now if this statement seems incredible to some, they should take into account the fact that we cannot properly judge the freedom of the ancients from avarice by the dishonest greed of present-day Romans. For in our lifetime this people has, it appears, acquired a strong tendency to want more and more.

Having just now called a good man to mind, I wish to speak briefly of the training of the Scipio who later destroyed Numantia, so that his success in after years may not appear incredible to some through ignorance of his youthful concern with the most noble pursuits.

Publius Scipio was by blood, as has already been stated, the son of the Aemilius who triumphed over Perseus, but having been given in adoption to Scipio, the son of the conqueror of Hannibal and the Carthaginians, he had as his adoptive grandfather Scipio, surnamed Africanus, the greatest Roman down to his own day. Sprung from such stock, and succeeding to a family and clan of such importance, he showed himself worthy of the fame of his ancestors. For having had from childhood up extensive training in Greek studies, he now, on attaining the age of eighteen in this year. devoted himself to philosophy, taking as his tutor Polybius of Megalopolis, the author of the *Histories.* Living in constant association with him, and proving a zealous adept of every virtue, he far outstripped not only his peers in age but all his elders as well in temperance, in nobility of character, in magnanimity, and generally in all good qualities. Yet earlier, before applying himself to philosophy, he was generally regarded as a sluggard and no adequate successor to and representative of the dignity of his house. Nevertheless, he began, as befitted his years, by winning first a name for temperance. Now the fashion of the time tended strongly to unbridled pleasures and excessive licentiousness among the younger men. Some had abandoned themselves to catamites, others to courtesans, others to all sorts of musical entertainments and banquetings, and, in general, to the extravagance that these things entail. For having spent considerable time in Greece during the war with Perseus, they soon affected the easygoing Greek attitude to such matters, the more so as they had acquired ample funds, so that their wealth made adequate provision for the costs of indulgence.

27. Scipio, however, embarking upon a contrary-course of conduct, and taking arms against all his natural appetites, as if they were wild beasts, in less than five years achieved a reputation, universally acknowledged, for discipline and temperance. Even as this reputation was being accorded him by common consent, and was exciting favourable attention in all quarters, he set out to distinguish himself by his magnanimity and his liberal conduct of financial affairs. For the attainment of this virtue he had in the character of his real father, Aemilius, an excellent model to follow, and, in general, his close association with his father had given him certain advantages and left its mark on him. Chance also co-operated to no small extent, providing opportunities for his generosity about money to become quickly well known.

Aemilia, for example, the wife of the great Scipio and sister of Aemilius, the conqueror of Perseus, died leaving a large estate, which he stood to inherit. Here he gave the first indication of his purpose, under the following circumstances. Long before the death of his father, his mother, Papiria, had been separated from her husband, but in her separate establishment her means were inadequate to her high station in life. The mother of Scipio's adoptive father, however, the woman who left him the inheritance, had possessed, apart even from the rest of her fortune, a great array of personal adornments, attendants and the like, as befitted one who had shared in the prestige of the great Scipio's life and fortunes. All these trappings, worth many talents, he now took and gave to his own mother. Since she employed this donated pomp and splendour in making conspicuous public appearances, the goodness and generosity of the young man and, in general, his filial piety towards his mother won the acclaim of the whole city, first among the women and then among the men. This would be regarded as a shining example and as a thing to marvel at in any city, but especially so at Rome, where no one readily and of his own free will parts with anything he has. Later, when a large sum of money to complete their dowries remained to be paid to the daughters of the great Scipio, although it is the practice of the Romans to pay off a dowry piecemeal within three years, he paid the money to them all in full and at once. Next, when Aemilius, his real father, died and left his property to him and to [Q] Fabius [Maximus Aemilanus], the sons he had given in adoption, Scipio performed a noble act, which deserves to be put on record. Seeing that his brother was less prosperous than himself he gave him as a supplement his own share of the inheritance, to the value of more than sixty talents, and thus equalised his entire holdings with those of his brother. This being greeted with approval and favourable comment on all sides, he did a thing even more remarkable. For when his brother Fabius, wishing to stage a gladiatorial show in honour of their father, was unable to assume the expense because of the great outlays involved, he gave him from his own pocket a half of the total cost. On the death of his mother, so far from taking for himself anything he had given her, he allowed his sisters to have not only that but the rest of her estate, although they had no legal claim to the inheritance. Increasingly he gained the admiration of the whole city, receiving uncontested praise for his goodness and magnanimity; yet it was not so much the amounts involved that brought this about as the timeliness of his gifts and the tact with which he carried out his proposals. The acquisition of temperance, on the other hand, required no outlay of money; indeed, abstinence from indulgence conferred the boon of bodily health and vigour, which, as it lasted all his life, brought him ample compensation and requital. One virtue remains, courage, which indeed is regarded as essential by all men and in particular by the Romans: this too he pursued with unusual vigour and made perfect, chance having provided him a great opportunity. For the Macedonian kings had always been especially devoted to the chase, and Scipio outdid everyone.

27a. When it became known that the Romans were ill disposed towards Demetrius, [161] not only the other kings but even some of the satraps subject to him regarded his kingship with scant respect. Of these satraps the most outstanding was a certain Timarchus. A Milesian by birth, and a friend of the previous king, Antiochus [IV], he had, in the course of a series of missions to Rome, worked serious detriment to the senate. Providing himself with large sums of money, he offered the senators bribes, seeking especially to overwhelm and lure with his gifts any senators who were in a weak financial position. By gaining in this way a large number of adherents and supplying them with proposals contrary to the public policy of Rome, he debauched the senate; in this he was seconded by Heracleides, his brother, a man supremely endowed by nature for such service. Following the same tactics he repaired to Rome on the present occasion, being now satrap of Media, and by launching many accusations against Demetrius persuaded the senate to enact the following decree concerning him: "To Timarchus, because of . . . to be their king." Emboldened by this decree he raised an army of considerable size in Media; he also entered into an alliance against Demetrius with Artaxias, the king of Armenia. Having, moreover, intimidated the neighbouring peoples by an impressive display of force, and brought many of them under his sway, he marched against Zeugma, and eventually gained control of the kingdom.

28. In the one hundred and fifty-fifth Olympiad [160] envoys arrived from Ariarathes, bringing with them a "crown" often thousand gold pieces, to inform the senate of the king's friendly attitude towards the Roman people, as well as of his renunciation, on their account, of an alliance of marriage and friendship with Demetrius. Since this was confirmed by the testimony of Gracchus and his fellow commissioners, the senate, expressing their approval of Ariarathes, accepted the crown and sent him the highest gifts that it was their custom to bestow.

29. At about the same time the envoys of Demetrius were also introduced. They too brought a "crown" of ten thousand gold pieces and had with them, in chains, the men responsible for the murder of Octavius. The senators were for a long time uncertain how to handle the situation. Finally, they accepted the crown but declined to accept custody of the men, Isocrates and Leptines, whose surrender was offered them together with the crown.

30. When Demetrius sent an embassy to Rome the senate gave him a devious and enigmatic reply, that he would receive kind treatment at their hands if in the exercise of his authority he gave satisfaction to the senate.

31. After vanquishing Perseus the Romans curbed some of those who had taken part in the war on the Macedonian side, and removed others to Rome. In Epirus Charops, who had gained control of the state on the strength of his reputation as a friend of the Romans, at the outset was guilty of but few crimes against his people and showed some caution; but proceeding further and further in lawless behaviour, he wrought havoc in Epirus. He incessantly brought false charges against the wealthy, and by murdering some, and driving others into exile and confiscating their property, he exacted money not only from the men but also, through his mother Philota (for she was a person with a gift for cruelty and lawlessness that belied her sex), from the women as well; and he haled many before the popular assembly on charges of disaffection to Rome: the sentence in all cases was death.

32. Orophernes, [158] having driven his brother Ariarathes from the throne, made no effort, far from it, to manage his affairs sensibly, and to elicit popular support by helping and serving his people. Indeed, at the very time when he was raising money by forced contributions and was putting numbers of people to death, he presented Timotheüs with a gift of fifty talents, and King Demetrius with a gift of seventy, quite apart from the payment to Demetrius of six hundred talents with a promise to pay the remaining four hundred at another time. And seeing that the Cappadocians were disaffected, he began to exact contributions on all sides and to confiscate for the privy purse the property of men of the highest distinction. When he had amassed a great sum, he deposited four hundred talents with the city of Prienê as a hedge against the surprises of fortune, which amount the citizens of Prienê later repaid.

32a. King Eumenes, grieved at the expulsion of Ariarathes and being eager for reasons of his own to check Demetrius, sent for a certain youth who in beauty of countenance and in age was exceedingly like Antiochus the late king of Syria. This man resided in Smyrna and stoutly affirmed that he was a son of King Antiochus [IV]; and because of the resemblance he found many to believe him. On his arrival at Pergamum the king tricked him out with a diadem and the other insignia proper to a king, then sent him to a certain Cilician named Zenophanes. This man, who had quarrelled for some reason with Demetrius, and had been assisted in certain difficult situations by Eumenes, who was then king, was accordingly at odds with the one, and kindly disposed to the other. He received the youth in a town of Cilicia, and spread the word abroad in Syria that the youth would reclaim his father's kingdom in his own good time. Now after the generous behaviour of their former kings the common peoples of Syria were ill pleased with the austerity of Demetrius and his drastic demands. Being therefore ready for a change, they were buoyed up with hopeful expectations that the government would shortly fall into the hands of another and more considerate monarch.

32b. While returning from Rome the envoys of Orophernes formed a plot during the voyage against Ariarathes, [157] but were themselves apprehended and put to death by Ariarathes at Coreyra. Likewise at Corinth when the henchmen of Orophernes laid plans against Ariarathes, he upset their calculations by eluding them, and got safe to Attalus at Pergamum.

33. Thanks to his large army the elder Ptolemy soon forced his brother [Physcon] to stand a siege and made him undergo every deprivation, 158/7]yet did not venture to put him to death, partly because of his own innate goodness and their family ties, partly through fear of the Romans. He granted him assurances of personal safety, and made with him an agreement according to which the younger Ptolemy was to rest content with the possession of Cyrenê, and was to receive each year a fixed amount of grain. Thus the relations of the kings, which had advanced to a state of serious estrangement and desperate frays, found an unexpected and humane solution.

417

34. As the situation worsened Orophernes was anxious to pay his men, for fear they might start a revolution, but being for the present without funds he was driven to plundering the temple of Zeus, which stands beneath the Mountain of Ariadnê, as it is called, though from remote times it had been held inviolable. This he robbed, and paid off the arrears of their wages.

35. King Prusias of Bithynia, [156] having failed in his design on Attalus, destroyed the sanctuary outside the walls, known as the Nicephorium, and despoiled the temple. He also carried off the votive statues, the images of the gods, and the famous statue of Asclepius, reputed to be by the hand of Phyromachus, a piece of extraordinary workmanship; and he plundered all the shrines. The divine power was quick to requite him in signal fashion. The army was stricken with dysentery, and the greater part of his soldiers perished. A similar fate overtook his naval forces: for when the fleet ran into a sudden storm in the Propontis, many of the vessels were swallowed up by the sea, men and all, while some were driven on the shore and wrecked. Such were the first returns he received for his sacrilege.

36. The Rhodians, thanks to their shrewdness and the uses to which they turned their prestige, kept receiving payments of voluntary tribute, so to speak, from the kings. For by honouring whatever men are in power with clever flatteries and public decrees, and doing this, moreover, with assurance and keen foresight, they gain favours and receive donations of many times the value from the kings. From Demetrius, for example, they received a gift of two hundred thousand measures of wheat and a hundred thousand of barley, and Eumenes still owed them thirty thousand at his death; this king had also promised to do over their theatre in marble. Thus the Rhodians, while maintaining the best government in Greece, induced many princes to vie with one another in conferring benefactions upon them.

37. But in general when he was put to the test of combat, like base coin he was found to be of other metal, and by his personal shortcomings he enlarged the war.

38. What happened to the Rhodians was rather like a bear hunt. For indeed these beasts, which in size and strength appear so fearsome, are very easily routed when hunters unleash against them little dogs that, though small, are active and brave. For since bears have tender and fleshy feet, the snapping at their heels from beneath compels them to sit still until one of the hunters gets in a blow that strikes home, their slow and cumbersome movements making it impossible for them to . . . the nimbleness of the dogs. So the Rhodians, though world-renowned for their superiority in naval warfare, when unexpectedly surrounded on all sides by a fleet of midget ships, "mice" and "goats," were plunged into the greatest distress.

39. There was in Celtiberia a small city named Begeda, [153] which, because of a great increase in population, they voted to enlarge. The Roman senate, viewing with suspicion their growth in strength, sent out a commission to stop them in accordance with the treaty, wherein it was stated, along with much else, that without the consent of the Romans the Celtiberians might not found a city. One of the elders, named Cacyrus, replied that the agreement prevented them from founding a city, but did not forbid them to enlarge their old homes; that they were not founding a city that had not previously been there, but were reconstructing the city already in existence, and so were doing nothing in violation of the treaty or of the common practice of all mankind. In all else, he said, they were obedient to the Romans, and were wholeheartedly their allies, whenever occasion required their help, but they would in no wise, he added, desist from building their city. When the assembly with one accord signified its approval of these words, the envoys returned with their answer to the senate. The senate then voided the treaty and began hostilities.

40. Whereas a single occasion decides the outcome of wars in Greece, in the Celtiberian wars night generally separated the combatants with vigour and energy still undiminished, and even winter did not bring the war to an end. Hence the term "fiery war," used by some, brings this war to mind before any other.

40a. Once again a popular uprising, due to the disaffection of the masses, threatened Demetrius with the loss of his throne. One of his mercenary troops, a man named Andriscus, bore a close resemblance to Philip, the son of Perseus, both in appearance and stature, and while at first it was only in jest and derision that his friends called him "son of Perseus," soon the statement won popular credence. Andriscus, boldly taking his cue from this talk, not only declared that he was indeed the son of Perseus, but adducing a fictitious story of his birth and upbringing, even approached Demetrius with a crowd of followers and called upon him to restore him to Macedonia and to the throne of his fathers. Now Demetrius at first regarded him as a crank, but when the populace had gathered, and many speakers declared that Demetrius should either restore Andriscus or, if he could not or would not play the king, should abdicate, Demetrius, fearing the quick temper of the mob, had Andriscus arrested during the night and sent him off straightway to Rome with a full report to the senate of the claims made for the man.

41. After this victory the Celtiberians, with a prudent eye to the future, sent envoys to the consul to treat for peace. The consul, however, feeling that it was incumbent upon him to maintain the proud Roman tradition, told them in reply either to place themselves entirely at the disposal of the Romans or to carry on the war in earnest.

42. Diodorus also calls the Iberians Lusitanians. [153] For he says that the praetor Mummius was sent with an army to Iberia and that the Lusitanians, gathering in force and catching him off guard as he came to land, defeated him in battle and wiped out the greater part of his army. When the news of the Iberian victory became known, the Arevaci, considering themselves far superior to the Iberians, made light of the enemy, and the people in their assembly, when they elected to enter the war against the Romans, acted chiefly for this reason.

43. Although the Rhodian people had been aroused to enthusiastic and eager preparations for the war, yet when they were unlucky in their ventures they lapsed into strange ways of thinking, like men long ill who lose heart. For when such men find themselves no better after observing the regimen prescribed by their physicians, they have recourse to those who deal in sacrifice and divination, while some countenance the use of spells and all sorts of amulets. So the Rhodians, suddenly failing in all their ventures, had recourse to the aid of men whom they ordinarily held in contempt, and took a course that was bound to make them ridiculous in the eyes of others.

44. It is not the equipment and size of the ships that bring victory, but the deeds and daring of the stout fighters aboard them.

45. The Cretans, putting in at Siphnos, assaulted the city and by intimidation and deceit gained admission within the walls. Having pledged their word to commit no wrong, but acting with customary Cretan faithlessness, they enslaved the city, and after sacking the temples of the gods (set sail) for Crete, laden with their spoil. Swiftly the gods inflicted upon them the penalty for their transgressions, and the divine power signally dealt with their impiety in unexpected fashion. For through fear of the enemy and his large ships they were forced to set sail at night, and, when a gale burst upon them, most of the men were swallowed up by the waves, while some were dashed to death against the rocky shore, and a mere remnant were saved: those who had had no part in the perfidy practised upon the Siphnians.

BOOK XXXII FRAGMENTS

1. The Carthaginians, by engaging Masinissa in war, [150] were considered to have violated their treaty with Rome. Upon sending an embassy, they were told that the Romans knew what ought to be done. Since the answer they received was so ambiguous, the Carthaginians were greatly disturbed.

2. Those whose object is to gain dominion over others use courage and intelligence to get it, moderation and consideration for others to extend it widely, and paralysing terror to secure it against attack. The proofs of these propositions are to be found in attentive consideration of the history of such empires as were created in ancient times as well as of the Roman domination that succeeded them.

3. When the envoys of the Carthaginians announced that they had punished those responsible for the war against Masinissa, a member of the senate exclaimed: "And why were those responsible for the dispute not punished then and there, instead of at the end of the war?" At this the Carthaginian envoys stood silent, having no honest or plausible reply to give. The senate then returned them an awkward and elusive answer, for they adopted the statement that the Romans well knew what they ought to do.

4. Philip, the son of Amyntas, having succeeded to the throne at a time when Macedonia was enslaved by the Illyrians, wrested his kingdom from them by force of arms and by his shrewdness as a military commander, but it was by the moderation that he displayed towards the vanquished that he made it the greatest power in Europe. When, for example, in a famous battle [Chaeronea] he defeated the Athenians who disputed his dominance in Greece, he took great pains with the funeral of those slain in the defeat and left behind unburied, while he released without ransom and sent back to their own land the captives, to the number of more than two thousand. As a result those who had taken up arms in the contest for leadership now, because of his clemency towards them, willingly resigned their authority over the Greek states; while he, who in many struggles and battles had failed to achieve that authority, through a single act of kindness received with the free consent of his opponents the leadership of all Hellas, and finally he secured the permanence of his kingdom by the use of fear, when he levelled to the ground a populous city, Olynthus. In like manner his son Alexander, after seizing Thebes, by the destruction of this city deterred from rebellion the Athenians and Lacedaemonians, who were starting to revolt; yet in his Persian campaigns, by treating prisoners of war with the greatest kindness, he made the renown of his clemency as well as his courage contribute to his success in making the Asiatics eager to be ruled by him.

In more recent times the Romans, when they went in pursuit of world empire, brought it into being by the valour of their arms, then extended its influence far and wide by the kindest possible treatment of the vanquished. So far, indeed, did they abstain from cruelty and revenge on those subjected to them that they appeared to treat them not as enemies, but as if they were benefactors and friends. Whereas the conquered, as former foes, expected to be visited with fearful reprisals, the conquerors left no room for anyone to surpass them in clemency. Some they enrolled as fellow citizens, to some they granted rights of intermarriage, to others they restored their independence, and in no case did they nurse a resentment that was unduly severe. Because of their surpassing humanity, therefore, kings, cities, and whole nations went over to the Roman standard. Once they held sway over virtually the whole inhabited world, they confirmed their power by terrorism and by the destruction of the most eminent cities. Corinth they razed to the ground, the Macedonians (Perseus for example) they rooted out, they razed Carthage and the Celtiberian city of Numantia, and there were many whom they cowed by terror.

5. The Romans make it a point to embark only upon wars that are just, and to make no casual or precipitate decisions about such matters.

6. When the Romans sent out an expeditionary force [149] against the Carthaginians and news reached Carthage that the fleet was already at Lilybaeum, the Carthaginians, abstaining from all acts of hostility, sent legates to Rome, who placed themselves and their country at the disposal of the Romans. The senate, accepting their surrender, made answer that inasmuch as the Carthaginians were well advised, the senate granted them their laws, territory, sanctuaries, tombs, freedom, and property (the city of Carthage, however, was nowhere mentioned, their intention to destroy it being suppressed): these mercies the Carthaginians were to obtain provided they gave three hundred hostages, senators' sons, and obeyed the orders of the consuls. The Carthaginians, thinking that they were quit of the war, sent the hostages, not without great lamentation. Then the Romans arrived in Utica. Carthage again sent envoys to learn if the Romans had further demands to make upon them. When the consuls told them to surrender, without fraud, their arms and artillery, they were at first cast down, inasmuch as they were at war with Hasdrubal; none the less (the Romans) received from them two hundred thousand weapons of all sorts and two thousand catapults. Thereupon the Romans again sent word to the Carthaginians, bidding them appoint a delegation of Elders, to whom they would make known their final directive. The Carthaginians dispatched thirty men of the highest rank. Manilius, the elder of the consuls, stated that the senate had decreed that they should abandon the city they now inhabited, and should found another at a distance of eighty stades from the sea. At this the envoys resorted to lamentation and appeals for pity, all easting themselves to the ground and mingling cries of grief with tears, and a great wave of emotion swept over the assembly. When the Carthaginians after a struggle recovered from their consternation, one man alone, a certain Blanno, uttered words appropriate to the occasion, and speaking with desperate courage yet with complete frankness aroused feelings of pity in all who heard him.

The Romans, being immovable in their resolve to destroy Carthage, ordered the envoys to return straightway to Carthage and to report to the citizens what had been decreed. Some of the envoys, considering it hopeless to return home, individually sought refuge as best they could, but the others, electing to return, made their way back, their fatal mission completed. As the populace thronged to meet them, they said not a word to them, but beating their heads, raising aloft their hands, and calling upon the gods for aid, they proceeded to the market-place and reported to the *gerousia* the orders imposed by the Romans.

7. Scipio (he who was later called Africanus but who at this time was a mere tribune of the soldiers), unlike the other (tribunes), who disregarding their pledged word broke faith with those who had reached sworn agreements with them, was most faithful in adhering to his promises to the besieged and was honest in his dealings with all who put themselves in his hands. For this reason, and because his reputation for justice was becoming known throughout Libya, no one under siege would give himself up unless Scipio was a party to the agreement.

8. Since three Romans who fell in this engagement [Nepheris] had remained unburied, [149/8] the whole army was distressed at the loss of the men and, above all, at their being deprived of burial. Scipio. with the consent of the consul, sent a written appeal to Hasdrubal to give them burial. He acceded to the appeal, performed the rites of burial with all due honour, and sent their bones to the consul; whereby Scipio advanced in esteem, as a man who was highly influential even with the enemy.

9. The Carthaginian women contributed their gold jewellery. For now that life clung to the last narrow foothold, the whole populace felt that they were not losing their wealth, but were by their gift re-establishing their own safety.

13. [The harbour of Carthage is known as Cothon. Of its several advantages we shall endeavour to give a full account at the appropriate time.]

14. He says that the wall of Carthage is forty cubits in height and twenty-two in breadth. Notwithstanding, the siege engines of the Romans and their martial exploits proved stronger than the Carthaginian defences, and the city was captured and levelled to the ground.

15. [Concerning him there is again an account elsewhere.] When King Demetrius sent on to Rome the self-styled son of Perseus, a young man named Andriscus, the senate ordered him to live in a certain city of Italy. But after a period he escaped and sailed off to Miletus. During his stay there he invented tales about himself purporting to demonstrate that he was the son of Perseus. He said that while still an infant he had been given to . . . the Cretan to rear, and that the Cretan had transmitted to him a sealed tablet, in which Perseus revealed to him the existence of two treasures, one at Amphipolis, lying beneath the highway at a depth of ten fathoms (?), containing one hundred and fifty talents of silver, and the other, of seventy talents, at Thessalonica, in the middle of the exedra of the colonnade, opposite the court. Since his story attracted much attention, it finally reached the ears of the magistrates of Miletus, who arrested him and placed him in prison. Certain envoys happening to visit the city, they referred the matter to them, seeking advice on what should be done. They scoffingly bade the magistrates let the fellow loose to go his own way. He, on receiving his release, set himself in earnest to act out and make a reality of his mummery. By constantly embroidering the story of his royal birth, he gulled many, even the Macedonians themselves. Having as his accomplice a certain harpist named Nicolaüs, a Macedonian by birth, he learned from him that a woman called Callippa, who had been a concubine of King Perseus, was now the wife of Athenaeus of Pergamum. Accordingly he made his way to her, and pouring out his romantic tale of kinship to Perseus procured from her funds for his travels, a regal costume, a diadem, and two slaves suited to his needs. From her he heard, moreover, that Teres, a Thracian chieftain, was married to a daughter of the late King Philip. Encouraged by this support he made for Thrace. On the way he stopped at Byzantium and was received with honour; a display of folly for which the citizens of Byzantium later paid the penalty to Rome. With more and more people flocking to him, he arrived in Thrace at the court of Teres. As a mark of honour Teres presented him with a troop of a hundred soldiers, and placed a diadem on his head. Recommended by him to the other chieftains, Andriscus received from them another hundred men. Proceeding to the court of the Thracian chieftain Barsabas, he prevailed upon him to take part in the expedition and to escort him home to Macedonia, for he was now asserting, on the grounds of inheritance, a legal claim to the Macedonian throne. Defeated in battle by Macedonicus this false Philip took refuge in Thrace. [148] . . . Finally he [Metellus?] gained the upper hand in the cities throughout Macedonia.

16. Masinissa, [149/8] the late king of Libya, who had winter, always maintained friendly relations with Rome, lived till the age of ninety, in full possession of his faculties, and at his death left ten sons, whom he entrusted to the guardianship of Rome. He was a man remarkable for his physical vigour, and had, from the days of his childhood, accustomed himself to endurance and strenuous activities: indeed, standing in his tracks he would remain motionless the whole day long, or sit all day until nightfall without stirring, busy with his affairs; and mounted on horseback he would even ride a whole day and a night, continuously, without growing faint. The following is a prime indication of his good health and vitality: though nearly ninety, he had at the time of his death a son aged four, who was a remarkably sturdy child. In the care of his fields Masinissa was so outstanding that he left each of his sons a farm of ten thousand plethra, well equipped with all necessary buildings. His distinguished career as a king-lasted sixty years.

17. 1. At his rendezvous with Phameas, Scipio, by holding out great hopes, [149/8] persuaded him to desert the Carthaginians, along with twelve hundred cavalry.

9a. The pseudo-Philip, after gaining a resounding victory over the Romans, shifted to a course of savage cruelty and tyrannical disregard for law. He put many wealthy persons to death, after first throwing out false and slanderous charges against them, and murdered not a few even of his friends. For he was by nature brutal, bloodthirsty, and arrogant in manner, and was, moreover, shot through with greed and every base quality.

Marcus Porcius Cato, a man widely acclaimed for sagacity, when asked by someone how Scipio was faring in Libya, said: "He alone has sense, the others flit about like shadows." Moreover, the populace conceived such a liking for the man that he became consul.

The populace conceived such a liking for Scipio that even though his age did not allow it nor the laws permit, they bent their best efforts to confer upon him the consulship.

9b. The false Philip appointed Telestes general. He, however, seduced by the promises of the Romans, revolted and went over with his cavalry to Caecilius. The pseudo-Philip, enraged at his conduct, arrested the wife and children of Telestes, and vented his anger on them.

17. 2. Fortune, embroiling the whole situation as if of set purpose, furnished alliances to first one and then the other of the contestants.

The Roman consul Calpurnius, after accepting the surrender of certain towns, razed them to the ground in disregard of his pledged word. Hence, being distrusted, he failed in all his undertakings, as if some divine agency were working against him. For though he attempted much his actions were ineffective.

19. Since King Prusias had repulsive features and had become physically effeminate through soft living, [149] he was detested by the Bithynians.

20. The senate dispatched a commission to Asia to settle the war between Nicomedes and his father Prusias, and selected for this service Licinius, a man afflicted with gout, Mancinus, who had had his head pierced by a falling tile so that most of the bones were removed, and Lucius, a person utterly without perception. Cato, the leader of the senate and a man of great sagacity, thereupon remarked in the senate: "We are sending out an embassy without feet, without head, and without heart." His shot was well aimed and became the talk of the town.

21. Nicomedes, having defeated his father Prusias in battle, put him to death after he took sanctuary in the temple of Zeus. Thus he succeeded to the throne of Bithynia, having gained this eminence by perpetrating a most sacrilegious murder.

22. While the Carthaginians lay beleaguered, [147] Hasdrubal sent and invited Gulussa to come to a colloquy. In accordance with the commands of the general, Gulussa offered Hasdrubal an asylum for himself and ten families of his choosing with a grant of ten talents and a hundred slaves. Hasdrubal replied that while his country was being ravaged with fire the sun would never behold him seeking safety for himself. Now in words he cut a brave figure, but his deeds exposed him as a renegade. For though his city was in desperate straits, he led a luxurious life, holding drinking parties at all hours, giving sumptuous banquets, and arrogantly serving second courses. Meanwhile his fellow citizens were perishing of starvation, but he, as the crowning insult, went about in purple robes and an expensive woollen cloak, as though revelling in his country's misfortunes.

23. At the fall of Carthage [146] the general [Hasdrubal], forgetting his proud courage, or rather his proud talk, abandoned the deserters and approached Scipio in the guise of a suppliant. Clasping Scipio by the knees and sobbing as he urged every possible plea, he moved him to compassion. Scipio exhorted him to take heart, and addressing the friends who sat with him in council, said: "This is the man who a while back was not willing to accept an offer of safety on highly favourable terms. Such is the inconstancy of Fortune and her power; unpredictably she brings about the collapse of all human pretensions."

24. When Carthage had been put to the torch and the flames were doing their awful work of devastation throughout the whole city, Scipio wept unabashedly. Asked by Polybius, his mentor, why he was thus affected, he said: "Because I am reflecting on the fickleness of Fortune. Some day, perhaps, the time will come when a similar fate shall overtake Rome." And he cited these lines from the poet, Homer:

> The day will come when sacred Ilium shall perish, with
> Priam and his people. *Il.* 6.448,9

25. After the capture of Carthage Scipio, showing the collected spoils to the envoys who had arrived from Sicily, bade them severally pick out whatever things had in times past been carried off from their particular cities to Carthage, and to take them home to Sicily. Many portraits of famous men were found, many statues of outstanding workmanship, and not a few striking dedications to the gods in gold and silver. Among them was also the notorious bull of Acragas: Perilaüs fashioned it for the tyrant Phalaris, and lost his life in the first demonstration of his device when he was justly punished by being himself made its victim.

26. Never in all the time that men's deeds have been recorded in history had Greece been a prey to such calamities. Indeed, so extreme were her misfortunes that no one could either write or read of them without weeping. I am not unaware how painful it is to rehearse the misfortunes of Greece, and through my writings to pass on to coming generations an enduring record of what then befell; but I note too that warnings drawn from experience of events and their outcome are of no little service to men in correcting their own shortcomings. Accordingly criticism should be directed not at the historians, but rather at those whose conduct of affairs has been so unwise. It was not, for example, the cowardice of the soldiers, but the inexperience of their commanders that brought the Achaean League crashing to its fall. For though it was a dreadful disaster that overtook the Carthaginians at about this same time, yet the misfortune that befell the Greeks was not less but even, in all truth, greater than theirs. For since the Carthaginians were utterly annihilated, grief for their misfortunes perished with them; but the Greeks, after witnessing in person the butchery and beheading of their kinsmen and friends, the capture and looting of their cities, the abusive enslavement of whole populations, after, in a word, losing both their liberty and the right to speak freely, exchanged the height of prosperity for the most extreme misery. Having so heedlessly allowed themselves to get into war with Rome, they now experienced the greatest disasters.

Indeed the frenzy that possessed the Achaean League and their surprising plunge into self-destruction had all the appearance of a divine visitation. The men responsible for all their troubles were the generals. Some of them, being involved in debt, were ripe for revolution and war, and proposed the cancelling of all debts; and since there were many helpless debtors who supported them, they were able to arouse the commons. There were other leaders who through sheer folly plunged into counsels of despair. Above all it was Critolaus [*Strategus*] who enflamed the sparks of revolution in the populace. Using the prestige that his position gave him he openly accused the Romans of high-handed behaviour and self-seeking: he said that he wished to be Rome's friend, but that he certainly did not choose, of his own free will, to hail the Romans as overlords. The assemblies were sweepingly assured that, if they showed themselves men, they would not lack allies; if slaves, that they would not lack masters; and in his speeches he created the impression that conversations had already been held with kings and free cities on the subject of a military alliance.

Having by his oratory inflamed the passions of the mob he brought forward a proposed declaration of war, nominally against Sparta, but in reality against Rome. Thus all too often vice prevails over virtue, and a declaration that leads to destruction over an appeal to refrain and be safe.

27. Of Corinth the poets had sung in earlier time:

> Corinth, bright star of Hellas.

This was the city that, to the dismay of later ages, was now wiped out by her conquerors. Nor was it only at the time of her downfall that Corinth evoked great compassion from those that saw her; even in later times, when they saw the city levelled to the ground, all who looked upon her were moved to pity. No traveller passing by but wept, though he beheld but a few scant relics of her past prosperity and glory. Wherefore in ancient times, nearly a hundred years later, Gaius Iulius Caesar (who for his great deeds was entitled *divus*), after viewing the site restored the city.

Their spirits were gripped by two opposite emotions, the hope of safety and the expectation of destruction.

In ancient times, nearly a hundred years later, Gaius Iulius Caesar (who for his great deeds was entitled *divus*), when he inspected the site of Corinth, was so moved by compassion and the thirst for fame that he set about restoring it with great energy. It is therefore just that this man and his high standard of conduct should receive our full approval and that we should by our history accord him enduring praise for his generosity. For whereas his forefathers had harshly used the city, he by his clemency made amends for their unrelenting severity, preferring to forgive rather than to punish. In the magnitude of his achievements he surpassed all his predecessors, and he deserved the title that he acquired on the basis of his own merits. To sum up, this was a man who by his nobility, his power as an orator, his leadership in war, and his indifference to money is entitled to receive our approval, and to be accorded praise by history for his generous behaviour. For in the magnitude of his deeds he surpassed all earlier Romans.

9c. Ptolemy Philometor entered Syria [146] intending to support Alexander [Balas] on the grounds of kinship. But on discovering the man's downright poverty of spirit, he transferred his daughter Cleopatra to Demetrius, alleging that there was a conspiracy afoot, and after arranging an alliance pledged her to him in marriage. Hierax and Diodotus, despairing of Alexander and standing in fear of Demetrius because of their misdeeds against his father, aroused the people of Antioch to rebellion, and receiving Ptolemy within the city, bound a diadem about his head and offered him the kingship. He, however, had no appetite for the throne, but did desire to add Coelê Syria to his own realm, and privately arranged with Demetrius a joint plan, whereby Ptolemy was to rule Coelê Syria and Demetrius his ancestral domains.

9d and **10.1.** Alexander, worsted in battle, [145] fled with five hundred of his men to Abae in Arabia, to take refuge with Diocles, the local sheikh, in whose care he had earlier placed his infant son Antiochus. Thereupon Heliades and Casius, two officers who were with Alexander, entered into secret negotiations for their own safety and voluntarily offered to assassinate Alexander. When Demetrius consented to their terms, they became, not merely traitors to their king, but his murderers. Thus was Alexander put to death by his friends.

10.2. It would be a mistake to omit the strange occurrence that took place before the death of Alexander, even though it is a thing so marvellous that it will not, perhaps, be credited. A short while before the time of our present narrative, as King Alexander was consulting an oracle in Cilicia (where [Seleucia] there is said to be a sanctuary of Apollo Sarpedonius), the god, we are told, replied to him that he should beware of the place that bore the "two-formed one." At the time the oracle seemed enigmatic, but later, after the king's death, its sense was learnt through the following causes.

There was dwelling at Abae in Arabia a certain man named Diophantus, a Macedonian by descent. He married an Arabian woman of that region and begot a son, named for himself, and a daughter called Heraïs. Now the son he saw dead before his prime, but when the daughter was of an age to be married he gave her a dowry and bestowed her upon a man named Samiades. He, after living in wedlock with his wife for the space of a year, went off on a long journey. Heraïs, it is said, fell ill of a strange and altogether incredible infirmity. A severe tumour appeared at the base of her abdomen, and as the region became more and more swollen and high fevers supervened her physicians suspected that an ulceration had taken place at the mouth of the uterus. They applied such remedies as they thought would reduce the inflammation, but notwithstanding, on the seventh day, the surface of the tumour burst, and projecting from her groin there appeared a male genital organ with testicles attached. Now when the rupture occurred, with its sequel, neither her physician nor any other visitors were present, but only her mother and two maidservants. Dumfounded at this extraordinary event they tended Heraïs as best they could, and said nothing of what had occurred. She, on recovering from her illness, wore feminine attire and continued to conduct herself as a homebody and as one subject to a husband. It was assumed, however, by those who were privy to the strange secret that she was an hermaphrodite, and as to her past life with her husband, since natural intercourse did not fit their theory, she was thought to have consorted with him homosexually. Now while her condition was still undisclosed, Samiades returned and, as was fitting, sought the company of his wife. When she, for very shame, could not bear to appear in his presence, he, they say, grew angry. As he continually pressed the point and claimed his wife, her father meanwhile denying his plea but feeling too embarrassed to disclose the reason, their disagreement soon grew into a quarrel. As a result Samiades brought suit for his own wife against her father, for Fortune did in real life what she commonly does in plays and made the strange alteration lead to an accusation. After the judges took their seats and all the arguments had been presented, the person in dispute appeared before the tribunal, and the jurors debated whether the husband should have jurisdiction over his wife or the father over his daughter. When, however, the court found that it was the wife's duty to attend upon her husband, she at last revealed the truth. Screwing up her courage she unloosed the dress that disguised her, displayed her masculinity to them all, and burst out in bitter protest that anyone should require her man to cohabit with a man. All present were overcome with astonishment, and exclaimed with surprise at this marvel. Heraïs, now that her shame had been publicly disclosed, exchanged her woman's apparel for the garb of a young man; and the physicians, on being shown the evidence, concluded that her male organ had been concealed in an egg-shaped portion of the female organ, and that since a membrane had abnormally encased the organ, an aperture had formed through which excretions were discharged. In consequence they found it necessary to scarify the perforated area and induce cicatrisation: having thus brought the male organ into decent shape, they gained credit for applying such treatment as the case allowed. Heraïs, changing her name to Diophantus, was enrolled in the cavalry, and after fighting in the king's forces accompanied him in his withdrawal to Abae. Thus it was that the oracle, which previously had not been understood, now became clear when the king was assassinated at Abae, the birthplace of the "two-formed one." As for Samiades, they say that he, a thrall still to his love and its old associations, but constrained by shame for his unnatural marriage, designated Diophantus in his will as heir to his property, and made his departure from life. Thus she who was born a woman took on man's courage and renown, while the man proved to be less strong-minded than a woman.

11. A change of sex under similar conditions occurred thirty years later in the city of Epidaurus. There was an Epidaurian child, named Callo, orphaned of both parents, who was supposed to be a girl. Now the orifice with which women are naturally provided had in her case no opening, but beside the so-called *pecten* she had from birth a perforation through which she excreted the liquid residues. On reaching maturity she became the wife of a fellow citizen. For two years she lived with him, and since she was incapable of intercourse as a woman, was obliged to submit to unnatural embraces. Later a tumour appeared on her genitals and because it gave rise to great pain a number of physicians were called in. None of the others would take the responsibility for treating her, but a certain apothecary, who offered to cure her, cut into the swollen area, whereupon a man's privates were protruded, namely testicles and an imperforate penis. While all the others stood amazed at the extraordinary event, the apothecary took steps to remedy the remaining deficiencies. First of all, cutting into the glans he made a passage into the urethra, and inserting a silver catheter drew off the liquid residues. Then, by scarifying the perforated area, he brought the parts together. After achieving a cure in this manner he demanded double fees, saying that he had received a female invalid and made her into a healthy young man. Callo laid aside her loom-shuttles and all other instruments of woman's work, and taking in their stead the garb and status of a man changed her name (by adding a single letter, N, at the end) to Callon. It is stated by some that before changing to man's form she had been a priestess of Demeter, and that because she had witnessed things not to be seen by men she was brought to trial for impiety.

12. Likewise in Naples and a good many other places sudden changes of this sort are said to have occurred. Not that the male and female natures have been united to form a truly bisexual type, for that is impossible, but that Nature, to mankind's consternation and mystification, has through the bodily parts falsely given this impression. And this is the reason why we have considered these shifts of sex worthy of record, not for the entertainment, but for the improvement of our readers. For many men, thinking such things to be portents, fall into superstition, and not merely isolated individuals, but even nations and cities. At the outset of the Marsian War, at any rate, there was, so it is reported, an Italian living not far from Home who had married an hermaphrodite similar to those described above; he laid information before the senate, which in an access of superstitious terror and in obedience to the Etruscan diviners ordered the creature to be burned alive. Thus did one whose nature was like ours and who was not, in reality, a monster, meet an unsuitable end through misunderstanding of his malady. Shortly afterwards there was another such case at Athens, and again through misunderstanding of the affliction the person was burned alive. There are even, in fact, fanciful stories to the effect that the animals called hyenas are at once both male and female, and that in successive years they mount one another in turn. This is simply not true. Both the male and the female have each their own sexual attributes, simple and distinct, but there is also in each case an adjunct that creates a false impression and deceives the casual observer: the female, in her parts, has an appendage that resembles the male organ, and the male, conversely, has one similar in appearance to that of the female. This same consideration holds for all living creatures, and while it is true that monsters of every kind are frequently born, they do not develop and are incapable of reaching full maturity. Let this much then be said by way of remedy to superstitious fears.

BOOK XXXIII FRAGMENTS

1. The Lusitanians, says Diodorus, were at first for lack of any adequate leader an easy prey in their war with Rome, but later, after they found Viriathus, inflicted heavy losses on the Romans. This Viriathus was one of the Lusitanians who dwell near the ocean, and having been a shepherd from boyhood was a practised mountaineer; to this mode of life, indeed, his physical endowment well suited him, since in strength of arm, in speed of foot, and in agility and nimbleness generally he was far superior to the other Iberians. Having accustomed himself to a regime of little food, much exercise, and a bare minimum of sleep, and in short by living at all times under arms and in constant conflict with beasts of the wild and with brigands, he had made his name a byword with the populace, was chosen to be their leader, and in a short while gathered about him a band of freebooters. By his success on the battlefield he not only won acclaim as a warrior but gained besides a reputation for exceptional qualities of leadership. He was, moreover, scrupulous in the division of spoils and according to their deserts honoured with gifts those of his men who distinguished themselves for bravery. As time went on he proclaimed himself chieftain, a brigand no more, and taking up arms against the Romans, he defeated them in many battles: the Roman general Vetilius, for example, he utterly crushed [147], with all his army, and taking the general himself captive, put him to death by the sword. He won many military successes besides, until Fabius was chosen to take charge of the war against him [145/4]. Thereupon his fortunes began to decline in no small measure. Then, rallying, he won new laurels at the expense of Fabius and forced him to subscribe to a treaty unworthy of the Romans [140]. But Caepio, on being picked to command the forces opposing Viriathus [140/39], annulled the treaty, and after first inflicting repeated reverses on Viriathus and then bringing him to utter defeat, so that he even sought a truce, got him assassinated by the man's own kinsmen. Then, having cowed Tautamus, who succeeded to the command, and his army, and having arranged a treaty such as he wished to impose, he granted them land and a city in which to dwell.

Viriathus, the Lusitanian robber-captain, was scrupulous in the division of spoils: he based his rewards on merit, making special gifts to those of his men who distinguished themselves for bravery, and took for his own use not one thing belonging to the common store. In consequence the Lusitanians followed him wholeheartedly into battle, and honoured him as their common benefactor and saviour.

2. In his provincial governorship Plautius, the Roman praetor [146], proved to be a poor leader. Found guilty on his return home on charges of *minuta maiestas,* he left Rome and went into exile.

3. In Syria King Alexander [145?], whose weakness of character rendered him incompetent to govern a kingdom, had turned over the administration of Antioch to Hierax and Diodotus.

4. Demetrius, now that the royal power of Egypt had been shattered and he alone was left [145], assumed that he was quit of all danger. Scorning, therefore, to ingratiate himself with the populace as was customary, and waxing ever more burdensome in his demands upon them, he sank into ways of despotic brutality and extravagantly lawless behaviour of every sort. Now the responsibility for his disposition lay not only in his nature, but also with the man [Lasthenes?] who was set over the kingdom. For he, being an impious knave, was the author of all these evils, since he flattered the youth and prompted him to deeds of utter infamy. In the first instance Demetrius chastened those who had been hostile to him in the war, not with mild censure, but visited them with outlandish punishments. Then, when the citizens of Antioch behaved towards him in their usual fashion, he arrayed against them a considerable body of mercenary troops and stripped the citizens of their arms; those who did not choose to hand them over he either slew in open combat or cut down, together with their wives and children, in their own homes; and when serious riots broke out over the disarming he set fire to the greater part of the city. After punishing many of those implicated, he confiscated their property to the royal purse. Many Antiochenes, in fear and hatred, fled the city and wandered all about Syria, biding their time to attack the king. Demetrius, now their avowed enemy, never ceased to murder, banish, and rob, and even outdid his father in harshness and thirst for blood. For in fact his father, who had affected, not a kingly equity, but a tyrant's lawlessness, had involved his subjects in irremediable misfortunes, with the consequence that the kings of this house were hated for their transgressions, and those of the other house were loved for their equity. Hence at any moment there were struggles and continual wars in Syria, as the princes of each house constantly lay in wait for one another. The populace, in fact, welcomed the dynastic changes, since each king on being restored sought their favour.

4a. A certain Diodotus, also called Tryphon, who stood high in esteem among the king's "Friends," perceiving the excitement of the masses and their hatred for the prince, revolted from Demetrius, and soon finding large numbers ready to join him (enlisted first?) the men of Larissa, who were renowned for their courage, and had indeed received their present habitation as a reward of valour (for they were colonists from Thessalian Larissa), and as loyal allies to the royal line descended from Seleucus Nicator (had always fought?) in the front ranks of the cavalry. He also made an ally of the Arab sheikh Iamblichus, who happened to have in his keeping Antiochus (styled Epiphanes), a mere child, the son of Alexander. Setting a diadem on his head and providing him with the retinue appropriate to a king, he restored the child to his father's throne. For he supposed, as was only natural, that the populace, eager for a change, would welcome him home because of the equity of the kings (of this house?) and because of the lawlessness of the present ruler. Having collected a modest host he first encamped around Chalcis, a city situated on the Arabian border and capable of supporting an army quartered there and assuring it safety; with this as his base he brought over the neighbouring regions and accumulated the supplies needed for war. Demetrius at first made light of him as a mere brigand, and ordered his soldiers to arrest the man, but later, when Tryphon had built up an army of unexpected size and taken as a pretext for his own venture the restoration of the boy to his kingdom, Demetrius resolved to dispatch a general against him.

5. The inhabitants of Aradus thought that the moment had come to destroy the city of Marathus. Sending secretly therefore to Ammonius, the prime minister of the realm, they persuaded him by a gift of three hundred talents to betray

Marathus to them. He sent Isidorus to Marathus, ostensibly on some other business, in reality to seize the city and hand it over to the Aradians. The Marathenes, ignorant of the doom pronounced against them and aware that the Aradians stood high in favour with the king, resolved not to admit into the city the soldiers sent by the king, and instead to appeal personally for help from Aradus. Accordingly they at once selected ten of their oldest citizens, men of the highest distinction, and sent them to Aradus bearing branches of supplication, and carrying with them the most ancient of the city's idols, hoping, by an appeal to the ties of kinship and to reverence for the gods, to effect a complete change in the attitude of the Aradians. The emissaries, following instructions, disembarked from their ship and addressed their appeals and supplications to the populace. The Aradians, keyed to a frenzy, paid no heed to the laws everywhere observed with respect to suppliants, and counted as nought the reverence due to the images and gods of a kindred people. So, dashing to pieces the divine images they wantonly trampled them under foot, and attempted to stone the envoys to death. When a few elderly men intervened to check the excited mob, the crowd reluctantly and in deference to the elders stopped throwing stones, but bade them lead the envoys off to prison.

The Aradians, keyed to a frenzy, showed no respect for the envoys. And when the hapless emissaries in protest invoked the sacred rights of suppliants and the inviolability assured to envoys, the most reckless of the young men in a fury ran them through. As soon as the unholy slaughter was ended, they rushed to the assembly, and compounding their offences contrived yet another impious plot against the Marathenes. Stripping the dead men of their rings, they sent a letter to the people of Marathus, ostensibly from the ambassadors, in which they informed them that the Aradians promised to send soldiers to their aid, hoping that, if the Marathenes believed that they had, in truth, allies on the way, their soldiers would be admitted to the city. They were not, however, able to carry through their wicked design, since a god-fearing and upright man took pity on their fate even as they were about to be utterly ruined. Though the Aradians had removed all boats, so that no one should be able to reveal to the intended victims the intrigue aimed at them, a certain seaman, well disposed towards the Marathenes and accustomed to ply the waterways thereabouts, swam by night across the strait (for his own bark had been taken away), safely accomplished the perilous mile-long crossing, and revealed to the Marathenes the plot against them. And when the Aradians learned through spies that their project had been made known, they gave up the villainous scheme of the letters.

5a. In Pisidia there was a man named Molcestes: native of Boubo [145/39], he stood first in esteem among all in those parts, and because of his prominence was chosen general. As his power grew, he obtained bodyguards, and then openly proclaimed himself tyrant. After a certain time his brother, Semias, who sought to transfer the power to himself and who was trusted as a brother would be, slew Moceltes and succeeded to his position. The sons of the murdered man, who at the time were still in their teens, were secretly taken by a kinsman to Termessus. There they were reared, and on reaching full manhood set out to avenge their father's murder. But after slaying the tyrant, they elected not to assume power themselves, but restored their country's popular government.

6. Ptolemy [VIII], the brother of Ptolemy Philometor, on becoming king [145] began his administration of the realm with flagrant breaches of the law.

There were many persons, for example, whom he ensnared on false charges of plotting against him, and cruelly and illegally put to death; others he falsely charged with crime on various counts, and driving them into exile confiscated their property. As these acts provoked dissatisfaction and resentment, he brought upon himself the wrath of the entire populace and soon became an object of hatred to his subjects. None the less he ruled for fifteen years.

6a. Diodorus says that the younger Ptolemy, succeeding his elder brother, ruled for fifteen years, and committed many lawless acts: he married his own sister, Cleopatra, falsely accused many of plotting against him, and putting some to death, drove others into exile by his charges and seized their property.

7. Viriathus, when many gold and silver cups and all sorts of embroidered robes had been set out for his wedding, supporting himself on his lance, regarded the lavish display with no sign of admiration or wonder, but showed rather a feeling of disdain. He also in a single remark spoke volumes of good sense, and he let fall many statements about ingratitude towards benefactors and about folly . . . at being puffed up over the unstable gifts of fortune: above all, that the much-touted wealth of his father-in-law was itself subject to the man who held the spear; further, that he owed him a greater debt than others, yet offered him, the true master of it all, no personal gift. Viriathus therefore neither bathed nor took his place at table, though importuned to do so, but when a table with viands of all sorts was set before him, he took bread and meat and gave it to those who had made the journey with him; then, after casually taking a few morsels himself, he ordered them to fetch the bride. Having offered sacrifice and performed the rites customary among the Iberians, he set the maiden on his mare and rode off at once to the place he had in readiness in the mountains. For he considered self-sufficiency his greatest wealth, freedom his country, and the eminence won by bravery his securest possession. He was a man who in conversation too went straight to the mark, since the words he uttered were the faultless outpouring of an untutored and unspoilt nature.

When many costly objects had been set out for his wedding, Viriathus, having looked his fill, said to Astolpas: "How is it, pray, that the Romans, who saw all this at your banquets, kept their hands off such valuables, though it was in their power to wrest them from you?" When Astolpas replied that no one had ever moved to seize or ask for them, though many knew of their existence, he said: "Then why in the world, man, if the authorities granted you immunity and the secure enjoyment of these things, did you desert them and choose to ally yourself with my nomadic life and my humble company?"

This was, indeed, a man who in conversation went straight to the mark, since his words flowed from an untutored and unspoilt nature. So, for example, *a propos* of the people of Tucca, who never stuck to the same course, but went over now to the Romans, now to him, and often repeated these moves, he told a story that subtly rallied, and at the same time rebuked their uncertainty of purpose. There was, he said, a certain middle-aged man who took two wives. The younger, eager to have her husband resemble her, pulled out his grey hairs, while the old woman pulled out the black ones, until between them he was soon left quite bald. A similar fate, he said, would be in store for the people of Tucca; for as the Romans put to death those who were at odds with them and the Lusitanians did away with their enemies, the city would soon be left empty. He is said to have made many other pithy remarks as well, for though he had had no formal education, he was schooled in the understanding of practical affairs. For the speech of one who lives according to nature is concise, being a by-product of virtuous pursuits; and when a thing is stated simply, briefly, and without frills, the speaker is credited with a pointed saying, while the hearer has something to remember.

8. Weakness and a lowly status in life foster a frugal self-sufficiency and honesty, but a lofty estate goes hand in hand with self-aggrandisement and a disregard for law that is rooted in dishonesty.

9. Demetrius, during his stay at Laodieeia [145/4], spent his time idly, giving drinking parties and lavishly indulging in the most costly pleasures. So too his public conduct remained unchanged, in that he continued to commit random outrages on many persons and was incapable of profiting by his reverses to mend his ways.

10. The men of Cnossos clung stubbornly to their primacy. What prompted them to ambitions of leadership was the ancient repute of their city and the widespread fame of their ancestors in the heroic age. For Zeus, as some tell the tale, was reared among them, and Minos, the sea-lord, who was a Cnossian, was educated by Zeus and far surpassed all other men in valiancy.

11. In keeping with the tale told about Agamemnon, how he laid a curse on the soldiers left behind in Crete, there is still current among the Cretans an ancient proverb, which in a single verse prophesies the unexpected disaster that now took place:

> Alas, the men of Pergamus were heedless of ruin.

12. The Egyptian populace cherished a deep hatred for Ptolemy because of his brutality towards his subjects and his lawless conduct. For when his character was considered side by side with that of Philometor it did not even admit of comparison, since each of the two went to an extreme, the one of equity, the other of bloodthirsty brutality. Therefore the populace was ripe for a change and awaited the proper moment to revolt.

13. While Ptolemy was being enthroned in his palace at Memphis in accordance with Egyptian custom [144], Cleopatra bore the king a son. Exceedingly pleased, he surnamed the child Memphites, after the city in which he was performing sacrifice when the child was born. During the birth festival, indulging his usual thirst for blood he ordered the execution of the Cyrenêans who had accompanied him on his return to Egypt, but were now under accusation for certain frank and honest statements because of his concubine, Irene.

14. When Diêgylis, the king of the Thracians, ascended the throne and the tide of fortune was flowing in his favour beyond all expectations, he ceased to govern his subjects as friends and comrades- in-arms, but lorded it over them harshly as if they were bought slaves or captive foes. Many were the fine, noble Thracians he tortured and put to death, and many were the victims of his abusive treatment and unbridled violence. There was no woman, no boy whose beauty he left intact, no rich store of possessions that was left undiminished: the whole realm was full of his lawlessness. He ravaged also the Greek cities along his borders, and the captives were subjected to his outrages or punished with terrible and exquisite tortures. Becoming master of Lysimacheia, a city subject to Attalus, he set the city afire, and picking out the most prominent of the captives visited them with peculiar and outlandish punishments. He would, for example, cut off the hands and feet and heads of children and hang them about their parents' necks to wear, or cut off the parts of husbands and wives and exchange them; at times, after lopping off his victims' hands, he would split them down the spine, and on occasion would even carry the hewn halves on the points of spears, whereby he surpassed in cruelty Phalaris and the tyrant of Cassandreia, Apollodorus. Even leaving out of account all the rest of his bloodthirstiness, one could judge of his surpassing cruelty by the single instance now to be related. In the course of celebrating his marriage according to ancient Thracian usage, he seized two young travellers, Greeks from the kingdom of Attalus, a pair of brothers, both strikingly handsome, one with the first down sprouting on his cheeks, the other just acquiring a suggestion of this bloom. Having garlanded them both like sacrificial victims he brought them in, and when he had had his attendants stretch out the younger at full length, as if to split him down the middle, he exclaimed that it was not right for kings and commoners to use the same kind of victims. When the older youth wailed, displaying a brotherly affection, and threw himself beneath the axe, the king ordered the attendants to stretch him out as well. His cruelty then redoubled, he aimed a single blow at each, and both times drove it home, while the spectators raised the paean to signal his success. Many other crimes as well did he commit.

15. Attalus [II], hearing how Diêgylis was hated by his subjects because of his rapacity and his extreme cruelty, affected a policy that was just the opposite. Accordingly, by treating the Thracians who were taken captive with humanity and setting them free, he enlisted many voices to proclaim his mercy. Diêgylis, on learning of this, inflicted terrible outrages and cruel tortures on the hostages left by any who absconded, among them children of very tender years and delicate constitution. For even these were torn limb from limb by every possible means, or had their heads, hands, and feet chopped off. Some of them were impaled on stakes, others exposed on trees. Women, and not a few only, were to be seen with bodies spread-eagled and offered for outrage in addition to the fate of death, being made to assume every shameful position that the arrogance of barbarians could suggest. Thus the victims were presented to their violators as the demonstration of a shameless savagery, but provoked many who were onlookers with a capacity for civilised reflection to feelings of pity for the hapless creatures.

16. When Numantia and Termessus sent envoys to the Romans [143+] to discuss the cessation of hostilities, the Romans granted them peace on the following terms: each city was to surrender to the Romans three hundred hostages, nine thousand cloaks, three thousand hides, eight hundred war-horses, and all their arms; this done, they would be "friends and allies." A day having been set for the cities to comply, they duly fulfilled all the terms of the agreement, but when last of all they were required to surrender their arms, there was an outburst of noble lamentation as a frenzy of independence swept over the crowd. It was an outrage, they complained to one another, if they were to strip themselves of arms, like so many women. Repenting of their decision, they engaged in mutual reproaches, and fathers accused sons, children their parents, wives their husbands. Reverting, therefore, to their original disposition and refusing to give up their arms, they renewed the conflict with the Romans.

17. When Pompeius advanced against the city called Lagni and laid it under siege [140], the Numantians, wishing to succour their countrymen, sent four hundred soldiers under cover of night. The inhabitants, welcoming them with delight, called them "saviours" and honoured them with gifts. A few days later, however, overcome with fear, they offered to yield the city and sought assurances of safety for their persons. Now when Pompeius replied that he would not make terms with them unless they first surrendered their allies, they at first held out, scrupling to wrong their benefactors, but as the situation grew desperate, they resumed negotiations and attempted to secure their own safety by the destruction of their friends. Their resolve did not, however, pass unnoticed by the intended victims, who, on learning what was afoot, prepared to defend themselves, and attacking the townsmen by night, spilled much blood. Pompeius, hearing the din, set ladders to the walls and seized the city. All the nobles he slaughtered, but he released from jeopardy the allies, two hundred in number, partly out of pity for their imperilled valour and for the mischance that had befallen these victims of ingratitude, and partly as a means of soliciting at long range the good will of the Numantians for the Romans. The city he razed to the ground.

18. King Arsaces [VI], by pursuing a set policy of clemency and humanity, won an automatic stream of advantages and further enlarged his kingdom. For he extended his power even to India, and without a battle brought under his sway the region once ruled by Porus. But, though raised to such heights of royal power, he did not cultivate luxury or arrogance, the usual accompaniments of power, but prided himself on the exercise of equity towards those who accepted his rule and courage towards those who opposed him. In short, having made himself master over many peoples, he taught the Parthians the best of the customs practised by each.

19. When Viriathus requested an interview [139], the consul Popillius decided to state one by one the Roman demands, for fear that if they were mentioned all at once, in desperation and fury he would be driven to implacable hostility.

20. A certain Galaestes, an Athamanian by birth and son of Amynander, the former king of the Athamanians, was a man far superior to his countrymen in birth, wealth, and renown; he became the friend of Ptolemy Philometor, and in the struggle against Demetrius had served as commander of the Alexandrian forces. Now after the defeat and death of Ptolemy false charges were levelled against him, that he had wilfully betrayed the Egyptian cause to the enemy, and when the Ptolemy who inherited the kingdom stripped him of his estates and showed himself ill-disposed towards him, he took fright and departed for Greece. As many others besides were being banished from Egypt because of the strife with the mercenary troops [140/39], he made the exiles welcome. Claiming that King Ptolemy Philometor had entrusted to him a son by Cleopatra to be reared as heir to the kingdom, he placed a diadem on the boy's head, and with a number of exiles as partisans of the cause made ready to restore him to his father's kingdom.

21. Audas, Ditalces, and Nicorontes, [139] men of the city of Orso, all three close kinsmen and friends, observing that Viriathus' prestige was suffering under the Roman blows and apprehensive on their own score, decided to establish some claim to favour with the Romans as a means of insuring their personal safety. Seeing that Viriathus was eager to bring the war to an end, they promised, to persuade Caepio to make peace, if Viriathus would send them as envoys to arrange a cessation of hostilities. When the chieftain gave his ready assent, they hastened to Caepio and easily persuaded him to arrant them assurances of safety on their promise to assassinate Viriathus. After an exchange of pledges, they quickly returned to the camp, and asserting that they had won the consent of the Romans to the peace aroused Viriathus to high hopes, for they were eager to distract his mind as far as possible from any suspicion of the truth. Since they were trusted by virtue of their friendship with Viriathus, they made their way unobserved into his tent by night, and having dispatched him with well-aimed strokes of the sword rushed at once from the camp, and by keeping to trackless mountain country escaped safely to Caepio.

21a. They [his army] accorded the body of Viriathus a marvellous and resplendent burial, and by the tomb, in honour of his far-famed courage, held funeral games in which two hundred pairs of gladiators participated. By common consent he was a most valiant fighter in battle, and a most able general in foreseeing what would be advantageous; most important of all, throughout his entire career as a general he commanded the devotion of his troops to a degree unequalled by anyone. In the distribution of booty he took no more than the share apportioned to the common soldiers, and from what was assigned to him he rewarded the soldiers who merited thanks and succoured those who were in need. He was sober, tireless, and alert to every difficulty and danger; and he was superior to every pleasure. The proofs of his ability are manifest: for in the eleven years that he commanded the Lusitanians his troops not only remained free of dissension but were all but invincible, whereas after his death the confederacy of the Lusitanians disintegrated, once it was deprived of his leadership.

22. Ptolemy . . . because of his cruelty and thirst for blood, and because of his unabashed enjoyment of the most shameful pleasures and his gross physical deformity (whence his nickname, "Pot-belly"). His general, Hierax, being a man of extraordinary talent in the arts of war, and having a gift for dealing with crowds, besides being open-hearted, held together the kingdom of Ptolemy. Thus, when Ptolemy's funds were low and the soldiers were inclined to go over to Galaestes because they were not paid, by providing for the army from his private purse he brought the movement to an end.

23. The Egyptians utterly despised Ptolemy, for they saw that he was childish in dealing with people, that he had abandoned himself to the most shameful pleasures, and that he had grown physically effeminate through self-indulgence.

24. The city known as Contobris sent envoys to the Romans [139/7], who, in accordance with their instructions, ordered the Romans to quit the region with all possible speed before some disaster befell them, inasmuch as all others who had had the temerity to invade those areas with a hostile army had perished to a man. The consul replied that though the Lusitanians and Celtiberians were much given to great threats and encroachments, the Romans made it their practice to punish wrongdoers and to disregard threats: accordingly, it would become them to demonstrate their valour not with threats but with actions, and, indeed, their valour would be put to the most precise test.

25. He considered it better for them to fight and meet death gloriously than to submit their persons, stripped of arms, to a most shameful slavery.

26. [D] Iunius [Brutus] exhorted his soldiers now [138/7], if ever, to acquit them like men and to show themselves worthy of their former successes. . . . Nevertheless, their hearts did not falter, for the power of reason prevailed over their physical weakness.

Word was spread abroad of the inexorable vengeance of the Romans on those who opposed them, and of their outstandingly fair treatment of those who obeyed their commands.

27. The consul Aemilius [137/6] was ineffectual in the pursuits of war because of his physical bulk and lack of agility, what with his excess of weight and his great rolls of flesh.

28. In Syria Diodotus, surnamed Tryphon [138], having murdered Antiochus, the son of Alexander, a mere child who was being reared as one destined to the throne, put on his own head the royal diadem and, having seized the vacant throne, proclaimed himself monarch and engaged in war on the satraps and generals of the legitimate king. For in Mesopotamia there was Dionysius the Mede, in Coelê Syria Sarpedon and Palamedes, and in Seleuceia-by-the-sea Aeschrion, who had with him Queen Cleopatra, the wife of Demetrius (whom Arsaces had taken captive).

28a. Tryphon, having risen from private estate to the kingship, was eager to strengthen his position by means of a senatorial decree. Accordingly, having prepared a golden statue of Victory, of the weight of ten thousand gold staters, he dispatched envoys to Rome to convey it to the Roman people. For he supposed that the Romans would accept the Victory, both because of its value and as an object of good omen, and would acclaim him as king. He found that the senators were more cunning than himself and that they shrewdly outmanoeuvred those who sought to mislead and deceive them. For the senate accepted the gift and secured the good omen together with the profit, but changed the attribution of the gift and in Tryphon's stead inscribed it with the name of the king whom he had assassinated. By this act the senate went on record as condemning the murder of the boy and as refusing the gifts of impious men.

28b. Scipio Africanus and his fellow ambassadors came to Alexandria to survey the entire kingdom. Ptolemy welcomed the men with a great reception and much pomp, held costly banquets for them, and conducting them about showed them his palace and-other royal treasures. Now the Roman envoys were men of superior virtue, and since their normal diet was limited to a few dishes, and only such as were conducive to health, they were scornful of his extravagance as detrimental to both body and mind. The spectacle of all that the king considered marvellous they regarded as a side show of no real account, but busied themselves in detail with what was truly worth seeing: the situation and strength of the city, the unique features of the Pharos, then, proceeding up the river to Memphis, the quality of the land and the blessings brought to it by the Nile, the great number of Egyptian cities and the untold myriads of their inhabitants, the strong defensive position of Egypt, and the general excellence of the country, in that it is well suited to provide for the security and greatness of an empire. When they had marvelled at the number of the inhabitants of Egypt and the natural advantages of its terrain, they apprehended that a very great power could be built there, if this kingdom should ever find rulers worthy of it.

Having surveyed Egypt, the envoys embarked for Cyprus, and thence for Syria. In sum they traversed the greater part of the inhabited world, and on all sides, since they conducted their visit in sober fashion, worthy of wonder, they received a warm welcome, and returned home with plaudits in which all concurred. For where there were parties in dispute, some they had reconciled one to the other, some they had persuaded to do justice to those who had brought complaint; some who could not be abashed they had put under restraint, and those whose cases admitted of no easy decision they had referred to the senate. They had had dealings with kings and with popular governments, and by renewing the existing ties of friendship with one and all had enhanced, in terms of good will, the leadership of Rome. As a result all, having now been won over to a friendly attitude, dispatched embassies to Rome and expressed appreciation that the Romans had sent out men of this stamp.

BOOKS XXXIV AND XXXV FRAGMENTS

1. When King Antiochus [VII], says Diodorus, was laying siege to Jerusalem [134], the Jews held out for a time, but when all their supplies were exhausted they found themselves compelled to make overtures for a cessation of hostilities. Now the majority of his friends advised the king to take the city by storm and to wipe out completely the race of Jews, since they alone of all nations avoided dealings with any other people and looked upon all men as their enemies. They pointed out, too, that the ancestors of the Jews had been driven out of all Egypt as men who were impious and detested by the gods. For by way of purging the country all persons who had white or leprous marks on their bodies had been assembled and driven across the border, as being under a curse; the refugees had occupied the territory round about Jerusalem, and having organised the nation of the Jews had made their hatred of mankind into a tradition, and on this account had introduced utterly outlandish laws: not to break bread with any other race, nor to show them any good will at all. His friends reminded Antiochus also of the enmity that in times past his ancestors had felt for this people. Antiochus, called Epiphanes, on defeating the Jews [169] had entered the innermost sanctuary of the god's temple, where it was lawful for the priest alone to enter. Finding there a marble statue of a heavily bearded man seated on an ass, with a book in his hands, he supposed it to be an image of Moses, the founder of Jerusalem and organiser of the nation, the man, moreover, who had ordained for the Jews their misanthropic and lawless customs. Since Epiphanes was shocked by such hatred directed against all mankind, he had set himself to break down their traditional practices. Accordingly, he sacrificed before the image of the founder and the open-air altar of the god a great sow, and poured its blood over them. Then, having prepared its flesh, he ordered that their holy books, containing the xenophobic laws, should be sprinkled with the broth of the meat; that the lamp, which they call undying and which burns continually in the temple, should be extinguished; and that the high priest and the rest of the Jews should be compelled to partake of the meat.

Rehearsing all these events, his friends strongly urged Antiochus to make an end of the race completely, or, failing that, to abolish their laws and force them to change their ways; but the king, being a magnanimous and mild-mannered person, took hostages but dismissed the charges against the Jews, once he had exacted the tribute that was due and had dismantled the walls of Jerusalem.

2. When Sicily, after the Carthaginian collapse [135?], had enjoyed sixty years of good fortune in all respects, the Servile War broke out for the following reason. The Sicilians, having shot up in prosperity and acquired great wealth, began to purchase a vast number of slaves, to whose bodies, as they were brought in droves from the slave markets, they at once applied marks and brands. The young men they used as cowherds, the others in such ways as they happened to be useful. They treated them with a heavy hand in their service, and granted them the most meagre care, the bare minimum for food and clothing. As a result most of them made their livelihood by brigandage, and there was bloodshed everywhere, since the brigands were like scattered bands of soldiers. The governors (*praetores*) attempted to repress them, but since they did not dare to punish them because of the power and prestige of the gentry who owned the brigands, they were forced to connive at the pillaging of the province. For most of the landowners were Roman knights (*equites*), and since it was the knights who acted as judges when charges arising from provincial affairs were brought against the governors, the magistrates stood in awe of them.

The slaves, distressed by their hardships, and frequently outraged and beaten beyond all reason, could not endure their treatment. Getting together as opportunity offered, they discussed the possibility of revolt, until at last they put their plans into action. There was a certain Syrian slave, belonging to Antigenes of Enna; he was an Apamean by birth and had an aptitude for magic and the working of wonders. He claimed to foretell the future, by divine command, through dreams, and because of his talent along these lines deceived many. Going on from there he not only gave oracles by means of dreams, but even made a pretence of having waking visions of the gods and of hearing the future from their own lips. Of his many improvisations some by chance turned out true, and since those which failed to do so were left unchallenged, while those that were fulfilled attracted attention, his reputation advanced apace. Finally, through some device, while in a state of divine possession, he would produce fire and flame from his mouth, and thus rave oracularly about things to come. For he would place fire, and fuel to maintain it, in a nut, or something similar, that was pierced on both sides; then, placing it in his mouth and blowing on it, he kindled now sparks, and now a flame. Prior to the revolt he used to say that the Syrian goddess [Atargatis] appeared to him, saying that he should be king, and he repeated this, not only to others, but even to his own master. Since his claims were treated as a joke, Antigenes, taken by his hocus-pocus, would introduce Eunus (for that was the wonder-worker's name) at his dinner parties, and cross-question him about his kingship and how he would treat each of the men present. Since he gave a full account of everything without hesitation, explaining with what moderation he would treat the masters and in sum making a colourful tale of his quackery, the guests were always stirred to laughter, and some of them, picking up a nice tidbit from the table, would present it to him, adding, as they did so, that when he became king, he should remember the favour. As it happened, his charlatanism did in fact result in kingship, and for the favours received in jest at the banquets he made a return of thanks in good earnest. The beginning of the whole revolt took place as follows.

There was a certain Damophilus of Enna, a man of great wealth but insolent of manner; he had abused his slaves to excess, and his wife Megallis vied even with her husband in punishing the slaves and in her general inhumanity towards them. The slaves, reduced by this degrading treatment to the level of brutes, conspired to revolt and to murder their masters. Going to Eunus they asked him whether their resolve had the favour of the gods. He, resorting to his usual mummery, promised them the favour of the gods, and soon persuaded them to act at once. Immediately, therefore, they brought together four hundred of their fellow slaves and, having armed themselves in such ways as opportunity permitted, they fell upon the city of Enna, with Eunus at their head and working his miracle of the flames of fire for their benefit. When they found their way into the houses they shed much blood, sparing not even suckling babes. Rather they tore them from the breast and dashed them to the ground, while as for the women, and under their husbands' very eyes, but words cannot tell the extent of their outrages and acts of lewdness! By now a great multitude of slaves from the city had joined them, who, after first demonstrating against their own masters their utter ruthlessness, then turned to the slaughter of others. When Eunus and his men learned that Damophilus and his wife were in the garden that lay near the city, they sent some of their band and dragged them off, both the man and his wife, fettered and with hands bound behind their backs, subjecting them to many outrages along the way. Only in the case of the couple's daughter were the slaves seen to show consideration throughout, and this was because of her kindly nature, in that to the extent of her power she was always compassionate and ready to succour the slaves. Thereby it was demonstrated that the others were treated as they were, not because of some "natural savagely of slaves," but rather in revenge for wrongs previously received. The men appointed to the task, having dragged Damophilus and Megallis into the city, as we said, brought them to the theatre, where the crowd of rebels had assembled. When Damophilus attempted to devise a plea to get them off safe and was winning over many of the crowd with his words, Hermeias and Zeuxis, men bitterly disposed towards him, denounced him as a cheat, and without waiting for a formal trial by the assembly the one ran him through the chest with a sword, the other chopped off his head with an axe. Thereupon Eunus was chosen king, not for his manly courage or his ability as a military leader, but solely for his marvels and his setting of the revolt in motion, and because his name seemed to contain a favourable omen that suggested good will towards his subjects.

Established as the rebels' supreme commander, he called an assembly and put to death all the citizenry of Enna except for those who were skilled in the manufacture of arms: these he put in chains and assigned them to this task. He gave Megallis to the maidservants to deal with as they might wish; they subjected her to torture and threw her over a precipice. He himself murdered his own masters, Antigenes and Pytho. Having set a diadem upon his head, and arrayed himself in full royal style, he proclaimed his wife queen (she was a fellow Syrian and of the same city), and appointed to the royal council such men as seemed to be gifted with superior intelligence, among them one Achaeus (Aehaeus by name and an Achaean by birth), a man who excelled both at planning and in action. In three days Eunus had armed, as best he could, more than six thousand men, besides others in his train who had only axes and hatchets, or slings, or sickles, or fire-hardened stakes, or even kitchen spits; and he went about ravaging the countryside. Then, since he kept recruiting untold numbers of slaves, he ventured even to do battle with Roman generals, and on joining combat repeatedly overcame them with his superior numbers, for he now had more than ten thousand soldiers.

Meanwhile a man named Cleon, a Cilician, began a revolt of still other slaves. Though there were high hopes everywhere that the revolutionary groups would come into conflict one with the other, and that the rebels, by destroying themselves, would free Sicily of strife, contrary to expectations the two groups joined forces, Cleon having subordinated himself to Eunus at his mere command, and discharging, as it were, the function of a general serving a king; his particular band numbered five thousand men. It was now about thirty days since the outbreak.

Soon after, engaging in battle with a general arrived from Rome, Lucius Hypsaeus, who had eight thousand Sicilian troops, the rebels were victorious, since they now numbered twenty thousand. Before long their band reached a total of two hundred thousand, and in numerous battles with the Romans they acquitted themselves well, and failed but seldom. As word of this was bruited about, a revolt of one hundred and fifty slaves, banded together, flared up in Rome, of more than a thousand in Attica, and of yet others in Delos and many other places. Thanks to the speed with which forces were brought up and to the severity of their punitive measures, the magistrates of these communities at once disposed of the rebels and brought to their senses any who were wavering on the verge of revolt. In Sicily, however, the trouble grew. Cities were captured with all their inhabitants, and many armies were cut to pieces by the rebels, until Rupilius, [132] the Roman commander, recovered Tauromenium for the Romans by placing it under strict siege and confining the rebels under conditions of unspeakable duress and famine: conditions such that, beginning by eating the children, they progressed to the women, and did not altogether abstain even from eating one another. It was on this occasion that Rupilius captured Comanus the brother of Cleon, as he was attempting to escape from the beleaguered city. Finally, after Sarapion, a Syrian, had betrayed the citadel, the general laid hands on all the runaway slaves in the city, whom, after torture, he threw over a cliff. From there he advanced to Enna, which he put under siege in much the same manner, bringing the rebels into extreme straits and frustrating their hopes. Cleon came forth from the city with a few men, but after an heroic struggle, covered with wounds, he was displayed dead, and Rupilius captured this city also by betrayal, since its strength was impregnable to force of arms. Eunus, taking with him his bodyguards, a thousand strong, fled in unmanly fashion to a certain precipitous region. The men with him, however, aware that their dreaded fate was inevitable, inasmuch as the general, Rupilius, was already marching against them, killed one another with the sword, by beheading. Eunus, the wonder-worker and king, who through cowardice had sought refuge in certain caves, was dragged out with four others, a cook, a baker, the man who massaged him at his bath, and a fourth, whose duty it had been to amuse him at drinking parties. Remanded to prison, where his flesh disintegrated into a mass of lice, he met such an end as befitted his knavery, and died at Morgantina. Thereupon Rupilius, traversing the whole of Sicily with a few picked troops, sooner than had been expected rid it of every nest of robbers.

Eunus, king of the rebels, called himself Antiochus, and his horde of rebels Syrians.

There was never a sedition of slaves so great as that which occurred in Sicily [135?], whereby many cities met with grave calamities, innumerable men and women, together with their children, experienced the greatest misfortunes, and all the island was in danger of falling into the power of fugitive slaves, who measured their authority only by the excessive suffering of the freeborn. To most people these events came as an unexpected and sudden surprise, but to those who were capable of judging affairs realistically they did not seem to happen without reason. Because of the superabundant prosperity of those who exploited the products of this mighty island, nearly all who had risen in wealth affected first a luxurious mode of living, then arrogance and insolence. As a result of all this, since both the maltreatment of the slaves and their estrangement from their masters increased at an equal rate, there was at last, when occasion offered, a violent outburst of hatred. So without a word of summons tens of thousands of slaves joined forces to destroy their masters. Similar events took place throughout Asia at the same period, after Aristonicus laid claim to a kingdom that was not rightfully his, and the slaves, because of their owners' maltreatment of them, joined him in his mad venture and involved many cities in great misfortunes.

In like fashion each of the large landowners bought up whole slave marts to work their lands; . . . to bind some in fetters, to wear out others by the severity of their tasks; and they marked all with their arrogant brands. In consequence, so great a multitude of slaves inundated all Sicily that those who heard tell of the immense number were incredulous. For in fact the Sicilians who had acquired much wealth were now rivalling the Italians in arrogance, greed, and villainy. The Italians who owned large numbers of slaves had made crime so familiar to their herdsmen that they provided them no food, but permitted them to plunder. With such licence given to men who had the physical strength to accomplish their every resolve, who had scope and leisure to seize the opportunity, and who for want of food were constrained to embark on perilous enterprises, there was soon an increase in lawlessness. They began by murdering men who were travelling singly or in pairs, in the most conspicuous areas. Then they took to assaulting in a body, by night, the homesteads of the less well protected, which they destroyed, seizing the property and killing all who resisted. As their boldness grew steadily greater, Sicily became impassable to travellers by night; those who normally lived in the country found it no longer safe to stay there; and there was violence, robbery, and all manner of bloodshed on every side. The herdsmen, however, because of their experience of life in the open and their military accoutrements, were naturally all brimming with high spirits and audacity; and since they carried clubs or spears or stout staves, while their bodies were protected by the skins of wolves or wild boars, they presented a terrifying appearance that was little short of actual belligerency. Moreover, each had at his heels a pack of valiant dogs, while the plentiful diet of milk and meat available to the men rendered them savage in temper and in physique. So every region was filled with what were practically scattered bands of soldiers, since with the permission of their masters the reckless daring of the slaves had been furnished with arms. The praetors attempted to hold the raging slaves in check, but not daring to punish them because of the power and influence of the masters were forced to wink at the plundering of their province. For most of the landowners were Roman knights in full standing, and since it was the knights who acted as judges when charges arising from provincial affairs were brought against the governors, the magistrates stood in awe of them.

The Italians who were engaged in agriculture purchased great numbers of slaves, all of whom they marked with brands, but failed to provide them sufficient food, and by oppressive toil wore them out . . . their distress.

Not only in the exercise of political power should men of prominence be considerate towards those of low estate, but so also in private life they should, if they are sensible, treat their slaves gently. For heavy-handed arrogance leads states into civil strife and factionalism between citizens, and in individual households it paves the way for plots of slaves against masters and for terrible uprisings in concert against the whole state. The more power is perverted to cruelty and lawlessness, the more the character of those subject to that power is brutalised to the point of desperation. Anyone whom fortune has set in low estate willingly yields place to his superiors in point of gentility and esteem, but if he is deprived of due consideration, he comes to regard those who harshly lord it over him with bitter enmity.

There was a certain Damophilus, a native of Enna, a man of great wealth but arrogant in manner, who, since he had under cultivation a great circuit of land and owned many herds of cattle, emulated not only the luxury affected by the Italian landowners in Sicily, but also their troops of slaves and their inhumanity and severity towards them. He drove about the countryside with expensive horses, four-wheeled carriages, and a bodyguard of slaves, and prided himself, in addition, on his great train of handsome serving-boys and ill-mannered parasites. Both in town and at his villas he took pains to provide a veritable exhibition of embossed silver and costly crimson spreads, and had himself served sumptuous and regally lavish dinners, in which he surpassed even the luxury of the Persians in outlay and extravagance, as indeed he outdid them also in arrogance. His uncouth and boorish nature, in fact, being set in possession of irresponsible power and in control of a vast fortune, first of all engendered satiety, then overweening pride, and, at last, destruction for him and great calamities for his country. Purchasing a large number of slaves, he treated them outrageously, marking with branding irons the bodies of men who in their own countries had been free, but who through capture in war had come to know the fate of a slave. Some of these he put in fetters and thrust into slave pens; others he designated to act as his herdsmen, but neglected to provide them with suitable clothing or food.

On one occasion when approached by a group of naked domestics with a request for clothing, Damophilus of Enna impatiently refused to listen. "What!" he said, "do those who travel through the country go naked? Do they not offer a ready source of supply for anyone who needs garments?" Having said this, he ordered them bound to pillars, piled blows on them, and arrogantly dismissed them. Because of his arbitrary and savage humour not a day passed that this same Damophilus did not torment some of his slaves without just cause. His wife Metallis, who delighted no less in these arrogant punishments, treated her maidservants cruelly, as well as any other slaves who fell into her clutches. Because of the despiteful punishments received from them both, the slaves were filled with rage against their masters, and conceiving that they could encounter nothing worse than their present misfortunes began to form conspiracies to revolt and to murder their masters. Approaching Eunus, who lived not far away, they asked whether their project had the approval of the gods. He put on a display of his inspired transports, and when he learned why they had come, stated clearly that the gods favoured their revolt, provided they made no delay but applied themselves to the enterprise at once; for it was decreed by Fate that Enna, the citadel of the whole island, should be their land. Having heard this, and believing that Providence was assisting them in their project, they were so keenly wrought up for revolt that there was no delay in executing their resolve. At once, therefore, they set free those in bonds, and collecting such of the others as lived near by they assembled about four hundred men at a certain field not far from Enna. After making a compact and exchanging pledges sworn by night over sacrificial victims, they armed themselves in such fashion as the occasion allowed; but all were equipped with the best of weapons, fury, which was bent on the destruction of their arrogant masters. Their leader was Eunus. With cries of encouragement to one another they broke into the city about midnight and put many to the sword.

There was in Sicily a daughter of Damophilus, a girl of marriageable age, remarkable for her simplicity of manner and her kindness of heart. It was always her practice to do all she could to comfort the slaves who were beaten by her parents, and since she also took the part of any who had been put in bonds, she was wondrously loved by one and all for her kindness. So now at this time, since her past favours enlisted in her service the mercy of those to whom she had shown kindness, no one was so bold as to lay violent hands upon the girl, but all maintained her fresh young beauty inviolate. And selecting suitable men from their number, among them Hermeias, her warmest champion, they escorted her to the home of certain kinsmen in Catana.

Although the rebellious slaves were enraged against the whole household of their masters, and resorted to unrelenting abuse and vengeance, there were yet some indications that it was not from innate savagery but rather because of the arrogant treatment they had themselves received that they now ran amuck when they turned to avenge themselves on their persecutors.

Even among slaves human nature needs no instructor in regard to a just repayment, whether of gratitude or of revenge.

Eunus, after being proclaimed king, put them all to death, except for the men who in times past had, when his master indulged him, admitted him to their banquets, and had shown him courtesy both in respect of his prophecies and in their gifts of good things from the table; these men he spirited away and set free. Here indeed was cause for astonishment: that their fortunes should be so dramatically reversed, and that a kindness in such trivial matters should be requited so opportunely and with so great a boon.

Achaeus, the counsellor of King Antiochus [Eunus], being far from pleased at the conduct of the runaway slaves, censured them for their recklessness and boldly warned them that they would meet with speedy punishment. So far from putting him to death for his outspokenness, Eunus not only presented him with the house of his former masters but made him a royal counsellor.

There was, in addition, another revolt of fugitive slaves who banded together in considerable numbers. A certain Cleon, a Cilician from the region about Taurus, who was accustomed from childhood to a life of brigandage and had become in Sicily a herder of horses, constantly waylaid travellers and perpetrated murders of all kinds. On hearing the news of Eunus' success and of the victories of the fugitives serving with him, he rose in revolt, and persuading some of the slaves near by to join him in his mad venture overran the city of Acragas and all the surrounding country.

Their pressing needs and their poverty forced the rebel slaves to regard everyone as acceptable, giving them no opportunity to pick and choose.

It needed no portent from the heavens to realize how easily the city could be captured. For it was evident even to the most simple-minded that because of the long period of peace the walls had crumbled, and that now, when many of its soldiers had been killed, the siege of the city would bring an easy success.

Eunus, having stationed his army out of range of their missiles, taunted the Romans by declaring that it was they, and not his men, who were runaways from battle. For the inhabitants of the city, at a safe distance (?), he staged a production of mimes, in which the slaves acted out scenes of revolt from their individual masters, heaping abuse on their arrogance and the inordinate insolence that had led to their destruction.

As for unusual strokes of ill fortune, even though some persons may be convinced that Providence has no concern with anything of the sort, yet surely it is to the interest of society that the fear of the gods should be deeply embedded in the hearts of the people. For those who act honestly because they are themselves virtuous are but few, and the great mass of humanity abstain from evil-doing only because of the penalties of the law and the retribution that comes from the gods.

When these many great troubles fell upon the Sicilians, the common people were not only unsympathetic, but actually gloated over their plight, being envious because of the inequality in their respective lots, and the disparity in their modes of life. Their envy, from being a gnawing canker, now turned to joy, as it beheld the once resplendent lot of the rich changed and fallen into a condition such as was formerly beneath their very notice. Worst of all, though the rebels, making prudent provision for the future, did not set fire to the country estates nor damage the stock or the stored harvests, and abstained from harming anyone whose pursuit was agriculture, the populace, making the runaway slaves a pretext, made sallies into the country and with the malice of envy not only plundered the estates but set fire to the buildings as well.

3. In Asia King Attalus, soon after his accession to the throne, [133?] adopted an attitude markedly different from that of his predecessors. For they, by practising kindness and benevolence, had prospered in their kingship; he, however, being cruel and bloodthirsty, visited on many of those subject to his rule irremediable disaster or death. Suspecting the most powerful of his father's friends of having formed designs against him, he decided that all must be put out of the way. Accordingly, he selected the most savagely murderous of his barbarian mercenaries, men who were also insatiate in their thirst for gold, and concealing them in certain chambers of the palace sent in turn for the friends who were under suspicion. When they appeared . . . he had them all killed, for his underlings were as bloodthirsty as himself, and he gave immediate orders to inflict the same harsh treatment on their wives and children also. Of the other friends, those who had been appointed to commands in the army or as governors of cities, he had some assassinated, while others he arrested and put to death with their entire households. Because of his cruelty he was hated not only by everyone subject to him but by the neighbouring peoples as well. Thus he stirred all his subjects to hope for a revolution.

4. Most of the captive barbarians, [133?] while they were being marched away, committed suicide or killed one another, being unwilling to tolerate the indignity of servitude. One, a mere lad, went up to his three sisters as they lay sleeping from exhaustion and cut their throats. Thwarted in his attempt to do away with himself as well, he was asked by his captors why he had killed his sisters. He replied that there was nothing worth living for left to them. He himself, by refusing to eat, ended his life by starvation.

These same captives, on reaching the boundaries of their land, threw themselves to the ground and with cries of lamentation kissed the earth and even collected some of the dust in the folds of their garments, whereat all the army was moved to pity and sympathy. Each man, touched by the emotions common to humankind, was overcome with a sense of divine awe as he perceived that even barbarians, brutish in spirit though they were, when fortune broke the customary bond between them and their native land, did not forget their fond affection for the sod that had reared them.

5. Tiberius Gracchus was a son of that Tiberius who had been twice consul, [133] had conducted brilliant and important military affairs, and had had an honourable political career. Through his mother he was also a grandson of Publius Scipio, the conqueror of Hannibal and the Carthaginians. Quite apart from his position as the scion of a distinguished family on both sides, even in his own right he towered above the men of his generation in sagacity, in skill as a speaker, and, in short, in every acquirement; and he was competent to hold his own in debate despite the greater prestige of his opponents.

6. The crowds poured into Rome from the country like rivers into the all-receptive sea. Buoyed up with the hope of effecting their own salvation, since the law was their leader and ally, and their champion a man subject neither to favour nor to fear - a man, moreover, who for the sake of restoring the land to the people was determined to endure any toil or danger, to his last breath. . . .

. . . while his was not a group just recently assembled and drawn from many tribes, but comprised the most politically alert and the well-to-do segments of the populace. Since, then, the strength on both sides was evenly balanced, and the scales tipped now this way, now that, the two parties, being assembled many thousands strong, clashed violently, and in the public assemblies there appeared billowing forms and patterns like waves of the sea.

7. [M] Octavius, after being deposed, though refusing to acknowledge that he was a private citizen, yet did not dare to exercise as a magistrate the tribunician powers, but stayed quietly at home. Yet before ever he reached this state, he too had the opportunity, when Gracchus first proposed the plebiscite on his removal from office, to agree to a simultaneous motion that would have embraced the removal of Gracchus from the tribunate. In that case, either they would both have become private citizens if the proposals were legal, or both would have continued in office if the proposals were adjudged unconstitutional.

Since he[Tiberius Gracchus] was heading straight for destruction, he speedily met with the punishment he merited. [P.] Scipio [Nascio Serapio], seizing a club that lay ready at hand, for his anger prevailed over any seeming difficulties. . . .

The news of the death of Gracchus reached the camp, and Africanus is said to have cried out:

> So perish any other besides, who does such deeds.

8. The runaway "Syrian" slaves [of Eunus] cut off the hands of their captives, but not content with amputation at the wrist included arms and all in the mutilation.

9. Those who ate of the sacred fish [of Arethusa] found no relief from their pains. For the Divine Power, as if with the intention of holding up an example to deter the others, left all those who had acted so madly to suffer un-succoured, and since in keeping with the retribution visited on them by the gods they have also received abuse in the pages of history, they have indeed reaped a just reward.

10. The senate, prompted by religious scruples, sent a delegation to Sicily in accordance with an oracle of the Sibylline Books. They visited throughout Sicily the altars set up to Aetnaean Zeus; here they offered sacrifice and fenced in the areas, and forbade access to them except in the case of those in each state who had traditional sacrifices to perform.

11. There was a certain Gorgus of Morgantina, [133/1] surnamed Cambalus, a man of wealth and good standing, who, having gone out hunting, happened upon a robber-nest of fugitive slaves, and tried to escape on foot to the city. His father, Gorgus, chancing to meet him on horseback, jumped down and offered him the horse that he might mount and ride off to the city, but the son did not choose to save himself at his father's expense, nor was the father willing to make good his escape from danger by letting his son die. While they were still pleading with one another, both in tears, and were engaged in a contest of piety and affection, as paternal devotion vied with a son's love for his father, the bandits appeared on the scene and killed them both.

12. Zibelmius, the son of Diêgylis, emulating his father's thirst for blood and nursing his anger at what the Thracians had done to Diêgylis, went to such lengths of cruelty and lawlessness that he exacted punishment from those who offended him together with all their households. On the most trivial provocation he tore men limb from limb, or crucified them, or burned them alive. He slaughtered children before the eyes of their parents or in a parent's arms, and carving up their bodies would serve them to the closest of kin, reviving the storied banquets of Tereus and Thyestes. Finally the Thracians laid hands on Ziselmius (sic), and though it was virtually impossible to retaliate upon him for his individual offences; for how could a single body make satisfaction for violence perpetrated against a whole nation? Nevertheless, within the range of what was possible, they exerted themselves to visit every indignity and punishment upon his person.

13. When the first King Attalus consulted the oracle on some matter the Pythia is said to have volunteered this response:

> Be of stout heart, thou of the bull horns, thou shalt bear
> kingly honour,
> Thou and thy children's children, but the children of these
> no longer.

14. Ptolemy [VIII], nicknamed Physcon [131/0], having discovered Cleopatra's estrangement from him and being unable to wound her in any other way, had the audacity to commit a most wicked deed. Copying the murderous savagery of Medea, he put to death, in Cyprus, his own son and hers, a mere boy who was known as Memphites. Not content with this act of impiety, he committed another, far more heinous, abomination. After mutilating the body of the boy and placing it in a chest, he ordered one of his servants to convey it to Alexandria: for since the birthday of Cleopatra was approaching, he had made arrangements to set the chest down in front of the palace on the eve of the occasion. This was done, and when the circumstance became known Cleopatra put on mourning and the populace went completely wild with rage against Ptolemy.

15. When spring with its warmth was melting the snow and crops were now [129], after the long period of frost, beginning to develop and grow, and men too were resuming their activity, Arsaces [VII], wishing to feel out his enemies, sent envoys to discuss terms of peace. In reply Antiochus told them that he would agree to the peace if Arsaces would release his brother Demetrius from captivity and send him home, if he would withdraw from the satrapies that he had seized by force, and if, retaining only his ancestral domain, he would pay tribute.

Arsaces, taking offence at the harshness of the reply, placed an army in the field against him.

16. His friends pleaded with Antiochus not to join battle with the far more numerous Parthian hordes, since they, by taking refuge in the mountainous country that overlooked them, with its rough terrain, could neutralise the threat of his cavalry. Antiochus, however, completely disregarded their advice, remarking that it was disgraceful for the victorious to fear any ventures of those whom they had previously defeated. So, exhorting his men to the fray, he awaited with stout heart the onslaught of the barbarians.

17. When Antioch received the news of Antiochus' death, not only did the city go into public mourning, but every private house as well was dejected and filled with lamentation. Above all, the wailing of the women enflamed their grief. Indeed, since three hundred thousand men had been lost, including those who had accompanied the army as supernumeraries, not a household could be found that was exempt from misfortune. Some were mourning the loss of brothers, some of husbands, and some of sons, while many girls and boys, left orphaned, wept for their own bereavement, till at last Time, the best healer of grief, dulled the edge of their sorrow.

Athenaeus, the general of Antiochus, who in billeting his soldiers had done many wrongs, was the first to take flight. Though he abandoned Antiochus, he met the end he deserved, for when in his flight he reached certain villages that he had mistreated in connection with quartering his men, no one would admit him to his home or share food with him, and he roamed the countryside until he perished of starvation.

18. Arsaces, king of the Parthians, having crushed Antiochus, was minded to advance upon Syria, thinking that it would fall an easy prey. He did not, however, find it in his power to make the campaign; far from it, for because of the magnitude of his successes, Fortune set in his way perils and misfortunes many times as great. It is, I think, true that no unmixed blessing is granted to man by god; as if on purpose the Divine Power sees that fortune and misfortune, good and evil, succeed one another. Of a certainty Fortune did not on this occasion forget her proper nature, but as if fatigued by the bestowal of continuous favour on the same men, she contrived so great a turn of the tide in the whole conflict that the hitherto successful side was now completely humbled.

19. Arsaces, king of the Parthians, was angry with the people of Seleuceia and bore them a grudge for the despites and punishments that they had inflicted on his general, Enius. When they sent a mission to him, pleading to win pardon for what had taken place, and pressed him for an answer, he led the envoys to the place where blind Pitthides sat on the ground, his eyes gouged out, and bade them report to the men of Seleuceia that they must all suffer the same fate. Thoroughly alarmed, they forgot their former troubles in view of the enormity of the horrors now anticipated, for men's new trouble's regularly tend to cast prior misfortunes into the shade.

20. Hegelochus, sent by the elder Ptolemy in command of an army against Marsyas [127/6], the general of the Alexandrians, captured him alive and wiped out his army. When Marsyas was brought before the king, and everyone anticipated that he would receive the most severe punishment, Ptolemy let the charges against him drop. For he was now beginning to suffer a change of heart, and by acts of kindness sought to remedy the hatred that the populace bore him.

21. Euhemerus, the king of the Parthians, was an Hyrcanian by race and surpassed in cruelty all Tyrants of whom we have record, so that there is no manner of punishment whatsoever that he did not employ. On the most casual pretexts he enslaved many of the Babylonians, together with all their families, and sent them to Media with orders that:hey should be sold as booty. He set fire to the agora of Babylon and to some of the temples, and destroyed the best part of the city.

22. When Antipater, Clonius, and Aeropus, leaders of note [128+], revolted and seized Laodiceia, Alexander (nicknamed Zabinas) successfully attacked the city. Behaving with magnanimity, he gave them a free pardon, for he was kindly and of a forgiving nature, and moreover was gentle in speech and in manners, wherefore he was deeply beloved by the common people.

23. When [C] Sextius [Calvinus], [124] after capturing the city of the Gauls, was selling its inhabitants as booty, a certain Crato, who had been a partisan of the Roman cause and for that reason had endured many outrages and tortures at the hands of the rebels, his fellow citizens, was being conducted in chains together with the rest of the captives. When he espied the consul at his duties, and disclosed who he was and that, as a supporter of Roman policy, he had gone through many and oft repeated perils at the hands of his fellow citizens, not only was he, together with all his kindred, released and their property restored, but because of his loyalty to Rome he was granted permission to exempt nine hundred of his fellows from slavery. Indeed, the consul treated him more generously even than he had anticipated, since he wished to give the Gauls a clear demonstration of Roman thoroughness, whether in dispensing mercy or in exacting reprisals.

24. The populace thronged about him [Gracchus] not only when he took office [123], but also when he was a candidate, and even before; and on his return home from Sardinia they met him, and, as he disembarked, greeted him with acclamations and applause: such was his extreme popularity with the common people.

25. Gracchus, having delivered public harangues on the subject of abolishing aristocratic rule and establishing democracy, and having won credit with all classes, had in these men no longer mere supporters but rather sponsors of his own daring plans. Each man, in fact, bribed by hope of private gains, was ready to face any risk on behalf of the proposed laws, quite as though they were a personal interest. By taking away from the senators the right to serve in the courts and designating the knights as jurors, he made the inferior element in the state supreme over their betters; by disrupting the existing harmony of senate and knights, he rendered the common people hostile towards both; then, by using this general dissension as a steppingstone to personal power, and by exhausting the public treasury on base and unsuitable expenditures and favours, he made everyone look only to him as leader; by sacrificing the provinces to the reckless rapacity of the tax farmers he provoked the subject peoples to well-merited hatred of their rulers; and by relaxing through legislation the severity of the old discipline, as a means of currying favour with the soldiers, he introduced disobedience and anarchy into the state: for a man who despises those in authority over him rebels also against the laws, and from these practices come fatal lawlessness and the overthrow of the state.

Gracchus reached such heights of power and arrogance that when the *plebs* voted to exile Octavius from the city he set him free, stating to the people that he did this as a favour to his own mother, who had interceded for the man.

26. Publius [Popillius Leanas] was escorted by weeping throngs as he departed from the city into exile. Indeed, the populace was not unaware that his banishment was unjust, but corrupted by bribery directed against him, it had deprived itself of the freedom to denounce evil.

27. Seventeen tribes voted against the law, and an equal number of others approved it. When the eighteenth was tallied, there was a plurality of one for those supporting the measure. While the decision of the people was narrowing down to so close a finish Gracchus was as overwrought as if he were fighting for very life, but when he realised that he had won by the addition of a single vote he cried out: "Now the sword hangs over the head of my enemies! As for all else, whatever the decision of Fortune, we shall be content."

28. Alexander [II], having no confidence in the masses because of their inexperience of the hazards of war and their readiness for any change, did not venture to join battle, but resolved to get together the royal treasures and steal the offerings dedicated to the gods, and with these to sail away by night to Greece. He made an attempt to plunder the temple of Zeus, employing for the purpose certain barbarians, but was detected, and together with his troops all but met with condign punishment on the spot. Having managed, however, to slip away with a few men, he attempted to make his escape to Seleuceia. The news, however, outran him, and when the Seleuceians heard about the temple robbery, they barred his entry into the city. Having failed in this attempt too, he rushed to seek refuge at Posideium, clinging to the sea-coast in his flight.

Alexander, after his temple robbery, tried to escape to Posideium, but all unseen, we may assume, a Divine Power was following at. his heels in close pursuit, and, co-operating to effect his punishment, forced him closer and ever closer to his proper doom. He was, in fact, apprehended and taken before Antiochus at his camp only two days after the temple robbery. In such wise does avenging justice inescapably pursue the rash deeds of impious men. Aye, vigilant Avengers track down the evil, and the punishment that they bring is swift. But yesterday he had been a king, and the leader of forty thousand men under arms. Now he was being led in chains to face insults and punishment at the hands of his foes.

When Alexander, the king of Syria, was being led in chains through the camp, it appeared incredible, not only to those who heard of it, but even to eyewitnesses, for the expectation that it could never happen strove to tip the balance against the plain evidence of the senses. When the truth was confirmed by actual sight, one and all marvelled as they turned from the scene, some applauding with frequent expressions of approval the manifestation of divine power, others commenting variously on the instability of fortune, the changeableness of human affairs, the sudden turns of the tide, and the mutability of human life, so far beyond all that a man would expect.

28a. Gracchus, [121] whose partisans were numerous, continued to resist; but as he was constantly and increasingly being humiliated, and had unexpected disappointments, he began to fall into a kind of frenzy and state of madness. Assembling the conspirators at his own house he decided, after consultation with [M. Fulvius] Flaccus, that they must overcome their opponents by force of arms and make an attack on the consuls and the senate. Accordingly he urged them all to wear swords beneath their togas, and as they accompanied him to pay close attention to his orders. Since Opimius was at the Capitol debating what should be done, Gracchus and his malcontents started for that place, but finding the temple already occupied and a large number of nobles collected, he withdrew to the portico behind the temple, a prey to agony of spirit and fiendish torments. While he was still in this frenzied state, a certain Quintus, a man on terms of familiarity with him, fell at his knees and besought him to take no violent or irreparable steps against the fatherland. Gracchus, however, acting now openly as a tyrant, knocked him headlong to the ground and ordered his companions to dispatch him, and to make this the beginning of reprisals against their opponents. The consul, aghast, announced to the senate the murder and the coming attack upon themselves.

29. After the death of Gracchus at the hands of his own slave, Lucius Vitellius, who had been one of his friends and was the first to come upon his body, not only did not grieve at what had befallen his dead friend, but having removed his head and carried it home, displayed a special ingenuity in exorbitant greed and a callousness that knew no bounds. The consul had made proclamation that he would give for the head its weight in gold to the man who brought it in. Lucius, therefore, bored through the neck, and having removed the brain, poured in molten lead. He then produced the head and received the gold, but was despised for the rest of his life for this betrayal of friendship. Like Gracchus, the Flacci also were killed.

30. Flaccus . . . to reveal his identity (?) for the sake of . . . running about . . . proscription (or confiscation) . . . expectation . . . this lawlessness. . . .

30a. The Cordisci, [119/05] having taken great quantities of booty, induced many others to adopt the same policy, and to consider the pillaging of others' property and the harrying of . . . the mark of manly behaviour: for it is but a confirmation of the law of nature when the strong ravage the property of the weak.

30b. Later the Scordisci, by refusing passage, demonstrated that even Rome's superiority rested not on her own strength but on the weakness of others.

30c. Understanding, which is thought to be master of all things, is weaker than one thing only, Fortune. Many a time her spitefulness unexpectedly ruins what a man (has mapped out) with intelligence and shrewdness . . ., and again, at times, contrary to all expectations she sets to right affairs which in our folly we have despaired of. As a result, one who finds her unfailingly propitious may succeed in almost all undertakings, while those to whom she is adverse fail in their individual actions, and some may be seen. . . .

31. In Libya when the kings met in combat [112], Jugurtha was victorious in battle and slew many of the Numidians. His brother Adherbal took refuge in Cirta, where, being beleaguered in a close siege, he sent envoys to Rome, begging the Romans not to ignore the jeopardy of a friendly and allied king. The senate dispatched legates to break the siege. When Jugurtha paid no heed, they sent a second legation of greater weight. After they too had returned empty-handed, Jugurtha surrounded the city with a trench and through privation wore down its inhabitants. His brother came out holding a suppliant's bough, and though he abdicated the kingship and begged only for life, Jugurtha slew him, without regard either to kinship or to the rights of a suppliant. He likewise tortured and put to death all the Italians who had fought on his brother's side.

32. Jugurtha, the king of the Numidians, marvelling at the manly courage of the Romans and praising their exploits, declared to his friends that with these men (?) he could traverse all Libya. . .

32a. When the news broke upon them of the death of . . . and of those who had perished with him . . . the city was filled with cries and lamentation. For many were the children left orphans, and not a few . . . brothers. . . .

33. The consul Nasica was a man distinguished in his own right and was, as well, esteemed for his noble lineage [111]. He belonged, in fact, to that *gens* whose scions had acquired the names Africanus, Asiaticus, and Hispanus; for since one of their number subdued Libya, another Asia, and the third Spain, each won for himself a cognomen signifying his achievements. In addition to the high repute of his ancestors generally, he had for father and grandfather two of the most prominent men in Rome. Both held the position of leader of the senate and of "first speaker," each to the time of his death, and in addition the grandfather was by decree of the senate adjudged the "best" man in the state. For it was found written in the Sibylline oracles that the Romans should establish a temple for the Great Mother of the Gods, that her sacred objects should be fetched from Pessinus in Asia, and be received in Rome by a muster of the whole populace going forth to meet them, that of the noblest men and women alike . . . the good woman . . . and that they should lead the welcoming procession, when it took place, and receive the sacred objects of the goddess. When the senate proceeded to carry out the instructions of the oracle, Publius Nasica was selected as the best of all the men and Valeria as the best of the women. Not only was he considered outstanding in piety towards the gods, but he was a statesman as well, and a man who spoke his mind in public debate shrewdly. After the Hannibalic War, for example, Marcus Cato (dubbed Demosthenes) made it his practice to remark on every occasion, when stating his opinion in the senate, "Would that Carthage did not exist," and he kept repeating this even when no relevant motion was before the house and different matters were in turn being considered. Nasica [Corculum], however, always expressed the contrary wish, "May Carthage exist for all time." Now though each point of view seemed to the senate to merit consideration, that of Nasica was regarded by the more intelligent members as being far and away the better. Rome's strength should be judged, they thought, not by the weakness of others, but by showing herself greater than the great. Furthermore, so long as Carthage survived, the fear that she generated compelled the Romans to live together in harmony and to rule their subjects equitably and with credit to themselves, much the best means to maintain and extend an empire; but once the rival city was destroyed, it was only too evident that there would be civil war at home, and that hatred for the governing power would spring up among all the allies because of the rapacity and lawlessness to which the Roman magistrates would subject them. All this did indeed happen to Rome after the destruction of Carthage, which brought in its wake the following: dangerous demagoguery, the redistribution of land, major revolts among the allies, prolonged and frightful civil wars, and all the other things predicted by Scipio. Now it was this man's son who, as an old man, and leader of the senate, killed with his own hands Tiberius Gracchus, after the latter had attempted to gain absolute power. The masses were angry, and raged against the perpetrators of the deed, while the tribunes even haled the senators, one by one, to the rostra and demanded to know who the actual murderer was. All the rest, fearing the impetuosity and violence of the crowd, denied any knowledge or gave devious and conflicting answers. Scipio alone admitted that the killing was done by him, adding that unbeknown to the rest of the city Gracchus had been aiming at tyranny, and that only he and the senate had not been deceived. The crowd, though disgruntled, subsided, awed by the dignity of the man and his frank statement. Now this man's son, too, who died in the year in question, remained incorruptible throughout his entire career, and since he took part in public affairs and proved himself a true lover of wisdom, not in words alone but in his way of life, his legacy of virtue was indeed in keeping with his noble lineage.

34. Shortly after Antiochus [IX] Cyzicenus gained the throne he lapsed into drunken habits, crass self-indulgence, and pursuits utterly inappropriate to a king. He delighted, for example, in mimes and pantomimic actors, and generally in all showmen, and devoted himself eagerly to learning their crafts. He practised also how to manipulate puppets, and personally to keep in motion silver-plated and gilded animals five cubits high, and many another such contrivance. On the other hand, he possessed no store of "city-takers" or other instruments of siegecraft that might have brought him high renown and performed some service worth recording. He was, moreover, addicted to hunting at odd and unseasonable hours, and many a time would slip away from his friends at night, and making his way to the country with two or three servants go in pursuit of lions, panthers, or wild boars, and since in grappling with brute beasts he was reckless, he frequently put his own life in extreme peril.

35. Micipsa, the son of the Numidian king Masinissa, had several other sons, but his favourites were Adherbal, the elder (*sic*) of his children, Iampsamus, and Micipsa. Now Micipsa was the most civilised of all the Numidian kings, and lived much in the company of cultivated Greeks whom he had summoned to his court. He took a great interest in culture, especially philosophy, and waxed old both in the exercise of power and in the pursuit of wisdom.

35a. There came to Rome a member of the royal family, [110] another Jugurtha, who was a contender for the throne of Numidia. Since he was extremely popular, Jugurtha hired murderers to assassinate him, then returned without let or hindrance to his kingdom.

36. Contoniatus, chieftain of the Gaulish city called Iontora, was a man of unusual sagacity and military ability, and was a friend and ally of the Roman people. This was natural, as he had previously spent much time in Rome, had come to share their ideals and way of life, and through Rome's support had succeeded to his chieftainship in Gaul.

38. Marius, though a member of the staff and a legate [109/8], received scant notice from the general, since he was least of the legates in repute. While the other legates, more prominent by virtue of the offices they had held and the nobility of their birth, received many marks of favour from the general, Marius, who was reputed to have been a tax farmer and had barely secured election to the lower ranks of office, was slighted whenever preferment was made to posts of honour. Whereas each of the others, avoiding all possible discomfort in the performance of their military duties, preferred a life of ease and indolence, Marius, when assigned, as he frequently was, to lead his men into the thick of battle, welcomed the disparagement shown therein, and applying himself eagerly to such services acquired much experience in warfare, and since he had a natural talent for combat and battle, and gladly exposed himself to their risks, he soon won great influence and a reputation for courage. Moreover, by treating his soldiers with consideration and by employing means designed to please those under his command, whether in bestowing gifts, in conversation, or in routine contacts with them, he gained great popularity among his men. In return for his favours they fought all the more zealously when in battle with him, in order to enhance his prestige; but if some other legate happened to be in command they played the coward deliberately and at the most crucial moments. So it came about that as a rule the Romans suffered setbacks under the command of the others, but always conquered if Marius was present.

39. Bocchus, who had a kingdom in Libya [Mauretania] [105], after hurling many reproaches at the men who had persuaded him to take up arms against the Romans, sent envoys to Marius; he besought pardon for his past offences and requested a pact of friendship, promising that he would be helpful to the Romans in many ways. When Marius told him to address his petitions to the senate, the king dispatched an embassy to Rome charged with these matters. The senate, however, returned them the answer that Bocchus would be granted complete satisfaction provided he won Marius' consent. Now Marius had in mind to capture King Jugurtha, and Bocchus met his wishes by sending for Jugurtha, ostensibly to discuss with him matters pertaining to their common advantage; and having seized and bound him, he then handed him over to Lucius Sulla, the quaestor appointed to escort him. Thus did Bocchus, securing his own safety at Jugurtha's expense, escape retribution at the hands of the Romans.

39a. While the elder Ptolemy [IX] was shut up in the city of Seleuceia, a plot against him was formed by one of his friends. He arrested and punished the offender, and henceforth did not trust his safety to "friends " indiscriminately.

37. . . . of Carbo and Silanus. Since so great a multitude had perished, some grieved for sons, others for brothers; children, left fatherless, bewailed the loss of a sire and the desolation of Italy; and large numbers of women, bereft of their husbands, were made acquainted with the sad fate of widowhood. The senate, with courageous fortitude in the face of disaster, sought to restrain the general mourning and the excessive lamentation, and bore their heavy load of grief without showing it.

BOOK XXXVI FRAGMENTS

1. In Rome [104] , at about the same time that Marius defeated the Libyan kings Bocchus and Jugurtha in a great battle and slew many tens of thousands of Libyans, and, later, took thence and held captive Jugurtha himself (after he had been seized by Bocchus who thereby won pardon from the Romans for the offences that had brought him into war with them), at the time, furthermore, that the Romans, at war with the Cimbri, were disheartened, having met with very serious reverses in Gaul, at about this time, I repeat, men arrived in Rome from Sicily bearing news of an uprising of slaves, their numbers running into many tens of thousands. With the advent of this fresh news the whole Roman state found itself in a crisis, inasmuch as nearly sixty thousand allied troops had perished in the war in Gaul against the Cimbri and there were no legionary forces available to send out.

2. Even before the new uprising of the slaves in Sicily there had occurred in Italy a number of short lived and minor revolts, as though the supernatural was indicating in advance the magnitude of the impending Sicilian rebellion. The first was at Nuceria, where thirty slaves formed a conspiracy and were promptly punished; the second at Capua, where two hundred rose in insurrection and were promptly put down. The third was surprising in character. There was a certain Titus Minucius, a Roman knight and the son of a very wealthy father. This man fell in love with a servant girl of outstanding beauty who belonged to another. Having lain with her and fallen unbelievably in love, he purchased her freedom for seven Attic talents (his infatuation being so compelling, and the girl's master having consented to the sale only reluctantly), and fixed a time by which he was to pay off the debt, for his father's abundant means obtained him credit. When the appointed day came and he was unable to pay, he set a new deadline of thirty days. When this day too was at hand and the sellers put in a claim for payment, while he, though his passion was in full tide, was no better able than before to carry out his bargain, he then embarked on an enterprise that passes all comprehension: he made designs on tile life of those who were dunning him, and arrogated to himself autocratic powers. He bought up five hundred suits of armour, and contracting for a delay in payment, which he was granted, he secretly conveyed them to a certain field and stirred up his own slaves, four hundred in number, to rise in revolt. Then, having assumed the diadem and a purple cloak, together with lictors and the other appurtenances of office, and having with the co-operation of the slaves proclaimed himself king, he flogged and beheaded the persons who were demanding payment for the girl. Arming his slaves, he marched on the neighbouring farmsteads and gave arms to those who eagerly joined his revolt, but slew anyone who opposed him. Soon he had more than seven hundred soldiers, and having enrolled them by centuries he constructed a palisade and welcomed all who revolted. When word of the uprising was reported at Rome the senate took prudent measures and remedied the situation. Of the praetors then in the city they appointed one, Lucius Lucullus, to apprehend the fugitives. That very day he selected six hundred soldiers in Rome itself, and by the time he reached Capua had mustered four thousand infantry and four hundred cavalry. Vettius, on learning that Lucullus was on his way, occupied a strong hill with an army that now totalled more than thirty-five hundred men. The forces engaged, and at first the fugitives had the advantage, since they were fighting from higher ground; but later Lucullus, by suborning Apollonius, the general of Vettius, and guaranteeing him in the name of the state immunity from punishment, persuaded him to turn traitor against his fellow rebels. Since he was now cooperating with the Romans and turning his forces against Vettius, the latter, fearing the punishment that would await him if he were captured, slew himself, and was presently joined in death by all who had taken part in the insurrection, save only the traitor Apollonius. Now these events, forming as it were a prelude, preceded the major revolt in Sicily, which began in the following manner.

2a. There were many new uprisings of slaves, the first at Nuceria, where thirty slaves formed a conspiracy and were promptly punished, and the second at Capua, where two hundred slaves rose in insurrection and also were promptly punished. A third revolt was extraordinary and quite out of the usual pattern. There was a certain Titus Vettius, a Roman knight, whose father was a person of great wealth. Being a very young man, he was attracted by a servant girl of outstanding beauty who belonged to another. Having lain with her, and even lived with her for a certain length of time, he fell marvellously in love and into a state bordering, in fact, on madness. Wishing because of his affection for her to purchase the girl's freedom, he at first encountered her master's opposition, but later, having won his consent by the magnitude of the offer, he purchased her for seven Attic talents, and agreed to pay the purchase price at a stipulated time. His father's wealth obtaining him credit for the sum, he carried the girl off, and hiding away at one of his father's country estates sated his private lusts. When the stipulated time for the debt came round he was visited by men sent to demand payment. He put off the settlement till thirty days later, and when he was still unable to furnish the money, but was now a very slave to love, he embarked on an enterprise that passes all comprehension. Indeed, the extreme severity of his affliction and the embarrassment that accompanied his failure to pay promptly caused his mind to turn to childish and utterly foolish calculations. Faced by impending separation from his mistress, he formed a desperate plot against those who were demanding payment. . . .

3. In the course of Marius' campaign against the Cimbri the senate granted Marius permission to summon military aid from the nations situated beyond the seas. Accordingly Marius sent to Nicomedes, the king of Bithynia, requesting assistance. The king replied that the majority of the Bithynians had been seized by tax farmers and were now in slavery in the Roman provinces. The senate then issued a decree that no citizen of an allied state should be held in slavery in a Roman province, and that the praetors should provide for their liberation. In compliance with the decree Licinius Nerva, who was at this time governor of Sicily, appointed hearings and set free a number of slaves, with the result that in a few days more than eight hundred persons obtained their freedom, and all who were in slavery throughout the island were agog with hopes of freedom. The notables, however, assembled in haste and entreated the praetor to desist from this course. Whether he was won over by their bribes or weakly succumbed in his desire to favour them, in any case he ceased to show interest in these tribunals, and when men approached him to obtain freedom he rebuked them and ordered them to return to their masters. The slaves, banding together, departed from Syracuse, and taking refuge in the sanctuary of the Palici canvassed the question of revolution. From this point on the audacity of the slaves was made manifest in many places, but the first to make a bid for freedom were the thirty slaves of two very wealthy brothers in the region of Halicyae, led by a man named Varius. They first murdered their own masters by night as they lay sleeping, then proceeded to the neighbouring villas and summoned the slaves to freedom. In this one night more than a hundred and twenty gathered together. Seizing a position that was naturally strong, they strengthened it even further, having received in the meantime an increment of eighty armed slaves. Licinius Nerva, the governor of the province, marched against them in haste, but though he placed them under siege his efforts were in vain. When he saw that their fortress could not be taken by force, he set his hopes on treason. As the instrument for his purpose he had one Gaius Titinius, surnamed Gadaeus, whom he won over with promises of immunity. This man had been condemned to death two years before, but had escaped punishment, and living as a brigand had murdered many of the free men of the region, while abstaining from harm to any of the slaves. Now, taking with him a sufficient body of loyal slaves, he approached the fortress of the rebels, as though intending to join them in the war against the Romans. Welcomed with open arms as a friend, he was even chosen, because of his valour, to be general, whereupon he betrayed the fortress. Of the rebels some were cut down in battle, and others, fearing the punishment that would follow on their capture, cast themselves down from the heights. Thus was the first uprising of the fugitives quelled.

4. After the soldiers had disbanded and returned to their usual abodes, word was brought that eighty slaves had risen in rebellion and murdered Publius Clonius, who had been a Roman knight, and, further, that they were now engaged in gathering a large band. The praetor, distracted by the advice of others and by the fact that most of his forces had been disbanded, failed to act promptly and so provided the rebels an opportunity to make their position more secure. He set out with the soldiers that were available, and after crossing the river Alba [Allava?] passed by the rebels who were quartered on Mount Caprianus and reached the city of Heracleia. By spreading the report that the praetor was a coward, since he had not attacked them, they aroused a large number of slaves to revolt, and with an influx of many recruits, who were equipped for battle in such fashion as was possible, within the first seven days they had more than eight hundred men under arms, and soon thereafter numbered not less than two thousand. When the praetor learned at Heracleia of their growing numbers he appointed Marcus Titinius as commander, giving him a force of six hundred men from the garrison at Enna. Titinius launched an attack on the rebels, but since they held the advantage both in numbers and by reason of the difficult terrain, he and his men were routed, many of them being killed, while the rest threw down their arms and barely made good their escape by flight. The rebels, having gained both a victory and so many arms all at once, maintained their efforts all the more boldly, and all slaves everywhere were now keyed up to revolt. Since there were many who revolted each day, their numbers received a sudden and marvellous increase, and in a few days there were more than six thousand. Thereupon they held an assembly, and when the question was laid before them first of all chose as their king a man named Salvius, who was reputed to be skilled in divination and was a flute-player of frenetic music at performances for women. When he became king he avoided the cities, regarding them as the source of sloth and self-indulgence, and dividing the rebels into three groups, over whom he set a like number of commanders, he ordered them to scour the country and then assemble in full force at a stated time and place. Having provided themselves by their raids with an abundance of horses and other beasts, they soon had more than two thousand cavalry and no fewer than twenty thousand infantry, and were by now making a good showing in military exercises. So, descending suddenly on the strong city of Morgantina, they subjected it to vigorous and constant assaults. The praetor, with about ten thousand Italian and Sicilian troops, set out to bring aid to the city, marching by night; discovering on his arrival that the rebels were occupied with the siege, he attacked their camp, and finding that it was guarded by a mere handful of men, but was filled with captive women and other booty of all sorts, he captured the place with ease. After plundering the camp he moved on Morgantina. The rebels made a sudden counterattack and, since they held a commanding position and struck with might and main, at once gained the ascendant, and the praetor's forces were routed. When the king of the rebels made proclamation that no one who threw down his arms should be killed, the majority dropped them and ran. Having outwitted the enemy in this manner, Salvius recovered his camp, and by his resounding victory got possession of many arms. Not more than six hundred of the Italians and Sicilians perished in the battle, thanks to the king's humane proclamation, but about four thousand were taken prisoner. Having doubled his forces, since there were many who flocked to him as a result of his success, Salvius was now undisputed master of the open country, and again attempted to take Morgantina by siege. By proclamation he offered the slaves in the city their freedom, but when their masters countered with a like offer if they would join in the defence of the city, they chose rather the side of their masters, and by stout resistance repelled the siege. Later, however, the praetor, by rescinding their emancipation, caused the majority of them to desert to the rebels.

5. In the territory of Segesta and Lilybaeum, and of the other neighbouring cities, the fever of insurrection was also raging among the masses of slaves. Here the leader was a certain Athenion, a man of outstanding courage, a Cilician by birth. He was the bailiff of two very wealthy brothers, and having great skill in astrology he won over first the slaves who were under him, some two hundred, and then those in the vicinity, so that in five days he had gathered together more than a thousand men. When he was chosen as king and had put on the diadem, he adopted an attitude just the opposite to that of all the other rebels: he did not admit all who revolted, but making the best ones soldiers, he required the rest to remain at their former labours and to busy themselves each with his domestic affairs and his appointed task; thus Athenion was enabled to provide food in abundance for his soldiers. He pretended, moreover, that the gods forecasted for him, by the stars, that he would be king of all Sicily; consequently, he must needs conserve the land and all its cattle and crops, as being his own property. Finally, when he had assembled a force of more than ten thousand men, he ventured to lay siege to Lilybaeum, an impregnable city. Having failed to achieve anything, he departed thence, saying that this was by order of the gods, and that if they persisted in the siege they would meet with misfortune. While he was yet making ready to withdraw from:he city, ships arrived in the harbour bringing a contingent of Mauretanian auxiliaries, who had been sent to reinforce the city of Lilybaeum and had as their commander a man named Gomon. He and his men made an unexpected attack by night on Athenion's forces as they were on the march, and after felling many and wounding quite a few others returned to the city. As a result the rebels marvelled at his prediction of the event by reading the stars.

6. Turmoil and a very Iliad of woes possessed all Sicily. Not only slaves but also impoverished freemen were guilty of every sort of rapine and lawlessness, and ruthlessly murdered anyone they met, slave or free, so that no one should report their frenzied conduct. As a result all city-dwellers considered what was within the city walls scarcely their own, and whatever was outside as lost to them and subject only to the lawless rule of force. And many besides were the strange deeds perpetrated in Sicily, and many were the perpetrators.

11. Not only did the multitude of slaves who had plunged into revolt ravage the country, but even those freemen who possessed no holdings on the land resorted to rapine and lawlessness. Those without means, impelled alike by poverty and lawlessness, streamed out into the country in swarms, drove off the herds of cattle, plundered the crops stored in the barns, and murdered without more ado all who fell in their way, slave or free alike, so that no one should be able to carry back news of their frantic and lawless conduct. Since no Roman officials were dispensing justice and anarchy prevailed, there was irresponsible licence, and men everywhere were wreaking havoc far and wide. Hence every region was filled with violence and rapine, which ran riot and enjoyed full licence to pillage the property of the well-to-do. Men who afore time had stood first in their cities in reputation and wealth, now through this unexpected turn of fortune were not only losing their property by violence at the hands of the fugitives, but were forced to put up with insolent treatment even from the free born. Consequently they all considered whatever was within the gates scarcely their own, and whatever was without the walls as lost to them and subject only to the lawless rule of force. In general there was turmoil in the cities, and a confounding of all justice under law. For the rebels, supreme in the open country, made the land impassable to travellers, since they were implacable in their hatred for their masters and never got enough of their unexpected good fortune. Meanwhile the slaves in the cities, who were contracting the infection and were poised for revolt, were a source of great fear to their masters.

7. After the siege of Morgantina, Salvius, having overrun the country as far as the plain of Leontini, assembled his whole army there, no fewer than thirty thousand picked men, and after sacrificing to the heroes, the Palici, dedicated to them in thank offering for his victory a robe bordered with a strip of sea-dyed purple. At the same time he proclaimed himself king and was henceforth addressed by the rebels as Tryphon. As it was his intention to seize Triocala and build a palace there, he sent to Athenion, summoning him as a king might summon a general. Everyone supposed that Athenion would dispute the primacy with him and that in the resulting strife between the rebels the war would easily be brought to an end, but Fortune, as though intentionally increasing the power of the fugitives, caused their leaders to be of one mind. Tryphon came promptly to Triocala with his army, and thither also came Athenion with three thousand men, obedient to Tryphon as a general is obedient to his king; the rest of his army he had sent out to cover the countryside and rouse the slaves to rebellion. Later on, suspecting that Athenion would attack him, given the opportunity, Tryphon placed him under detention. The fortress, which was already very strong, he equipped with lavish constructions, and strengthened it even more. This place, Triocala, is said to be so named because it possesses three fine advantages: first, an abundance of flowing springs, whose waters are exceptionally sweet; second, an adjacent countryside yielding vines and olives, and wonderfully amenable to cultivation; and third, surpassing strength, for it is a large and impregnable ridge of rock. This place, which he surrounded with a city wall eight stades in length, and with a deep moat, he used as his royal capital, and saw that it was abundantly supplied with all the necessities of life. He constructed also a royal palace, and a market place that could accommodate a large multitude. Moreover, he picked out a sufficient number of men endowed with superior intelligence, whom he appointed counsellors and employed as his cabinet. When holding audience he put on a toga bordered in purple and wore a wide-bordered tunic, and had lictors with axes to precede him; and in general he affected all the trappings that go to make up and embellish the dignity of a king.

8. To oppose the rebels the Roman senate assigned Lucius Licinius Lucullus, [103] with an army of fourteen thousand Romans and Italians, eight hundred Bithynians, Thessalians, and Acarnanians, six hundred Lucanians (commanded by Cleptius, a skilled general and a man renowned for valour), besides six hundred others, for a total of seventeen thousand: with these forces he occupied Sicily. Now Tryphon, having dropped the charges against Athenion, was making plans for the impending war with the Romans. His choice was to fight at Triocala, but it was Athenion's advice that they ought not to shut themselves up to undergo siege, but should fight in the open. This plan prevailed, and they encamped near Scirthaea, no fewer than forty thousand strong; the Roman camp was at a distance of twelve stades. There was constant skirmishing at first, then the two armies met face to face. The battle swayed now this way, now that, with many casualties on both sides. Athenion, who had a fighting force of two hundred horse, was victorious and covered the whole area about him with corpses, but after being wounded in both knees and receiving a third blow as well, he was of no service in fighting, whereupon the runagate slaves lost spirit and were routed. Athenion was taken for dead and so was not detected. By thus feigning death he made good his escape during the coming night. The Romans won a brilliant victory, for Tryphon's army and Tryphon himself turned and fled. Many were cut down in flight, and no fewer than twenty thousand were finally slain. Under cover of night the rest escaped to Triocala, though it would have been an easy matter to dispatch them also if only the praetor had followed in pursuit. The slave party was now so dejected that they even considered returning to their masters and placing themselves in their hands, but it was the sentiment of those who had pledged themselves to fight to the end and not to yield themselves abjectly to the enemy that at last prevailed. On the ninth day following, the praetor arrived to lay siege to Triocala. After inflicting and suffering some casualties he retired worsted, and the rebels once more held their heads high. The praetor, whether through indolence or because he had been bribed, accomplished nothing of what needed doing, and in consequence he was later haled to judgement by the Romans and punished.

9. Gaius Servilius, sent out as praetor to succeed: Lucullus, likewise achieved nothing worthy of note. Hence he, like Lucullus, was later condemned and sent into exile. On the death of Tryphon, Athenion succeeded to the command, and, since Servilius did nothing to hinder him, he laid cities under siege, overran the country with impunity, and brought many places under his sway.

The praetor Lucullus, on learning that Gaius Servilius, the praetor appointed to succeed him in the war, had crossed the Strait, disbanded his army, and set fire to the camp and the constructions, for he did not wish his successor in the command to have any significant resources for waging war. Since he himself was being denounced for his supposed desire to enlarge the scope of the war, he assumed that by ensuring the humiliation and disgrace of his successor he was also dispelling the charge brought against himself.

10. At the end of the year Gaius Marius was elected consul at Rome for the fifth time [101/0], with Gaius Aquillius as his colleague. It was Aquillius who was sent against the rebels, and by his personal valour won a resounding victory over them. Meeting Athenion, the king of the rebels, face to face, he put up an heroic struggle; he slew Athenion, and was himself wounded in the head but recovered after treatment. Then he continued the campaign against the surviving rebels, who now numbered ten thousand. When they did not abide his approach, but sought refuge in their strongholds, Aquillius unrelentingly employed every means till he had captured their forts and mastered them. A thousand were still left, with Satyrus at their head. Aquillius at first intended to subdue them by force of arms, but when later, after an exchange of envoys, they surrendered, he released them from immediate punishment and took them to Rome to do combat with wild beasts. There, as some report, they brought their lives to a most glorious end; for they avoided combat with the beasts and cut one another down at the public altars, Satyrus himself slaying the last man. Then he, as the final survivor, died heroically by his own hand. Such was the dramatic conclusion of the Sicilian Slave War, a war that lasted about four years.

12. Saturninus the tribune [104/3],1 who was a man of licentious pursuits, had as quaestor been charged with the transport of grain from Ostia to Rome, but since his idle and frivolous behaviour encouraged the judgement that he had not been a success as director of the operation, he was duly rebuked. The senate, in fact, stripped him of his authority and transferred his charge to others. Once he had corrected his former loose habits and adopted a sober manner of life, he was raised by the people to the tribunate.

13. A certain man named Battaces [102], a priest of the Great Mother of the Gods, arrived, says Diodorus, from Pessinus in Phrygia. Claiming that he had come by command of the goddess, he obtained an audience with the consuls and with the senate, in which he stated that the temple of the goddess had been defiled and that rites of purification to her must be performed at Rome in the name of the state. The robe he wore, like the rest of his costume, was outlandish and by Roman standards not to be countenanced, for he had on an immense golden crown and a gaudy cape shot with gold, the marks of royal rank. After addressing the populace from the rostra, and creating in the crowd a mood of religious awe, he was granted lodging and hospitality at the expense of the state, but was forbidden by one of the tribunes, Aulus Pompeius, to wear his crown. Brought back to the rostra by another of the tribunes, and questioned as to what ritual purity for the temple required, he couched his answers in words evocative of holy dread. When he was thereupon attacked in a partisan spirit by Pompeius, and was contemptuously sent back to his lodgings, he refused to appear again in public, saying that not only he, but the goddess as well, had been impiously treated with disrespect. Pompeius was straightway smitten with a raging fever, then lost his voice and was stricken with quinsy, and on the third day died. To the man in the street it seemed that his death was an act of Divine Providence in requital for his offences against the goddess and her priest, for the Romans are very prone to fear in matters of religion. Accordingly Battaces was granted a special dispensation in regard to his costume and the sacred robe, was honoured with notable gifts, and when he started homeward from Rome was escorted on his way by a large crowd, both men and women.

14. The Roman soldiers had a custom that when a general of theirs who with them joined battle against an enemy had slain six thousand of the foe, they hailed and acclaimed him imperator, that is to say, "king."

15. Envoys of King Mithridates [VI] arrived in Rome [101], bringing with them a large sum of money with which to bribe the senate. Saturninus, thinking that this gave him a point of attack on the senate, behaved with great insolence towards the embassy. At the instigation of the senators, who promised to lend their support, the outraged envoys preferred charges against Saturninus for his insulting treatment. The trial, held in public, was of great import because of the inviolability attaching to ambassadors and the Romans' habitual detestation of any wrongdoing where embassies were concerned; it was therefore a capital charge of which Saturninus stood accused, and since his prosecutors were men of senatorial rank, and it was the senate that judged such cases, he was thrown into great fear and great danger. Alarmed by the serious nature of the issues at stake, he had recourse to pity, the common refuge of the unfortunate: laying aside his costly attire he donned instead a shabby garb, and letting his hair and beard grow, canvassed the urban proletariat; falling at the knees of some, and grasping others by the hands, he begged and besought them with tears to aid him in his distress. He told them that he was being made a victim of the senate's partisanship in violation of all justice, and pointed out that it was because of his concern for the common people that he was being treated in this way, and that, moreover, his enemies were at one and the same time his accusers and his judges. The populace, aroused to a man by his prayers, massed many thousands strong at the place of judgement, and he was unexpectedly acquitted. Having the support of the people, he was again proclaimed tribune.

16. For two years the exile of Metellus was discussed in the public assemblies. His son, letting his hair and beard grow and wearing a shabby garb, went about the Forum beseeching the citizens, and falling at their knees in tears begged them one by one to grant his father's return. The people, though unwilling to give the exiles a foothold that would enable them to return in violation of the laws, nevertheless through pity for the young man and because of his zeal in his father's cause recalled Metellus, and gave the son, in tribute to his devotion to the cause of his sire, the cognomen Pius.

BOOK XXXVII FRAGMENTS

1. In all the time that men's deeds have been handed down by recorded history to the memory of posterity the greatest war known to us is the "Marsic," [Social War] so named after the Marsi. [91] This war surpassed all that preceded it both in the valorous exploits of its leaders and in the magnitude of its operations. The Trojan War, to be sure, and the merits of its heroes were so dramatically depicted by the most renowned of poets, Homer, that their glory is supreme; and since in that war Europe and Asia were locked in battle and the greatest continents were contending for victory, the exploits of the combatants were such that for all succeeding generations the dramatic stage has been filled with the tragic stories of their various ordeals. Nevertheless, those heroes were ten years in subjugating the cities of the Troad, whereas the Romans of a later age conquered Antiochus the Great in a single engagement and emerged the masters of all Asia. After the Trojan War the king of Persia led an army against Greece, and so vast a host accompanied him that even perennial streams were dried up. Yet the military genius of Themistocles and the valour of the Greeks brought down those Persians in defeat. At about the same time the Carthaginians conducted an army of three hundred thousand men against Sicily, but by a single stratagem Gelon the Syracusan commander set fire in a moment to two hundred ships, and cutting to pieces in pitched battle one hundred and fifty thousand of the enemy took as many more captive. Nevertheless, the descendants of those who did these mighty deeds were defeated by the people who fought the Marsic War, the Romans. Next in order comes Alexander of Macedon, whose surpassing genius and courage enabled him to overthrow the Persian Empire; yet in more recent times Roman arms took Macedonia itself captive. Carthage waged war with Rome over Sicily for four and twenty years, but after numerous mighty battles fought on land and sea was at last beaten back by the weight of Rome's military power. Soon after, however, Carthage set afoot the so-called Hannibalic War, and since her general was Hannibal, a man of the very highest ability, she was victorious on land and sea and won wide acclaim for her many achievements, only at the end to be brought down in defeat by the prowess of the Romans and Italians and the valour of Scipio. The Cimbri, giantlike in appearance and unexcelled in feats of strength . . . for though they had cut to pieces many large Roman armies and had four hundred thousand men poised for an attack on Italy, they were utterly cut to pieces by the valorous Romans.

Since, therefore, on the basis of actual results, the palm for manly valour in war was awarded to the Romans and to the peoples who inhabit Italy, Fortune as if of set purpose put these two at variance and set ablaze the war that surpassed all in magnitude. Indeed when the nations of Italy revolted against Rome's domination, and those who from time immemorial had been accounted the bravest of men fell into discord and contention, the war that ensued reached the very summit of magnitude. Since the Marsi took the lead in the revolt, it was called the Marsic War.

2. Diodorus declares that the so-called Marsic War, which fell in his lifetime, was greater than any war in the past. He says that it was called Marsic after those who led the revolt, for certainly it was the united Italians who went to war against Rome. The primary cause of the war, he says, was this, that the Romans abandoned the disciplined, frugal, and stern manner of life that had brought them to such greatness, and fell into the pernicious pursuit of luxury and licence. The *plebs* and senate being at odds as a result of this deterioration, the latter called on the Italians to support them, promising to admit them to the much coveted Roman citizenship, and to confirm the grant by law; but when none of the promises made to the Italians was realised, war flared up between them and the Romans. This occurred when Lucius Marcius Philippus and Sextus Iulius were consuls at Rome, [91] in the course of the one hundred and seventy-second Olympiad. In this conflict all sorts and manner of sufferings, including the storming of cities, severally befell the two parties in the war, since Victory tipped the scales in turn now this way, now that, as if of set purpose, and remained securely in the possession of neither, though after innumerable casualties on either side it was belatedly and with difficulty brought about that Rome's power was firmly established.

Engaged in the war with the Romans were the Samnites, the people of Asculum, the Lucanians, the Picentines, the people of Nola, and other cities and nations. Their most notable and important city was Corfinium, recently established as federal capital of the Italians, and there they had set up, among other symbols of political and imperial might, a spacious forum and council hall, abundant store of money and other supplies of war, and a plentiful supply of food. They also set up a joint senate of five hundred members, from whose number men worthy to rule the country and capable of providing for the common safety were to be selected for promotion. To them they entrusted the conduct of the war, giving the senators full power to act. The latter accordingly ordained that two consuls should be chosen annually, and twelve praetors.

The men installed as consuls were Quintus Pompaedius Silo, a Marsian by birth and first of his nation, and secondly, of Samnite blood, Gaius Aponius Motylus, likewise a man of outstanding reputation and achievements in his nation. Dividing all Italy into two parts, they designated these as consular provinces and districts. To Pompaedius they assigned the region from what is known as the Cercola to the Adriatic sea, that is, the section to the northwest, and subordinated six praetors to him; the rest of Italy, to the southeast, they assigned to Gaius Motylus, providing him likewise with six praetors. When they had so ably disposed their affairs and had organised a government, which for the most part copied the time-honoured Roman pattern, they devoted themselves henceforth to the energetic prosecution of the war, having given their federal city the new name Italia [Italica].

Their struggle with the Romans went [89], for the most part, to their advantage up to the time when Gnaeus Pompeius was elected consul and took command of the war, and he, together with Sulla, legate under the other consul Cato, won notable victories, not once but repeatedly, over the Italians, and - shattered their cause to bits. Yet still they fought on, but after Gaius Cosconius was sent to take command in Iapygia they were defeated again and again. Thereupon, reduced in strength and left a mere remnant of their original numbers, by common consent they abandoned their federal capital, Corfinium, since the Marsi and all the neighbouring peoples had yielded to the Romans. They established themselves, however, at the Samnite town of Aesernia, and put themselves under five praetors, to one of whom in particular, Quintus Pompaedius Silo, they entrusted the supreme command because of his ability and reputation as a general. He, with the common consent of the praetors, built up a large army, so that, including the men they already had, their numbers now totalled some thirty thousand. In addition, by freeing the slaves and, as occasion offered, providing them with arms, he assembled not far short of twenty thousand men and a thousand horsemen. Meeting in battle a Roman force under Mamercus [88], he slew a few Romans but lost over six thousand of his own men. At about the same time Metellus took by siege Venusia in Apulia, an important city with many soldiers, and took more than three thousand captives. Since the Romans were increasingly gaining the upper hand, the Italians sent to King Mithridates of Pontus, whose military power and means were now at their height, asking him to bring an army into Italy against the Romans; for if they should join forces the might of Rome would easily be overthrown. Mithridates replied that he would lead his armies to Italy when he had brought Asia under his sway, for he was now occupied with this. In consequence the rebels were downcast and in utter despair, for they had left to them only a few Samnites and Sabellians, who were at Nola, and besides these, the remnants of the Lucanians under Lamponius and Clepitius.

Now, since the Marsic War was virtually at an end, the intestine disputes that, had earlier occurred in Rome took on new life, inasmuch as many prominent men were rival claimants for the command against Mithridates in view of the rich prizes it offered. Gaius Iulius and Gaius Marius (the man who had been six times consul) were pitted against one another, and the populace was divided in sentiment for one side or the other. Other disturbances occurred as well. The consul Sulla, [88] however, quitted Rome and joined the armies gathered about Nola, and by striking fear into many of the neighbouring peoples forced them to surrender their persons and their cities. Once Sulla had set out for Asia to make war upon Mithridates, since Rome was now distracted by great disturbances and intestine bloodshed, Marcus Aponius and Tiberius Clepitius, and also Pompeius, the generals of the Italian remnant, who were now in Bruttium, laid siege for a long time to Isiae, a strongly fortified city. They did not succeed in capturing it, but leaving a part of their army to continue the siege, strongly invested Rhegium with the rest, expecting that if they once got it into their hands they would at their ease transport their armies to Sicily and win control of the richest island under the sun. Gaius Norbanus, the governor of Sicily [87], by prompt use of his large army and military resources struck fear into the Italians by the magnitude of his preparations and rescued the people of Rhegium. [82?] Then, with the rekindling of the civil strife at Rome between Sulla and Marius, some fought for Sulla and some for Marius. Most of them perished in the conflict, and the survivors went over to the victorious Sulla. Thus the flames of civil strife were quenched, and at the same time the greatest of wars, the Marsic, finally came to an end.

3. In days of old the Romans [91], by adhering to the best laws and customs, little by little became so powerful that they acquired the greatest and most splendid empire known to history. In more recent times, when most nations had already been subjugated in war and there was a long period of peace, the ancient practices gave way at Rome to pernicious tendencies. After the cessation of warfare the young men turned to a soft and undisciplined manner of life, and their wealth served as purveyor to their desires. Throughout the city lavishness was preferred to frugality, a life of ease to the practice of warlike pursuits, and he who was regarded as happy by the populace was not the man distinguished for his high qualities of character, but rather one who passed his whole life in the enjoyment of the most gratifying pleasures. Hence elaborate and costly dinner parties came into fashion, with marvellously sweet-scented unguents, the use of expensive coloured draperies, and the making of dining couches with ivory, silver, and the other most expensive materials by workmen of rare skill. Of wines, any that gave but moderate pleasure to the palate were rejected, while Falernian, Chian, and all that rival these in flavour were consumed without stint, as were the fish and other choice foods that were most highly prized as delicacies. Following this standard the young men would appear in the Forum wearing garments of exceptional softness, and so sheer as to be transparent, quite like women's attire. Since they were busy acquiring the appurtenances of pleasure and of fatal ostentation, they soon raised the prices of these articles to incredible peaks. A jar of wine, for example, sold for a hundred drachmas, a jar of Pontic smoked fish for four hundred drachmas, chefs who were especially gifted in the culinary arts at four talents, and male concubines of striking physical beauty for many talents. Although the appetite for evil could not be corrected, some officials in the provinces attempted to remedy the craze for this kind of life and to make their own conduct, placed as it was in the limelight by rank and position, a model of noble pursuits for all to imitate.

Marcus Cato, a man distinguished for his probity and good conduct, when denouncing before the senate the prevalence of luxury at Rome, stated that only in this city were jars of Pontic smoked fish valued more highly than teamsters, and catamites than farmlands.

4. I shall make mention of certain men to serve as models, both because they merit my praise and for the good it does to society, in order that the denunciations of History may lead the wicked to turn from their evil course, and the praises that its enduring glory confers may persuade the good to aspire to high standards of conduct.

5. Quintus Scaevola applied very great energy to correcting by his personal integrity the perversion of men's ideals. When sent out to Asia as governor, he selected as his legate the noblest of his friends, Quintus Rutilius, and kept him at his side when taking counsel, issuing orders, and giving judgement about provincial matters. He resolved that all expenses for himself and his staff should come from his own purse. Furthermore, by his observance of frugality and simplicity, and by allowing nothing to warp his honesty, he enabled the province to recover from its former misery. For his predecessors in Asia, being in partnership with the publicans, the very men who sat in judgement on public cases at Rome, had filled the province with their acts of lawlessness.

Mucius Scaevola, by maintaining the administration of justice incorruptible and exact, not only relieved the provincials from all legal chicanery, but in addition redressed the unjust exactions of the publicans. He assigned scrupulously fair tribunals to hear all who had been wronged, and in every case found the publicans guilty; he forced them to reimburse the plaintiffs for financial losses they had suffered, while he required those who were accused of having put men to death to stand trial on capital charges. Indeed, in the case of the chief agent for the publicans, a slave who was ready to pay a great sum for his freedom and had already made an agreement with his masters, he acted promptly before the man was manumitted, and on his being found guilty had him crucified.

This same man [?] gave judgement against the publicans and handed them over to those whom they had wronged. So it came about that men who in their contempt for others and their desire for gain had a short while before often flouted the law were unexpectedly taken into custody by the men they had wronged and were led off to join the condemned. Since he furnished from his own purse the expenses normally provided for the governors and their staffs, he soon restored the good will of the allies towards Rome.

6. The governor's wisdom and virtue, together with the assistance he was enabled to render, served as a corrective to the hatred that had previously arisen against the ruling power. He himself was accorded quasi-divine honours among those he had benefited, and from his fellow citizens he received many tributes in recognition of his achievements.

5a. . . . he was minded. But as some say, because in his will he had left the greater part of his property to the other son, he nearly lost everything. For the young man, rash and impetuous to excess, setting a diadem on his head and proclaiming himself "King of the Macedonians" exhorted the populace to rise in revolt against Rome and restore the traditional kingdom once held by the Macedonians. Many flocked to his standard in anticipation of the looting that would take place. Execestus, however, in deep distress sent someone to inform Sentius, the governor, of his son's mad folly. He sent also to Cotys, the king of the Thracians, asking him to summon the young man and persuade him to desist from his enterprise. Cotys, being on friendly terms with Euphenes, sent for him and after detaining him for some days handed him over to his father, and he was acquitted of the charges placed against him.

7. We must speak also of the men who started from a quite humble level of repute, but set their sights on a goal no different from those mentioned. Indeed, the pursuit of virtue is found in equal measure among men of high rank and those of more lowly estate.

8. Lucius Asyllius [Syllius], son of a man who had risen only to the rank of quaestor, on being sent out as governor of Sicily found the province ruined, but by the excellence of the measures he employed succeeded in restoring the island. Like Scaevola, he selected the finest of his friends as legate and adviser, a certain Gaius, surnamed Longus, an ardent partisan of the sober, old-fashioned way of life, and together with him a man named Publius, the most highly esteemed member of the equestrian order resident in Syracuse. The latter, indeed, was a man of exceptional personal qualities, quite apart from the gifts of fortune. His piety is attested by the sacrifices, the improvements made to temples, and the dedications offered in his name, his sobriety by the fact that he retained his faculties unimpaired to his dying day, and his culture and humanity by the special consideration he showed to men of learning; in general he was the benefactor of practitioners of any of the esteemed arts, whom he assisted from his personal fortune without stint. These then were the two men on whom Syllius relied, and having constructed adjoining houses to accommodate them, he kept them by him as he worked out the details of the administration of justice and devised means to further the rehabilitation of the province.

This same man, . . . aspiring (to reform) the administration of justice for the common good, banished sycophancy from the market place and made it his major concern to succour the weak. Whereas other governors had been wont to appoint guardians for orphaned children and women without kinsmen, he designated himself as the one to care for them; and since he investigated for himself any disputes among them and took great care in making a decision, he rendered to all victims of oppression such assistance as was fitting. In general he devoted his entire term of office to redressing private and public wrongs, and thereby restored the island to its former state of generally acclaimed prosperity.

9. When the senate was threatening Gracchus with war because of his transfer of the courts, he resolutely exclaimed: "Even though I perish, I shall not cease . . . the sword wrested from the grasp of the senators." This utterance, as though it had been some divine oracle, found fulfilment in accordance with the words spoken, inasmuch as Gracchus, having arrogated to himself tyrannical power, was put to death without trial.

10. Marcus Livius Drusus, though young in years [91], was endowed with every advantage. His father was a man of very great distinction, whose nobility and virtues had won him the particular affection of his fellow citizens. Drusus himself was the most competent orator of his generation, and was the wealthiest man in the city; he was highly trustworthy, and most faithful to his promises; he was, moreover, imbued with a generous magnanimity. Hence it was thought that he alone was destined to become the champion of the senate.

The family of the Drusi wielded very great influence because of the nobility of its members and the kindness and consideration that they displayed to their fellow citizens. Hence when a certain law was brought forward and had just received approval, one citizen added the facetious amendment: "this law is binding on all citizens, except the two Drusi."

When the senate pronounced his legislation invalid Drusus declared that the laws were within his sphere of competency and that he had the power, in his own person, to veto the senatorial decrees; this, however, he would not willingly do, since he knew full well that the offenders would in any case soon meet with the retribution they deserved; but if the laws drawn up by him were invalidated, so likewise, he claimed, would the law relating to the courts be null and void; and while, under this law, had it been put into effect, no one whose life had remained untainted by bribery would be liable to accusations, those who had plundered the provinces would be haled up to give an accounting before special courts for cases of bribery; thus the men who through jealousy were engaged in demolishing his reputation were in effect the assassins of their own decrees.

11. "I swear by Jupiter Capitolinus, by Vesta of Rome, by Mars her ancestral god, by Sol [Indiges] the founder of the race, and by Terra the benefactress of animals and plants, likewise by the demigods who founded Rome and by the heroes who have contributed to increase her empire, that I will count the friend and foe of Drusus my friend and foe, and that I will spare neither property nor the lives of my children or parents except as it be to the advantage of Drusus and of those who have taken this oath. If I become a citizen by the law of Drusus, I shall consider Rome my country and Drusus my greatest benefactor. This oath I will transmit to as many citizens as I can. If I swear faithfully may all good things come to me; if I am forsworn, the reverse."

12. It so happened that a festival was being celebrated and that the theatre was filled with Romans who had turned out for the spectacle; when a comedian on the stage gave vent to his indignation they lynched him right in the theatre, declaring that he was not playing his part as the situation required. The festive occasion having thus been transformed into one of glowering hostility and utter panic, at this juncture Fortune introduced on the scene a droll Satyr-like figure. This was a certain Latin named Saunio, a buffoon with a wonderful gift for gaiety. Not only could he stir up laughter by what he said, but even without a word his slightest motion would bring smiles to all who watched him, so winning was his natural appeal. In consequence he was enthusiastically welcomed by the Romans in their theatres, but the Picentines, wishing to deprive the Romans of this enjoyment and pleasure, had resolved to put him to death. Foreseeing what was about to happen he came on the stage soon after the comedian had been killed, and said: "Members of the audience, the omens are favourable. May the evil that has been done bring good fortune! Know that I am no Roman, but, subject to the *fasces* as you yourselves are, I travel around Italy, peddling my graces in quest of merriment and laughter. Spare then the swallow that belongs to all men alike, to whom God has given the privilege of building her nest without risk in any man's house. It would be unfair for you to bring bitter tears upon yourselves." Continuing at length in a conciliatory and humorous vein, by the persuasive charm of his discourse he wheedled them out of their bitter and vengeful mood and thereby escaped the danger that threatened.

13. The Marsic leader Pompaedius embarked on a grandiose and fantastic venture. Assembling ten thousand men drawn from the ranks of those who had occasion to fear judicial investigations, he led them on Rome, with swords concealed beneath their garb of peace. It was his intention to surround the senate with armed men and demand citizenship, or, if persuasion failed, to ravage the seat of empire with fire and sword. Encountering Gaius Domitius, who asked him, "Where are you going, Pompaedius, with so large a band?" he said, "To Rome, to get citizenship, at the summons of the tribunes." Domitius retorted that he would obtain the citizenship with less risk and more honourably if he approached the senate in a manner which was not warlike; the senate, he said, was in favour of granting this boon to the allies, if instead of violence a petition was presented. Pompaedius took the man's advice as in some way sacred, and persuaded by what he said returned home. Thus by his prudent words Domitius rescued his country from grave danger, having proved far more effective in this interchange than the praetor Servilius in his dealings with the Picentines. For the latter did not speak with them as to free men and allies, but treated them despitefully as slaves, and by his threats of fearful punishments spurred the allies to seek vengeance on him and the other Romans. Domitius, however, by speaking with moderation converted the unthinking impulses of spirited rebels into a sentiment of goodwill.

14. They shared the booty with the soldiers, so that by getting a taste of the profits of war the men who had experienced its perils would undertake the struggle for freedom with a willing heart.

15. Marius led his army into Samnite territory and encamped over against the enemy [90]. Pompaedius, who had assumed full command of the Marsic forces, also advanced with his troops. As the armies came close to one another their grim belligerency gave way to peaceful feelings. For as they reached the point where features could be distinguished, the soldiers on both sides detected many personal friends, refreshed their memory of not a few former comrades in arms, and identified numerous relatives and kinsmen, that is to say, men whom the law governing intermarriage had united in this kind of friendly tie. Since their common bonds compelled them to give voice to friendly greetings, they called one another by name and exchanged exhortations to abstain from murdering men bound to them by close ties. Laying aside their weapons, which had been placed in hostile poses of defence, they held out their hands in sign of friendly greeting. Seeing this, Marius himself advanced from the battle line, and when Pompaedius had done the like they conversed with one another like kinsmen. When the commanders had discussed at length the question of peace and the longed-for citizenship, in both armies a tide of joyous optimism surged up and the whole encounter lost its warlike air and took on a festive appearance. Inasmuch as the soldiers too had in private conversations been urging peace, they were all glad to be relieved of the necessity of mutual slaughter.

16. There was at Asculum, where he had been remanded by the Romans for confinement, a certain Cilician named Agamemnon, who through a sudden reverse in which his accomplices were cut down had been taken alive. Having been released from prison by the Picentines, he was now, in gratitude, cheerfully serving in their army, and since he had much experience in brigandage, he overran the enemy's country with a band of soldiers his equals in lawlessness.

17. Despite the lack either of distinguished ancestry or of any personal advantages that might lead to success, he unexpectedly arrived at the pinnacle of dignity and fame.

Fortune is wont to veer towards what is morally fitting, and to involve those who have contrived some injustice against others in the same difficulties themselves. . . . . Perhaps for the present they exercise tyrannical power, but later they will have to render an accounting for their tyrannical crimes.

18. A Cretan came to the consul [L.] Iulius with an offer of betrayal and said: "If I enable you to conquer the enemy, what reward will you give me for my services?" The general said: "I will make you a Roman citizen, and you will be honoured in my sight." Convulsed with laughter at this remark, the Cretan said: "In the eyes of the Cretans citizenship is just high-sounding claptrap. Gain is what we aim at, and as we range over land and sea, every arrow we shoot is for ourselves and for the sake of money. So I too am here now to get money. Grant your reward of citizenship to the men who are now quarrelling over that very thing, and who are purchasing with blood this empty word for which men fight." The other laughed and said to him: "If our attempt is successful, I shall give you a thousand drachmas."

19. The people of Aesernia, pressed by starvation, employed a ruse of some sort to get the slaves out of the city. Indeed, their particular situation drove them to stop at nothing, and to procure their own safety even at the cost of destroying others. The slaves, however, on being plunged into a strange and dreadful predicament, withdrew and found a remedy for the brutality of their masters in the consideration shown them by the enemy.

The people of Aesernia fed on dogs and other animals, for the compelling needs of nature drove them to disregard all proprieties, and forced them to accept the uncouth food which they had previously spurned.

Men's souls have in them some admixture of a divine nature, whereby on occasion they have forebodings of the future, and through certain natural means of calling up images foresee what is about to happen. This is precisely what happened to the women of Pinna, who bewailed in advance the calamity that was still in the future.

The Italians brought all the children of Pinna before the city walls, and threatened to slaughter them if the city would not revolt from Rome. The men of Pinna, however, steeled themselves and replied that if deprived of their children they should easily beget others, provided they were true to their Alliance with Rome.

The same Italians, despairing of resolving the situation by persuasion, perpetrated an act of surpassing cruelty. They brought the children up close to the walls and ordered them, as they were about to be killed, to beseech their fathers to take pity on the children they had begotten, and with hands raised towards heaven to invoke the sun, who watches over all human affairs, to save the lives of helpless young children.

20. The people of Pinna were caught in a dreadful dilemma. Since they had a hard and fast alliance with Rome, they were compelled to detach themselves from their natural emotions and stand idly by while their children were put to death before the eyes of those who had begotten them.

21. Their desperate courage throughout the struggle was such that it left posterity no hope of surpassing them in the endurance of horrors, and though the besiegers outnumbered them many times over, the townsmen made up for their deficiency in numbers by an excess of courage.

22. The Italians, who so many times before had fought with distinction on behalf of Rome's empire, were now risking life and limb to secure their own, and their feats of bravery went far beyond those of their former victories. The Romans, on the other hand, being engaged in a struggle against their former subjects, considered it a disgrace to appear inferior to their inferiors.

23. Lamponius rushed headlong at Crassus, for he believed that it was appropriate, not that the masses should fight on behalf of their leaders, but rather that the leaders should fight for the masses.

24. The Romans and the Italians contested which were to harvest the crops. In skirmishes and hand-to-hand fighting the mutual slaughter continued without let up. Since the ripe ears were there before them, ready to be reaped, they settled with their blood the question who was to have the essential food. No one waited on the urging of his commander: nature itself, confronting them with the cold logic of deprivation, spurred them on to bravery. Each man stoutly faced the prospect of dying by the sword because he feared death by privation.

25. Sulla's conduct of affairs was effective and energetic [89], and he gained fame and a good reputation in Rome. The populace considered him worthy to be elected consul, and his name was on everyone's lips as a result of his courage and military skill. In short, it was quite evident that he was a man who would be elevated to some higher pinnacle of glory.

26. Mithridates, having been victorious over the Roman command in Asia, [88] and having taken many prisoners, presented them all with clothes and supplies for travel and sent them back to their own lands. As the fame of this generous conduct was spread abroad, the cities were swept by an impulse to attach themselves to the king. Embassies were to be seen from all the cities, bearing decrees inviting him to their lands and hailing him as their "god and saviour." So, too, wherever the king appeared the cities poured forth bodily to meet him, their people clothed in festive garb and rejoicing greatly.

27. While Mithridates was gaining the ascendancy in Asia, and the cities, out of control, were revolting from Rome, the Lesbians decided not only to align themselves with the king, but also to arrest Aquillius, who had sought refuge in Mitylenê and was under medical treatment, and hand him over to Mithridates. They accordingly selected some of their most valiant young men and sent them to his lodgings. They descended upon the place in a group, and seizing Aquillius put him in fetters, thinking that he would be a magnificent and welcome gift for them to send to the king.

He, however, though a very young man, had the courage to perform an heroic deed. Forestalling the men who were about to arrest him, he chose death in preference to ill-usage and a shameful execution. He slew himself, and by this frightful act so stunned his assailants that they had no heart to appear near him. With utter fearlessness he departed this life with its approaching ills, and thereby gained widespread renown for his good courage.

28. In the fighting by sea the Rhodians enjoyed, in general, great superiority in everything but numbers: in the skill of their pilots, the marshalling of their ships, the experience of their oarsmen, the ability of their commanders, and the bravery of their marines. On the Cappadocian side, however, there was a lack of experience, a lack of training, and (the accessory cause of all troubles) a lack of discipline. In zeal, to be sure, they did not fall short of the Rhodians, inasmuch as the king was present in person to supervise and observe the fighting, and they were eager to demonstrate their loyalty to him. Since it was only in the number of their ships that they excelled, they swarmed about the enemy ships and sought to encircle and cut them off.

29. Marius walked every day to the Campus Martius and engaged in military exercises, for he was concerned to correct the weakness and sluggishness of old age by daily and industrious participation in athletics.

In his younger days Gaius Marius, a man who attained the highest prominence, had aspired to noble achievements and had rigorously avoided all avarice; and both in Libya and Europe he accomplished great deeds, whereby he won for himself far-famed distinction and renown. In his extreme old age, seized with a desire to bring into his own hands the wealth of King Mithridates and the riches of the Asiatic cities, he suffered total ruin, for he brought disgrace on the high good fortune he had previously enjoyed, and in the attempt to wrest illegally from Cornelius Sulla the province assigned to him brought down appropriate misfortune upon himself. Not only did he not obtain the wealth he coveted, but lost in addition what he already had, since as a result of his excessive greed all he possessed was confiscated. Condemned to death by his fatherland, he did indeed escape immediate execution but only to wander alone and hunted about the country, and was finally driven out of Libya to seek refuge in Libyan Numidia, without attendants, without means, without friends. Later, when Rome became involved in civil dissensions [87], he assisted the enemies of his country, and not content merely to return home from exile, kindled the flames of war. Though he obtained a seventh consulship, [86] he did not venture to tempt Fortune further, his serious reverses having brought him to a realisation of her fickle nature. Foreseeing that an attack upon Rome by Sulla was impending, he departed from life of his own volition. Yet since he left in his wake abundant seeds of war, he brought upon both his son and his fatherland the most dire calamities. The son, compelled to do battle against superior forces, perished miserably after seeking vain refuge in the underground tunnel. [Praenestê, 82] Rome and the cities of Italy plunged into the long impending conflict, and suffered the disasters that stood ready and waiting for them. For example, the most outstanding men of Rome, I mean Scaevola and Crassus, were cruelly murdered without trial in the senate house, and their private misfortunes provided a foretaste of the great woes that were to descend upon all Italy. Indeed, the majority of the senators and men of distinction were put to death by Sulla and his party, and in the course of the struggles and dissensions no fewer than a hundred thousand soldiers were slain. All this befell mankind because of the wealth that Marius had so coveted at the beginning.

30. Wealth, which is so great a source of contention to mankind, sometimes brings grievous misfortunes upon those who covet it. It prompts men to dark and lawless deeds, panders to every licentious pleasure, and guides the heedless into unworthy conduct. Accordingly we see men of this sort involve themselves in great calamities, and also bring down disasters upon their cities. So great is wealth's power for evil when it is fondly esteemed above all else! Yet in their excessive eagerness to possess it men constantly recite these verses of the poets:

> O gold, fairest gift received by mortals!
> Such delights neither a mother . . .

or again:

> Let me be called a scoundrel, so I but gain;

and the lyric verses:

> Gold, offshoot of earth,
> What passion you kindle among mortals,
> Mightiest of all, monarch of all!
> For men at war your strength
> outstrips the strength of Ares;
> All things feel your spell. At Orpheus' songs
> Trees followed and
> the witless race of beasts:
> You, however, draw after you the whole earth
> and sea and all-devising Ares.

Yet how much better it would be to cull from the poets lines that have just the opposite message:

> Lady Wisdom, be my delight.
> May the gods not bestow upon me,
> Sooner than wisdom's self, tyranny
> Or the bright gleam of golden riches.
> Farthest from Zeus stands he
> To whom fair treasure has come nigh.

BOOKS XXXVIII AND XXXIX FRAGMENTS

5. Then came the outbreak of the civil war [88], in the 662nd year, soon after the . . . which gave rise to Rome's hatred for Mithridates. The onset of the impending troubles was portended, as Livy and Diodorus relate, by many signs; in particular, out of a clear and cloudless sky the sound of a great trumpet was heard, prolonging a shrill and mournful note. All who heard it were beside themselves with fear, and the Etruscan soothsayers declared that the portent betokened a change in the race and a new world order. There were, they said, eight races of men, each different from the others in manners and customs. To each of them God has assigned an age, whose completion coincides with the period of a great year. Whenever the old period draws to an end and a new one is coming to birth, some wondrous sign is sent forth from earth or heaven, whereby it is at once evident to those who are learned in such matters that men have now appeared on earth whose ways and manners are different, and who are of less concern to the gods. Whether this is so or not I omit to inquire, though the argument gains a certain plausibility from the sequel of events. For indeed, if one considers the history of Rome from this point on, the body politic changed altogether for the worse and men of evil ways flourished.

1. Emissaries of the Roman people were sent to Cinna to arrange a settlement [87]. He replied, however, that since he had left the city as its consul he did not expect to return in the status of a private citizen.

2. Later Metellus with such forces as he still possessed approached the encampment of Cinna, and after conferring with him agreed to recognise Cinna as consul, Metellus being the first to address him by that title. Both men were subjected to renunciation on this score. Marius, on encountering Cinna, told him to his face that with victory all but won he ought not to be undermining the power that the gods had granted them, while Metellus, on his return, had a violent disagreement with [Cn.] Octavius, who called him a traitor to the consuls and to his country. Octavius declared that under no circumstances would he allow himself and the city of Rome to fall a prey to Cinna, and even if everyone deserted him, he would still remain true to his high office, and with men of like mind would. . . . But if he lost all hope he would set fire to his own house and perish in the flames together with all his personal effects, and with honour intact would submit voluntarily to death while still enjoying liberty.

3. Merula, the man who had been chosen consul to replace Cinna, was considered to have acted as a thoroughly good citizen would, once the agreement had been reached that he should no longer hold the consulship. Speaking both in the senate and before the people on the best course of action for the state, he offered his services as promoter of concord: as it had been against his wishes that he was made consul, so now of his own free will he would cede the office to Cinna. So in an instant he returned to private life. The senate then dispatched emissaries to conclude the agreement and to escort Cinna into the city as its consul.

4. Cinna and Marius met with the most eminent riders to consider how to establish the peace on a firm basis. The decision at which they finally arrived was to put to death the most prominent of their opponents, all in fact who were capable of challenging their power. Thus, when their own party and faction had been purged, they and their friends could thenceforth conduct their administration without fear and to suit themselves. Accordingly they immediately disregarded their sworn agreements and pledges, and the men marked for death were slaughtered right and left without a hearing. Quintus Lutatius Catulus, who had triumphed signally over the Cimbri and was held in particular affection by his fellow citizens, found himself accused before the people by a certain tribune of a capital crime. Fearing the risk involved in this legal trumpery, he turned to Marius with a request for aid. Marius, though in times past his friend, had now, because something aroused his suspicion, turned against him, and gave as his only answer: "You must die." Catulus, left with no hope of survival, but anxious to end his days without being subjected to base indignities, took his departure from life in a quite original and extraordinary manner. Locking himself in a freshly plastered room, he intensified the fumes from the lime with fire and smoke, and by suffocating himself in the noxious vapours ended his days.

6. In consequence of their butchery of the citizens and their monstrous crimes a divinely appointed Nemesis pursued Cinna and Marius. For Sulla, their one surviving opponent, after cutting to pieces the forces of Mithridates in Boeotia and forcing Athens to capitulate, made an ally of Mithridates, and taking over the king's fleet returned home to Italy. In a trice he smashed the forces of Cinna and Marius and brought the whole of Rome and Italy into his power. He had the whole murderous crew of Cinna's men put to the sword, and utterly wiped out the Marian brood. Hence many of the moderates imputed the punishment of the men who had inaugurated the reign of terror to the workings of divine Providence, inasmuch as a most excellent object lesson had been bequeathed to those who elect an impious course, to turn them from the ways of wickedness.

7. Sulla, being in need of money, laid hands on three sanctuaries that possessed a wealth of offerings in gold and silver: those consecrated to Apollo at Delphi, to Asclepius at Epidaurus, and to Zeus at Olympia. His largest haul was at Olympia, since that sanctuary had remained inviolate through the ages, whereas most of the treasures at Delphi had been plundered by the Phocians during the so-called Sacred War." Sulla, by appropriating large amounts of gold and silver, and any other objects of value, amassed ample funds for the anticipated war in Italy, and though he showed no scruples in seizing the sacred treasures, in their stead he did consecrate land to the gods to provide them an annual revenue. He would say in jest that his supremacy in battle was assured, since the gods, by their large contributions to his war chest, were aiding his cause.

8. During the march Fimbria [86/5], being far in advance of Flaccus, found an opportunity to attempt great ventures, and in the interest of winning the affections of his troops gave them licence to plunder the territory of the allies as if it were enemy country, enslaving anyone they encountered. The soldiers, receiving this permission with delight, within a few days amassed much wealth. Those who had been despoiled waited upon the consul with their tale of woe. He was distressed and told them to come along with him so that they might recover their goods, and he himself ordered Fimbria, with threats, to make restitution of the plunder to those who had suffered the losses. Fimbria attempted to shift all the blame to his men, saying that they had done all they did without his approval, but privately he passed word along to his troops to pay no attention to the orders, and not to surrender what they had acquired by force of arms and under the rules of war. When Flaccus gave even more urgent orders to return the stolen goods, and the soldiers still paid no heed, disorder and mutiny spread rampant among the host.

Once across the Hellespont, Fimbria incited the troops to acts of violence and rapine, exacted money from the cities, and divided the proceeds among his men. They, raised to a position of irresponsible power and stirred by the prospect of gain, held him dear as a public benefactor. If any cities failed to comply, he forced their surrender and turned them over to his men for plunder. Nicomedeia, for example, he handed over to his troops to be plundered.

This same Fimbria, after entering Cyzicus, [85] ostensibly as a friend, brought complaints against the wealthiest men in town, charging them with certain capital offences. In order to strike fear and horror into the rest he found two of them guilty, and had them scourged and beheaded. Then, having confiscated their property, and cowed the others by the fate meted out to his first victims, he compelled the remaining defendants to purchase their lives by surrendering their entire property to him.

In a short while Fimbria brought such disasters un the province as one might expect from a man who had resorted to such impious methods to win the power to do as he pleased. Devastating Phrygia like a hurricane, he swooped down upon the cities and overturned all who came in his path. When at last he died by his own hand, he died but once who should have died a thousand deaths.

9. Gnaeus Pompey, having chosen for his career the life of a soldier, [83] put up with its day-by-day discomforts, and soon won the highest honours for the practice of the military arts. Declining all ease and leisure, he busied himself day and night with whatever would stand him in good stead as a warrior. He kept to a spare diet, and avoided the bath and any society that entailed luxurious habits. He took his food seated, and apportioned less time for sleep than nature requires, working at night on the problems he faced by day, and spending his sleepless hours in the study of works on strategy. By this constant rehearsing of unlikely contingencies he became a master of warfare and the art of combat. Consequently, in far less time than another man would need to take over command of an army that stood ready, he assembled an army, equipped it and put it in battle array [at Picenum]. When his achievements were reported in Rome, everyone at first took them lightly, considering his years rather than his ability, and assuming that the bringers of the news were idly inflating the tale with heroic pomp. When events demonstrated the truth of the reports, the senate sent out Iunius, whom he routed and overcame.

10. Gnaeus Pompey, whose virtues had been so richly rewarded and whose manly spirit had won him the highest laurels, achieved further success after the pattern so laid down and apprised Sulla by letter of his growing strength. Sulla, who had on many other occasions expressed admiration for the young man, castigated the men of senatorial rank who happened to be present, holding them up to shame and at the same time exhorting them to a like zeal. It was astonishing, he said, that a mere youth could have wrested so large an army from the foe, while they, who were so far ahead of him in years and rank, had not been able to command the unfeigned support even of their own servants.

16. When the men, bribed and corrupted, had all deserted, and Scipio was left alone without hope of survival, Sulla sent horsemen to escort him safely to whatever place he desired. Thus Scipio, who in a single moment had been forced to lay aside the dignity of office for private life and a lowly status, by the mercies of Sulla was escorted to the city of his choice. Thereupon he assumed again the insignia of office and once more was in command of a large army.

11. Hadrianus, the propraetor in command at Utica, [82] was burnt alive by the Uticans. The deed, terrible though it was, occasioned no denunciations because of the wickedness of the victim.

12. When Marius the son of Marius became consul, not a few who had already completed their term of military service as set by law hastened of their own accord to join the young man in the conflict, and despite their years to demonstrate to their juniors how effective long training in warfare and familiarity with battlefields and other hazards of war can be.

13. City by city and nation by nation harsh tests were applied, and attempts of many sorts to find out where men stood in regard to them. Of necessity the people were constrained to shift the pretended loyalty that they assumed from one side to the other, and to incline toward whichever party was at hand. For representatives of the opposing belligerents assigned to the task of enlisting recruits kept appearing in person, and since they were striving to outdo one another, their highly exacting investigations brought the preference of the cities into the open.

14. As a result of the scarcity of all necessities Marius had been deserted by his troops. Only Marcus Perpenna, the praetor of Sicily, though approached by Sulla and urged to come over to his side, was so far from complying that he not only persisted in his loyalty to Marius, but even affirmed with passion that he would cross from Sicily with all the strength at his command and rescue Marius from Praenestê.

15. Just as the Marsic War was coming to a close, a great civil war broke out, headed by Sulla and by Gaius Marius, the young son of the Marius who had been so many times (seven, in fact) consul. In this strife many tens of thousands of men perished, but Sulla prevailed, and on becoming dictator he assumed the name of Epaphroditus [favourite of Aprodite], a boast in which he was not belied, since he was victorious in war and died a natural death. Marius put up a valiant struggle against Sulla, but was nevertheless defeated and sought refuge in Praenestê with fifteen thousand men. Hemmed in and subjected to a long siege, at last, when all had deserted him and he could discern no way to save himself, he was forced to call on the aid of a single faithful slave to release him from his troubles. The slave consented, and with a single stroke dispatched his master, then slew himself. Thus did the civil war end, though a few remnants of the Marian party, surviving the war, carried on the conflict with Sulla for a while, until they too perished like the rest.

17. As a result of malicious denunciations the leading men of Rome were murdered in cold blood. Even Scaevola, who was at this time *pontifex maximus* and was held in the highest popular esteem, met a fate that ill matched his noble nature. In one respect, at least, the Roman people were highly fortunate, namely that the supreme pontiff failed, though barely, to reach the holy of holies [temple of Vesta]; for granted the savagery of his pursuers he would have been murdered right at the altar of the innermost sanctum, and his blood would have extinguished the fire that through the ages has been kept alive with sleepless scrupulosity.

18. The praise of good men and the denunciation of the wicked have very great power to guide men towards noble deeds.

Men who are capable of making a wise decision and of carrying their resolves to fulfilment. . . .

19. When the proscription lists were posted in the Forum, large crowds hurried to read them, and for the most part they sympathised with the men who were obliged to submit to death. One fellow in the gathering, however, a man of unusual baseness and arrogance, ridiculed the intended victims and reviled them with many a gross insult. Then and there the retribution of some divinity imposed upon the man who mocked the lot of these unfortunates a punishment that indeed fitted his offence. Finding his own name written at the very end of the list, he at once veiled his head and rushed away through the crowd, hoping not to be noticed by those around and to make good his escape by flight. He was recognised, however, by one of the bystanders, and when the truth of his plight was disclosed he was arrested and executed, while all rejoiced at his death.

20. Inasmuch as Sicily had been without courts of law for a long period, Pompey applied himself to the administration of justice. In dealing both with public disputes and with matters of private contract he rendered his decisions with such unerring skill and such incorruptibility that no one could hope to surpass him. Though only twenty-two (*sic*) years old, at an age when youth itself invites to the irrational pleasures, he lived during his stay on the island with such austerity and sobriety that the Sicilians were astounded, and marvelled at the young man's display of character.

21. The barbarian Spartacus, on receiving a certain favour from someone, [73] showed him his gratitude. Indeed, nature is self-schooled, even among barbarians, to repay kindness for kindness to those who give assistance.

22. A victory won by force of arms brings honour and glory to officers and soldiers alike, but successes obtained through a general's skill redound only to the credit of the commander.

An irrepressible impulse swept over the barbarians to revolt to the Romans.

As a general rule the sufferings of others serve as a warning to those who find themselves amid similar perils.

Book 37. 22a. Sertorius, seeing that the movement among the natives could not be held in check, [73/2] behaved harshly towards his allies: some he arraigned and put to death, others he imprisoned, and the wealthiest he stripped of their estates. Though he amassed much gold and silver he did not deposit it in the common war chest, but hoarded it for his own use; nor did he provide pay for the soldiers therefrom, nor share it with the other leaders. In capital cases he did not sit down with the council or with his advisers, but appointing himself sole judge heard the evidence and pronounced sentence in private. At his banquets he refused to admit the commanders and failed to show any consideration for his friends. In general, exasperated by the progressive deterioration in his position, he behaved tyrannically towards everyone. He won the hatred of the people, and his friends plotted to take his life. They succeeded in doing away with him in the following way. The leaders of highest standing, Perpenna and Tarquitius, made common cause and resolved to do away with Sertorius because of his tyranny. Perpenna, chosen to head the conspiracy, invited Sertorius to dinner, and included among his guests the others who were privy to the plot. When Sertorius arrived the conspirators set upon him, and since he had been placed at the table between Tarquitius and Antonius, it was they who slew him.

Book 37. 22b. As a result of a plot Mithridates barely escaped falling into the hands of the Cyzicenes. It was a Roman centurion, working with them in their tunnelling operations, who attempted to bring this about. Since these operations were being conducted on both sides and gave frequent occasion for encounters and conversations, he had become known to the king's men from his frequent talks with them. It happened once that he was left all alone on guard in the mines, and when one of the royal overseers of the work approached him with the proposition that he betray the city, he pretended to be receptive. The proposal was reported to the king, and he, in his eagerness to win control of the city, offered the man rewards and set a time for them to meet to discuss the matter. When the Roman asked to have guarantees to these promises, the king sent men to give them in his name. The man, however, insisted that he would not accept them unless he had the oaths from the king himself. The king felt that it ill became his royal dignity to descend into the mines, but since the betrayer said he would not listen to any other proposition, and the attempt to get possession of the city was a pressing concern, Mithridates was forced to accede to the demand. The king would actually have fallen into his hands, had not one of his friends, astutely surmising the Roman's intentions, devised a mechanism of just the right size that could be quickly opened and closed. This was placed in the tunnel, and when Mithridates and his friends had entered, the centurion . . . the men with him who were to attack the king . . . drawing his sword he rushed upon the king, but the king got the door closed in time, and escaped safely out of danger.

BOOK XL FRAGMENTS

1. Marcus Antonius [Creticus] came to terms with the Cretans [71], and for a while they observed the peace. Later, however, when the question was brought forward how they might best look to their own advantage, the oldest men, and the most prudent, counselled them to send an embassy to Rome to offer a defence against the crimes imputed to them, and to attempt by fair words and petitions to appease the senate. Accordingly they dispatched thirty of their most eminent men as ambassadors [69?]. These men, by going about individually to the houses of the senators and voicing every possible plea for mercy, won over the pillars of the senate. Brought before the senate itself, they argued their case discreetly, and enumerated in detail their good services to the ruling power, and the military support they had rendered it; this said, they called upon the senators to restore them to favour and re-establish the alliance that had existed earlier. The senate, giving their explanations a ready welcome, attempted to pass a decree wherein they absolved the Cretans of the offences charged against them, and proclaimed them friends and allies of the state; but Lentulus, surnamed Spinther, vetoed the measure. Thereupon the Cretans departed. The senate, upon being informed time after time that the Cretans were in league with the pirates and sharing the booty, decreed that the Cretans should send to Rome all their ships, even to those of only four oars, should furnish three hundred hostages, all men of great prominence, should hand over Lasthenes and Panares, and should pay jointly an indemnity of four thousand talents in silver. When the Cretans learned of the senatorial decisions they met to deliberate on the news. The more prudent said that they ought to comply with all the demands, but Lasthenes and his supporters, being liable to conviction on these charges, and fearing that if they were sent to Rome they would be punished, stirred up the populace with exhortations to preserve the liberty handed down to them from time immemorial.

1a. Certain of the Antiochenes, [67/6] emboldened against King Antiochus [XIII] as a result of his defeat, stirred up the populace and proposed that he be banished from the city. There was a great uprising, but when the king prevailed, the ringleaders of the sedition fled in alarm from Syria; gathering in Cilicia they proposed to restore Philip [II], son of the Philip whose father was Antiochus Grypus. Philip proved receptive to the proposal and arranged a meeting with Azizus the Arab, who gave him a ready welcome, set a diadem on his head, and restored him to the kingship.

1b. Pinning all his hopes on the alliance with Sampsiceramus, he [Antiochus] sent for him to come with his army. He, however, having made a secret agreement with Azizus to do away with the kings, came with his army and summoned Antiochus to his presence. When the king, knowing nothing of this, complied, Sampsiceramus acted the part of a friend but placed him under arrest, and though for the time being he merely held him closely guarded in chains, he later had him put to death. So too, in accordance with the agreement to divide up the kingdom of Syria, Azizus intended to assassinate Philip, but Philip learned of the plot and fled to Antioch.

2. During Pompey's stay in Damascus of Syria [63], (Aristobulus, the king of the Jews, and Hyrcanus his brother came to him with their dispute over the kingship. Likewise the leading men, more than two hundred in number, gathered to address the general and explain that their forefathers, having revolted from Demetrius, [161] had sent an embassy to the senate and received from them the leadership of the Jews, who were, moreover, to be free and autonomous, their ruler being called High Priest, not King. Now, however, these men were lording it over them, having overthrown the ancient laws and enslaved the citizens in defiance of all justice; for it was by means of a horde of mercenaries, and by outrages and countless impious murders that they had established themselves as kings. Pompey put off till a later occasion the settlement of their rival claims, but as to the lawless behaviour of the Jews and the wrongs committed against the Romans he bitterly upbraided the party of Hyrcanus. They deserved, he said, some graver and harsher visitation; nevertheless, in the spirit of Rome's traditional clemency, he would, if they were obedient henceforward, grant them pardon.

3. Now that we are about to record the war against the Jews, we consider it appropriate to give first a summary account of the establishment of the nation, from its origins, and of the practices observed among them. When in ancient times a pestilence arose in Egypt, the common people ascribed their troubles to the workings of a divine agency; for indeed with many strangers of all sorts dwelling in their midst and practising different rites of religion and sacrifice, their own traditional observances in honour of the gods had fallen into disuse. Hence the natives of the land surmised that unless they removed the foreigners, their troubles would never be resolved. At once, therefore, the aliens were driven from the country, and the most outstanding and active among them banded together and, as some say, were cast ashore in Greece and certain other regions; their leaders were notable men, chief among them being Danaüs and Cadmus. The greater number were driven into what is now called Judaea, which is not far distant from Egypt and was at that time utterly uninhabited. The colony was headed by a man called Moses, outstanding both for his wisdom and for his courage. On taking possession of the land he founded, besides other cities, one that is now the most renowned of all, called Jerusalem. In addition he established the temple that they hold in chief veneration, instituted their forms of worship and ritual, drew up their laws and ordered their political institutions. He also divided them into twelve tribes, since this is regarded as the most perfect number and corresponds to the number of months that make up a year. But he had no images whatsoever of the gods made for them, being of the opinion that God is not in human form; rather the Heaven that surrounds the earth is alone divine, and rules the universe. The sacrifices that he established differ from those of other nations, as does their way of living, for as a result of their own expulsion from Egypt he introduced an unsocial and intolerant mode of life. He picked out the men of most refinement and with the greatest ability to head the entire nation, and appointed them priests; and he ordained that they should occupy themselves with the temple and the honours and sacrifices offered to their god. These same men he appointed to be judges in all major disputes, and entrusted to them the guardianship of the laws and customs. For this reason the Jews never have a king, and authority over the people is regularly vested in whichever priest is regarded as superior to his colleagues in wisdom and virtue. They call this man the high priest, and believe that he acts as a messenger to them of god's commandments. It is he, we are told, who in their assemblies and other gatherings announces what is ordained, and the Jews are so docile in such matters that straightway they fall to the ground and do reverence to the high priest when he expounds the commandments to them. At the end of their laws there is even appended the statement: "These are the words that Moses heard from God and declares unto the Jews." Their lawgiver was careful also to make provision for warfare, and required the young men to cultivate manliness, steadfastness, and, generally, the endurance of every hardship. He led out military expeditions against the neighbouring tribes, and after annexing much land apportioned it out, assigning equal allotments to private citizens and greater ones to the priests, in order that they, by virtue of receiving more ample revenues, might be undistracted and apply themselves continually to the worship of god. The common citizens were forbidden to sell their individual plots, lest there be some who for their own advantage should buy them up, and by oppressing the poorer classes bring on a scarcity of manpower. He required those who dwelt in the land to rear their children, and since offspring could be cared for at little cost, the Jews were from the start a populous nation. As to marriage and the burial of the dead, he saw to it that their customs should differ widely from those of other men. But later, when they became subject to foreign rule, as a result of their mingling with men of other nations (both under Persian rule and under that of the Macedonians who overthrew the Persians), many of their traditional practices were disturbed. Such is the account of Hecataeus of Abdera in regard to the Jews.

4. Pompey had inscribed on a tablet [61], which he set up as a dedication, the record of his achievements in Asia. Here is a copy of the inscription: "Pompey the Great, son of Gnaeus, Imperator, having liberated the seacoast of the inhabited world and all islands this side Ocean from the war with the pirates, being likewise the man who delivered from siege the kingdom of Ariobarzanes [I], Galatia and the lands and provinces lying beyond it, Asia, and Bithynia; who save protection to Paphlagonia and Pontus, Armenia and [Sythian] Achaia, as well as Iberia, Colchis, Mesopotamia, Sophenê, and Gordyenê; brought into subjection Darius king of the Medes, Artoles king of the Iberians, Aristobulus king of the Jews, Aretas king of the Nabataean Arabs, Syria bordering on Cilicia, Judaea, Arabia, the province of Cyrenê, the Achaeans, the Iozygi, the Soani, the Heniochi, and the other tribes along the seacoast between Colchis and the Maeotic Sea, with their kings, nine in number, and all the nations that dwell between the Pontic and the Red Seas [Black Sea and Persian Gulf]; extended the frontiers of the Empire to the limits of the earth; and secured and in some cases increased the revenues of the Roman people; he, by confiscation of the statues and the images set up to the gods, as well as other valuables taken from the enemy, has dedicated to the goddess twelve thousand and sixty pieces of gold and three hundred and seven talents of silver."

5. At Rome a certain insolvent debtor named Catiline and Lentulus surnamed Sura gathered a mob and fomented sedition against the senate, as follows [63]. A certain festival was approaching when it was customary for the clients of prominent men to send gifts, and for this reason houses were kept open all through the night. The conspirators agreed, therefore, to use this opportunity to introduce into the houses of their intended victims men whose business it would be to lay violent hands upon them. With swords concealed at their girdles they were to gain entry without rousing suspicion, ostensibly for the purpose of bringing gifts, and, distributed a few to each house, at one and the same time to do away with virtually the entire senate. Though the plot had been thus carefully planned, by a miracle the victims escaped assassination. For among the more than four hundred men who were detailed to do the killing, there was one [Fulvia] who was in love with a certain girl and who, on being slighted by her, remarked more than once that within a few days her very life would be in his power. The remark puzzled her, and she could not guess what grounds he had for his threat, but still the young man remained insistent. When they were together, therefore, and drinking, she feigned extreme delight at his company and asked him to tell her what in the world his remark meant, and he, wishing in his infatuation to please her, disclosed the whole truth. She pretended to have taken what was said sympathetically and joyfully, and held her peace, but on the morrow went to the wife of Cicero the consul, and speaking privately with her about the matter reported what the young man had said. Thus was the conspiracy brought to light, and the consul, by using now threats and terror, now kindly exhortations, learned from them full details of the plot.

5a. Lucius Sergius, surnamed Catiline [Nov. 8, 63], on finding himself deep in debt had fomented an insurrection, and the consul Marcus Cicero was composing a speech on the anticipated disturbance. Catiline, on being openly named and accused to his face, declared that under no circumstances would he condemn himself to voluntary exile without a trial. Cicero put the question to the senators, whether it was their wish to banish Catiline from the city. When the majority, abashed by the man's presence, remained silent, Cicero, wishing as it were to probe their sentiments exactly, turned the question and asked the senators next whether they would order him to banish Quintus Catulus from Rome. When with one voice they all shouted their disapproval and showed their displeasure at what was said, Cicero, reverting to Catiline, remarked that when they considered a man not deserving of banishment they shouted with all their might; hence it was evident that by silence they were agreeing to his banishment. Catiline, after stating that he would think it over in private, withdrew.

According to the proverb the less is the enemy of the more.

6. This Cleopatra is mentioned by Virgil, Lucian, Galen, along with Plutarch, and by Diodorus and George the chronicler among others.

7. [. . . the beginning of the Gallic War, which we have made the end of our history.]

[This part of the inhabited world and that about the British Isles and the arctic regions have fallen least of all within the range of men's common knowledge. As for the northern latitudes adjacent to the region that is uninhabited because of the cold, we shall discuss them when we come to write of the deeds of Gaius Caesar; for it was he who extended the Roman Empire farthest in that direction, and brought all the area that was previously unknown within the scope of history.]

[In our own times Gaius Caesar, who by his deeds won the title *divus,* was the first on record to have conquered the island, and by defeating the Britons in war compelled them to pay fixed tribute. As for these matters we shall record the particulars of his enterprise at the appropriate times.]

[As for their customs and other peculiarities we shall record them in detail when we come to Caesar's campaign against Britain.]

8. Some of the books were pirated and published before being corrected and before they had received the finishing touches, at a time when we were not yet fully satisfied with the work. These we disown. In order that these books, by getting before the public, may not mar the general plan of our history, we have deemed it necessary to publish a statement that will expose any misconception. Our subject matter is contained within forty books, and in the first six we have recorded the events and legends prior to the Trojan War. In these we have not fixed the dates with any precision, since no chronological record of them was at hand. . . .

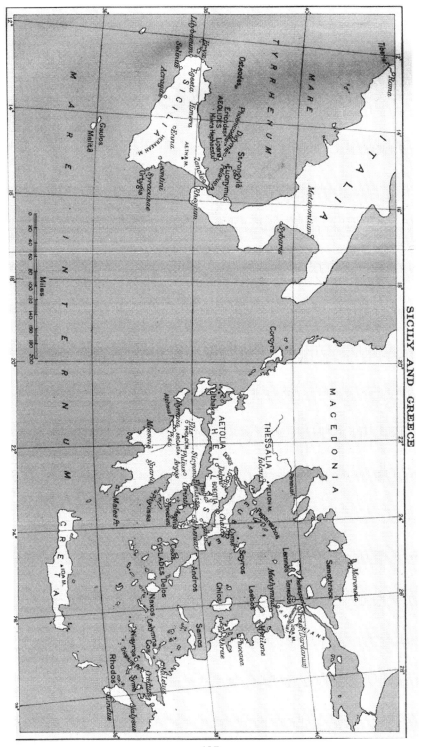

SICILY AND GREECE

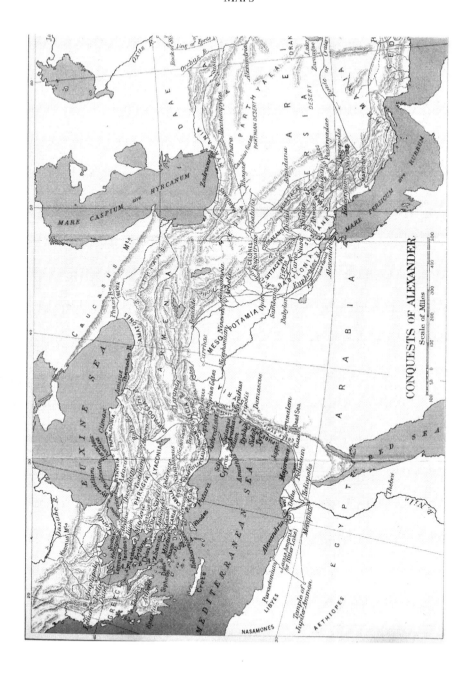

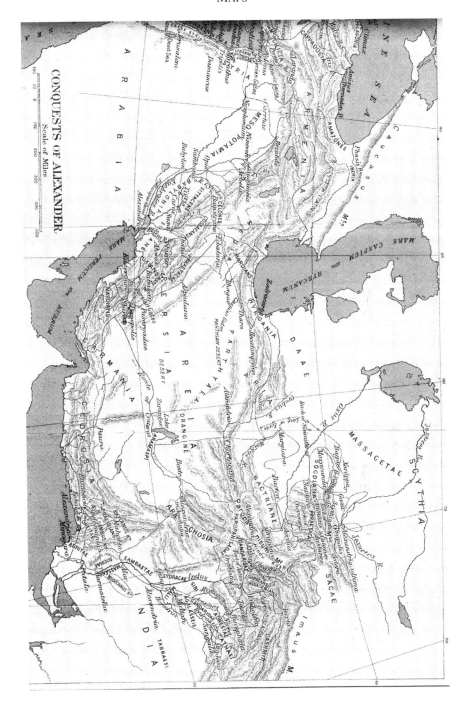

489

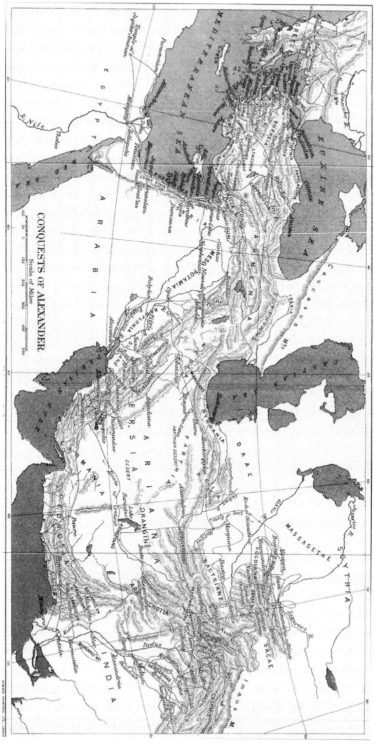

CONQUESTS OF ALEXANDER

Scale of Miles

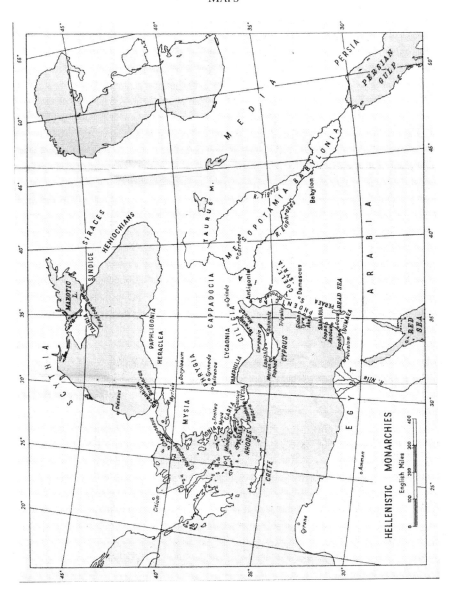

HELLENISTIC MONARCHIES

491

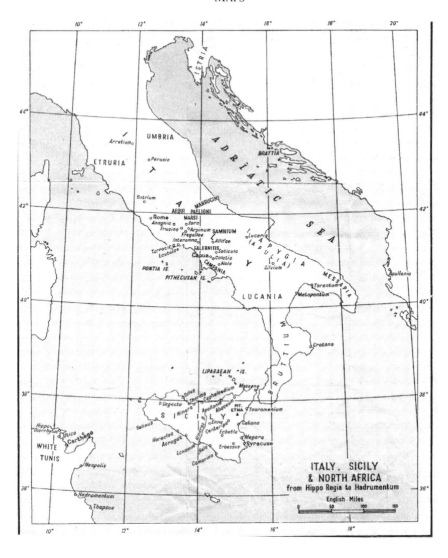

ITALY , SICILY
& NORTH AFRICA
from Hippo Regia to Hadrumentum

English Miles

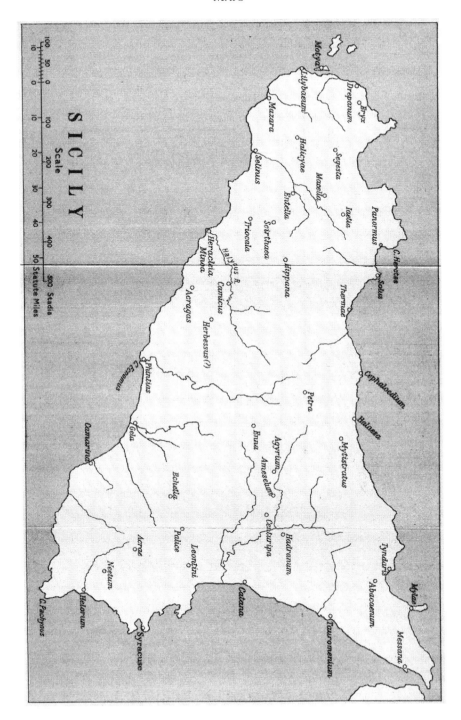

SOPHRON CATALOGUE

2014

Caesar's Commentaries: The Complete Gallic War. Revised. 8vo., xxiv,507 pp.; Introduction, Latin text of all eight Books, Notes, Companion, Grammar, Exercises, Vocabularies, 17 Maps, illus. all based on Francis W. Kelsey. ISBN 978-0-9850811 1 9 . . . . $19.95

Virgil's Aeneid Complete, Books I-XII. With Introduction, Latin text and Notes by W. D. Williams. 8vo., xxviii, 739 pp., 2 maps, Glossary, Index.   ISBN 978-0-9850811 6 4 . . . . $27.95

Praxis Grammatica. **A New Edition.** John Harmer. 12 mo., xviii, 116 pp.; Introduction by Mark Riley.   ISBN 978-0-9850811 2 6. . . . . , $3.95

The *Other* Trojan War. Dictys & Dares. 12 mo., xxii,397 pp.; Latin/English Parallel Texts; Frazer's Introduction & Notes, Index.   ISBN 978-0-9850811 5 7. . . . . $14.95

The Stoic's Bible: *a Florilegium for the Good Life. EXPANDED.* Giles Laurén. 8vo., xxvi,653 pp., 2 illus., Introduction, Bibliography.   ISBN 978-1-4538162 2 6. . . . . $24.95

Why Don't We Learn from History? B. H. Liddell Hart. 12 mo., 126 pp.   ISBN 978-0-9850811 3 3. . . . . $4.95

Quintilian. Institutionis Oratoriae. Liber Decimus. Text, Notes & Introductory Essays by W. Peterson. Foreword by James J. Murphy. 8vo., cvi,291 pp., Harleian MS facsimile, Indexes.   ISBN 978-0-9850811-8-8 . . . . $19.95

Schools of Hellas. Kenneth Freeman. 12 mo., xxi,279 pp., illus., Indexes.   ISBN 978-0-9850811-9-5 . . . . $14.95

Cornelius Nepos Vitae. 12 mo., xviii,314 pp., 3 maps, notes, exercises, & vocabulary by John Rolf. ISBN 978-0-9850811-7-1 . $14.95

Greek Reader. Mark Riley. Based on the selection of Wilamowitz-Moellendorff, with notes and a vocabulary. 12 mo., vi,286 pp.   ISBN 978-0-9897836-0-6 . . . . $12.95

Quintilian: *A Roman Educator and his Quest for the Perfect Orator*. Revised Edition, George A. Kennedy. 12 mo., 188 pp. Index.
ISBN 978-0-9897836-1-3 . . . . $9.95

Diodorus Siculus. I *The Library of History* in Forty Books. Vol. I. (books I-XIV). 8vo., 620 pp., maps. ISBN 978-0-9897836-2-0 . . . . .$19.95

Diodorus Siculus. II *The Library of History* in Forty Books. Vol. II. (books XV-XL). 8vo., 512 pp., maps. ISBN 978-0-9897836-3-7. . . . $19.95

Foulquié, Paul. *La Dialectique*. in-8, 160 pp.
ISBN 978-1-4954688-3-4 . $6.95

Available from SOPHRON EDITOR (CreateSpace and Amazon worldwide)

In Preparation:
Isocrates by Richard Enos.